WELCOME TO *CORRECTIONS: AN INTRODUCTION,* the first introduction to corrections text written by an author who is both an accomplished scholar and a former corrections professional. The following pages will introduce you to what we do in corrections, why we do it, and what challenges face contemporary correctional staff.

It takes experience to write a great textbook, and Richard P. Seiter served more than twenty years as a correctional professional. In 1976, Seiter began his career with the Federal Bureau of Prisons (BOP) and after five years was appointed warden at the Federal Prison Camp in Allenwood, PA. In 1983, he was appointed Director of the Ohio Department of Rehabilitation and Correction, supervising the entire state prison system with 30,000 inmates and 7,000 staff.

He eventually returned to the Federal Bureau of Prisons as the Assistant Director for Industries, Education and Training, and became Chief Operating Officer of Federal Prison Industries, with sales of over $400 million per year of prison-made products. His next position was warden of the Federal Correctional Institution in Greenville, IL. Seiter retired from the Federal Bureau of Prisons in January 1999 and is currently Associate Professor and Director of the Criminal Justice Program at Saint Louis University.

With his knowledge and more than 100 of his **original photos**, Seiter brings the real world of corrections to today's students in a way no one else could.

Practical Perspective

AN INSIDER'S EXPERIENCE . . . I Thought I Would Get Fired

I was awakened about 3:00 A.M. As I sleepily answered, a correctional supervisor in Ohio's maximum-security prison was on the telephone, saying, "I am sorry to have to wake you up, but we just had an inmate die here at the prison after an altercation with staff. The warden is out of town, and the associate warden is on his way, but said I should call and inform you." I was now fully awake, got more information, and asked the supervisor to tell the associate warden that I would be at the prison in about two hours. I called my deputy director, and we soon left for the hundred-mile drive to the prison.

When we arrived, we received more details. An inmate with a history of mental health problems who had a history of violence and was isolated in a cell identified for mental-health-troubled inmates, had started to destroy his cell and act out about 11:00 P.M. He also jumped headfirst from the top bunk to the floor and appeared to be injured. The supervisor in charge at the time ordered a group of correctional officers to assemble, remove the inmate from his cell, and move him to another cell where he could be restrained, medicated, and checked for injuries.

When the group of eight officers was assembled, they discussed how to move the inmate. The inmate staff member had threatened to fire him from his job unless he improved his work performance.

The staff member's death rocked the spirit and morale of the prison staff. They questioned the leadership of the prison and the department, they complained that there were not enough staff for security and safety, and they threatened a union action of some type if things didn't improve. The prison was in the district of the most powerful member of the state legislature (the speaker of the house of representatives), and he had to do something to respond to his constituents. So there was already an emotional and inflamed environment at the prison at the time of the inmate's death.

When the circumstances of the inmate's death became public, there were cries from the black community and many media sources of racism and retaliation by prison staff. Another very powerful state legislator and leader of the black elected officials in the state called on the governor for action, including criminal prosecution and the firing of all officers responsible for the death. The racial issue was even more inflamed by the fact that about one month before, a black woman who was director of the department of mental retardation was fired by the governor

An Insider's Experience

The author shares his personal thoughts and observations on events and circumstances he experienced firsthand during his career.

YOUR CAREER IN CORRECTIONS   WARDENS

The author of this textbook is a career correctional administrator and was warden of two federal prisons. He thoroughly enjoyed these jobs and often described a warden's job as similar to that of a city manager, in that wardens are responsible for many service functions (food service, health care, sanitation and maintenance, policing, construction, human resources, and budget management), as well as the correctional aspects of security, inmate programs, and legal issues.

In 2001, there were almost 1,400 state and federal prisons, each having a warden as the chief executive of the prison. On January 1, 2001, it was reported that a warden's pay ranged from $33,492 to $133,591,[10] with the average approximately $70,000. The average time that wardens had worked for their correctional agency was 15.3 years,[11] indicating that they are experienced when taking a position as warden. In most states, there is no minimum educational level, although most wardens have a college degree. There is also no specific requirement for education or experience, as wardens can begin their correctional careers in almost any discipline, including security, counseling, or any other area of corrections.

College students do not usually plan a career toward the job of warden. In fact, most college students do not plan to go to work in a prison. Many who end up in institutional corrections often plan to be a social worker or counselor, and later find opportunities to work in prisons both exciting and challenging. Warden is a job that takes many years of training and experience. As noted previously, the average correctional job experience for wardens was more than fifteen years. No matter how much education, how much experience in management, or how much willingness to work a person has, nothing is more important to prepare someone to be a warden than working in a prison at a variety of levels. Most decisions that come to a warden's desk are not simple, and there are no easy or obvious solutions. Many have multiple problems and risks, and the difficulty lies in selecting a solution that has the least likelihood of dire consequences. There are always so many varying impacts from what a warden does (if it helps security, it may hurt treatment; if it is something positive for inmates, it may be problematic for staff; if it has great potential for a positive outcome, it may not be affordable within the budget) that each decision must be thoughtfully considered as to how it affects different groups or other prison functions.

Some of these problems are what makes a job as a warden enjoyable for most. Surveys have pointed out that prison wardens have much greater job satisfaction than all but a few other professions. There is never a boring day, and each day brings something different. It takes skills in every different area of management (budget, human resources, security and treatment, and facility maintenance). But most important, being a warden is a very people-oriented job. Wardens get things done by dealing with people—staff and inmates—and must enjoy and be good at getting others to implement and follow what has been decided.

Your Career in Corrections

These career boxes note the types of jobs available to individuals entering this field, the requirements of the job, life on the job, and the pay and work conditions they can expect.

YOU MAKE THE DECISION . . .   SHOULD I REVOKE HIM?

One of the most difficult challenges for a probation officer is deciding whether to initiate a revocation process for a probationer. To some, it may seem very clear-cut: if probationers violate the conditions of their supervision, their probation should be revoked. Most probation agency policies require that violations be brought to the attention of the court for action to either revoke or modify probation conditions. Yet courts do not want to see every technical violation of a probationer, and officers have considerable discretion in how to handle most minor infractions. For instance, a probationer may be required to report several times per month to the officer, and is usually very responsible in doing so. If the offender misses one appointment, agencies do not want officers reporting it as a violation to the court. Yet all criminal activities should be reported.

The officer must decide whether to initiate a revocation process for a thousand different situations between these two extremes. It is easy for officers to take the "hard line" and report al-

You Make the Decision

Students take on the role of the decision maker to decide how to handle issues that someone working in the field might encounter.

Case Studies

Real, practical situations and challenges faced in correctional operations allow students to put history, theory, facts, and research into a practice-meets-theory perspective.

THE EFFECTIVENESS OF UNIT MANAGEMENT

When I worked at the U.S. Penitentiary in Leavenworth, Kansas, two incidents occurred that illustrated the positive impact unit management can have on the operations of a prison. When I first arrived at Leavenworth, it was not operated under the unit management concept. There were correctional counselors, but instead of being assigned to housing units, they were assigned to areas of the prison, such as industries, the dining room, the main corridor, the recreation yard, and the segregation building. Their duties were to be accessible to inmates in those areas and help out in the management as necessary.

About a year after I began working there, we had a work strike. Several inmates were upset with a change in the telephone policy (how they were allowed to make telephone calls) and decided to organize a work strike to get the attention of the administration and try to force a change in the policy. Early on a Monday morning, when inmates were on their way to work, groups of inmates blocked them in some of the main work areas, showing knives or other prison-made weapons, and threatening inmates who did not comply with their demands to go back to their cells and not work.

We quickly discovered what was going on, and to avoid putting inmates in danger, we ordered all inmates to return to their cells. We locked down the prison and began to try to identify the organizers of the work strike. We began by interviewing inmates, and called all the correctional counselors together to see whether they had an idea of which inmates were behind the work strike. Unfortunately, we discovered the counselors did not really know the inmates and could not put together a credible list of suspects.

About six months later, we implemented unit management at Leavenworth and assigned unit managers, case managers, and correctional counselors to each of the housing units. Their offices were in the housing units, and they spent most of their day observing and talking to inmates.

DEALING WITH THE MENTALLY ILL PROBATIONER

The Bureau of Justice Statistics estimated that at midyear 1998, there were 547,800 mentally ill offenders on probation. It is estimated that 13 percent of all probationers had a condition requiring mental health treatment, yet in a 1997 survey of these probationers, only 43 percent of those required to participate in such treatment had done so.[11] Historically, mentally ill offenders in the community were spread out among standard caseloads of non–mentally ill offenders. Recently, most probation and parole agencies have created special caseloads for managing the mentally ill offender. These caseloads are usually smaller than standard caseloads, averaging between fifty and fifty-five offenders. Most offenders are placed on a special caseload by an order of the court as a condition of their probation. Otherwise, probation officers may identify an offender as possibly having a mental illness and request his or her placement on a special caseload. The following is a description by a probation officer of his approach to dealing with mentally ill probationers.

The supervision philosophy of this probation officer is to build trust with clients, particularly because he is concerned about the client's risk of suicide or violence to others. The officer notes that he would not know these things unless offenders tell him, and they must believe that they can share sensitive information with their probation officer without fear of immediate violation (return to prison). The officer states that after a few crises with offenders, this trust often develops.

Mentally ill probationers report more frequently than standard probationers; weekly contact is not unusual. This frequency of contact often continues even when offenders' behavior is good and they are eligible for less intensive supervision. This is because these probationers may become unstable at any time. Every time the officers sees his probationers, he asks them if they are taking their psychotropic medication, if they are having any thoughts of harming themselves or others, and if they know the date and time of their next psychiatric appointment. He notes that it is very important not just to ask them these questions and accept their answers, but to "pry and push" them. He gave an example of an offender under his supervision who had a history of serious suicide attempts through overdoses of psychotropic drugs. The offender called the probation officer (PO) one day and said his roommate was using drugs, and he was afraid he would get caught up in it. The PO advised him to move as soon as possible, but as they continued to talk, it became clear that something else was bothering him. After some prodding, the probationer finally admitted that he was thinking of harming himself. In fact, he then admitted that he had already begun to take his medicine in a suicide attempt, and had called the PO in hopes that the PO would get him to admit what he was doing without his volunteering the information. When asked why someone attempting suicide would not admit it, the PO noted that this is not unusual, as the person planning suicide is often embarrassed and sometimes even concerned about upsetting the PO. Some of his clients become very apologetic about the trouble they cause the PO. In this situation, the PO called emergency medical services (EMS) and continued to talk to the probationer on the phone until the paramedics arrived. He then directed the probationer to go out to meet the EMS workers when they drove up. However, the probationer had kept some pills in his hand, and on the way to the hospital, he took some more pills. The EMS workers were able to treat and save him, and the probationer is now doing very well, both physically and psychologically.

A Look Into...

Students see through the eyes of professionals in the real correctional world and learn how their experiences provide insight into career decisions, how to effectively handle crises, and how to deal with specific offender issues.

SHOULD PAROLE BE SAVED?

Parole has been commonly acknowledged to aid prisoner reentry in several ways, and with the indeterminate sentencing structure, parole served many positive functions. First, extremely dangerous inmates were often maintained in prisons longer than they would have been under a determinate sentence structure. Determinate sentences are usually shorter than indeterminate sentences, and parole boards regularly require dangerous, high-risk inmates to serve the maximum sentence. The State of Colorado abolished parole as a release mechanism in 1979, but reinstated it after finding out that the length of prison sentences served was decreasing, particularly for high-risk offenders.

Second, parole boards do act as a gatekeeper to ensure that inmates have solid release plans when they return to the community. Parole boards always ask inmates questions such as, "Where will you live when you get out of prison?" and "What job opportunities are available to you?" The boards also have reports available to them from parole officers who have investigated the inmates' release plans. Third, the existence of parole is an incentive for good behavior by inmates and an incentive for program participation that can be beneficial, even if not truly voluntary. There is no evidence that nonvoluntary program participation is less effective than participation with some coercion, and there is recent data indicating the benefit of a variety of prison program participation (cognitive skills training, drug treatment programs, education and work programs, and treatment of sex offenders) on reducing recidivism.[50]

Finally, parole consideration sets the framework for supervision and treatment needs following release. Parole boards create conditions under which parolees must be supervised and attend treatment programs from which they would benefit. Without parole, supervision is less individualized and based on risk rather than need, setting supervision levels based primarily on offenders' history of criminal behavior.

A Question of Policy

These boxes provide students insight and perspective into the dilemmas facing elected officials and correctional administrators trying to create policies that are effective and efficient and contribute significantly to the accomplishment of correctional goals.

Contemporary Issues

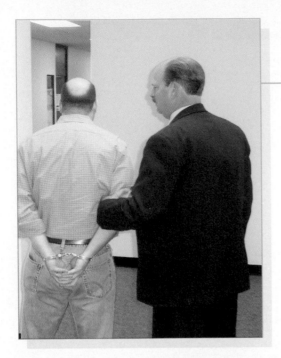

Pretrial Correctional Activities

One of the few introductory textbooks to explain the role of pretrial services in decisions regarding bail and release on recognizance and the use of pretrial supervision to enhance the reduction of jail populations.

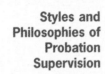

Styles and Philosophies of Probation Supervision

Addresses the struggle between casework and surveillance styles of supervision of probationers.

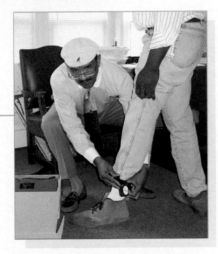

Issues in Jail Operations

Highlights critical issues that face the nation's jails, including jail classification systems, dealing with mentally ill offenders, legal issues, and preventing suicides.

YOU MAKE THE DECISION...

USE THE PRIVATE SECTOR TO OPERATE PRISONS?

You are the director of a state department of corrections with no history of contracting entire prison operations to the private sector. Several of your fellow state administrators have used the private sector to house their inmates, and no one has expressed a serious concern about price or quality. You are aware of several serious incidents (riots, escapes, and inmate brutality) that have occurred in a few private prisons across the country and are sensitive to the negative publicity that these incidents brought. You are also aware of all of the studies that are inconclusive in terms of the benefits of the private sector in comparison to the public sector for cost and outcome.

Yet your legislative budget committee is pushing for the state to try privatization. They cite tightening budgets and the need to find better and less expensive ways to manage the burgeoning correctional population in the state. At the same time, you have had a good relationship with the labor union representing state correctional officers, and they are firmly opposed to privatization, as none of the private prisons allow collective bargaining. You feel caught in the middle of the positions of the budget committee and the labor union in terms of where you come down on supporting privatization. You are going to make one of them very unhappy with whatever decision you make.

The Role of Private Correctional Agencies

Includes the most recent research and trends regarding privatization of corrections.

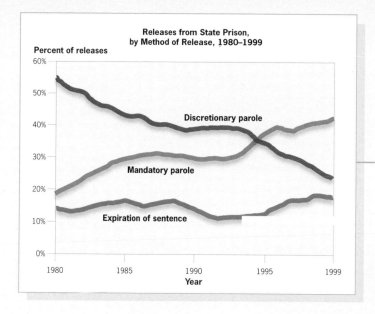

**Releases from State Prison,
by Method of Release, 1980–1999**

Percent of releases

- Discretionary parole
- Mandatory parole
- Expiration of sentence

Year

Postrelease Supervision and Prisoner Reentry

Addresses questions such as: Should parole continue (or be reinstated in some states)? and What can correctional officials do to better prepare inmates to return to their communities as successful, law-abiding citizens?

Juveniles Managed by Traditional or Punitive Methods

Asks students to consider whether past concepts of juvenile justice or developing philosophies will better serve our society in the future.

YOU MAKE THE DECISION . . .

SHOULD JUVENILES BE TRIED AS ADULTS?

As described previously, more juveniles arrested for serious crimes are being bound over to adult courts to be tried as adults and, if convicted, to serve an adult sentence. Since serious crimes are those handled in the criminal justice system, the sanctions usually include imprisonment. Three models of incarceration of juveniles tried and convicted as adults are used. Most states place these juvenile offenders in adult prisons with adult inmates. A few states house juveniles with adults, but require them to be housed and programmed separately. Some states place juveniles in juvenile institutions until they reach age 18, and they then are transferred to adult prisons.

In 1997, there were 5,400 juveniles in adult prisons, 92 percent were male, 61 percent were committed for violent crimes, and the average maximum sentence was 82 months. Fifty-eight percent were black, another 15 percent were Hispanic, and 2 percent were of other races. However, by 2002, the number of juveniles in adult prisons declined to 3,055 (almost all males). The original punitive attitude of the late 1990s has lessened, and many people are reconsidering the reasons for prosecuting juvenile offenders as adults.

Current Practices and Issues Regarding the Death Penalty

Presents the most recent statistics regarding the use of the death penalty and the emergence of a concern for error in death sentences.

People in the System

Prison Staff on the Job

A practical view of prison workers, including the "daily grind," stress, danger, and challenges of managing inmates.

Special Offenders

Expanded and contemporary coverage of the challenges facing today's corrections professional.

Prison Life for Inmates

A realistic view of the life of prisoners.

Female Offenders

Strategies to meet the special needs and circumstances of the increasing number of women in the correctional system.

Corrections

An Introduction

Richard P. Seiter, Ph.D.
Director, Criminal Justice Program
Saint Louis University

Upper Saddle River, New Jersey 07458

Library of Congress Cataloging-in-Publication Data

Seiter, Richard P.
    Corrections: an introduction / Richard P. Seiter.
        p. cm.
    Includes bibliographical references and index.
    ISBN 0-13-142131-X
        1. Corrections—United States. I. Title.

HV9471.S45 2005
364.6'0973—dc22

                        2004044299

Executive Editor: Frank Mortimer, Jr.
Assistant Editor: Korrine Dorsey
Development Editor: Susan Beauchamp
Full-Service Project Management: Ann Mohan/WordCrafters
    Editorial Services, Inc.
Production Liaison: Barbara Marttine Cappuccio
Director of Manufacturing and Production: Bruce Johnson
Managing Editor: Mary Carnis
Manufacturing Buyer: Cathleen Petersen
Creative Director: Cheryl Asherman
Cover Design Coordinator: Miguel Ortiz
Interior Design: Amanda Kavanagh

Cover Designer: Ruta Fiorino
Cover Image: Eric Larrayadieu/STONE/Getty Images
Editorial Assistant: Barbara Rosenberg
Marketing Manager: Tim Peyton
Director, Image Resource Center: Melinda Reo
Manager, Rights and Permissions: Zina Arabia
Interior Image Specialist: Beth Brenzel
Cover Image Specialist: Karen Sanatar
Image Permission Coordinator: Craig Jones
Photo Researcher: Teri Stratford
Composition: Carlisle Communications, Ltd.
Printing and Binding: Banta/Menasha

Photo Credits: p. 2, Historical Picture Archive, CORBIS-NY; p. 34, © Royality-Free/CORBIS; pp. 32, 98, 206, 240, 268, 302, 338, 368, 400, 442, Richard P. Seiter; p. 130, Ohio Department of Rehabilitation and Correction; p. 162, AP/Wide World Photos; p. 478, Brad Markel/Getty Images, Inc.-Liaison; p. 506, © Liaison/Tim Chapman/Newsmakers/Online USA. Credits for all other photos appear on the appropriate pages within the text.

Pearson Prentice Hall™ is a trademark of Pearson Education, Inc.
Pearson® is a registered trademark of Pearson plc
Prentice Hall® is a registered trademark of Pearson Education, Inc.

Pearson Education LTD.
Pearson Education Singapore, Pte. Ltd
Pearson Education, Canada, Ltd
Pearson Education–Japan
Pearson Education Australia PTY, Limited
Pearson Education North Asia Ltd
Pearson Educaçion de Mexico, S.A. de C.V.
Pearson Education Malaysia, Pte. Ltd

10 9 8 7 6 5 4 3 2
ISBN 0-13-142131-X

DEDICATED TO

All the correctional staff that I have worked with over the years. You are dedicated, professional public servants.

Brief Contents

Preface xvii
Acknowledgments xxi
About the Author xxiii

Part I: Putting Corrections in Perspective

CHAPTER 1: The History of Crime and Corrections 2
CHAPTER 2: Sentencing and the Correctional Process 34

Part II: Correctional Policy and Operations

CHAPTER 3: Jails 62
CHAPTER 4: Probation and Intermediate Sanctions 98
CHAPTER 5: Prison Systems 130
CHAPTER 6: Parole and Prisoner Reentry 163

Part III: Correctional Clients

CHAPTER 7: The Clients of Adult Correctional Agencies 206
CHAPTER 8: The Juvenile Correctional System 240
CHAPTER 9: Special Offenders 268

Part IV: Prison Life

CHAPTER 10: The Management of Prisons 302
CHAPTER 11: Prison Life for Inmates 338
CHAPTER 12: The World of Prison Staff 368
CHAPTER 13: Custody and Treatment 400
CHAPTER 14: Legal Issues and the Death Penalty 442

Part V: Correctional Challenges

CHAPTER 15: Issues in Corrections 478
CHAPTER 16: Questions Regarding the Future of Corrections 506

Glossary 535
Index 545

Contents

Preface xvii
About the Author xxi
Acknowledgments xxiii

Part I: Putting Corrections in Perspective

CHAPTER 1: The History of Crime and Corrections 2

Introduction 4
Defining Corrections 4
    What Is Corrections? 4
    The Mission of Corrections 5
    Corrections as a Part of the Criminal Justice System 6
    The Correctional Funnel and Correctional Policy 8
Why Should Students Study Corrections? 9
Theories of Crime and Punishment 16
Early Responses to Crime 17
The Development of the Prison 20
    The Walnut Street Jail 20
    The Pennsylvania System 21
    The Auburn System 22
Prisons throughout the Last Two Centuries 22
The Sentencing Goals of Corrections 25
    Punishment 26
    Deterrence 27
    Incapacitation 27
    Rehabilitation 29
    Restitution 30

Chapter Review
Summary 32
Review Questions 32
Endnotes 33

CHAPTER 2: Sentencing and the Correctional Process 34

Introduction 36
Pretrial Correctional Activities 36
    Diversion from the Criminal Justice System 37
    Pretrial Detention in Jail 38
    Release from Pretrial Detention on Bail 39
    Alternatives to Bail 40
    Pretrial Service Programs 41
The Role of Plea Bargaining and Sentencing 42
Presentencing Correctional Activities 43

Purposes of the PSI 44
Collecting Information for the PSI 45
Contents of the PSI 46
The Sentencing Decision 47
Sentencing Options 47
Sentencing Models 50
Judicial Discretion in Sentencing 52
Drug Courts: A Creative Sentencing Option 56

Chapter Review
Summary 60
Review Questions 60
Endnotes 61

Part II: Correctional Policy and Operations

CHAPTER 3: Jails 62

Introduction 64
The History of Jails 64
Current Jail Operations 65
Role and Functions of Jails 65
The Organization of Jails 65
Jail Populations 66
The Increasing Use of Jails 69
Admissions and Length of Stay 70
The Jail Process and Daily Operations 70
Jail Classification 73
Jail Staffing 74
Design and Supervision in Jails 75
Creating a Secure Setting Inside the Jail 77
Issues in Jails 84
Responding to Jail Crowding 86
Legal Issues for Jails 89
Dealing with Mentally Ill Offenders 90
Preventing Suicides 92

Chapter Review
Summary 95
Review Questions 96
Endnotes 96

CHAPTER 4: Probation and Intermediate Sanctions 98

Introduction 100
The History of Probation 100

Modern Probation Operations 101
    Supervision 102
    Conditions of Probation 103
    Revocation of Probation 106
Issues Regarding Probation 109
    Effectiveness 109
    A Changing Style of Supervision 110
    Probation Classification Systems 111
Intermediate Sanctions 115
    Defining Intermediate Sanctions 115
    Types of Intermediate Sanctions 115
    The Effectiveness of Intermediate Sanctions 125

Chapter Review
Summary 127
Review Questions 127
Endnotes 128

CHAPTER 5: Prison Systems 130

Introduction 132
Current Status of Prisons in the United States 132
    The Role and Mission of Prisons 133
    Growth of the Prison Population 135
Adult Prison Systems in the United States 142
    The Federal Prison System 143
    State Prison Systems 148
    Other Public Correctional Systems 153
    Private Correctional Systems 154
A Question of Policy 159

Chapter Review
Summary 159
Review Questions 160
Endnotes 160

CHAPTER 6: Parole and Prisoner Reentry 162

Introduction 164
The History of Parole 164
    Maconochie and the Mark System 165
    Walter Crofton and the Irish System 165
Parole Begins in the United States 167
    Parole and the Medical Model 167
    Attacks on the Medical Model and Parole 170

    Alternatives to Indeterminate Sentencing 172

    Problems with Moving Away from Indeterminate Sentences 175

The Current Status of Parole in the United States 175

Operations of Parole 176

    The Organization of Parole Boards 176

    The Parole Hearing 180

    Supervision and Conditions of Parole 182

Terminating Parole Supervision 188

    Revoking Parole 188

    Legal Issues Regarding Revocation 191

Effectiveness of Parole 191

Prisoner Reentry: A Changing Phenomenon 194

    Changes over the Past Two Decades 196

    Issues Faced by Offenders Returning to the Community 196

    What Can Be Done to Improve Prisoner Reentry? 201

Chapter Review

Summary 202

Review Questions 203

Endnotes 203

Part III: Correctional Clients

CHAPTER 7: The Clients of Adult Correctional Agencies 206

Introduction 208

Overview of Adult Offenders 209

    Gender, Race, and Ethnicity 210

    Age of Offenders 214

    Types of Offenses and Length of Confinement 215

Male Offenders 218

    Male Offenders and Violence 218

    Male Prisoners 220

Female Offenders 223

    Women in Prison 226

    Special Issues and Needs of Female Inmates 227

    Legal Issues Regarding Parity for Female Inmates 233

    Alternatives to Prison for Women Offenders 234

Chapter Review

Summary 237

Review Questions 238

Endnotes 238

CHAPTER 8: The Juvenile Correctional System 240

Introduction 242
The Problem of Juvenile Crime 242
Development of the Juvenile Justice System 247
   Waiver of Juvenile Offenders 249
Categories of Juvenile Offenders 250
The Juvenile Justice Process 253
   Steps in the Juvenile Justice Process 254
Legal Issues Affecting the Juvenile Justice System 259
Issues in Juvenile Corrections 261
   Juvenile Gangs and Juvenile Crime 262
   Responding to Juvenile Drug Crime 263

Chapter Review
Summary 266
Review Questions 266
Endnotes 267

CHAPTER 9: Special Offenders 268

Introduction 270
Juvenile Offenders in Adult Criminal Courts 270
Drug Offenders 273
Mentally Ill Offenders 276
Aging Offenders 281
Violent Offenders 283
Sex Offenders 288
   Treatment and Management of Sex Offenders 290
   Sex Offender Recidivism 291
Offenders with Infectious Diseases 292
   HIV/AIDS 292
   Tuberculosis 296

Chapter Review
Summary 297
Review Questions 299
Endnotes 300

Part IV: Prison Life

CHAPTER 10: The Management of Prisons 302

Introduction 304
The Organization of Prisons 304
    State Departments of Corrections 305
    Prison Staff Organization 313
Unit Management 317
Controlling Inmate Behavior 322
    Policies and Procedures 322
    Inmate Classification 324
    Inmate Discipline 329
The Role of Staff in a Prison 332
    Recruiting and Hiring Correctional Staff 332
    Collective Bargaining within Correctional Agencies 334

Chapter Review
Summary 336
Review Questions 337
Endnotes 337

CHAPTER 11: Prison Life for Inmates 338

Introduction 340
Prison Life for Male Offenders 340
    Prison Culture and the Inmate Code 342
    Violence in Prisons 346
    Gangs in Prisons 348
    Homosexual Behavior in Male Prisons 353
    Drugs in Prisons 355
    The Function of Humor in Prison 357
Prison Life for Female Offenders 359
    The History of Women's Prisons 359
    Culture in Women's Prisons 362

Chapter Review
Summary 364
Review Questions 365
Endnotes 365

CHAPTER 12: The World of Prison Staff 368

Introduction 370
The Jobs of Prison Staff 371
The Organization of a Prison 372

Prison Chain of Command 372
The Warden 374
    The Role of Modern Wardens 375
Life for a Correctional Officer 379
    The Daily Grind 380
    Stress and Danger 382
    Gaining Compliance of Inmates 383
    Correctional Officer Careers 384
The Roles of Other Prison Staff 386
    Other Security Personnel 387
    Treatment and Program Staff 387
    Services Staff 387
The Prison Culture for Staff 389
Female Correctional Officers in Men's Prisons 392

Chapter Review
Summary 397
Review Questions 398
Endnotes 398

CHAPTER 13: Custody and Treatment 400
Introduction 402
Security and Custody within a Prison 402
Security and Custody Functions 404
    Inmate Accountability 405
    Control of Contraband 409
    Special Housing Units 412
Inmate Riots and Disturbances 414
    Planning for Emergency Situations 418
    Emergency Response Teams 418
Treatment and Programs within a Prison 422
Identifying Inmate Needs 423
Types of Prison Programs 424
    Educational and Vocational Programs 424
    Mental Health Programs 428
    Substance Abuse Programs 431
    Prison Work Programs 433
    Religious Programs 436
    Recreation Programs 436

Chapter Review
Summary 439
Review Questions 439
Endnotes 440

CHAPTER 14: Legal Issues and the Death Penalty 442

Introduction 444
Legal Issues Regarding Inmates 444
The Development of Inmate Legal Rights 445
The Bill of Rights and Congressional Actions Providing Inmate Rights 446
Specific Rights of Prisoners 448
   Conditions of Confinement 449
   Religious Freedom 450
   Medical Care 452
   First Amendment Rights 453
   Access to the Courts 454
   Fourth Amendment Rights 454
   Inmate Discipline 455
Limiting Litigation by Inmates 456
Capital Punishment 458
The History of Capital Punishment in the United States 459
Legal and Statutory Provisions for the Death Penalty 460
Current Statistics Regarding Capital Punishment 465
   Death Row Prisoners 465
   Executions 467
   Operational Problems 469
Reasons for Capital Punishment 470
   Deterrence 471
   Retribution 471
   Incapacitation 471
   Cost 472
Public Opinion Regarding the Death Penalty 472
The Potential for Error 472

Chapter Review
Summary 475
Review Questions 476
Endnotes 476

Part V: Correctional Challenges

CHAPTER 15: Issues in Corrections 478

Introduction 480
Prison and Jail Populations 480
Politics and Policy 484
Tightening Budgets 488
   Reducing the Inmate Population 490
   Developing Community Alternatives to Prison 491

    Creating Revenues by Correctional Agencies 491
    Contracting with the Private Sector 492
Accreditation of Correctional Programs 495
Importance of Staff Diversity 497
Effectiveness of Treatment Programs 501

Chapter Review
Summary 502
Review Questions 503
Endnotes 503

CHAPTER 16: Questions Regarding the Future of Corrections 506
Introduction 508
Can Our Current Approach to Sentencing and Corrections Be Successful
    and Continue? 508
Will Rehabilitation Continue as a Primary Correctional Goal? 511
Will Supervision of Offenders in the Community Change in Approach? 515
Do We Need a New Paradigm for Sentencing and Corrections? 518
Can We Reduce the Impact of Prisonization and Improve the Successful Reentry
    of Prisoners to the Community? 522
Is Corrections a Good Career Choice for Me? 526

Chapter Review
Summary 529
Review Questions 531
Endnotes 531

Glossary 535
Index 545

As an author and a former correctional practitioner, I am very excited about this introductory textbook on corrections. I have spent most of my life working in the correctional field and have had the opportunity to work in many different situations and with many dedicated people. I am pleased to be able to pass on some of my experiences and information, gathered over twenty-five years, to students studying corrections and perhaps considering corrections as a career.

The goal of *Corrections: An Introduction* is to provide students with a practical understanding of today's corrections operations. Correctional history and theory are included; however, the focus is on what we do in corrections, why we do it, and what challenges face contemporary correctional staff and administrators. The text also presents case studies, information on careers, and real examples of situations to help students understand the practical aspects of working in corrections.

Organization of the Text

The text has five parts and sixteen chapters. In Part 1, students learn about theories of crime and how society responded to crime before the eighteenth century, the development of formal correctional practices, and the theories that are embraced by various correctional approaches. In addition, students are presented with the processes (pretrial diversion, bail, jail, finding of guilt) that lead up to sentencing, various sentencing approaches and options, postsentencing processes for managing offenders, and the activities and decision points surrounding the actual sentencing decision.

In Part 2, students learn how the various elements of the correctional processes operate, including jails and detention facilities, probation and intermediate sanctions, prisons, parole, and prisoner reentry. Chapter 3 addresses the operations and issues surrounding contemporary use of jails. Included are issues of management, jail crowding, legal liabilities, and offender issues such as suicide prevention, mentally ill offenders, and classification. Chapter 4 reviews the operation of probation, including conditions, supervision styles, and revocation; the entire range of intermediate sanctions between probation and prison is described and issues are addressed. Chapter 5 deals with the role and mission of prisons, the increasing reliance on prisons as a criminal sanction and the resulting challenge of increased capacity and crowding, and the various prison systems within the United States. The various levels of security and operations within American prisons are described. Chapter 6 reviews the mechanisms for release from prison. The history and current operations of parole, preparation for release, challenges facing ex-prisoners as they return to the community, supervision requirements, revocation processes, and successful completion of supervision are described.

In Part 3, perspectives regarding various categories of correctional clients are presented. Chapter 7 provides general background information regarding male and female adult offenders including the offenses they commit, the needs they have, and the special circumstances they face while fulfilling their sentences. Chapter 8 describes the system and processes for handling juvenile offenders separately from the adult system. The history, theories, practices, and issues of juvenile correctional systems are presented. Chapter 9 covers offenders with special characteristics that require management or processing outside the "norm" of typical correctional operations. It includes descriptions of these issues as they relate to drug offenders, the mentally ill, aging offenders, violent offenders, sex offenders, and offenders with serious infectious diseases.

Part 4 describes life in prison through the eyes of inmates and staff, while addressing how correctional administrators organize and manage prisons, how custody and treatment are provided, how legal rights of inmates have been developed and are managed, and how the death penalty is carried out in the United States. In Chapter 10, the overall approach that administrators take to create a prison environment that is safe, secure, and provides rehabilitative opportunities is presented. In Chapter 11, the world of inmates is described, and many issues such as violence, drug use, homosexuality, and the inmate culture are discussed. Chapter 12 describes the life of those who work in a prison and the challenges and stresses they deal with on a daily basis. In Chapter 13, the sometimes conflicting areas of custody and treatment are explained. Chapter 14 details the historical development of legal rights for inmates, citing legal cases and illustrating the way case law has built modern expectations for standard operations within prisons. The controversial use of the death penalty is also presented, including its history in the United States, the legal debates, the processes used to carry it out, and the pros and cons of the death penalty as a sentencing option.

Finally, in Part 5, the challenges facing corrections now and in the future are presented. Chapter 15 addresses issues regarding the management of correctional processes, including accreditation, privatization, staff diversity, overcrowding, tightening budgets, program effectiveness, and political intervention. Chapter 16 details the challenges that face correctional administrators over the next several years. This chapter asks several questions that reflect issues surrounding our current sentencing approach, rehabilitation as a correctional goal, community supervision, prisonization, and corrections as a career.

To give students a realistic and practical understanding of modern corrections, this textbook includes several features and approaches that are designed to heighten the learning process and make it interesting for students. Chapters include realistic experiences and insights into the world of today's correctional operations.

Features

This text includes several pedagogical features that should make it interesting and informative for students.

- Chapters include a brief segment on history and theory, but focus on the actual operations of prisons, community corrections, and jails. Students are able to experience the challenges that correctional workers face and the practical applications they use to meet these challenges.
- Several **Case Studies** of real issues that have confronted staff who try to manage today's correctional populations are presented. Some of these case studies describe how certain people look at their jobs or issues facing them, and others are a brief interview with someone working in the field described in the chapter.
- Each chapter includes a feature titled **A Look Into . . .** , which provides students with additional practical examples of the world of corrections through interviews and in-depth examinations of real-life correctional situations.
- Students will also enjoy and benefit from a feature titled **Your Career in Corrections**. Every chapter includes descriptions of jobs that students may carry out as a specific correctional application is described. For instance, in a discussion of halfway houses, a career box notes the types of jobs available to

staff entering this field, what they do, the requirements of the job, and the possible pay and work conditions they will face.

■ Another interesting feature in every chapter is **You Make the Decision**, which presents real situations that someone working in the field may encounter. For instance, in a discussion of probation, students have to struggle with the decision of whether to revoke a person's probation for failing to follow all conditions of supervision; the chapter regarding parole presents several scenarios for prisoners appearing before the parole board, and students must decide whether to grant parole.

■ A valuable learning approach of the book is to focus on the policy implications of different theories and perspectives regarding corrections. All chapters address the practical issues of modern correctional policy development, and some chapters include a feature titled **A Question of Policy**. By addressing policy, students gain insight into the critical policy challenges that result from today's practice of corrections. The dilemmas that face elected officials and correctional administrators in trying to create a policy that is most effective and efficient and contributes significantly to the accomplishment of correctional goals are presented.

■ To take advantage of my many years of practical experience, every chapter includes a feature titled **An Insider's Experience**. In this unique feature, I describe events or circumstances that I had to address during my career and share some very personal thoughts and observations.

■ Each chapter also includes Key Terms, Chapter Objectives, and Review Questions. As students begin to read a chapter, it will be helpful to read the objectives; after reading the chapter, they can use the questions to reinforce the most important aspects of the chapter.

I hope that students enjoy this textbook and find it easy to read and study, and that the practical perspectives motivate students to consider a career in corrections. Even if students decide that a career opportunity in corrections is not for them, corrections is such an important component in today's criminal justice system that an understanding of how programs operate and how much they cost is important to taxpayers who must support their operation.

Richard P. Seiter, Ph.D.

I am a very fortunate person. I was able to write this book because I have a tremendous group of people who help and support me in my personal life as well as in my working life. I would first like to thank the many correctional colleagues who assisted me by granting interviews, providing advice, and giving me information that was used both for the general information in the book and to make the book come to life for students through their personal stories and situations. I also want to thank my colleagues at Saint Louis University, who are an outstanding group of educators and academics, which they demonstrate every day in their classrooms and offices as they interact with and guide students.

Our staff and student workers at the university have also been a great help on this project. Cindy Lennox, our department secretary, provided assistance in many ways. The primary student worker who assisted throughout the project was Kim Fowler. She conducted background research, created the glossary, and assisted with several other administrative details of preparing the manuscript. Jennifer Dienhart assisted with preparation of the Instructor's Manual, and Julia Ferguson, Brett Ramsey, and Lisa Eyberg also provided assistance.

I thank the criminal justice and marketing group at Pearson/Prentice Hall, especially Frank Mortimer, Executive Editor for the Criminal Justice Section, who encouraged me to write this book and provided guidance regarding the targeted audience and and how to distinguish the book from other introductory texts. I also thank Susan Beauchamp, Development Editor, who worked with me throughout the preparation, review, and revision of the manuscript. In addition, I thank the following reviewers selected by Pearson/Prentice Hall to give me feedback throughout the writing process: Bruce Bikle, California State University–Sacramento, Sacramento, California; Robert Bing, University of Texas–Arlington, Arlington, Texas; Vicky Dorworth, Montgomery College, Rockville, Maryland; David Graff, Kent State University–Tuscarawas, New Philadelphia, Ohio; David McElreath, Washburn University, Topeka, Kansas; and David Streater, Catawba Valley Community College, Hickory, North Carolina. Their advice was always thoughtful, on point, and helpful in improving the text and making it more readable and useful for students of corrections.

I also thank the correctional agencies that were so helpful in giving me the opportunity to take pictures of their programs and facilities. Of greatest assistance was the Ohio Department of Rehabilitation and Correction. Several individuals helped arrange the photo sessions and cooperated as I took pictures. Anne Diestel, archivist at the Federal Bureau of Prisons, provided several pictures from that agency. In addition, staff members at the Correctional Corporation of America David L. Moss Criminal Justice Center and the Cimarron Correctional Facility were extremely helpful and cooperative. I also appreciate the assistance of the St. Louis County Justice Center and the St. Louis City Jail for allowing pictures to be taken of their facilities.

Finally, I thank my family and friends, who encouraged and supported me throughout the process. My wife, Riffi O'Brien (along with Meg and Mike), encouraged, sympathized, and tolerated me when I ran the gamut of emotions from excited to discouraged to just tired of all the work. My son Matt has been through this process with me before, and he continues to provide his commonsense advice and humor as I get bogged down in the work of preparing a book of this magnitude.

His personal work ethic is a constant motivation when I think I am working too hard. At age twenty-one, he amazes me with his energy, drive, ambition, and the sacrifices he makes to reach his goals. I only hope to achieve his level of commitment some day.

Thanks to all of you. I am a very lucky person.

Richard P. Seiter, Ph.D.

Richard P. Seiter has twenty-five years of experience as a correctional administrator. He worked in two Federal Bureau of Prisons institutions (the Federal Correctional Institution in Pleasanton, California, and the U.S. Penitentiary in Leavenworth, Kansas), served as warden of two others (the Federal Prison Camp in Allenwood, Pennsylvania, and the Federal Correctional Institution in Greenville, Illinois), and was both Assistant Director for Industries, Education, and Training and Chief Operating Officer of Federal Prison Industries.

Dr. Seiter was Director of the Ohio Department of Rehabilitation and Correction, responsible for an annual budget of $400 million, twenty prisons, 8,000 staff members, and 30,000 inmates. He also oversaw the construction of 12 new state prisons at a cost of more than $500 million.

Dr. Seiter was the first Superintendent of the National Academy of Corrections and is currently director of the Criminal Justice Program at Saint Louis University.

Corrections

Chapter 1

Published by William Miller Albemarle Street, Jan'y 1803. Nº 30.

The History of Crime and Corrections

KEY TERMS

penology
penitentiary
corrections
penal code
Cesare Beccaria
Classical School
Jeremy Bentham
hedonistic calculus
Positive School
Cesare Lombroso
Neoclassical School
John Howard
Walnut Street Jail
Pennsylvania system
Auburn system
Irish System
Reformatory Era
Industrial Prison Era
Period of Transition
hands-off doctrine
Rehabilitative Era
medical model
reintegration
"Nothing works"
Retributive Era
punishment
retribution
test of proportionality
specific deterrence
general deterrence
incapacitation
selective incapacitation
rehabilitation
recidivism
restitution
restorative justice

Introduction

What is corrections, how does it relate to the other components of the criminal justice system, how does it operate, how well does it work, and why should it be studied? This textbook is designed to answer these questions. While these questions are worded as if "corrections" is a clearly defined and well-bounded activity, this is far from the case. Corrections includes a wide variety of activities, each with a wide variety of emphases and goals; some of the components have direct relationships with other correctional or criminal justice activities, and others operate almost independently. Corrections has been described as a system of fully integrated services and functions, and it has been described as a nonsystem with no coordination or shared mission by any of its components.

Throughout this text, students will learn how government, private, and not-for-profit agencies all contribute to corrections and the correctional process. The text covers history, theories, operations, costs, and effectiveness. It goes beyond providing students a historical perspective, an encyclopedia of terms, and general information regarding corrections. In addition, the text emphasizes practice as well as theory; the challenges to accomplishing the mission of correctional agencies; and the roles of the people who work in, are supervised by, or are affected by the correctional process. The goal of this textbook is to help students understand (1) how various factors throughout the historical development of corrections influenced the basic operating foundations of today, (2) the linkage of theory and practice, and (3) the difficulty in carrying out the functions of correctional agencies in a cost-efficient manner.

Defining Corrections

What is meant by "corrections"? Why do we even use the term *corrections* to refer to the legal punishment of criminal offenders? Does the use of the term *corrections* mean that it is the principal function of the management of criminals after sentencing? In this section, we define *corrections;* address these questions; and look at the historical development of terms, titles, and corresponding philosophies as our current practices evolved from the earliest approaches to punishing criminals. Terminology in any discipline usually comes from the role, mission, and expectations of the activities that are described. For our study of corrections, we examine the use of various terminology over time, how it relates to the mission of corrections, and how corrections fits into the larger activities of the criminal justice system.

WHAT IS CORRECTIONS?

Corrections is an interesting term to use to describe the punishment of offenders for the crimes they have committed. However, *corrections* offers a broader perspective on how agencies deal with criminal offenders. Previously, the term **penology** was used instead of corrections. *Penal* is defined as pertaining to or imposing punishment, and is a derivation of the Latin term *peonalis,* meaning "punishment." Penology is simply the study of punishment. Until the 1950s, the functions, components, and actions of carrying out criminal sanctions regularly used the term *penal,* and penal institutions (prisons) and penal systems (organizations to carry out punishment) emphasized the principal function of implementing punishment for agencies handling criminal offenders after their sentencing.

However, ever since the birth of the United States and the creation of the prison as a method for punishment in the late eighteenth century, prisons and other correctional agencies have played a broader role. The Walnut Street Jail, established in 1790 as the first prison designed to house sentenced offenders in the United States, had reformation of the offender as its primary objective. Inmates were expected to

Penology

the study of the use of punishment for criminal acts

read the Bible, reflect on their wrongdoing, and do penance for their crimes. Hence, **penitentiary** was established as the term used for secure facilities used to hold offenders serving a criminal sentence.

Penology is the study of punishment. However, this term generally included a much broader focus than simply punishment, and effectively covered the theories, activities, and operations of carrying out the criminal sentence, whether in a prison or in the community. During the 1950s, the nation's penal system evolved such that the rehabilitation of offenders replaced punishment as its primary objective. This philosophical change affected theory and practice, and the term *penology* was replaced by the term **corrections**. For purposes of this textbook, *corrections* is defined as the range of community and institutional sanctions, treatment programs, and services for managing criminal offenders. As such, corrections includes functions such as the supervision and monitoring of offenders in the community, the secure holding of inmates in prisons, the provision of treatment for problems such as drug addiction or mental illness, and residential and other services provided to inmates as a transition from prison to the community.

In most diagrams of the criminal justice system, corrections is illustrated as the functions for dealing with criminal offenders after a court sentences them. However, the boundaries of corrections have expanded, and corrections now also relates to the detention in jails of offenders charged with crimes, as well as pretrial services such as supervising offenders released on bail. This broader characterization of corrections acknowledges that correctional agencies are often required to deal with offenders who have not yet been found guilty and sentenced to a punishment. This broader definition also makes the establishment of a mission for corrections difficult and complex.

THE MISSION OF CORRECTIONS

A mission is the statement of what an organization is to accomplish. Eadie defines the mission of an organization as "a statement of its basic purposes, often in terms of broad outcomes that it is committed to achieving or the major functions it carries out."[1] The mission of corrections has traditionally been to implement court-prescribed sentences for criminal violators or to carry out the sentence of the

Penitentiary
the term first used to describe secure facilities used to hold offenders serving a criminal sentence. Still used today for some older or highly secure prisons.

Corrections
the range of community and institutional sanctions, treatment programs, and services for managing criminal offenders

Corrections includes counseling and offender treatment programs, as well as prisons, concrete, and bars.
Photo by Richard P. Seiter.

court. This mission statement is rather narrow and seems to indicate a lack of control or initiative by correctional agencies as to their functions and how they are to carry them out. However, most contemporary correctional administrators recognize a much broader mission and responsibility. The more complete mission of corrections is to protect society. Protection of society is accomplished through a combination of surveillance and control of offenders, of treatment and rehabilitative services, and of incapacitation during the service of a prison sentence.

In practice, correctional agencies fulfill their mission by assisting courts in the decision to grant bail, by providing the courts with information to guide sentencing, by supervising offenders in the community under court jurisdiction, by imprisoning offenders who receive a sentence of incarceration from the courts, and by overseeing inmates' reentry to the community. The short-term protection of society occurs as correctional agencies either detain offenders in jail or incarcerate them in prison, thus separating them from society and keeping them from further victimizing citizens in the community. The longer-term protection of society results from correctional agencies providing treatment and services to help offenders become less likely or less motivated to return to a life of crime, and more likely to become productive and law-abiding citizens.

CORRECTIONS AS A PART OF THE CRIMINAL JUSTICE SYSTEM

Figure 1.1 is an illustration of the criminal justice system. There are generally thought to be three major components of the criminal justice system: the police, courts, and corrections. In the ideal process of criminal justice, the police investigate crimes and arrest suspects, handing over the results of their efforts (investigative information and evidence) to the court system. Prosecutors determine whether a crime has been committed and whether there is probable cause to believe that the suspect has committed the crime. If so, the courts then oversee a determination of guilt for the suspect. If the offender is found guilty, the courts sentence him or her to an appropriate sentence within the state **penal code**, the legislative authorization to provide a specific range of punishment for a specific crime. Once the offender is sentenced, correctional agencies carry out the sentence.

Penal code

a legislative authorization to provide a specific range of punishment for a specific crime

However, where the correctional system begins and ends is not as clear as indicated in Figure 1.1. The figure illustrates probation, prison, parole, residential community placement, and revocation of probation and parole, appropriately depicted as part of the "corrections" section of the criminal justice process. However, supervision during bail, detention in jail, diversion programs, and intermediate sanctions are not included as part of corrections. Yet these functions are acknowledged as legitimate components of corrections, especially over the past decade, as corrections (as well as other criminal justice components) has expanded its activities and functions across traditional lines and boundaries. Today, correctional agencies supervise offenders released during the pretrial process; police assist probation officers in supervising community offenders; and courts maintain jurisdiction and supervise offenders even after their release from prison. All of this makes a simple illustration of the criminal justice system and delineation of the major components almost impossible.

Even within the grouping of activities that are referred to as corrections, there are differences among jurisdictions. No one system of corrections exists across the country. There are three governmental levels of correctional systems: federal, state, and thousands of local (county and city) correctional systems. In each state, the role distinctions between what is done at the state versus the local level are different. Some state correctional systems operate all probation activities, while in other states, counties carry out probation. Some states have a sentencing structure that includes release on parole; others do not. And in some states, there are statewide

FIGURE 1.1

THE CRIMINAL JUSTICE SYSTEM

7

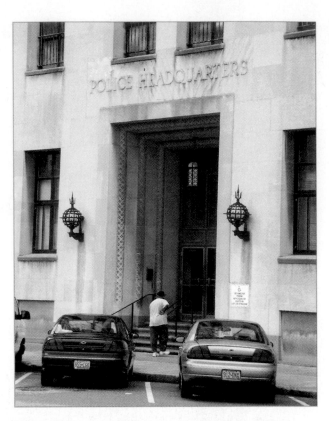

Corrections is one of the three elements of the criminal justice system. Police and courts are the other two.
Photo by Richard P. Seiter.

or regionally operated jails, and in others jails are solely within the domain of the city or county.

THE CORRECTIONAL FUNNEL AND CORRECTIONAL POLICY

As one of the three major components of the criminal justice system, corrections is believed to be responsible for administering punishment to criminals, thereby preventing future crimes through deterrence and incapacitation, limiting offenders' opportunity to commit further crimes, or reducing their inclination to commit crimes as a result of correctional treatments. The fallacy in this expectation is that the correctional system in reality handles an extremely small percentage of criminals. The "correctional funnel" shown in Figure 1.2 illustrates this phenomenon; there is a large numerical difference between the number of crimes reported and the number of offenders convicted and facing any specific correctional sanction.

As illustrated in Figure 1.2, of approximately 10 million felony crimes reported in 2000, only about 1 million individuals (10 percent) were convicted, only about 400,000 (4 percent of the number of crimes) were sent to prison, and only about 6 percent received a sentence of jail or probation. The public often believes that adopting a policy of lengthening prison sentences will deter offenders, and that keeping them in prison longer will significantly reduce crime. However, the relatively small number of crimes that result in a sentence of imprisonment makes it unlikely that even major modifications of prison sentences will have a significant impact on crime rates.

The last few sections included a description of the mission of corrections, the role of corrections within the criminal justice system, and a discussion of the cor-

THE CORRECTIONAL FUNNEL

FIGURE 1.2

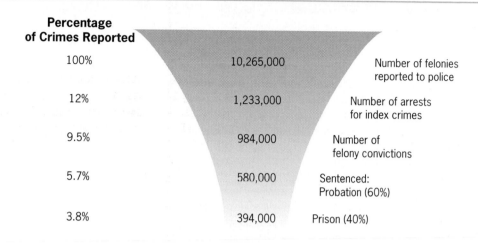

Percentage of Crimes Reported		
100%	10,265,000	Number of felonies reported to police
12%	1,233,000	Number of arrests for index crimes
9.5%	984,000	Number of felony convictions
5.7%	580,000	Sentenced: Probation (60%)
3.8%	394,000	Prison (40%)

Source: Adapted from Bureau of Justice Statistics, *Sourcebook of Criminal Justice Statistics, 2001* (Washington, D.C.: U.S. Department of Justice, 2003); and Matthew R. Durose and Patrick A. Langan, *Felony Sentences in State Courts, 2000* (Washington, D.C.: U.S. Department of Justice, Bureau of Justice, Statistics, June 2003).

rectional funnel. These three topics do not, at first reading, appear to have a common theme among them. However, they all relate to correctional policy development. The development of correctional policy, for discussion purposes in this text, is the process that includes considering the mission and role, relevant information, and the best interests of the public (in terms of issues such as safety and cost), and then deciding what broad approaches to take to best meet the goal of protecting society. The correctional funnel is a good example of how, with thoughtful examination, it can be seen that extending sentences significantly may have a deterrent and incapacitative effect on those in prison. However, since they represent such a small percentage of the overall population that commits crimes, the direct impact on a reduction of crime rates is questionable.

Throughout this textbook, the "A Question of Policy" boxes encourage discussion of some of the difficult policy issues facing public officials and correctional administrators. Staff that work in corrections to aid in the policy development process are correctional policy analysts. These positions represent interesting and valuable potential jobs for students majoring in criminal justice and corrections. The "Your Career in Corrections" box presents the role of policy analysts.

Why Should Students Study Corrections?

The criminal justice system and corrections is a "booming business." The number of clients processed and managed by the system continues to climb every year. The amount of money directed to criminal justice agencies has expanded exponentially. The availability of jobs for those seeking a profession in the criminal justice system has increased significantly. And the interest in corrections by the general public and elected officials has grown tremendously. Today, few citizens of the United States do not have some understanding and knowledge of the criminal justice system, and almost everyone has an opinion of how the system should operate or be changed. Crime and corrections have gone through a metamorphosis from an almost invisible public function to one that seems to be on the mind of almost all members of society.

The number of clients under the supervision of correctional agencies has been increasing for the past three decades. The number of offenders on probation, in prison, and parole has increased significantly. By the end of the twentieth century, more than 6 million offenders were either in prison, in jail, or under supervision in

YOUR CAREER IN CORRECTIONS — POLICY ANALYSTS

It may seem odd to start out the "Your Career in Corrections" boxes by describing the job of a policy analyst. Students seldom consider this job, and seldom do they begin a career track to achieve it. However, it is very important to "good government" that correctional policy be thoughtfully considered with full information regarding cost, effectiveness, and impact. American taxpayers contribute almost $35 billion to maintain our correctional system, while much of what we do is not based on such a consideration. This textbook emphasizes the policy choices that must be made as we reform, modify, and update correctional practices, and policy analysts can play a key role in this process.

A policy analyst who works on correctional issues can work for a variety of agencies. Most state (and some large county) correctional departments have a policy and research bureau. Their job is to conduct research and gather statistics that can assist the agency in making policy decisions, provide justification for funding, and assist in creating future strategies and directions for the agency. Legislative bodies always employ policy analysts, and some are assigned to criminal justice or correctional committees. They also conduct research on the effectiveness of correctional programs, usually to aid the legislative body in funding decisions. Some nonprofit agencies employ analysts to examine correctional issues. Groups that are interested in issues such as drug treatment, sentencing, or employment issues for offenders conduct studies to assist in their lobbying efforts to urge that certain policies be implemented. Finally, universities or other research groups often receive grants to conduct correctional research and employ researchers and analysts to examine an issue and write reports as requested by the funding agencies.

There are no reports regarding how many people work in these areas. However, at any one time, easily more than a thousand people are doing the work we have described. Depending on the sophistication of the issue, some will have a doctorate and be experts in research methodology, possibly with some educational emphasis in corrections or criminal justice research. Many others have a master's degree in sociology, criminal justice, business, or public administration, and have skills to develop research and policy analysis criteria to be able to provide answers to questions regarding effectiveness or budget impact.

These jobs are not highly visible, yet can have a tremendous impact on the development of good public policy, and save taxpayers millions of dollars. A key criterion for someone desiring to work in this field is to be ethically and professionally grounded. Many of the employing agencies noted above may have an "answer" they are looking for to move forward on a policy they would like to see adopted, and just want the analyst to give them evidence to use in their arguments in favor of their preferred policy. However, it is critical for analysts to be above justifying a preferred position, without the true data and information to do so. Research and policy analysis should be unbiased, and show the true impact of a program or practice. Truly professional analysts will never shortcut their examination or not cite evidence contrary to their agencies desired outcome.

---

the community. Table 1.1 illustrates the growth from 1980 until 2001, during which there was a 251 percent increase in the number of offenders on probation, a 243 percent increase in the number of offenders in jail, a 316 percent increase in the number of inmates in prison, and a 231 percent increase in the number of offenders on parole.

This growth has been the most dramatic over the past five years (see Figure 1.3), and is expected to continue to grow, but at a slower pace, over the next decade. This continued growth in offenders under correctional supervision will generate a comparable growth in the amount of money required to operate correctional agencies.

In fiscal year 1991, state and federal adult correctional agency budgets totaled just $18.1 billion. By fiscal year 2001, these budgets almost doubled to $35.6 billion and represented 4.3 percent of the total budget of the jurisdiction.[2] Figure 1.4

TABLE 1.1	Number of People under Correctional Supervision				
	Probation	**Jail**	**Prison**	**Parole**	**Total**
1980	1,118,097	183,988	319,598	220,438	1,842,100
1981	1,225,934	196,785	360,029	225,539	2,008,300
1982	1,357,264	209,582	402,914	224,604	2,194,400
1983	1,582,947	223,551	423,898	246,440	2,476,800
1984	1,740,948	234,500	448,264	266,992	2,690,700
1985	1,968,712	256,615	487,593	300,203	3,013,100
1986	2,114,621	274,444	526,436	325,638	3,241,100
1987	2,247,158	295,873	562,814	355,505	3,461,400
1988	2,356,483	343,569	607,766	407,977	3,715,800
1989	2,522,125	395,553	683,367	456,803	4,057,800
1990	2,670,234	405,320	743,382	531,407	4,350,300
1991	2,728,472	426,479	792,535	590,442	4,537,900
1992	2,811,611	444,584	850,566	658,601	4,765,400
1993	2,903,061	459,804	909,381	676,100	4,948,300
1994	2,981,022	486,474	990,147	690,371	5,148,000
1995	3,077,861	507,044	1,078,542	679,421	5,342,900
1996	3,164,996	518,492	1,127,528	679,733	5,490,700
1997	3,296,513	567,079	1,176,564	694,787	5,734,900
1998	3,670,441	592,462	1,224,469	696,385	6,134,200*
1999	3,779,922	605,943	1,287,172	714,457	6,340,800*
2000	3,826,209	621,149	1,316,333	723,898	6,445,100*
2001	3,932,751	631,240	1,330,980	731,147	6,592,800*

*Totals for 1998 through 2001 exclude probationers in jail or prison.

Source: U.S. Department of Justice, Bureau of Justice Statistics, "Key Facts at a Glance: Correctional Populations," http://www.ojp.usdoj.gov/bjs/glance/tables/corr2tab.htm (accessed November 8, 2002).

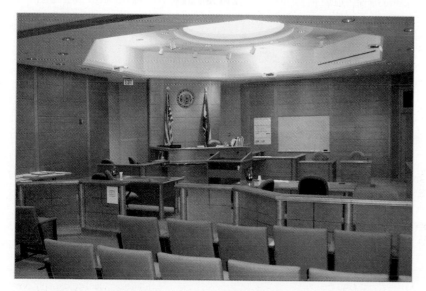

Most offenders are sentenced to probation and supervised by probation or parole officers in the community, even though most of the public thinks of prisons and jails regarding criminal offenders.
Photo by Richard P. Seiter.

ADULT CORRECTIONAL POPULATIONS, 1980–2001

FIGURE **1.3**

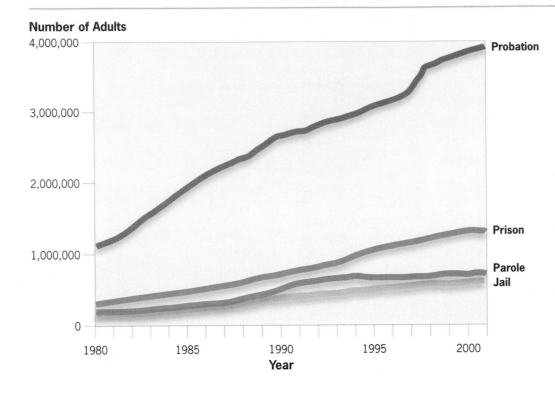

Number of Adults

Source: Data from Bureau of Justice Statistics Correctional Surveys (The Annual Probation Survey, National Prisoner Statistics, Survey of Jails, and The Annual Parole Survey) as presented in *Correctional Populations in the United States, Annual, Prisoners in 2001* and *Probation and Parole in the United States, 2001.*

DIRECT EXPENDITURES FOR CRIMINAL JUSTICE FUNCTIONS, 1982–1999

FIGURE **1.4**

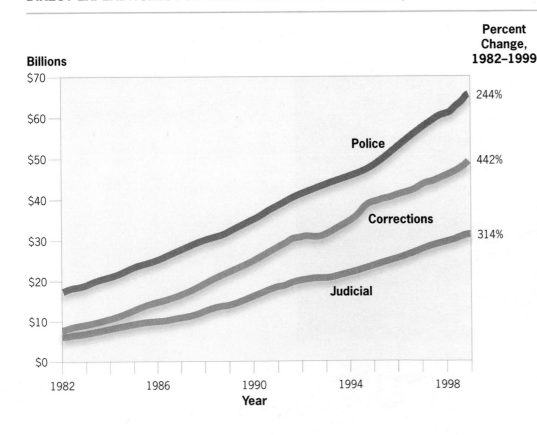

Source: U.S. Department of Justice, Bureau of Justice Statistics, "Justice Expenditure and Employment Extracts," http://www.ojp.usdojp.gov/bjs/glance/exptyp.htm (accessed November 8, 2002).

illustrates the direct expenditure for all criminal justice functions from 1982 through 1999. Spending for police increased 244 percent, and spending for the judiciary increased 314 percent. However, expenditures for corrections increased 442 percent, far exceeding the increase in police and judicial spending. It is interesting to note the factors driving the increase in overall spending for adult correctional agencies. Inflation and increases in employee salaries and benefits cause some of the budget increase. The cost per inmate per day has increased only from $48.07 in 1990[3] to $61.04 in 2000.[4] During this period, the inmate population for these agencies increased 84 percent, from 750,000 to 1,380,000.[5] The increase in demand for services (housing more inmates) has almost entirely triggered the increased costs.

Just as budgets for prison operations have increased, the budgets for probation and parole functions have also increased. The average budget for state probation and parole agencies more than doubled from $34.3 million in 1992 to $74.2 million in 2001.[6] On January 1, 2001, these state agencies supervised 2.55 million offenders on probation or parole, at an average cost per day of community supervision of $4.37.[7] These average costs include regular probation and parole supervision, intensive supervision with more contacts by the officer with the offender than regular probation, special supervision with programs such as a boot camp, substance abuse treatment, and electronic monitoring of offenders using such devices as an ankle bracelet or some other electronic technology used to ascertain the offenders' whereabouts.

Correctional agency spending is expected to continue to increase for the next several years. There were 41,368 new prison beds under construction in 1999, 47,476 in 2000, and 58,000 in 2001.[8] As these new beds are put to use at an average cost of over $60 per inmate per day in 2001, the budget figures will climb dramatically over the next five years. The increase in the number of correctional clients and correctional expenditures will result in more availability of criminal justice and correctional jobs for students now studying corrections.

Over the past two decades, the need has increased for staff to supervise the increasing number of criminal offenders. In 1992, there were 556,500 correctional employees throughout the United States.[9] The *Sourcebook of Criminal Justice Statistics, 2001* reports almost a 30 percent increase since that time, as there were 715,573 correctional staff working at the federal, state, and local levels in the United States in 2001.[10] Many people unfamiliar with corrections believe that only a few types of jobs are held by correctional staff. They understand what correctional officers and wardens do, and perhaps even a probation or parole officer. However, those are only a few of the types of jobs available to those seeking a career in corrections. Spertzel lists the following as examples of correctional jobs.[11] It is obvious from this list that the variety of correctional jobs both is extensive and offers opportunities for employment for students in many fields of study.

Budget administrator	Juvenile caseworker
Chaplain	Medical officer
Computer specialist	Ombudsman
Correctional officer	Personnel manager
Employee development specialist	Probation/parole officer
Facility manager	Psychologist
Financial manager	Recreation specialist
Food service manager	Safety manager
Health system administrator	Teacher
Industrial specialist	Training instructor
Institution administrator	

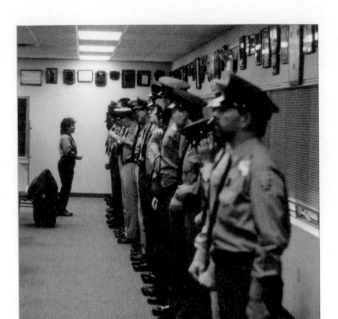

The growth in corrections has caused growth in the number of correctional staff. Here, correctional officers complete training in preparation to begin their new duties.
Courtesy of the Pennsylvania Department of Corrections.

Citizens and elected officials continue to increase their interest and oversight of the criminal justice and correctional systems. Much of this is due to the misperception that crime is increasing. From 1991 to 2000, crime decreased significantly, from a Crime Index rate of 5,897 to 4,124 offenses per every 100,000 citizens (a decrease of 30 percent), a rate not seen since 1975.[12] However, thanks to continuous media coverage of crime and criminals, when citizens were asked in polls conducted over the past ten years whether there is more crime in the United States now than one year ago, they indicated a belief that crime is increasing (see Table 1.2).

Because of citizens' general concern about crime, public officials will continue to legislate or regulate responses to the perceived crime problem. They will expand

TABLE	1.2	Attitudes toward the Crime Level in the United States: Selected Years, 1989–2000

Gallup Polling Question: "Is there more crime in the United States than there was a year ago, or less?"

	More	Less	Same*	No opinion
1989	84%	5%	5%	6%
1990	84	3	7	6
1992	89	3	4	4
1993	87	4	5	4
1996	71	15	8	6
1997	64	25	6	5
1998	52	35	8	5
2000 (August 29–Sept. 5)	47	41	7	5

*Response volunteered.

Source: The Gallup Organization, *The Gallup Poll (Online)*, http://www.gallup.com/pol/indicators/indcrime.asp.2. (accessed March 2, 2001).

penalties for offenders, increase the numbers of police, and authorize more money to be spent by the criminal justice system. This increased activity results in increased visibility for criminal justice agencies. As crime and corrections remains on the minds of the public and their elected officials, and there are demands to improve the system and find new ways of operations, those who work in the field will have to create new paradigms to make the system more efficient and enhance the level of support from the citizens whose tax dollars support it.

The question of why we should study corrections makes me recall my own career in corrections. Every chapter of this textbook contains a box titled "An Insider's Experience," in which students get a firsthand look at issues that I had to confront while working in correctional institutions and settings for more than twenty years. The first "An Insider's Experience" box is an overview of this career, with some hindsight of things that relate to why we should study corrections. As you read later features on this topic, you will better understand the jobs I had and the issues I faced.

AN INSIDER'S EXPERIENCE: Twenty Years of Correctional Work

When I was an undergraduate, I did not plan to work in the criminal justice field. In fact, I was having a tough time deciding what I wanted to major in and wanted to do after graduation. I received my B.A. in community analysis, which was a major in the College of Business at The Ohio State University that focused on a combination of sociology, urban geography, and public management of cities and towns. I went to graduate school to receive a master's degree in public administration, with plans to be a city manager. I was attracted to the idea of managing a large, complex organization, requiring communications with many different people, and serving the public good.

In graduate school, my advisor was doing some evaluative work for the Ohio department of corrections. As I worked with him on these evaluations, I came to understand that managing a correctional environment (especially a prison) had responsibilities very similar to what I found attractive in city management. I decided to focus on corrections and see where it took me. I continued my academic studies and received a Ph.D. in public administration, and then went to work for the Federal Bureau of Prisons (BOP).

I was first assigned to the research division within the BOP and was asked to conduct an evaluation of the federal halfway houses, since I had completed a similar study of Ohio's halfway houses. While I was willing to do this, I wanted to get practical experience working in a prison; I asked my bosses if I could get the evaluation started, but soon move to a prison. They were accommodating, and I became a case manager at the federal correctional institution in Pleasanton, California. It was a "co-correctional" prison holding both male and female inmates, and I was assigned to a female unit. I was nervous about working with female inmates, and quickly found that there was no limit to the issues they faced and the program needs they had. I received valuable experience in dealing with inmates with all types of problems. One of the best experiences was working with the U.S. Parole Board as they held hearings at the prison each month. The case managers wrote reports for the board with recommendations for release decisions, and I was allowed to sit in on their deliberations and see the criteria they used. Before I left, I became a unit manager and supervised an inmate housing unit and case managers, counselors, and correctional officers.

I was transferred as an assistant to the warden at the U.S. Penitentiary in Leavenworth, Kansas, a maximum-security prison holding violent and dangerous inmates. I quickly discovered the importance of security and control, as there were several acts of violence and an inmate disturbance while I was assigned to the prison. From Leavenworth, I became director of a training academy for new employees with the BOP, and learned the importance of developing skills and transferring organizational culture to new correctional employees. A major change occurred when I became the warden of a minimum-security prison, with no fences and very sophisticated white-collar offenders. Community programs such as furloughs home were used extensively at this time (late 1970s), and some of my most difficult decisions were

(continued)

whether to approve inmates to leave the prison to go home for short stays.

I then became the chief of the National Academy of Corrections, which trained state and local correctional officials in many emerging national topics. I was fortunate to be appointed director of the Ohio department of corrections in 1983, and led an agency with a budget of $400 million per year, 30,000 inmates, and 8,000 staff. The department had a poor public image, morale was low, and it was extremely overcrowded. While I was there, we designed and built ten new prisons and four community release centers, implemented unit management and objective classification, opened a training academy, and improved our image with the public, the state legislature, and the media. There were many positive outcomes of this job, but also many challenges such as the beginning of collective bargaining in the state, several hostage situations, and the murder of a staff person.

I returned to the BOP as an assistant director responsible for inmate education, training, and prison industries. The biggest challenge was overseeing the growth of prison industries to meet the growing prison population, to the point where we had annual sales of more than $400 million and employed more than 25,000 inmates. The private sector and labor unions made several complaints that prisoners should not produce products sold to the federal government, because their production meant free citizens lost jobs. This was a difficult argument to counter, so we worked hard to educate Congress about the advantages of prison industries.

I ended my career with the BOP by "activating" FCI-Greenville (Illinois), a new medium-security prison, as warden. I was the first employee and was able to oversee the hiring and training of all staff, the establishment of policies and procedures, and the development of inmate programs. There were many enjoyable parts of the activation, but soon after we opened, we had a serious riot. The riot damaged staff morale and made all of us question the physical security, procedures, and leadership style. I am pleased to say that all of these areas improved with much hard work by all staff involved. I learned from every experience I had during my correctional career, and you will read about many of them in the "An Insider's Experience" boxes presented in each chapter.

Theories of Crime and Punishment

To begin a study of corrections and its historical development, it is important to understand the evolution of theories of crime and its causes. If the purpose of the punishment is to "correct," the punishment must adequately match the reasons why the person committed the crime. There has been considerable thinking and speculation regarding crime and the response to it over the years. Many authors note the contribution of the French thinkers Montesquieu and Voltaire for encouraging thinking about crime and the then-brutal response to it.[13] However, **Cesare Beccaria**, an Italian theorist, first suggested linking crime causation to punishments in the eighteenth century, and his 1764 book *Essays on Crimes and Punishments* is often credited as the driving force in shaping contemporary thinking about crime and corrections.

Beccaria is known as the founder of the **Classical School** of criminology, the first organized theory of crime causation linked to appropriate punishments. Beccaria suggested that the purpose of punishment is utility, or the prevention of crime. Included in his principles are that crime is an injury to society, prevention (deterrence of crime) is more important than punishment, that the accused have the right to speedy trials and humane treatment, that there should be no secret accusations or torture, that certainty and swiftness of punishment (more than severity) best deter crime, and that imprisonment should be more widely used as a punishment.

Underlying Beccaria's principles was an emphasis on free will and hedonism. For punishment to deter, individuals must have freedom to choose their actions of committing crime or not. As well, they would judge the impact of that punishment on their own well-being, and make a choice regarding the seeking of pleasure and

Cesare Beccaria

an Italian theorist who in the eighteenth century first suggested linking crime causation to punishments and became known as the founder of the Classical School of criminology

Classical School

the theory linking crime causation to punishment, based on offenders' free will and hedonism avoidance of pain (hedonism). Building on these principles, **Jeremy Bentham** (1748–1832) created the concept of **hedonistic calculus,** the idea that the main objective of an intelligent man is to achieve the most pleasure and the least pain, and that individuals are constantly calculating the pluses and minuses of their potential actions. Bentham therefore theorized that to prevent crime, criminal laws should be organized so that the punishment for any act would outweigh the pleasure that would be derived from the act. Potential offenders would therefore (in line with the Classical School idea of free will) consider the consequences of their actions and be deterred from the commission of crimes.

In reaction to the development of the Classical School emphasizing free will, others began to suggest that not every criminal has complete choice over his or her criminal actions. The **Positive School** was created by **Cesare Lombroso** (1835–1909), with the suggestion that people sometimes commit acts beyond their control. Lombroso, an Italian physician, conducted research into the links between criminality and physical traits. He concluded that criminals had traits that made them throwbacks to earlier stages of evolution: they were not sufficiently developed mentally and had long arms, large amounts of body hair, prominent cheekbones, and large foreheads. This **atavism,** or the existence of features common in the early stages of human evolution, implied that criminals are born, and criminal behavior is *predetermined.*

While several later tests failed to prove Lombroso's theories of atavism, some still support the idea that some factors result in a level of predetermination (not total free will) that influences the chance that someone will commit crimes. Proponents of this approach cite the early work by Dugdale and Goddard suggesting that there are "criminal families" with a high number of members involved in crime, indicating the possibility of bad genetic influences;[14] the identification by Sheldon of certain body types that are most prone to aggression and violence;[15] or several studies addressing the possibility that chemical imbalances in the body contribute to crime.[16]

A more recent theory that has developed somewhat as a compromise to the Classical and Positive Schools is the **Neoclassical School** of criminology. Suggested by Gabriel Tarde in 1890, the Neoclassical School recognized there was much ground between total free will and determinism. Tarde argued that no one has complete free will and is uninfluenced by factors such as gender, age, or social and economic environments, yet everyone is still the "author" of his or her own action.[17] The key factors are that while the Classical School approach to holding offenders accountable makes sense, there should be some consideration of mitigating and aggravating circumstances in consideration of the criminal activities of any individual. Some authors suggest that the current "get tough" philosophies and transition to determinate sentences are most illustrative of the Neoclassical School in practice today.[18]

Modern theories seem to include a variety of factors that influence people toward criminal behavior. Several theories address the importance of psychological and social factors in determining criminality.[19] Today, however, policy regarding how to punish criminals most often follows the Classical School, emphasizing free will. It is generally believed that offenders must be held accountable and receive just punishments for their crimes. The underlying concept behind this approach is that offenders choose to commit crimes, and that punishments must be dire enough to make them consider the result (in both pleasure and pain) that will result from their criminal behavior.

Early Responses to Crime

The types of public responses to crime varied based on the beliefs regarding the causes of crime. The earliest responses to crime were extremely brutal and included torture, beatings, branding, and mutilation. These corporal punishments

Jeremy Bentham

creator of the hedonistic calculus suggesting that punishments outweigh the pleasure criminals get from committing their crime

Hedonistic calculus

the idea that the main objective of an intelligent person is to achieve the most pleasure and the least pain, and that individuals are constantly calculating the pluses and minuses of their potential actions

Positive School

the belief that criminals do not have complete choice over their criminal actions and may commit acts that are beyond their control

Cesare Lombroso

the Italian physician who in the nineteenth century founded the Positive School

Atavism

the existence of features common in the early stages of human evolution, implied the idea that criminals are born, and criminal behavior is *predetermined*

Neoclassical School

a compromise between Classical and Positive Schools; while holding offenders accountable for their crimes, allowing for some consideration of mitigating and aggravating circumstances were often an attempt to relate the punishment as closely as possible to the crime. For instance, liars had their tongues ripped out; thieves had fingers or a hand cut off; adulterers had a scarlet A branded in their foreheads to reduce their attractiveness and discourage any further adultery. Besides corporal punishment, removing the offender from the group was regularly used. Banishing someone from the tribe into the wilderness not only resulted in no likelihood of a repeat of the offense, but also often resulted in death as the person could not survive alone in the wilderness. Another way to remove offenders from society was through **transportation** or deportation. Transportation started in England and was used throughout the seventeenth and eighteenth centuries to send undesirables to the colonies in America.

Transportation

used in England during the seventeenth and eighteenth centuries to remove criminals from society by sending them to British colonies such as America

The first response to crime in the American colonies was based on the English criminal codes and incorporated the Puritans' linking of crime with sin in developing a rigid and strict system of punishments. Violations of expected community behavior were dealt with severely, using corporal and capital punishment carried out in public to deter both individual offenders and the broader community. Whipping at the town center whipping post or placement in stocks and pillories were common punishment for minor offenses such as drunkenness, slander, or stealing something of minor value. *Pillories* were wooden frames with holes for offenders' hands and head. Offenders had to stand while their hands and head were secured. *Stocks,* similar to pillories, allowed offenders to sit while their hands, head, and feet were all secured in the wooden frame. These punishments were not just for ridicule, as passersby often threw rotten vegetables or even rocks at the offender to aid in the punishment.

Branding was also a popular way to punish offenders, as their forehead, face, or hands would be branded, labeling the offender as a certain type of criminal. Adul-

Historical punishments were both painful and shameful. Stocks and pillories were used both as physical punishment and to ridicule offenders in front of their fellow townspeople, in hopes that they would end their criminal ways.
Courtesy of Corbis/Bettmann.

terers had the letter A carved into their foreheads; thieves had a T carved on their hands; blasphemers were stamped with a B, or perhaps had a hole drilled in their tongues. Torture could also include cutting a hand or finger off thieves or pickpockets; placing gossips in a *brank,* similar to a birdcage placed over their head with a sharpened shaft with barbs placed in their mouths; or subjecting other minor violators to the *ducking stool,* in which they were lowered underwater until they almost drowned. More serious offenses resulted in brutal torture such as stretching and breaking the offender's body on the rack, or in capital punishment by hanging or burning at the stake.

In colonial times, prisons were not yet developed as punishment for crimes. The colonists did use jails, copying the English system of *gaols,* for holding defendants awaiting trial or those already convicted and waiting for their corporal or capital punishment to be carried out. These jails had deplorable conditions, in which poor men, women, and children all lived together in filth, with little food or sanitary conditions. Offenders who could afford it could avoid jail via the *fee system,* an early bail system that enabled the rich to pay a fee and be released. The conditions in both English and colonial jails during the 1600s and 1700s was so deplorable that few doubted the need for reform.

The most famous jail reformer was **John Howard**, who was the sheriff of Bedfordshire, England. Howard himself, while on an English ship, was taken captive by a French privateer and subsequently imprisoned. He was later paroled to England

John Howard

the sheriff of Bedfordshire, England, who encouraged reform of English jails in the late 1700s

John Howard (1726–1790) was one of the earliest prison and jail reformers. He was appointed sheriff of Bedfordshire in 1773 and pushed for the passage of the English Penitentiary Act of 1779 to require minimum standards for jail conditions.
Courtesy of the American Correctional Association.

but never forgot the horrendous conditions resulting in the death of several English prisoners. Once he became sheriff, he was responsible for the operation of the jail, and was disturbed over the conditions and the fact that some people were there for weeks because they were unable to pay the fee required for release. He encouraged legislation to do away with the fee system and became a jail reformer, visiting gaols throughout England to observe conditions. In 1777, he wrote *The State of the Prisons in England and Wales,* which educated the public and Parliament to the problem. As a result, Parliament passed the Penitentiary Act in 1779, providing for "secure and sanitary structures, systematic inspections, abolition of fees for basic services, and a reformatory regime."[20] Howard coined the term *penitentiary* to emphasize the purpose of offenders doing penance while reflecting on their sins, rather than simply being punished brutally. These ideas not only had an effect on gaols in England, but also influenced the development of penitentiaries in America.

The Development of the Prison

As a result of the brutality and extensive use of corporal and capital punishment, some were dissatisfied with these methods of responding to criminal behavior. One reform-minded individual was William Penn, the governor of Pennsylvania. The Quakers, who settled Pennsylvania, were hardworking and economical people. They realized that the criminal codes were both inhumane and inefficient in that judges often did not follow the criminal codes because they did not want to inflict more severe punishments on relatively minor offenders. The Quakers had also been the victims of religious persecution, and freedom to choose their way of life was the reason they came to America and settled the Pennsylvania colony. Under the leadership of Penn, the Quakers replaced the current criminal code with a new one that included the following:

- The abolition of capital punishment for all crimes other than homicide
- The substitution of imprisonment at hard labor for bloody corporal punishments
- The provision of free food and lodging to inmates
- The replacement of the stocks and pillory with houses of detention[21]

THE WALNUT STREET JAIL

In the late 1700s, Dr. Benjamin Rush (one of the original signers of the Declaration of Independence) became leader of the Philadelphia Society for Alleviating the Miseries of the Public Prisons. He revived the Quaker code, which had been repealed when Penn died in 1718, and the Philadelphia Society established the first prison in the United States in 1790 by converting a wing of the Walnut Street Jail for use in housing sentenced offenders as an alternative to corporal punishment. As in John Howard's concept of the penitentiary, the **Walnut Street Jail** created a regimen of hard work and doing penance for their offenses.

Walnut Street Jail

the first penitentiary in America

Inmates were kept in individual cells and had to remain silent in order to avoid moral contamination among prisoners. Administrators of the jail did not want prisoners to even know the identity of other inmates, and would often put masks on inmates as they moved through the prison to avoid identification that would detract from the reform of prisoners in case they met each other after release. Prisoners were given work such as making handicrafts in their cells during the day, and were encouraged to read the Bible and do penance in the evenings. The overall operating theme was one of hard labor, strict discipline, solitary and silent confinement, and religious study.

THE PENNSYLVANIA SYSTEM

When the State of Pennsylvania opened its first two prisons (the Western State Penitentiary in Pittsburgh in 1826 and the Eastern State Penitentiary in Cherry Hill just outside Philadelphia in 1829), the Walnut Street Jail served as the model for their design and operation. The Western Penitentiary was an architectural nightmare, built in an octagon with small, dark cells inside the cellblocks to provide solitary confinement and no labor. It was soon modified in 1833 to provide cells on the outside of the blocks to allow light in through windows and increasing cell size to allow for inmate labor within the cell. The mistakes of the Western Penitentiary influenced and improved the design of the Eastern Penitentiary, built with seven cellblocks extending from a hub in the center of the prison walls. Each cellblock was long and narrow, with cells on the outside and a corridor down the middle. The cells had a door through the wall into a small recreation yard, in which prisoners had brief exercise periods by themselves each day.

The basis of these two prisons' operation was the same as the Walnut Street Jail: to emphasize the opportunity for prisoners to reform themselves through hard work while reflecting on their crimes. The **Pennsylvania system** was known as the "separate and silent" system, with silence enforced and inmates not allowed to see or talk with each other. Through this approach, it was believed that offenders would not be morally contaminated and be trained in crime by other prisoners. There were several problems with the Pennsylvania system. First, it was almost impossible to keep inmates from seeing and communicating with each other. Second, it was very expensive to operate, as the requirement to keep inmates separate increased the number of staff needed. Third, there was very limited productivity by inmates, as the requirement to work alone in their cells did not allow for as much production of goods for resale as was desired. Fourth, opponents of the operation of the Pennsylvania prisons suggested that the solitude imposed on inmates made many of them mentally ill. Finally, the planned operation was modified almost immediately. Two inmates were placed in a cell together so one could learn a trade from the other and increase the production of goods. The warden of the Eastern Penitentiary, Samuel Wood, used inmates as servants in his home and allowed them to communicate. The Pennsylvania system seemed doomed from

Pennsylvania system
the "separate and silent" system of prison operations emphasizing reformation and avoidance of criminal contamination

As illustrated in the design of early prisons, it would be very difficult to operate in the Pennsylvania model and keep inmates isolated from one another throughout the day.
Courtesy of the Ohio Department of Rehabilitation and Correction.

its beginning and forced prison operators in other states to search for new approaches to overcome the problems. While there was great interest in the Pennsylvania system, only two states (New Jersey and Rhode Island) adopted its "separate and silent" system. However, both soon abandoned the Pennsylvania system in favor of the improved system that was created in Auburn, New York.

THE AUBURN SYSTEM

New York opened a prison in Auburn in 1817 that was originally designed around the Pennsylvania model. Cells were back to back and stacked five tiers high to make it easier to keep inmates separate. However, this design did not allow for the use of individual recreation yards, as did the Eastern Penitentiary. The Auburn prison originally adopted the "separate and silent" system of Pennsylvania, but soon determined that the problems that plagued Pennsylvania were too serious to overcome. In 1823, a modification of the prison began, to change its unwieldy design and make it more efficient to operate.

The major change was in the Pennsylvania emphasis on keeping inmates separate. Auburn officials determined that they would continue to keep inmates in separate cells at night; however, they would allow them to congregate during the day to work in factories to improve the production of goods, which would be resold and cover some of the prison operational costs. The **Auburn system** became known as the "congregate and silent" system, as officials continued to reduce the spread of criminal ideas by inmates through silence and strict discipline. Barnes and Teeters describe the enforcement of the system through lockstep marching with eyes downcast, hard work and activity while outside cells, and prohibitions of inmates even being face to face.[22]

Auburn system

the congregate and silent operation of prisons, in which inmates were allowed to work together during the day, but had to stay separate and silent at other times

After the operation of Auburn was copied at Sing Sing prison in New York as well as at prisons in other states, the Auburn system was recognized as better than the Pennsylvania system. The prisons were cheaper to build and operate, the congregate style allowed production of goods and more income for the state, and fewer inmates developed mental health problems. Other prisons being built across the country adopted the Auburn system. The operation of prisons for sentenced offenders received international attention, and many countries sent representatives to examine the operation of both the Pennsylvania-style and Auburn-style prisons. Although the Pennsylvania style of prisons was seldom favored in the United States, most international visitors found advantages in both, and many preferred the Pennsylvania system because of its effort to avoid contamination among prisoners. During the first half of the nineteenth century, the Auburn style of silence, hard labor, separation at night and congregation during the day to maximize production of goods, and strict discipline was the approach used for most American prisons.

Prisons throughout the Last Two Centuries

During the first half of the 1800s, several large prisons were built and operated on the Auburn model. However, driven by a need to respond to the overcrowding of prisons by building new ones, U.S. prison administrators began to look for reform, and watched the early work of Captain Alexander Maconochie, who in 1840 took over the British penal colony on Norfolk Island, and Sir Walter Crofton, who built on the ideas of Maconochie as head of the Irish penal system. These two men used the concept of indeterminate sentencing, emphasizing preparing offenders for release, giving inmates an opportunity to gradually reduce control and work their way to a less restricted environment, and releasing offenders on a conditional basis when administrators determined that they were prepared to return to the community (the first effort to have conditional release that led to the development of

During the Reformatory Era, prisons were often built using imposing "gothic" style architecture, to remind inmates of their need to reform their ways.
Courtesy of the Ohio Department of Rehabilitation and Correction.

parole). This operation of the **Irish system** was seen as more humanitarian, placing an emphasis on training and preparation for release, and was believed to do more to return offenders to the community with a greater chance for success.

In 1870, a group of prison administrators, politicians, and interested citizens met in Cincinnati and formed the National Prison Association, now known as the American Correctional Association. They adopted the principles of the Irish system, emphasizing reformation rather than suffering, rewards for good behavior, and the use of indeterminate sentences to release prisoners when they were best prepared to become industrious free citizens.[23] At this point, corrections entered the **Reformatory Era**, which lasted from 1870 to 1910. To replace the emphasis on punishment and reflection on the past as with the Auburn system, the Reformatory Era provided an environment that expanded education and vocational programs and focused offenders' attention on their future.

As sensible as the Reformatory Era seemed, tremendous growth in the U.S. prison population forced another change after the turn of the century. During the first three decades of the twentieth century, the number of inmates in U.S. prisons grew more than 170 percent,[24] resulting in the construction of several new prisons designed to hold large numbers of inmates in harsh work-oriented environments. The emphasis was on having inmates work and produce products that could help make the prisons economically self-supporting. Using their free labor, prisons became very successful at this, prison management emphasized production as much as security and rehabilitation, and the volume of prison-made products sold on the open market increased considerably. Thus the **Industrial Prison Era**, from 1910 to 1935, led to the first major interest in the management of prisons by external parties.

The production and sale of prison-made products resulted in challenges to these practices from organized labor. As the country entered the Great Depression with the crash on Wall Street in 1929, Congress passed two laws to restrict competition from inmate-made goods with the private sector. The Hawes-Cooper Act in 1929 and the Ashurst-Sumners Act in 1935 and amended in 1940, severely limited the sale of prison-made products on the open market. These statutes tolled the death knell for industrial prisons, which suddenly had no

Irish system

a four-stage system of graduated release from prison and return to the community; the stages were solitary confinement, special prison, open institutions, and ticket of leave

Reformatory Era

an environment emphasizing reformation that expanded education and vocational programs and focused offenders' attention on their future

Industrial Prison Era

prison operations with emphasis on having inmates work and produce products that could help to make the prisons self-sustaining

Prisons built and operated in the first part of the 1900s were designed to hold large numbers of inmates, in tiers of cells stacked one on top of another.
Courtesy of the Federal Bureau of Prisons.

Period of Transition

an era of prison operations in which enforced idleness, lack of professional programs, and excessive size and overcrowding of prisons resulted in an increase in prisoner discontent and prison riots

Hands-off doctrine

an avoidance by the U.S. Supreme Court of judicial intervention in the operations of prisons and the judgment of correctional administrators

Rehabilitative Era

an era of prison management emphasizing the professionalizing of staff through recruitment and training and implementation of many self-improvement programs of prison management

Medical model

a theory of corrections that offenders were sick, inflicted with problems that caused their criminality, and needed to be diagnosed and treated, and that rehabilitative programs would resolve offenders' problems and prepare them for release to the community able to be productive and crime-free

Reintegration

a belief that after offenders complete their treatment in prison they need transitional care, and that the community must be involved in their successful return to society

marketplace for their goods. Thousands of inmates who had previously been working were idled, and prison administrators had to find another approach to operating prisons.

From 1935 until 1960, corrections entered the **Period of Transition**, during which enforced idleness, a lack of professional programs and the excessive size and overcrowding of prisons resulted in an increase in prisoner discontent and prison riots. Between 1950 and 1966, more than 100 riots and major disturbances occurred in American prisons.[25] Prison managers were constrained in what they could do with the large facilities designed to maximize production they had inherited, and they struggled to find alternative approaches to maintain control of large concentrations of idle prisoners. This era was greatly impacted when the U.S. Supreme Court decided *Cooper v. Pate* (1964) and ended its **hands-off doctrine**, which had restricted judicial intervention in the operations of prisons and the judgment of correctional administrators. By accepting inmate-filed cases alleging cruel and inhumane punishment under the Fourteenth Amendment to the U.S. Constitution, the Court opened Pandora's box, and federal courts were flooded with requests by inmates to improve the conditions in most prisons.

Resulting reforms included the professionalizing of staff through recruitment and training, and implementation of many self-improvement programs to take the place of the industrial work programs, ushering in the **Rehabilitative Era** (1960–1980). In the early 1960s, corrections adopted what was called the **medical model**, which became the dominant theory influencing prison and other correctional practices. Under the medical model, offenders were believed to be "sick," inflicted with problems that caused their criminality; they needed to be diagnosed and treated, and rehabilitative programs would resolve their problems and prepare them for release as "well" into the community, able to be productive and crime-free.

A minor "adjustment" to the medical model was the recognition of the need to strengthen the links between prisons and the community. **Reintegration** was added to the emphasis on rehabilitation. After offenders completed their treatment in prison, they needed transitional care. Reintegration includes the community in the medical model, with a recognition that the transition from prison to free

During the Retributive Era, some prisons and jails returned to making inmates wear stripes, a tradition that goes back to the 1800s. While the argument was for security in case of escape, the real reason was to punish inmates in every way legally allowable.
Courtesy of the Maricopa County (Arizona) Sheriff.

citizen is difficult. Community correctional programs were expanded, and halfway houses and special parole programs became an important element in the correctional process.

The medical model came under attack during the 1970s. In the early 1970s, Robert Martinson and his colleagues completed a review of correctional research to determine "what worked."[26] In the review of more than two hundred studies, the researchers concluded that while there were a few isolated correlations between a treatment program and a reduction in recidivism, no consistent findings indicated that any single treatment program significantly reduced recidivism. Therefore, the Martinson review concluded that **"nothing works."** For public officials looking for a way to reduce costs and make corrections more punitive, this study provided statistical support and was the death knell for the medical model. Rehabilitative programs lost funding, and parole was eliminated in several states.

With the increase in crime, especially violent crimes, over much of the 1980s, crime and corrections became very important to the public and elected officials. Throughout the 1980s and 1990s, constant media coverage of violent crime created fear and anger toward the crime issue. Political rhetoric emphasized holding offenders accountable for their acts, and the current **Retributive Era** came into being, emphasizing the need to be tough on criminals while keeping them isolated from law-abiding citizens and make them serve "hard" time. With this model, correctional sanctions are tough, offer few amenities, and emphasize public safety over all else. The Retributive Era is also a return to the Classical School of criminality, in which offenders have free choice to commit their crimes, and a response of lengthening and toughening punishments is believed to deter and prevent crime.

The Sentencing Goals of Corrections

The sentencing goals of corrections are punishment, deterrence, incapacitation, rehabilitation, and restitution. As one might imagine, it is very difficult to attempt

Nothing works

a conclusion by Robert Martinson that no correctional treatment programs reduce recidivism; it effectively spelled the end to the medical model

Retributive Era

an era of corrections that emphasized holding offenders accountable for their acts and being tough on criminals while keeping them isolated from law-abiding citizens and making them serve "hard" time these seemingly conflicting goals at the same time. Can corrections punish at the same time as it rehabilitates? Can prisons incapacitate offenders, and at the same time try to get them to repay the victim or society for the damage they have done? Even though correctional officials may admit that these conflicting demands create a management challenge, society continues to expect corrections to pursue all five of these goals.

PUNISHMENT

Punishment

the correctional goal emphasizing the infliction of pain or suffering

While different correctional goals have been emphasized in varying degrees over time, the most dominant correctional goal has historically been **punishment**, the infliction of pain or suffering. As a society, we believe that punishment for inappropriate behavior is not only allowable, but also advisable. We use punishment to teach children right from wrong. We believe that punishment helps maintain moral order, with the focus on society rather than on the individual who committed the crime. Criminal offenders are brought to justice by the state, acting for society. Through punishment, society can maintain order and show fairness to those who do not violate the law. Some think of the role of punishment within society as a catharsis, a way for society to feel good about the punishment of offenders. People need to see that those who demonstrate inappropriate behavior receive their "just deserts," or what is coming to them.

Retribution

infliction of punishment on those who deserve to be punished

Punishment for criminal acts is sometimes referred to as **retribution**, which implies the infliction of punishment on those who deserve to be punished. The idea of *lex talionis* (Latin for "law of retribution") is similar to the biblical adage of "an eye for an eye," and indicates that offenders get the punishment they deserve. The idea of punishment and retribution is primarily focused on the past, in that it is in exchange for the commission of a criminal violation. However, it is closely linked to more future-oriented correctional goals such as deterrence or rehabilitation. Punishment is necessary for deterrence, and the presence of punishment encourages rehabilitation. Punishment is also reactive in that it focuses on the act or crime, rather than on the offender's particular circumstances or needs. Society believes that it is only fair and just that criminal offenders receive punishment for their crimes.

It is difficult for a democratic society to determine how much punishment is necessary for the commission of a crime. The U.S. Supreme Court addressed this issue in *Bell v. Wolfish,* when the Court established the "punitive intent standard."[27] The case dealt with conditions and practices at a federal jail for short-term offenders in New York City. Inmates alleged that overcrowded conditions and restrictive security procedures were a violation of the Eighth Amendment, which states that "Excessive bail shall not be required, nor excessive fines imposed, nor cruel and unusual punishment inflicted." The Court ruled that the case should turn only on whether the practices in question violated detainees' right to be free from punishment, using a standard of whether the individual restrictions were punitive or merely regulatory restraints; whether the practice is reasonably related to a legitimate goal other than punishment; and whether it appears to be excessive in relation to that alternative purpose.

Test of proportionality

the result of the 1983 case of *Solem v. Helm;* a test used to guide sentencing based on the gravity of the offense and consistency of the severity of punishment

The Court also addressed punishment and created the **test of proportionality** in the 1983 case of *Solem v. Helm,* by declaring that "a criminal sentence must be proportionate to the crime for which the defendant has been convicted. . . . and be guided by objective criteria, including (i) the gravity of the offense and the harshness of the penalty; (ii) the sentences imposed on other criminals in the same jurisdiction; and (iii) the sentences imposed for commission of the same crime in other jurisdictions. . . ."[28]

DETERRENCE

Deterrence is a correctional goal focused on future actions (or the avoidance of certain actions) by both individuals and society. The expectation is that as a result of offenders receiving punishment, both they and others will be deterred or discouraged from committing crimes in the future. Jeremy Bentham, in his 1789 concept of hedonistic calculus, argued that if the sanction for committing a crime inflicted a greater amount of pain than the pleasure resulting from the offense, crime would be prevented. When an individual commits a crime and receives a punishment, the punishment is designed to result in **specific deterrence** of that offender from committing further crimes. The idea is that the punishment the offender received created such an unpleasant situation that he or she will not want to experience it again. This certainly seems logical, but requires that offenders receive punishment that is swift, certain, and specifically linked to the criminal act. Unfortunately, justice today often does not end with these results.

Specific deterrence
the effect of punishment on an individual offender that prevents that person from committing future crimes

Deterrence philosophies are also expected to have an effect on the general society. **General deterrence** presumes that others in society will not commit crimes, because they see that there is a punishment for such acts and that individuals do receive those prescribed punishments. For general deterrence to be effective, the punishment must be visible and the public must believe that if they commit a crime they will be caught and punished, the punishment must be carried out uniformly, and the benefits of the crime will not outweigh the punishment. This requires logic and rationality. The theory often breaks down, as criminals do not believe they will get caught, think they can get out of trouble with a good lawyer, or do not fear the available punishment enough for it to deter them from the criminal act.

General deterrence
the recognition that criminal acts result in punishment, and the effect of that recognition on society that prevents future crimes

Over the past two decades, legislators have operated under a misconception that if they continue to enhance (increase) penalties for certain crimes, the commission of those crimes will go down. Public relations campaigns have sought to educate potential criminals regarding the penalties for drug offenses or for using a gun in the commission of a crime. However, research has failed to indicate that such penalty modifications have a significant deterrent effect. However, those who increasingly favor using prison rather than probation and increasing the length of current prison sentences argue that even if such enhancements do not have a deterrent effect, they will have an incapacitative effect.

INCAPACITATION

Incapacitation is thought of as reducing offenders' ability or capacity to commit further crimes. Correctional sanctions restrict offenders' opportunity to continue their criminality, and through this restriction, society is protected from potential criminals. Some suggest that incapacitation is reactive in that it is a punishment for past crimes. Others contend that "sentences based on incapacitation are future oriented, . . . [as they look] at the offender's potential future actions."[29] Others imply that incapacitation is both reactive and proactive. Carlson and colleagues argue, "Like retribution, incapacitation is reactive, and yet, like deterrence, it attempts to predict and influence future behavior."[30]

Incapacitation
reducing offenders' ability or capacity to commit further crimes

There are two ways to define and view the correctional goal of incapacitation. The most narrow is that incapacitation (through a sentence of imprisonment or death) makes it literally impossible for offenders to commit future crimes. In this view, incapacitation serves to [avert crimes] in the general society by isolation of the identified offenders during periods of incarceration."[31] Thus incapacitation is believed to reduce crime by focusing on the offender who is being incapacitated or imprisoned, while the person is under control of the authorities carrying out the punishment. Incapacitation is based on the belief that most criminals commit

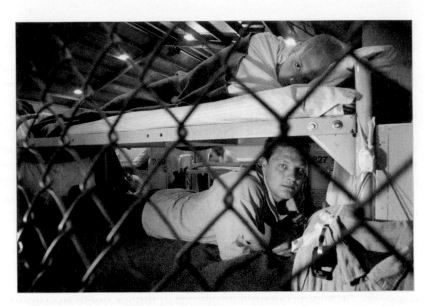

Incapacitation is focused on securing inmates in prisons so they cannot commit further crimes against society.
Courtesy of AP/Wide World Photos.

several crimes over their lifetimes, and therefore, during the time of their criminal sanction, crime is being prevented by their reduced opportunity. Blumstein notes that incapacitation operates on the assumption that "punishment can take a slice out of an individual criminal career."[32] However, even a person who is in prison or on death row is capable of committing crimes against victims. In prison, inmates commit crimes of assault against other inmates or prison staff. Offenders in prison still use or deal drugs. However, society is protected, even while those who work or live in prison are still potential victims of crime.

The second way to consider incapacitation is under a broader definition whereby offenders' opportunities to commit further crimes is lessened by the imposition of the criminal sentence. For instance, house arrest using electronic monitoring to ensure that an offender remains at home at prescribed times reduces the opportunity for criminal activity. Whenever an offender serving a sanction while in the community is under the supervision or monitoring of correctional staff, his or her opportunity to commit crime is reduced.

As noted above, incapacitation is based on a belief that most criminals repeat their criminality. Several studies, beginning with Wolfgang and Sellin's classic work on cohort groups in Philadelphia, have shown that most offenders commit more that one crime, and a small group of offenders commit a large percent of crimes. A review of this work found the following:

> Career criminals, though few in number, account for most crime. Even though chronic repeat offenders (those with five or more arrests by age 18) make up a relatively small proportion of all offenders, they commit a very high proportion of all crimes . . . In Wolfgang's Philadelphia study, chronic offenders accounted for 23% of all male offenders in the study, but they had committed 61% of all crimes. Of all crimes by all members of the group studied, chronic offenders committed: 61% of all homicides; 76% of all rapes; 73% of all robberies; and 65% of all aggravated assaults.[33]

Selective incapacitation

incarceration of high-risk offenders for preventative reasons based on what they are expected to do, not what they have already done

These findings led to efforts to identify offenders with the greatest potential of committing a high number of crimes and sentence them to long prison terms, an approach referred to as **selective incapacitation**. During the 1980s, the RAND Corporation, recognizing that prison cells were an expensive and therefore scarce resource, created the concept of selective incapacitation. In this work, Greenwood argued that in order to maximize the incapacitating result (preventing future crimes) of imprisonment, scarce prison and jail space should be reserved for the most dangerous, violent, and repeat offenders.[34] It had earlier been concluded that if selected offenders who commit repetitive crimes were imprisoned and incapacitated for three or even five years, significantly fewer crimes would have been committed.[35] Therefore, a model of selective incapacitation advocates incarcerating, for preventive reasons, high-risk people for what they are expected to do, not what they have already done.

Selective incapacitation remains hotly debated and has several critics. Gottfredson and Hirschi have challenged the methodological approach and conclusions of the RAND studies.[36] Others have raised the issue of "false positives" and the fairness of incarcerating for long periods of time those who are wrongly expected to commit future crimes. As Allen and Simonsen noted, "the evidence is that we would probably incarcerate numerous noneligible (a "false positive" problem) persons and release to lesser confinement many of those eligible (a "false negative" problem) persons. Whatever benefits might accrue to this sentencing doctrine have thus far eluded corrections."[37]

REHABILITATION

The next goal of corrections is to rehabilitate offenders, or return them to society better able to avoid criminality and less likely to commit further crimes. **Rehabilitation** means returning someone to a prior state. It is assumed that this refers to the life of offenders before they began to commit crimes. However, for most offenders, rehabilitation does not take them back, but to a new and better state, one in which they are self-restrained and not motivated to commit crime. The emphasis of rehabilitation is clearly proactive and focused on preventing future crimes. Correctional officials believe this may be their most important function, protecting society in the long term by reducing **recidivism** (a return to crime). However, it is questionable whether the effectiveness of correctional programs should be judged solely by the recidivism rate. No person or program can force offenders to change their behavior or to make good decisions to avoid crime, especially months after they leave the supervision of correctional officials. The situations and environments facing offenders differ from case to case. Even though recidivism may not be the most appropriate measure of the success of rehabilitation programs, it is likely to remain the one most often examined and used.

Corrections attempts to rehabilitate offenders in many ways. First, correctional programs are aimed at trying to reduce offenders' motivation to commit further crimes. Although there are many reasons why people commit crimes, correctional agencies offer psychological counseling to help offenders understand the factors that trigger certain behaviors, anger management and other programs to help offenders recognize dangerous situations in which they may act wrongfully, and sensitivity training to get offenders to understand the impact of their criminal actions on victims and their families. Second, correctional programs try to build competencies in offenders that may help them avoid problems that heighten their likelihood of committing crime. Such programs are designed to help offenders to increase their educational level, develop a vocational skill, or reduce the use of drugs or alcohol. Finally, correctional programs may simply have a goal of improving offenders' decision making. Why do offenders choose selling drugs over getting a legitimate job? Why do offenders choose to act out violently rather than avoid confrontation or seek nonviolent resolutions to problems? Or why do offenders steal others' property to try to make an easy buck? Some correctional programs help offenders improve their decision-making skills while considering the values and potential outcomes of their criminal actions.

Rehabilitation
a programmed effort to alter the attitudes and behaviors of inmates and improve their likelihood of becoming law-abiding citizens

Recidivism
the state of relapse that occurs when offenders complete their criminal punishment and then continue to commit crimes

While the importance of rehabilitation has experienced ebbs and flows throughout the history of corrections, public attitudes have consistently supported rehabilitating criminal offenders. In the National Opinion Survey of Crime and Justice, respondents indicated support for rehabilitative programs; 93 percent support prisoners' learning a skill or trade and 94 percent support requiring offenders to be able to read and write before release from prison. Similarly, 88 percent support inmate work programs to construct buildings, make products, or perform services.[38]

RESTITUTION

Restitution

acts by which criminals make right or repay society or their victims for their wrongs

The first four goals of corrections are acknowledged by almost every author and in almost every textbook. Less mentioned, but currently gaining in popularity, is the goal of **restitution,** or making right by repaying society or victims for the wrongs created by offenders. This is not a new goal in the way it is carried out. Criminal sentences have historically included fines and victim restitution. And it can be argued that the chain gangs of the early twentieth century were public works programs in which inmates had to build roads or clear trails to improve the public good. During more contemporary times, the principle of "restoration" of the damage resulting from crime has increased in importance, and many more criminal sentences include the opportunity for restitution as the sanctions are carried out.

As society took over responsibility for bringing a criminal to justice and removed victims from the process to avoid their seeking revenge, the pendulum swung too far, and the victim became the forgotten participant in the criminal justice process. After police took victims' statements, victims often did not hear anything else official unless they were required to testify at trial. Victims played no role in sentencing, few sentences sought to repair the damages they incurred, and they seldom received any progress reports such as when a criminal would appear before a parole board or was to get out of prison.

Victims' movement

the criminal justice system's recognition that victims should be involved in the process of sentencing criminals

As the **victims' movement** became popular during the 1980s, the criminal justice system made many adjustments to include victims. Victim assistance programs advised them during the adjudication process, and sometimes even arranged transportation to the trial if necessary. Sentencing decisions often considered victim statements of their losses. Notifications regarding a change in status in the sentence of a criminal (such as a move from one prison to another) were initiated. Victims were informed of parole hearings and told how they could provide input if desired. And the plan for an inmate after release would be provided the victim to ensure that they saw no conflicts or felt threatened by the proposed release.

Restorative justice

models of sentencing that shift the focus away from punishment of the offender and emphasize the victim by holding offenders accountable for the harm they caused and finding opportunities for them to repair the damage

All of these activities were positive in getting offenders to repay the state or the victim for the damage done by their crime. However, they still failed to satisfy the needs of most victims, the community, and even the offender. Over the past two decades, an alternative to traditional criminal sentencing, called **restorative justice**, emerged; it more fully implements the overall philosophy of the goal of restitution. Described more fully in Chapter 16, restorative justice models of sentencing shift the focus away from reactive, punishment-oriented sentencing and without concern for the victim. These models emphasize involving the victim while holding offenders accountable for the harm they caused and finding opportunities for them to repair the damage. Freeman describes restorative justice as "a process that focuses on the injury resulting from the crime and works to repair the injury by shifting the role of the offender from passive recipient of punishment to active participant in reparation."[39] Meanwhile, public opinion surveys conclude that "the process of mediating conflict between crime victims and offenders provides many benefits to the parties involved, the community, and the justice sys-

Offenders are regularly required to do some type of community service to help pay back society for their crimes.
Courtesy of the Georgia Department of Corrections.

tem."[40] Because of the current recognized value of holding offenders responsible for "making right" the harm they have done with their crimes, and the importance of involving the victim in the criminal justice process, restitution is now recognized as a goal of corrections with comparable importance to the other four goals. In fact, and because of these reasons, this goal will probably continue to be seen as important in sentencing criminal offenders.

The "You Make the Decision" box asks you to compare and contrast the five goals of sentencing. While these goals can all be accomplished in any jurisdiction's penal code and sentencing practices, the exercise makes students think about the relative importance they put on each goal.

YOU MAKE THE DECISION . . .

RATING THE IMPORTANCE OF CORRECTIONAL GOALS

No jurisdiction has to formally rate the importance of the five goals or corrections; however, the following exercise asks students to do just that. It can be done individually, but will be more fun in a small group and a better learning exercise.

Your instructions are to consider each of the five goals of sentencing and create a list of the favorable and unfavorable consequences of focusing on each one. For instance, someone might suggest that focusing on punishment can slowly undermine society's emphasis on fair and just treatment. Or, emphasizing incapacitation may result in positively impacting the crime rate, as incapacitated offenders cannot commit crimes in the community. After creating and discussing the list for each goal, go about the difficult task of rating the importance of each goal. There are no guidelines as to what "importance" means, and this should be a very individual decision. Does one person believe that the most important purpose of a criminal sanction is to punish an offender, while another believes it should first focus on rehabilitation? Each person should create his or her list, and then the group should discuss the lists and come to a group conclusion about the rating of goals by importance to society. The discussions, debates, and even arguments that result from this exercise should be both fun and a valuable learning opportunity.

Chapter Review

SUMMARY

This chapter includes several topics as we begin our study of corrections. Students receive an overview of what corrections is, how it links to the rest of the criminal justice system, and why it is important to study corrections. As the criminal justice system has expanded over the past several decades, the correctional system has grown at the most rapid pace, with elected officials authorizing extensive funds and resources to meet the growing demand for services. As this demand has grown, employment and advancement opportunities have increased, and more students are considering corrections as a career field.

The causes of crime are presented, from the earliest theories based on a range of belief that offenders exhibit "free will" to the idea that some offenders are "predetermined" and have no choice in becoming involved in crime. More modern theories, while not discounting any possible cause of crime, emphasize holding offenders accountable and weighing more heavily on the free will concepts than on predetermination. Understanding the theories regarding the causes is critical to determining how to respond to crime. Early approaches included severe corporal punishment, torture, and public humiliation; capital punishment for several crimes; and removing offenders by transporting them out of society. Today we have settled on the use of prisons to punish, deter, incapacitate, and rehabilitate criminals.

The Quakers of Pennsylvania, who opened the Walnut Street Jail in Philadelphia as the first penitentiary for convicted offenders in 1790, are credited for the creation of prisons to house sentenced offenders in the United States. For two hundred years since that time, prisons have undergone many transitions regarding their emphasis on varying correctional goals from punishment to rehabilitation. Each correctional goal is described in the chapter, and students can realize how correctional practices and various sentences emphasized certain goals over others during various eras of prison and community correctional operations.

The purpose of this chapter is to create a foundation of history and theory, so that as current policies and practices are described, students can link those to theories and goals in order to critically consider the overall effectiveness and public value of correctional policy. In the next several chapters, the operations of the major components of the correctional system are described, beginning with a description of the types of sentences that offenders receive. In Chapter 2 the first stage of correctional operations, including the processes (pretrial diversion, bail, jail, finding of guilt) that lead up to sentencing, is described, as well as various sentencing approaches and options and postsentencing processes for handling the offender and making the actual sentencing decision.

REVIEW QUESTIONS

1. How did the term *corrections* evolve from the earlier use of the term *penology*?
2. What is the mission of corrections?
3. Describe the correctional funnel.
4. List the principles of the Classical School of criminology.
5. What is Bentham's hedonistic calculus?
6. List the principles of the Positive School of criminology.
7. Describe the operation of the Walnut Street Jail.
8. Describe the differences in the Pennsylvania and Auburn systems.
9. How did the Irish system contribute to modern correctional operations in the United States?
10. How did abandonment of the "hands-off doctrine" impact prison operations?
11. In what ways does corrections attempt to rehabilitate offenders?
12. How does reintegration differ from rehabilitation?
13. Differentiate between specific and general deterrence.
14. What is selective incapacitation?
15. How has the victims' rights movement impacted correctional policies and operations?
16. Describe restorative justice.

ENDNOTES

1. Douglas C. Eadie, "Strategic Management by Design," in *Strategic Planning for Local Government: A Handbook for Officials and Citizens,* edited by Roger L. Kemp (Jefferson, N.C.: McFarland, 1993), p. 85.

2. Camille Graham Camp and George M. Camp, *The Corrections Yearbook, 2001* (Middletown, Conn.: Criminal Justice Institute, 2002), pp. 99–100.

3. Camille Graham Camp and George M. Camp, *The Corrections Yearbook, 2001* (Middletown, Conn.: Criminal Justice Institute, 2002), p. 91.

4. Camp and Camp, 2002, p. 106.

5. Camp and Camp, 1998, p. 5.

6. Camp and Camp, 2002, p. 205.

7. Ibid., pp. 188 and 207.

8. Camille Graham Camp and George M. Camp, *The 2000 Corrections Yearbook: Adult Corrections* (Middletown, Conn.: Criminal Justice Institute, 2000), pp. 76, 83–85; Camp and Camp, 2002, p. 88.

9. Bureau of Justice Statistics, *Sourcebook of Criminal Justice Statistics, 1994* (Washington, D.C.: U.S. Department of Justice, 1995), p. 26.

10. Bureau of Justice Statistics. *Sourcebook of Criminal Justice Statistics, 2001* (Washington, D.C.: U.S. Department of Justice, 2003), p. 19.

11. Jody K. Spertzel, "A Correctional Career Guide," *Corrections Today* 55, no. 1 (1993): 37.

12. Frank Schmalleger, *Criminal Justice Today,* 7th ed. (Upper Saddle River, N.J.: Prentice Hall, 2003), p. 46.

13. Harry Elmer Barnes and Negley K. Teeters, *New Horizons in Criminology,* 3rd ed., (Upper Saddle River, N.J.: Prentice Hall, 1959), p. 322.

14. See Richard Louis Dugsdale, *The Jukes: A Study in Crime Pauperism, Disease, and Heredity,* 3rd ed. (New York: G. P. Putnam's Sons, 1985); and Henry Herbert Goddard, *The Kallikak Family: A Study in the Heredity of Feeblemindedness* (New York: Macmillan, 1912).

15. For more information, see Richard Herrnstein, "Crime File: Biology and Crime" (study guide, National Institute of Justice, n.d.).

16. For an overview of this issue, see Schmalleger, pp. 101–102.

17. Gabriel Tarde, *Penal Philosophy,* translated by R. Howell (Boston: Little, Brown, 1912). Originally published in 1890.

18. Randy Martin, Robert J. Mutchnick, and W. Timothy Austin, *Criminological Thought: Pioneers Past and Present* (New York: Macmillan, 1990).

19. A good overview of these theories of crime can be found in Hugh D. Barlow, *Criminal Justice in America* (Upper Saddle River, N.J.: Prentice Hall, 2000), pp. 84–117.

20. *The American Prison: From the Beginning . . . A Pictorial History* (College Park, Md.: The American Correctional Association, 1983), p. 16.

21. Ibid., p. 24.

22. Barnes and Teeters.

23. For the complete list of principles of the 1870 National Prison Association, see Enoch C. Wines, ed., *Transactions of the National Congress on Penitentiary and Reformatory Discipline* (Albany, N.Y.: Argus, 1871).

24. Margaret Calahan, *Historical Corrections Statistics in the United States: 1850–1984* (Washington, D.C.: U.S. Department of Justice, 1986), p. 36.

25. *The American Prison,* p. 208.

26. Douglas Lipton, Robert Martinson, and Judith Wilks, *The Effectiveness of Correctional Treatment and What Works: A Survey of Treatment Evaluation Studies* (New York: Praeger, 1975).

27. *Bell v. Wolfish,* 441 U.S. 520 (1979).

28. *Solem v. Helm,* 463 U.S. 277 (1983).

29. Todd R. Clear and George R. Cole, *American Corrections,* 5th ed. (Belmont, Calif.: West/Wadsworth, 2000), p. 59.

30. Norman A. Carlson, Karen M. Hess, and Christine M. H. Orthmann, *Corrections in the 21st Century* (Belmont, Calif.: West/Wadsworth, 1999), p. 16.

31. Alfred Blumstein, "Selective Incapacitation as a Means of Crime Control," *American Behavioral Scientist* 27, no. 1 (1983): 93.

32. Ibid., p. 94.

33. Marianne W. Zawitz, ed., *Report to the Nation on Crime and Justice* (Washington, D.C.: U.S. Department of Justice, Bureau of Justice Statistics, 1983), p. 35.

34. Peter Greenwood, *Selective Incapacitation* (Santa Monica, Calif.: RAND Corporation, 1983).

35. Stuart Miller, Simon Dinitz, and John Conrad, *Careers of the Violent* (Lexington, Mass.: Lexington Books, 1982).

36. Michael R. Gottfredson and Travis Hirschi, "The Methodological Adequacy of Longitudinal Research on Crime," *Criminology* 25 (1987): 581–614.

37. Harry E. Allen and Clifford E. Simonsen, *Corrections in America: An Introduction,* 9th ed. (Upper Saddle River, N.J.: Prentice Hall, 2001), pp. 58–59.

38. Barbara A. Sims, "Questions of Corrections: Public Attitudes toward Prison and Community-Based Programs," *Corrections Management Quarterly* 1, no. 1 (1997): p. 55.

39. Robert M. Freeman, *Correctional Organization and Management: Public Policy Challenges, Behavior, and Structure* (Boston: Butterworth-Heinemann, 1999), p. 397.

40. Myron Steele and Thomas J. Quinn, "Restorative Justice: Including Victims in Community Corrections," in *The Dilemmas of Corrections: Contemporary Readings,* edited by Kenneth C. Haas and Geoffrey P. Alpert (Prospect Heights, Ill.: Waveland Press, 1995), p. 530.

Chapter 2

AFTER READING THIS CHAPTER, YOU SHOULD BE ABLE TO:

1. Explain the operation of pretrial activities and understand how they can be considered a part of corrections.

2. Specify the reasons for preventive detention and describe the forms of release from jail pending trial.

3. Discuss how the Manhattan Bail Project operates and how it expands the number of offenders eligible for release on recognizance.

4. Identify the role that plea bargaining plays in criminal sentencing.

5. List the purposes of the presentence investigation.

6. List and describe the six sentencing options available as criminal sanctions.

7. Compare indeterminate and determinate sentencing models.

8. Explain the use of sentencing guidelines.

9. Suggest how drug courts are a positive development in the sentencing of criminal offenders.

Sentencing and the Correctional Process

KEY TERMS

sentencing
felony
misdemeanor
pretrial diversion
preventive detention
bail
surety
release on recognizance
Manhattan Bail Project
supervised pretrial release programs
plea bargaining
presentence investigation
economic sanctions
community service
probation
intermediate sanctions
short-term confinement
imprisonment
capital punishment
concurrent sentences
consecutive sentences
indeterminate sentences
determinate sentences
good time
truth in sentencing
judicial form of sentencing
administrative form of sentencing
legislative form of sentencing
mandatory minimum sentences
three-strikes laws
presumptive sentencing
sentencing guidelines
drug courts

Introduction

Sentencing

imposition of a criminal
sanction by a judicial
authority

Felony

a crime that is punishable
by a year or more of
incarceration

Misdemeanor

a crime that is punishable
by less than a year of
incarceration

Once a criminal offender has either pleaded guilty or been found guilty of a crime, a judge must determine the sentence to be received. **Sentencing** is the imposition of a criminal sanction by a judicial authority. Before a judge can prescribe a sentence, the range of allowable sanctions must be enacted by the legislature and listed in the state or federal penal code. Each year, hundreds of thousands of criminals appear before judges to be sentenced for their crimes. This chapter describes the process, the correctional activities that accompany the process, and the sentencing options and approaches available to judges.

Sentencing descriptions are primarily for **felony** offenses, or those punishable by a year or more of incarceration. **Misdemeanors** are crimes punishable by less than a year of incarceration, and have a significantly shorter process for handling offenders. Misdemeanor (lower) courts usually handle all of the steps in the court process in one hearing, and are often referred to as "assembly-line justice." Offenders charged with a misdemeanor appear in court for their preliminary hearing, usually plead guilty, and receive a sentence of a fine, probation, community service, a short jail term, or a combination of some or all of these. The entire court process may take only a few minutes.

Felony sentencing is much more complicated because the potential sanctions are much more severe. Correctional activities begin even prior to the determination of guilt, as offenders are evaluated for potential release from jail on bail or under some alternative release mechanism. After a finding of guilt, a process of information gathering begins, to provide judges with a more complete picture of offenders and the crimes they committed. At the time of sentencing, judges must consider complicated sentencing laws for each individual case and offender. Today, judges have significantly less discretion in sentencing options than in the past. Mandatory minimum sentences, three-strikes laws, and sentencing guidelines frequently require specific sentences, with little consideration of personal factors regarding offenders, their crimes, and the victims. Various sentencing options and approaches usually available in today's criminal courts are presented next.

Pretrial Correctional Activities

The criminal justice system is said to have three major components: the police, who investigate crimes and arrest suspects; the court system, which includes prosecutors who determine whether to charge suspects with crimes and negotiate plea bargains, and courts that oversee the trial process and sentence guilty offenders; and corrections, which carries out the sentences imposed by the courts. Typically, corrections is considered to begin after the sentencing of criminal offenders. However, the past thirty years have seen many innovations and improvements in the criminal justice management of offenders just after the booking (the formal identification of a suspect arrested for a crime) and the first appearance (at which charges against suspects are read, they are advised of their rights, and they are afforded the opportunity for bail) but before the trial or a guilty plea and sentencing. These innovations include diversion from the criminal justice system, alternatives to traditional bail, and other nontraditional handling of those charged with crimes prior to their sentencing.

These innovations to the pretrial and presentence activities within the criminal justice system have expanded the traditional boundaries of corrections. Today, many consider the diversion of offenders from the criminal justice system into treatment and supervision programs a correctional practice. As well, pretrial services activities, including investigating the potential for offenders' release from pretrial detention on bail, release on recognizance, other alternatives to bail, and supervision in the community of those not detained in jail, are also considered part of corrections. Some authors describe these activities as part of a chapter on probation. However, these functions are pretrial and have a great effect on the sentencing process and decision. Therefore, these pretrial activities are discussed in conjunction with, and described in terms of how they lead to, the sentencing decision in this chapter.

DIVERSION FROM THE CRIMINAL JUSTICE SYSTEM

Pretrial diversion provides the opportunity for a criminal offender to be diverted from processing in the criminal justice system, by suspending criminal processing while offering offenders the chance to participate in treatment programs and avoid further criminal activity. Diversion occurs without (before) a finding of guilt; therefore, if offenders are successful in the diversion program, the charges against them are dismissed and they will not have a formal criminal record of the offense. Diversion programs are usually used for minor offenders of laws against public intoxication or minor property crimes who have little if any prior criminal record and appear to be candidates for some type of treatment in the community.

> **Pretrial diversion**
> the suspension of criminal process while the offender is provided the chance to participate in treatment programs and avoid further criminal activity

Pretrial diversion programs are sometimes referred to as *deferred prosecution* or *probation without adjudication*. Many court systems have bail and diversion staff, separate from the probation staff, who interview suspects in jail and then recommend to the court whether they should get bail or release on recognizance, or whether they are good candidates for diversion. If offenders are charged with a nonviolent crime, have a limited prior criminal record, and possibly have a treatment need such as drug or alcohol abuse, the pretrial staff are likely to recommend that the judge grant the offender the opportunity for diversion. The recommendation will also include certain conditions that must be met over a specified period of time for the offender to successfully complete the diversionary program. Pretrial conditions are very similar to those for probationers (avoidance of additional criminality, reporting to the supervising officer as required, maintaining employment, and participating in the identified treatment program). Pretrial services staff then supervise the diverted offender in the community while making periodic reports to the court.

The following practices are considered to define a pretrial diversion program:

- It offers people charged with criminal offenses alternatives to traditional criminal justice or juvenile justice proceedings.
- It permits participation by the accused only on a voluntary basis.
- The accused has access to defense counsel prior to a decision to participate.
- It occurs no sooner than the filing of formal charges and no later than a final adjudication of guilt.
- It develops service plans in conjunction with the defendant that address the needs of that defendant and are structured to assist that person in avoiding behavior likely to lead to future arrests.
- It results in dismissal of charges or the equivalent, if the divertee successfully completes the diversion process.[1]

One of the first and most notable diversion programs was Treatment Alternatives to Street Crimes (TASC).[2] TASC is focused on offenders with a drug problem that is believed to be the cause of their criminal involvement. With these type of programs, offenders may participate in a drug treatment program and avoid traditional processing through the criminal justice system. TASC and other diversionary drug treatment programs operate under the philosophy that if offenders become involved in a treatment program for their addiction and successfully deal with their drug problem, their chance of avoiding future criminal activity is improved.

There are no conclusive data to indicate that pretrial diversion programs are more effective than formal criminal processing, even though diverted individuals typically have a lower recidivism rate than those who are not diverted. However, this is to be expected, as they are less serious offenders, and few evaluations control for the different levels of seriousness when examining such program models.[3] However, diversionary treatment programs have several advantages:

1. They reduce the demands on the court and prosecutors to process the case as a criminal activity. When an offender is diverted from criminal handling, prosecutors save considerable time by not having to prepare the case for trial and not having to assemble evidence to prove the offender guilty beyond a reasonable doubt. Even if the crime is likely to result in a plea bargain instead of a trial, it still reduces the prosecutors' time requirements. As well, it eliminates several appearances before the court and clogging of the court docket.

2. They cost considerably less than criminal justice processing. Diversion generally moves the offender into community treatment programs (mental health, drug treatment, alcohol treatment) instead of more costly correctional-based programs. The reduction of prosecution and court time previously described also represents considerable cost savings.

3. Offenders avoid the stigma associated with a criminal conviction. For the type of offenders involved in pretrial diversion (nonviolent and usually first-time offenders), this is a significant advantage. It is generally believed that the further offenders penetrate into the correctional process (from probation to imprisonment), the more likely they are to be involved in crime in the future.

For these reasons, pretrial diversion programs are experiencing a resurgence of interest from criminal justice and court agencies that cannot keep up with their workloads. Today's emphasis on punishment and accountability of offenders has resulted in overcrowded jails and prisons and has overextended the resources available to justice agencies. The emphasis of diversionary programs on rehabilitation and reduction of recidivism is considered a bright light in the otherwise dreary environment of the criminal justice system. The National Association of Pretrial Services Agencies Diversion Committee writes:

> Pretrial diversion is a strong, viable alternative that provides an important service for defendants and the communities in which they live. For defendants, diversion provides an opportunity to make significant changes in their lives and prevent further penetration into the criminal justice system. For communities, the programs assist the courts, prosecutors, and victims in addressing serious problems caused by growing criminal and juvenile justice populations through reducing reliance on traditional case processing and working to stem the "revolving door" syndrome.[4]

PRETRIAL DETENTION IN JAIL

After arrest, booking, and a reading of their charges, many offenders are detained in jail until their trial or guilty plea. This occurs even though our justice system is based on the belief of "innocent until proven guilty," and there has yet to be a finding of guilt. Offenders are detained for one (or both) of two reasons. First, they are detained if considered a flight risk, in order to ensure that they will appear at all future court proceedings. Second, they are detained if considered dangerous, in order to protect the public from their committing further crimes.

There are many alternatives to pretrial detention. It is generally believed that a variety of bail options (such as pledging money or property) will work for most individuals to reduce the likelihood of flight and ensure their appearance at court

The St. Louis County Jail holds more than eight-hundred inmates, most there on pretrial detention, because they either do not have the funds to make bail or are too high a risk to release to the community pending trial.
Photo by Richard P. Seiter.

processes. The issue of danger and avoidance of risk to the community is much more difficult to predict and manage. Theoretically, we regularly hold charged yet still innocent offenders in jail for crimes they may possibly commit. This **preventive detention** is detaining an accused person in jail to protect the community from crimes he or she is likely to commit if set free pending trial.

In an effort to reduce the release from jail of high-risk offenders, the 1984 Comprehensive Crime Control Act authorized holding allegedly dangerous suspects in jail without bail if a judge finds no conditions that would ensure that the defendant will appear at trial and at the same time ensure the safety of the community. And the U.S. Supreme Court, in the 1987 decision of *United States v. Salerno,* upheld the ability of a magistrate to confine an offender on a presumption that he or she was dangerous.[5] While some question holding defendants in custody for something they *may* do as a violation of their due process rights, most states have established laws that allow it to occur. Preventive detention can be criticized both in terms of violating one's right to due process and in terms of its effectiveness. Of all defendants released while awaiting trial, only 16 percent are arrested and less than half of those are convicted of a new crime committed during the release period.[6] And there is a strong correlation between denial of bail and a conviction.

If not granted bail, offenders are held in jails, temporary holding facilities that primarily house offenders before trial. At any time, more than half of the inmates housed in jails are not yet convicted of the crime for which they are being held. Almost every county in the United States has a jail, and many municipalities also operate jails. In the next chapter, operations and issues surrounding contemporary use of jails, jail management, jail crowding, legal liabilities, and offender issues such as suicide prevention, mentally ill offenders, and classification are described.

RELEASE FROM PRETRIAL DETENTION ON BAIL

After criminal suspects are arrested and booked, they (usually within hours of their arrest) have a *first appearance* before a judge or magistrate, the charges against them are read, they are advised of their rights, and they are considered for bail or some other method of release from detention. In most cases, release requires the use of **bail**, the pledge of money or property in exchange for a promise to return for

Preventive detention
detaining an accused person in jail to protect the community from crimes the person is likely to commit if set free pending trial

Bail
the pledge of money or property in exchange for a promise to return for further criminal processing

further criminal processing. Offenders on bail remain under the jurisdiction and supervision of the courts and must stay in the community while they await adjudication, but in most circumstances they have no contact with court personnel other than at formal hearings.

The history of pretrial release programs can be traced to medieval England, when those accused of crimes were often detained for months in local jails until the traveling magistrate arrived for trial. These early jails were not designed to hold offenders securely for long periods of time; problems of idleness, sanitation, and disruptive behavior resulted, and many offenders escaped. To avoid these problems, when the offenders were not charged with a serious crime or seen as dangerous, sheriffs began to turn defendants over to willing friends, relatives, or employers. These third parties would offer themselves or money as **surety** (a person who is legally liable for the conduct of another) for the accused person's appearance in court. If the defendant did not appear, the surety could be imprisoned or forced to pay a sum of money to the sheriff. The concept of releasing a defendant before trial with a personal or financial guarantee thereafter developed into today's concept of bail.

Unfortunately, the practice of bail was often abused and misused from its inception. Therefore, in 1275, specific offenses in England were established as "bailable" and other crimes as "not bailable." As well, the authority to set bail was moved from the sheriff to justices of the peace. To discourage unreasonably high bails, the English Bill of Rights in 1689 stated that excessive bail should not be required, a stipulation later incorporated into the U.S. Constitution, which states in the Eighth Amendment (ratified in 1791) that excessive bail may not be required.

Many times, offenders, their families, or their friends do not have personal funds or property to pledge as bail. As a result, the posting of bail bonds moved away from friends and family and became commercialized, as the bond amount could be purchased for a fee. *Bail bondsmen* are independent businesspeople who usually charge a fee of from 5 to 10 percent of the bond to provide it as bail. If offenders fail to appear for future criminal proceedings, the bond is forfeited. If they do appear, the full bond is returned to the person or business placing it. However, the percentage of the bond given to the commercial bondsman is not returned to the individual if he or she appears; it is just a fee for the posting of the bond.

There are many problems with the system of bail as a requirement for release. First, the availability of financial resources and the ability to "make bail" is not related to the risk of the offender or the chance of successful criminal processing. Second, the bail process discriminates against the poor. A recent survey found that of all offenders for whom bail was allowable yet who did not post bail, 94 percent remained incarcerated only because they could not afford bail or even the bondsman's fee.[7] Finally, many find the idea that "freedom can be bought for a price" unfair and antithetical to our system of justice for all. Because of these problems, several alternatives to financial bail developed.

ALTERNATIVES TO BAIL

To respond to the concerns noted previously, several options to traditional bail have been created. For minor offenses such as misdemeanors, summonses are used instead of arrest warrants. A *summons* is a legal order for an individual to appear at a future court proceeding. For felonies, a variety of bond options have been created. Options used by U.S. courts include the following:

- *Personal recognizance:* The defendant is released upon personal or own recognizance (promise to appear in court) without an appearance bond.

Surety

a person who is legally liable for the conduct of another; someone who guarantees the accused person's appearance in court

- *Unsecured bond:* The defendant is released on an unsecured appearance bond with a monetary amount that is secured only by the signature of the defendant.
- *Percentage bond:* The defendant is required to execute an appearance bond in a specific amount with the clerk of the court, in cash or other security as directed by the judicial officer.
- *Surety bond:* The defendant is required to execute a bail bond by the deposit of cash or the posting of a bail bond.
- *Collateral:* The defendant is required to execute the bail bond by posting property of a value equal to or greater than the bail set by the judicial officer.
- *Third-party custody:* The court may place the person in the custody of another person or organization.

With the first three options, individuals do not have to place the entire bond amount, but only an unsecured bond or a percentage of the bond required. A recent survey found that 62 percent of defendants are released from jail pending trial (25 percent on financial release [bail], 36 percent on nonfinancial release, and 1 percent on emergency release). The other 38 percent remain detained pending trial.[8]

PRETRIAL SERVICE PROGRAMS

The most frequent mechanism for releasing from jail offenders awaiting trial is **release on recognizance (ROR),** or with the defendants' personal promise to appear. Historically, not many felony offenders were granted this level of trust, and by the middle of the twentieth century, jails were becoming increasingly overcrowded with nonsentenced offenders. To improve this situation, the Vera Institute of Justice in New York City created the **Manhattan Bail Project (MBP)** in the 1960s. The purpose of the MBP was to help judges identify individuals who were good candidates to be released on their own recognizance without commercial or monetary bond. The Vera Institute had determined that even though judges had the authority to release offenders without bail, it was not being used to a great extent.

The staff of the MBP interviewed defendants in jail and contacted their references to verify interview statements. They worked on the assumption that offenders with strong community ties were most likely to appear for trial, and they created criteria to "score" offenders and recommend to judges those who they believed were most suitable for release on recognizance. Because of its positive impact on the detention and bail process, the MBP was replicated by many jurisdictions across the United States. By the 1980s, more than two hundred cities had such pretrial release programs to reduce jail crowding. Their goal was to decrease the number of offenders detained in jail awaiting trial while providing a more equitable form of release than simple bail.

The expansion of the Manhattan Bail Project led to the development of a broader form of ROR program. **Supervised pretrial release programs (SPTR)** were subsequently developed to enable individuals who were considered poor risks for ROR to be released under community supervision prior to trial. In the 1980s, the SPTR began to serve a second purpose. They provided a means to respond to growing public safety concerns by monitoring pretrial releases in the community. In the 1984 Federal Bail Reform Act, the safety of other people was included as a criterion to determine the pretrial release decision. The pretrial services report addresses this factor and weighs community risk as well as appearance at trial.

For offenders determined to pose no risk of nonappearance or danger, there is simple release on recognizance. For those who pose some risk, many jurisdictions have created SPTR programs to supervise offenders. Under pretrial supervision, offenders must follow certain conditions (no criminal activity, no drug use, and

Release on recognizance (ROR) release from jail based only on the defendant's promise to appear for further court procedures

Manhattan Bail Project (MBP) a program started in the 1960s to help judges identify individuals who were good candidates to be released on their own recognizance without commercial or monetary bond

Supervised pretrial release programs (SPTR) programs in which offenders are supervised while released on their own recognizance, similar to supervision while on probation

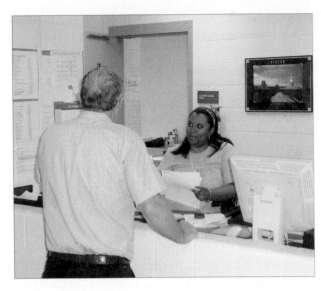

Pretrial release officers interview inmates after they are booked into jail and make a recommendation to the court as to whether the inmate should be granted bail or release on recognizance.
Photo by Richard P. Seiter.

steady employment), must report to a pretrial supervision officer, and can be violated (returned to jail) if they do not follow the conditions.[9] ROR and SPTR programs are considered successful and usually result in only a small percentage of releasees being arrested while on pretrial release status.

Pretrial services are continually growing as more jurisdictions look for safe and effective ways to reduce jail overcrowding, and so there is a growing need for pretrial services staff. The "Your Career in Corrections" box explains the role and responsibilities of these jobs.

The Role of Plea Bargaining and Sentencing

More than 90 percent of felony cases result in a guilty plea by the defendant instead of a trial to determine guilt or innocence. **Plea bargaining** is an agreement in which the defendant enters a plea of guilty in exchange for a reduced sentence in comparison to the sentence allowable for the charged offense. In practical terms, offenders usually plead guilty to an offense less serious than indicted by the prosecution. For example, instead of first-degree murder, the offender may plead guilty to second-degree murder; instead of armed robbery, he or she may plead guilty to theft. Prosecutors are willing to accept a plea in exchange for a lesser sentence for many reasons. Trials are time-consuming and costly, and if fewer offenders pleaded guilty, the court resources would be overwhelmed. In addition, even if the prosecution believes it has a sound case against the offender, there is a risk in trying it before a jury, as the jury must be convinced of the offender's guilt "beyond a reasonable doubt." Offenders often plead guilty if they know they are guilty and believe that the evidence against them is overwhelming, and they wish to get a lighter sentence than is possible for the crime they committed.

Plea bargaining is primarily a function of the prosecution and the court system, yet it has many implications for corrections and the sentencing process. Upon a plea of guilty, the court (if accepting the plea agreement) moves immediately to the sentencing process and sentences the offender to the agreed-on sentence. Usually the court, once the plea is negotiated, will ask the probation office to conduct a presentence investigation, in order to have more information to ensure that the

Plea bargaining

an agreement in which the defendant enters a guilty plea in exchange for a reduced sentence in comparison to the sentence allowable for the charged offense

YOUR CAREER IN CORRECTIONS

PRETRIAL SERVICES OFFICERS

Pretrial services officers are officers of the court, serving the court system in most states, most large cities, and thirty-six federal districts. Their job is twofold: investigation and supervision. In most situations, newly arrested offenders are investigated, and recommendations are made to the court regarding their release or detention. The investigation is completed through the creation of a social history regarding the person's life, including family ties, health, mental health status, employment history, financial assets, and other community relationships. The purpose of this history is to determine the strength of the offender's ties to the community, which is critical in the assessment of risk of flight and failure to appear at future court hearings. The social history is created through interviewing the individual, calling family members or other significant parties, doing a credit check, and searching official records. As well, pretrial services officers examine the individual's prior criminal history, using computer networks to check prior offenses, gang affiliations, other court histories, and other confinement records. The report usually must be done very quickly, because the hearing to determine bail occurs early in the criminal justice process. In fact, in the federal court system, officers must do the report and make a recommendation within about two hours. The recommendation usually focuses on whether the person should be released or detained. The officer may also address any need for alternatives to detention, such as the use of a halfway house, an inpatient or outpatient drug or mental health treatment center, or electronic monitoring.

If the individual is released, specific conditions are placed on his or her release, and a pretrial services officer supervises the person in a similar way to probation. Many jurisdictions use a "least restrictive" model of supervision, because the individual has a presumption of innocence. This means that supervision conditions are placed according to the individual case, with the fewest conditions possible to ensure that the offender will show up for court and is not a danger to others. Supervision is similar to probation and each case has a separate plan covering the requirements for supervision, including the frequency of contact and other conditions. Almost always, the officer must visit the residence and walk through every room to ensure that the home is an acceptable placement and that there is no evidence of any criminal activity. After this initial home inspection, the supervision begins, and offenders are reminded of court dates and requirements of supervision.

Supervision typically lasts three to six months, until a trial or plea agreement. It can be extended if the conviction is appealed and the person is granted release status. Some individuals are seen daily, while others must only make a monthly telephone report. Many contacts are in the field rather than in the office. Officers who do community contacts are usually allowed to carry a weapon, receive special training in personal protection, and wear bulletproof vests for their personal safety. They also make contacts with treatment providers, such as for drug abuse, sex offenders, and mental health. The supervision usually includes urine testing for drug use.

If there is a violation of supervision, the officer reports to the court with a recommendation to either continue supervision as is, change the supervision conditions, or violate and revoke the release status. A detention hearing is held, and the court must show that there are no conditions that can be supervised in community and still ensure that the person will show up at court. For the hearing, the officer presents a report detailing evidence of the violations, and may have to testify.

---

agreement is within realistic expectations for an offender with this type of background and criminal involvement. Upon sentencing, the offender is then turned over to correctional authorities to carry out the sentence, whether it be probation with certain conditions or a period of imprisonment.

Presentencing Correctional Activities

Following a finding or plea of guilt, criminal courts must determine sentences that will be imposed on criminal offenders. A critical tool used by judges during the sentencing process is the **presentence investigation (PSI).** The PSI is a report

Presentence investigation (PSI)

a report used during the sentencing process that details the background of a convicted offender, including criminal, social, education, employment, mental and physical health, and other significant factors detailing the background of a convicted offender, including criminal history, social background, education, employment, mental and physical health, and other factors valuable to consider in the sentencing process. The PSI often also provides judges the range of sanctions allowable for the crime, and recommendations for sentencing based on the risk of the offender and the chance for success if he or she is granted probation and remains in the community.

Most states require a PSI to be completed for felony cases that allow the possibility of probation. When judges have discretion regarding the sentence they will grant offenders, the recommendation within the PSI is followed 80 to 90 percent of the time. The PSI is usually prepared by probation officers working for the court. Probation departments usually have a dual responsibility of investigation (preparation of the PSI) and supervision of offenders placed on probation. Some departments have separate groups of probation officers that do only PSIs or only supervision. Others mix officer responsibilities to do some of both these tasks.

PURPOSES OF THE PSI

While the purpose of the PSI is to assist courts in the sentencing decision, it is valuable in many other ways, including the following:

1. *For use in sentencing by the court.* As noted, the information provided by the PSI is critical in the sentencing decision. The PSI provides judges specific factors about the offender that are considered to determine his or her risk to the community and mitigating and aggravating circumstances regarding the offense.
2. *For use in determining supervision needs during probation.* If the offender is granted probation, the information in the PSI is helpful in determining the type of supervision needed and the types of programs that could help the offender succeed in the community. Similarly, if the offender is sentenced to prison with a period of supervision after release, the PSI is valuable in determining postincarceration community supervision needs.
3. *For use by prison officials in classifying offenders and determining program needs.* For offenders given prison sentences, the PSI is very valuable to prison officials in determining the level of prison security (minimum, medium, or maximum) required and the types of programs that should be available to the inmate.
4. *For use by the parole board in making release decisions.* In states that still use indeterminate sentences (described shortly) with release by a parole board, information regarding the current offense, past history of crime, and personal background are critical in deciding when an inmate is to be released from prison and put in the community.
5. *For research purposes.* Research studies of the effectiveness of correctional sanctions or programs usually measure outcome as recidivism or return to criminal activity. This outcome variable is much more valuable if it can be correlated with specific factors relative to offenders, such as problems of drug abuse or mental illness, lack of education, or a history of violence.

Throughout the correctional process, officials continually use the PSI to assess the dual needs of offenders for security and supervison and for rehabilitative treatment. Offenders must be placed in a level of supervision (whether in the community or in prison) that is commensurate to their risk of violence or escape. As well, offenders must have the opportunity to participate in programs that can be beneficial in dealing with their problems and treatment needs. Information critical to both of these categories of decisions is collected and included in the PSI.

COLLECTING INFORMATION FOR THE PSI

Shortly after a finding or plea of guilt, the judge sets a date for sentencing of the offender. In addition, the probation office will assign a probation officer to conduct the PSI for presentation to the court to consider for the sentencing decision. The first step in collecting information begins with an interview of the offender. Most states and the federal government provide a worksheet used by probation officers to collect preliminary information during the initial interview. The worksheet includes several questions regarding offenders' criminal history, family situation including marital status and children, physical and mental condition, substance abuse, education and vocational background, and employment record.

Information from the interview is then verified by checking the sources provided by the offender. For instance, all of the past employers named by offenders are contacted to verify the accuracy of the information. In addition, the investigating officer often interviews other people who can provide additional information or collaborate information provided by the offender. Offenders' spouses or parents are usually interviewed to determine their perspective of the offender and identify other problems not mentioned by the offender. Finally, investigating officers search for official records such as a copy of the offender's birth certificate, social security card, military records, or verification of high school graduation.

While the types of information necessary to complete the PSI are generally clear, the detailed information required is not. As noted earlier, correctional officials are continually trying to balance the goal of risk management with the need for rehabilitation. The investigating officer must keep this balance and the end use of the PSI in mind while collecting information. For example, the officer may note that the offender has a poor employment history and a record of constantly changing jobs. These facts are important, yet are much more valuable if the officer continues to pursue the reasons for the job changes. Did they result from the offender being fired for failure to get along with co-workers, for stealing from employers, or for drug use on the job? Or does the offender simply lack responsibility in finding

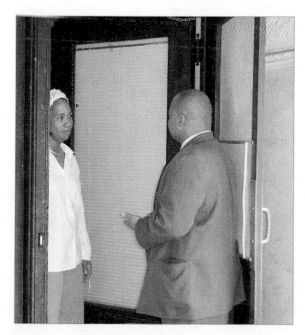

An important part of the creation of a PSI occurs when the officer visits the family and interviews them regarding the offender.
Photo by Richard P. Seiter.

and maintaining employment? The more detailed the PSI regarding the reasons behind the facts, the more useful the PSI is to correctional officials.

CONTENTS OF THE PSI

The categories of information noted previously have historically been included in a PSI. However, the approach to writing the PSI has changed significantly. Historically, the PSI was a lengthy narrative of these categories, including many subjective conclusions by the investigating officer. The advantage of this type of report was that it often told a story about the offender, in a way that the reader almost got to know the offender and the types of issues and problems that contributed to his or her involvement in crime. PSIs, with their many subjective statements, were considered the property of the court, and offenders were not allowed to see them. This lack of disclosure was supported in the 1949 case of *Williams v. New York,* in which the U.S. Supreme Court upheld a decision to deny the defense access to the PSI, even though the sentencing judge used evidence in the confidential PSI to give a death penalty over the recommendation of a life sentence by the jury.[10] Since the *Williams* case, many courts have modified their decisions and disclose the PSI, and many state legislatures have passed laws requiring full disclosure of the PSI to the defendants' lawyers.

With these changes, PSIs have undergone an expected change in the style in which they are written. Many PSIs are now much shorter, factual without opinion, and designed to avoid legal challenges by the defense. In federal courts, the PSI is provided to the defense attorney before sentencing, so that any defense objections to facts or statements in the PSI can be noted to the judge. The defense may even point out inaccuracies or provide new information that results in the PSI being changed before it is sent to the judge. Figure 2.1 illustrates the current format suggested for use by federal courts.

Most of the sections in the PSI are fairly clear. However, two important areas that need further explanation are the victim impact statement and the recommendation. As a result of the recent emphasis of including the victims in the criminal justice process, and emphasizing restitution of the victim as a goal of sentencing, victim impact statements have been added to many states and to federal presentence investigations. Victim impact information provides the sentencing judge details regarding both the financial loss and emotional trauma that resulted to the victim of the crime. This information then helps the judge set a required amount of money as a fine or for the offender to pay as victim compensation, when the offender has the potential to pay these costs. Victim statements also sometimes reflect the victims' desire for the type of sentences offenders should receive. Initially, there was concern that including statements of the victims' preferences during sentencing, would unduly influence judges in their sentencing decision or assignment of monetary payments to the victim. However, studies have indicated that these statements do not overstate victim losses or result in harsher sentencing.[11]

Another key component of the PSI is the recommendation of a sentence by the investigating officer. Because of the recent disclosure of PSIs, some states no longer have the officer make a sentencing recommendation in the PSI. However, it is still believed that a recommended sentence is valuable to the sentencing process. First, the recommendation section often identifies the range of sanctions available to the judge. Second, the officer's recommendation is based on fact and offender background, and is seen as both professionally developed and without any biases that may have come about during the trial or other court hearings. Third, judges respect these recommendations and follow them in 80 to 90 percent of cases in which recommendations are made. However, with the high level of concurrence by the judge, it can be argued that allowing a probation officer to make a

FORMAT FOR PRESENTENCE INVESTIGATIONS IN U.S. COURTS

Face Sheet
- Pedigree information
- Court information
- Offense information
- Release status
  1. Personal recognizance
  2. Unsecured bond
  3. Percentage bond
  4. Surety bond
  5. Collateral
  6. Third-person custody
- Detainers
- Codefendants
- Related cases

The Offense
- Charges
- Plea or verdict
- Plea agreement
- Motion for substantial assistance
- Co-defendants
- Related cases
- Pretrial adjustments

Victim Impact
- Financial
- Social
- Psychological
- Medical
- Costs

Adjustment/Obstruction of Justice
- Any attempt to impede prosecution

Acceptance of Responsibility
- Does the offender accept responsibility?

Criminal History
- Arrests
- Convictions
- Pending charges
- Other law enforcement contacts
- Juvenile adjudications

Offender Characteristics
- Personal and family data
- Physical condition
- Mental and emotional health
- Substance abuse
- Educational and vocational skills
- Employment history

Financial Ability to Pay
- Assets
- Unsecured debt
- Net worth
- Income
- Necessary expenses
- Net monthly cash flow
- Analysis

Sentencing Options
- Impact of plea agreement
- Custody options
- Probation options—necessary conditions
- Fines
- Restitution

Recommendations

sentencing recommendation gives the officer authority to make a sentence via the judge. Finally, the recommendation is useful during the judicial consideration of the plea bargain agreement. When the defense and prosecution negotiate a specific sentence in exchange for a guilty plea, the judge can compare that sentence to the recommendation by the probation officer to determine whether the agreement is reasonable based on the risk and treatment needs of the offender.

The Sentencing Decision

At this point in the correctional and sentencing process, offenders have either pleaded or been found guilty, a presentence investigation has been provided to the court, and it is time for the sentencing decision. The judge assigned to preside over each criminal case determines the sentence. The range of sentences that can be used by a judge for any criminal case is identified in the state penal code, a statute passed by the legislature. In the following sections, various sentencing options, models of sentences, and discretion provided to judges are described.

SENTENCING OPTIONS

Six general categories of sentencing options are authorized in state penal codes and therefore available to judges. These include the following:

- **Economic sanctions**: a requirement that an offender pay a fine or restitution to the victim as a part of his or her sentence, or do **community service** (a

Economic sanction

a requirement that an offender pay a fine or restitution to the victim as a part of his or her sentence

Community service

a requirement that an offender provide his or her personal time to do some public good

Probation

a prison sentence that is suspended on the condition that the offender follow certain prescribed rules and commit no further crimes

Intermediate sanctions

midrange dispositions that fall between probation and imprisonment

Short-term confinement

a sentence in a jail for one year or less

Imprisonment

a sentence in a prison of a year or more

Capital punishment

punishment for the most serious crimes (generally first-degree murder); most states and the federal government provide for the death penalty

requirement that an offender provide personal time to do some public good). In most cases, economic sanctions are a condition of probation; however, in some instances, these are stand-alone sentences without probation.

- **Probation**: a prison sentence that is suspended on the condition that the offender is supervised in the community, follows certain prescribed rules, and commits no further crimes. If offenders who receive probation meet all the requirements of probation and complete the time they are to be supervised in the community, the suspended sentence is never invoked. Standard conditions of probation include avoiding further crime, maintaining employment, and reporting as required to the probation officer. Additional conditions to have more intensive monitoring or respond to a certain need of the offender (such as substance abuse or mental illness) may be added to standard conditions. Conditions that add monitoring or treatment requirements are sometimes referred to as intermediate sanctions.
- **Intermediate sanctions**: midrange dispositions that fall between probation and imprisonment. Intermediate sanctions (such as intensive probation supervision or house arrest with electronic monitoring) provide more supervision and monitoring than standard probation, yet are less than a sentence of confinement to a jail or prison.
- **Short-term confinement**: a sentence in a jail for one year or less. Minor offenders (those who have committed misdemeanors or less serious felonies) may receive a sentence of less than one year. With sentences of this length, offenders often are sentenced to stay in the local community jail rather than being transferred to a state prison.
- **Imprisonment**: a sentence in a prison for a year or more to a life sentence. Offenders receiving sentences of more than one year are usually ordered into the custody of the state (or federal) department of corrections for placement in a suitable prison.
- **Capital punishment**: for the most serious crimes (generally first-degree murder), most states and the federal government provide for the death penalty.

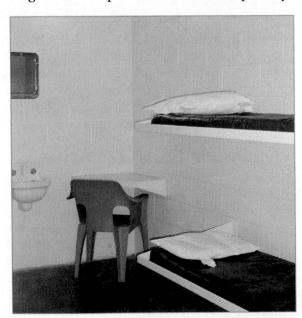

If offenders receive a sentence of short-term confinement, they serve the sentence in a jail and spend much of their time idle in a small cell usually holding two inmates.
Photo by Richard P. Seiter.

SUPERVISION CONTINUUM SENTENCING OPTIONS IN MISSOURI

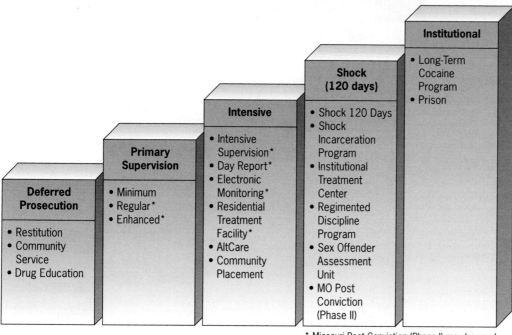

Institutional
- Long-Term Cocaine Program
- Prison

Shock (120 days)
- Shock 120 Days
- Shock Incarceration Program
- Institutional Treatment Center
- Regimented Discipline Program
- Sex Offender Assessment Unit
- MO Post Conviction (Phase II)

Intensive
- Intensive Supervision*
- Day Report*
- Electronic Monitoring*
- Residential Treatment Facility*
- AltCare
- Community Placement

Primary Supervision
- Minimum
- Regular*
- Enhanced*

Deferred Prosecution
- Restitution
- Community Service
- Drug Education

* Missouri Post Conviction (Phase I) may be used in conjunction with these programs.

Source: Missouri Department of Corrections, 2000.

Over the past two decades, there has been an emphasis on creating a broad array of sentencing options to meet the varying needs and requirements of different types of crimes and different types of criminals. Figure 2.2 is an example of the sentencing options available for crimes committed in the State of Missouri. These options illustrate how increasing levels of supervision are provided for more serious criminals.

Even with the "tough on crime" approaches resulting in more prison sentences for longer periods of time for many offenders, the largest proportion of offenders remain on probation or are supervised in the community. As indicated in Table 2.1, the estimated number of people under correctional supervision increased from 1.84 million in 1980 to 6.59 million by 2001. Of these, 3.93 million (60 percent) were on probation, 631,000 (9.6 percent) were in jail, 1.33 million (20 percent) were in prison, and 732,000 (10.4 percent) were on parole.

One important consideration during sentencing comes in the sequencing of sentences. In a large percentage of criminal cases, offenders are charged with more than one crime, or with several counts of the same crime. Penal codes allow the sentences for each crime or count to be aggregated separately. As a result, sentences can be either concurrent or consecutive. **Concurrent sentences** are assigned to run at the same time. For example, if an offender is found guilty of three counts of larceny, and each count carries a sentence of three years, the total time of the sentences would be nine years. Concurrent sentences would have all three counts begin at the same time, and the offender in the example would then complete the three sentences in three years. However, **consecutive sentences** run one after the other. If sentenced to the three counts in the example to be served consecutively, the offender would have to finish each of the three-year sentences before beginning the next, and would complete the sentences in nine years (3 + 3 + 3 = 9 years). The use of concurrent and consecutive sentencing options is usually a consideration during plea bargain negotiations.

Concurrent sentences
sentences that run at the same time

Consecutive sentences
sentences that run one after the other

TABLE	2.1	Adults on Probation, In Jail or Prison, and on Parole in the United States, 1980–2001

Year	Total estimated correctional population[a]	Probation	Jail	Prison	Parole
1980	1,840,400	1,118,097	182,288[b]	319,598	220,438
1981	2,006,600	1,225,934	195,085[b]	360,029	225,539
1982	2,192,600	1,357,264	207,853	402,914	224,604
1983	2,475,100	1,582,947	221,815	423,898	246,440
1984	2,689,200	1,740,948	233,018	448,264	266,992
1985	3,011,500	1,968,712	254,986	487,593	300,203
1986	3,239,400	2,114,621	272,735	526,436	325,638
1987	3,459,600	2,247,158	294,092	562,814	355,505
1988	3,714,100	2,356,483	341,893	607,766	407,977
1989	4,055,600	2,522,125	393,303	683,367	456,803
1990	4,350,300	2,670,234	405,320	743,382	531,407
1991	4,535,600	2,728,472	424,129[c]	792,535	590,442
1992	4,762,600	2,811,611	441,781[c]	850,566	658,601
1993	4,944,000	2,903,061	455,500[c]	909,381	676,100
1994	5,141,300	2,981,022	479,800	990,147	690,371
1995	5,342,900	3,077,861	507,044	1,078,542	679,421
1996	5,490,700	3,164,996	518,492	1,127,528	679,733
1997[d]	5,734,900	3,296,513	567,079	1,176,564	694,787
1998[d]	6,134,200	3,670,441	592,462	1,224,469	696,385
1999[d]	6,349,800	3,779,922	605,943	1,287,172	714,457
2000	6,445,600	3,826,209	621,149	1,316,333	724,486
2001	6,594,000	3,932,751	631,240	1,330,980	732,351
Percent change 2000 to 2001	2.3%	2.8%	1.6%	1.1%	1.1%

Note: Counts for probation, prison, and parole populations are for December 31 of each year; jail population counts are for June 30 of each year. Counts of adults held in jail facilities for 1993 and 1994 were estimated and rounded to the nearest 100. Data for jail and prison are for inmates under custody and include those held in private facilities. Totals for 1998–2001 exclude probationers reported to have been in jail or prison. These data have been revised by the Source based on the most recently reported counts and may differ from previous editions of *Sourcebook*.

[a]A small number of Individuals have multiple correctional statuses: consequently, the total number of persons under correctional supervision is an overestimate. The total is rounded to the nearest 100.
[b]Estimated.
[c]Includes an unknown number of persons supervised outside jail facilities.
[d]Coverage of probation agencies was expanded. For counts based on the same reporting agencies, use 3,266,837 in 1997 (to compare with 1996); 3,417,613 in 1998 (to compare with 1997); and 3,773,624 in 1999 (to compare with 1998).

Source: Bureau of Justice Statistics, *Sourcebook of Criminal Justice Statistics: 2001* (Washington, D.C.: U.S. Department of Justice, 2001), p. 478.

SENTENCING MODELS

As noted earlier, nonincarceration sentences include economic sanctions, probation, and intermediate sanctions; incarceration sentences include both short-term and long-term confinement. As described in the next two chapters, short sentences are sometimes linked with an intermediate sanction, so that offenders spend part of their sentence in jail or prison, and part of their sentence under supervision in the community. Finally, there are sentences of death. For sentences of incarceration, indeterminate and determinate sentences are the two primary models used throughout the United States, although there are many variations to each of these.

Indeterminate sentences blend the decision by the sentencing judge and a later decision by a release authority to determine the actual time served. At the time of sentencing, judges sentence offenders to indeterminate sentences, with a minimum and maximum amount of time to be served (for example, two to five years or ten to twenty years). After serving the minimum term, offenders are eligible to be released and their cases are reviewed by a parole board. The parole board determines the release date any time between the minimum and maximum sentence. If a parole board never grants parole, the offender serves the maximum sentence and then must be released. The parole decision and postrelease supervision in the community is described in Chapter 6.

As the Reformatory Era of prison operations was initiated in the United States around 1870, many states and prisons began to implement the concepts of rehabilitation and preparing inmates for return to the community. By the beginning of the twentieth century, preparation for release was considered an important part of the prison experience, and correctional systems were organized to provide programs to prepare inmates for the community transition. During the mid-twentieth century, all states used indeterminate sentences with release by parole boards, and by 1977 release on parole reached its peak, as 72 percent of all prisoners were released on parole.[12]

For almost twenty years preceding this high-water mark, the focus of incarceration was rehabilitation, as parole boards reviewed inmates' cases and determined their release dates based on the best judgment of their readiness for successfully returning to the community. Emphasizing rehabilitation made it almost impossible for judges to make a good decision about when offenders should be released at the time of sentencing. Critical to the release decision were efforts by offenders to improve themselves, as demonstrated by their personal status after they had served their minimum sentence. When believed "reformed" and ready to face life in free society, prisoners were released from prison.

The "Case Study" box illustrates some of the costs and other issues that result from changes in sentencing without a thoughtful investigation of the impact of changes.

Determinate sentences are sentences of fixed terms. Offenders are eligible for release following the completion of the time to be served (for example, five years). Determinate sentences are not reviewed by any body, or subject to release by parole boards. When offenders complete their sentence terms, they are released. Determinate sentences were used throughout the eighteenth century in the United States. Sentencing judges were believed to have the most informed knowledge of offenders and the amount of time needed to punish them and deter them from further crimes. Therefore, judges were granted considerable discretion in determining the prescribed sentence.

An early reform in determinate sentences was the use of **good time**. The concept of good time was initiated first by Captain Alexander Machonchie, who created a system of marks when he was superintendent of the British penal colony on Norfolk Island in the 1840s. By earning marks, inmates could earn time off their sentence through good behavior and efforts toward personal reform. Good time is now the number of days subtracted from the required time to be served due to good behavior and following prison rules. Good time is used in both determinate and indeterminate sentences and affords inmates the opportunity to reduce the time until their eligibility for release. Good time is seen as a critical tool for prison staff to maintain order, as it is a valued reward that can be granted to inmates who behave, or not awarded to those who fail to follow the rules of the prison.

A form of determinate sentences that has gained popularity over the past decade is **truth in sentencing**. Recent enactments by Congress have encouraged states to adopt truth-in-sentencing (TIS) statutes and allowed states enacting such laws to qualify for federal funds to aid in prison construction. TIS statutes are

Indeterminate sentences sentences that have a minimum and maximum time to be served; a decision by a release authority determines the actual time served within that range

Determinate sentences sentences of fixed terms

Good time a reward that affords inmates the opportunity to reduce the time until their eligibility for release by good behavior in prison

Truth in sentencing a sentencing model that requires completion of 85 percent of the sentence before prisoners are eligible for release

---

MINOR CHANGES CAN HAVE MAJOR BUDGET IMPLICATIONS

A state experiencing a rapid increase in the number of offenders in prison examined the impact of several suggestions to reduce overcrowding in the prison system. The state used indeterminate sentences, but had greatly increased the minimum time to be served before inmates were eligible for parole. These sentences were often increased from one to two years, from five to seven years, or from ten to fifteen years. It is interesting that when sentences are increased, it is usually by some increment of years, rather than months or even days. It is easy to decide to extend the minimum sentence for some crime, especially if the decision to lengthen the sentence comes shortly after a serious crime has occurred that received a lot of media attention, and there is too much emotion and anger involved in the decision.

One of the arguments for stopping the increase by annual increments is that there is not much consideration of the cost of such jumps. In a study in the state of the cost of such increases, it was determined that if every inmate in the state were serving a sentence that was only ninety days shorter, it would save the state $500 million over thirty years! Legislators were shocked by these figures. The state held approximately 20,000 inmates, and reducing the sentence served by each for three months would over time reduce the population by five-hundred inmates. To build a five-hundred-bed prison cost approximately $50 million, and it is estimated that construction costs represent only 10 percent of the overall operating costs of a prison over thirty years, or a total of $500 million. This represents how minor adjustments in time served can save state governments massive amounts of money.

---

determinate sentences, and also limit to 15 percent of the sentence the amount of good time that prison officials may grant inmates as incentives for good behavior or program participation.[13] Inmates under truth-in-sentencing statutes must complete 85 percent of the sentence before they are eligible for release. By the end of 2000, twenty-nine states and the District of Columbia had adopted truth-in-sentencing statutes.[14] From 1980 to 1996, the number of prisoners in state and federal prisons grew from 330,000 to 1,054,000, a more than threefold increase,[15] and reached 1,440,655 at the end of 2002.[16]

The reduction in good time—so that offenders do not get out of prison sooner than the public expects and they are held accountable for their crimes—seems warranted. However, the "An Insider's Experience" box illustrates how important the discretion to award good time can be for correctional administrators attempting to keep prisons from becoming too overcrowded and to save their agency money.

JUDICIAL DISCRETION IN SENTENCING

In addition to the return to determinate sentencing over the past twenty years, there has also been a move to reduce the amount of discretion granted to sentencing judges and administrative bodies. As noted, early in the history of U.S. sentencing practices, judges were granted considerable discretion in determining the length and severity of criminal sentences. However, reforms to indeterminate sentencing and a "tough on crime" movement also brought about efforts to reduce discretion by judges and parole boards in modifying sentences. There are three forms of sentencing, based on where discretion resides within the system.

The first is the **judicial form of sentencing**, in which judges are granted considerable discretion in sentencing decisions. Under this form, penal codes create broad ranges of allowable sentences for each crime; allow judges to decide whether to grant a sentence of probation or incarceration; and, if sending the offender to prison, define a broad range of the length of time to be served. The second is the **administrative form of sentencing**, which grants considerable dis-

---

Judicial form of sentencing

a sentencing model in which judges have primary discretion in creating the sentence

Administrative form of sentencing

a sentencing model in which administrative bodies (correctional officials and parole/release boards) have primary discretion in granting good time and determining the release time of offenders

AN INSIDER'S EXPERIENCE: Increasing Good Time Opportunities

When I was director of corrections in Ohio, we were facing severe overcrowding resulting from a legislative change in sentencing that occurred just before I assumed the position. The change kept the use of indeterminate sentencing but lengthened many sentences, significantly reduced good time that could be awarded to inmates, and initiated determinate sentences for some felonies. After I had been director for about three years, we received a grant from the National Institute of Corrections to form an "Overcrowding Committee" made up of judges, prosecutors, legislators, and many officials from local and state government. Our purpose was to review the sentencing laws and correctional approaches and make any recommendations that we believed could safely reduce the level of prison overcrowding. With the differing opinions and backgrounds of our members, it was difficult to come up with recommendations that we all supported.

One area we proposed was to increase good time, but only if inmates truly "earned" it. There was genuine concern that the previous sentencing structure had allowed inmates to earn too much good time (they would serve only about one-third of their maximum sentence before being eligible for parole). However, the change in sentencing made good time so limited that it took all incentive for good behavior away. We proposed specific awards of good time based on completion of programs in prison. If inmates completed their GED, a substance abuse program, or vocational training, they could be granted thirty to sixty days of good time. We knew (from the preceding case study) how much these days could add up to and save money for the entire state correctional system.

Presenting the proposal to the legislature was not so easy, however. While this proposal seemed exceedingly rational to me, many legislators did not want to do anything that would seem to be reversing what they believed to be the proper public policy of holding offenders accountable for their crimes by increasing the level of punishment received. We were successful in getting this proposal passed, but not without a lot of educating of members of the legislature, and by carefully posturing the message. The key selling point was that this proposal made inmates "earn" their way out of prison, by working hard to compete programs that would ultimately assist their successful return to the community. Good time would not be given just for good behavior; they had to affirmatively complete something before they received it. Overall, it did make a difference in the number of inmates in prison, and did save the state money.

cretion to officials of the executive branch of government. This includes prison officials in the award of good time and parole board members in determining when inmates will be released. More recently, the **legislative form of sentencing** has come to dominate sentencing across many states and the federal government. This approach grants most of the discretion to the legislative branch of government, as legislative bodies create penal codes with determinate sentences and little (or no) discretion available to judges. Legislative forms of sentencing include mandatory minimum sentences, presumptive sentencing, and the use of sentencing guidelines.

Mandatory Minimum Sentences

During the 1980s there was a concern that certain categories of offenders should be sentenced to prison without the opportunity for probation. Since that time, mandatory minimum sentences were adopted by forty-eight states and the federal government. **Mandatory minimum sentences** require that for certain crimes (violent crimes, crimes using a gun, distribution of narcotics) or for certain types of offenders (habitual criminals, sexual predators), there must be a sentence to prison for a set minimum term. The sentencing judge may not impose a sentence of probation, assess a fine, or suspend the prison sentence.

As with many criminal justice policy reforms, while the theory behind mandatory minimum sentences makes sense, the practical application results in many

Legislative form of sentencing

a sentencing model in which legislative bodies create very structured sentencing codes and therefore have primary discretion in the length of time served by offenders

Mandatory minimum sentences

a requirement that for certain crimes or for certain types of offenders, there must be a sentence to prison for at least a minimum term unintended consequences. The lack of discretion provided to judges often results in their sentencing offenders to prison that they believe warrant only being supervised in the community. Mandatory minimum sentences for drug crimes are particularly telling in this regard. Twenty years ago, 22 percent of the federal prison population were drug offenders, and today drug offenders make up 55 percent of federal inmates.[17] New York has also enacted mandatory prison sentences for drug offenders, and as a result, the percentage of violent offenders in New York prisons decreased from 63 percent in 1982 to 34 percent in 1992.[18] Many experts are questioning the value of incarcerating large numbers of drug offenders, many with no prior history, thereby requiring the construction and operation of hundreds of new prisons to hold this population.

Three-Strikes Laws

Three-strikes laws

a legislative mandate that judges sentence third-time felons to extremely long or life prison sentences

Another form of mandatory minimum sentence is called **three-strikes laws**, which require judges to sentence third-time felons to extremely long prison sentences (often twenty years, thirty years, or life). These laws were intended to incapacitate habitual and dangerous law violators who commit three felonies, so that they could not continue to prey on law-abiding citizens. The initial passage of such a law by the state of Washington in 1993 was intended to target repeat violent offenders. In 1994, California expanded the definition of those who come under the law, and allowed some second-felony offenders to be included. At this time, twenty-three states have passed three-strikes laws. As with other mandatory minimum sentences, three-strikes laws are often an overreaction to crime-control efforts.[19]

An often-cited case of overreach of mandatory prison terms was the 1995 sentencing under the California three-strikes law of Jerry Williams. Williams had a record of two prior felony convictions involving violence when he stole a piece of pizza (without a weapon) from four children. The judge, under the mandatory California law, had to sentence Williams to twenty-five years in prison. The cost to the state for his incarceration for stealing a piece of pizza is estimated to be $500,000. An unintended problem resulting from the California three-strikes law is that offenders with two prior convictions are refusing to plea bargain. For offenders with two prior convictions, any new felony results in their receiving either a twenty-five-year sentence or a life sentence, eliminating the likelihood of a plea and resulting in a demand for a trial. The court systems are being engulfed in trials for relatively simple cases. Cases like the Williams sentence and the overall impact on cost and court delays resulting from the California three-strikes law have raised considerable questions about the value of such laws.

There has been much debate about the effectiveness of three-strikes laws and the impact of such laws on crime rates and costs to the correctional system. Since California has one of the oldest of such laws in effect and has used the law more extensively than many other states, it has been the most studied.[20] The most important issue is whether three-strikes laws reduce crime. California's crime rates have decreased since the three-strikes law was adopted. However, the impact of three-strikes laws on this decline is questionable. In one of the most thorough analyses of the California law, Zimring, Kamin, and Hawkins concluded that "declines in crime observed after the effective date of the three-strikes law were not the results of the deterrent impacts of the (the three-strikes) statute."[21]

Presumptive Sentencing

Presumptive sentencing

a predetermined range of a minimum, average, and maximum term for a specific crime for a "typical" offender, with allowances for mitigating and aggravating circumstances to be considered

Presumptive sentencing is a predetermined range of a minimum, average, and maximum term for a specific crime. Judges are directed to sentence the "typical" offender committing a crime to the presumptive term. The sentencing judge is then granted limited discretion in determining whether there are *mitigating* cir-

Three-strikes laws and other mandatory minimum sentences have resulted in prisons becoming extremely overcrowded.
Photo by Richard P. Seiter.

cumstances (those that indicate reasons for leniency) that should be considered and used to reduce the sentence to below the presumptive term, or *aggravating* circumstances (those that indicate that the offender deserves more than the average) resulting in a sentence of more than the presumptive term. Most presumptive sentences include a minimum and maximum sentence, with very limited ranges of discretion. For example, in one presumptive sentencing model, the presumptive sentence is fifty-four months, the minimum sentence is fifty months, and the maximum sentence is fifty-eight months.

Sentencing Guidelines

Sentencing guidelines combine both minimum mandatory and presumptive sentencing approaches. **Sentencing guidelines** are structured sentences, based on measures of offense severity and criminal history, to determine the length of the term of imprisonment. Figure 2.3 is the Minnesota sentencing guideline grid. It was one of the earliest enacted sentencing guidelines, adopted in 1983. The left side of the grid is a list of crime categories in order of increasing severity. Across the top, offenders' criminal histories are scored on factors such as the number of prior offenses, age at first offense, history of violence, or escape from a prison or absconding from community supervision.

Sentencing guidelines
a system of structured sentences, based on measures of offense severity and criminal history, that is used to determine the length of the term of imprisonment

States have adopted sentencing guidelines for several reasons. First, it was believed that judges might not be harsh enough on certain criminals, and required guidelines ensure that dangerous criminals are sent to prison. Second, sentencing guidelines provide uniformity, ensuring that offenders who commit similar crimes receive similar sentences. Sentencing guidelines provide planners (using projections of crime rates) with a better idea of what future sentences may mean to the number of inmates in prison or offenders under probation supervision. Most important, sentencing guidelines (by combining factors of offense severity and criminal history) provide a rational approach to determining a sentence.[22] In some states, judges have very little discretion and cannot vary from the guidelines. In other states, the guidelines are just "guidelines," and judges are not required to follow them. Finally, some jurisdictions allow judges to sentence above or below the sentencing guidelines, if the judge includes a written explanation as to the reason for the deviation.

The "A Look Into" box provides a good indication of the types of decisions and the process used in sentencing and the struggles that judges face in trying

MINNESOTA SENTENCING GUIDELINE GRID

Severity level of conviction offense	Criminal History Score						
	0	**1**	**2**	**3**	**4**	**5**	**6 or more**
• Unauthorized use of motor vehicle • Possession of marijuana	12	12	12	15	18	21	24 *23–25*
• Theft-related crimes ($150–$2,500) • Sale of marijuana	12	12	14	17	20	23	27 *25–29*
• Theft crimes ($150–$2,500)	12	13	16	19	22 *21–23*	27 *25–29*	32 *30–34*
• Burglary—felony intent • Receiving stolen goods ($150–$2,500)	12	15	18	21	25 *24–26*	32 *30–34*	41 *37–45*
• Simple robbery	18	23	27	30 *29–31*	38 *36–40*	46 *43–49*	54 *50–58*
• Assault, 2nd degree	21	26	30	34 *33–35*	44 *42–46*	54 *50–58*	65 *60–70*
• Aggravated robbery	24 *23–25*	32 *30–34*	41 *38–44*	49 *45–53*	65 *60–70*	81 *75–87*	97 *90–104*
• Assault, 1st degree • Criminal sexual conduct, 1st degree	43 *41–45*	54 *50–58*	65 *60–70*	76 *71–81*	95 *89–101*	113 *106–120*	132 *124–140*
• Murder, 3rd degree	97 *94–100*	119 *116–122*	127 *124–130*	149 *143–155*	176 *168–184*	205 *195–215*	230 *218–242*
• Murder, 2nd degree	116 *111–121*	140 *133–147*	162 *153–171*	203 *192–214*	243 *231–255*	284 *270–298*	324 *309–339*

Note: Italicized numbers within the lighter boxes denote the range within which a judge may sentence without the sentence being deemed a departure. First-degree murder is excluded from the guidelines by law and is punished by life imprisonment.

Source: Minnesota Sentencing Guidelines Commission, *Report to the Legislature* (St. Paul: Minnesota Sentencing Guidelines Commission, 1983), p. 14.

to fit a criminal sentence for a particular individual into fairly limited sentencing options.

Drug Courts: A Creative Sentencing Option

Drug courts

an alternative to traditional court models to deal with the underlying drug problem as the basis of the offenders' criminality

One promising innovation regarding sentencing is the use of drug courts. **Drug courts** are an alternative to traditional court models in many ways. First, the overall philosophy is not to punish but to change behavior. Drug courts deal with offenders experiencing a drug problem as the basis of their criminality. Offenders are held accountable and must accept responsibility. Drug courts still oversee the criminal processing, yet all the court players (judges, prosecutors, defense counsel, probation officers, and treatment professionals) acknowledge the need for drug treatment (usually in the community), and therefore the adversarial nature of most criminal court proceedings is replaced with a much more collaborative one. The intent is to quickly and nonbureaucratically get the offender into drug treatment. Identification of the offender as needing intervention immediately after arrest is believed to improve offenders' motivation for change.[23]

A LOOK INTO . . .

SENTENCING: AN INTERVIEW WITH A SENTENCING JUDGE

The following is an interview with Robert H. Dierker, Jr., Circuit Judge of the 22nd Judicial Circuit of Missouri (St. Louis). The Circuit Court in Missouri is the sentencing court for adult felons and misdemeanants. Judge Dierker, who received his law degree from the University of Missouri at Kansas City and an LL.M. from Harvard University, has been a judge since 1986. He has presided over numerous civil and criminal trials, including nine capital murder trials.

Q: Thank you, Judge Dierker, for agreeing to be interviewed regarding criminal sentencing. Can you briefly describe your career as a judge?

A: I was appointed a circuit judge in 1986. The circuit court handles all types of criminal and civil cases. I have served in all divisions of the circuit court except probate and juvenile. I have been in the criminal trial division, holding criminal trials, for three years, and also served as the assignment judge to assign criminal cases to courts and judges for two years. I have also sat by designation on the Missouri Court of Appeals and Supreme Court.

Q: Can you describe the sentencing model and process in Missouri?

A: In criminal trials in which the defendant has no prior convictions, the initial punishment is "assessed" by the jury, which means that the jury decides on the sentence ceiling and the judge can use that sentence or depart downward from that sentence. When the defendant has prior convictions or there is a plea, the judge determines the sentence. The sentence, however, must be within the statutory sentencing code. The Missouri code classifies felonies into level A, B, C, or D. Each of these levels has a range of sentencing options. There is also first-degree murder, which carries a penalty of death or life without parole. There are also some mandatory sentences for career criminals or consistent offenders. Offenders that have previously been committed to the custody of the department of corrections must serve a mandatory minimum portion of their sentence prior to release. Certain dangerous felonies also carry a mandatory minimum term of imprisonment. The sentencing judge has discretion to determine the sentence within prescribed ranges. There are advisory sentencing guidelines that judges can consider, but they are not mandated to use them.

Q: How has the role of a judge changed regarding the sentencing process over the past several years?

A: Without doubt, the most significant change has been the mandatory minimum sentences for dangerous felons, persistent offenders, or those previously committed to prison.

Q: How do judges feel about these changes and the mandatory sentence requirement?

A: Many judges feel these mandatory minimum sentences simplify the sentencing task, and most are sympathetic to the policy need of the legislature to provide "truth in sentencing." Previously, the parole board had the authority to release an offender after serving considerably less time than the full sentence, and the public often questioned the credibility of such sentences. The Missouri legislature has discussed the adoption of a sentencing model similar to the federal sentencing guidelines, thus making the "advisory" guidelines mandatory, with no discretion for the judge to attempt to individualize a sentence to make the punishment best fit the crime and the offender. I personally testified against this change, and very few judges support this total lack of sentencing discretion.

Q: What are the key issues or circumstances that you consider when deciding on a criminal sentence?

(continued)

A ■ The paramount consideration is the nature of the crime. The next most important is the defendant's criminal history. Of some importance is the offender's social history. It is also valuable to consider the consequences, impact, and opinions of the victim.

Q ■ Is it usual to have a wide disagreement between the prosecutor and the defense attorney on what the sentence should be? Or are most cases plea bargained?

A ■ There is considerable difference between Missouri and the federal model of sentencing in this regard. In Missouri, there is considerable bargaining over the sentence between the prosecution and the defense. In federal court, the only bargaining is in regard to the charges to be filed by the prosecutor, since the sentencing guidelines dictate the sentence once a plea is reached. Therefore, when there is a plea bargain, the Missouri trial judge has a limited range of options, and may either accept or reject the plea and the agreed-upon sentence. In that sense, most plea bargaining sentences are not decisions as much as agreements.

Q ■ What is the most difficult thing, or the thing you struggle most with, in deciding a criminal sentence?

A ■ It is interesting that as I grow older, the sentencing process seems to become more difficult for me. As I have more experience in sentencing and the people involved, I see or am more conscious of the impact on a specific sentence for the offender and the victim and their family members. While it seems easy to invoke a sentence, it really is difficult to consider all these individual aspects and make the punishment fit the crime and the sentence make sense from the standpoint of what the criminal justice system is trying to accomplish. Many cases are not all that difficult, and I have no problem sentencing someone to a severe sentence or even death when the crime warrants it. But there are times when the options available in the statutory sentencing code just do not seem to fit the crime or meet the needs of the individuals involved.

Q ■ What other general comments would you make about the sentencing process?

A ■ I have great concern about the efficacy of the sentencing structure for narcotics offenses. I believe we have made progress on sentencing for drug offenses, as the treatment aspects have become much more prominent. Yet we need to continue to be thinking of creative ways to deal with drug offenders and looking for sentencing alternatives such as a greater range in treatment options for drug offenders. While the drug courts receive much attention, I am not yet persuaded that they are the best approach.

Drug courts are usually a unit within the court system, and drug-addicted offenders are diverted from traditional criminal processing. Courts sentence offenders to treatment programs, recognizing that sanctions that merely increase in punitiveness for repeat offenses do not work for drug addicts.[24] The judge continues to oversee the sentence and holds regular status review hearings with the offender to determine progress and compliance with conditions of the sentence. Drug courts have proven very promising; as of 1998 there were 275 drug courts in operation throughout the United States, serving approximately 90,000 offenders.[25] A recent review of recidivism of drug court graduates for 1999 and 2000 found that 16.4 percent were arrested and charged with a serious offense within one year of graduation, and 27.5 percent within two years of graduation.[26] These rates, however, have not been compared with a similar group of drug offenders who did not go through a drug court.

While it is too early in the existence of drug courts to make total claims of success, preliminary evaluations have shown some success in reducing drug use and future criminal activity. An evaluation of one of the first drug courts initiated in

Drug courts have received positive preliminary evaluations for diverting substance abusers from prisons and getting them involved in treatment to deal with underlying problems that are often the cause of their criminality.
Courtesy of Richard Hutchings/PhotoEdit Inc.

Dade County, Florida, in 1989 indicates that drug court offenders experienced lower incarceration rates, longer time to rearrest, and less frequent rearrest.[27] A more recent evaluation of the success of drug courts published in 2000 found that graduates of drug court programs are less likely to be rearrested than a comparison group of those who do not graduate from the program.[28] While drug courts are still in their relative infancy in the criminal justice system, they have proven very popular and serve as a model for alternative sentencing approaches.[29]

As we conclude our study of sentencing, you must decide what type of sentencing model you prefer. In the "You Make the Decision" box, you are asked to choose between determinate and indeterminate sentencing for your state.

YOU MAKE THE DECISION . . .

DETERMINATE OR INDETERMINATE SENTENCES

As noted, the history of sentencing for criminal offenses has been a combination of determinate and indeterminate sentences. Determinate sentences were used throughout the 1800s, and indeterminate sentences for most of the 1900s. Over the past twenty years, disillusionment with the concept of rehabilitation, the medical model, and parole prompted a tough-on-crime philosophy that resulted in an apparent swing back to determinate sentencing and limited discretion with the imposition of mandatory sentencing and truth in sentencing. However, states have more recently become concerned about the increasing costs and prison overcrowding that have resulted from abandoning indeterminate sentences, and some have reversed themselves and returned to using an indeterminate sentencing structure. There has even been a question as to whether public safety is reduced through the use of determinate sentences, since the parole board

(continued)

cannot act as a gatekeeper for those inmates that are a high risk to repeat their crimes, yet must be released under determinate sentence structures.

Your task is to decide which of these two sentencing models you think is best and you want implemented in your home state. List all the pros and cons for each model. Consider the benefits of each model you think are most important, and then decide which model you favor. If you are changing from a current model, think through the types of consequences that are likely to occur, and list the outcomes that are expected as well as those which are unknown. But make a choice: Should your state use determinate or indeterminate sentencing?

Chapter Review

SUMMARY

Criminal sentencing is one of the most complicated, yet obviously one of the most critical, components of the criminal justice process. Sentencing attempts to meet several distinct yet often overlapping goals, and must take into account a variety of factors, laws, and situations. Some consider sentencing the linchpin of the criminal justice system, in that all of the presentence activities are designed to lead up to the sentencing decision, while all of the postsentence activities are designed to carry out the sentence.

As described in this chapter, the functions of corrections no longer just begin after sentencing. Many critical pretrial functions are now considered a part of the correctional process. Correctional personnel help identify offenders who are good risks for release on recognizance. They may also conduct community supervision of offenders not detained while waiting for their trial dates. Probation officers investigate the background of offenders, conduct a presentence investigation that is extremely valuable for the sentencing decision, and provide information throughout the correctional system to classify and assign offenders to prisons or programs.

Sentencing models and forms have changed significantly over the past several decades. During the nineteenth century, judges had significant discretion in sentencing offenders. During most of the twentieth century, parole boards made decisions regarding offenders' readiness and time of release. Over the past two decades, however, legislatures have taken discretion away from most correctional and court personnel and replaced it with mandatory minimum sentencing, three-strikes laws, truth in sentencing, and sentencing guidelines. While some argue that this provides for uniformity and fairness, others suggest that this "cookie cutter" form of sentencing, in which all offenders committing similar crimes are treated in a "one size fits all" approach, is not a reform, but a step backward into an overly excessive and inefficient system of justice.

Following this chapter describing sentencing are four chapters that describe the theoretical approaches, operations, and issues surrounding the various sentencing alternatives. The use of jails and detention facilities is described in Chapter 3; probation and intermediate sentencing options are described in Chapter 4; the rapidly expanding use of prison sentences and the operation of prisons is discussed in Chapter 5; and the release on parole for offenders serving indeterminate sentences and the difficult transition from prison to the community are presented in Chapter 6. By the end of Part 2 of this text, students will have an understanding of the major components that make up the correctional systems of the United States.

REVIEW QUESTIONS

1. Differentiate between a felony and misdemeanor.
2. Describe the types of diversion programs currently used.
3. List some of the problems with using bail as a requirement for release from jail pending prosecution.
4. Describe the Manhattan Bail Project and how it has expanded and influenced current detention practices.
5. List the pros and cons of plea bargaining.
6. List the five purposes of the presentence investigation.
7. What are economic sanctions and community service?
8. Differentiate between concurrent and consecutive sentences.
9. Describe how truth-in-sentencing legislation works.

10. Differentiate between judicial, administrative, and legislative forms of sentencing.

11. What are mandatory minimum sentences?

12. List the pros and cons of three-strikes laws.

13. Describe how sentencing guidelines work.

14. How do drug courts operate, and what are their advantages?

ENDNOTES

1. National Association of Pretrial Services Agencies Diversion Committee, *Pretrial Diversion Abstract: Information Report*, http://www.napsa.org/docs/divabst.htm (accessed September 25, 2002), pp. 2–3.

2. For a discussion of TASC, see "Treatment Alternatives to Street Crimes," *Bureau of Justice Assistance Fact Sheet* (Washington, D.C.: U.S. Department of Justice, 1992).

3. For a discussion of diversion and recidivism, see Dean J. Champion, *Probation, Parole, and Community Corrections*, 4th ed. (Upper Saddle River, N.J.: Prentice Hall, 2002), p. 162.

4. National Association of Pretrial Services Agencies Diversion Committee, pp. 3–4.

5. *United States v. Salerno*, 481 U.S. 739 (1987).

6. William Rhodes, Raymond Hyatt, and Paul Scheiman, "Predicting Pretrial Misconduct with Drug Tests of Arrestees," in *Research in Brief* (Washington, D.C.: National Institute of Justice, 1996), pp. 1–6.

7. Wayne Welsh, "Changes in Arrest Policies as a Result of Court Orders Against County Jails," *Justice Quarterly* 10, no. 1 (March 1993).

8. B. A. Reaves, *Felony Defendants in Large Urban Counties, 1994* (Washington, D.C.: Bureau of Justice Statistics, 1998).

9. For a good description of pretrial supervision programs, see Thomas J. Wolf, "What United States Pretrial Service Officers Do," *Federal Probation* 61, no. 1 (March 1997): 19–24.

10. *Williams v. New York*, 337 U.S. 241 (1949).

11. Robert C. Davis and Barbara E. Smith, "The Effects of Victim Impact Statements on Sentencing Decisions: A Test in an Urban Setting," *Justice Quarterly*, 11, no. 3 (September 1994): 453–470.

12. As cited in Joan Petersilia, "Parole and Prisoner Reentry in the United States," in Michael Tonry and Joan Petersilia (Eds.), *Prisons* (Chicago, Ill.: University of Chicago Press, 1999), pp. 489–490.

13. P. Ditton and D. J. Wilson, *Truth in Sentencing in State Prisons* (Washington, D.C.: U.S. Department of Justice, Bureau of Justice Statistics, 1999).

14. Timothy A. Hughes, Doris James Wilson, and Allen J. Beck, *Trends in State Parole, 1990–2000* (Washington, D.C.: U.S. Department of Justice, Bureau of Justice Statistics, October 2001).

15. J. Furniss, "The Population Boom," *Corrections Today* 58, no. 1 (1996): 38–43.

16. Paige M. Harrison and Allen J. Beck, "Prisoners in 2002," *Bureau of Justice Statistics Bulletin*, July 2003, p. 1.

17. Bureau of Prisons, Website: www.bop.gov. (November 2003).

18. Walter J. Dickey, *Evaluating Mandatory Minimum Sentences* (Washington, D.C.: Campaign for Effective Crime Policy, 1993), p. 3.

19. For an overview of three-strikes laws across the country, see Walter J. Dickey and Pam Hollenhorst, "Three-Strikes Laws: Five Years Later," *Corrections Management Quarterly* 3, no. 3 (1999): 1–18.

20. For a good review of the three-strikes law in California, see Kevin E. Meehan, "California's Three-Strikes Law: The First Six Years," *Corrections Management Quarterly* 4, no. 4 (2000): 22–33.

21. F. Zimring, S. Kamin, and G. Hawkins, *Crime and Punishment in California* (Berkeley, Calif.: Institute of Government Studies Press, 1999), p. 83.

22. For a discussion of sentencing guidelines, see Bureau of Justice Statistics, *Report to the Nation on Crime and Justice*, 2nd ed. (Washington, D.C.: U.S, Department of Justice, 1988), p. 92.

23. Drug Court Programs Office, *Defining Drug Courts: The Key Components* (Washington, D.C.: U.S. Department of Justice, Office of Justice Programs, 1997).

24. John A. Fagan, "Do Criminal Sanctions Deter Drug Crimes?" in *Drugs and Crime: Evaluating Public Policy Initiatives*, edited by Doris L. MacKenzie and C. D. Uchida (Thousand Oaks, Calif.: Sage, 1994).

25. Drug Court Programs Office, *Drug Court Activity* (Washington, D.C.: U.S. Department of Justice, Office of Justice Programs, 1998).

26. John Roman, Wendy Townsend, and Avinash Singh Bhati, *Recidivism Rates for Drug Court Graduates: Nationally Based Estimates, Final Report* (Washington, D.C.: U.S. Department of Justice, National Institute of Justice, July 2003).

27. J. S. Goldkamp, "Miami's Treatment Drug Court for Felony Defendants: Some Implications of Assessment Findings," *Prison Journal* 74, no. 2 (1994): 110–157.

28. R. H. Peters and M. R. Murrin, "Effectiveness of Treatment-Based Drug Courts in Reducing Criminal Recidivism," *Criminal Justice and Behavior* 27, no. 1 (2000): 72–96.

29. A good overview of the drug court model can be found in Shelly Johnson, Dana Jones Hubbard, and Edward J. Latessa, "Drug Courts and Treatment: Lessons to Be Learned from the 'What Works' Literature," *Corrections Management Quarterly* 4, no. 4 (2000): 70–77.

Chapter 3

AFTER READING THIS CHAPTER, YOU SHOULD BE ABLE TO:

1. Describe the historical development of jail design and operations.

2. List the categories of offenders that are housed in jails.

3. Define regional jails and explain their role.

4. Explain the reasons for the increased incarceration rate in jails over the past two decades.

5. Discuss the daily operations of a jail.

6. Identify the staff roles and functions in a modern jail.

7. Compare the various jail designs and explain the positive benefits of direct supervision.

8. Describe efforts to reduce jail overcrowding.

9. Explain the approaches that jails take to reduce the likelihood of inmate suicides.

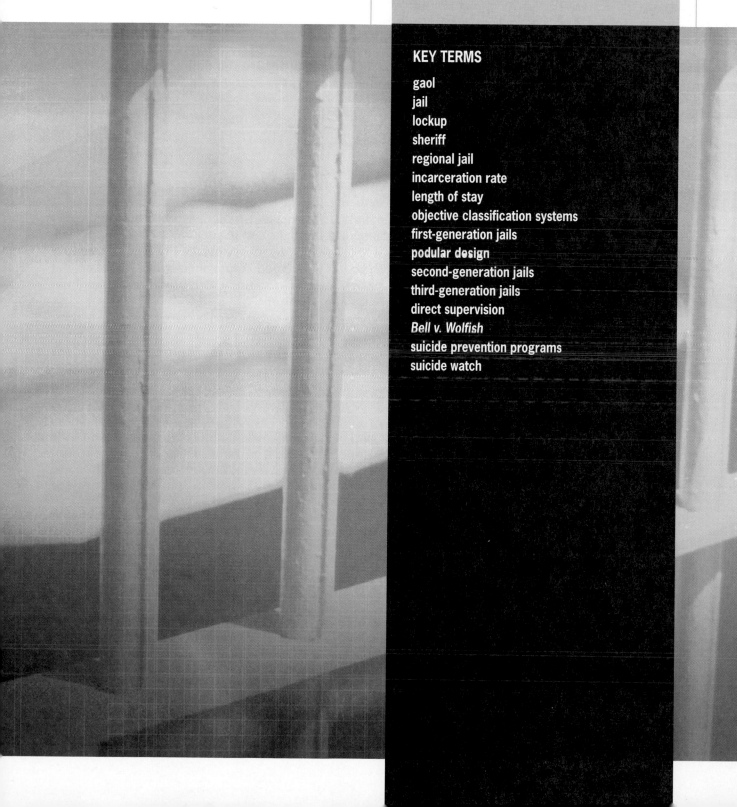

Jails

KEY TERMS

gaol
jail
lockup
sheriff
regional jail
incarceration rate
length of stay
objective classification systems
first-generation jails
podular design
second-generation jails
third-generation jails
direct supervision
Bell v. Wolfish
suicide prevention programs
suicide watch

Introduction

Probably no major segment of the criminal justice system is less studied, evaluated, or understood than the nation's jails. Yet no segment of the criminal justice system touches more people's lives. Jails hold only about one-tenth of all offenders under correctional supervision, yet admit approximately four times as many offenders each year as all other correctional components combined.[1] Jails are often misunderstood, as the general public regularly confuses prisons and jails. We have all heard someone say something like, "For that crime, I hope the criminal spends years in jail," when jails are not used to hold sentenced offenders for long terms of confinement.

Jails are the watershed of the correctional system. The American jail is the oldest of the correctional components, initiated well before prisons, probation, parole, or halfway houses. Yet the jail still has a diverse and difficult mission and role. Few offenders won't pass through a jail as they enter the correctional system. Jails hold a variety of offenders (those who have been arrested, have been detained pending trial, have been sentenced to short terms of confinement for minor crimes, are awaiting transfer to another facility, and are being held administratively for a criminal justice agency). They may hold offenders arrested for public drunkenness or for multiple murders.

Some jail systems are larger than all but a few state prison systems, and some are extremely small (four or five beds). Jails face unique issues such as dealing with unknown offenders, detoxification, and medical problems and serving the court with security and prisoner transportation. Jails can have budgets in the hundreds of millions of dollars per year, or they may have budgets of only a few hundred thousand dollars. Jails may have sophisticated management and professional training of staff, or they may have poor management with patrol deputies with no specialized training assigned to watch prisoners.

This chapter provides an overview of the nation's jail systems, to include their historical development, current operations with the make-up and characteristics of offenders, their organization and physical design, and current issues such as overcrowding, legal issues, dealing with mentally ill offenders, and preventing suicides. Students will find how the diverse make-up of jail clients makes the job of jail staff complex and difficult. Jail inmates may be incarcerated from only a few hours to several months. They hold inmates charged with drunkenness to serial murder, and many are violent and impulsive. These multifaceted challenges of the nation's jails can make other components of the criminal justice system seem simple in their operation and management. By the end of the chapter, students will understand the approaches that jail officials take to deal with these issues and the continuing problems they will face into the next several years.

The History of Jails

Gaol

an early English term for a jail

The first jails were created in England. The first **gaol**, as jails were then called, was ordered built by King Henry II in 1166. Originally for use in detaining offenders awaiting trial, as vagrancy became a problem between the fourteenth and eighteenth centuries, the jails were used to house displaced persons, the poor, and sometimes even the mentally ill. These early jails had deplorable conditions of filth, violence, poor food and little medical care. These conditions came to the attention of John Howard, who was appointed sheriff of Bedfordshire in 1773. While inspecting the local jails, Howard was shocked by the conditions of disease, lack of discipline, and lack of sanitation that he discovered. He visited prisons in other European countries to find models that could be replicated in England and worked with members of the English House of Commons to draft the Penitentiary Act of

1779. This act created four requirements for English prisons and jails: (1) secure and sanitary structures, (2) systematic inspections, (3) abolition of fees charged to inmates, and (4) a reformatory regime in which inmates were confined in solitary cells but worked in common rooms during the day. The act also detailed the requirements for diet, uniforms, and hygiene for prisoners.

Early jails in the American colonies followed the English model and were primarily used to house those awaiting trial. Instead of cells, they often had as many as thirty inmates housed in one large room.[2] As punishment for crimes, offenders were often fined. Those too poor to pay their fines were confined until they worked off their debts. "Workhouses" and jails were sometimes different facilities, and sometimes jails held both populations. It was not until the end of the eighteenth century that the concept of confinement for punishment and rehabilitation of convicted offenders came to America. The first prison for this purpose was established in 1790 in a wing of the Walnut Street Jail in Philadelphia, and the function of confining sentenced criminals was established in penitentiaries that were built in most states over the next fifty years. Jails continued their role of housing primarily pretrial inmates, and by the end of the nineteenth century, almost every American city had constructed and operated a jail for this purpose.

Current Jail Operations
ROLE AND FUNCTIONS OF JAILS

Jails are locally operated correctional facilities that confine people before or after adjudication. Jails serve a variety of functions, and hold a variety of categories of offenders, including the following:

- Individuals pending arraignment and awaiting trial, conviction, or sentencing
- Probation, parole, and bail bond violators and absconders
- Juveniles, pending transfer to juvenile authorities
- Mentally ill people, pending their movement to appropriate mental health facilities
- Individuals held for the military, for protective custody, for contempt, and for the courts as witnesses
- Inmates pending transfer to federal, state, or other criminal justice authorities
- Inmates held for federal, state, or other authorities because of crowding of their facilities
- Offenders assigned to community-based programs such as day reporting, home detention, or electronic monitoring
- Inmates sentenced to short terms (generally less than one year).

This multiple mission makes the operation of contemporary jails very complex, and requires systems, staff, and facilities that are flexible enough to meet these various demands. While several different terms are now used to describe facilities that carry out these functions (*correctional center, house of correction, detention facility,* and even *prison*), the role is similar. Jails are full-service facilities that offer security, food service, medical care, and offender programs, and are therefore different from **lockups**, which are commonly located in police stations and hold people only for a short time, usually no more than forty-eight hours.

THE ORGANIZATION OF JAILS

The county government almost always operates jails, and almost every county has a jail. It is estimated that there are approximately 3,350 jails in the United States. In some counties in which there is a large metropolitan area, the county and city may

Jails
locally operated correctional facilities that confine people before or after adjudication

Lockup
A few cells, commonly located in police stations, that hold people for only a short time, usually no more than 48 hours

Most police departments and even some court buildings have a few cells that are called a lockup. However, these are not full-service jails and cannot be used to hold offenders for more than a few hours.
Photo by Richard P. Seiter.

Sheriff

the elected official who oversees both policing activities within the county and the operation of the jail

Regional jail

a jail that serves more than one county and is overseen by a regional jail commission

combine the jail function and possibly jointly contribute to the jail budget and management. In rural counties, jails are the responsibility of the **sheriff**, the elected official who oversees both policing activities within the county and the operation of the jail. In some metropolitan areas, the sheriff only supervises the jail and a county police force takes care of typical law enforcement activities.

A fairly new development is that of **regional jails**. As the operation of jails became increasingly complex and interventions by the courts required a full-range of security and services for all jails, some small counties found it increasingly difficult to provide adequate funding for their jail operation. As a solution, sometimes several small counties form coalitions to jointly fund, build, and operate a regional jail that would serve all the counties and result in economies of scale that make its operation more financially reasonable. A regional jail commission oversees these regional jails, with each county having one representative to serve on the commission. The commission hires a jail administrator to supervise the jail, approves the budget and the proportionate contribution of funds from each county, and approves the general policies and operating practices for the facility. In some cases, the management (and sometimes the construction and ownership) of the regional jail is contracted to the private sector. On June 30, 1999, there were forty-seven privately operated jails in the United States.[3] The role of the private sector in prison and jail operations is discussed in Chapter 5 and 16.

JAIL POPULATIONS

At midyear 2002, the nation's 3,367 local jails held 665,475 inmates,[4] up from 631,240 at midyear 2001 and 621,149 at midyear 2000[5] (see Table 3.1). From midyear 2001 to midyear 2002, the twelve-month increase of 5.4 percent in the jail population was larger than the average annual increase of 4.0 percent since 1995.

Regional jails are more efficient for small counties that cannot afford the high cost of modern jail-operating requirements.
Photo by Richard P. Seiter

TABLE 3.1		Midyear Populations in the Nation's Jails				
1983	1988	1993	1999	2000	2001	2002
223,551	343,569	459,804	605,943	621,149	631,240	665,475

Source: James J. Stephan, *Census of Jails, 1999*, NCJ 186633 (Washington, D.C.: U.S. Department of Justice, Bureau of Justice Statistics, August 2001). Updated from Bureau of Justice Statistics, *Jail Census, Mid-Year Reports*, 2000, 2001, and 2002.

The number of people in the nation's jails has clearly risen significantly over the past twenty years. The **incarceration rate** is defined as the number of people per 100,000 U.S. residents who are incarcerated in either a jail or a prison. Figure 3.1 shows that the jail incarceration rate more than doubled between 1983 and 1999. The incarceration rate in jails has continued to rise sharply; on June 30, 2002, the jail incarceration rate rose to 231 per 100,000 U.S. residents.[6]

Incarceration rate

The number of people per 100,000 residents who are in jail or prison

The incarceration rate is significantly different by race and ethnicity. Table 3.2 shows that the jail incarceration rate in 1990 for white non-Hispanics was only half that of Hispanics of any race, and was less than one-fifth that of black non-Hispanics. At midyear 2002, of all jail inmates, 43.8 percent were white, 39.8 percent were black, 14.7 percent were Hispanic, and 1.6 percent were other.[7] It is interesting to examine the makeup of the jail population in the United States. The U.S. Department of Justice, Bureau of Justice Statistics, does a complete survey of the nation's jails approximately every five years. As a part of this survey, a sample of inmates is interviewed. The survey represents a "snapshot" examination of inmates in jails on a specific day. The 1996 survey resulted in interviews with more than 6,000 inmates in 431 jails, and created the following description of jail inmates:

- They are predominantly male (90 percent), nonwhite (64 percent), and young (68 percent are under age 35), and have a high school education or less (86 percent).

JAIL INCARCERATION RATE, 1983–1999

FIGURE **3.1**

Number of jail inmates per 100,000 residents

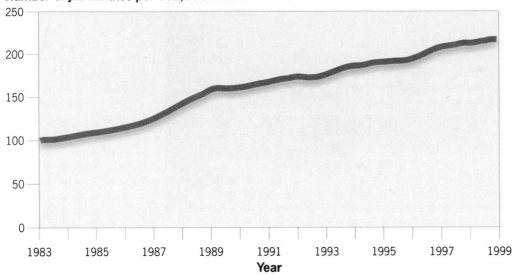

Source: James J. Stephan, *Census of Jails, 1999*, NCJ 186633 (Washington, D.C.: U.S. Department of Justice, Bureau of Justice Statistics, August 2001), p. iii.

TABLE	3.2	Jail Incarceration Rates by Race and Ethnicity, 1990–2000	
	Number of jail inmates per 100,000 U.S. residents		
Year	**White non-Hispanic**	**Black non-Hispanic**	**Hispanic of any race**
1990	89	560	245
1991	92	594	247
1992	93	618	251
1993	94	633	262
1994	98	656	274
1995	104	670	263
1996	111	640	276
1997	117	706	293
1998	125	716	292
1999	127	730	288
2000	132	736	280

Sources: Jail inmate populations, 1990–1997, from *Correctional Populations in the United States, 1997*, T-2.3. Jail inmate populations, 1998–1999, from *Prison and Jail Inmates at Midyear 1998*, p. 7., and *Prison and Jail Inmates at Midyear 1999*, p. 6. (Preceding sources published by the Bureau of Justice Statistics.) Resident population of the United States, estimates by sex, race, and Hispanic origin, from Population Estimates Program Division, U.S. Census Bureau Internet release, December 23, 1999, with adjustments for census undercount.

- The vast majority (74 percent) are in jail on a charge or conviction of a nonviolent offense.
- Most (73 percent) have previously been on probation or in jail or prison.
- Most had prior drug use (82 percent) and had been involved in substance abuse treatment (42 percent).
- A significant number (41 percent) were under the influence of alcohol at the time of their crime.
- They are poor, with almost half reporting an annual income of less than $7,200.
- Over one-third reported a physical or mental disability.[8]

This description does not paint a pretty picture of the jail population. Inmates in jail are a troubled lot and experience many problems (poverty, substance abuse, mental illness) that contribute to their criminal behavior and must be managed by jail staff. It is also troubling to note that such a high percentage are sitting in jails having been charged with or convicted of a nonviolent crime. This fact is borne out by other studies of jail populations. In Texas, a review of the state's jail population found that more than half of the jail inmates were there for drug offenses (36.4 percent for possession of a controlled substance and 16.9 percent for delivery of a controlled substance), and almost another 30 percent for other property crimes (15.2 percent for theft/larceny, 8.8 percent for unauthorized use of a motor vehicle, 8.4 percent for forgery, 8.2 percent for burglary of a building, and 3.2 percent for other property offenses).[9]

THE INCREASING USE OF JAILS

While there is no question that the jail population and incarceration rate has been increasing, several theories suggest reasons for the increase. In reality, several factors may underlie this growth. First, the "tough on crime" mentality of the public affects the percentage of offenders who receive bail or release on recognizance. Judges do not want to put potentially dangerous offenders back on the streets, and are more likely to set higher bail amounts and less likely to grant release without bond requirements. One review of those arrested for crimes and their release on bail indicated that 61.6 percent of people arrested and jailed for violent offenses were released pending disposition of charges in 1990; this dropped to 57 percent in 1992 and 53.9 percent in 1994.[10] The number of jail inmates who were awaiting trial (not yet convicted of the charged offense) increased from 228,900 in 1993 to 331,000 in 1999, an increase of 40 percent.[11] This resulted in an increase from 50 to 54 percent of all jail inmates (from 1993 to 1999) awaiting trial rather than serving a sentence. By 2002, 59.9 percent of jail inmates were unconvicted.[12]

Second, the number of arrests increased 20 percent from 1983 to 1993.[13] Since that time, the arrest rate has remained fairly constant. There were 13,980,297 estimated arrests in 2000 in the United States.[14] Much of this increase is the result of the war on drugs and an emphasis by law enforcement agencies on targeting drug crimes; the increase in the number of police officers; and the subsequent increase of a large number of drug offenders. In 1983, only 9 percent of jail inmates had been arrested for drug offenses; this increased to 22 percent in 1996,[15] but dropped to 11 percent in 2000.[16] Yet a recent review of Texas jail inmates found that more than 50 percent of the population in jail was being held for drug offenses.[17]

Third, with extensive overcrowding of state and federal prisons over the past decade, more jail inmates are being held by jails as they await transfer to prison. On January 1, 2001, state and federal prisons were operating at 107 percent capacity.[18] In 1991, only 28,600 offenders were held in local jails for state or federal jurisdictions. This figure rose to 48,435 by January 1, 2001, and 16.2 percent of inmates in local jails were awaiting transfer to a prison.[19]

Finally, there has been increasing use of a split sentence, or the sentencing of adult felons to a short stay in jail in addition to release to probation. The percentage of felons receiving a jail sentence increased from 25 to 31 percent from 1988 to 1996.[20] These reasons influenced the increase in the jail populations over the past decade. However, while the nation's jail populations continue to increase, the growth has been slowing, increasing only 1.6 percent from 2000 to 2001. It is projected that the growth of jails will continue to slow over the next five to ten years.

ADMISSIONS AND LENGTH OF STAY

One factor that truly differentiates jails from prisons is in the number of admissions and length of stay. During 2000, 728,296 inmates were admitted to state and federal prisons, 596,191 inmates were released, and the average length of stay for released inmates was 30.6 months.[21] These figures are decidedly different for jails. While jails do not report all admissions and releases every year, estimates are that the 3,367 jails process between 9 million and 11 million admissions each year.

In each of the years between the full censuses of jails, the Bureau of Justice Statistics does a sample survey of jails to estimate baseline characteristics of the jails and the inmates housed in the jails. In 1993, it was estimated that there were more than 9 million new admissions to jails.[22] As well, findings from the *Census of Jails, 1999* found that 219,000 offenders were admitted to the nation's jails during the week preceding the 1999 survey.[23] These figures can include fewer individuals admitted to jail multiple times. A recent study found that approximately 25 percent of the bookings into the Cook County (Illinois) jail were multiple admissions of the same person.[24] Therefore, the 9 million to 11 million admissions noted earlier probably represent between 7 million and 8.5 million different offenders.

Length of stay

the time served in a jail or prison by any inmate

The average **length of stay** for a jail is fifteen to twenty days, much less than the average thirty-month length of stay within a prison. This average length of stay for jails is misleading, however, as a very large percentage of arrested and jailed offenders make bond and are released within forty-eight hours. Those who do not make bail are likely to spend seventy-five to ninety days in jail awaiting trial, while sentenced offenders can serve up to one year in jail. O'Toole, in pointing out the difficulty in looking at average length of stay as it pertains to jail populations, notes the following:

> In fact the reality of jail population dynamics is that the vast majority of inmates are released within a few days, and those who are not released early tend to remain in custody throughout the adjudication process. This tends to create two trends in inmate average length of stay (ALOS) figures. One is considerably less than the arithmetically calculated ALOS and the other considerably longer.[25]

The fact that so many jail inmates are released shortly after arrest creates a logistical nightmare of jail operations in terms of bookings and releases. The sheer volume of these admissions and releases often results in mistakes. Unfortunately, it is not uncommon for jails to be plagued with releasing the wrong person or making errors in identification of offenders.[26] These problems seem to continue, no matter what steps are taken by jails to improve their booking and release processes and their record keeping. And mistaken releases of offenders undermine the public confidence in the ability of jail staff to do a professional job.

THE JAIL PROCESS AND DAILY OPERATIONS

What occurs on a daily basis in a typical jail? A number of activities and functions are a part of the daily jail routine. The first major function is admissions and releases. Jails have a central area for booking, admitting, and releasing inmates. Police officers or county sheriff deputies bring arrested offenders to the jail, where they are identified and fingerprinted and their property is inventoried and stored. They receive a brief physical and mental health screening, and usually talk to a social worker about the process and how potential release on bail or personal recognizance works. If they are there for a minor offense, they may be quickly released on bond. Offenders sit in a relatively unsecured part of the jail booking area until someone comes to the jail to post their bond. If they are arrested for a felony, they will have to wait until their initial appearance before a magistrate (usually within

Offenders are arrested and brought to a jail by the police, where they are booked into the jail.
Photo by Richard P. Seiter.

Within the jail booking area is space for minor offenders to wait until someone comes to post their bond or bail.
Photo by Richard P. Seiter.

twenty-four hours) to see if they are granted bail. During this time, they are placed in a general holding area within the jail, in which they are housed with several other newly arrived offenders.

Offenders not released on bail or personal recognizance are moved to more permanent housing within the jail. They are first placed in a very secure housing unit, often in cells holding only one person, until they can be further interviewed and some preliminary information can be collected regarding their crime and past criminal history. This classification process (described shortly) identifies the dangerousness and risk of the offender and determines whether there are other offenders from whom they should be separated. In addition, any major problems such as a need for detoxification, potential of suicide, or potential threats by other jail inmates are identified and considered in the classification and assignment of housing. Once classified, inmates are moved to the housing unit that holds inmates of similar risk of violence or escape.

In their housing unit, inmates begin the normal routine of the jail. Days are filled with boredom, as there is usually little to do. Depending on the jail design, inmates may be let out of their cells and into a common area in which they can talk to other inmates or watch television. Prepared food is delivered to the common area, where inmates eat their meals. If inmates receive visits, they go to the visiting area, which is often adjacent to the housing unit. Visits with family or friends are usually *noncontact*, meaning that inmates and their visitors talk on a telephone or through sound ports between secure glass to prevent the passing of items that are not allowed in the jail. If visited by their attorney, a probation or parole officer, or some other law enforcement official, inmates usually are provided a small, yet secure area, with direct contact with their visitor, so they can talk in private and sign any necessary papers.

Jails have limited programs, such as education, substance abuse counseling, or work. However, these types of programs and activities are usually welcomed by inmates, as the boredom of a regular day is extremely difficult for most offenders. Some programs are provided in the common areas of the housing units, but inmates generally are transported to another location in the jail for these programs.

Jail inmates have noncontact visiting and have to talk to their visitors through sound ports in the secure glass.
Photo by Richard P. Seiter.

Jail inmates can have contact visiting with their attorneys, so they can review and sign papers. Note, however, the handcuffs attached to the wall to prevent inmates from attacking their attorney or trying to escape out the visitors' entrance.
Photo by Richard P. Seiter.

Inmates who are awaiting trial and not yet sentenced may volunteer, but are not required to work. Work opportunities include cleaning the areas of the jail or assisting in food preparation and service. Even for the few inmates who work, there is normally only enough to do to keep them busy a few hours per day.

JAIL CLASSIFICATION

As noted earlier, an important aspect of the operation of jails is the classification of inmates. Sophisticated classification systems for jails are a relatively recent phenomenon, having been used extensively only over the past two decades. During the early history of jails, all inmates were mixed together. There was later some segregation of inmates, as "separation by sex came first, then separation by age, followed by separation by problem."[27] Brennan notes that "Before 1870, . . . classification was based primarily on type of offense . . . In the latter part of the 19th century, . . . classification . . . emphasized offenders' personal pathologies."[28]

Objective classification systems have more recently superceded these subjective classification processes. Objective systems identify offenders' criminal history and personal characteristics (number of violent offenses, history of violence, age, marital status) that have been found to be statistically linked to dangerousness or escape potential; they result in an actuarial assessment of risk that is used in assigning inmates to a type of housing unit or recommending certain mental health or substance abuse programs.

Jail classification systems are plagued with problems not inherent in prison classification systems. First, there is often little information available for jail inmates. Jail social service staff interview inmates to collect information, but usually do not have time to confirm the accuracy of the information. Second, the

Objective classification systems

statistical approaches to considering the risk of escape and violence by inmates short stay complicates the process for most inmates, and there is no time for thorough medical or psychological assessments that could aid in the classification process. Finally, Brennan notes that jail classification has "suffered from benign neglect," in that jail administrators have "not accorded classification a central role in management."[29]

However, effective jail classification systems are important for many reasons:

- They provide a guide for separating violent, predatory inmates from potential inmate victims. One of the most challenging problems for jails is to protect inmates who could be preyed on by dangerous inmates. With little prior information, and many housing arrangements in which numerous inmates live together, it is critical to try to separate inmates by risk of assault against one another.
- They provide a guide for identifying and managing differently inmates with special needs, such as the emotionally disturbed or those at risk for suicide.
- They provide a guide for identifying inmates with a high risk of escape and housing them in more secure settings than those with a low risk of escape. Such systems allow jails to have a variety of housing assignments, rather than all maximum-security areas that are very expensive to build and operate.

Jail staff use classification systems to make decisions on the housing assignment for inmates, the types of programs they should participate in, the number of staff assigned to various housing areas, the type of supervision to provide inmates, and whether inmates should be allowed to work or participate in diversion programs. In this regard, classification is an important and valuable tool in jail management.

JAIL STAFFING

One way in which jails and prisons are extremely similar is the importance of professional staff. In both types of correctional facilities, staff are more important than any other element in the operations and policies—more important than the facility, the physical security, the services provided, and the programs offered. Poor-quality or poorly performing staff undermine all of these other factors, while

Staff who work in jails include jail officers, counselors, and transportation officers who move inmates from the jail to the courthouse for hearings.
Photo by Richard P. Seiter

professional and well-trained staff can overcome other problems in the jail or its operations.

The *Census of Jails, 1999* reported an estimated 210,600 total staff employed by jails on June 30, 1999.[30] As indicated in Table 3.3, the largest proportion of jail staff (151,200 of the total staff, or 72 percent) are correctional officers. Most jail correctional officers are assigned to housing units, but others act as transportation officers and move inmates from the jail to the courthouse to attend hearings. The percentage of correctional officers of the total jail staff is higher than in prisons because jails do not offer extensive programs or services, and their primary function is to hold inmates in a secure setting. The next largest categories of staff are clerical and maintenance (12 percent), administrative (6.9 percent), and professional and technicians (5.4 percent).

Jail staff are always extremely outnumbered by the inmates in any correctional setting. There is no way to "rule" a correctional facility through force; jails must be managed through clear procedures, a consistent routine of operations, and professional staff. In 1999, the number of inmates per correctional officer was 4.3.[31] However, this number is misleading, as all correctional officer's are not employed at the jail at any single time. Since correctional officers must supervise the jail twenty-four hours per day, seven days per week, only about one-sixth of the total officer workforce is likely to be on duty at any one time. Therefore, on a typical day, there would be one correctional officer for more than twenty-five (4.3 times 6) inmates. Yet correctional officers are assigned throughout the jail, and a typical jail housing unit has approximately seventy-five inmates with one correctional officer. While the number of inmates in jails increased significantly over the past twenty years, the number of jail employees grew at an even faster rate. In 1983, the average number of inmates per all jail staff (not just correctional officers) was 3.5, but this number declined to 2.9 in 1999.[32]

Another change in jail staff has come in the diversity of employees. In 1999, women constituted approximately 34 percent (up from 30 percent in 1993) of all jail employees, and 28 percent (up from 24 percent in 1993) of all jail correctional officers.[33] In addition, the percentage of white jail staff decreased to 66 percent in 1999 from 71 percent in 1993, while during the same period black employees increased from 22 to 24 percent, and Hispanic employees from 6 to 8 percent.[34] This increase in minority employees is important to the management of jails, as in 1999, 42 percent of all jail inmates were black, and 15 percent Hispanic. It is commonly acknowledged that management of a correctional facility is benefited when the facility has a like proportion of minority employees to the proportion of minority inmates. See the following "Your Career in Corrections" box for a discussion of the opportunities for jobs as jail officers.

Design and Supervision in Jails

Contemporary jails are very different from the earliest jails in the United States. As most can recall from watching old television westerns, every small town had a sheriff's office with a few jail cells to hold those arrested for committing serious crimes or getting drunk in the local saloon. This idea of combining the sheriff's office with the local jail continued into the twentieth century. In many rural counties, the sheriff and his family lived in the second floor of a county-owned house, the main floor was the sheriff's office, and the basement included cells for housing inmates. Most of these jails have now been replaced with more modern facilities. In major metropolitan areas, it is desirable to locate the jail next to the county court building, creating problems for both architectural and security concerns.

Urban leaders do not want a jail to "look like a jail" and ruin the aesthetics of the area in which it is located. Yet jails must be very secure and as escape-proof as

TABLE 3.3	Jail Staff by Occupational Category, June 30, 1999

Region and jurisdiction	Total staff	Administrative	Correctional officers	Clerical and maintenance	Educational	Professional and technical[a]	Other
National estimate[b]	210,600	14,600	151,200	25,400	2,100	11,500	5,800
State estimate[b]	207,600	14,400	149,600	25,300	2,100	10,700	5,500
U.S. total	197,375	13,722	141,663	23,772	1,969	10,764	5,485
Federal	3,110	253	1,685	93	30	715	334
State	194,265	13,469	139,978	23,679	1,939	10,049	5,151
Northeast	40,899	1,819	31,269	3,995	579	2,270	967
Maine	800	55	608	70	18	38	11
Massachusetts	4,617	370	3,007	611	100	448	81
New Hampshire	546	47	420	29	10	36	4
New Jersey	5,538	143	4,559	484	24	276	52
New York	21,454	717	16,707	2,093	317	928	692
Pennsylvania	7,944	487	5,968	708	110	544	127
Midwest	32,821	2,741	23,190	4,281	320	1,585	704
Illinois	2,936	233	2,091	383	17	76	136
Indiana	3,443	440	2,155	563	46	141	98
Iowa	1,566	176	1,212	155	1	13	9
Kansas	1,950	262	1,430	222	4	28	4
Michigan	4,738	311	3,199	755	73	304	96
Minnesota	2,600	203	1,804	364	40	136	53
Missouri	3,047	259	2,152	409	19	131	77
Nebraska	1,141	109	858	111	5	28	30
North Dakota	344	30	266	13	7	20	8
Ohio	7,007	415	5,072	805	68	540	107
South Dakota	479	50	346	61	0	7	15
Wisconsin	3,570	253	2,605	440	40	161	71
South	82,245	5,019	62,227	8,878	507	3,398	2,216
Alabama	2,919	394	2,044	266	6	55	154
Arkansas	1,813	175	1,393	200	5	18	22
Dist. of Col.	696	9	589	75	3	20	0
Florida	15,618	481	11,186	2,432	98	860	561
Georgia	8,188	653	6,229	891	32	184	199
Kentucky	2,632	181	2,115	231	19	45	41
Louisiana	6,100	371	4,255	798	40	337	299
Maryland	4,284	221	3,007	548	50	433	25
Mississippi	2,015	186	1,496	207	20	61	45
North Carolina	3,717	263	3,077	223	12	85	57
Oklahoma	1,995	199	1,452	203	47	24	70
South Carolina	2,420	104	1,989	202	15	82	28
Tennessee	6,177	354	4,471	651	40	426	235
Texas	15,477	965	12,744	1,124	58	463	123
Virginia	7,457	414	5,595	759	59	284	346
West Virginia	737	49	585	68	3	21	11
West	38,300	3,890	23,292	6,525	533	2,796	1,264
Alaska	79	20	37	11	0	1	10
Arizona	3,118	152	2,191	447	25	275	28
California	20,217	2,737	10,679	3,808	436	1,746	811
Colorado	3,660	242	2,791	365	12	166	84
Idaho	786	91	493	161	3	23	15
Montana	639	65	479	64	2	16	13
Nevada	1,997	83	1,178	483	0	49	204
New Mexico	1,218	93	885	126	16	82	16
Oregon	2,431	130	1,638	379	8	235	41
Utah	854	87	553	142	18	45	9
Washington	2,880	145	2,074	496	11	128	26
Wyoming	421	45	294	43	2	30	7

Note: A total of 228 reporting units were unable to provide data on staff by gender or occupation. Total staff includes full-time, part-time, payroll and nonpayroll staff, and excludes contract staff, and community volunteers.

[a]Includes psychiatrists, psychologists, social workers, counselors, medical doctors, nurses, paramedics, chaplains, and legal specialists.

[b]National estimates were obtained by summing the item values from reporting units and then multiplying by a nonresponse adjustment factor. All estimates for type of staff were rounded to the nearest 100.

Source: James J. Stephan, *Census of Jails, 1999*, NCJ 186633 (Washington, D.C.: U.S. Department of Justice, Bureau of Justice Statistics, August 2000), p. 25.

JAIL OFFICERS

As noted in this chapter, there is much less attention, much less research, and much less interest by the public regarding the staffing and operation of county jails than for prisons. While there are almost three times as many jails as prisons, the nation's jails employ less than half as many staff as state and federal prisons. According to the *Census of Jails, 1999,* jails employed an estimated 207,600 people at midyear 1999. Just as with prisons, the number of staff in jails is increasing. While the number of inmates in jails increased by 32 percent between 1993 and 1999, the number of staff increased by 25 percent.[35]

The largest percentage of jail staff (about seven out of ten) are jail correctional officers, who supervise inmates or provide facility security. In 1999, there were 149,600 jail correctional officers. Other occupational categories in jails include administrators, clerical and maintenance workers, professional and technical employees, and educational employees. Jails have few inmate programs but most jails offer limited education, counseling, vocational training, religious programming, and health services for inmates. In 1999, women constituted 28 percent of jail correctional officers, and 26 percent of officers were black.

Jail officers do much of the same work as prison correctional officers. Their primary responsibilities are supervising inmates to maintain order and compliance with rules, and performing security procedures such as searching for contraband. However, with most of the staff being officers, and with most inmate programs (visiting, education) and services (food, medical) coming to the inmates in housing units rather than inmates going to the program or service, the function of officers often extends into the provision or supervision of these functions. Food service staff bring meals to the housing area, but the cell block officer supervises the meal service. As well, visitors come to visiting rooms adjacent to the housing unit, and the cell block officer moves the inmates to a noncontact visiting area and maintains some surveillance over the visit.

Similar to prison staff, jail staff work in stressful and sometimes dangerous environments. Between July 1, 1998, and June 30, 1999, there were 9,276 inmate physical or sexual assaults on jail employees in 848 jail jurisdictions. The total number of assaults compared to the average daily population translated into 17.8 assaults per 1,000 inmates or 48.8 assaults per 1,000 staff during the twelve-month period.[36] Despite this fact, many individuals find work as jail correctional officers challenging and rewarding. As well, just as in prisons, an officer position is usually the entry-level job, and staff later have the opportunity for advancement and other types of jobs.

possible. They must take into account requirements for lighting and airflow, for offering inmate programs, and for movement of inmates within the jail and between the jail and the courthouse. Architects take great pride in meeting these sometimes conflicting demands of a jail being secure, yet fitting into the current landscape of the urban environment. The new St. Louis city jail, that opened in early 2003 illustrates this effort. A jury of the American Institute of Architects Committee on Architecture for Justice reviewed the design and appearance and stated, "We found this multi-level solution to be sensitive to its urban context and the fabric of the façade while providing good operational solutions."[37] The following "An Insider's Experience" box illustrates my personal challenge of fitting a correctional institution design into an urban setting.

CREATING A SECURE SETTING INSIDE THE JAIL

Not only must designers of jails make the facility attractive to fit into the city skyline, they must also make it functional and secure. Jail functionality begins with the fact that inmates are kept in their housing areas most of the time and are seldom moved to other locations in the jail. Therefore, services (food, laundry, medical), programs (education, counseling), and even visitors must be brought to the

This sheriff's office from the 1950s was the standard in most county seats, in which the sheriff's family lived upstairs, the administrative office was on the main floor, and the jail was in the basement.
Courtesy of the Ohio Department of Rehabilitation and Correction.

The St. Louis City Jail is a good example of modern jail architecture, in which the jail is conveniently located next to the courthouse, yet fits into the urban look of the other buildings.
Photo by Richard P. Seiter.

AN INSIDER'S EXPERIENCE: Siting an Urban Correctional Facility

I know how difficult it is to try to find an urban site for a jail and get community support for the design and location. When I was director of the Ohio department of corrections, we had a major construction program of more than $500 million to build just more than 15,000 beds. One of the authorized construction projects was a replacement for the Ohio Penitentiary (OP), which opened before 1850 and was located in the center of downtown Columbus, just a few blocks from the state capitol building. The statutory authorization provided for a prison hospital, a central state reception center, and a reintegration center (a community correctional institution) to replace the OP, and required that it be located within Franklin County, the county in which Columbus was located. The city fathers were excited about demolishing the OP, as they knew it was a valuable piece of property, and getting rid of the eyesore old prison was a goal of the entire downtown business and government group.

One of the first activities after I received the job was to be placed on a site selection committee with one state senator and one state representative, both from Franklin County, with the charge of finding a site for the new prison. We looked all over the county and just couldn't find a suitable site that was large enough to hold the facility. I had what I thought was a good idea. Instead of looking for some thirty acres, why not change the design from campus-style, spread out over several acres, to a high-rise design, built as many urban jails are now constructed. My idea was to use the back half of the current site of the OP, which was eighteen acres, and free up the front of it for development. I had seen many of the new high-rise jails and knew they could be very attractive and that five

or six acres was more than enough space. The role of this facility was for short terms of confinement, and I believed that could easily be accomplished in a high-rise facility. I was so excited about the prospect that I leaked the information to a reporter for the local newspaper.

The next day the article was front-page news, and the reaction was all bad. Everyone from the governor down thought it was a bad idea. I was invited to the office of the CEO of a large national insurance company based in Columbus, and looked out over the area around their headquarters. They had developed about three sides of their property into beautiful office and shopping buildings, and the fourth side was . . . the OP. He couldn't believe I would even suggest putting a prison on that location, and the nice pictures of the high-rise jails I showed him did little to change his mind.

Even though no one liked my idea, it did at least generate some effort to help us find a site. The legislature changed the construction bill language to put the reception center outside of Franklin County, and we built it on a state-owned site just two miles outside the county line. The City of Columbus provided us (at no cost) a ten-acre site in the city to build the reintegration center and the hospital. Today Ohio has three excellent facilities in convenient locations that serve the state and the department of corrections well to this day. I learned two valuable lessons. First, it is very difficult to get the key players behind any location for a jail or prison in an urban area. Second, even when you make a mistake and do not handle a sensitive political and community issue very well, you sometimes get lucky and something good comes from it.

inmate housing area. The design of the housing areas has evolved and changed significantly over the past several decades.

Historically, **first-generation jails** housed inmates using a linear design, in which cells are aligned in long, straight rows, with walkways in the front of the cells for jail correctional officers to walk intermittently to observe what is going on in the cells. As illustrated in Figure 3.2, this linear approach did not allow officers to observe and supervise inmates from a single location, and resulted in little if any communication between officers and inmates as officers patrolled the corridors and looked into cells. The design of the cells and furnishings was very secure. Cell fronts were open bars (allowing no privacy and increasing the noise level), beds and other furniture were solid metal, and toilets and sinks were often stainless steel and difficult to destroy. There was little space for recreation or programs, and therefore inmates remained in their cells and grew restless and irritated. Food had

First-generation jails
jails in which a linear design was used for housing inmates; cells are aligned in long, straight rows, with walkways in the front of the cells for jail correctional officers to walk intermittently to observe what is going on in the cells

LINEAR DESIGN OF JAIL HOUSING UNITS

FIGURE **3.2**

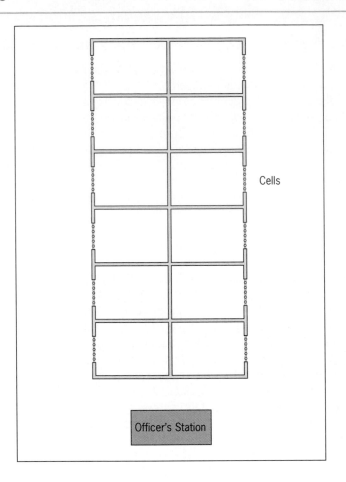

Cells

Officer's Station

Podular designs

a design of prisoner housing that provides common dayroom areas in the center of the unit to allow inmates to get out of their cells, reducing idleness and tension; podular designs make it easier for officers to view inmate activities in the cells and the dayrooms from one central location

Second-generation jails

jails that use podular housing designs and remote supervision; officers are located in a secure control room overlooking the cells and dayroom, with electronic controls to open and close individual cell doors

to be delivered to each cell, taking extensive staff time and making it difficult to maintain quality in food service.

To improve the supervision and resolve some of the program and service issues, jail designers introduced a podular style of housing in the 1970s. These **podular designs**, as illustrated in Figure 3.3, have several advantages over linear designs. They usually house smaller numbers of inmates, resulting in a better inmate-staff ratio. They provide common areas in the center of the unit (called dayrooms) in which inmates can watch television or play table games during the day, getting out of their cells and reducing idleness and tension. Podular designs make it easier for officers to view inmate activities in the cells and the dayrooms from one central location.

The creation of the podular design was an improvement from the linear jails. They resulted in the development of **second-generation jails**, using podular designs with remote supervision. Remote supervision placed officers in a secure control room overlooking the cells and dayroom, with electronic controls to open and close individual cell doors. There was extensive use of secure glass instead of bars

First-generation jails had long rows of cells, and jail personnel saw inmates only as they walked the tier and looked into cells.
Courtesy of the Federal Bureau of Prisons.

PODULAR DESIGN OF JAIL INMATE HOUSING UNITS

FIGURE **3.3**

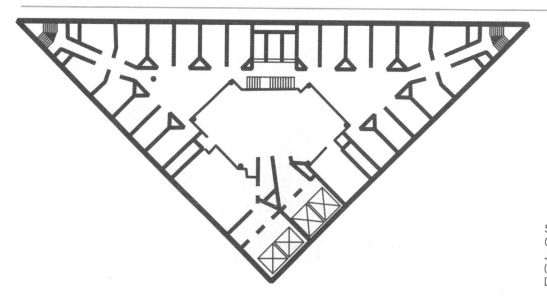

Source: National Institute of Corrections, *Direct Supervision Jails Information Packet* (Washington, D.C.: U.S. Department of Justice, 1993).

Podular jail designs allow for dayrooms in the center, in which officers can easily view inmates allowed out of their cells and into the dayrooms.
Photo by Richard P. Seiter.

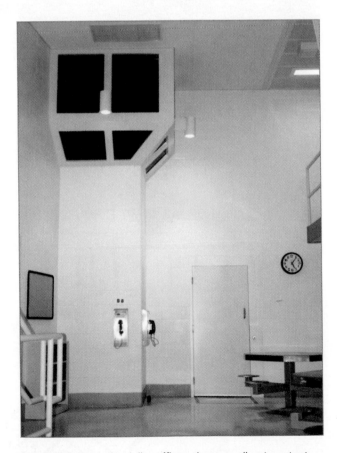

In second-generation jails, officers have no direct contact with inmates, as they oversee activities in the cellhouse from a remote location, similar to a perimeter tower within the building.
Photo by Richard P. Seiter.

From their remote location in second-generation jails, officers could open and close cell doors electronically simply by pushing a button.
Photo by Richard P. Seiter.

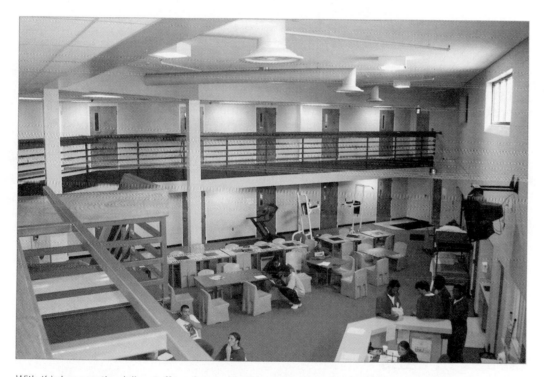

With third-generation jails, staff are located in the cellhouse in direct contact with inmates.
Photo by Richard P. Seiter.

to improve visibility. While second-generation jails had several advantages over first-generation jails, the disadvantage was that with this indirect supervision, jail staff had limited contact with inmates, and there was no communication or ability to talk to inmates, find out issues that were developing, and respond to them in a proactive manner.

To improve the problems resulting from the indirect supervision in second-generation jails, jail officials began to design **third-generation jails**, with the remote control center for staff removed and correctional officers placed in the

Third-generation jails
jail designs without remote control centers, in which correctional officers are located in the housing unit in direct contact with inmates

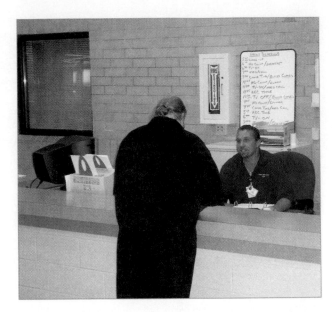

Staff interact directly and continuously with inmates in third-generation jails.
Photo by Richard P. Seiter.

Direct supervision

a style of inmate supervision with staff located in direct contact with inmates; requires staff to continuously supervise and communicate with inmates, reducing tension and avoiding the development of conflicts between inmates or inmates and staff

housing unit in direct contact with inmates. This requires staff to continuously supervise and communicate with inmates, reducing tension and avoiding the development of conflicts among inmates or between inmates and staff. The design also allows food to be brought to and served in the common area and there are often laundry facilities in the unit, allowing inmates to take responsibility for these functions rather than staff having to do it for them.

While officials initially feared for staff safety, **direct supervision** of jails was found to be better controlled, less violent, and safer for staff and inmates. A study of the behavior of inmates that covered many new direct-supervision jails that replaced old indirect-supervision facilities found a reduction in fifty-one of seventy categories of negative conduct by inmates when the direct-supervision jails opened.[38] Since the first podular direct-supervision jail was constructed in 1981 in Contra Costa County, California, more than one hundred jails across the country use direct supervision, and most new jails are constructed and managed on this concept.

Issues in Jails

The nation's jails face many significant challenges. With the increased reliance on jails described previously, jails have become increasingly overcrowded, and many new jails have been constructed to accommodate the increasing numbers of inmates. Some jurisdictions have opted to contract with the private, for-profit sector to build and manage a new jail. Jails also receive and hold people with many problems that can require immediate identification and attention. Detained offenders may suffer from mental illness or drug or alcohol addictions, or be suicidal. As well, jails are increasingly called on to house juvenile offenders who, because of the severity or nature of their crimes, will be processed through the adult court and correctional systems. These issues will be addressed after the following "A Look Into" box.

A LOOK INTO . . .

ISSUES FACING JAIL ADMINISTRATORS

Administrators of large urban jails face many serious challenges in trying to manage their facilities. Herbert L. Bernsen, assistant director of the St. Louis County Department of Justice Services and former administrator of the St. Louis County Jail, has a national reputation as a knowledgeable and professional jail administrator, and his thoughts on issues facing jail administrators are valuable for students.

Q: What are the major challenges facing you as a jail administrator?

A: There are many, but include (1) hiring competent staff, and training them in the multiple competencies required of individuals in this field; (2) communicating the philosophy of our agency and the criminal justice field in general in terms of what we are trying to do as far as our mission; and (3) to bring the community into our mission by contacting social service as well as law enforcement agencies, and integrating them into not just how we intake and hold prisoners, but what we do with them to prepare for release.

Q: What are the characteristics essential for staff to work successfully in a large jail?

A: It is not necessary that they have prior criminal justice experience, but valuable to have a combination of education and work experience that lends itself to the qualities that are needed in this facility. These include dependability, discipline, and the ability to communicate and work with others. Most importantly, individuals must have good skills in communicating with individuals from a variety of backgrounds, and the ability to not only work under supervision, but also independently, being able to think on their feet and make decisions in line with the mission and philosophy we want to achieve.

Q: How do you find people with the abilities to perform well in a jail setting?

A: You have to put the jail out there, in a variety of places where those individuals that are apt to become interested may see or hear about you. You have to do more than just advertise; you have to explain the organization, how it operates professionally, and the critical skills you are looking for. We are looking for more than what the public perceives as a correctional officer, and you emphasize the talent and skill required, and the career opportunities that exist. You look at universities, the military, and even use Internet sites, so that your message is received by a wide variety of people. Also critical is that your personnel department and administrators that may talk to applicants have a good understanding of what to look for, and represent the agency well.

Q: Talk more about the mission of a jail.

A: As a correctional agency, we have a mandate to hold (detain) people that have been assigned to us because of violating a statute or ordinance, and we have to provide a safe, secure, and humane environment for them. Our goal is to provide an environment where staff, inmates, and visitors are free from emotional or physical danger. Inmates must have the opportunity to participate in programs, and improve themselves while they are here. This environment should also foster a well-trained staff, capable of direct-supervision management. Direct supervision is the philosophy that we use to manage our jail; we believe it creates a better environment for staff, improves our ability to manage inmates, and increases their chances of successful return to the community.

(continued)

It is important to get others to understand this mission, and the media can play an important role in this. With a jail setting, there are always negative things that can occur, and the media will want to know why these things happen. Even when mistakes or omissions occur, it is an opportunity to get the message of your mission before the public. You may have a tragic incident such as a suicide, but you can also discuss the type of suicide prevention program you have, and the plans you have to improve it. It is important to develop a rapport with the media and invite them to learn about the successful programs within the jail. We need to get agencies to be partners in what we do. An example is the mental health court, in which the community was brought into the facility as a partner with us to get other phases of the community mental health groups to determine how best to handle and provide services to offenders with mental health problems. These can develop into grant opportunities and involvement by other agencies.

Another part of what we can do is to get the courts, judges, and prosecutors involved in what we are trying to do. Any one of these components can block programs from being successful. We have regular meetings to discuss issues of mutual interest. The courts want to be partners with the jail, and through discussions of issues as mundane as how we transport inmates, doors are opened for further discussions.

Q: Tight budget times always force reducing or ending programs or services you see as valuable. How do you determine what you are going to cut when cuts are needed?

A: We look for other funding opportunities, such as grant opportunities that can be found through universities or social service agencies. There may be a source of getting funds to develop a program we would otherwise not be able to afford. Another way is to have contacts to begin doing things in house you did not realize you could do, such as using intern students, which provides assistance and recruits staff. Social service agencies may decide they should be providing services at the jail, such as our local school board determining they have a responsibility to offer education classes to our population. It is very important that we have an environment that welcomes outside participation, because even though it takes more time and work, the potential payoff is tremendous. As a result of an active use of volunteers, we have more programs and have a calmer institution.

Q: Looking to the future, do you foresee a "new paradigm" for jails?

A: I do, because hopefully organizations like the American Jail Association, the National Institute of Corrections, and the American Correctional Association are getting the word out to national and state decision makers that jails are areas that need assistance and are worth investing in. When you look at the number of individuals that come through jails and go out into the community, jails touch many more offenders than prison or community supervision, and many of the individuals they touch have mental, medical, and emotional problems in need of intervention.

RESPONDING TO JAIL CROWDING

As noted earlier, the jail incarceration rate has more than doubled, and the population of the nation's jails has almost tripled over the past twenty years. Much of the growth has resulted from the increased numbers of minority inmates. As indicated in Figure 3.4, between 1990 and 2000, the number of Hispanic jail inmates increased at the fastest annual rate, followed by whites and then by blacks.[39] While some jail officials attempted to deal with the increasing number of offenders by in-

JAIL POPULATION BY RACE AND ETHNICITY, 1990–2000

FIGURE **3.4**

Number of jail inmates (one-day count)

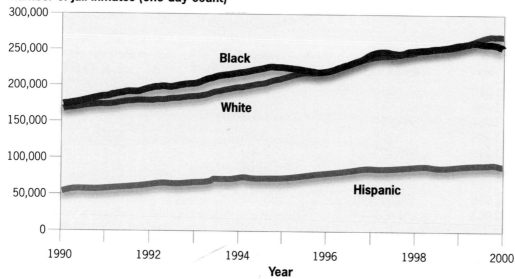

Source: Bureau of Justice Statistics Correctional Surveys (The National Probation Data Survey, National Prisoner Statistics, Survey of Jails, and The National Parole Data Survey) as presented in *Correctional Populations in the United States, 1997*. Data from 1998 to 2000 are presented in *Prison and Jail Inmates at Midyear*.

creasing the pretrial release and diversion programs, the problem usually resulted in the need to construct new jails or add onto the existing jail to increase capacity. During the 1990s approximately 150 additional jails were built (not including new jails constructed to replace old jails), and the capacity of the nation's jails increased from approximately 350,000 to more than 600,000.[40]

Table 3.4 illustrates the rated capacity of jails, the amount of capacity that was added each year, and the percentage of the overall capacity of jails that was occupied. Since the major construction boom in the last decade, America's jails have been able to add enough capacity to stay ahead of the increasing population, and the population has not been over 97 percent of capacity in the last ten years.[41] However, in 1999, the jail population exceeded the rated capacity in seven states and the District of Columbia. Table 3.5 indicates the level of crowding in each of these jurisdictions.

Another approach for dealing with jail overcrowding has been to contract out for the detention of jail inmates with a private correctional company. A private correctional facility is any correctional facility, operated by other than a governmental agency and usually in a "for-profit" manner, that contracts with a governmental entity to provide security, housing, and programs for offenders. According to most reports, the first jail contract with a private company was in 1984, for a 250-bed facility operated by Corrections Corporation of America under contract with Hamilton County, Tennessee. Privatizing the operation of prisons or jails has been very controversial, and arguments surround the issues of benefits and costs, ethics and corruption, quality of service, security and public protection, and liability.[42]

Today, there are dozens of privately operated jails across the country, and privatization of jail construction or management is seen as a viable option for counties that need a new jail and do not have the funds available to build one. Between 1993 and 1999, the number of private jails in the United States increased from seventeen to forty-seven, and the number of offenders supervised in them grew from 3,229 to 16,659. Even with this increase, private jails held only 2.4 percent of jail inmates in 1999.[43] Many of the concerns about privatization can be dealt with through the contracting process between the government and the private entity. The county can agree on a contract with a private company, which will build a jail

TABLE	3.4	Rated Capacity of Jails and Percentage of Capacity Occupied, 1983, 1988, and 1993–1999

		Number of jail inmates	
Year	Rated capacity[a]	Amount of capacity added[b]	Percent of capacity occupied[c]
1999	652,321	39,541	93
1998	612,780	26,216	97
1997	586,564	23,593	97
1996	562,971	17,208	92
1995	545,763	41,439	93
1994	504,324	29,100	96
1993	475,224	26,027	97
1988	339,949	38,751	101
1983	261,556	—	85

Years	Average annual percent change	Average annual amount of change
1993–1999	5.4%	29,516
1983–1993	6.2	21,367

Note: Capacity data for 1994–1998 were estimated from the Annual Survey of Jails.

—Not available.

[a]Rated capacity is the number of beds or inmates assigned by a rating official to facilities within each jurisdiction.

[b]The number of beds added during the 12 months ending each midyear.

[c]The number of inmates divided by the rated capacity times 100.

Source: James J. Stephan, *Census of Jails, 1999*, NCJ 186633 (Washington, D.C.: U.S. Department of Justice, Bureau of Justice Statistics, August 2001), p. 4.

TABLE	3.5	Percentage of Overcrowding in Jurisdictions over Capacity, 1999

State	Percent of capacity occupied
District of Columbia	120%
Virginia	118
New Jersey	110
Massachusetts	108
Kentucky	105
Washington	105
California	103
Indiana	102

Source: James J. Stephan, *Census of Jails, 1999*, NCJ 186633 (Washington, D.C.: U.S. Department of Justice, Bureau of Justice Statistics, August 2001), p. 5.

to meet the county needs and charge the county on a per-day basis for each inmate the private jail holds. Many of these contracts require the private company to meet established professional standards for jail operations, to provide certain specified programs, and to ensure that the cost per day does not exceed the average cost per day for jail inmates held by the publicly operated jail.

LEGAL ISSUES FOR JAILS

One of the primary reasons for increased capacity through new jail construction over the past decade has been the increase in the number of successful legal challenges by jail inmates against jails for either overcrowding or other conditions of confinement. Jail inmates file lawsuits over a variety of things: lack of privacy, privileges (or lack thereof), food, brutality by staff, access to their attorneys, or general conditions of overcrowding. While most lawsuits are not successful, the courts recognize that most jail inmates are not yet convicted, and afford them more privileges that the typical prison inmate.

Jails are expected to provide a constitutionally acceptable environment, which means they must meet all the requirements of health and safety codes, adequately control violence, provide an acceptable level of privacy as allowed by security concerns, and meet basic inmate needs such as medical care and a nutritious diet. When a jail does not meet the expected level and an inmate files a legal action in federal court, the court can impose requirements for action by the jail to remedy the concerns and bring the jail environment up to constitutional standards.

One of the first major cases in which the U.S. Supreme Court addressed jail conditions was the 1979 case of **Bell v. Wolfish**, in which the Court established the "punitive intent standard."[44] The case dealt with conditions and practices at a

Bell v. Wolfish
a 1979 U.S. Supreme Court case in which the punitive intent standard was adopted for considering violations of the Eighth Amendment regarding jail operations

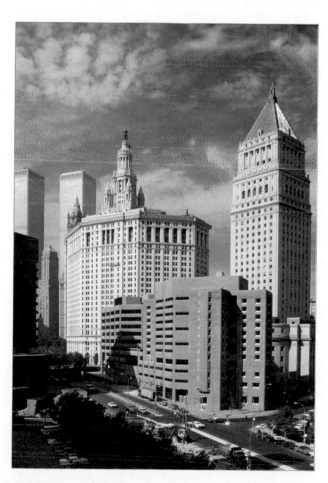

The Metropolitan Correctional Center in New York City, operated by the U.S. Bureau of Prisons, was the location of one of the major inmate lawsuits regarding jail operations.
Courtesy of the Federal Bureau of Prisons.

federal jail in New York City. The jail, although newly constructed, was already overcrowded and "double-bunked," housing two inmates in cells designed for one. The lawsuit by inmates challenged the crowded conditions as well as practices at the jail of not allowing inmates to observe searches of their cells and of requiring them to submit to visual searches of body cavities after visits with family members or friends. The lawsuit alleged violations of the Eighth Amendment of the Constitution, which states: "Excessive bail shall not be required, nor excessive fines imposed, nor cruel and unusual punishment inflicted."

The Supreme Court ruled that the case should turn only on whether the practices in question violated jail inmates' right to be free from punishment (since they were not yet convicted of a crime), using a standard of whether the individual restrictions were punitive or merely regulatory restraints, whether the practices were reasonably related to a legitimate goal other than punishment, and whether the practices appeared excessive in relation to that alternative purpose. This decision is guidance for jails in what is expected by the courts in operating in a safe and secure manner, yet one that does not overly infringe on the rights of yet-to-be-convicted offenders.

Since the *Bell* decision, courts regularly have ruled against the operating conditions at a jail and required jail administrators to make changes or even build a new jail. In a 1999 survey, approximately 15 percent of the reporting jurisdictions reported that they were under a court order or consent decree for crowding or other confinement conditions, and 11 percent were under a court order to limit their population so that it would not be overcrowded.[45] These numbers, however, are lower than in 1993, as many new jails have been constructed and procedures have been improved to avoid the likelihood of inmate suits.

DEALING WITH MENTALLY ILL OFFENDERS

Over the last thirty years, the number of criminal offenders with mental illness has been rising. In the 1960s, new antipsychotropic drugs were created and prescribed for people with mental illness, allowing many mentally ill individuals to remain in the community rather than be placed in mental hospitals. As a result, states closed their hospitals, and the number of mentally ill patients went from a high of 559,000 in 1955 to 69,000 in 1995.[46] When these community patients stop taking their medication, the symptoms of the mental illness return; many commit crimes and become clients of the criminal justice system. A report by the National Coalition for the Mentally Ill in Criminal Justice indicates that there are 33 percent more mentally ill people in jails than in mental hospitals.[47]

In another report issued by the U.S. Department of Justice, the Bureau of Justice Statistics estimated that 283,800 mentally ill offenders were being held in state and federal prisons and local jails at midyear 1998, and an additional 547,800 mentally ill individuals were on probation. The report further estimated that 16 percent of all jail inmates have a mental illness.[48]

Upon arrival in a jail, offenders are usually screened to detect mental illness or the potential for suicide. These assessment instruments are very short, but can accurately indicate a problem that requires immediate attention. The assessment instruments rely on the offenders' honesty and ask them about histories of mental illness, taking of psychotropic medication, and thoughts of suicide. Although most jails (78 percent) do an initial screening, very few offer intensive mental health programs. Of jails surveyed in 1999, 66 percent provide psychotropic medication, 47 percent provide twenty-four-hour care, 46 percent provide routine care and counseling, and 38 percent provide full psychiatric evaluations.[49] Table 3.6 illustrates the number of jail inmates receiving these services by state and region.

TABLE 3.6 Jail Inmates Receiving Mental Health Services, June 30, 1999

		Number of inmates who were receiving—		
Region and jurisdiction	Number of inmates in jurisdictions reporting data	24-hour mental health care[a]	Mental health therapy or counseling	Psychotropic medication[b]
U.S. total	490,710	11,323	41,029	44,337
Federal	—	0	—	—
State	490,710	11,323	41,029	44,337
Northeast	84,869	2,395	11,057	9,937
Maine	1,113	20	59	276
Massachusetts	10,623	152	497	550
New Hampshire	1,422	40	151	140
New Jersey	14,267	346	415	894
New York	31,219	1,141	6,107	4,286
Pennsylvania	26,225	696	3,828	3,791
Midwest	68,134	1,078	4,552	5,914
Illinois	5,819	130	337	422
Indiana	9,140	105	371	410
Iowa	2,217	12	132	263
Kansas	2,078	35	93	315
Michigan	13,685	144	867	1,328
Minnesota	2,671	21	199	306
Missouri	4,996	101	592	636
Nebraska	1,887	12	61	160
North Dakota	310	2	67	27
Ohio	13,479	310	1,044	1,186
South Dakota	817	3	45	80
Wisconsin	11,035	203	744	781
South	223,580	4,175	16,477	19,944
Alabama	7,852	274	297	576
Arkansas	2,407	12	75	130
Dist. of Col.	1,653	108	45	142
Florida	47,253	1,090	3,889	4,435
Georgia	22,881	382	2,905	2,052
Kentucky	6,446	84	210	495
Louisiana	17,000	284	1,238	1,030
Maryland	10,889	194	860	844
Mississippi	4,978	58	117	274
North Carolina	8,211	44	285	456
Oklahoma	4,619	28	108	247
South Carolina	7,103	78	396	399
Tennessee	17,982	202	1,198	2,465
Texas	45,641	1,088	2,997	4,278
Virginia	17,228	238	1,779	1,902
West Virginia	1,437	11	78	219
West	114,127	3,675	8,943	8,542
Alaska	6	0	0	2
Arizona	10,083	168	176	116
California	71,712	2,963	6,119	5,598
Colorado	6,627	62	231	288
Idaho	2,209	18	108	315
Montana	777	5	86	81
Nevada	4,671	96	639	395
New Mexico	4,380	64	611	636
Oregon	5,442	238	556	452
Utah	1,796	8	117	225
Washington	5,523	46	252	370
Wyoming	901	7	48	64

—Not available.

[a]In special housing or a psychiatric unit on or off jail grounds.

[b]Drugs having a mind-altering effect, such as antidepressants, stimulants, sedatives, tranquilizers, and other antipsychotic drugs.

Source: James J. Stephan, *Census of Jails, 1999*, NCJ 186633 (Washington, D.C.: U.S. Department of Justice, Bureau of Justice Statistics, August 2001), p. 40.

Mental health staff do assessments of inmates as they enter jails to determine whether they are a serious suicide risk.
Photo by Richard P. Seiter.

PREVENTING SUICIDES

As noted earlier, jails do a preliminary screening upon an offender's entry to the jail to determine whether there are immediate concerns about an attempted suicide. Of the total number of inmate deaths (919) while in jail reported in the *Census of Jails, 1999,* 35.3 percent of them (324) were a result of suicide.[50] This is approximately the same proportion as in the previous national jail census in 1993. This is by far the greatest cause of death for inmates in jail other than deaths resulting from illness or natural causes (41.8 percent). Homicides accounted for only 3 percent of jail deaths, and AIDS accounted for 8.5 percent of jail deaths.

Suicide prevention programs

jail and prison programs that include early detection of suicide risks, staff education to recognize signs of potential suicide, and procedures for managing inmates who are now suicidal

Since suicide represents a significant concern for jail administrators, most jails have **suicide prevention programs**. As indicated in Table 3.7, less than 3 percent of jails reported that they did not have specific procedures for suicide prevention (84 of 2,866 jails). Suicide prevention programs include risk assessment at admission, special staff training, counseling for inmates, and monitoring and special watches of high-risk inmates. Inmates who indicate some risk during the assessment are noted and receive specific counseling from mental health professionals regarding their thoughts of suicide. All staff receive training on the signs of potential suicide among inmates. These include sleeping a lot, depression, staying by oneself, giving away property to other inmates, or confiding their thoughts to family or friends.

Suicide watch

management of suicidal inmates who are placed in a specially designed cell and have constant supervision

If inmates are deemed a high risk for suicide as a result of the assessment or staff observations, they may be specially monitored. Some of the monitoring may include **suicide watch** programs, in which inmates are placed in a specially equipped cell without materials that could be used for a suicide attempt (blankets, sheets, belts, shoestrings, places in the cell to hang something from). Some suicide watch cells then have constant supervision by either a camera or a person so that staff can quickly react if the inmate begins any dangerous activity. Others require officers to check on the offender every thirty minutes to ensure his or her safety. Even with all of these programs, it is difficult to prevent suicides of inmates truly committed to ending their lives.

TABLE 3.7 Jail Procedures for Suicide Prevention

Region and jurisdiction	Jail jurisdictions have specific procedures for suicide prevention* No	Yes	Jail jurisdictions with suicide prevention procedures involving— Suicide risk assessment at admission	Staff training in suicide prevention	Counseling or psychiatric services	Monitoring of high risk inmates	Suicide watch cell or special location	Inmate suicide prevention teams	Other procedures
U.S. total	84	2,782	2,499	1,997	1,764	2,085	2,403	215	151
Federal	0	1	1	1	1	1	1	1	0
State	84	2,781	2,498	1,996	1,763	2,084	2,402	214	151
Northeast	2	180	176	171	173	155	169	24	11
Maine	0	15	15	15	15	11	14	0	0
Massachusetts	0	14	13	14	14	14	13	4	2
New Hampshire	0	10	9	10	9	8	10	1	1
New Jersey	0	21	21	17	20	16	19	4	2
New York	1	56	56	56	56	52	54	6	2
Pennsylvania	1	64	62	59	59	54	59	9	4
Midwest	36	854	786	635	554	680	742	54	35
Illinois	1	84	77	59	68	60	75	8	4
Indiana	1	83	77	51	48	71	76	4	2
Iowa	1	91	89	81	37	83	74	7	1
Kansas	2	87	73	60	45	69	73	4	1
Michigan	3	77	76	62	68	69	74	3	1
Minnesota	5	71	69	60	58	49	62	7	4
Missouri	17	92	70	40	38	63	79	3	7
Nebraska	4	54	52	40	27	36	41	0	2
North Dakota	1	21	20	19	11	19	18	2	0
Ohio	0	95	90	76	77	73	78	9	7
South Dakota	0	29	24	25	13	23	22	2	3
Wisconsin	1	70	69	62	64	65	70	5	3
South	41	1,347	1,161	892	762	939	1,161	110	72
Alabama	9	128	102	67	48	107	105	16	16
Arkansas	3	80	59	40	30	54	66	2	2
Dist. of Col.	0	1	1	1	1	1	1	0	0
Florida	1	68	62	45	57	56	61	4	4
Georgia	6	176	144	91	94	102	150	15	8
Kentucky	3	69	62	52	44	45	62	1	4
Louisiana	5	80	68	51	38	49	65	7	4
Maryland	0	25	25	23	24	19	24	3	1
Mississippi	9	70	52	36	30	38	59	3	5
North Carolina	1	89	76	55	46	66	78	7	3
Oklahoma	3	86	74	58	26	64	71	6	3
South Carolina	1	46	39	37	27	30	42	3	0
Tennessee	0	93	74	52	55	55	85	13	5
Texas	0	237	229	202	160	171	203	21	12
Virginia	0	76	72	67	66	62	69	7	3
West Virginia	0	23	22	15	16	20	20	2	2
West	5	400	375	298	274	310	330	26	33
Alaska	0	8	6	6	3	7	6	0	0
Arizona	0	14	14	12	14	12	13	2	0
California	1	75	70	62	52	51	58	7	12
Colorado	0	53	50	32	36	38	43	6	4
Idaho	0	38	36	27	20	35	30	1	2
Montana	4	31	27	19	15	26	22	0	4
Nevada	0	20	18	15	13	14	19	2	1
New Mexico	0	31	28	20	22	21	29	0	1
Oregon	0	31	30	24	26	27	29	4	3
Utah	0	23	22	20	17	17	20	0	0
Washington	0	54	52	41	38	41	40	2	5
Wyoming	0	22	22	20	18	21	21	2	1

*A total of 218 jail jurisdictions did not indicate whether specific procedures were followed for suicide prevention.

Source: James J. Stephan, *Census of Jails, 1999*, NCJ 186633 (Washington, D.C.: U.S. Department of Justice, Bureau of Justice Statistics, August 2001), p. 41.

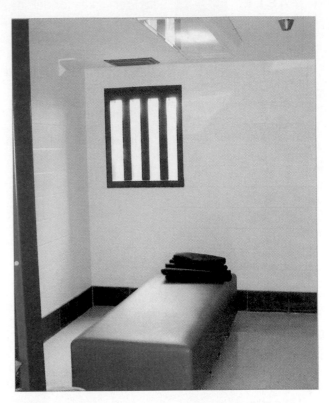

Suicide prevention cells have little that inmates can use to harm themselves and are monitored continuously through cameras or personal supervision.
Photo by Richard P. Seiter.

In 2003, Maury Travis, an alleged serial killer, was arrested and jailed in the St. Louis County Jail for the brutal rape and murder of multiple victims. Because of the nature of the crimes, he was housed in the jail isolation block and placed on a suicide watch, with trained inmates assigned to sit outside his cell and watch him to prevent the possibility of a suicide attempt. The jail had a policy that inmates housed in the isolation block would be allowed to come out of their cells and walk on the short range immediately outside their cell for one hour per day. Therefore, the inmate "watcher" had to move back behind another wall, from which he did not have a direct view of the entire cell. Within thirty minutes after the inmate watcher moved from the cell front, Travis tied his bed sheet around his neck and a ventilation grill in the cell and hanged himself to death. The suicide resulted in the county jail hiring several more staff just to conduct the suicide watch instead of using inmates.

In the "You Make the Decision" box, students consider several factors in a suicide prevention program and decide how they want to structure a prevention policy.

YOU MAKE THE DECISION . . .

PREVENTING JAIL SUICIDES

The story of Maury Travis is troubling for many reasons. First, a life was lost, even though there was significant evidence of his guilt in kidnapping and brutally murdering several women in the St. Louis metropolitan region. Second, with his death, there are still missing women that fit the description of other Travis victims, and law enforcement personnel are disappointed that they cannot question him for information regarding those disappearances. And finally, the county jail failed in its responsibility to safely house Travis and prevent him from harming himself during the investigation and pending prosecution for his alleged acts.

It seems as if preventing suicides in a jail would be easy. After all, the inmates are locked up in cells. But if someone really wants to commit suicide, it takes only a few minutes, and almost any piece of clothing, sheet, or shoestring can be used to hang oneself. Suicide prevention screenings upon admission are only as good as the information provided by the offender. And, as in the Travis case, even when an inmate is identified as a risk and placed on suicide watch, weaknesses in the procedures can result in a suicide.

The issues to consider when developing a suicide prevention policy include the following: (1) whom to place on suicide watch; (2) what clothing and bedding are allowed; and (3) whether to use inmate watchers. Keep in mind that it is expensive to place someone on suicide watch, and there are always limited funds for operation. It is easy to decide to place an offender on suicide watch if he or she admits consideration of suicide. But if someone has a minor history or no history yet faces a long sentence or the death penalty, such as Travis, should he or she be on suicide watch? If the person is placed on the watch, do you strip the inmate and not allow any clothing or bedding? This seems harsh, but keep in mind that almost any item can be used as a noose to hang oneself. Finally, many jurisdictions do use inmates trained as suicide watchers. They cost nothing and have proven to be good companions to suicidal inmates. Through their communications, inmates often end their suicidal thoughts quicker than if a correctional officer is watching them. But if something goes wrong, as in the Travis case, it is difficult to justify the use of inmates as watchers to the public. Consider all these issues and develop your own suicide prevention program.

Chapter Review

SUMMARY

Jails today represent one of the most challenging operations in the nation's criminal justice process. Jails not only hold more than 600,000 inmates at any one time, but they also admit more than ten times that number per year, hold a wide variety of categories of offenders, house inmates with several unique problems and needs, and must maintain constitutional standards and protect the rights of offenders charged yet not convicted of a crime.

As a result of this multitasked mission, jails are extremely difficult to administer and operate. With the high turnover of offenders, jails sometimes make a mistake by releasing the wrong inmate. With many inmates having mental health, drug abuse, and physical problems, there are regularly cases of suicide, assault, and alleged mistreatment. Located in the center of cities and rural communities, jails get much more public attention than most prisons or other correctional facilities. In many counties, jails are operated by an elected official (the sheriff); sometimes hiring decisions result from political connections or campaign contributions rather than the professional or technical skills or knowledge of the applicant.

Through all of these challenges, jails continue to operate almost nine hundred years after the first jail was opened in medieval England. The jail serves a critical role as an offender intake point to the criminal justice system. Even with major efforts to reform, improve, and reinvent the way jails are operated, few major changes have been made in the basic system of operating jails.

And while efforts continue to improve and professionalize the nation's jails, it is not expected that the public's perceptions of how jails run will change.

Jails primarily hold offenders before trial, in addition to some offenders serving short terms of confinement. For more serious inmates who are sentenced to longer periods of incarceration, America's early colonists invented the prison. Chapter 5 describes the current status of prisons in the United States, how they operate, the types of jurisdictions that oversee them, and the assignment of inmates to various security levels. After reading Chapter 5, students will have a clear understanding of the differences in policies and practices between jails and prisons.

REVIEW QUESTIONS

1. What role did John Howard play in the early development of jails?
2. What are the advantages of a regional jail?
3. List potential reasons for the increase in the jail incarceration rate over the past decade.
4. Compare the average length of stay in a jail to that in a prison.
5. Describe the normal booking process in a jail.
6. Describe the problems associated with the use of classification systems in jails.
7. How are podular jail designs an improvement over linear jail designs?
8. Describe direct supervision.
9. Describe the impact of the *Bell v. Wolfish* decision on modern jail operations.
10. What steps do jails take to reduce the likelihood of suicide by inmates?

ENDNOTES

1. Data from the Bureau of Justice Statistics indicates that a total of 2.4 million offenders were admitted to probation (1.5 million), prison (0.5 million), and parole (0.4 million) in 1993, while 9.8 million were admitted to jails. See *Sourcebook of Criminal Justice Statistics 1994* (Washington, D.C.: U.S. Government Printing Office, 1995), pp. 524, 533, 537, 575.

2. David Rothman, *The Discovery of the Asylum: Social Order and Disorder in the New Republic* (Boston: Little, Brown, 1971) p. 56.

3. Bureau of Justice Statistics, *Census of Jails, 1999* (Washington, D.C.: U.S. Department of Justice, 2001), p. 6.

4. There were 3,367 jails in the United States on June 30, 1999, according to Bureau of Justice Statistics, *Sourcebook of Criminal Justice Statistics, 2001* (Washington, D.C.: U.S. Department of Justice, 2003), p. 82.

5. James J. Stephan, *Census of Jails, 1999*, NCJ 186633 (Washington, D.C.: Department of Justice, Bureau of Justice Statistics, August 2001), p. 5. Updated from Bureau of Justice Statistics, *Jail Census, Mid-Year Reports, 2002.*

6. BJS Bulletin, *Prison and Jail Inmates at Midyear 2002* (Washington, D.C.: U.S. Department of Justice, March 2003).

7. Ibid., p. 8.

8. C. W. Harlow, *Profile of Jail Inmates, 1996*, Bureau of Justice Statistics Special Report NCJ 16444620 (Washington, D.C.: U.S. Government Printing Office, 1998).

9. Criminal Justice Policy Council, *The State Jail System Today* (Austin, Texas: Criminal Justice Policy Council, September 1998).

10. D. Alan Henry, "The Impact of Financial Conditions of Release on Jail Populations," *Corrections Management Quarterly* 3, no. 2 (1999): 30.

11. Stephan, p. 4.

12. BJS Bulletin, p. 8.

13. Craig Perkins, James J. Stephan, and Allen J. Beck, *Jails and Jail Inmates, 1993–94* (Washington, D.C.: Bureau of Justice Statistics, U.S. Department of Justice, April 1995), p. 13.

14. Bureau of Justice Statistics, 2003, p. 342.

15. Harlow, op. cit.

16. Bureau of Justice Statistics, 2003, p. 342.

17. Criminal Justice Policy Council, op. cit.

18. Camille Graham Camp and George M. Camp, *The 2001 Corrections Yearbook: Adult Systems* (Middletown, Conn.: Criminal Justice Institute, 2002), p. 86.

19. Ibid., p. 15.

20. J. M. Brown, P. A. Langan, and D. J. Lenin, *Felony Sentences in State Courts, 1996*, NCJ 173939 (Washington, D.C.: Bureau of Justice Statistics, 1999).

21. Camp and Camp, pp. 55, 71.

22. Perkins, Stephan, and Beck.

23. Stephan, p. 7.

24. See James Austin, "An Overview of the Nation's Jails," *Corrections Management Quarterly* 3, no. 2 (1999): 3.

25. Michael O'Toole, "The Numbers Say They Are More Different Than Normally Assumed," *American Jails* May-June 1997, p. 37.

26. During 2002, the St. Louis City Jail had serious problems in this regard; five individuals were released

mistakenly, and the jail received considerable negative media attention as a result.

27. Vernon Fox, *Correctional Institutions* (Englewood Cliffs, N.J.: Prentice Hall, 1983), p. 61.

28. Tim Brennan, "Implementing Organization Change in Criminal Justice: Some Lessons from Jail Classification Systems," *Corrections Management Quarterly* 3, no. 2 (1999): 12.

29. Ibid., p. 14.

30. Stephan, p. 25.

31. Ibid., p. 10.

32. Ibid.

33. Ibid., p. 9.

34. Ibid.

35. Ibid.

36. Ibid.

37. As cited in Robert W. Duffy, "City's $101 Million Justice Center Is State-of-the-Art in Jail Design," *St. Louis Post-Dispatch,* November 17, 2002, p. B5.

38. G. J. Bayens, J. Williams, and J. O. Smykla, "Jail Type Makes a Difference: Evaluating the Transition from a Traditional to a Podular Direct Supervision Jail across Ten Years," *American Jails* (May/June 1997): 33–39.

39. Bureau of Justice Statistics Correctional Surveys, *Correctional Populations in the United States* and *Prison and Jail Inmates at Midyear* (Washington, D.C.: U.S. Department of Justice, various years).

40. Darrell Gilliard, *Prison and Jail Inmates at Midyear 1998* (Washington, D.C.: US Department of Justice, 1999), p. 7.

41. Stephan, p. 4.

42. For a good overview of the issues regarding privatization, see Charles Logan, *Private Prisons: Cons and Pros* (New York: McGraw-Hill, 1996).

43. Stephan, p. 6.

44. *Bell v. Wolfish,* 441 U.S. 520 (1979).

45. Stephan, p. 5.

46. "Prisons Replace Hospitals for the Nation's Mentally Ill," *New York Times,* March 5, 1998, p. A26.

47. William M. DiMascio, *Seeking Justice: Crime and Punishment in America* (New York: Edna McConnell Clark Foundation, 1997), p. 22.

48. Paula M. Ditton, *Mental Health and Treatment of Inmates and Probationers* (Washington, D.C.: U.S. Department of Justice, Bureau of Justice Statistics, 1999).

49. Stephan, p. 10.

50. Ibid., p. 8.

Chapter 4

AFTER READING THIS CHAPTER, YOU SHOULD BE ABLE TO:

1. Describe the history and development of probation during the nineteenth century.

2. Explain the organization and operation of modern probation.

3. Compare a casework and surveillance style of supervision.

4. Contrast regular, intensive, and special caseloads.

5. Define and give examples of standard and special conditions of probation.

6. Discuss the development of case law regarding due process requirements for probation revocation.

7. Outline the results of evaluations regarding the effectiveness of felony probation.

8. Define "broken windows" probation strategies.

9. Describe intermediate sanctions and how they are used for criminal sentencing.

10. Describe how intensive supervised probation operates.

11. Contrast active and passive electronic monitoring systems.

12. Describe the operation and effectiveness of shock incarceration or boot camp programs.

13. Explain the concept of "net widening" and the problem it creates in the efficient use of intermediate sanctions.

Probation and Intermediate Sanctions

KEY TERMS

community corrections
John Augustus
probation supervision
casework style of supervision
surveillance style of supervision
regular caseload
intensive-supervision caseload
special caseload
standard conditions of probation
special conditions of probation
technical violations
new-crime violations
Gagnon v. Scarpelli
community classification systems
fines
offender restitution
victim compensation
cost of supervision
asset forfeiture
intensive supervised probation
house arrest
electronic monitoring
community residential centers
split sentence
shock incarceration/boot camp
shock probation
net widening

Introduction

Historically, felony offenders were sentenced to either probation or prison. Over the past fifty years, however, the sentencing options available to judges have increased, with the addition of many other sanctions—some that supervise offenders in the community, and some that supervise offenders in some type of institutional confinement. In the 1960s, many alternative sanctions to incarceration were developed, and the term **community corrections** was initiated. Community corrections or community-based corrections are criminal sanctions that involve community supervision of offenders, use correctional and program resources available in the community, and require offenders to abide by specified conditions to remain in the community.

Community corrections gained prominence as an adaptation of the Rehabilitative Era of corrections. During this period, offender problems were identified that required treatment to improve and prepare them for a productive and crime-free lifestyle. Most of the treatment was within institutional settings (prisons). However, it was soon recognized that for these treatments to maximize their effectiveness, the community must be a part of the provision of treatment. In the restrictive prison environment, offenders could not test their readiness to return to the community or build relationships with community programs that could be continued as they lived in society. Therefore the Reintegrative Era developed, with the distinct provision that the community is an essential part of the correctional process.

Today, even as corrections becomes more retributive, there is still an emphasis on community corrections. However, the current emphasis on community corrections has changed from the 1960s and 1970s in that the focus is not on the offender and his or her rehabilitation or reintegration but on public safety. Driving this trend is the realization that we cannot afford to continue to increase the number of offenders in prisons, and therefore safe and cost-effective community alternatives to incarceration must be developed.

This chapter describes the history, evolution, and current operations of community sanctions. Probation has been a part of community corrections for more than 150 years. In many ways, probation has changed little from its original philosophies and practices. In many other ways, however, probation has changed significantly, and some experts even describe a "new paradigm" for probation supervision. However, over the past thirty years, a dissatisfaction with standard probation as a sanction for criminal offenders, combined with a recognition of the need for alternatives to incarceration, has led to an expansion of intermediate sanctions in order to provide greater supervision than regular probation, while still monitoring offenders in the community.

The History of Probation

The earliest history of probation in the United States began in Boston in 1841, when a shoemaker named **John Augustus** posted bail for a man charged with public drunkenness. Augustus had become very interested in the court system and concerned about the dire situation of people charged with crimes who had to spend time in poor jail conditions. While visiting a court hearing, Augustus heard a defendant state than he would drink no more if saved from a sentence in the house of correction, and Augustus asked the judge to defer sentencing and release the man into his custody. In doing so, he became the nation's first probation officer.[1] Augustus began to help others in the same way, bailing them out, helping them find work and a residence, and keeping the court apprised of their progress. By the time of his death in 1859, Augustus had bailed out more than 1,800 offend-

Community corrections

criminal sanctions that involve community supervision of offenders, use correctional and program resources available in the community, and require offenders to abide by specified conditions to remain in the community

John Augustus

the Boston shoemaker who became the "father" of probation

ers. His records on the first 1,100 offenders that he bailed out revealed that only one forfeited bond.[2] Augustus's work had great impact on how many jurisdictions handled criminal offenders, and he became known as the "father of probation." Unfortunately, while he was alive, he received little recognition for his efforts; he died destitute, having used all his funds to help others.

As the successes of Augustus became known, jurisdictions began to recognize that not every offender needs to be sentenced to jail or prison. In 1878, Massachusetts passed the first probation statute for juveniles, and probation was officially recognized. Not until 1901, however, did New York pass the first statute authorizing the use of probation for adult felons. Other states quickly followed New York's lead, and by 1938 thirty-seven states, the District of Columbia, and the federal government had passed juvenile and adult probation laws.[3] By 1907, the first directory of probation officers in the United States listed 795 juvenile and adult probation officers.

Augustus's acts of supervising offenders slowly crept into the formalization of the role of probation officers. Augustus himself came up with the term *probation* (based on the Latin term *probatio* meaning "a period of proving oneself") as well as ideas for requiring offenders to meet conditions of supervision, reporting to the courts, and revoking probation when the conditions were not met.[4] In addition, Augustus's idea of investigating offenders' situations prior to sentencing resulted in the concept of presentence investigations being assigned to probation officers. Although probation has become much more sophisticated in its operation over the years, most of the original concepts created by Augustus continue to this day.

Modern Probation Operations

Probation is a prison sentence that is suspended on the condition that the offender follow certain prescribed rules and commit no further crimes. Even though probation currently suffers from a perception of being "soft on crime," the public and elected officials recognize that not every offender can be sent to prison, and probation is still a sanction regularly used in the United States. In fact, since 1975 the number of offenders under community supervision has risen from less than 1 million to almost 4 million by 2001.[5] However, since that time, the operations of probation have changed significantly. In 1976, a U.S. Comptroller General's Office report criticized probation operations, calling probation a failure due to a lack of adequate resources and recommending a total reevaluation of its operations and practices.[6] As a result, several probation programs such as intensive probation supervision, house arrest, boot camps, and shock probation have been created to enhance supervision, increase effectiveness and increasingly limit offenders' freedom.

Today, probation in the United States is a federal, state, and local activity, administered by more than 2,000 separate agencies; there is considerable diversity of operations and no uniform structure. Although probation began as a service to the judiciary and an arm of the court, today, in all but eleven of the states, adult probation is located in the executive branch of government. In more than half of the states, probation operations are centralized in the state department of corrections. This move to the executive branch and toward centralization stems from the need for training, professionalism, and uniformity of standards, which can be better accomplished in larger administrative systems; there can also be better coordination with other correctional services. In approximately eight states and the federal government, probation and parole services are provided by the same state agency, which supervises both probationers and parolees.

Even though prisons and issues focusing on incarceration receive much of the attention and most of the resources, probation operations have a tremendous

Probation supervision

the role of a probation or parole officer in monitoring an offender's behavior through office visits; contacts with family, friends, bosses, or treatment providers; and visits to the offender's home or place of work

Casework style of supervision

a style of supervising community offenders that places emphasis on assisting the offender with problems, providing counseling, and ensuring that the offender successfully completes supervision

Surveillance style of supervision

a style of supervising community offenders that emphasizes monitoring and enforcing compliance with the rules of supervision and detecting violations leading to revocation and return to custody

impact on the correctional systems within the United States. In 2001, the Bureau of Justice Statistics reported a total of 6,592,800 adults under correctional supervision. Of those, 3,932,751 were on probation, 731,147 were on parole, 631,240 were in jail, and 1,330,980 were in prison.[7] Even with the "tough on crime" mentality gripping the country, probation remains an important component of the correctional process, and the number of people on probation has remained relatively steady for the past several years.

SUPERVISION

Once offenders are granted probation, it is the responsibility of probation officers to supervise them and get them to comply with conditions of their probation. Officers have a dual, and sometimes conflicting, responsibility. The primary purpose of **probation supervision** is to maintain surveillance, enforce conditions of probation, and guide offenders into treatment to protect the public from further crimes. To fulfill this purpose, officers first monitor probationers' activities through a combination of office visits (probationers report to the officer at the probation office), verification of probationers' activities by visiting their homes and contacting their employers or program providers, and monitoring activities such as drug testing of probationers. Second, officers help offenders succeed by determining program or treatment needs and placing probationers in social service programs that address their needs for education, mental health counseling, vocational training, or substance abuse programming.

It has been suggested that officers develop a supervision style that falls into either a casework or a surveillance approach. A **casework style of supervision** emphasizes helping the offender with problems, providing counseling, and ensuring that the offender completes supervision. A **surveillance style of supervision** emphasizes monitoring and enforcing compliance with the rules or supervision and the detection of violations leading to revocation and return to custody. In a recent survey of probation and parole officers in St. Louis, Missouri, officers were asked what they considered the most important roles for probation officers, and how they spent their time in supervising offenders in the community. Officers responded that the primary role of probation and parole officers is to ensure public

Part of supervision of offenders in the community is through office visits in which probation and parole officers get updates on the activities of their clients.
Photo by Richard P. Seiter.

safety, to supervise and offer resources to help the client readjust to society, to prevent recidivism, to steer offenders in the right direction, to monitor offenders, and to hold offenders highly accountable for their actions and responsibilities.

Results indicated that officers spend an average of 55.9 percent of their time on casework activities during supervision, and 41.4 percent of their time on surveillance activities.[8] These results indicate that officers must do both surveillance (monitoring compliance with conditions) and casework (helping offenders with their problems) in order to enforce conditions of probation and guide offenders to a status that improves their likelihood of success in the community. The types of services that most probation and parole agencies provide include referral services, individual counseling, substance abuse counseling, job development, and family counseling.[9]

Probation agencies generally organize caseloads into three types: regular, intensive, and special. **Regular caseloads** are those for standard probationers who may have a significant risk of reoffending or several program needs but do not warrant assignment to one of the other two types of caseloads. **Intensive-supervision caseloads** (described in more detail later in this chapter) are for offenders with too high a risk or a need to be on regular supervision, and were created as an alternative to sending these offenders to prison. Intensive-supervision caseloads are significantly less in number, and required contacts between officers and probationers are significantly higher. Most jurisdictions also use **special caseloads**, whereby an officer's entire caseload is made up of probationers with a specific type of problem, such as substance abuse, mental illness, or a history of sex offenses. Such specialization allows the officer to become knowledgeable and proficient in dealing with this particular problem. On January 1, 2001, 89.8 percent of probationers were on regular caseloads, 6.7 percent were on special caseloads, 3.2 percent were on intensive caseloads, and 0.3 percent were on a caseload using electronic monitoring.[10] The "A Look Into" box gives a good idea of the challenges of managing a special caseload.

Average caseload sizes vary considerably from jurisdiction to jurisdiction. *The 2001 Corrections Yearbook* reports that the average size of probation officer caseloads is very large. During 2000, the average caseload size for regular probation supervision was 133, and ranged from 320 cases per officer in Rhode Island to 60 cases per officer in Arizona.[11] Caseload size by type of supervision is illustrated in Table 4.1. The large average caseload size occurs because government agencies continue to recognize the importance of probation, but fail to financially support it in line with the large number of offenders. This lack of funding and large caseload sizes make it very difficult for probation to be an effective sanction in providing services to offenders, monitoring their behavior, and reducing recidivism.

The number of face-to-face contacts officers have with probationers varies considerably, depending on caseload sizes and the type of supervision. The average number of face-to-face contacts by type of caseload for 1999 is illustrated in Table 4.2. As indicated, the higher the caseload size, the fewer contacts possible. As well, more contacts are needed for special caseloads, and still more for intensive-supervision caseloads.

CONDITIONS OF PROBATION

The key to probation supervision is that offenders must meet certain conditions in order to complete their period of probation and avoid having their supervision suspended and being sent to prison. Jurisdictions have **standard conditions of probation** that must be followed by every probationer; judges usually have the authority to impose **special conditions of probation** tailored to meet the needs for a

Regular caseload
a caseload made up of standard probationers requiring no special program or supervision

Intensive-supervision caseload
a caseload for offenders with too high a risk or need to be on regular supervision; created as an alternative to sending these offenders to prison

Special caseload
a caseload made up of offenders with a particular type of problem, such as substance abuse, mental illness, or a history of sex offenses

Standard conditions of probation
conditions that must be followed by every probationer

Special conditions of probation
conditions of probation tailored to meet the needs of a particular offender; they can be imposed to meet specific risks or needs

A LOOK INTO . . .   DEALING WITH THE MENTALLY ILL PROBATIONER

The Bureau of Justice Statistics estimated that at midyear 1998, there were 547,800 mentally ill offenders on probation. It is estimated that 13 percent of all probationers had a condition requiring mental health treatment, yet in a 1997 survey of these probationers, only 43 percent of those required to participate in such treatment had done so.[12] Historically, mentally ill offenders in the community were spread out among standard caseloads of non–mentally ill offenders. Recently, most probation and parole agencies have created special caseloads for managing the mentally ill offender. These caseloads are usually smaller than standard caseloads, averaging between fifty and fifty-five offenders. Most offenders are placed on a special caseload by an order of the court as a condition of their probation. Otherwise, probation officers may identify an offender as possibly having a mental illness and request his or her placement on a special caseload. The following is a description by a probation officer of his approach to dealing with mentally ill probationers.

The supervision philosophy of this probation officer is to build trust with clients, particularly because he is concerned about the client's risk of suicide or violence to others. The officer notes that he would not know these things unless offenders tell him, and they must believe that they can share sensitive information with their probation officer without fear of immediate violation (return to prison). The officer states that after a few crises with offenders, this trust often develops.

Mentally ill probationers report more frequently than standard probationers; weekly contact is not unusual. This frequency of contact often continues even when offenders' behavior is good and they are eligible for less intensive supervision. This is because these probationers may become unstable at any time. Every time the officers sees his probationers, he asks them if they are taking their psychotropic medication, if they are having any thoughts of harming themselves or others, and if they know the date and time of their next psychiatric appointment. He notes that it is very important not just to ask them these questions and accept their answers, but to "pry and push" them. He gave an example of an offender under his supervision who had a history of serious suicide attempts through overdoses of psychotropic drugs. The offender called the probation officer (PO) one day and said his roommate was using drugs, and he was afraid he would get caught up in it. The PO advised him to move as soon as possible, but as they continued to talk, it became clear that something else was bothering him. After some prodding, the probationer finally admitted that he was thinking of harming himself. In fact, he then admitted that he had already begun to take his medicine in a suicide attempt, and had called the PO in hopes that the PO would get him to admit what he was doing without his volunteering the information. When asked why someone attempting suicide would not admit it, the PO noted that this is not unusual, as the person planning suicide is often embarrassed and sometimes even concerned about upsetting the PO. Some of his clients become very apologetic about the trouble they cause the PO. In this situation, the PO called emergency medical services (EMS) and continued to talk to the probationer on the phone until the paramedics arrived. He then directed the probationer to go out to meet the EMS workers when they drove up. However, the probationer had kept some pills in his hand, and on the way to the hospital, he took some more pills. The EMS workers were able to treat and save him, and the probationer is now doing very well, both physically and psychologically.

The PO noted that an important part of his job is to be just one part of the mental health treatment team, with the probationer's psychiatrist, the case manager (who acts as community support to help the person keep track of appointments and monitor medication), the probationer's family (although most mentally ill probationers do not have significant family support), and other treatment providers.

One thing that is very different for a PO who specializes in managing mentally ill offenders is the number of hospital visits. The PO indicated that seven probationers out of his caseload of fifty-three were in a mental institution or a psychiatric wing of a hospital. He noted that he also has to work much more closely with the court and judges to educate them regarding the special circumstances of mentally ill offenders. Sometimes he has to be an advocate for the needs of these offenders and suggest that the court show more tolerance for minor violations of probation. Other times, the PO must act in an unconventional manner and have good relationships with court officials in order to get them to act beyond their normal operations. He gave the example of a female probationer who had stopped taking her psychotropic medication, had just had a baby, and was psychotic and delusional. During an evening telephone conversation with the PO in which he was urging her to go to a hospital for inpatient care, the woman threatened to kill her mother and stated that she did not want to go to the hospital. The PO asked her to hold for a minute, called the probation duty officer, obtained an immediate arrest warrant from the court, and asked the police to arrest the probationer immediately. Within half an hour, the police were at her front door to arrest her.

In closing, the PO indicated that in order to manage a caseload of mentally ill probationers, a person must have a strong desire to do it and must be compassionate and understanding, as these probationers do not respond in the typical manner to threats of a probation violation. If they want to die and are planning to commit suicide, the PO cannot simply demand compliance. He noted that even for most compassionate individuals, this work could lead to a great deal of frustration.

TABLE 4.1 Average Caseload Size by Type of Supervision, 2000

Type of supervision	Average caseload size
Regular caseloads	133
Special caseloads	50
Intensive-supervision caseloads	28
Electronic monitoring	15

Source: Adapted from Camille Graham Camp and George M. Camp, *The 2001 Corrections Yearbook: Adult Corrections* (Middletown, Conn.: Criminal Justice Institute, 2002), p. 192.

TABLE 4.2 Average Caseload Size and Annual Contacts by Type of Supervision, 1999

Type of Supervision	Average caseload size	Annual contacts
Regular caseloads	139	12
Special caseloads	45	47
Intensive-supervision caseloads	29	83

Source: Adapted from Camille Graham Camp and George M. Camp, *The 2000 Corrections Yearbook: Adult Corrections* (Middletown, Conn.: Criminal Justice Institute, 2001), pp. 176–177.

particular offender, and these conditions can be imposed to meet an individual offender's specific risks or needs. During the probation period, judges may modify conditions as they determine that offenders are performing satisfactorily and no longer need certain conditions, or are performing poorly and require added conditions as a part of their supervision.

Standard conditions of probation usually include the following:

1. The probationer shall not leave the judicial district without permission of the probation officer or the court.
2. The probationer shall report to the probation officer as directed and shall submit truthful and complete reports.

One way to monitor compliance with conditions of no illegal drug use is through random drug testing. Inmates submit urine samples that are sent to a lab for testing.
Photo by Richard P. Seiter.

3. The probationer shall answer truthfully all inquiries by the probation officer and follow his or her instructions.
4. The probationer shall maintain employment.
5. The probationer shall notify the probation officer of all changes of address within seventy-two hours.
6. The probationer shall refrain from the excessive use of alcohol and is prohibited from the use of controlled substances.
7. The probationer shall not associate with criminals.
8. The probationer shall not commit any crimes.

Examples of special conditions of probation may include requiring drug or alcohol counseling, drug testing, mental health counseling, vocational training, avoiding a particular person or group, staying out of bars or poolrooms, or imposition of any of the intermediate sanctions described shortly. Judges have considerable discretion in imposing special conditions of probation. If offenders meet the conditions of their probation, the supervising probation agency may recommend that the sentencing court end the period of probation, terminate supervision, and close the case. In 2000, there were 612,647 successful terminations from probation, meaning that probationers satisfied the requirements of their supervision (completing the number of visits, passing drug tests, receiving counseling, or meeting other conditions required of their supervision). For those who were successfully terminated, the average time under probation supervision was twenty-five months.[13]

REVOCATION OF PROBATION

If probationers violate or fail to meet any conditions of their probation, they are subject to having their probation revoked and their original prison sentence im-

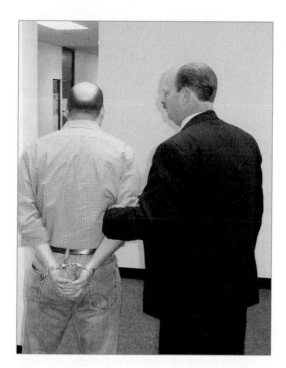

When a probationer commits a serious technical
violation or a new crime, the probation office
usually issues an arrest warrant and the offender
is taken into custody.
Photo by Richard P. Seiter.

posed. Probationers can have their probation revoked for either **technical viola-tions** (not meeting all the conditions of their supervision) or **new-crime violations** (violating the condition of not committing additional crimes). For minor viola-tions of technical conditions, it is unlikely that probation will be revoked, but for continued violations, serious technical violations, or commission of a new crime, probation most likely will be revoked. One exception resulted from a 1983 U.S. Supreme Court ruling in *Bearden v. Georgia,* as the Court decided that failure to make restitution payments due to unemployment is not sufficient reason to re-voke probation.[14]

For minor technical violations, probation officers usually have the discretion to determine how they will handle the infraction. They may warn probationers or in-tensify their own supervision of the case by making more community visits or in-creasing the reporting requirements. In most jurisdictions, officers cannot impose new conditions without requesting modification by the court. If these actions do not change behaviors or if the violation is serious, probation officers begin the for-mal probation revocation process.

The revocation process begins with a report of the violation and a recommen-dation for action by the supervising probation officer. The report goes to the sen-tencing court, and the probationer is given a copy of the alleged violations and directed to appear for a preliminary hearing. The probationer may be arrested and detained in jail until the preliminary hearing. The preliminary hearing is to deter-mine whether there is probable cause to believe that the probationer has com-mitted the violations. If so, a full revocation hearing is scheduled. The probationer may be taken into custody or released on bail or personal recognizance. The probationer may waive the full hearing and plead guilty to the violation at the pre-liminary hearing, and the judge will decide how to handle the violation at that time.

Technical violations

violations of conditions of community supervision with-out commission of a new crime

New-crime violations

violations of a condition of probation that prohibits the commission of any addi-tional crimes

Gagnon v. Scarpelli

a 1973 U.S. Supreme Court decision that created the due process requirements for revoking probation

If the case proceeds to a full revocation hearing, the probation officer bringing the charges and presenting evidence of the violation prepares a full report, and the probationer is given a copy. At the revocation hearing, the officer presents the violation report; the probationer may be represented by legal counsel and have the opportunity to testify and present evidence of his or her innocence of the violations.

In the 1970 case of *United States v. Birnbaum,* the U.S. Supreme Court determined that probation is a privilege and not a right.[15] Once probation is granted, however, the probationer has a liberty interest in avoiding incarceration, and probation cannot be revoked without limited due process requirements. In *Mempa v. Rhay* (1967), probationers were granted the right to legal counsel during the revocation hearing.[16] In 1972, the U.S. Supreme Court decided *Morrissey v. Brewer,* which spelled out the due process rights for parole violations hearings.[17] The next year, the Court decided **Gagnon v. Scarpelli**, which extended the *Morrissey* due process rights to probationers.[18] These include the following rights: (1) to be informed in writing of the alleged violations; (2) to have written notice in advance of the revocation process; (3) to have a preliminary hearing to determine whether there is probable cause; (4) to have a revocation hearing prior to the final decision; (5) to attend the hearings and present witnesses on their behalf; (6) to confront and cross-examine adverse witnesses; and (6) to receive a written decision noting the reasons for the decision.

If there is a finding of a violation, the court has three options: (1) reprimand and restore to supervision; (2) add conditions and restore to probation; (3) revoke probation and order imprisonment under the original sentence. A serious concern is the increase in the number of violations of probation and parole over the past decade. In 1974, the percentage of the U.S. prison population admitted for probation or parole violations was 17 percent, but by 1991 that figure had increased to 45 percent.[19] A review of probationers returned to custody for cause in 2000 found that of the 63,404 probationer violators imprisoned, 35,580 (56.1 percent) were for technical violations alone, and 25,835 (40.7 percent) were for violations and commission of a new crime; for the rest, the reason for the return was not clear.[20] The "tough on crime" attitude and interest in public safety and avoiding risk of further criminality encourages probation officers to report more violations to the court than previously, and encourages the courts to violate probationers and send them to prison at a higher level than in past years.

In the "You Make the Decision" box, you are asked to consider whether to revoke the probation of an offender who is not complying with all of the conditions of his probation.

YOU MAKE THE DECISION . . .   SHOULD I REVOKE HIM?

One of the most difficult challenges for a probation officer is deciding whether to initiate a revocation process for a probationer. To some, it may seem very clear-cut: if probationers violate the conditions of their supervision, their probation should be revoked. Most probation agency policies require that violations be brought to the attention of the court for action to either revoke or modify probation conditions. Yet courts do not want to see every technical violation of a probationer, and officers have considerable discretion in how to handle most minor infractions. For instance, a probationer may be required to report several times per month to the officer, and is usually very responsible in doing so. If the offender misses one appointment, agencies do not want officers reporting it as a violation to the court. Yet all criminal activities should be reported.

The officer must decide whether to initiate a revocation process for a thousand different situations between these two extremes. It is easy for officers to take the "hard line" and report almost any violation. They can never be criticized if the offender later commits a serious crime. However, research findings indicate that recidivism is not reduced by only surveillance techniques of probation, but by a combination of casework and surveillance, and by the officer's getting offenders to take responsibility for their crimes and the behaviors that lead to criminal acts. The best officers use this discretion wisely and counsel offenders or issue agreements to modify supervision conditions as intermediate actions. Many probation agencies now give officers limited authority to add requirements to be better able to hold the offender accountable, such as drug testing, additional reporting to the officer, or even (in a few situations) residence in a halfway house or electronic monitoring. The following is a scenario for students to consider and decide how to handle the case.

You are the probation officer for John Smith. Smith is a 32-year-old offender with a serious history of drug use, three misdemeanor theft offenses, and one prior felony conviction for breaking and entering. The current offense is auto theft and possession of cocaine. He received a sentence of two years of probation with standard conditions and a requirement to participate in drug abuse counseling and random drug testing. Smith did rather well the first eight months of supervision, but his behavior began to deteriorate since then. In month nine, he missed two of his four appointments with you, with excuses that his car broke down and that there was a family emergency. He also lost his job and has yet to find another. His sister called and told you that Smith was again using drugs. You had him come in immediately for a random drug test, which proved negative.

In month ten, he missed two of his drug counseling sessions, claiming that he was not using drugs and the sessions were a waste of time. He said he would rather spend his time trying to find a job. In month eleven, he tested positive for cocaine use. You had not notified the court before this time, but had counseled Smith repeatedly and told him that continued failure to meet the conditions of his probation could result in revocation and a prison sentence. You believe that Smith is not a dangerous person, as he does not have a violent history. You also believe that if he could stay in the community and conquer his drug use, he could stay out of trouble. Yet he has not been honest with you and seems to not respond to your more intensive counseling (and threats). You now must report the violations to the court and recommend how to deal with Smith. You can recommend continuation of probation with current conditions, added conditions as an intermediate sanction, or revocation and implementation of Smith's eighteen-month prison sentence. What do you recommend, and why?

Issues Regarding Probation

Many issues are discussed when describing the current system of probation operations and determining how the system should be changed or improved. First, does probation work? Many studies have resulted in serious questions as to whether probation is effective. The true answer depends on what probation is expected to do and what is determined to be success. How are offenders supervised in the community, and what is the role of the probation officer? Probation officers' roles have changed over the past few years, yet there is still little understanding of what they do and how they should do it. Finally, how do you allocate resources for probation supervision? Most jurisdictions use some method of classifying offenders by risk and need in order to both create supervision guidelines and expectations, and to determine how many offenders a probation officer will supervise.

EFFECTIVENESS

Studies of regular probation (without some type of enhanced supervision) have demonstrated mixed results in probation's effectiveness in protecting society from future crimes. A 1986 review of 79,000 felons sentenced to probation in thirty-two counties across seventeen states revealed that within three years of sentencing, while still on probation, 43 percent were rearrested for a felony.[21] A 1985 RAND study followed California adult felons on probation in Los Angeles and Alameda counties over a forty-month period. Of the sample of 1,672 probationers in 1980, 65 percent were rearrested, 51 percent were reconvicted, and 34 percent were reincarcerated.[22] While these studies question the effectiveness of probation, other studies show some success of probation in reducing recidivism, depending on the seriousness of the offender population, the length of the follow-up, and the type of surveillance provided.

One review of probation outcomes gives conflicting data. Clear and Braga examined the success of a group of both felony and misdemeanor probationers and found that 80 percent completed their terms without a new arrest.[23] However, Langan and Cunniff examined the same data, but only for felony probationers, and found that 43 percent were rearrested within three years.[24] A review of seventeen evaluations of felony probation found rearrest rates as low as 12 percent and as high as 65 percent.[25] This review concluded that probation without adequate surveillance and treatment is not effective. However, well-managed and adequately funded probation programs do reduce recidivism.

All of the preceding evaluations only cite success rates, with no comparison of alternative sentencing outcomes. In some evaluations, probation success rates are compared to the success of ex-inmates. Probationers' recidivism is consistently lower, but that is expected because offenders who receive probation are a less serious group than those who are sentenced to prison. However, in a study with groups of 511 probationers and 511 parolees matched to have an equal likelihood of recidivism, the results over a two-year follow-up indicated that probationers were more successful; 72 percent of parolees and 63 percent of probationers were rearrested, 53 percent of parolees and 38 percent of probationers had new charges filed, and 47 percent of parolees and 31 percent of probationers were incarcerated in jail or prison.[26] This finding suggests that while probationers have high rates of recidivism, prison parolees do even worse.

Some studies also cite the low cost of probation compared to other sanctions. Estimates of the cost of constructing a maximum-security prison are approximately $83,000 per bed, and the annual cost of maintaining and housing an inmate is approximately $22,200.[27] Costs for regular probation were reported to be an average of only $3.03 per day in 2000.[28] Therefore, particularly during tight budget times, elected officials and correctional administrators continue to support the use of probation, even while looking for ways to increase its effectiveness to protect society and deter crime.

A CHANGING STYLE OF SUPERVISION

Even while the public recognizes that not every criminal offender can be sent to prison, there has been an increasing public dissatisfaction with the use of probation, spurred by a belief that those under probation received minimal supervision, and therefore society was not protected against the likelihood of repeat crimes by those who were allowed to remain in the community. However, the manner in which a parolee or probationer is supervised receives relatively little attention, even though its importance was recognized almost forty years ago. In the classic review of prisons and parole, Glaser notes, "The principal functions of parole supervision have been procurement of information on the parolee . . . and facilitating and graduating the transition between imprisonment and complete freedom . . . these functions presumably are oriented to the goals of protecting the public and rehabilitating the offender."[29] Soon thereafter, Alberty analyzed the comparison between styles of parole supervision and violation rates, and defined supervision as "the means used to accomplish the goals of protecting society and rehabilitating the offender."[30]

Until the late 1960s, probation and parole supervision focused on the casework style of supervision, or restoring offenders to the community.[31] However, over the past twenty years, there has been an increasing reliance on surveillance, or closely monitoring offenders in order to catch them when they fail to meet all required conditions. Rhine, in describing this change in supervision style, suggests that it brings about a new paradigm in the supervision of offenders in the community:

> Despite their importance to public safety, the past 20 years have witnessed a marked devaluation of traditional probation and parole supervision. Acknowledging this trend, many administrators in the field have adopted a set of practices and a discourse that represent a discernible shift toward risk management and surveillance. This shift in the mission and conduct of supervision reflects a new narrative, the plausibility of which has yet to be established.[32]

The transition from casework to the surveillance style of supervision could be less of a philosophical than a pragmatic change, as caseload sizes have been increasing, and with less time to provide individual attention to probationers, officers must resort to surveillance tactics. As an example, caseloads in California over the last few decades of the twentieth century increased dramatically; in the early 1990s they reached 500 per officer, and "some 60 percent of Los Angeles probationers were tracked solely by computer and had no face-to-face contact with a probation officer."[33]

Perhaps the most promising reform of probation has been a concept called "broken windows" probation. This concept mimics the philosophy of community policing, in that all "broken windows" in a neighborhood are to be promptly repaired, as this small indication of a lack of community concern leads to a larger instability and criminal activity in the community. As such, probation supervision follows the lead of community policing by partnering with citizen groups, churches, and other neighborhood organizations to take joint responsibility for supervising offenders. Emphasizing public safety first, "broken windows" probation also allocates resources according to risk and need assessments, locates probation officers in the probationers' neighborhoods, and uses graduated sanctions such as house arrest, electronic monitoring, and mandatory substance abuse treatment.[34]

One important function of community supervision officers is to visit offenders' residences or places of employment. These visits lead to concerns about the safety of officers. Therefore, most agencies allow officers to carry a weapon when doing a home visit, and some require them to go with a partner. While the safety of officers is a serious and real concern, there is also a concern that the arming of officers moves supervision even further away from a casework model to more of a policing or surveillance model.

PROBATION CLASSIFICATION SYSTEMS

One of the important issues in supervising offenders in the community is classifying them in terms of risk to the community and need for treatment programs. Such classification identifies offender risks and provides appropriate supervision, in order to maximize the distribution of resources and focus on public safety. Models of risk assessment were first developed for probation in the mid-1970s and quickly gained support. In 1976, the U.S. Comptroller General tested the predictive power of community risk-prediction models and concluded that "probation prediction models could improve probation systems operations by allocating resources to

Officers going into the field to conduct home visits usually are armed, wear a protective vest, and carry other equipment similar to a police officer.
Photo by Richard P. Seiter.

offenders who most need help . . . Model sources appeared to be useful in determining supervision levels and more successfully selected probationers for early release."[35] A National Institute of Corrections report titled *Directions for Community Corrections in the 1990s* noted, "In general, one effective way to increase decision reliability is to make visible the criteria for decisions. For that reason, we advocate the use of statistically based devises to classify offenders according to relative risk."[36]

Community classification systems score offenders based on their offense background and personal characteristics. Figures 4.1 and 4.2 illustrate the current Missouri model used to determine levels of community supervision. Probation and parole officers initially complete the Client Analysis Scale-Risk for the offender (Figure 4.1). Each case is scored on the number of prior convictions, employment status, age, present offense, and whether the present offense is a felony. The scores are combined to determine the permanent risk score, which is used to determine the classification of risk and the supervision level.

The highest risk level, *intensive supervision*, applies to offenders posing a significant risk of committing a new offense. They are assigned to smaller caseloads, must report at least once per week to the supervising officer, and are visited two to three times per month at home or at work. Most probationers are placed on *regular supervision*, with larger caseloads and fewer reporting requirements. For offenders who pose little risk to the community, *minimum supervision*, with caseloads as high as three-hundred offenders, may be satisfactory. These offenders often have

Community classification systems

risk assessments that predict the chance of new crimes being committed; they are used to determine the level of supervision an offender will receive in the community

MISSOURI CLIENT ANALYSIS SCALE-RISK, FOR USE WITH PROBATIONERS AND PAROLEES

FIGURE 4.1

STATE OF MISSOURI
DEPARTMENT OF CORRECTIONS
CLIENT ANALYSIS SCALE-RISK

OFFICER CODE

NAME	NUMBER	DATE

PRIOR CONVICTIONS (ADULT-FELONY, MISDEMEANOR, CRIMINAL ORDINANCE INCLUDING SIS)

☐ 1   ☐ 2   ☐ 3

NONE   1 OR 2 PRIORS   3 OR MORE

EMPLOYMENT/VOCATION

☐ 0   ☐ 1   ☐ 2

FULL TIME WORK   PART TIME WORK   UNEMPLOYED

AGE (AT ASSIGNMENT)

☐ 0   ☐ 1   ☐ 2

30 YEARS OR OVER   22 TO 29 YEARS   21 YEARS OR YOUNGER

PRESENT OFFENSE (CHARGE FOR WHICH CONVICTED) (ROBBERY, BURGLARY, STEALING, FORGERY, SEXUAL ASSAULT AS PER RSMo 589.015)

☐ 0   ☐ 1

NO   YES

PRESENT OFFENSE A FELONY (OFFICIAL CHARGE)

☐ 0   ☐ 1

NO   YES

RISK SCORE

Source: Missouri Department of Corrections, 1991.

STATE OF MISSOURI
DEPARTMENT OF CORRECTIONS
BOARD OF PROBATION AND PAROLE
MONTHLY SUPERVISION REPORT

OFFICE USE ONLY
☐ INITIAL SCALE
☐ ENTER

OFFICER NAME AND NUMBER

SUPERVISION NUMBER

NAME

PHONE NUMBER

ADDRESS   (CITY)   (STATE)   (ZIP CODE)

WITH WHOM DO YOU LIVE? (NAME AND RELATIONSHIP)

YOUR SOCIAL SECURITY NUMBER

NAME OF PRESENT EMPLOYER, ADDRESS, CITY, ZIP CODE

EMPLOYER'S PHONE NUMBER

NAME OF SUPERVISOR   IS EMPLOYER AWARE OF PROBATION/PAROLE?
☐ YES   ☐ NO

TOTAL INCOME FOR PAST 30 DAYS

MODEL   YEAR   MAKE

DO YOU OWN A VEHICLE?   ☐ YES   ☐ NO

DESCRIPTION/COLOR

LICENSE NUMBER

HAVE YOU BEEN ARRESTED DURING PAST 30 DAYS?   ☐ YES   ☐ NO   IF YES, DATE OF ARREST _____

ARRESTING DEPARTMENT   CHARGE

SIGNATURE   ACCEPTED BY   DATE   TIME   ☐ A.M.
☐ P.M.

DO NOT WRITE BELOW THIS LINE

____ **EMPLOYMENT/EDUCATIONAL VOCATIONAL**
0 - FULL-TIME FOR PAST 3 MONTHS
1 - PART-TIME; SCHOOL; TRAINING; FULL-TIME LESS
    THAN 3 MONTHS; UNEMPLOYMENT COMPENSATION
2 - UNEMPLOYED
   DATE EMPLOYED _____

____ **LEGAL (EXCLUDES PRESENT OFFENSE)**
1 - NO ARRESTS IN THE PAST 3 MONTHS
2 - NO CONVICTIONS, 1 ARREST IN PAST 3 MONTHS
3 - 2 OR MORE ARRESTS, PENDING CHARGE, OR
    CONVICTION IN PAST 3 MONTHS
   DATE OF ARREST/CONVICTION _____

____ **TECHNICAL VIOLATIONS**
1 - NO TECHNICAL VIOLATION REPORT IN PAST 6 MONTHS
2 - TECHNICAL VIOLATION REPORT IN PAST 6 MONTHS
3 - TECHNICAL VIOLATION IN PAST 3 MONTHS OR
    PENDING REVOCATION
   DATE OF LAST TECHNICAL VLTN. RPT. _____
   CONDITIONS CITED _____

____ **SUBSTANCE ABUSE**
1 - NO DRUG USE/ALCOHOL ABUSE WITHIN 6 MONTHS
2 - DRUG USE/ALCOHOL ABUSE IN PAST 4-6 MONTHS
3 - DRUG USE/ALCOHOL ABUSE IN PAST 3 MONTHS
   DATE OF LAST USE/PROBLEM _____

PROBLEM CODES: 1 = NO PROBLEM   2 = IDENTIFIED HISTORY
                 3 = PROBLEM PAST 4–6 MONTHS   4 = PROBLEM PAST 3 MOS

____ **SOCIAL**
0 - NO PROBLEM
1 - PROBLEM NOT REQUIRING INTERVENTION
2 - PROBLEM REQUIRING INTERVENTION
   DATE OF LAST OCCURRENCE _____

SUBSTANCE ABUSE   ____ # UA'S   ____ # POSITIVE
____ ALCOHOL
____ MARIJ/HASHISH   ____ STIM/COCAINE   ____ INHALENTS/SOLVENTS
____ OPIATES   ____ DEPRESSANTS   ____ HALLUCINOGENS

SOCIAL
____ MENTAL PROBLEMS   ____ FINANCIAL   ____ PHYSICAL
____ FAMILY PROBLEMS   ____ ASSAULT/AGGRESSIVE ____ REPORTING

RISK SCORE _____   NEED SCORE _____

ISP/EMP/RF SCREEN FOR PLACEMENT IF RISK
IS 10 OR NEED IS 11 OR MORE

SCORE OVER-RIDES (If scored minimum; check only most serious one)

LEVEL OF SUPERVISION

SPECIAL CONDITIONS
_____ SEXUAL OFFENDER   _____ FINANCIAL   _____ COMMUNITY SERVICE

MONTHLY ACTIVITIES
_____
_____
_____
_____

MO 931-3698 (2-96)

Source: Board of Probation and Parole, Missouri Department of Corrections, 1991.

contact with their probation officer only every few months, and are basically themselves responsible for following the conditions of their supervision. Some jurisdictions also have *administrative supervision,* under which offenders have no contact with a parole or probation officer. However, they still must meet their conditions and commit no further crimes, or their original parole or probation will be revoked. Administrative supervision is used only after low-risk offenders demonstrate a good adjustment to supervision.

After the initial classification of risk, each offender is scored on the Monthly Supervision Report (Figure 4.2) to review the status of the supervision and determine the need for changes.

In Missouri, offenders with a risk score of 10 or more and a need score of 11 or more are automatically assigned to participate in intensive supervision or another special-supervision caseload. If the review indicates that considerable supervision time has passed without a violation, a lower level of supervision will likely be assigned. Classification processes are extremely valuable to match resources to offenders' risk and needs, and help officers make decisions regarding supervision level, revocation, or successful termination of supervision.

Intermediate Sanctions

DEFINING INTERMEDIATE SANCTIONS

Intermediate sanctions are midrange dispositions that fall between probation and imprisonment. Until the past few decades in many American jurisdictions, judges imposing sentences for any but the most trivial of crimes had to choose between what seemed to be "doing something" (imprisonment) and "doing nothing" (probation). However, the problems of prison and jail crowding forced policymakers to develop punishments that fall between these two sanctions. Intermediate sanctions are commonly referred to as *midlevel punishments* and are designed to fill the gap that is widely perceived to exist between probation and prison.

Several factors have been cited in support of intermediate sanctions:

1. Unhappiness with regular probation supervision
2. An increase in the number in prisons and prison overcrowding
3. Tightening of budgets by states and an inability to continue to fund high numbers of offenders sentenced to prison
4. A belief that intermediate sanctions are more effective in providing effective rehabilitative programs
5. A realization that solid ties in the community are critical to the success of offenders, and the knowledge that keeping offenders in the community helps them maintain these ties
6. Proportionality of sentencing, in that with a continuum of sanctions, the sentence can be crafted to better fit the crime and offender

Intermediate sanctions include economic sanctions, community service, intensive supervised probation, house arrest, community residential centers, split sentences, shock incarceration (boot camps), and shock probation. Electronic monitoring often accompanies some of these midrange punishments.

TYPES OF INTERMEDIATE SANCTIONS

Economic Sanctions

Economic sanctions use money as the means of carrying out criminal sanctions, such as fines, restitution, or forfeiture of assets. In most cases, economic sanctions

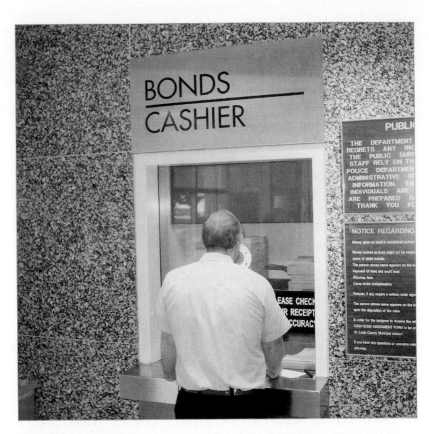

Fines are a common condition of probation and are paid through the court cashier.
Photo by Richard P. Seiter.

are attached as a condition of probation; however, for minor offenses they may stand alone as punishments for crimes. When people think of economic sanctions, they usually consider small fines for minor offenses. However, fines and forfeiture of assets can be of very large amounts. For instance, during the 1980s, junk bond king Michael Milken defrauded investors of what was estimated to be hundreds of millions of dollars. As a result, in addition to a short prison term, Milken was fined $600 million, although it was believed to be far less than he made from his illegal trading.

Fines are a requirement that offenders pay some dollar amount to the court as punishment for committing the offense. Fines can be a set amount for each type of crime or can be more creative, and reflect the individual situation of each offense and offender. Courts usually consider both the seriousness of the offense and the economic gain by the offender to determine the amount of a fine. For instance, fines may be appropriate for white-collar offenders, who have a minimal risk of future criminality and perhaps no need for any rehabilitative programs; the sanction focuses on pure punishment, deterrence, and opportunity to repay the victims or society for the wrong done by the offense.

While fines are usually paid to the court, a second type of economic sanction is **offender restitution**, which requires offenders to repay society for the harm created by the offense. Restitution can take several forms. One type of offender restitution is **victim compensation**, in which offenders repay their victims directly for their losses and harm caused by the offense. As noted in the discussion of presentence investigations, federal and many state courts allow victims to submit victimization statements to detail the amount of loss they incurred from

---

Fines

money that offenders must pay to the court as punishment for committing the offense

Offender restitution

a requirement that offenders repay society for the harm created by the offense

Victim compensation

a form of restitution in which offenders repay their victims directly for their losses and harm caused by the offense the crime. Sentencing judges take this into account when sentencing offenders, and often use the submitted amount for assigning a level of victim compensation. Offenders can also pay restitution through *community service.* Community service can include cleaning up trash in a public area or counseling teenagers about the negative results of drug use. Community service is included here as an economic sanction, as it is often used when offenders do not have funds from which to pay a fine or make restitution. It is then referred to as a "fine on their time," so that indigent offenders do not have to serve prison or jail time merely because they lack the fiscal ability to pay a fine. Offenders may also be required to pay for their **cost of supervision**, by paying to the court the costs affiliated with their supervision such as drug testing, counseling, or electronic monitoring, reducing the cost to the taxpayers.

Another extremely effective economic sanction is **asset forfeiture**, the authorized seizure by the government of money, negotiable instruments, securities, or other things of value that were obtained through illegal activities. Created over the past thirty years, asset forfeiture enables courts to punish offenders by taking away assets they accumulated as a result of their criminal activity, ensuring that "crime doesn't pay." Asset forfeiture was first authorized in the RICO (Racketeer Influenced and Corrupt Organization) statute, a part of the federal Organized Crime Control Act of 1970. RICO statutes were created to aid law enforcement in investigating and prosecuting organized crime figures, making it unlawful for anyone involved in a pattern of racketeering to derive any income or proceeds from that activity and allowing the government to seize anything of value that can be shown to have been acquired through the racketeering activity.

Asset forfeiture is also regularly used in the prosecution and punishment of drug offenders. When the federal government expanded its powers and more aggressively targeted the arrest and prosecution of drug offenders during the 1980s, asset forfeiture became a valuable strategy. As property assets are seized, they are auctioned off and the proceeds are divided among the federal and local law enforcement agencies that participated in the criminal investigation. Local law enforcement agencies use these funds to enhance their own capabilities to target drug crimes, leading to more arrests and prosecution.

Intensive Supervised Probation

When regular probation supervision is not considered satisfactory monitoring of offenders who either are high risk or have high treatment needs, yet still do not require incarceration, intensive supervised probation is a viable alternative. **Intensive supervised probation (ISP)** was initiated in Georgia in 1974 to increase the amount of supervision provided to selected felony probationers. ISP programs are now actively used in every state, and more than 50,000 probationers were on intensive caseloads on January 1, 2001.[37] The intent of ISP is to identify offenders who need supervision greater than that available through regular probation, yet are not such a risk to the community that they should be in prison.

Offenders placed in an ISP program are supervised by probation officers who have smaller caseloads (an average of twenty-eight per officer in 2000),[38] and provide more frequent contacts through a combination of office reporting by offenders and home and work visits by the officer. The intensity of supervision allows for enhancing the goal of incapacitation, since the additional contacts reduce the opportunity for slipping into criminal behavior. As well, ISP is more of a punishment and deterrence as the number of contacts required disrupts the daily lives of offenders. Equally, it can enhance rehabilitation, as officers with smaller caseloads can provide counseling or follow up on treatment plans for the offenders they supervise.

Cost of supervision
costs, associated with their supervision in the community, that offenders must pay for, such as drug testing or electronic monitoring

Asset forfeiture
the authorized seizure by the government of money, negotiable instruments, securities, or other things of value that were obtained through illegal activities

Intensive supervised probation (ISP)
supervision of community offenders with higher-than-average risk, through smaller caseloads and very close monitoring of activities

In a review of the effectiveness of intensive supervision for both probationers and parolees, the findings were mixed in terms of the positive results from ISP programs. In a review of fourteen counties in nine states, Petersilia and Turner found that judges placed high-risk probationers in the programs rather than diverting offenders from prison. The ISP participants were watched more closely (having more contacts with their supervising officers), and while this did not result in more arrests, there were significantly more technical violations (70 percent for the ISP group and 40 percent for regular probationers), which resulted in 27 percent of the ISP participants being returned to prison or jail compared to only 19 percent of regular probationers at the end of one year.[39] However, if the ISP supervision combined drug treatment, community service, and employment programs with surveillance, recidivism rates were 10 to 20 percent lower than those who did not participate in such activities. Another analysis of 175 evaluations of ISP programs also found that combining surveillance with treatment resulted in reduced recidivism.[40]

House Arrest

An even greater level of supervision, even while sanctioned offenders remain in the community, results from house arrest, sometimes referred to as community control. With **house arrest**, offenders are allowed to avoid a prison sentence, yet must be detained or incapacitated in their own homes, while they may remain employed, earn an income, support their families, and pay for their own upkeep and usually the cost of supervision for their house arrest. Offenders under house arrest live at home, and must be at home except for times they are to be at work or participating in other activities previously approved by their probation officer. House arrest has the potential benefits of being economical, imposing severe restrictions on the offender's freedom and opportunity to commit crimes, and allowing for participation in community-based treatment programs.

Although not always necessary, house arrest is commonly used in conjunction with **electronic monitoring**, or the use of technology to monitor an offender's location. Electronic monitoring requires offenders to wear a tamperproof bracelet around their ankle. The bracelet acts as a receiver for a radio wave sent off by a transmitter that is placed in the offender's home. There are two types of systems, active and passive, both of which are monitored from a central location. With active systems, the central location maintains a computerized schedule of when offenders should be in their homes, and automatically "alarms" or sends a notice when the signal is not communicated between the transmitter and receiver during those times. This indicates to the monitor or probation officer that the offender has violated the conditions of his or her house arrest, and someone will be dispatched to check on or arrest the offender. The passive system requires random telephone calls during times the offender should be in the home. When a monitoring telephone call is received, offenders have a certain amount of time to place the receiver against the transmitter, proving that they are in the home as required.

Electronic monitoring is not a criminal sanction; it is a method of supervision. The use of electronic monitoring has increased greatly throughout the United States; the first systems were activated in 1986, more than 40,000 units were in use by 1992, and their use continued to grow throughout the 1990s.[41] The use of electronic monitoring is also believed to be cost-effective, particularly as many states require offenders using the monitors to pay for the cost of supervision. However, on January 1, 2001, less than 1 percent of probationers were reported to be under electronic monitoring, at an average cost per day of $10.32 for 2000.[42]

Generally, house arrest using electronic monitoring is considered effective. Evaluations of programs in Illinois[43] and in several other states[44] indicated good re-

House arrest

a form of supervision in which offenders live at home and must be at home except when they are to be at work or participating in other activities approved by their probation officer

Electronic monitoring

the use of technology to monitor an offender's location

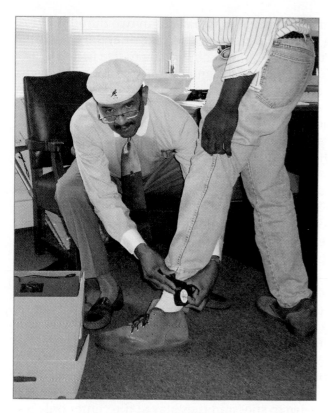

Electronic monitoring involves placing a bracelet around an offender's ankle. The bracelet acts as a receiver and notifies surveillance officers if the offender is not at home at designated times.
Photo by Richard P. Seiter.

sults, and a 1989 survey on telemonitoring of offenders noted, "There were no significant differences in successful terminations among probationers, offenders on parole, or those in community corrections. All had successful terminations rates ranging between 74 and 86 percent."[45]

Community Residential Centers

Community residential centers (CRCs) have been commonly known as halfway houses, which began as programs to help ex-inmates make the transition between prison and the community. Today, CRCs play a much broader role than simply helping in the postprison transition. As an intermediate sanction, CRCs provide a combination of supervision, structure, accountability, and programming to aid in the community supervision of probationers who require more than standard probation in response to their risk of reoffending and program needs. Governor du Pont of Delaware identified the role of CRCs as an adjunct to traditional community supervision, while providing an increase in supervision leading to enhanced public safety in the management of offenders.[46] CRCs are less expensive than the operation of a prison. Camp and Camp report that the average cost per inmate per day in a state or federal prison in 2000 was $61.04;[47] the average cost for 2000 for a halfway house operated by the department of corrections was $46.20 per day, and for contracted halfway houses the cost was $48.60.[48] In most halfway houses or CRCs, residents must pay a portion of the cost of their stay through wages they earn while in the community.

Community residential centers (CRCs)

houses in which offenders live in the community that provide supervision, room and board, and some treatment as an alternative to prison

The use of CRCs as an intermediate sanction can occur in two different ways. First, at the time of sentencing, judges can determine that offenders need the services of a residential center, and can require probationers to live in a CRC as a condition of their probation. However, CRC placement more commonly occurs later in the period of probation supervision, after probationers are failing under their current supervision requirement. Probation officers may determine that offenders have violated minor conditions of supervision and require more structure and accountability, or need a place to live or additional program assistance. The officer then recommends that the court add a CRC requirement as a condition of probation.

CRCs are usually an old boarding house, a YMCA, or some other large residential structure in an urban area. They range in size from thirty to two hundred residents. Resident rooms often hold two people, although some rooms are large enough to accommodate six or eight residents in a dormitory-style environment. The CRCs operate their own kitchen and provide meals to residents. While CRCs have limited physical security to keep residents from leaving (usually standard residential locks, with cameras throughout the center to assist in supervision), residents are not free to come and go as they please. Residents must stay at the center unless they are approved to go to work or attend an authorized program. If they are complying with center rules, they may receive a weekend pass to visit family or friends.

The stay at CRCs is usually only a few months, and may be as short as thirty days. There are sometimes emergency placements to provide room and board for probationers who do not have a place to stay, and they stay at the center only until they find another place to live. Other probationers may need supervision or programs that require a longer stay, perhaps up to six months. During this time, many CRCs have stages of privileges, and residents earn the opportunity for more time away from the center as they follow rules and appear successful in their adjustment. In general, CRCs are only for temporary placement when either the need arises for housing or the probationer exhibits less than responsible behavior that requires a period of additional supervision.

Halfway houses are usually large, older homes located in an area close to the central city so that public transportation and other services are readily available.
Photo by Richard P. Seiter.

A bedroom of a halfway house is dormitory-style, typically shared by three to six residents.
Photo by Richard P. Seiter.

There is no or very minimal physical security at halfway houses. The security relies on offenders taking responsibility for being at the house when they are required to be, and staff ensuring that they are accounted for when they come and go from the house. The "Your Career in Corrections" box illustrates some of the roles of halfway house staff in this regard.

YOUR CAREER IN CORRECTIONS

HALFWAY HOUSE STAFF

Most students do not think of working in a halfway house or CRC as they begin a career in corrections. However, in 2001, state and federal correctional agencies operated 57 halfway houses, and contracted with another 564. On January 1, 2001, there were 22,832 inmates living in these houses.[49] So there are many job opportunities in these facilities. Historically, since most of the contracted houses were operated by church-affiliated or other not-for-profit agencies, the program mission of helping offenders was the primary emphasis, salaries were quite low, and staff turnover was high. To a great extent, that is still the case. Yet halfway houses have improved their professionalism in the management of these programs, salaries have improved somewhat, and there is less turnover, at least in the higher management of the houses. However, the lack of a career track or promotional opportunities still makes this more likely to be a short-term entry-level job than a career.

Most individuals enter one of two positions when beginning work at a halfway house. The first is a paraprofessional position often called *desk monitor*. Desk monitors control access into and out of the facility. Most houses have a nonsecure control point at the front door, and residents must sign a logbook when they go in or out. The monitor ensures that they do this, and controls residents to be sure they are in the house when required. In many ways, it is equivalent to the role of a correctional officer in a prison. If someone leaves when not permitted or fails to return when required,

(continued)

desk monitors notify management and the police and probation or parole officers are likely to be called. When not watching the desk, monitors do room checks to make sure there is no contraband (items not allowed in the possession of residents) or activities such as drinking or drug use. They also search for contraband in rooms or other locations throughout the house. These positions are often paid between $8 and $12 per hour and have limited benefits. However, they are very good part-time positions for students preparing for a corrections career and good entry-level jobs to get experience working in a criminal justice agency and with offenders. This experience is very good preparation for work as a police officer, probation or parole officer, or correctional officer.

The second category of halfway house jobs is professional positions such as counselor, case manager, or substance abuse specialist. Counselors and case managers are assigned a case-load of residents and are responsible for guiding them through their stay by suggesting (or requiring) participation in certain programs, initiating disciplinary action for violation of probation or parole when required, and overseeing the collection of fines or costs for staying at the house. A college degree in criminal justice, social work, psychology, or one of the other social sciences is usually required. These jobs are very interesting and very challenging. These staff must be directive with residents and hold them accountable for following the rules. They must be knowledgeable of programs and job-finding resources to assist residents. And they must deal with the difficult situation of offenders being restricted in their activities and movements, yet in a nonsecure facility in which they go into the community on almost a daily basis.

The overall organization of a halfway house for approximately seventy-five residents would include a director, an assistant director, two to three professional staff, and ten to fifteen desk monitors. Therefore, there is limited opportunity for advancement, and most staff who want a career in corrections must go to another agency for a promotion. Yet students are encouraged to consider these jobs to get experience and help them decide what type of future jobs they would like. Halfway house staff interact with several categories of criminal justice and social service professionals, and get the opportunity to see what they do and network to develop contacts that can help them in future job-finding efforts. While the pay is low and career opportunities limited, the work is challenging and provides a great training opportunity.

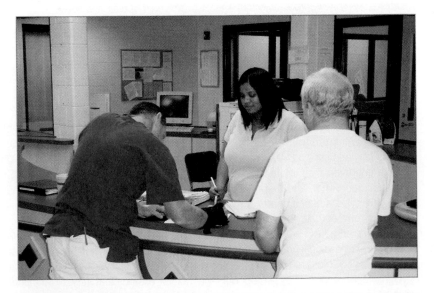

The main security of a halfway house is the role of desk monitor, in which staff check residents in and out of the house.
Photo by Richard P. Seiter.

Split Sentences

Split sentences are a combination of a short jail sentence and then return to the community on probation. The jail sentence can be anywhere from 30 to 180 days. The purpose of a split sentence is to provide a clear combination of punishment and rehabilitation for offenders who have not committed crimes serious enough to require a sentence of imprisonment. However, when offenders' behavior is seen as particularly irresponsible, judges may use a short jail term to get their attention and expose them to the uncomfortable environment of jail to encourage a change of attitude. The jail sentence is simply to add punishment to a sentence of standard probation, and once completed, the offender returns to the community under probation supervision—hence the term *split sentence,* as the sentence is divided between a term in jail and a period of probation.

The jail part of a split sentence is sometimes served on weekends. This lessens the negative impact of serving time in jail, and offenders are able to keep their jobs and maintain ties to family. They must check into the jail on Friday evenings and are released Sunday nights until the total number of days of their sentence has been met. Split sentences have become more common over the past twenty years, as the "tough on crime" mentality has emphasized punishment as well as rehabilitation for even minor offenders. The Bureau of Justice Statistics reports that percentages for felony convictions by type of sentence in 1998 included 44 percent prison, 32 percent probation, and 24 percent of a combination of local jail and probation.[50] A split sentence was the most frequently imposed sentence for felony offenders in California in 2001.[51]

Split sentence

a combination of a short jail sentence and then return to the community on probation

Shock Incarceration

An interesting correctional sanction that has developed since the mid-1980s is **shock incarceration** or **boot camp**. The first boot camps were initiated in Georgia in 1983 and Oklahoma in 1984. Quickly gaining in popularity, boot camps were implemented in many other states over the next ten years. This development is interesting in regard to the accomplishment of correctional goals, as boot camps were created with the purpose of holding offenders accountable for their crimes, with a harsh punishment and deterrent effect. Correctional boot camps are operated similar to a military boot camp; offenders are required to have short hair, shine their shoes, wear uniforms, do extensive physical exercise, and perform hard physical labor. At times, these activities are complemented with education or drug programming, but the major components of boot camps remain military regimentation, discipline, exercise, and hard work. Boot camps appeal to both liberals and conservatives, as they focus on being tough on crime and tough on the offender, but are also a community alternative to traditional imprisonment. If offenders complete boot camp, they receive a shorter sentence than if they had received a traditional prison sentence.

Boot camps are usually reserved for young, first-time prisoners who are deemed likely to benefit from structure and discipline while gaining self-control with the rigorous daily routine. Evaluations in some states have indicated that offenders who complete boot camp programs leave with more positive attitudes.[52] However, boot camps have been criticized as expensive and less than effective. Boot camps are more expensive to operate than probation and many prisons because they require a high staff to inmate ratio, and they are especially expensive compared to minimum-security prisons, where most of the boot camp offenders would otherwise be incarcerated. In fact, daily per-inmate costs for operating boot camps in thirty-one states and the federal system in 2000 were $61.45, even higher than the average cost for all prisons during 2000 of $61.04.[53]

Shock incarceration/ boot camp

alternatives to traditional incarceration that are operated similar to a military boot camp; offenders are required to have short hair, shine their shoes, wear uniforms, do extensive physical exercise, and perform hard physical labor; at times, these are complemented with education or drug programming, but the major components of boot camps are military regimentation, discipline, exercise, and hard work

Graduation from the boot camp illustrates the regimentation and discipline gained by participants over their stay.
Courtesy of the Georgia Department of Correction.

Several recent findings have been very critical of the impact of boot camps on reducing recidivism.[54] A review by the U.S. General Accounting Office (GAO) reported that boot camps only marginally reduce recidivism, and the differences between boot camp and non–boot camp offenders diminish over time.[55] While the GAO study found an improvement in attitudes, it determined the impact on recidivism to be "at best negligible."[56] As a result of the negative findings, several states are questioning their efficacy and reconsidering the concept, and New Hampshire, Connecticut, and Arizona have all closed their boot camp operations.

Shock Probation

Shock probation

a short period of imprisonment to "shock" the offender, with a return to the community within a few weeks to continue supervision on probation

A final intermediate sanction is **shock probation**, a short period of imprisonment to "shock" the offender, with a return to the community within a few weeks to continue supervision on probation. The concept originated in Ohio, as 1965 legislation authorized the sentencing judge to reconsider a sentence of imprisonment within 90 to 130 days after incarceration of the offender. If the offender meets the criteria (a nonviolent offense with no prior offense history), and the judge believes that the punitive and deterrent value of the sentence has already been met, the sentence can be modified and the offender released to regular probation. Shock probation is based on a specific deterrence model, with a belief that the shock of the sentence and admission to prison shows offenders the punishment they will receive if they continue to commit crimes. The theory is that as a result of placement in prison for a short period of time, offenders granted shock probation will be deterred from commission of further crimes.

In an evaluation of the effectiveness of shock probation, this theory proved to be true, as Vito concluded:

1. The shock experience should not be limited to first-time offenders; eligibility should properly include those with prior records, as deemed eligible by the judge.
2. The length of incarceration necessary to secure the deterrent effect could be much shorter, probably thirty days or less.

3. Reincarceration rates have never exceeded 26 percent and, in Ohio, have been as low as 10 percent. The level of these rates clearly indicates that the program has potential for reintegration.

4. Shock probation has considerable potential to reduce institutional overcrowding characteristics of contemporary corrections.[57]

Shock probation is generally believed to be a low-cost and effective intermediate sanction for less serious felons, and many states have implemented shock probation as a part of their sentencing structure.

THE EFFECTIVENESS OF INTERMEDIATE SANCTIONS

The use of intermediate sanctions has increased significantly over the past two decades. However, there are still a fairly limited number of research studies from which to evaluate the effectiveness of these programs against their desired outcomes. The following list suggest some reasons for the limited number of studies of effectiveness and the lack of use of these evaluations for correctional policymaking:

1. Political, ethical, and programmatic reasons may not permit random assignment of clients to either the treatment or control group.
2. Treatment or program effects "bleed over" to the control group, or the intended treatment is inappropriately or unevenly applied.
3. It is rare to have only one treatment in operation at a time, thus contaminating the impact of the measure of outcome.
4. Varying measures of success and failure make it difficult to generalize across studies and program results.[58]

In the preceding descriptions of the intermediate sanctions, some outcome studies were identified, with mixed conclusions as to their overall effectivenss. To fully evaluate their success, intermediate sanctions should be analyzed against their desired goals. Examples of such analyses follow.

Goal 1: Intermediate sanctions should be used to divert offenders from prison. Most experts would agree that one of the goals of intermediate sanctions is to manage more offenders in the community who would (without intermediate sanctions) have to be sentenced to prison. However, it is generally concluded that intermediate sanctions are not always used with high-risk probationers, and therefore add to the supervision of probationers who would not have been sent to prison even if the intermediate sanction did not exist. This phenomenon is called **net widening**, the overlapping of criminal sanctions and added supervision for community-placed offenders, rather than diversion of offenders from prison.

Goal 2: Intermediate sanctions should reduce the cost of corrections. Common sense would seem to indicate that it would be less expensive to maintain offenders in the community rather than sentence them to prison. However, most offenders who are assigned to intermediate sanctions would, if sentenced to prison, be assigned to minimum-security prisons and sentenced to short terms of confinement. If offenders are maintained in the community and net widening occurs, the overall cost of supervision could end up being more than if they are sent to a minimum-security prison. For instance, placement in a boot camp or community residential center costs more per day than placement in a minimum-security prison.

Goal 3: Intermediate sanctions should reduce the level of recidivism for offenders. The studies noted earlier provide mixed indications of the effectiveness of intermediate sanctions in reducing recidivism. However, the most consistent conclusion is

Net widening
the overlapping of criminal sanctions and added supervision for community-placed offenders, rather than diversion of offenders from prison

that recidivism is not significantly impacted by mere community surveillance unless it is combined with participation in treatment programs. Petersilia, in reviewing studies of intermediate sanctions concluded, "The empirical evidence regarding intermediate sanctions is decisive: without a rehabilitation component, reductions in recidivism are elusive."[59] When these two components are combined in a quality fashion, intermediate sanctions have proven effective in reducing recidivism.

It is not easy to implement intermediate sanctions in a cost-effective manner. The "An Insider's Experience" box illustrates this difficulty.

AN INSIDER'S EXPERIENCE: Implementing Intermediate Sanctions

When I was director of the Ohio department of corrections, we were given the authority to spend approximately $15 million to build community-based facilities, and additional funds to encourage counties to implement community sanctions that would divert offenders from prison and keep them in their local county. We would fund some construction and pay some of the operational fees as an incentive for the counties to supervise felons in their community rather than sending them to prison and making the state cover the cost of their incarceration. It was a reasonable plan, and one that should work for all parties.

The department had a bureau that was responsible for approving plans for these community programs. After they worked with the counties to come up with an acceptable plan, it came to me for final approval and to authorize funding. The bureau staff brought me the first two at one time. I was surprised and disappointed that they really did not seem to be diverting offenders from prison, but just added supervision to those already in the community. For instance, one county wanted to add electronic monitoring for their highest-risk group of probationers, and the other wanted to build a community correctional institution to place youthful offenders for a short period of time before they were placed on probation. These pro-

grams were definitely what would be termed "net widening." I was angry with myself for not being more involved in the early stages, and angry with the bureau staff that seemed to allow plans to move forward that really did not divert offenders from prison. The staff told me that these were the programs the county judges wanted, and they were not eager to take risks and keep felons in the community rather than sending them to prison. While I hated to not approve these plans "at the eleventh hour," I felt I could not in good faith approve them and spend taxpayer money that did not meet the intent of the legislation.

I did disapprove the plans, and meekly told the judges I was sorry, but the intent was to divert offenders from prison, and I did not see that their proposal did that. In the end, we compromised on a few operational issues, so that these programs met some of the needs for diversion and still provided the judges with the additional sanctions that they wanted. But from then on, we included a requirement that the plan had to show how many offenders the community corrections program would divert from prison and how it would do so. And we funded almost a dozen more, that fully met the design to divert offenders. It was a good lesson in how difficult it is to get local officials to take the risk and keep offenders in the community, even when someone else is paying for it.

Chapter Review

SUMMARY

This chapter has described the first set of sentencing sanctions in the correctional process: probation and intermediate sanctions. The least intrusive and least intensive sentencing option is probation. Probation has the advantages of maintaining offenders in the community so that family and employment ties are maintained, of being less costly than imprisonment, and of focusing on offender rehabilitation to a greater extent than does imprisonment. For many minor offenders who have a low risk of reoffending and little or no history of violence, probation is a viable sanction.

For offenders who have a greater risk of reoffending or treatment needs that cannot be met through regular probation, intermediate sanctions can provide additional supervision and program opportunities. When they are used for offenders who (without their availability) would be sent to prison, intermediate sanctions have all the benefits of probation and are generally less expensive than imprisonment. Intermediate sanctions add proportionality to the sentencing process, in that

they provide a wide range of alternative supervision and treatment options and can be more appropriately matched to the crime committed and to the offenders' risks and needs. Research has also determined that if surveillance is combined with treatment, intermediate sanctions can effectively reduce recidivism.

Probation and intermediate sanctions represent community-based alternatives to institutional-based sentences. The next chapter continues the discussion of modern correctional operations by moving further into the continuum of correctional sanctions and describing the theories and operational approaches of U.S. prisons. We will then complete our overview of correctional operations by describing the postprison programs of supervision and reentry to the community. At the end of Part 2 of this textbook, students will have a thorough understanding of the major correctional components used today, and we can move into a more detailed examination of correctional perspectives, issues, and challenges.

REVIEW QUESTIONS

1. Approximately how many people were on probation in the United States in 2001?

2. What are the primary emphases of probation supervision?

3. Differentiate between the casework and surveillance styles of probation supervision.

4. Differentiate between standard and special conditions of probation.

5. What are the two types of probation violations?

6. What were the important findings in the *Gagnon v. Scarpelli* decision regarding revocation of probation?

7. Describe the philosophy of the "broken windows" approach to the operation of probation.

8. How do community classification systems work, and what is their impact on probation supervision?

9. List the four levels of probation supervision and define each.

10. Differentiate between offender restitution and victim compensation programs.

11. What is asset forfeiture and why can it be called an economic sanction?

12. Describe the results of evaluations regarding intensive supervised probation.

13. How is electronic monitoring used to enforce the requirements of house arrest?

14. Differentiate passive and active electronic monitoring systems.

15. What are the two ways that community residential centers are used as intermediate sanctions?

16. Describe the operation of a boot camp.

17. How can "net widening" reduce the effectiveness of an intermediate-sanctions program?

ENDNOTES

1. David Dressler, *Practice of Probation and Parole* (New York: Columbia University Press, 1962).

2. Ibid., p. 18.

3. Joan Petersilia, *Reforming Probation and Parole in the 21st Century* (Lanham, Md.: American Correctional Association, 2002), p. 20.

4. Dressler, op. cit.

5. Bureau of Justice Statistics, *Sourcebook of Criminal Justice Statistics, 2001 Edition* (Washington, D.C.: U.S. Department of Justice, 2003), p. 478.

6. Comptroller General of the United States, *State and County Probation: Systems in Crisis, Report to the Congress of the United States* (Washington, D.C.: U.S. Government Printing Office, 1976.)

7. Bureau of Justice Statistics, "Key Facts at a Glance: Correctional Populations," http://www.ojp.usdoj.gov/bjs/glance/tables/corr2tab.htm (accessed November 8, 2002).

8. Richard P. Seiter and Angela West, "Supervision Styles in Probation and Parole: An Analysis of Activities," *Journal Of Offender Rehabilitation* (forthcoming).

9. Camille Graham Camp and George M. Camp, *The 2001 Corrections Yearbook: Adult Systems* (Middletown, Conn.: Criminal Justice Institute, 2002), p. 241.

10. Ibid., p. 192.

11. Camp and Camp, p. 195.

12. Paula M. Ditton, *Mental Health and Treatment of Inmates and Probationers* (Washington, D.C.: U.S. Department of Justice, Bureau of Justice Statistics, 1999).

13. Ibid., p. 196.

14. *Bearden v. Georgia,* 461 U.S. 660 (1983);

15. *United States v. Birnbaum,* 421 F.2d 993 (1970).

16. *Mempa v. Rhay,* 389 U.S. 128 (1967).

17. *Morrissey v. Brewer,* 408 U.S. 271 (1972).

18. *Gagnon v. Scarpelli,* 411 U.S. 778 (1973).

19. R. I. Cohen, *Probation and Parole Violators in State Prison, 1991* (Washington, D.C.: U.S. Department of Justice, 1995) p. 2.

20. Camp and Camp, p. 59.

21. *Bureau of Justice Statistics National Update* (Washington, D.C.: U.S. Department of Justice, 1994), p. 10.

22. Joan R. Petersilia, Susan Turner, James Kahan, and Joyce Peterson, Executive Summary of *Granting Felons Probation: Public Risks and Alternatives* (Santa Monica, Calif.: RAND, 1985), p. 1.

23. Todd Clear and Anthony Braga, "Community Corrections," in *Crime* edited by James Q. Wilson and John R. Petersilia (San Francisco, Calif.: Institute for Contemporary Studies, 1995), pp. 421–444.

24. Patrick Langan and Mark A. Cunniff, *Recidivism of Felons on Probation, 1986–89* (Washington, D.C.: U.S. Department of Justice, Bureau of Justice Statistics, 1995).

25. Michael Geerken and Hennessey D. Hayes, "Probation and Parole: Public Risk and the Future of Incarceration Alternatives," *Criminology* 31, no. 4 (1993): 549–564.

26. Joan R. Petersilia and Susan Turner, *Prison versus Probation in California: Implications for Crime and Offender Recidivism* (Santa Monica, Calif.: RAND, 1986), pp. 27–33.

27. Camp and Camp, p. 106.

28. Ibid., p. 206.

29. Daniel Glaser, *The Effectiveness of a Prison and Parole System* (New York: Bobbs-Merrill, 1964), p. 423.

30. P. T. Alberty, *A Study of the Relationship between Styles of Supervision and Parole Officer's Violations Rate* (master's thesis, University of Missouri, 1969), 3.

31. David I. Rothman, *Conscience and Convenience: The Asylum and Its Alternatives in Progressive America* (Boston: Little, Brown, 1980).

32. Edward E. Rhine, "Probation and Parole Supervision: In Need of a New Narrative," *Corrections Management Quarterly* 1, no. 2 (1999): 72.

33. Dan Richard Beto, Ronald P. Corbett, Jr., and John J. DiIulio, Jr., "Getting Serious about Probation and the Crime Problem," *Corrections Management Quarterly* 4, no. 2 (2000): 3.

34. Reinventing Probation Council, " 'Broken Windows' Probation: The Next Step in Fighting Crime," *Civil Report* 7 (1999): 2.

35. General Accounting Office, *State and County Probation Systems in Crisis* (Washington, D.C.: U.S. Government Printing Office, 1976), p. 53.

36. Vincent O'Leary and Todd R. Clear, *Directions for Community Corrections in the 1990s* (Washington, D.C.: U.S. Department of Justice, June 1984), p. 11.

37. Camp and Camp, p. 190.

38. Ibid., p. 195.

39. Joan Petersilia and Susan Turner, "Intensive Probation and Parole," in *Crime and Justice: An Annual Review of Research*, edited by Michael Tonry (Chicago: University of Chicago Press, 1993).

40. Paul Gendreau and Tracy Little, *A Meta-Analysis of the Effectiveness of Sanctions on Offender Recidivism* (University of New Brunswick, 1993).

41. A good description of the current use of electronic monitoring can be seen in Randy R. Gainey and Brian K. Payne, "Understanding the Experience of House Arrest with Electronic Monitoring: An Analysis of Quantitative and Qualitative Data," *International Journal of Offender Therapy and Comparative Criminology* 44, no. 1 (February 2000): 84–96.

42. Camp and Camp, pp. 192, 207.

43. Michael Brown and Preston Elrod, "Electronic House Arrest: An Examination of Citizen Attitudes," *Crime and Delinquency* 41, no. 3 (1995): 332–346.

44. A. W. Cohn, L. Biondi, L. C. Flaim, M. Paskowski, and S. Cohn, "Evaluating Electronic Monitoring Programs," *Alternatives to Incarceration* 3, no. 1 (January–February 1997): 16–24.

45. Voncile Gowdy, *Intermediate Sanctions* (Washington D.C.: U.S. Department of Justice, 1993), pp. 6–7.

46. P. duPont, *Expanding Sentencing Options: A Governor's Perspective* (Washington, D.C.: U.S. National Institute of Justice, 1985).

47. Camp and Camp, p. 106.

48. Ibid., p. 143.

49. Ibid., pp. 142–143.

50. Matthew R. Durose, David J. Levin, and Patrick A. Langan, *Felony Sentences in State Courts, 1998* (Washington, D.C.: U.S. Department of Justice, 2001).

51. California Department of Justice, *Crime and Delinquency in California, 2001* (Sacramento, Calif.: California Department of Justice, 2001).

52. D. MacKenzie and C. Souryal, "Multisite Evaluation of Shock Incarceration," in *National Institute of Justice: Research Report* (Washington, D.C.: U.S. Department of Justice, 1994).

53. Camp and Camp, pp. 106, 140.

54. For an overview of evaluations of correctional boot camps, see Jeanne B. Stinchcomb, "Recovering from the Shocking Reality of Shock Incarceration— What Correctional Administrators Can Learn from Boot Camp Failures," *Corrections Management Quarterly* 3, no. 4 (1999): 43–52.

55. U.S. General Accounting Office, *Prison Boot Camps: Short-Term Prison Costs Reduced, but Long-Term Impact Uncertain* (Washington, D.C.: U.S. Government Printing Office, 1993).

56. MacKenzie and Souryal, p. 28.

57. Gennaro Vito, "Developments in Shock Probation: A Review of Research Findings and Policy Implications," *Federal Probation* 50, no. 1 (1985): 23–25.

58. Edward J. Latessa and Harry E. Allen, *Corrections in the Community* 2nd Edition (Cincinnati, OH: Anderson, 1999), pp. 403–404.

59. Joan Petersilia, "A Decade of Experimenting with Intermediate Sanctions: What Have We Learned," *Corrections Management Quarterly* 3, no. 4 (1999): 23–24.

Chapter 5

AFTER READING THIS CHAPTER, YOU SHOULD BE ABLE TO:

1. Describe how the role and prevailing philosophies of prison operations have changed significantly over the past century.

2. Explain the mission of a prison.

3. Explain the reasons for the dramatic increase in the number of prisoners since 1980.

4. Discuss how the construction of new prisons paralleled the growth of the inmate population.

5. Explain the changing makeup of the inmate population regarding age, gender, race, and ethnicity.

6. Describe the creation and development of the federal prison system.

7. Compare and contrast the federal and state prison systems.

8. Suggest the reasons for the development of private prisons, and speculate regarding their role in the future.

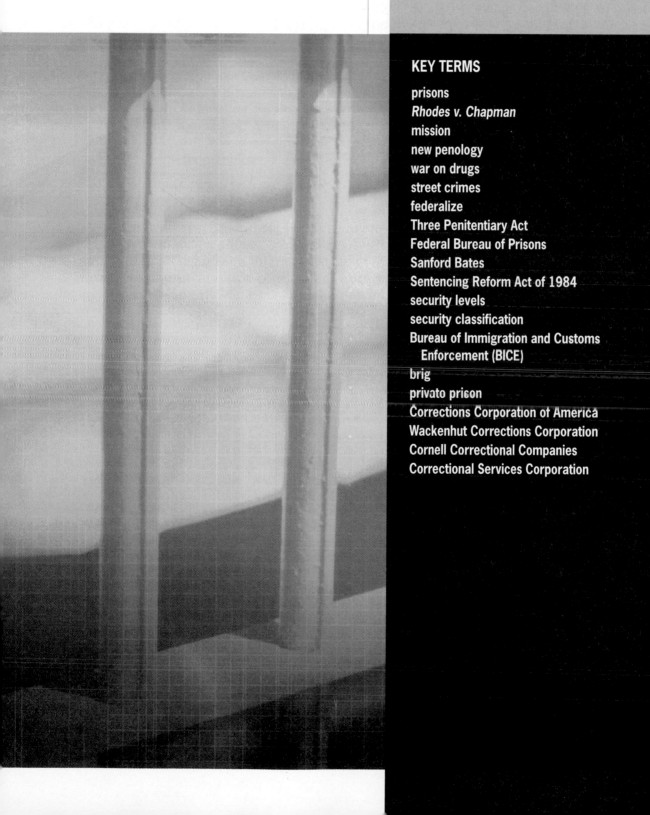

Prison Systems

KEY TERMS

prisons
Rhodes v. Chapman
mission
new penology
war on drugs
street crimes
federalize
Three Penitentiary Act
Federal Bureau of Prisons
Sanford Bates
Sentencing Reform Act of 1984
security levels
security classification
Bureau of Immigration and Customs
   Enforcement (BICE)
brig
private prison
Corrections Corporation of America
Wackenhut Corrections Corporation
Cornell Correctional Companies
Correctional Services Corporation

Introduction

We now turn our study of corrections to **prisons**, institutions designed to house convicted, adult felons serving a sentence of one year or more. Prisons are relatively new phenomena in criminal justice and corrections. As described in Chapter 1, the early sanctions for convicted offenders were primarily corporal and capital punishment, mixed with public humiliation. It was not until the end of the eighteenth century that the Quakers of Pennsylvania decided that a more humane and efficient way to punish and reform criminals was needed, and the penitentiary was first established in Philadelphia.

Over the next two hundred years, prisons have evolved with a variety of theoretical foundations influencing policies and practice. Over the past twenty-five years, a toughening public attitude toward crime and criminals has helped prisons emerge as the sanction believed to most effectively meet the correctional goals of punishment, deterrence, and incapacitation. Unfortunately and inaccurately, the public has come to believe that probation and intermediate sanctions do not successfully meet their concern for public safety, and increasingly, more offenders are sentenced to prisons, many for extremely long periods of time.

This change in philosophy and practice has resulted in an unprecedented level of prison construction, a burgeoning industry of prison operations, and a significant percentage of federal and state budgets going toward construction and operation of prisons. In 1980, almost two hundred years after prisons were first used as a criminal sanction, there were only 316,000 sentenced prisoners under state or federal jurisdiction. In only twenty years, from 1980 to 2000, the number of prisoners increased by almost 500 percent, to more than 1.5 million inmates. This chapter describes recent trends in the makeup of the prison population in the United States, the construction of prisons to keep up with the increase in inmate numbers, the types of prison systems in the United States, and the way in which prisons are organized by security levels to manage the different levels of offender risk.

Current Status of Prisons in the United States

As noted previously, there has been tremendous growth in the role of prisons in the U.S. criminal justice system over the past twenty-five years. As an example of the difference in philosophy regarding the operation of prisons, the 1967 report by the President's Commission on Law Enforcement and Administration of Justice, Corrections Section, recommended the following:

1. Long sentences are self-defeating in regard to rehabilitation.
2. Most offenders do not need to be incarcerated, and could function in the community under supervision.
3. Most inmates derive maximum benefit from their incarceration during the first two years.
4. Community-based corrections are less expensive than and at least as effective as incarceration.
5. Corrections must encompass all aspects of rehabilitative service, including mental health, employment services, education, and social services.
6. Because of their dangerousness, some offenders will require extensive incarceration in secure institutions.
7. Most inmates are not mentally ill but suffer from a variety of educational, medical, maturational, economic, and interpersonal handicaps that are seldom reduced or resolved in prison.
8. Inmates must be given the opportunity and capability to earn a living wage to compensate their victims and support their families.

9. The pay for inmates is too low. The rates of pay should be at least the minimum wage for similar labor.
10. The private sector should be used to provide training and work programs that are realistic to develop employable workers at the end of their sentence.[1]

As is obvious, public opinion and the purpose of prisons in the criminal justice system have changed significantly since this report was written. In 1967, state and federal prisons held less than 300,000 inmates. The medical model, with an emphasis on rehabilitating offenders, was the prevailing philosophy. Shichor noted that rehabilitation was strongly emphasized as the goal of prisons until the 1970s, when this emphasis began to diminish as the United States experienced large increases in crime rates, resulting in rising numbers of prison commitments.[2] Before that time, however, prisons were reserved for the most violent and dangerous offenders, while property offenders were usually granted probation and supervision in the community. As well, prisons held a generally homogeneous groups of offenders, with very similar histories of criminality, sentences, age, and treatment needs.

Today, the role and prevailing philosophies of prison operations have changed significantly. The tough-on-crime mentality of the public and elected officials has forced prisons to become a catchall for all types of offenders, as punishment became favored over rehabilitation.[3] Property offenders are now as likely to be imprisoned as violent offenders. Drug offenders, even those with no prior involvement in crime, often receive mandatory prison sentences of five to ten years. The prison population is much more heterogeneous in terms of prior criminal history, sentence, age, and treatment needs. By the end of 2002, the number of prisoners under the jurisdiction of federal or state adult correctional authorities had risen dramatically to 1,440,655.[4]

THE ROLE AND MISSION OF PRISONS

The primary function of prisons is to hold convicted felons, usually serving a sentence of a year or more, while convicted felons serving shorter sentences usually serve their time in local jails. Inmates consider jail sentences very "hard time,"

Inmates are now very diverse in terms of age, race, gender, and ethnicity.
Courtesy of A. Ramey/PhotoEdit.

since jails do not have the full range of education, vocational training, work, recreational, or other treatment programs that are available in prisons. Therefore, jail inmates spend most of their time just sitting in their cells, watching television, or playing cards with other inmates. Since prisons are designed to hold inmates for longer terms, they need to provide a full range of programs, both for rehabilitative purposes and to keep inmates productively busy.

Many people perceive that prison inmates just sit in cells. This could not be further from the truth. For both management and legal reasons, prison administrators develop activities to keep inmates out of their cells and busy as much of the day as possible. During the "Period of Transition" of prisons described in Chapter 1, prison administrators discovered how difficult it was to operate prisons without the ability to let inmates out of their cells and keep them busy. When Congress passed laws in the 1930s restricting the sale of inmate-made goods on the open market, prisons constructed with large factory operations emphasizing production had to find another way to manage large prison inmate populations (many prisons during that time housed 3,000 to 4,000 inmates). Fearful of violence and tension erupting from the forced idleness, prison administrators tightened security and kept inmates locked in their cells for much of the day. This resulted in even more tension, and after a series of prison riots, officials were forced to find better methods to operate modern prisons.

Prison administrators now understand the problems that can result if inmates are confined to housing units for long periods of time. While not specifically stating that inmates had to be out of cells and involved in work and program activities for any particular number of hours, the federal courts have also encouraged this type of operation through their decisions regarding prison operations. In *Rhodes v. Chapman* (1981), the U.S. Supreme Court decided that overcrowded conditions resulting from two inmates housed in cells designed for one person at the Southern Ohio Correctional Facility (SOCF) was not a violation of the Eighth Amendment right of protection from cruel and unusual punishment.[5] Very important in the decision was the Court's consideration of the "totality of conditions" at SOCF, finding that inmates were out of their cells for much of the day, and no other problems such as poor medical care or food service resulted from the crowded conditions. If prison officials attempted to keep inmates locked in their cells without adequate programs and work activities, the Court would likely reconsider the *Rhodes* decision.

The federal courts have allowed inmates to be locked in cells for all but five hours per week in the case of *Brucino v. Carlson*.[6] However, this case did not involve the operations of a traditional prison. *Brucino* is based on a lockdown of a U.S. penitentiary (USP) in Marion, Illinois, and the elimination of inmate programs outside cells resulting from continued violent acts by inmates that culminated in the murder of two correctional officers in the same day. The Court considered the fact that inmates were placed in USP-Marion because they were unmanageable and had violated rules at other prisons. There was a process for reviewing their assignment to and their removal from USP-Marion. A federal judge, in denying a motion by inmates to stop the lockdown, stated that "the Court is of the firm conviction that this litigation was conceived by a small group of hard-core inmates who are bent on the disruption of the prison system in general and of USP-Marion in particular."[7] However, it is unlikely that the federal courts would accept this type of lockdown for a standard prison not designated for the most violent and dangerous inmates.

Currently, prison officials keep inmates locked in cells (or confined to their housing areas in dormitory-style facilities) for only about eight hours per day, generally from 11:00 P.M. to 7:00 A.M. During the day, inmates work or participate in educational or vocational programs. In the evening (from dinner until lockdown time), inmates participate in recreational activities or other treatment programs

Rhodes v. Chapman
a 1981 U.S. Supreme Court decision that overcrowded conditions resulting in two inmates housed in cells designed for one person was not a violation of the Eighth Amendment right of protection from cruel and unusual punishment

such as substance abuse programs, religious activities, or counseling. The key to a successfully operated prison is to keep inmates productively occupied and under the supervision of staff for the sixteen hours per day that inmates are not confined to their housing units.

A **mission** is a statement of what an organization is to accomplish, or a "statement of its basic purposes, often in terms of broad outcomes that it is committed to achieving or the major function it carries out."[8] In many cases, the mission is the statement of why an agency exists. For most state prison systems, the mission is legislatively created. State legislatures, in creating the agencies that operate prisons, often include the purpose or function of the agency in the authorizing legislation. A common mission statement for a prison is "to supervise criminal offenders during the period of their sentence, protect the public, and offer programs that assist in the rehabilitation of criminals." When a mission statement is not created by the legislative body, agencies regularly generate their own mission statement. The mission statement for the Federal Bureau of Prisons (BOP) appears on its Web site: "It is the mission of the Federal Bureau of Prisons to protect society by confining offenders in the controlled environments of prisons and community-based facilities that are safe, humane, cost-efficient, and appropriately secure, and that provide work and other self-improvement opportunities to assist offenders in becoming law-abiding citizens."[9]

As is clear from both the example of a legislatively created mission and the BOP mission, most prisons have a dual-purpose mission statement. First, prisons are to be safe and secure, protecting inmates and staff from harm while they live and work in the prison environment, and protecting the public from further criminality by not allowing inmates to escape and further prey on society. Second, prisons provide programs that assist in the management of prisons by keeping inmates busy—but, more important, prepare offenders for release and the transition to the community. By concentrating on the rehabilitation of offenders in addition to simple incapacitation, prisons further protect society by improving the chance of inmates' successful return to society and reduction of the long-term likelihood of further criminal activity.

Creating a safe and secure prison environment, and one that encourages inmates to participate in meaningful treatment programs, is a difficult balance. This balancing act usually falls on the shoulders of the warden, who must set the tone and ensure that both security and treatment get the appropriate level of attention. Not many students go through college studying to be a warden. Yet the warden's job is one of the most challenging and interesting in the public management arena. The "Your Career in Corrections" box illustrates some of these challenges.

GROWTH OF THE PRISON POPULATION

Currently, the American public believes that confinement facilities are the most effective sanction to protect the public, punish criminals, and deter them from committing further crimes after release. We continue to increase the number of offenders sentenced to correctional institutions. By the end of 2002, there were 2,166,260 offenders incarcerated in prisons and other detention facilities. Table 5.1 illustrates the makeup of offenders housed in the various types of correctional facilities. Whenever criminal justice policymakers have a concern about the risk of placing offenders in the community, they shift to a policy of increased use of confinement. While this option undoubtedly maximizes community safety, in many cases it does so marginally and comes at a great expense to taxpayers.

It is interesting that from the invention of the prison in 1790 until about 1980 (almost two hundred years), the state and federal prison population rose from zero to only about 300,000. In just over twenty more years, the prison population grew

Mission

a statement of an organization's major function and what it is to accomplish, or its basic purposes, including general outcomes that it is committed to achieving

YOUR CAREER IN CORRECTIONS — WARDENS

The author of this textbook is a career correctional administrator and was warden of two federal prisons. He thoroughly enjoyed these jobs and often described a warden's job as similar to that of a city manager, in that wardens are responsible for many service functions (food service, health care, sanitation and maintenance, policing, construction, human resources, and budget management), as well as the correctional aspects of security, inmate programs, and legal issues.

In 2001, there were almost 1,400 state and federal prisons, each having a warden as the chief executive of the prison. On January 1, 2001, it was reported that a warden's pay ranged from $33,492 to $133,591,[10] with the average approximately $70,000. The average time that wardens had worked for their correctional agency was 15.3 years,[11] indicating that they are experienced when taking a position as warden. In most states, there is no minimum educational level, although most wardens have a college degree. There is also no specific requirement for education or experience, as wardens can begin their correctional careers in almost any discipline, including security, counseling, or any other area of corrections.

College students do not usually plan a career toward the job of warden. In fact, most college students do not plan to go to work in a prison. Many who end up in institutional corrections often plan to be a social worker or counselor, and later find opportunities to work in prisons both exciting and challenging. Warden is a job that takes many years of training and experience. As noted previously, the average correctional job experience for wardens was more than fifteen years. No matter how much education, how much experience in management, or how much willingness to work a person has, nothing is more important to prepare someone to be a warden than working in a prison at a variety of levels. Most decisions that come to a warden's desk are not simple, and there are no easy or obvious solutions. Many have multiple problems and risks, and the difficulty lies in selecting a solution that has the least likelihood of dire consequences. There are always so many varying impacts from what a warden does (if it helps security, it may hurt treatment; if it is something positive for inmates, it may be problematic for staff; if it has great potential for a positive outcome, it may not be affordable within the budget) that each decision must be thoughtfully considered as to how it affects different groups or other prison functions.

Some of these problems are what makes a job as a warden enjoyable for most. Surveys have pointed out that prison wardens have much greater job satisfaction than all but a few other professions. There is never a boring day, and each day brings something different. It takes skills in every different area of management (budget, human resources, security and treatment, and facility maintenance). But most important, being a warden is a very people-oriented job. Wardens get things done by dealing with people—staff and inmates—and must enjoy and be good at getting others to implement and follow what has been decided.

---

by 500 percent, to approximately 1.5 million. In one-tenth the time, the population multiplied five times over. This growth illustrates a remarkable shift in the policies that had previously influenced the use of prisons as a criminal sanction throughout our history. Why the tremendous increase? Several factors have predisposed the increase.

First, since 1980, the public has become more fearful of crime, less tolerant of criminals, and more demanding of tougher sentencing laws. This was understandable during the 1980s, when crime rates (particularly for violent crime) were increasing. According to Gallup polls, in 1989, 84 percent of citizens polled felt there was more crime in the United States that the year before. Since that time, crime rates have been declining, and have gone down in almost every category of felonies every year since 1993. However, more recent Gallup polls still indicate a concern, as 41 percent of citizens polled during 2001 still believed that there was more crime now than the year before.[12] As a result of this belief and the resulting fear of crime, the public demands that criminals be sentenced for longer periods

TABLE 5.1	Number of Offenders Housed in U.S. Correctional Facilities
Federal and state prisons	1,361,258[a]
Territorial prisons	16,206
Local jails	665,475
Bureau of Immigration and Customs Enforcement facilities	8,748[b]
Military facilities	2,377
Jails in Indian country	1,912[c]
Juvenile correctional facilities	110,284[d]

[a]This excludes state and federal prisoners held in local jails.
[b]Formerly the U.S. Immigration and Naturalization Service.
[c]At midyear 2001.
[d]Juvenile total is as of October 2000.
Source: Paige M. Harrison and Allen J. Beck, *Prisoners in 2002* (Washington, D.C.: U.S. Department of Justice, Bureau of Justice Statistics, July 2003), p. 1.

of time, and wants punishment and offender accountability to be the primary focuses of such sentences.

Elected officials have responded and continually lengthened sentences. With every high-visibility, heinous crime, elected officials respond by proposing an increase in criminal sanctions for that crime or type of criminal. As a result, the average length of incarceration has increased significantly since 1990. The average length of stay for inmates released during 1990 was 23.7 months. By 1996, the average time served for inmates released was 30.0 months (an increase of more than 25 percent). Since then, the average time served has leveled off and was 30.6 months for inmates released in 2000.[13]

Unfortunately, elected officials do not have many crime policy alternatives that they believe will have a short-term impact, while demonstrating to voters that they are serious about the crime problem. Therefore, these officials continue to emphasize an increased use of incarceration, rather than alternative sanctions or preventive approaches. Crime has now become a partisan political issue, and both Republicans and Democrats try to show they are tough on crime by using "sound bites" that fit into thirty-second commercials, rather than thoughtfully debating the substance and effectiveness of crime policy alternatives. Tonry, in analyzing reasons for the increase in incarceration rates in the United States, suggests that the partisan political approach to crime policy results in "widespread adoption of broadly defined three-strikes laws, mandatory minimum-sentence laws, sexual psychopath laws, and the federal sentencing guidelines . . . [These laws] are too rigid and often result in unjustly harsh penalties . . ."[14]

Sentencing practices have also changed. During the mid-1900s, all states used indeterminate sentences, and release on parole peaked in 1977, as 72 percent of all prisoners were released on parole.[15] But with the demise of the medical model, the tough-on-crime attitude of the public and elected officials, and the belief that rehabilitation did not work, fifteen states and the federal government moved to the use of determinate sentences, and only 28 percent of offenders were released on parole in 1997.[16] As well, twenty-seven states have adopted truth-in-sentencing (TIS) statutes, requiring inmates to serve 85 percent of a determinate sentence before release.[17] These sentencing changes have resulted in an unprecedented level of the prison population.

This toughening of philosophical approaches has influenced not only sentencing decisions, but also supervision in the community. For most of the 1990s,

New penology

an emphasis on rational and efficient deployment of control strategies for managing and confining high-risk criminal populations

community supervision (probation and parole) underwent a transition from helping and counseling offenders to risk management and surveillance. This resulted in the allocation of resources for increased monitoring rather than counseling and rehabilitative programs for offenders on probation and parole. In this **new penology** perspective, Rhine writes, "The traditional corrections objectives of rehabilitation and the reduction of offender recidivism give way to the rational and efficient deployment of control strategies for managing (and confining) high-risk criminal populations."[18]

As a result, there is more strident parole and probation monitoring with little tolerance for risk of crime by offenders, and increasing numbers of offenders are sent to prison as community supervision violators. During 2000, there were 182,100 parole violators and 63,404 probation violators admitted to adult prisons. Together, parole and probation violators represented one-third of the 728,296 admissions to prisons in that year.[19] Even more alarming than this high number is the fact that 81 percent of all parole violators and 56 percent of all probation violators had their community supervision revoked for a technical violation only, without the commission of a new crime.[20] Courts and parole boards do not want to risk keeping uncertain offenders in the community. If minor violators later commit a serious crime, those deciding to allow them to continue in the community face criticism or even legal action. This "risk-free" approach has a tremendous impact on prison populations and the commitment of taxpayer dollars to the prison systems of the United States.

In addition, since the 1980s, society has operated on the premise that illicit drug use and trafficking create a serious danger to our society and way of life, and we

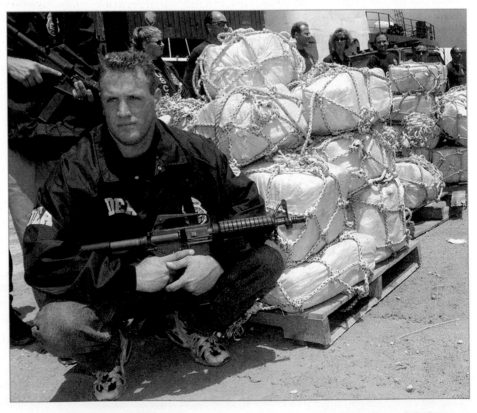

The federalization of drug laws has had the greatest impact on the increase in the number of drug offenders in prisons.
Courtesy of AP/Wide World Photos.

have declared a **war on drugs**. The U.S. Department of Justice reports that "there is extensive evidence of the strong relationship between drug use and crime,"[21] noting that drug users report more involvement in crime, people with criminal records are more likely than those without criminal records to report being drug users, and crime rises as drug use increases.

In 1991, the federal government drug control budget was $10.9 billion, which grew to $18.8 billion in 2002.[22] Of this amount, 67 percent went to supply reduction such as interdiction, international reduction efforts, and domestic law enforcement, and only 33 percent went toward demand reduction such as treatment programs. With the continued increase in the dollars directed toward law enforcement efforts to find and arrest drug dealers and users, the increased "federalization" of drug crimes, and the enactment of federal criminal statutes requiring either five- or ten-year mandatory sentences for drug offenders, more than two-thirds of Federal Bureau of Prisons inmates are currently serving sentences for drug crimes. These statutory and policy or operational changes have resulted in not only an increase in the total number of prisoners, but also in a continuous and dramatic rise in the incarceration rate of the United States. In 1980, the United States incarcerated 139 individuals per 100,000 population; by 2002, the rate had reached 476 people per 100,000 population.[23]

Likelihood of Going to Prison

A 1997 report by the Bureau of Justice Statistics (BJS) indicated that an estimated 5.1 percent of all people in the United States would be confined in a state or federal prison during their lifetime.[24] However, this estimate was made on the assumption that 1997 incarceration rates would remain unchanged since 1991 (the base year for estimates). However, since 1991, incarceration rates have increased from 312 per 100,000 population to 476 per 100,000 population in 2002.[25] Therefore, the estimated percent of the population likely to go to prison has also increased. The report also indicates that men (9.0 percent) are much more likely to go to prison than women (1.1 percent), and blacks (16.2 percent) and Hispanics (9.4 percent) are much more likely than whites (2.5 percent) to go to prison.

Lifetime chances of incarceration are very different from the basic incarceration rates. The BJS report also notes that at year-end 1995, about half of 1 percent of the nation's adult population was confined in a state or federal prison—approximately 1.1 million adults.[26] Lifetime incarceration rates summarize the chances of going to prison over an entire lifetime, rather than just looking at a "snapshot" of those in prison at any one time. The chance of going to prison at some time was about ten times that of the snapshot percentage of the population. These lifetime numbers bring another reality to most individuals. Many people do not know anyone who has gone to prison. But this report estimates that one in every twenty Americans will go to prison at some time during their life, and makes the use of incarceration as a response to crime seem much bigger than snapshot numbers indicating "only" about 1.3 million people in state or federal prison.

Meeting Growth Demands

To respond to the major increase in prison population over the past two decades, most jurisdictions have expanded capacity by building new prisons. As the inmate population increased, state legislatures and the U.S. Congress responded with financial support to construct hundreds of thousands of new prison beds. *Corrections Compendium* reported that during the fiscal year 1994–1995, 135 new state and federal prisons were under construction, costing $5.1 billion and adding more than 100,000 new beds to prison capacity.[27] An earlier survey of federal and state prison systems regarding fiscal year 1991–1992 construction reported

War on drugs

an initiative by President Reagan to reduce the availability of and dependence on illicit drugs through interdiction, criminal sanctions, and treatment

TABLE	5.2	Number of New Prisons Opened (1993–2000)

Year	Number of prisons opened
1993	48
1994	49
1995	70
1996	31
1997	31
1998	35
1999	24
2000	24

Source: Adapted from Camille Graham Camp and George M. Camp, *The 2001 Corrections Yearbook: Adult Systems* (Middletown, Conn.: Criminal Justice Institute, 2002), p. 87.

approximately $6.8 billion allocated for new facilities or additions, which is a leveling off from the large jump reported by a similar survey of construction during fiscal year 1989–1990.[28]

Table 5.2 reports the number of new prisons opened from 1993 to 2000. The twenty-four new prisons opened in 2000 added 18,526 beds at a total cost of $1,231,139,180, or an average cost of $66,021 per bed.[29] In 2000, there were also 10,243 prison beds added through renovation of existing facilities, at a total cost of $296,774,145 and an average cost per bed of $28,973.[30] And on January 1, 2001, thirty-nine new prisons were under construction and sixty-two existing prisons were being renovated to add a total of 58,422 new beds at a cost of $3.4 billion.[31]

When building new prisons, there are many options for designs, and the way a prison is built will influence the style of management for years to come. The "An Insider's Experience" box tells of how I was faced with one of these decisions.

Over the past two decades, billions of dollars have been spent to construct new prisons to keep up with the increase in the number of inmates.
Courtesy of the Federal Bureau of Prisons.

AN INSIDER'S EXPERIENCE: Throwing Out a $2 Million Prison Design

When I was appointed director of the Ohio Department of Rehabilitation and Correction in 1983, we faced many challenges, among them a rapidly growing inmate population and the need for significant prison expansion. Fortunately, the state legislature had just approved a $550 million prison construction program. The outgoing administration had hired an architect to begin the design for the first new prison, a 1,250-bed medium-security facility with a construction budget of $60 million. The state had not built a new prison in almost twenty years, and the last prison (a maximum-security prison) was a telephone-pole design with a linear array of cells in the cellblocks. The same architectural firm had done the design for the new prison, an almost identical telephone-pole-style design.

Unfortunately, that design was not at all what I thought was state of the art, nor the style of prison that I considered consistent with the management approach I wanted for our new prisons. I wanted to change to a campus-style design, but in meetings with the architects I was told that they could not modify the design work that was already completed. The design work (with a $2 million fee) was almost complete. I was faced with a decision of how to get the type of design consistent with the management approach that I wanted to instill in the department, without wasting the $2 million already spent on design work. Complicating the decision was the fact that the architectural firm was very "politically connected" and was marketing itself nationally as a firm that could efficiently build this type of prison. So they did not want to change and admit they were not "state of the art." Even more seriously complicating the decision was the contract signed just days before I took over that gave this firm the opportunity to design every new Ohio prison. I just did not think they were the right architects to meet our long-term needs, and wanted to give more firms the opportunity to be involved in our design process.

I sought the advice of associates who had designed campus-style prisons in other states and the Federal Bureau of Prisons, asking them if they thought the completed design could be modified and what the

additional design and construction cost might be. What the design architects had told me was confirmed—that a change from the telephone-pole design to campus style would be almost impossible and very expensive. So I asked these associates for their estimates of cost for design and construction if the entire plan started from scratch, incorporating a campus style.

The rough estimates were that the design costs would again be close to $2 million, but the prison could probably be constructed for $54 million. Even with starting over, the total cost would be approximately $58 million. Although it was both a financial risk (we could not be sure until bids were received if the prison could in fact be constructed for $54 million) and a public relations/political risk, I decided to scrap the first design and commission a new design for a campus-style prison. The original architects were committed to the telephone-pole design, and were not supportive of the decision. They complained to friends in the governor's office and state legislature about the director's decision to "throw out $2 million of design fees."

However, I did not back down, and the governor supported my decision and let me proceed with the new design. I also voided the overall state contract for design services and brought in many talented architectural firms to design the other institutions with a campus-style approach. In the end, the new prison was built for $54 million, both saving money and resulting in the style of prison consistent with direct supervision and unit management. Needless to say, I was very relieved. When the decision was final, the entire department staff welcomed it, knowing that I was in a strong enough position with the governor to handle pressure from politically influential groups, and that the campus design would allow for progressive changes in how the state managed its prisons. The remainder of the new prisons were built on this campus model. Twenty years later, the department considers this change in design and philosophy a turning point in its administration and management, from a very traditional to a more progressive and professional style.

DIRECT EXPENDITURES FOR POLICE, CORRECTIONS, AND COURTS (1982–1999)   F I G U R E   **5 . 1**

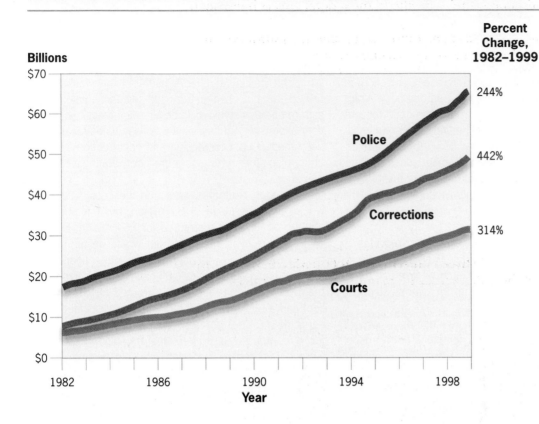

Source: U.S. Department of Justice, Bureau of Justice Statistics, "Justice Expenditure and Employment Extracts," http://www.ojp.usdoj.gov/bjs/glance (accessed September 2002).

This tremendous increase in the number of inmates and new prisons has also required constant increases in the operating budget of state and federal correctional agencies. As illustrated in Figure 5.1, the budgets for all three areas of the criminal justice system (police, courts, and corrections) have increased dramatically. However, neither police nor court budgets have increased as much as corrections budgets, with a 442 percent increase in direct expenditures between 1982 and 1999. Most of this is due to the increasing number of prisons, and not increased use of community supervision. State and federal adult correctional agencies alone increased their total budgets from $21.1 billion in 1993 to $35.6 billion in 2001.[32]

Adult Prison Systems in the United States

While most people think that only the federal and state governments operate prisons for adult offenders, there are actually several other correctional systems and agencies in the United States. These include private companies that contract to house offenders for other jurisdictions, immigration facilities that hold noncitizens subject to deportation to their home country, and military prisons that house violators of the military justice system. However, by far the largest numbers of prisoners are housed in state and federal prisons. On January 1, 2001, there were 1,384 state and federal prisons in the United States, with a capacity of housing (without overcrowding) 1,169,700 prisoners.[33] However, the Bureau of Justice Statistics reported that state and federal prisons confined 1,355,748 inmates on June 30, 2002, operating at 109.6 percent of capacity.[34]

Historically, there has been a significant difference between federal and state prison systems. Each holds offenders convicted under the jurisdiction's specific criminal statutes. State penal codes usually include the standard "**street crimes**," such as murder, robbery, burglary, assault, and theft. In the past, federal crimes in-

Street crimes

crimes with little sophistication required, such as murder, robbery, burglary, assault, and theft cluded fraud and other white-collar offenses, movement of criminal activity across state or national boundaries, and crimes specific to the federal government such as postal fraud or treason. However, over the past several decades, Congress has continually **federalized** crimes such as bank robbery, kidnapping, murder of public officials, drug distribution, and certain crimes using a weapon. As a result, there is now less distinction between the types of inmates in state and federal prisons than in the past.

THE FEDERAL PRISON SYSTEM

Until the late 1800s, offenders convicted of federal crimes were housed in state prisons if their sentence was for more than one year, and in local jails if they were to serve less than one year. After the establishment of the U.S. Department of Justice in 1870, an official of the department was charged with the responsibility for the "care and custody" of all federal prisoners. However, as state prisons became more overcrowded, the states became reluctant to house federal offenders and pressured the Department of Justice to create facilities to maintain federal inmates.

As a result, Congress passed the **Three Penitentiary Act** on March 3, 1891, authorizing the construction of three penitentiaries to house federal offenders.[35] The act included the construction and operation of federal prisons in Leavenworth, Kansas (construction beginning in 1896[36]); McNeil Island, Washington (constructed from 1892 to 1895); and Atlanta, Georgia (construction completed in 1899). These three prisons served the needs of the federal government and housed almost all federal inmates for several decades. As these facilities became more crowded, however, the Department of Justice sought the authority to construct additional prisons. As a result, Congress in 1925 authorized the construction of a reformatory for male prisoners between ages 17 and 30 at Chillicothe, Ohio, and a federal prison for women was opened in Alderson, West Virginia, in 1927.

Federalize
to make a crime a federal rather than a state offense; results when Congress decides that it desires federal law enforcement and prosecution of certain offenses

Three Penitentiary Act
the 1891 act of Congress that authorized the construction of the first three federal prisons

The U.S. Penitentiary in McNeil Island, Washington (c. 1909) was one of the first three federal prisons authorized and built under the Three Penitentiary Act of 1891.
Courtesy of the Federal Bureau of Prisons.

Establishment of the Federal Bureau of Prisons

By the end of the 1920s, officials in the Department of Justice determined that a separate agency within the department was needed to oversee the operation of the growing number of prisons. The Congressional Special Committee on Federal Penal and Reformatory Institutions agreed, and recommended the establishment of a central agency to administer federal prisons. In 1930, Congress passed an act to establish the **Federal Bureau of Prisons (BOP)** to "provide more progressive and humane care for Federal inmates, to professionalize the prison service, and to ensure consistent and centralized administration of the 11 Federal prisons in operation at that time."[37] President Herbert Hoover signed the act into law on May 14, 1930, and **Sanford Bates** was appointed the first director of the Bureau of Prisons. Bates had been chief of the Massachusetts prison system, and his appointment began a trend (that continues today) of the director of the BOP being an experienced correctional administrator rather than a political appointment. Since its origination, the BOP has had only seven directors:

Sanford Bates	1930–1937
James V. Bennett	1937–1964
Myrl E. Alexander	1964–1970
Norman A. Carlson	1970–1987
J. Michael Quinlan	1987–1992
Kathleen Hawk Sawyer	1992–2003
Harley G. Lappin	2003–present

Growth of the Bureau of Prisons

It is interesting to examine the growth of the BOP over its history. Since federal offenders are those who commit crimes that Congress has placed under federal jurisdiction, growth comes primarily as a result of such acts of Congress. The growth of the federal prison population, from the establishment of the BOP to current

The U.S. Bureau of Prisons has been fortunate to have had only seven directors since its creation in 1930. The First three Bureau directors are shown here.
Courtesy of the Federal Bureau of Prisons.

times, resulted from passage of criminal statutes extending the authority of the federal government to prosecute new crimes that were difficult for local law enforcement agencies to handle. Early examples of these acts include the following:

- The *White Slave Act* in 1910 (interstate commerce of prostitution)
- The *Harrison Narcotic Act* in 1914 (taxing and records must be kept on controlled substances)
- The *Volstead Act* in 1918 (prohibition of the sale and consumption of alcohol)
- The *Dyer Act* of 1919 (interstate transportation of stolen vehicles)[38]

By the end of the year the bureau was established (1930), there were fourteen federal prisons housing just over 13,000 inmates. By 1940, the bureau had grown to twenty-four institutions with 24,360 inmates. This total population did not change significantly between 1940 and 1980. However, the bureau decided that large institutions (averaging more than 1,000 inmates) were difficult to manage, and several new prisons were opened to reduce the average prison size. By 1980 there were forty-four federal prisons, just over 24,500 inmates, and approximately 10,000 employees.

During the 1980s, the bureau experienced the beginning of a tremendous population growth, the result of the **Sentencing Reform Act of 1984**, which abolished parole, established determinate sentencing, and reduced the amount of good time available to federal offenders. Other acts of Congress in 1986, 1988, and 1990 created mandatory minimum sentences for various crimes. Between 1980 and 1989, the inmate population more than doubled from just over 24,000 to almost 58,000,[39] and the number of staff by 1990 was approximately 19,000 employees.

At the end of the 1980s, the federal government acted again, declaring the war on drugs and passing several new laws to prosecute drug offenders under federal statutes. These included federalizing drug possession and distribution (the federal role had previously been limited to the prosecution of importers of illegal drugs), imposing mandatory minimum sentences of five and ten years for any offenders distributing illegal drugs, and lengthening other drug crime sentences. About the same time, federal government efforts to crack down on illegal immigration resulted in placement of more illegal aliens in federal prisons. As a result, the federal prison population again more than doubled, reaching approximately 136,000 at the end of 1999.[40] During the late 1990s, Congress ordered the District of Columbia to close its prison system, and the Bureau of Prisons was directed to house District of Columbia felons. This transfer was completed in 2001, and on December 31, 2001, the federal prison system held 6,930 District of Columbia inmates.[41]

During the early years of the 2000s, some state prison systems actually reduced their prison populations, and the growth of state prisoners was only 0.3 percent during 2001. However, with the federalization of many offenses and increased BOP responsibility for housing District of Columbia and immigration offenders, the federal prison system in 2001 grew 9.2 percent, adding 11,465 sentenced prisoners, and had a prison population of 156,993 on December 31, 2001.[42] The number of staff grew to approximately 34,000 employees at that time. The Bureau of Prisons Web site reported a total of 171,724 inmates in BOP custody for the week of September 4, 2003.[43] Table 5.3 breaks this population into categories in terms of the type of facilities in which they are held.

The Bureau of Prisons Today

The federal prison system is a nationwide system of prisons and detention facilities for the incarceration of inmates sentenced for federal crimes and for the detention of individuals awaiting trial or sentencing in federal court. In September 2003, the BOP consisted of 103 prisons.[44] Institutions are classified as one of five

Sentencing Reform Act of 1984

an act of Congress that abolished parole, established determinate sentencing, and reduced the amount of good time available to federal offenders

TABLE 5.3	U.S. Bureau of Prisons Population on September 4, 2003

Type of facility	Number of inmates
BOP-operated prisons	155,452
Long-term contract facilities	7,148
Community correctional centers	6,377
Home confinement	1,457
Jails/short-term detention	1,003
Contract juvenile facilities	251
Total	171,724

Source: Federal Bureau of Prisons Web site, http://www.bop.gov (accessed September 4, 2003).

Security levels

levels such as minimum, low, medium, high, or administrative; they are distinguished by features such as the presence of towers and other perimeter security barriers (fences or walls) with detection devices, the type of housing for prisoners (cells or dormitory), and the staff-to-inmate ratio

different **security levels** (minimum, low, medium, high, or administrative), with each level holding inmates with similar risks of violence and escape. Security levels are distinguished by such security features as towers and other perimeter security barriers (fences or walls) with detection devices, the type of housing for prisoners (cells or dormitory), and the staff-to-inmate ratio.

Minimum-security institutions (federal prison camps) have dormitory housing, a relatively low staff-to-inmate ratio, and limited or no perimeter fencing. Low-security prisons (federal correctional institutions) have double-fenced perimeters, mostly dormitory housing, strong work and program components, and a staff-to-inmate ratio higher than in minimum-security facilities. Medium-security prisons (also called federal correctional institutions) have double fences with electronic detection systems, mostly cells for housing, and an even higher staff-to-inmate ratio than low-security prisons.

High-security institutions (U.S. penitentiaries) have highly secure perimeters (featuring walls or reinforced fences), cell housing, high staff-to-inmate ratios, and close control of inmate movement within the prison. The fifth category of federal prisons, administrative facilities, comprises institutions with special missions, such as detention of pretrial offenders, treatment of inmates with serious or chronic medical problems, or containment of extremely dangerous, violent,

Dormitory housing, in which beds are lined up next to one another and inmates are not locked into cells, is used for minimum-security prisons.
Photo by Richard P. Seiter.

CURRENT LOCATIONS OF PRISONS IN THE FEDERAL PRISON SYSTEM

FIGURE 5.2

MAP LEGEND

■ REGIONAL OFFICE

○ FPS TRAINING CENTER

◀ UNITED STATES PENITENTIARY

● FEDERAL CORRECTIONAL INSTITUTION

▼ FEDERAL PRISON CAMP

* INTENSIVE CONFINEMENT CENTER

□ DETENTION FACILITIES (METROPOLITAN CORRECTIONAL CENTER OR METROPOLITAN/FEDERAL DETENTION CENTER)

△ FEDERAL MEDICAL CENTER

C FEDERAL PRISON COMPLEXES:

ALLENWOOD, PA - HIGH
   MEDIUM
   LOW
   MINIMUM

BUTNER, NC - MEDIUM
   LOW
   MEDICAL

BEAUMONT, TX - HIGH
   MEDIUM
   LOW

COLEMAN, FL - HIGH
   MEDIUM
   LOW

FLORENCE, CO - ADMIN MAX
   HIGH
   MEDIUM

LOMPOC - HIGH
   LOW
   CC

VICTORVILLE - MEDIUM

Courtesy of the Federal Bureau of Prisons.

147

or escape-prone inmates. The BOP also houses prisoners under the jurisdiction of the U.S. Marshals Service, and therefore must build and operate detention facilities (jails) to house these inmates in several cities across the country. The Administrative-Maximum (ADX) U.S. Penitentiary in Florence, Colorado, is an example of a BOP administrative facility; it is a "supermax" prison designed to hold federal inmates who have proven unmanageable by being violent or attempting escape at other secure prisons.

The BOP also operates three intensive confinement centers (boot camps) for minimum-security, nonviolent offenders with no significant history of prior incarceration. These facilities feature physical training, labor-intensive work assignments, education, vocational training, and treatment programs in a highly structured and disciplined, no-frills environment. As noted in Table 5.3, the BOP makes extensive use of community correctional centers (halfway houses), placing many inmates in these facilities thirty days to six months prior to their release from prison to help them adjust to life in the community. Some of these offenders are then placed in home confinement at the end of their halfway house terms. The number of offenders in community correctional centers grew from 7,622 at the end of 2000 to 7,689 at the end of 2001, an increase of 3.7 percent. Approximately 24,000 inmates were referred to halfway houses from institutions during fiscal year 2001, and about 90 percent successfully completed the program.[45] However, the number of federal halfway house inmates dropped to 6,377 by September 2003, as the U.S. Department of Justice determined that the statutory authority of the BOP does not allow placement of inmates in halfway houses until they have completed their full sentence and been released from prison.

In some ways, the federal prison system is similar to most state prison systems. However, as a result of the federal system's unique role in federal law enforcement, its historical development, congressional actions to expand its mission, and the creation of new criminal statutes, there are also many differences between the two systems. In comparing the federal and state correctional systems, the Bureau of Justice Statistics noted the following:

- In 1997, federal inmates were more likely than state inmates to be women (7 percent versus 6 percent), Hispanic (27 percent versus 17 percent), age 45 or older (24 percent versus 13 percent), at least partly college educated (18 percent versus 11 percent), or noncitizens (18 percent versus 5 percent).
- In 2000, an estimated 57 percent of federal inmates and 21 percent of state inmates were serving a sentence for a drug offense; about 10 percent of federal inmates and 49 percent of state inmates were in prison for a violent offense.
- Violent offenders accounted for 53 percent of the growth in state prisons from 1990 to 2000; drug offenders accounted for 59 percent of the growth in federal prisons.[46]

STATE PRISON SYSTEMS

Most adult prisoners serving more than one year are housed in facilities operated by the fifty states. As of January 1, 2001, the states operated almost 1,200 prisons holding approximately 1.24 million inmates.[47] Just as the states are very different in terms of size and demographics of their populations, the state prison systems vary dramatically as well. Prison populations in 2001 ranged from California with 162,765 inmates to North Dakota with 1,161,[48] and the number of prisons ranged from ninety-three in Texas to two prisons in Utah.[49] Each state adopts its own penal code, specifying what acts are considered felonies, what range of sentences are available for each category of crime, and what type of sentencing structure it will have. As noted in earlier chapters, this results in considerable differences in the incarceration rates and therefore in the prison populations among states.

The Organization of State Prison Systems

Over the past decades, state correctional agencies have gone through a slow but deliberate transformation. The early eras of state prison operations were similar to the pre-1930s for the federal prison system, with no central control of prisons and legislatures allocating budgets and personnel directly to each individual prison. State prison wardens were often said to have their own individual "fiefdoms," with complete control over the hiring and firing of staff and the management and discipline of inmates.

Even as late as the first half of the twentieth century, many wardens of state prisons were appointed by governors, with no cabinet-level agency to oversee prison operations. However, as prison systems became larger, as their missions became more complex resulting from the increasing intervention of courts defining expected constitutional standards, and as prisons became more visible and accountable to the public, many states formed cabinet-level departments specifically to oversee the state prisons. Riveland writes, "Today, 32 states are organized with separate Departments of Corrections reporting to the Executive; 11 as separate departments reporting to boards or commissions; 5 under a Department of Public Safety umbrella, and 1 under a social services umbrella. Twenty-four of the separate departments have been so organized since 1979."[50] These state correctional agencies have become very large and very complex. Of the fifty state adult correctional systems, eight are also responsible for juvenile corrections, twenty-one have some probation responsibility, twenty-eight supervise parole functions, and twenty-five manage community corrections programs.[51]

The most common organizational model (twenty-four states) has the director, commissioner, or secretary of corrections as a cabinet-level officer, appointed by and reporting directly to the governor. In eleven other state correctional agencies, the corrections chief reports to a board or commission. The purpose behind this type of organizational model is to have some separation between politics and correctional policy.

The members of the corrections boards or commissions are appointed by the governor, and usually must be made up of individuals from different political parties (often a like number of Republicans and Democrats) and serve overlapping terms. Therefore, governors are not able to immediately replace the board or commission with their own appointees, having to wait until terms end to replace members. The boards and commissions are relatively stable as a result, maintaining consistency of policy and leadership in the correctional agency. Figure 5.3 illustrates three models of reporting by correctional agencies. In the first, the corrections director reports directly to a governor. In the second, the director reports to

THREE MODELS OF CORRECTIONAL AGENCY RELATIONSHIP TO THE CHIEF EXECUTIVE

FIGURE **5.3**

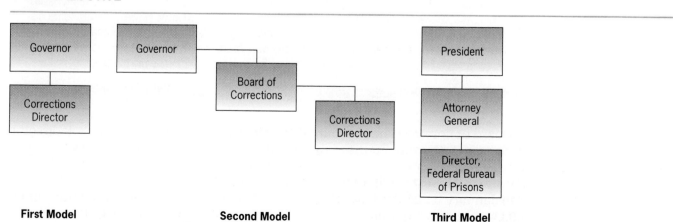

First Model   **Second Model**   **Third Model**

A CASE STUDY   APPOINTING CORRECTIONAL DIRECTORS

A very important issue is how directors of state and federal prison systems are appointed. As noted previously, there are three types of organizational structures for departments of corrections: reporting to a governor, a state board of corrections, or the U.S. Attorney General. The most relevant factor is the stability of the director in the position, how often there is a change of leadership, and the continuity of leadership that results. As noted in the discussion of the U.S. Bureau of Prisons (BOP), the agency has had only seven directors since 1930. In Ohio, I was one of only five state directors since 1970. However, many states have governors that serve only one four-year term, and with each turnover of governors, there is a new director of corrections. Such rapid turnover usually results in a lack of continuity of programs, operations, and leadership that reduce the quality of the overall operation of the correctional agency.

There are three scenarios in which directors of corrections are appointed. The first is the career correctional professional, in which the politics of the governor or the attorney general have little impact on the selection of the corrections chief. With the federal prison system, there has never been a "political" change of directors, even though there have been dozens of attorneys general and changes in political parties throughout the seven centuries of the BOP. A few states are similar in that the corrections director survives changes in governors and political parties, as the professionalism and competence of the leader is considered more important than being of the same political party or the person that the governor wants in the position. This, in most people's opinions, is the best situation, allowing for competent leadership and a long-term shaping of the department's culture and organization to best accomplish its mission. As well, staff see the agency as a career and strive to work to the top of the agency, without fear that promotion will at some point lead to dismissal.

The second scenario is that in which a professional correctional person is appointed as director of a state correctional agency, but the leadership turns over with every new governor. Most states unfortunately fall into this category, although a few state directors prove themselves so accomplished at their jobs that the governor decides to keep that person rather than replace him or her with someone new just for the sake of change. I have several close associates and friends who have been directors of state correctional agencies in several states, moving on as they are replaced in one state, but with the knowledge and reputation to get a job in another state almost immediately (as governors are elected at the same time in many states). Even with professional leadership, this lack of continuity is usually a negative in the ability for the agency to reach its maximum potential.

The third scenario is, in most professional correctional administrators minds, the worst. As correctional agencies become more of a political concern to elected officials, they sometimes decide not to appoint a correctional professional, but instead to appoint someone with a strong political background. This occurs when governors believe there is more danger to their re-election from making political than correctional management mistakes. These governors sometimes look to the state legislature to select someone who they know supports their criminal justice policies, or sometimes select a sheriff who may have some correctional background in running a jail but has also stood for election for the office of sheriff. One of the worst examples of this scenario occurred in a state in which the governor had originally appointed a professional correctional administrator who was extremely well respected throughout the country. However, after some disagreement between the governor and director regarding some issues of correctional policy (such as whether to have a chain gang), the director was fired. The governor appointed a funeral director as head of corrections, whose only experience was as a member of the state legislature.

a board or commission. The third is the federal model, in which the BOP director is appointed by and reports to the Attorney General of the United States.

Inmates in State Prison Systems

On January 1, 2001, the makeup of prison inmates was predominantly male (93.4 percent),[52] minority (38.5 percent white, 46.2 percent black, 12.8 percent

TABLE	5.4	Percentage of Sentenced State Inmates by Type of Crime, 1990 and 2000	
	Type of crime	**1990**	**2000**
	Violent	46%	49%
	Property	25	20
	Drug	22	21
	Public order	7	10

Source: Paige M. Harrison and Allen J. Beck, *Prisoners in 2001* (Washington, D.C.: U.S. Department of Justice, Bureau of Justice Statistics, July 2002), p. 12.

Hispanic, and 2.5 percent other minority),[53] and serving an average sentence of 5.31 years.[54] A large percentage of state prison inmates are serving time for violent offenses. Table 5.4 illustrates the percentage of sentenced state inmates by type of crime in 1990 and 2000. The Bureau of Justice Statistics reports that "[in] absolute numbers, an estimated 589,100 inmates in state prison at year-end 2000 were held for violent offenses, 158,700 for robbery, 156,300 for murder, 116,800 for assault, and 113,900 for rape and other sexual assaults."[55]

The largest growth of state prison inmates between 1990 and 2000 was among violent offenders. This is very different from the growth by offense category (predominantly drug offenses) within federal prisons. As many drug crimes were federalized, the federal prison population grew, resulting in more than two-thirds of all federal prison inmates serving sentences for drug offenses. In 1980, in both state and federal prisons, drug offenders made up less than 10 percent of the nation's prisoners, and violent offenders almost 60 percent. By 1993, the number of drug offenders had risen to 26 percent of the total, and the number of violent offenders had dropped to 45 percent of the total.[56] By 1995, there were 52,782 drug offenders in federal prisons, and by 2001, 78,501 federal prisoners were drug offenders.[57] Therefore, the growth of violent offenders in state prisons comes about from two phenomena. First, violent offenders are receiving much longer sentences than in the past, and therefore as more are admitted to prison without others being released, the overall number increases. Second, the percentage of the total inmates that are serving sentences for violent offences increases as many drug offenders are diverted to federal prisons.

A recent phenomenon among state prison systems is the decline in the growth of inmates. After almost two decades of dramatic increases, the growth has begun to slow and the level of overcrowding in state prisons has decreased. Table 5.5 illustrates the growth in the number of state inmates over the past decade. State prison populations grew only 0.3 percent during 2001, the lowest annual rate recorded since 1972,[58] and even declined by 6,200 inmates (0.5 percent) during the last six months of 2000.[59] This decline was the first measured decline in the state prison population since 1972.

There is debate over what issues have most influenced the declining increase in the number of state prison inmates, and several possible reasons exist for the drop. The first possibility is that demographics have changed; fewer Americans are in the high-crime age and have enough criminal history to be sent to prison. Second, crime rates have been dropping. But the most likely reason is that more crimes are being prosecuted at the federal level, and offenders who would have otherwise been in state prisons are now in federal prisons. The decline in rate of increase of the state prison population is counterbalanced by an increase in federal inmates. The Bureau of Justice Statistics reports, "Over 40% of the growth in the Nation's prison population during the 12 months ending June 30, 2002, was accounted for by the 8,893 additional inmates under jurisdiction of the Federal system."[60]

TABLE	5.5	Number of State Prison Inmates on December 31, Selected Years	

Year	Number of inmates	Percent of capacity
1990	708,393	115%
1995	1,025,624	114
1999	1,228,455	101
2000	1,245,845	100
2001	1,249,038	101

Source: Adapted from Paige M. Harrison and Allen J. Beck, *Prisoners in 2001* (Washington, D.C.: U.S. Department of Justice, Bureau of Justice Statistics, July 2002), p. 1.

Classification within State Prison Systems

State prison systems use similar security-level classifications, as does the federal prison system. One major difference, however, is that many states have central reception centers at which all inmates are initially placed until they are classified. Upon their arrival at the reception center, state inmates receive a **security classification** to determine to which prison they will be assigned. The purpose of a security classification is to match offenders to institutions that have the physical security and staff resources to prevent escapes and control their behavior. However, also important for the assignment to a prison is the need for specific programs for the inmate. Both security and program need determinations are the result of several factors. Inmates go through psychological, educational, or vocational testing, and their past records are reviewed. The presentence investigation (PSI) provides much of the information regarding criminal history, family and social history, education and vocational achievement, and employment history.

Objective classification systems, or actuarial methods to score past criminal behavior and program needs and predict offenders' risk of violence and escape, are used in most states to determine security classification. Points are assigned based on offenders' history, and the point totals indicate the level of security (minimum, medium, maximum) that is required for each inmate. In addition to security classification, inmates' program needs and home are also considered in the decision of prison assignment. Most states have many similar-security-level prisons (for instance, Michigan has twenty-five medium-security prisons), and inmates are assigned both geographically (as close to home as possible) and to meet specific program needs (some prisons may have specialized mental health or substance abuse programs).

The states use somewhat different terminologies of security classifications. In *The 2001 Corrections Yearbook,* the classifications were generalized as maximum, close/high, medium, minimum, and community.[61] On January 1, 2001, inmates were classified as follows:

Maximum security	11.3%
Close/high security	15.1%
Medium security	33.6%
Minimum security	29.8%
Community security	4.8%
Unclassified	5.4%

These distributions have been relatively constant over the past two decades. The highest proportion of inmates are classified as medium and minimum security. However, prisoners above medium security (to include close/high security and maximum security) have been rising as a percentage of the total prison population over

Security classification

a system for matching offenders to institutions that have the physical security and staff resources to prevent escapes and control their behavior

TABLE 5.6 Inmate Prison Assignments as of January 1, 2001		
Assignment	**Number of inmates**	**Percent of total**[a]
Prison industry	77,380	7.1%
Prison farm	30,856	3.1
Other work	536,722	49.4
Full-time education or vocational	128,535	13.0
Part-time education or vocational[b]	113,265	14.2

[a]The total will not be 100%, as some inmates are unassigned and some states have other assignments not included in these categories.

[b]Part-time includes release preparation, adult continuing education, parenting, and fitness and wellness programs.

Source: Adapted from Camille Graham Camp and George M. Camp, *The 2001 Corrections Yearbook: Adult Systems* (Middletown, Conn.: Criminal Justice Institute, 2002), p. 117.

the past several years. That is because the actuarial methods used by most objective classification systems put much weight on the length of time to be served before release. As sentences lengthen, an inmate with the same criminal history and background may be increased in security level, only because he or she is serving a longer sentence. Higher-security-level prisons have higher building and operating costs.

After assignment, inmates are transferred from the central reception center to the prison at which they begin serving their sentence. This assignment is seldom permanent, as inmates are often transferred as their security level (described in Chapter 10) or their program needs change.

At their assigned prison, inmates go through an orientation regarding rules and regulations, policies and procedures, and processes such as adding people to their visiting or telephone list. Inmates then go through another classification process to determine what type of prison job they will have and what type of programs they will be assigned. This classification and assignment process uses the results of the education, vocational, and mental health tests and assessments that were completed in the reception center. These are discussed with inmates, who state their preference for work and program assignments. In most states, all inmates must have a job unless they receive a full-time program assignment. Most programs (education and substance abuse) are voluntary, although in some states and under certain sentences, education (up to the level of basic literacy) and substance abuse programs may be mandatory. Table 5.6 illustrates the types of assignments inmates receive in prisons. After assignment, inmates begin their daily routine they carry out throughout their sentence. These routines and inmate activities are described in Chapters 12 and 13.

OTHER PUBLIC CORRECTIONAL SYSTEMS

State and federal prisons by far hold most of the adult prisoners housed in correctional facilities in the United States. However, as noted in Table 5.1, there are almost 9,000 inmates in immigration facilities, almost 2,400 inmates in military facilities, and more than 16,000 inmates in territorial facilities at year-end 2002. The U.S. **Bureau of Immigration and Customs Enforcement (BICE)**, formerly the U.S. Immigration and Naturalization Service (INS), is responsible for housing illegal aliens pending a hearing or deportation back to their home country. Offenders are usually detained in two ways: first, if caught while attempting to illegally enter the United States, and second, if they commit a crime and are arrested while not a citizen of the U.S. and are subject to potential deportation. The number of BICE detainees has been increasing over the past few years (see Table 5.7),

Bureau of Immigration and Customs Enforcement (BICE)

formerly the U.S. Immigration and Naturalization Service (INS); responsible for housing illegal aliens pending a hearing or deportation back to their home country

| TABLE 5.7 | Number of Detainees under the Jurisdiction of the Bureau of Immigration and Customs Enforcement (BICE), by Type of Facility, Year-End 1995, 2001, and 2002 |

Facility type	Number of detainees			Percent change 2001–2002	Percent of all detainees	
	2002	2001	1995		2002	1995
Total[a]	21,065	19,137	8,177	10.1%	100%	100%
BICE-operated facilities	5,087	4,550	3.776	11.8	24.1	48.2
Private facilities under exclusive contract to BICE	1,936	1,947	652	−0.6	9.2	8.0
Federal Bureau of Prisons	1,100	1,276	1,282	−13.8	5.2	15.7
Other Federal facilities	130	162	181	−19.8	0.6	2.2
Intergovernmental agreements	12,812	11,201	2,286	14.4	60.8	28.0
State prisons	453	419	8	8.1	2.2	0.1
Local jails	9,764	8,681	1,984	12.5	46.4	24.3
Other facilities	2,595	2,101	294	23.5	12.3	3.6

[a]Detail does not sum to total due to unknown facility type for 1 detainee in 2001.

Source: Paige M. Harrison and Allen J. Beck, "Prisoners in 2002," *Bureau of Justice Statistics Bulletin,* July 2000 (revised August 27, 2003), p. 8.

as enforcement efforts to catch and detain individuals attempting to enter the United States illegally have increased. By the end of 2002, there were 21,065 detainees held under BICE jurisdiction.

As illustrated in Table 5.7, BICE detains only about a quarter of its total detainees. The remainder are housed by the Federal Bureau of Prisons or other federal facilities, under contract to private facilities, or under intergovernmental agreements in state prisons or local jails. Among the BICE detainees at year-end 2002, just over 50 percent (10,763) had been convicted of a criminal offense. Of those convicted, 31.6 percent were for violent offenses, 31.4 percent for drug offenses, 14.7 percent for property offenses, and 12.6 percent for public-order offenses.[62]

Brig

a military term meaning a correctional facility

The U.S. military services also operate prisons or **brigs** to house offenders convicted of violating the military justice codes. The Army operates six correctional facilities, the Navy operates eleven, the Marine Corps operates six, and the Air Force operates thirty-six. The total capacity of these fifty-nine facilities is 3,249.[63] Table 5.8 illustrates the number of detainees held by the various military branches. Fifty-seven percent of these detainees are serving sentences of one year or more.

The final category of public correctional institutions described is that of territorial prisons. The five U.S. territories and commonwealths operate correctional facilities that serve as jails and prisons for these jurisdictions. Each has a court and correctional system similar to those of a state, and these correctional populations are also growing. Since 1995, the number of sentenced prisoners in U.S. territories has grown by 31 percent, and three-fourths of the territorial prison population (12,296) was serving a sentence of more than one year.[64] Table 5.9 illustrates the number of inmates in custody in the five territories.

PRIVATE CORRECTIONAL SYSTEMS

While the use of private facilities to house prisoners is a recent phenomenon, the private sector has been involved in the administration of various correctional aspects almost since the origination of penal codes. During the 1960s, the use of halfway houses as a transition from prison to the community grew rapidly. Most of the halfway houses were privately operated, although most were owned by faith-

| TABLE | 5.8 | Prisoners under Military Jurisdiction, by Branch of Service, Year-End 1995, 2001, and 2002 |

Branch of service	Total			Percent change 2001–2002	Sentenced to more than 1 year			Percent change, 2001–2002
	2002	2001	1995		2002	2001	1995	
To which prisoners belonged								
Total	2,377	2,436	2,838	−2.4%	1,361	1,332	1,845	2.2%
Air Force	450	480	486	−6.3	264	267	382	−1.1
Army	860	804	1,207	7.0	610	600	995	1.7
Marine Corps	565	628	612	−10.0	265	236	249	12.3
Navy	489	516	520	−6.2	219	226	213	−3.1
Coast Guard	13	8	13	62.5	3	3	6	0.0
Holding prisoners								
Total	2,377	2,436	2,838	−2.4%	1,361	1,332	1,845	2.2%
Air Force	128	126	—	1.6	14	14	—	0.0
Army	966	981	1,582	−1.5	767	822	1,403	−6.7
Marine Corps	478	428	591	11.7	171	77	188	122.1
Navy	805	901	665	−10.7	409	419	254	−2.4

—Not reported.

Source: Paige M. Harrison and Allen J. Beck, "Prisoners in 2002," *Bureau of Justice Statistics Bulletin,* July 2000 (revised August 27, 2003), p. 8.

| TABLE | 5.9 | Prisoners in Custody of Correctional Authorities In the U.S. Territories, Year-End 2001 and 2002 |

U.S. territory	Total			Sentenced to more than 1 year			
	2002	2001	Percent change 2001–2002	2002	2001	Percent change, 2001–2002	Incarceration rate, 2002[a]
Total	16,206	15,871	2.1%	12,296	11,933	3.0%	286
American Samoa	169	155	9.0	143	125	14.4	208
Guam	542	585	−7.4	261	297	12.1	162
Commonwealth of the Northern Marlana Islands	123	102	20.6	76	72	5.6	98
Commonwealth of Puerto Rico	14,725	14,539	1.3	11,371	11,020	3.2	294
U.S. Virgin Islands	647	494	31.0	445	419	6.2	360

[a]The number of prisoners with a sentence of more than 1 year per 100,000 persons in the resident population. Midyear population estimates were provided by the U.S. Bureau of the Census. International Data Base.

Source: Paige M. Harrison and Allen J. Beck, "Prisoners in 2002," *Bureau of Justice Statistics Bulletin,* July 2000 (revised August 27, 2003), p. 8.

based or not-for-profit charitable organizations such as the Salvation Army. By the 1980s, almost every state had contracts with privately operated halfway houses to provide residential services, supervision, and transitional programs for inmates leaving prison and returning to the community.[65] As well, many states with very small juvenile offender populations have often found it cost-effective to contract with privately operated facilities rather than to open state-run juvenile facilities. In 1984, it was reported that 65 percent of all juvenile facilities were private, housing approximately 32,000 offenders.[66]

While these uses of the private sector in corrections have not been found controversial, contracting to house adult prisoners in private "for-profit" prisons raised serious ethical and practical questions, resulting in a slow beginning to the use and role of private prisons. A **private prison** is any secure correctional facility, operated by an organization other than a governmental agency and usually in a "for profit" manner, which contracts with the government to provide security, housing, and programs for adult offenders. In a private prison, staff are not public employees, but are employees of the company that owns and operates the prison. Such prisons can be administered without cumbersome governmental purchasing and personnel policies, although they are still held to the same constitutional standard for treatment of inmates as a public prison.

The first private contract to house adult offenders was in 1984, for a small, 250-bed facility operated by **Corrections Corporation of America** under contract with Hamilton County, Tennessee. Soon thereafter, additional contracts with the private sector to house illegal aliens (contracted with the U.S. Immigration and Naturalization Service) and youthful offenders (with the Federal Bureau of Prisons) were established. The growth over the next few decades in the privatization of correctional facilities was spurred by the increasing number of inmates and the rapid need to build new prisons, the budgetary challenges required to fund these new prisons, and the Reagan-era support of using the private sector to help downsize the scope of government: Welch notes,

> At that time, the prevailing political and economic philosophy encouraged government officials to turn to the private sector to administer public services, such as sanitation, health care, security, fire protection, and education. As a result of the introduction of free-market principles into the administration of public services, . . . the privatization of corrections appeared to be a new and novel approach to some old problems (i.e., overcrowding and mounting costs).[67]

By 1990, Logan reported that private prisons held just over 9,000 adult inmates,[68] but by year-end 2001 there were 91,828 state and federal prisoners held in private prisons, accounting for 5.8 percent of state and 12.3 percent of federal prisoners.[69] Table 5.10 illustrates the numbers and percentage of all inmates held in private prisons by each state and the federal government.

Private Correctional Companies

The use of private prisons has continued to expand, and on January 1, 2001, there were 101 private prisons contracting to hold adult criminal offenders. The average population of these facilities was 698 prisoners, and the average cost per inmate per day was $43.62.[70] By year-end 2002, thirty-one states and the federal system had 93,771 inmates held in privately operated facilities.[71] Table 5.11 illustrates the number of contracted private facilities and number of inmates held by security level.

While several companies contract with government agencies to house adult offenders, only four have a significant market share. Table 5.12 lists each of the major companies (Corrections Corporation of America, **Wackenhut Corrections Corporation**, **Cornell Correctional Companies**, and **Correctional Services Corporation**) by their size and approximate revenues.

The private sector's ability to operate quality correctional institutions no longer seems to under question, although definitive conclusions have not been reached about how their costs and outcomes compare to public-sector prisons. However,

Private prison

any secure correctional facility operated by other than a governmental agency and usually in a "for profit" manner that contracts with a governmental entity to provide security, housing, and programs for adult offenders

Corrections Corporation of America

the largest of the private prison corporations, which opened the first private, for-profit correctional facility in 1984 in Tennessee; currently operates seventy correctional facilities

Wackenhut Corrections Corporation

a private correctional company that operates fifty-seven correctional facilities

Cornell Correctional Companies

a private correctional company that operates sixty-nine correctional facilities

Correctional Services Corporation

a private correctional company that operates thirty-three correctional facilities

TABLE	5.10	State and Federal Prisoners Held in Private Prisons

Region and jurisdiction	Private facilities		Region and jurisdiction	Private facilities	
	Number	Percent of all inmates[a]		Number	Percent of all inmates[a]
U.S. total	91,828	6.5%	Delaware	0	0
Federal	19,251	12.3	Dist. of Columbia	986	35.9
State[b]	72,577	5.8	Florida	3,995	5.5
Northeast	3,131	1.8%	Georgia	4,561	9.9
Connecticut	0	0	Kentucky	1,028	6.7
Maine	11	0.6	Louisiana	2,928	8.2
Massachusetts	0	0	Maryland	128	0.5
New Hampshire	0	0	Mississippi	3,634	16.9
New Jersey[c]	2,620	9.3	North Carolina	191	0.6
New York	0	0	Oklahoma	6,658	29.2
Pennsylvania	500	1.3	South Carolina	6	0
Rhode Island[c]	0	0	Tennessee	3,678	15.5
Vermont[c]	0	0	Texas	16,331	10.1
Midwest	6,920	2.9%	Virginia	1,566	5.0
Illinois	0	0	West Virginia	0	0
Indiana	915	4.4	**West**	16,836	6.2%
Iowa	0	0	Alaska	1,441	31.7
Kansas	98	1.1	Arizona	1,429	5.2
Michigan	449	0.9	California	4,452	2.8
Minnesota	0	0	Colorado	2,390	13.7
Missouri	0	0	Hawaii	1,251	22.9
Nebraska	0	0	Idaho	1,348	22.4
North Dakota	44	4	Montana	1,087	32.7
Ohio	1,924	4.2	Nevada	478	4.7
South Dakota	35	1.2	New Mexico	2,484	43.8
Wisconsin	3,455	16.0	Oregon	0	0
South	45,690	8.1%	Utah	0	0
Alabama	0	0	Washington[c]	0	0
Arkansas	0	0	Wyoming	476	28.3

[a]Based on the total number of inmates under state or federal jurisdiction.

[b]Includes 6,515 federal inmates in nonsecure privately operated facilities.

[c]Inmates held in other state facilities include interstate compact cases.

Source: Adapted from Paige M. Harrison and Allen J. Beck, *Prisoners in 2001*, (Washington, D.C.: U.S. Department of Justice, Bureau of Justice Statistics, July 2002), p. 8.

it is expected that private correctional operations will continue to remain strong, due to a number of factors. While the increase in the number of state and federal prisoners is slowing, demographics lead one to expect that it is only a temporary slowdown, and that the need for private prisons will continue. Tightening government budgets force public officials to increasingly look for alternatives to the traditional approaches. And the continued lack of public confidence in the public sector leads many citizens to support giving the private sector a chance. Even with no substantial evidence to support a wholesale move to contracting with the private sector for correctional services, Gowdy notes:

> Nonetheless, the public's unsatisfactory view of today's penal system in terms of its costs and high recidivism rates are two factors that are likely to encourage further expansion of the private sector's role.[72]

TABLE	5.11	Number of Privately Operated Prisons by Security Level, January 1, 2001

Security level	Number of prisons	Number of inmates housed
Low	4	4,381
Minimum	25	15,367
Minimum/medium	9	3,490
Medium	44	34,262
Medium/maximum	5	2,186
Close/medium	2	1,442
Multilevel	8	7,011
High/maximum	3	768

Source: Adapted from Camille Graham Camp and George M. Camp, *The 2001 Corrections Yearbook: Adult Systems* (Middletown, Conn.: Criminal Justice Institute, 2002), pp. 112–113.

TABLE	5.12	Major Private Correctional Companies

Company	Number of facilities	Revenues for 2001
Corrections Corporation of America	70	$981 million
Wackenhut Corrections Corporation	57	$562 million
Cornell Correctional Companies	69	$265 million
Correctional Services Corporation	33	$160 million

Source: Corrections Corporation of America Web site, http://www.correctionscorp.com; Wackenhut Corrections Web site, http://www.wackenhutcorrections.com; Cornell Companies Web site, http://www.cornellcorrections.com; Correctional Services Corporation Web site, http://www.correctionalservices.com.

This private prison owned by the Corrections Corporation of America is one of many private prisons now operated throughout the United States.
Courtesy of the Corrections Corporation of America.

A Question of Policy

The increase in the number of inmates of the past two decades and the resultant cost to construct new prisons to keep up with this growth leads to an important question of policy. The "You Make the Decision" box asks students to consider the policy of construction and cost implications of this option to respond to the constant expansion of the prison population and the increasing resources necessary to operate new prisons.

YOU MAKE THE DECISION . . .

IS INCARCERATION WORTH THE COST?

The question that must be asked is whether the changes in laws resulting in an increase in the number of inmates, constructing new prisons, renovating existing facilities, and spending tens of billions of dollars to house prison inmates is good public policy. As noted previously, the absolute number of violent and dangerous offenders in prison is not increasing significantly. The largest portion of the growth has come from the long-term incarceration of drug offenders. Whether our nation can withstand another decade of a policy to try to build our way out of prison overcrowding is a question that must be addressed in a thoughtful and fact-based manner by corrections and elected officials.

The somewhat dramatic differences in the incarceration rates of various states require the review of perhaps the most important policy issue regarding corrections in the United States: Does the increase in the use of incarceration reduce the risk to citizens of being victimized, and if so, is that reduction of risk worth the additional cost of such incarceration? This is an important issue for students of corrections to confront. Look at the states with the highest incarceration rates (Louisiana, Oklahoma, Alabama, and Mississippi). Compare these states with those having the lowest incarceration rates (Minnesota, Maine, North Dakota, Massachusetts, and New Hampshire). Do trends in crimes rates provide any parallels to increases in rates of incarceration?

Students should examine many factors and then come to their own conclusion as to whether the increased use of incarceration is worth the cost. Factors that should be considered include the trends in crime rates (particularly violent crime), the cost of building and operating new prisons, the available alternatives to incarceration, the mission and goals of corrections, and the effectiveness of both imprisonment and community correctional programs. Students should weigh the cost of the incarceration alternative to the impact it has on crime trends, while considering the potential for other uses of these funds. Unfortunately, this policy deliberation does not occur in the public policy debate among legislative bodies or most elected officials. It is a critical public policy dilemma that deserves a thorough debate.

Chapter Review

SUMMARY

Although prisons have been an important component in the criminal justice system since shortly after the creation of the U.S. Constitution and the formation of our current system of justice, they have changed in scope and role only minimally during their first two-hundred years of operation. However, over the past two decades, there have been major changes in their role, mission, and scope; the attributes of inmates; and the length of time that inmates serve. This chapter has described

these trends and discussed our nation's current approach of constructing new prisons to avoid severe overcrowding of correctional facilities. This policy decision, however, has been at great cost to the taxpayers, as direct expenditures to correctional agencies are now greater than $50 billion per year.

This chapter has also presented the different correctional agencies that operate prisons, including states, the Federal Bureau of Prisons, the U.S. Bureau of Immigration and Customs Enforcement, the military, U.S. territories, and private correctional companies. Major changes in policies and populations within the public agencies were described, specifically how changes in federal laws regarding crimes impact the federal and state prison systems. As well, the controversial issues surrounding "for-profit" private companies operating correctional institutions were described.

Much of the challenge in operating prisons under today's approach of construction of new facilities to keep up with the increasing number of inmates has to do with finding the budgetary resources to continue to operate correctional agencies. In the final two chapters of this textbook, this challenge and the future approaches and alternatives to our current overreliance on prisons are addressed. It is critical to examine and consider alternative methods of managing offenders, and to search for preventive approaches to offenders becoming involved in crime. We must also consider diversion from the criminal justice system for minor, first-time offenders and juveniles and using alternatives to incarceration that do not seriously endanger public safety as reasonable sanctions for minor property and drug offenses. Our society cannot continue to fund the growth of imprisonment to the detriment of other important government functions.

The next chapter examines what happens to inmates as they get out of prison. The declining use of parole and indeterminate sentences and the changing issues that confront prisoners as they leave prison and return to the community are reviewed. The past two decades have witnessed not only a change in the prison population, but also a change in the makeup of those being released. These changes require a renewed examination of how we prepare inmates for release, and the ability of the community to readily accept them upon their return.

REVIEW QUESTIONS

1. How did the Period of Transition influence modern correctional practices in terms of inmate "out-of-cell" time?
2. What is the general mission of most correctional agencies?
3. How do prison programs help protect society?
4. How does the new penology affect the increase in the use of incarceration?
5. Describe recent trends in terms of the inmate population, commission of violent crimes, and length of sentence.
6. What three prisons were included in the Three Penitentiary Act of 1891?
7. What was the result of the Sentencing Reform Act of 1984?
8. What factors influenced the continued significant growth of the Bureau of Prisons into the 2000s?
9. Describe the physical security factors that go with prison security levels (minimum, medium, maximum).
10. What factors have influenced a recent decline in the number of prison inmates in some states?
11. What state prison security level has the highest percentage of inmates?
12. When and where was the first private prison opened under contract to house adult offenders?
13. Describe the most controversial issues in the use of "for-profit" private companies to house inmates.

ENDNOTES

1. President's Commission on Law Enforcement and Administration of Justice, *The Challenge of Crime in a Free Society* (Washington, D.C.: U.S. Government Printing Office, 1967), p. 165.
2. David Shichor, *Punishment for Profit* (Thousand Oaks, Calif.: Sage, 1995), p. 9.
3. Pete Wittenberg, "Power, Influence, and the Development of Correctional Policy," *Federal Probation* 60, no. 2, (1996): 46.
4. Paige M. Harrison and Allen J. Beck, *Prisoners in 2002*, NCJ 200248 (Washington, D.C.: U.S. Department of Justice, Bureau of Justice Statistics Bulletin, July 2003), p. 1.
5. *Rhodes v. Chapman*, 29 Cr. L. Rptr. 3061 (1981).
6. *Brucino v. Carlson* (Civil Action No. 84-4320), D.C.S.D. III (1987).
7. Cisco Lassiter, "Roboprison," *Mother Jones* (September/October 1990): 76.
8. Douglas C. Eadie, "Strategic Management by Design," in *Strategic Planning for Local Government: A Handbook for Officials and Citizens*, edited by Roger L. Kemp (Jefferson, N.C.: McFarland, 1993), p. 85.
9. Federal Bureau of Prisons Web site, http://www.bop.gov (accessed November 2002).
10. Camille Graham Camp and George M. Camp, *The 2001 Corrections Yearbook: Adult Systems* (Middletown, Conn.: 2002), p. 149.
11. Ibid.
12. The Gallup Organization, "The Gallup Poll," http://www.gallup.com/pol/releases/pr011022.asp (accessed October 24, 2001).

13. Camille Graham Camp and George M. Camp, *The Corrections Yearbook, 1998* (Middletown, Conn.: Criminal Justice Institute, 1998), p. 57; and Camp and Camp, (2002), p. 70.

14. Michael Tonry, "Why Are U.S. Incarceration Rates So High?" *Crime and Delinquency* 45, no. 14 (October 1999): 445.

15. Bureau of Justice Statistics, *National Prisoner Statistics* (Washington, D.C.: U.S. Department of Justice, 1977).

16. Bureau of Justice Statistics, *National Prisoner Statistics* (Washington, D.C.: U.S. Department of Justice, 1997).

17. P. Ditton and D. J. Wilson, *Truth in Sentencing in State Prisons* (Washington, D.C.: U.S. Department of Justice, Bureau of Justice Statistics, 1999).

18. Edward E. Rhine, "Probation and Parole Supervision: In Need of a New Narrative," *Corrections Quarterly* 1, no. 2 (1997): 73.

19. A. Beck and C. Mumola, *Prisoners in 1998* (Washington, D.C.: U.S. Department of Justice, Bureau of Justice Statistics, 1999).

20. Camp and Camp, 2002, pp. 59–62.

21. Bureau of Justice Statistics, *Drugs, Crime and the Justice System* (Washington, D.C.: National Institute of Justice, 1993), p. 2.

22. Office of National Drug Control Policy, *National Drug Control Strategy: FY 2001 Budget Summary* (Washington, D.C.: Executive Office of the President, 2001), p. 13; Office of National Drug Control Policy, *National Drug Control Strategy: FY 2003 Budget Summary* (Washington, D.C.: Executive Office of the President, 2003), pp. 10–11.

23. U.S. Department of Justice, Bureau of Justice Statistics, "Key Facts at a Glance," http://www.ojp.usdoj.gov/bjs/glance/tables/incrttab.htm (accessed July 27, 2003).

24. Thomas P. Bonczar and Allen J. Beck, *Lifetime Likelihood of Going to State or Federal Prison* (Washington, D.C.: U.S. Department of Justice, March 1997).

25. "Key Facts at a Glance" (accessed July 27, 2003).

26. Ibid.

27. "Survey of Planned Construction: 1994–1995," *Corrections Compendium* 19, no. 5 (May 1994): 7–14.

28. "Survey of Planned Construction: 1991–1992," *Corrections Compendium* 16, no. 3 (March 1991): 9–17.

29. Camp and Camp, 2002, p. 87.

30. Ibid., p. 88.

31. Ibid., p. 89.

32. Ibid., p. 100.

33. Ibid., pp. 80, 84.

34. Paige M. Harrison and Jennifer C. Karberg, *Prison and Jail Inmates at Midyear 2002* (Washington, D.C.: U.S. Department of Justice, April 2003), p. 2.

35. This act was officially known as "An Act for the Erection of United States Prisons and for the Imprisonment of United States Prisoners, and for Other Purposes."

36. The U.S. Penitentiary in Leavenworth was built with convict labor, from inmates housed at the U.S. Disciplinary Barracks for Military Prisoners in Leavenworth, and took several years to complete. It was finally finished in 1928, but it housed inmates shortly after the beginning of the twentieth century.

37. Federal Prison System, *The Bureau in Brief,* http://www.bop.gov/ (accessed April 2002).

38. Harry E. Allen and Clifford E. Simonsen, *Corrections in America: An Introduction,* 8th ed. (Upper Saddle River, N.J.: Prentice Hall, 1998), p. 538.

39. *About the Federal Bureau of Prisons* (Washington, D.C.: U.S. Department of Justice, July 2001), p. 3.

40. Ibid.

41. Harrison and Beck, 2003, p. 4.

42. Ibid., pp. 3–4.

43. Federal Bureau of Prisons Web site, http://www.bop.gov/ (accessed September 4, 2003).

44. Ibid.

45. *State of the Bureau of Prisons, 2001,* (Washington, D.C.: U.S. Department of Justice, 2002), p. 8.

46. Bureau of Justice Statistics, "Criminal Offender Statistics," http://www.ojp.usdoj.gov/bjs/crimoff (accessed January 8, 2003).

47. Camp and Camp, 2002, pp. 3, 80.

48. Ibid., pp. 2–3.

49. Ibid., pp. 79–80.

50. Chase Riveland, "The Correctional Leader and Public Policy Skills," *Corrections Management Quarterly* 1, no. 3 (1997): 23.

51. Camp and Camp, 2002, p. 5.

52. Camp and Camp, 2002, p. 20.

53. Ibid., p. 21.

54. Ibid., p. 16.

55. Harrison and Beck, 2003, p. 12.

56. Allen Beck and Darrell Gilliard, *Prisoners in 1994* (Washington, D.C.: U.S. Department of Justice, 1995), p. 10.

57. Harrison and Beck, 2003, p. 11.

58. Ibid., p. 2.

59. U.S. Department of Justice, Bureau of Justice Statistics, "Prisoners in 2000," http://www.ojp.usdoj.gov/bjs (accessed January 8, 2003).

60. Harrison and Karberg, 2003, p. 3.

61. Camp and Camp, 2002, p. 30.

62. Paige M. Harrison and Allen J. Beck, "Prisoners in 2002," *Bureau of Justice Statistics Bulletin,* July 2000 (revised August 27, 2003), p. 8.

63. Ibid.

64. Ibid., p. 9.

65. Harry Allen, Evelyn Parks, Eric Carlson, and Richard Seiter, *Program Models, Halfway Houses* (Washington, D.C.: U.S. Department of Justice, 1978).

66. Edmund R. McGarrell and Timothy Flanagan, *Sourcebook of Criminal Justice Statistics, 1984* (Washington, D.C.: U.S. Department of Justice, 1985).

67. Michael Welch, *Corrections: A Critical Approach* (New York: McGraw-Hill, 1996), p. 416.

68. Charles Logan, *Private Prisons: Cons and Pros* (New York: Oxford University Press, 1990), p. 20.

69. Harrison and Beck, 2003, p. 7.

70. Camp and Camp, 2002, p. 112.

71. Harrison and Beck, 2003, p. 9.

72. Voncile B. Gowdy, "Should We Privatize Our Prisons? The Pros and Cons," *Corrections Management Quarterly* 1, no. 2 (1997): 61.

Chapter 6

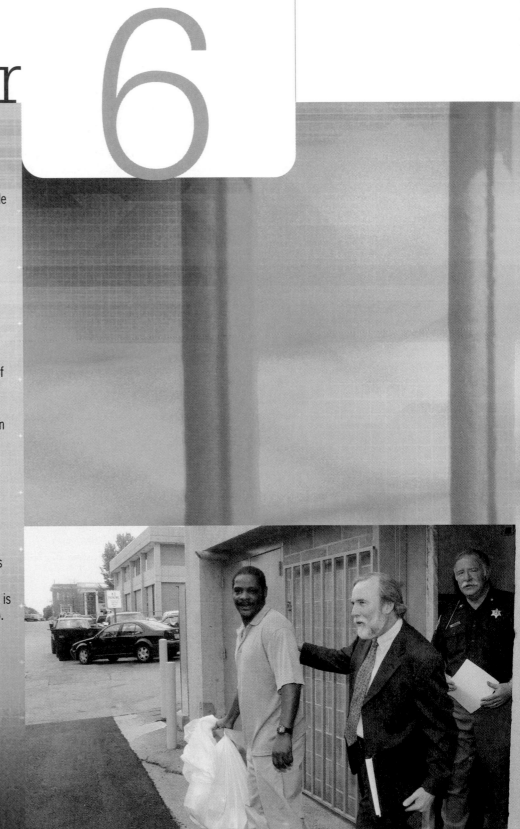

AFTER READING THIS CHAPTER, YOU SHOULD BE ABLE TO:

1. Describe the historical development of parole in America, and specify the role played by Maconochie and Crofton.

2. Explain the importance of the Elmira Reformatory in the early development of parole in America.

3. Discuss the operation of the medical model as it relates to the use of rehabilitation, indeterminate sentences, and parole in the United States.

4. Describe alternatives proposed to the use of parole and indeterminate sentences during the 1970s.

5. Compare and contrast the ways inmates can be released from prison, including parole, supervised mandatory release, and unconditional mandatory release.

6. Outline the use of parole guidelines using salient factor scores to determine parole readiness.

7. Describe the process of parole revocation and list the due process rights for offenders during this process.

8. Identify how the process of prisoner reentry is different today than it was twenty years ago.

9. List the collateral consequences of imprisonment, and discuss how they affect successful prisoner reentry.

Parole and Prisoner Reentry

KEY TERMS

parole
Alexander Maconochie
mark system
ticket of leave
Sir Walter Crofton
Zebulon R. Brockway
Elmira Reformatory
justice model
just deserts model
discretionary parole
supervised mandatory release
unconditional mandatory release
parole guidelines
salient factor score
hearing officers
presumptive parole date
positive contact
violation
Morrissey v. Brewer
prisoner reentry

Introduction

Throughout the history of the United States, prisons have held criminal offenders sentenced to their authority under many different sentencing structures. During the 1800s, prisoners served set amounts of time in crowded prisons, with little emphasis on rehabilitation or preparation for release. During the first half of the twentieth century, criminals continued to be confined in prisons under determinate sentences; however, there was a developing emphasis on work and some rehabilitative programs. By the middle of the twentieth century, prison sentences began to be for indeterminate terms, prisons accentuated rehabilitation programs, and parole board experts decided when prisoners would be released based on their readiness for returning to the community. This move to the use of parole was a major change in philosophy as well as sentence structure, and impacted not only prison operations, but the type of supervision that offenders received after release. This approach continued until the last two decades of the twentieth century.

Over the past twenty years, parole and indeterminate sentences have been abandoned in many states, and there has been a return to set, determinate sentences. Offenders are often limited in the amount of good time they can earn during their sentences, as truth-in-sentencing laws requiring the completion of 85 percent of the sentence before prisoners are released have been enacted and implemented in many states. This emphasis on holding offenders accountable through tough sentencing laws results in a focus on punishment, incapacitation, and deterrence. Prison rehabilitation programs are often reduced in importance, both to save money and to avoid making prisons too soft a punishment for crime. Many offenders are now released without the review of a parole board to determine readiness or consider the soundness of their release plans.

These changes make the status of prisoner reentry to the community very different from that of only a few decades ago. The number of releasees is greater, the majority are not released through parole, and they serve longer sentences. As well, they are less prepared to return to their communities, and their communities are less able to accommodate them. A large number of releasees are subsequently returned to prison, many for violating the technical conditions of their parole or release supervision rather than for the commission of a new crime.

This chapter reviews the development of parole in the United States and how it is administered for those states in which it is still in use. The release decision, supervision on parole, the violation process when offenders fail to meet their parole conditions, and the overall effectiveness of parole and indeterminate sentences are discussed. The challenge of reentry to the community is also described, and the types of challenges faced by returning prisoners is illustrated. There is also a review of the types of programs that help prisoners reenter the community, and examples of the types of programs that are used to both supervise and aid offenders as they leave prison and return to the community.

The History of Parole

The term *parole* is from the French word *parol,* meaning "word of honor." It was first used in the 1700s as a means of releasing prisoners of war upon their promise not to resume arms in the current conflict. This evolved to the modern meaning of **parole** as a conditional release of inmates by a parole board prior to the expiration of their sentence. While it is often thought that parole had no history in U.S. prisons until the mid-1900s, a much earlier use of conditional release influenced the development of parole as currently used. In colonial America, there was a shortage of labor, leading to the transportation of children and pardoned criminals from England to the American colonies to provide a ready workforce. As the pardoned criminals returned to England after serving their indentured time, specific condi-

Parole

the conditional release of inmates by a parole board prior to the expiration of their sentence tions for their freedom had to be created. Even with the end of the transportation of children and convicts to America after the Revolutionary War, the idea of a period of punishment and work followed by a requirement to meet conditions of freedom was established.

MACONOCHIE AND THE MARK SYSTEM

The more formal use of conditional release from prison most likely had its roots in 1840, when **Alexander Maconochie** became superintendent of the British penal colony on Norfolk Island, about 1,000 miles off the coast of Australia. Maconochie had been captured by the French while serving as a British naval officer, and was sensitive to the brutal way prisoners were often treated. Upon his appointment as superintendent, he decided to initiate a revolutionary philosophy of reforming the prisoner by instilling self-discipline with an emphasis on "punish for the past, and train for the future."

Since the amount of time necessary to instill self-discipline could not be estimated in advance, Maconochie advocated open-ended (indeterminate) sentences and a **mark system**. Instead of sentences for a specific amount of time, Maconochie required offenders to earn a specific number of marks based on the severity of the crime, and they would be released once they earned the required level of marks through work and good behavior. His system consisted of four stages on the way to release, each providing more personal liberty to the prisoner.[1] The *penal stage* emphasized punishment, and included solitary confinement and a diet of bread and water. The *associated stage* allowed inmates to associate and begin to earn marks through work, program participation, and good behavior. Poor behavior resulted in an increase in the number of marks required for release. The third stage was the *social stage*, in which inmates were grouped and held jointly responsible for the conduct of each other, as a way to begin the process of living responsibly in society. The final stage was a **ticket of leave**, in which prisoners earning the required level of marks received a conditional pardon and were released to the community.

Norfolk Island had deplorable conditions prior to the arrival of Maconochie. Hughes described conditions as so bad that "convicts would choose two men by drawing straws: one to die, the other to kill him . . . the killer and witnesses would have to be sent to Sydney for trial . . . a boon to the prisoners, who yearned for the meager relief of getting away from the ocean of hell."[2] The mark system worked well on Norfolk Island and brought tranquility to what had been a violent prison with regular riots. Unfortunately, his English overseers saw Maconochie's approach as "coddling" criminals, and he was relieved of his duty in 1844. After his return to England, Maconochie continued to write and encourage prison reform. In a review of some of Maconochie's writings, Morris noted that Maconochie desired to maintain a sanitary prison with adequate diet and decent treatment for prisoners. In his view, "punishment, allowing for and facilitating redemption, dignifies society, makes prison service a constructive occupation, and enhances public safety. By contrast, vengeance-based punishment, posing as effective deterrence, demeans society, makes torturers of prison guards, and lessens public safety."[3] Word of Maconochie's approach and system became widely known even after his dismissal, and influenced others, particularly Sir Walter Crofton.

WALTER CROFTON AND THE IRISH SYSTEM

Even though Maconochie was dismissed as superintendent of Norfolk Island, some of his ideas were later accepted, and the Penal Servitude Act, enacted by the British Parliament in 1853, enabled prisoners to be released on a ticket of leave and supervised by the police. In 1854, **Sir Walter Crofton** was appointed director of the

---

Alexander Maconochie

the superintendent of the British penal colony on Norfolk Island from 1841 to 1844 who created a system of marks for good behavior that could lead to a graduated release from prison

Mark system

credits against a sentence that allowed inmates to be released once they earned the required level of marks through work and good behavior

Ticket of leave

a form of release used by Maconochie; once prisoners earned the required level of marks, they received a conditional pardon and were released to the community

Sir Walter Crofton

the director of the Irish prison system, appointed in 1854, who began to implement many of the ideas of Maconochie's work

The concept of indeterminate sentences and parole were developed while Alexander Maconochie served as superintendent of the British penal colony on Norfolk Island between 1840 and 1844.
Courtesy of Hulton Archive/Getty Images.

Irish prison system and began to implement many of the ideas of Maconochie's work. He created the following four-stage system of graduated release from prison and return to the community:[4]

1. *Solitary confinement* of approximately nine months. Much like the first stage of Maconochie, it included an emphasis on punishment, little interaction with other prisoners, silence, chapel, and work.
2. *Special prison* in which the offender worked with other inmates and earned marks to gain privileges and move further toward release. Inmates also had to complete three conduct classes, taking up to twelve months.
3. *Open institution*—a transitional stage to society, with training on the freedoms and requirements of release and continued earning of marks to reach the fourth stage.
4. *Ticket of leave*—conditional release for the remainder of the sentence, and the first use of parole as it is known today. The police supervised offenders in rural Ireland, but Dublin had a civilian employee who worked with the police, but also secured employment for the released prisoners, visited their homes, and had them report to him. If they disobeyed the rules, the ticket of leave could be revoked.

These ideas and stages worked well. A report regarding 557 prisoners released during the 1850s noted that only seventeen had their tickets of leave revoked.[5] These stages of release and subsequent supervision in the community are the forerunners to the modern indeterminate sentence, parole officer supervision, and focus on finding employment as a key criterion for success. The Irish System was well received internationally, and many American penologists were soon campaigning to bring these ideas and procedures to the United States.

Parole Begins in the United States

With parole and indeterminate sentences still decades away, the idea of rewarding good behavior with reductions in the time served was initiated in 1817 when the New York legislature authored the first "good time" statute, allowing up to a 25 percent reduction in time served for good behavior and industrious work. Over the next fifty years, twenty-three states passed similar statutes authorizing the use of good time, which was seen as important in encouraging good behavior and preparing for successful release.[6]

In 1869, New York passed an act to build a reformatory in Elmira for youthful offenders, which would use indeterminate sentences and hold offenders until "reformed." In 1870, the American Prison Association was formed and held its first meeting in Cincinnati, Ohio. The major discussion was about the use of indeterminate sentences and the Irish parole system. One of the leading U.S. penologists, **Zebulon R. Brockway** of Michigan, presented a paper on the Irish System. The Association adopted a Declaration of Principles, promoting the use of the Irish System, parole, good time, and assistance to released prisoners in the United States. These reforms, when made public, were well received across the country. When the **Elmira Reformatory** opened in 1876, Brockway was appointed its superintendent. A system of classification allowing inmates to earn privileges for their work and behavior was implemented, and the reformatory was organized so that inmates spent much of their day in education programs and learning trades. Once inmates demonstrated reformation, prison administrators had the authority to conditionally release them to be supervised by state agents in the community.[7]

Over the next several decades, the use of parole increased, with many states adopting prison programs similar to those of the Elmira Reformatory. By 1900, twenty states had begun to use indeterminate sentences and to have correctional officials determine dates of inmate release by parole. In 1930, New York was the first state to develop an independent parole authority to make release decisions separate from the state department of corrections.[8] Even though the idea was solidly supported, the Great Depression was the real impetus for expansion of parole, as unemployment and Prohibition created a crime wave resulting in an increasing number of people being sent to prison. As prison populations grew and prisons became more overcrowded, states could not afford their operation, and looked to parole as a less expensive way to manage offenders. The number of offenders released annually on parole increased from 21,632 in 1923 to 37,794 in 1936.[9] By 1944, all states had adopted the use of parole and indeterminate sentences.[10]

Zebulon R. Brockway a leading American penologist in the mid-1800s who was a proponent of adopting the Irish System in the United States and who became the first superintendent of the Elmira Reformatory

Elmira Reformatory the first reformatory in the United States; it was opened in 1876 and used the principles of the Irish System, indeterminate sentences, and parole

PAROLE AND THE MEDICAL MODEL

As indicated in Chapter 1, after World War II, the country began to recognize the value of the scientific approach to solving problems, and incorporated this model into dealing with crime and criminals. The medical model of corrections was adopted as the dominant theory influencing prison practices. The medical model assumed that offenders were inflicted with an environmental or psychosocial condition that was the underlying reason for their criminality. Under the belief that offenders were sick, when they were sentenced to prison, their problems were diagnosed and a treatment plan was developed by prison officials who were experts in a variety of areas, such as education, vocational training, and mental health issues. The prison treatment continued until another group of experts (the parole board) determined that the "patient" could no longer benefit from institutional treatment and was ready for release and return to the community.

The medical model perfectly fit the use of indeterminate sentences and parole. Offenders were sentenced to open-ended sentences, with the minimum term

Rehabilitative programs with conditional release was a key element of the operation of the Elmira Reformatory under superintendent Zebulon Brockway.
Courtesy of Corbis/Bettmann.

As reformatories were opened, they stressed education of youthful offenders.
Courtesy of the Ohio Department of Rehabilitation and Correction.

determined to meet society's need for punishment, deterrence, and incapacitation. After they met this threshold level of the sentence term, their release depended on how well their treatment plan worked to remedy their deficiencies and prepare them for successful return to the community. A parole board of rehabili-

With the medical model of corrections, classification of inmates involved many professionals to evaluate the inmate and plan a treatment program.
Courtesy of the Federal Bureau of Prisons.

tative experts was believed well suited to determine when inmates' treatments were complete and what would be optimal times for release from prison and supervision in the community. In most cases, treatment continued in the community under the supervision of parole officers.

Under this indeterminate sentencing structure, parole served many positive functions. First, dangerous inmates could be incarcerated for longer periods of time than if they had a determinate sentence, which would usually be shorter than the maximum time allowable under an indeterminate sentence. Parole boards regularly require dangerous, high-risk inmates to serve the maximum sentence. Colorado abolished parole as a release mechanism in 1979, but reinstated it after finding out that the length of prison sentences served was decreasing, particularly for high-risk offenders. Second, parole boards act as gatekeepers to ensure that inmates have sound release plans for their return to the community. For inmates to be released they must have a place to live and address their possibilities of finding a job. If they have no community contacts, inmates are often released to a halfway house or given more time to develop a release plan. However, when a determinate sentence ends, there is usually no way to delay a release due to an insufficient plan.

Third, the fact that a parole board will review inmates is an incentive for good behavior and program participation by inmates. Opponents of parole criticize program participation that is done to impress the parole board, and suggest that program participation with no implied coercion will be more effective. Halleck argued that it was almost impossible to distinguish between fully voluntary and coercive treatment participation, especially in a correctional setting in which decisions affecting offenders' parole considered such participation.[11] Morris, in *The Future of Imprisonment*, asserted that rehabilitation is a valuable correctional goal, yet it could not be effective if seen as coercive by offenders, or if they saw it as an element of the punishment they were receiving for their criminal offenses.[12] And Irwin argued that inmates viewed decisions of the parole board as arbitrary, capricious, prejudicial, unpredictable, and not subject to review by an external body.[13] However, there has been no evidence that nonvoluntary program participation was less effective than participation with some coercion.

A final positive function of parole is that consideration for release begins the process and creates guidelines for supervision and treatment needs in the community. Parole boards consider inmates' levels of risk and chances for success, and create conditions for supervision and treatment to respond to these risks and needs. Without parole, even with mandatory supervision following determinate sentencing release, supervision is often less individualized and based primarily on risk rather than need. Abadinsky suggests that the medical model is based on two questionable assumptions:

- Criminals are "sick" and can thus benefit from treatment/therapy.
- The behavioral sciences can provide the necessary treatment/therapeutic methods.[14]

Unfortunately, these two premises were seriously questioned during the 1970s.

ATTACKS ON THE MEDICAL MODEL AND PAROLE

The medical model came under attack during the early 1970s, partly precipitated after Robert Martinson and his colleagues attempted to determine what worked in correctional treatment. They reviewed 231 studies of correctional treatment programs, and while they found a few isolated correlations between a treatment program and a reduction in recidivism, there were no consistent findings of the effect of any single treatment program significantly reducing recidivism.[15] Therefore, the Martinson review concluded, "nothing works," which was just the support that opponents of the medical model and parole were looking for. For public officials desiring to reduce costs and make corrections more punitive, this study provided statistical support, and their arguments for a return to determinate sentences gained momentum.

New models for sentencing and release to replace parole began to be proposed by a variety of individuals with varied philosophical rationale. In 1975, David Fogel, a liberal former correctional official, argued that treatment in prison was a myth, and parole board discretion was unpredictable and unfair to inmates. He proposed the **justice model** as an alternative, in which he suggested the following:

- A return to flat, determinate sentences, with procedural rules to limit sentencing discretion.
- The elimination of parole boards and parole agencies.
- Making all treatment programs strictly voluntary.[16]

In 1976, conservative Andrew von Hirsch proposed the **just deserts model**, with a return to the classical model of criminology, letting the punishment fit the seriousness of the crime.[17] In this model, indeterminate sentences would be replaced with fixed sentences based solely on the severity of the crime, and not on any individual offender characteristics. Also in 1976, the Twentieth Century Task Force on Sentencing proposed presumptive sentencing.[18] A presumptive sentencing system provides a sentence for each category of crime that would be imposed for a typical first-time offender (similar to the just deserts model). However, with this model, the sentencing judge has limited discretion to consider mitigating and aggravating circumstances that would reduce or increase the presumptive sentence.

The "nothing works" findings of Martinson and the criticism of parole by both the political right (for being too soft on crime) and left (for unpredictability and unfairness) created momentum toward abolishing parole and indeterminate sentences. In 1977, the use of parole reached its peak, as more than 70 percent of prisoners were released on discretionary parole.[19] Over the next two decades, fifteen

TABLE	6.1	Abolition of Discretionary Parole

Jurisdiction abolishing parole	Year abolished
Maine	1975
Indiana	1977
Illinois	1978
Minnesota	1980
Florida	1983
Washington	1984
Federal government	1984
Oregon	1989
Delaware	1990
Kansas	1993
Arizona	1994
North Carolina	1994
Mississippi	1995
Virginia	1995
Ohio	1996
Wisconsin	1999

states and the federal government ended the use of indeterminate sentencing and **discretionary parole**, in which the decision to release the offender is made by a parole board (see Table 6.1). As well, twenty other states severely limited the parole-eligible population. Only fifteen states still have full discretionary parole for inmates. The move to determinate sentences was a primary reason why the prison population grew more rapidly than in any other period in the history of prisons.[20] From 1980 to 1996, the number of prisoners in state and federal prisons went from 330,000 to 1,054,000, a threefold increase,[21] and reached 1.38 million on January 1, 2001.[22]

Parole has gone through several changes and transitions in its support, operations, and processes. Today there are at least three major methods (or statuses) in which inmates are released from prison. No consistent terminology is used to describe the three release statuses from jurisdiction to jurisdiction. The first is the use of discretionary parole, or release from prison to community supervision by the decision of a parole board, after completing the minimum portion of an indeterminate sentence. Parolees are required to meet certain conditions as a stipulation of their release, and are subject to being returned to prison if they violate the conditions or commit another offense. A second status of inmate release is **supervised mandatory release** (also referred to as mandatory parole), the release of inmates after they have served a determinate sentence, but with a period of supervision in the community. Supervised mandatory release is a conditional release, as there are still requirements and conditions that must be met or fulfilled or offenders can be returned to prison. Finally, inmates can serve the full portion of their sentence, pay their full "debt to society," and have no supervision after release from prison. This status is often referred to as **unconditional mandatory release** or expiration of sentence.

The Bureau of Justice Statistics reports that the percentage of releasees from state prisons on discretionary parole has continued to decline since 1980, as mandatory parole and expiration of sentence releases increased (see Figure 6.1). In 1999, only 24 percent of inmates were released on discretionary parole, 41 percent were released conditionally under mandatory parole with supervision to follow, and 18 percent were unconditionally mandatory released after the expiration of their sentence with no supervision in the community.[23]

Discretionary parole

release of inmates in which the decision to release is made by a parole board

Supervised mandatory release

a type of release in which inmates serve a determinate sentence and then are released but with a period of supervision to follow

Unconditional mandatory release

a form of release in which inmates serve the full portion of their sentence and have no supervision after release from prison

RELEASES FROM STATE PRISON, BY METHOD OF RELEASE, 1980–1999

FIGURE **6.1**

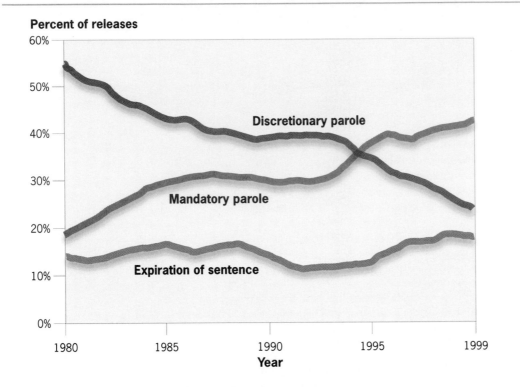

Source: Timothy A. Hughes, Doris James Wilson, and Allen J. Beck, *Trends in State Parole, 1990–2000* (Washington, D.C.: U.S. Department of Justice, Bureau of Justice Statistics, October 2001), p. 4.

ALTERNATIVES TO INDETERMINATE SENTENCING

The major emphasis of the move away from parole and indeterminate sentencing has been to limit discretion and to focus sentences more on offender accountability than on rehabilitation. Many of the states maintaining parole created mechanisms to ensure the consideration of community safety in parole board decisions. **Parole guidelines** were created as a means to reduce disparity and make decision making more understandable to the public and inmates. Parole guidelines, like sentencing guidelines, use predictive factors to determine the offenders' risk to the community and chance for success. Guidelines are then used to prescribe a presumptive time to be served based on the seriousness of the crime and the factors predictive of success for each inmate. The guidelines suggest a projected parole date after the inmate has served a set number of months, assuming good behavior during the prison term. Since guidelines are based on the severity of the sentence as well as factors predicting success, they focus on the "just deserts" form of sentencing.

The U.S. Parole Commission was the first to investigate the possibility of using guidelines during the mid-1970s, and was required to use guidelines beginning in 1976 by the Parole Commission and Reorganization Act (Public Law 94-233). To develop the guidelines, the commission hired a group of researchers to identify the factors available to parole board members that are most salient to success on parole. The researchers found several factors regarding the past history of offenses that are most predictive of success (or failure) after release. These factors are combined to find the **salient factor score** for inmates. The salient factors have been continually reviewed and validated. Figure 6.2 illustrates the most recent (1998)

Parole guidelines

similar to sentencing guidelines; guidelines that use predictive factors to determine offenders' risk to the community and chance for success; they prescribe a presumptive time to be served based on the seriousness of the crime and the factors predictive of success for each inmate

Salient factor score

a point determination for each inmate for use with parole guidelines; the score is based on factors predictive of success on parole

U.S. PAROLE COMMISSION SALIENT FACTOR SCORE SHEET　　　　　F I G U R E　**6 . 2**

SALIENT FACTOR SCORE (SFS 98)

Item A.　PRIOR CONVICTIONS/ADJUDICATIONS *(ADULT OR JUVENILE)* . . . .
None = 3; One = 2; Two or three = 1; Four or more = 0

Item B.　PRIOR COMMITMENT(S) OF MORE THAN 30 DAYS *(ADULT/JUVENILE)* . . . .
None = 2; One or two = 1; Three or more = 0

Item C.　AGE AT CURRENT OFFENSE/PRIOR COMMITMENTS . . . .

26 years or more	Three or fewer prior commitments	= 3
	Four prior commitments	= 2
	Five or more commitments	= 1
22–25 years	Three or fewer prior commitments	= 2
	Four prior commitments	= 1
	Five or more commitments	= 0
20–21 years	Three or fewer prior commitments	= 1
	Four prior commitments	= 0
19 years or less	Any number of prior commitments	= 0

Item D.　RECENT COMMITMENT FREE PERIOD *(THREE YEARS)* . . . .
No prior commitment of more than 30 days (adult or juvenile) or released to the community from last such commitment at least 3 years prior to the commencement of the current offense = 1; Otherwise = 0

Item E.　PROBATION/PAROLE/CONFINEMENT/ESCAPE STATUS VIOLATOR THIS TIME . . .
Neither on probation, parole, confinement, or escape status at the time of the current offense; nor committed as a probation, parole, confinement, or escape status violator this time = 1; Otherwise = 0

Item F.　OLDER OFFENDERS . . . .
If the offender was 41 years of age or more at the commencement of the current offense (and the total score from Items A–F above is 9 or less) = 1; Otherwise = 0

TOTAL SCORE . . . .

Source: U.S. Parole Commission, *Rules and Procedures Manual* (Washington, D.C.: U.S. Parole Commission, 1998).

listing of six elements used to predict success. Each inmate is scored on the list of salient factors. The sum of the six factors is the score predicting success, with higher scores indicating a lower probability of recidivism.

The salient factor score is then inserted into the guidelines table (Figure 6.3). The categories of offenses are based on the severity of the crime. The combination of the offense severity and parole prognosis (salient factor score) then gives a guideline range of the number of months that should be served before release. As an example, for an offender in Category Five (which includes bank robbery and intent to sell hard drugs) who had a salient factor score of 6, the guidelines suggest a range of 36 to 48 months served before release. The parole board can consider other mitigating or aggravating circumstances of the offense or offender to set the release date within the guideline range.

After the federal government developed and began using guidelines, many states adopted similar guidelines for their parole decision making. Guidelines continually focus on the risk of the offender and make it more difficult to release offenders on parole. This overprediction of dangerousness results in the buildup of prison populations by increasing the amount of time that inmates serve prior to release.[24]

U.S. PAROLE COMMISSION GUIDELINES FOR DECISION MAKING

GUIDELINES FOR DECISION MAKING
[Guidelines for Decision Making, Customary Total Time
to Be Served before Release (Including Jail Time)]

OFFENSE CHARACTERISTICS	OFFENDER CHARACTERISTICS: Parole Prognosis (Salient Factor Score 1998)			
Severity of Offense Behavior	Very Good (10–8)	Good (7–6)	Fair (5–4)	Poor (3–0)
Category One	Guideline Range <=4 months	<=8 months	8–12 months	12–16 months
Category Two	Guideline Range <=6 months	<=10 months	12–16 months	16–22 months
Category Three	Guideline Range <=10 months	12–16 months	18–24 months	24–32 months
Category Four	Guideline Range 12–18 months	20–26 months	26–34 months	34–44 months
Category Five	Guideline Range 24–36 months	36–48 months	48–60 months	60–72 months
Category Six	Guideline Range 40–52 months	52–64 months	64–78 months	78–100 months
Category Seven	Guideline Range 52–80 months	64–92 months	78–110 months	100–148 months
Category Eight*	Guideline Range 100+ months	120+ months	150+ months	180+ months

*Note: For Category Eight, no upper limits are specified due to the extreme variability of the cases within this category.

Source: U.S. Parole Commission, *Rules and Procedures Manual* (Washington, D.C.: U.S. Parole Commission, 1998).

PROBLEMS WITH MOVING AWAY FROM INDETERMINATE SENTENCES

While there are some valid reasons to adopt determinate sentences, there are also many problems with moving away from parole and indeterminate sentences, and often a poor fit between theory and practice in regards to "getting tough on criminals." These include the following:

1. With determinate sentences, inmates often serve shorter sentences and smaller portions of the sentence than with parole. Parole boards consider the dangerousness of offenders and often hold them in prison well beyond their minimum eligibility for parole.
2. Without parole, there are few ways to hold inmates accountable for misconduct in prison. Prison administrators miss the control and emphasis on prison discipline that resulted from inmates trying to have a good record to take before the parole board.
3. While elimination of parole does reduce discretionary release decisions, prosecutorial discretion is just substituted for correctional discretion. One of the problems with prosecutorial discretion is that it is exercised in private, and there is no review or public consideration of the use of plea bargaining.
4. One of the advantages of the use of parole boards is that they can reduce disparity in sentencing decisions by individual judges if there are no sentencing guidelines.
5. Parole boards, while they do not admit to consciously trying to do so, can act as a safety valve for prison overcrowding. In more formal ways, parole boards have been used to identify the most deserving inmates for release when there is a need to do so due to prison crowding.[25]
6. In some states (such as Maine), abolishing parole has also included abolishing supervision after release.

The Current Status of Parole in the United States

Parole and community supervision is still a very important function in several states. In fact, the number of offenders under state parole or mandatory release supervision at year-end 2002 was 753,141, which was almost a fourfold increase in the number of parolees or other postrelease supervision offenders in 1980,[26] and a 2.8 percent increase over the year-end 2001 total.[27] Nearly all of these offenders (96 percent) had been convicted of a felony and sentenced to incarceration of more than 1 year. Similar to the makeup of the adult prison population, a high percentage of minorities are under community supervision, with approximately 39 percent of parolees white, 42 percent black, and 18 percent Hispanic at the end of 2002. Women made up about 14 percent of all parolees. The percentage of women in the parole population in 2002 increased significantly since 1990, when women represented 8 percent of the parolee population.

This 2.8 percent growth during 2002 is larger than the average annual growth (1.5 percent) in the number of parolees since 1995 (see Table 6.2). For the year ending December 31, 2002, twelve states reported an increase of 10 percent or more in their parole populations, led by North Dakota with a 27 percent increase, followed by New Mexico (26 percent), Kentucky (23 percent), and Oklahoma (21 percent). In 2001, Oklahoma had an 87 percent increase, which is highly unusual and resulted from a change in law in 2000 that previously required the governor to personally sign parole certificates, resulting in a slow level of parole release and a severe budget problem with keeping inmates in prison several extra months before the parole certificate was signed. Eighteen states reported a decrease in their adult parole populations during 2002, with Washington declining by 39 percent, and three other states (South Carolina, Florida, and Vermont) declining by between 10 and 14 percent.[28]

TABLE	6.2	Change in the Number of Adults on Parole, 1995–2002

	Annual increase	
Year	**Number**	**Percent change**
1995	−10,950	−1.6%
1996	312	0.0
1997	15,054	2.2
1998	1,598	0.2
1999	18,072	2.6
2000	9,441	1.3
2001	8,435	1.2
2002	20,808	2.8
Total increase, 1995–2002	73,720	11.0%
Average annual increase, 1995–2002	8,967	1.5%

Source: Lauren E. Glaze, *Probation and Parole in the United States, 2002* (Washington, D.C.: U.S. Department of Justice, Bureau of Justice Statistics, August 2003), p. 5.

Table 6.3 illustrates the number of adults on parole, the entries and exits, the percent change during 2002, and the number of parolees per 100,000 population in state and federal jurisdictions during 2002.

Operations of Parole

The sentencing and release process for discretionary parole includes three major steps: (1) an indeterminate sentence with a minimum time to serve before parole eligibility and a maximum term to be served if not paroled; (2) consideration of release by a parole board authorized to conditionally release offenders; and (3) supervision in the community under specific conditions. When inmates complete their minimum term, there is no guarantee that they will be released from prison. In fact, in the 1979 case of *Greenholz v. Inmates of the Nebraska Penal and Correctional Complex,* the U.S. Supreme Court determined that parole was legally considered a privilege and not a right, and full due-process rights need not be afforded.[29] If offenders are not granted parole at their first eligibility, the parole board continues them until a later time, when they will again receive a hearing and consideration of release. This process can be repeated until an inmate either is paroled or reaches the maximum sentence term.

THE ORGANIZATION OF PAROLE BOARDS

Parole authorities can cover either or both of the two major parole functions: the release decision and postrelease supervision. In some states, two separate agencies are responsible for each of these parole functions. In others, the state department of corrections assumes responsibility for both functions. A third model is a separate parole decision-making authority, with parolees supervised by the state department of corrections. An important feature in the organization of parole decision making is that the parole board is independent from the administrators of the prisons. This can create problems if parole board members do not understand the programs provided within the prisons and what certain actions by prison officials may mean regarding an inmate's behavior and readiness for release. However, it would be a much greater problem if the parole board were overly influenced by prison staff opinions of the inmate. Boards are to independently consider the seriousness of the crime, the risk to the community, the

TABLE	6.3	Adults on Parole, 2002

Region and jurisdiction	Parole population, 1/1/2002	2002 Entries	2002 Exits	Parole population, 12/31/2002	Percent change, 2002	Number on parole per 100,000 adult residents 12/31/2002
U.S. total	732,333	468,506	447,991	753,141	2.8%	350
Federal	78,113	32,200	27,985	82,972	6.2%	39
State	654,220	436,306	420,006	670,169	2.4	311
Northeast	162,971	69,473	58,624	173,803	6.6%	421
Connecticut	2,126	2,060	1,931	2,255	6.1	86
Maine	31	1	0	32	3.2	3
Massachusetts[a]	3,718	3,715	3,698	3,718	—	—
New Hampshire[b]	953	480	470	963	1.0	101
New Jersey	11,931	10,812	10,829	11,914	−0.1	183
New York	56,719	24,416	25,145	55,990	−1.3	384
Pennsylvania[c]	86,238	27,245	15,771	97,712	13.3	1,037
Rhode Island	355	459	392	422	18.9	52
Vermont[b]	900	285	388	797	−11.4	171
Midwest	104,705	92,549	83,764	113,490	8.4%	234
Illinois[d]	30,148	33,498	28,188	35,458	17.6	377
Indiana	5,339	6,364	5,826	5,877	10.1	128
Iowa	2,614	2,574	2,278	2,910	11.3	131
Kansas[d]	3,991	4,528	4,529	3,990	0.0	199
Michigan	16,501	11,175	10,028	17,648	7.0	236
Minnesota	3,156	3,577	3,330	3,403	7.8	91
Missouri	12,864	10,515	9,846	13,533	5.2	320
Nebraska	530	763	719	574	8.3	45
North Dakota	117	373	341	149	27.4	31
Ohio	17,885	11,828	11,860	17,853	−0.2	209
South Dakota	1,437	1,131	896	1,672	16.4	299
Wisconsin[e]	10,123	6,223	5,923	10,423	3.0	256
South	224,269	94,772	97,917	220,409	−1.7%	285
Alabama[b]	5,663	2,162	2,516	5,309	−6.3	158
Arkansas	11,357	6,285	5,964	11,678	2.8	577
Delaware	530	262	241	551	4.0	91
District of Columbia[b]	4,506	2,668	1,877	5,297	—	1,147
Florida	5,891	4,369	4,732	5,138	−12.8	40
Georgia	20,809	10,376	9,948	20,912	0.5	331
Kentucky[d]	4,885	3,434	2,316	6,003	22.9	194
Louisiana	23,330	13,573	13,486	23,417	0.4	715
Maryland	13,415	7,478	7,622	13,271	−1.1	325
Mississippi[d]	1,788	912	884	1,816	1.6	87
North Carolina	2,954	3,341	3,490	2,805	−5.0	44
Oklahoma[b]	3,406	1,827	1,113	4,120	21.0	159
South Carolina	4,161	857	1,456	3,562	−14.4	116
Tennessee	8,074	3,023	3,164	7,933	−1.7	181
Texas[b]	107,688	30,506	35,126	103,068	−4.3	654
Virginia	4,873	3,006	3,349	4,530	−7.0	82
West Virginia	939	693	633	999	6.4	71

(continued)

TABLE	6.3	Continued				

Region and jurisdiction	Parole population, 1/1/2002	2002 Entries	2002 Exits	Parole population, 12/31/2002	Percent change, 2002	Number on parole per 100,000 adult residents 12/31/2002
West	162,275	179,512	179,701	162,467	0.1%	336
Alaska	522	305	319	508	−2.7	112
Arizona[b]	5,143	6,928	4,130	7,941	—	198
California	117,903	149,234	154,335	113,185	−4.0	439
Colorado	5,733	4,738	4,256	6,215	8.4	184
Hawaii	2,608	1,065	1,148	2,525	−3.2	268
Idaho	1,657	1,274	968	1,961	18.3	204
Montana[d]	710	681	546	845	19.0	124
Nevada	4,025	2,203	2,257	3,971	−1.3	246
New Mexico	1,562	2,305	1,905	1,962	25.6	146
Oregon	18,290	8,233	7,216	19,307	5.6	727
Utah	3,410	2,245	2,273	3,382	−0.8	213
Washington[b]	155	10	70	95	−38.7	2
Wyoming	557	291	278	570	2.3	154

Note: Because of incomplete data, the population on December 31, 2002, does not equal the population on January 1, 2002, plus entries, minus exits.

—Not calculated.

[a]Data were not reported for 2002. All counts were based on data for 2001.

[b]All data were estimated.

[c]Data for entries and exits were estimated for nonreporting agencies.

[d]Excludes parolees in one of the following categories: absconder, out of State, or inactive.

[e]Data are for the year ending November 30, 2002.

Source: Lauren E. Glaze, *Probation and Parole in the United States, 2002* (Washington, D.C.: U.S. Department of Justice, Bureau of Justice Statistics, August 2002), p. 5.

chance for success, and institutional conduct and program participation as elements of their decision.

For the past several decades, almost all parole boards consist of full-time employees of the state, and in most states, the governor appoints parole board members. The size of the parole board can vary, from two members in Minnesota to nineteen in New York.[30] Historically, governors would appoint experts in criminology, social work, or community reintegration to best determine when offenders were rehabilitated and able to return to the community. In fact, the 1967 report of the President's Crime Commission recommended the appointment of parole board members on merit, including qualifications for prospective members of "broad academic background, especially in the behavioral sciences."[31] However, with the era of "tough on crime" attitudes and offender accountability, this has changed, and over the past twenty years the appointment of parole board members has become much more of a political decision.

As a result of parolees committing highly publicized crimes in the community, governors became very concerned about the impression of being soft on crime and letting dangerous criminals out of prison too early. Therefore, they often began to appoint less qualified (in terms of having a background in corrections or rehabilitation), yet politically connected individuals who can represent the governor's views on crime and community safety rather than focusing on inmate preparation for release. While this may be perceived as very reasonable, the practical problem is that there is no guarantee that any offender will be successful and avoid further criminality, and therefore every parole decision represents a political and community safety risk. As a result of the change in philosophy by parole boards, they are less likely to approve offenders for parole, and the average sentence served has increased as a result. In fact, inmates receiving parole in 1999 had served an average of thirty-five months when first paroled, while those paroled in 1990 served an average of twenty-nine months.[32] The "An Insider's Experience" box illustrates the unique situation in Ohio regarding parole board appointments.

The Ohio Parole Board is an example of a parole board whose members have historically been appointed on the basis of their correctional qualifications instead of political contacts.
Courtesy of the Ohio Department of Rehabilitation and Correction.

AN INSIDER'S EXPERIENCE: Appointing Parole Board Members

One unusual organizational approach in the appointment of parole board members exists in Ohio, in which the director of the department of corrections appoints the parole board members, and there is a statutory requirement that members have a background and be qualified in corrections and criminal justice. When I was the director of the Ohio Department of Rehabilitation and Correction during the 1980s, there had been a few instances of parolees committing serious crimes when under state supervision, and parole was coming under attack. A staff person for the Ohio governor solicited my opinion as to whether the statute should be changed to have parole board members appointed by the governor. I believed that it was better to have the board continue to be ap-

pointed by and report to the director of corrections. This would continue the practice of having a professional parole board with less concern for the political fallout of their decisions. I advised the governor's representative of this, but also made the point that in the current system, since I appointed the parole board, the public saw me as responsible for parolees that failed. If the governor appointed the board members, crimes committed by parolees would then be seen as the responsibility (and fault) of the governor. Any outcry for heinous crimes committed would be the responsibility of the governor to resolve. This got the attention of the staff person, and the governor decided to continue the practice of the director appointing board members. This practice continues to this day.

THE PAROLE HEARING

In some states, the actual parole board members hold parole hearings in the prisons, while in other states, **hearing officers** conduct the hearings and recommend decisions to the parole board, which confirms or modifies the decision. A few weeks after the hearing, the parole decision is communicated to the inmate in writing through the prison staff. While it is unusual to have the final decision made and announced to the inmate at the hearing, some procedures allow the hearing officers or board members conducting the hearing to immediately inform the inmate of their recommendation.

The hearing procedures vary by state. While inmates are not provided full due process during a parole hearing, a few states allow inmates to have legal representation. At the beginning of the hearing, the board members or hearing officers review the file or records regarding the inmate, and complete the parole guidelines if they are used in the jurisdiction. The prison staff usually provide a summary report of the inmate's background, criminal history, and performance while in prison. In most states, they do not make a recommendation regarding parole. The board also considers outside opinions from the inmate's family, law enforcement professionals, or victims regarding the inmate's parole. Some states allow victims to appear at the hearing, while others provide victims the chance to provide input in writing or through a personal meeting with board members prior to the parole hearing.

During hearings, inmates are asked to provide some background as to why they committed the crime, what they have done while in prison, and why they believe they are now ready to return to the community as productive and law-abiding citizens. The board also reviews and questions inmates regarding their release plans. The board is primarily interested in the inmates' plans for housing, employment, and continued participation in necessary treatment programs. Prior to the hearing, prison staff assist inmates in developing release plans, and these plans are forwarded to field parole offices for investigation into the validity of the plan.

After reviewing all material, hearing from the inmate, and receiving any outside input, parole boards decide whether to grant inmates parole at that time, or "continue" them (to serve a longer period of time) until a later date. Some parole boards

Hearing officers

correctional professionals who are not appointed members of the parole board, yet for efficiency they hold parole hearings and make a recommendation to the parole board regarding inmates' release

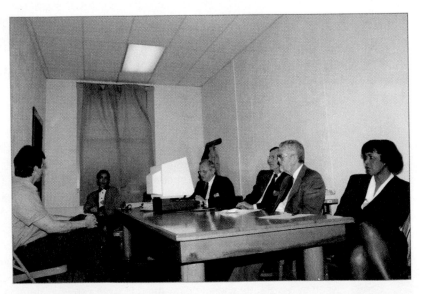

Inmates appear before a parole board, and board members question them to determine whether they are ready to be released to the community.
Courtesy of the Ohio Department of Rehabilitation and Correction.

give presumptive parole dates at the first hearing in many states; they hold the first hearing shortly after the inmate's incarceration, even before parole eligibility. A **presumptive parole date** is a date the inmate can expect to be released on parole, even if it is several years later than the hearing. The presumption is that if inmates have good institutional conduct and program participation, they will be granted parole at that date. As the date nears, the prison staff provide the parole board a report as to the inmate's conduct and program participation. If the behavior and programming are as expected, the board confirms the date in writing without another hearing. If the board has some concerns regarding the inmate's prison performance, it may schedule a hearing and thereafter make a decision as to whether to parole or continue the inmate. If performance has been poor, the board may do a continuance without a hearing, and either reset another presumptive date or set a date for a later hearing.

Decisions regarding parole are seldom simple. The "You Make the Decision" box illustrates this point.

Presumptive parole date
a date on which the inmate can expect to be released on parole, even if it is five or ten years later than the hearing

YOU MAKE THE DECISION . . .

PAROLE OR NOT?

The following scenarios represent the types of cases that can come before a parole board. Students should consider the situation in each case and determine what decision they would make regarding the individual's parole.[33]

Inmate A was convicted of vehicular manslaughter and received a sentence of seven years. He killed two teenagers in a head-on collision. He had been drinking, but his blood-alcohol content was below the limit. The inmate has never been arrested for any other offenses. He is 21 years old and was a senior in college when the offense occurred. He has been an excellent inmate and is a tutor in school. The victims' families are opposing parole. He has served ten months on the sentence. The minimum time he must serve is thirteen months. His conditional release date is fifty-six months. How much time should he serve?

Inmate B is a 31-year-old male who committed two burglaries and received two ten-year sentences running concurrently. He has two prior prison incarcerations. One is for stealing and the other is first degree burglary. He is a severe drug addict who has strong family ties. He has received his GED while incarcerated. His minimum mandatory prison term is five years, and he has served three years. His conditional release date is at seven years. How much time should he serve in all?

Inmate C is a 19-year-old female who has sold a large quantity of cocaine with no prior incarcerations. She has a prior probation for possession of drugs and is pregnant. She indicated that she is not a drug user but sold drugs because she needed money. She has a ninth-grade education and is going to school to get her GED. She has a five-year sentence with a minimum eligibility of twenty months. The conditional release date is at forty months and she has served six months. How much time should she serve in all?

Inmate D has a five-year sentence for felony DWI. He has two prior convictions and served time in jail for one of the offenses. He was on probation for DWI and this probation was revoked for the commission of this present DWI. He is 35 years old, married with two children. He works steadily when he is in the community. He has been in an inpatient alcohol treatment program before and also attends AA in prison. He states that he had been sober for 1 year when this present DWI occurred. He is illiterate, is attending school, but is having a difficult time grasping the work. He has served six months and his minimum eligibility is nine months. The conditional release date is at forty months. How much time should he serve in all?

Inmate E has a ten-year sentence for rape after being found guilty by a jury. He has never been in trouble before and the victim of the offense was a woman that he took out on a date and then raped. He denies it was rape and indicated that she consented. He is divorced with two

(continued)

children. He has never been in trouble before and is in business for himself. His family is taking care of his business. He has had difficulty adjusting in prison and has had a few minor violations. He has a tenth-grade education. He refuses to go to school. He has served six years and has a minimum eligibility of eight and a half years. How much time should he serve?

Inmate F has a thirty-year sentence for killing her husband. She states that her husband had beaten her during their fifteen-year marriage and there was some evidence that she had called the police and stated her husband had hit her but denied the accusations when the police came. She is 34 years old and has three children, who are being cared for by relatives. She has a college education. She has no prior arrests and no indication of prior assaultive behavior. She has served eight years and the minimum eligibility is ten years. There is opposition by the victim's family. Her conditional release date is at twenty-five years. How much time should she serve in all?

Inmate G has a twenty-five-year sentence for first-degree robbery. He was 16 years old when the offense occurred and was certified as an adult. He has a juvenile record and was in a juvenile institution for assaultive behavior for six months. He does not use drugs and there is family support. He has received his GED while incarcerated and is working in the furniture factory. He has had some minor violations and two major violations for assault. He has served ten years and his minimum eligibility has passed. His conditional release date is at twenty years. How much time should he serve in all?

Inmate H has a ten-year sentence for child molestation and the victim was his son. He was on probation for this offense when he was violated for failure to go to treatment. He is married and has the support of his wife, who is not the mother of his son. He is a high school graduate and is working in food service. He has served three years and his conditional release date is at seven years. How much time should he serve?

SUPERVISION AND CONDITIONS OF PAROLE

If the board grants parole (or if the inmate is granted supervised mandatory release), the inmate will also receive a list of conditions that must be followed during the period of supervision in the community. The list of conditions is similar to a contract between the parole board and the inmate. Inmates meeting the conditions can expect to be released from supervision successfully. However, if they violate conditions of supervision, they can expect to receive additional conditions or be returned to prison to serve more time on their sentence. There are two general types of parole conditions: *standard conditions* that are applicable to all parolees, and *special conditions* pertaining to that particular parolee. Standard conditions of parole are usually the same as the standard conditions for probation described in Chapter 4, including reporting to their parole officers and keeping them informed of any changes in employment, residence, or other status. Figure 6.4 represents the conditions for community supervision for the State of Ohio for offenders released after serving a term in prison. After the statement of conditions, there is a brief statement of the supervision plan or activities required during the period of supervision. At the bottom of the form, releasees sign the conditions, indicating that they have received and understand the expectations of their supervision.

Special conditions of parole are again similar to special conditions of probation, such as a requirement for drug or alcohol counseling and testing, vocational training, mental health counseling, other treatment programs, avoiding a particular person or group of people, residing in a halfway house, or being placed under electronic monitoring. The parole board considers the specific characteristics of each inmate when imposing special conditions that can add to the monitoring of the parolee, improve his or her rehabilitation and chance for success, or increase community safety.

STATE OF OHIO
Department of Rehabilitation and Correction
Adult Parole Authority
CONDITIONS OF SUPERVISION

In consideration of having been granted supervision on ____ /____ /____ , I agree to report to my supervising officer according to the instructions I have received and the following conditions:

1. I will obey federal, state and local laws and ordinances, including Chapter 2923 of the Revised Code relating to conduct involving firearms and other deadly weapons, and all orders, rules and regulations of _____ County Common Pleas Court or the Department of Rehabilitation and Correction. I agree to conduct myself as a responsible law abiding citizen. I understand that if I am convicted of a new felony offense while under Post Release Control, the Court may impose an additional prison term consecutive to any prison sentence imposed for the new felony offense.

2. I will always keep my supervising officer informed of my residence and place of employment. I will obtain permission from my supervising officer before changing my residence or my employment. I understand that if I am a releasee and abscond supervision, I may be prosecuted for the crime of escape, under section 2921.34 of the Revised Code.

3. I will not leave the State of Ohio without written permission of the Adult Parole Authority.

4. I will not enter the grounds of any correctional facility nor attempt to visit any prisoner without the written permission of my supervising officer. I will not communicate with any prisoner in any manner without obtaining permission from my supervising officer.

5. I will follow all orders verbal or written given to me by my supervising officer or other authorized representatives of the Court or the Department of Rehabilitation and Correction.

6. I will not purchase, possess, own, use or have under my control, any firearms, ammunition, dangerous ordinance or weapons, including chemical agents, electronic devices used to immobilize, pyrotechnics and/or explosive devices.

7. I will not purchase, possess, use or have under my control any narcotic drug or other controlled substance or illegal drugs, including any instrument, device or other object used to administer drugs or to prepare them for administration, unless it is lawfully prescribed for me by a licensed physician. I agree to inform my supervising officer promptly of any such prescription and I agree to submit to drug testing if required by the Adult Parole Authority.

8. I will report any arrest, citation of a violation of the law, conviction or any other contact with a law enforcement officer to my supervising officer no later than the next business day. I will not enter into any agreement or other arrangement with any law enforcement agency which might place me in the position of violating any law or condition of my supervision, unless I have obtained permission in writing from the Adult Parole Authority, or from the Court.

9. I agree to a search, without warrant, of my person, my motor vehicle, or my place of residence by a supervising officer or other authorized representative of the Department of Rehabilitation and Correction at any time. *Notice: Pursuant to section 2967.131 of the Revised Code, Officers of the Adult Parole Authority may conduct warrantless searches of your person, your place of residence, your personal property, or any property which you have been given permission to use if they have reasonable grounds to believe that you are not abiding by the law or terms and conditions of your supervision.*

10. I agree to sign a release of confidential information from any public or private agency if requested to do so by a supervising officer.

11. I agree not to associate with persons having a criminal background and/or persons who may have gang affiliation, or who could influence me to engage in criminal activity, without the prior permission of my supervising officer.

12. I agree to comply with all financial obligations, including child support and/or supervision fees as ordered by any court and/or the Department of Rehabilitation and Correction.

13. I agree to give all information regarding my financial status to assist in determining my ability to pay specific financial obligations, to my supervising officer.

DRC 3019 (Rev 02/03)

(continued)

14. I agree to follow all rules and regulations of treatment facilities or programs of any type in which I am placed or ordered to attend while under the jurisdiction of the Court, and/or Department of Rehabilitation and Correction.

15. I agree to fully participate in, and successfully complete, the following indicated Sanctions/Special conditions:

16. I agree and understand that if I am arrested in any other state or territory of the United States or in any foreign country, my signature as witnessed at the end of the page will be deemed to be a waiver of extradition and that no other formalities will be required for an authorized agent of the State of Ohio to bring about my return to this state.

I understand that I am required to pay the Financial Obligations listed. Failure to do so will negate any eligibility for an early termination of supervision and result in civil suit by the Attorney General's Office.

Financial Obligations

Type	Supervision Fees	Fines	Restitution	Court Costs	Child Support	Other
Amount						
Payment Frequency						
Completion Date						

I understand that I have a grievance process available to me and may request a grievance form from my supervising officer at any time, *However,* I also understand that I may not grieve Parole Board or Court Ordered Special Conditions and/or Sanctions, being arrested for supervision violations, failure to follow directions/instructions of my supervising officer, the final decision of previous grievances, complaints unrelated to supervision, e.g., legislative action, judicial proceedings and sentencing, or any matter exclusively within the jurisdiction of the courts or other agencies, e.g. Human Services. The grievance procedure has been read and/or explained to me and I am indicating by my signature that I understand this process.

I have read or had read to me the conditions of my _____ . I fully understand these conditions and I agree to follow them. I understand that a violation of any of these conditions may result in the revocation of my _____ which may result in additional imposed sanctions, including imprisonment.

In addition, I understand that I must follow these conditions until notified by my supervising officer. By my signature I acknowledge that I have received a copy of these conditions of supervision. I further understand that I may request a meeting with my supervising officer or his/her supervisor if I feel any of the conditions or instructions are causing problems. I shall make this request in writing if at all possible.

I further acknowledge I understand that I am under the supervision of the Adult Parole Authority until I receive a certificate or journal entry terminating my period of supervision. Be advised, ORC 2967.16 (B) establishes the categories for final release from post release control as "favorable" or "unfavorable." If you receive an *unfavorable* final release from your post release control, this could result in an enhancement of any future felony sentence.

Witness:	Date:	Offender Signature:	Date:

Source: Ohio Department of Rehabilitation and Correction, Policy Manual 3019, revised August 2003.

Once offenders begin their terms of supervision, they are classified to determine their risk and needed frequency of contacts with their parole officer, the types of programs in which they should be involved, and any specific monitoring (such as intensive caseload or electronic monitoring) requirements. The purpose of classification is to assess the risk of the offender to commit further crimes and the need for treatment programs to improve their chance for success. Most states and the federal government use some type of objective classification instrument as a guide for supervision strategies. Figure 6.5 is an example of risk assessment for community supervision and the variety of characteristics regarding history of crime, employment, and alcohol or drug use that affect classification. Each characteristic is scored, and the total score then determines the classification level. A serious history of substance abuse, mental illness, or some other treatment need may result in an immediate designation to an intensive caseload.[34] Otherwise, the supervision level is based on their assessment score as follows:

Basic high	Risk score of 28 and above
Basic medium	Risk score of 11 to 27
Basic low	Risk score of 10 or below

Based on the classification level, supervision policy often requires a certain minimum frequency of contacts, but additional contacts can be required if they are deemed necessary to meet the supervision needs of the individual offender:

Intensive: Five contacts per month, with at least one positive contact. For substance abusers, there should also be four drug tests per month.

Basic High: Three contacts per month with at least one positive contact. Substance abusers should be tested three times per month.

Basic Medium: One contact per month. Substance abusers should be tested twice per month.

Basic Low: No contacts required, but the offender completes and submits a form listing his or her activities related to jobs, residences, and so on. For substance abusers, there is one drug test per month.[35]

A **positive contact** is a face-to-face contact with the offender by the officer, and other contacts are those in which significant information is collected (from the offender or an ancillary service such as a treatment provider or employer). Currently, however, many parole agencies no longer specify a set number of contacts per risk level. Instead, the parole officer develops a supervision plan unique to the individual need of the offender.

Positive contact
face-to-face contact between a parole officer and an offender

Similar to probation, parolees are placed on a special caseload, regular caseload, or intensive caseload. Special caseloads are for offenders with a special treatment need, such as mental health, substance abuse, or sex offenses. Intensive caseloads are also for offenders with a special treatment need; however, they are more commonly used for offenders with a high level of risk for reoffending. In addition, some states use electronic monitoring for a small portion of their parolees. In most jurisdictions, those under electronic monitoring are placed on a caseload with others under electronic monitoring. On January 1, 2002, 83.2 percent of parolees were on regular caseloads, 11.2 percent on intensive caseloads, 4.3 percent on special caseloads, and 1.3 percent on electronic monitoring.[36] Table 6.4 lists the average size for each of these four types of caseloads. The average size of intensive, special, and electronic monitoring parole caseloads are almost equal to the same caseload types for probation. However, there is a significant difference between the average regular caseload size for parole (73) and that for probation (133) during 2000. It seems reasonable that parole caseloads be smaller, since they are made up of more serious offenders who received a sentence of prison rather than probation. "Your Career is Connections" box describes the job of parole officers.

ASSESSMENT OF OFFENDER RISK

Offender Name:		Offender #:
Date:	F.U. Date:	Unit Location:
Officer (Last, First):		

Select the appropriate answer and enter the associated weight in the score column. Total all scores to arrive at the risk assessment score.

SCORE

Number of Prior Felony Convictions: ....
(or Juvenile Adjudications)
- 0 None
- 2 One
- 4 Two or more _____

Arrested Within Five (5) Years Prior to Arrest ....
for Current Offense (exclude traffic):
- 0 None
- 4 Yes _____

Age at Arrest Leading to First Felony Conviction: ....
(or Juvenile Adjudications)
- 0 24 and over
- 2 20–23
- 4 19 and under _____

Amount of Time Employed in the Last 12 Months:
(Prior to Incarceration for Parolees/PRC Offenders) .....
- 0 More than 7 months
- 1 5 to 7 months
- 2 Less than 5 months
- 0 Not applicable _____

Alcohol Usage Problems (Prior to Incarceration
for Parolees/PRC Offenders): ....
- 0 No interference with functioning
- 2 Occasional abuse; some disruption of functioning
- 4 Frequent abuse; serious disruption; needs treatment _____

Other Drug Usage Problems (Prior to Incarceration
for Parolees/PRC Offenders): ....
- 0 No interference with functioning
- 2 Occasional abuse; some disruption of functioning
- 4 Frequent abuse; serious disruption; needs treatment _____

Number of Prior Adult Incarcerations in a State
or Federal Institution: ....
- 0 0
- 3 1–2
- 6 3 and above _____

Age at Admission to Institution or Probation/Community
Control for Current Offense: ....
- 0 30 and over
- 3 18–29
- 6 17 and under _____

Number of Prior *Adult* Supervisions: ....
- 0 None
- 4 One or more _____

Number of Prior Probation/Community Control/Parole/
PRC Revocations Resulting in Imprisonment
(Adult or Juvenile): ....
- 0 None
- 4 One or more _____

TOTAL: _____

CLASSIFICATION CODE:

_____

1 INTENSIVE
2 BASIC HIGH (28 & above)
3 BASIC MEDIUM 11–27)
4 BASIC LOW (10 & below)
5 MONITORED TIME

OVERRIDE CODE:

_____

1 HIGHER
2 LOWER
3 NONE

IF OVERRIDE, SUPERVISORS INITIALS:

_____

DRC 3001 (7/97)   DISTRIBUTION: WHITE–Central Records   CANARY–District File

Source: Ohio Department of Rehabilitation and Correction, Policy Manual 3019, revised July 1997.

TABLE	6.4	Average Caseload per Officer during 2000 by Type of Caseload

Type of caseload	Average size of caseload
Regular	73
Intensive	25
Special	49
Electronic	33

Source: Adapted from Camille Graham Camp and George M. Camp, *The 2001 Corrections Yearbook: Adult Systems* (Middletown, Conn.: Criminal Justice Institute, 2002), p. 195.

YOUR CAREER IN CORRECTIONS

PAROLE OFFICERS

Parole officers are the line-level employees responsible for supervising parolees in the community from the time of their release until they either successfully leave supervision or have their parole revoked. Even though many states have abolished parole, almost all states still provide supervision after release. If not on parole, supervised offenders are often called mandatory releasees, and the supervision (by whatever the supervising officer is called) is the same as if on parole. The only difference is that the authority over the offender during supervision is usually held by the sentencing court, rather than by the parole board.

Officers usually have two primary tasks, supervision and investigations, with supervision making up approximately 80 percent of their responsibilities. Investigations determinate the adequacy of the proposed release plans. A prison staff member transmits the proposed plan (including residence, job possibilities, program needs) to the officer, who interviews the person the inmate proposes to live with, prospective employers, and potential program providers. A report on the plan is then sent to the parole board. If the plan is not satisfactory, the parole officer usually suggests an alternative plan (such as living at a halfway house) to allow the inmate to have an adequate plan upon release.

In many jurisdictions, supervision of both parolees and probationers is done jointly by the same agency, and many times by the same officers. Supervision entails scheduling offenders for office visits, visiting them in the community at their residence or job/program site, and interviewing significant individuals regarding offenders' progress and conduct. As well, officers may place offenders into needed programs, such as substance abuse, parenting classes, or vocational training, and some officers run counseling groups. If offenders violate the conditions of their supervision, the officer must begin the revocation process by preparing a report of the violation and possibly an arrest warrant. Later in the process, the officer may have to testify at a revocation hearing regarding offenders' behavior during supervision.

There are almost 6,000 parole officers in the United States, and another 15,000 who complete a combination of probation and parole officer tasks.[37] While a forty-hour week is standard, almost all officers (82.4 percent) report receiving overtime pay or compensatory time for hours in excess of the normal workweek.[38] Most states require a college degree, but no specific major is usually designated. The average starting salary for parole officers on January 1, 2001, was $31,465, and the average salary was $38,585.[39]

Parole officer jobs are challenging, yet can be very rewarding. There is considerable flexibility in hours worked and significant autonomy on how the job is done. Officers can have a major impact on the success of a parolee in the community. While many officers enjoy their jobs and maintain them throughout their working career, others see their jobs as great work experience and use them to move into other criminal justice career tracks.

Terminating Parole Supervision

The length of parole supervision following release from prison can vary from six months to several years. Parolees can either successfully or unsuccessfully terminate their period of supervision. *The Corrections Yearbook* reports a total of 155,951 parolees successfully terminated from supervision during 2000, with twenty-two months as the average time under supervision for successful terminations.[40] Most states allow for release from supervision before the end of the supervision period and before the date that ends the full maximum term of the inmate's sentence. In order for this to occur, the parole officer must write a recommendation detailing why the supervision should be terminated; the report is considered by the full board, which can agree and terminate supervision or disagree and continue the parolee's supervision. Unsuccessful terminations of parole result from revocation as a result of offenders' violating the conditions of their supervision.

Table 6.5 illustrates the percentage of successful parole discharges by various characteristics of the parolees. Overall, the rate of successful discharges increased from 33 percent in 1990 to 39 percent in 1999.[41] As would be expected, parolees granted parole at first consideration are more successful than those released at later consideration, and the longer time they serve in prison, the less their success rate following release. Very interesting, and discussed shortly, is the fact that inmates released under discretionary parole have a significantly higher success rate than those under mandatory parole. Another interesting point is the impact that California has on these rates. Figure 6.6 illustrates the change if California parole discharges are excluded from these rates.

REVOKING PAROLE

If offenders do not meet the required conditions of their parole or mandatory release supervision, the violations will be reported to the parole board, which will consider what action to take. For released prisoners under mandatory release supervision, some states have created an authority similar to a parole board to review success during supervision, while in other states the sentencing court continues to have jurisdiction during postprison supervision. There are two types of parole violations: *technical violations* of a standard or special condition of parole, and *new crime violations* when a conviction of a new crime occurs. When offenders commit

---

EXCLUDING CALIFORNIA PAROLE DISCHARGES

FIGURE **6.6**

Rates of successful termination higher when California is excluded

The size and make-up of California's parole population, combined with the low percent of successful terminations (25% in 1999), affect the national rate of success for parole discharges. If data from California are removed from the analysis, the comparative rates of success for discretionary and mandatory parole change dramatically.

Overall, California accounted for nearly 30% of all State parole discharges during 1999. Discretionary parole, though available as a method of release, is rarely used in California. In 1999 more than 99% of California's parole discharges had received mandatory parole.

When California data are excluded, the success rate for all parole discharges rises to 53% (from 42%), and the rate for mandatory parolees increases to 64% (from 33%) in 1999.

Percent successful among parole discharges in California and all other States, 1995–99

Year	California All parole	Parole in all other States		
		All	Mandatory	Discretionary
1995	22.7%	52.8%	64.0%	54.2%
1996	23.8	56.6	71.6	55.8
1997	22.8	55.9	67.2	55.8
1998	24.3	54.5	65.7	55.2
1999	25.2	53.3	63.9	53.9

Note: Based on prisoners with a sentence of more than 1 year who were released from State prison.

Source: Timothy A. Hughes, Doris James Wilson, and Allen J. Beck, *Trends in State Parole, 1990–2000,* (Washington, D.C.: U.S. Department of Justice, Bureau of Justice Statistics, October 2001), p. 12.

TABLE	6.5	Percentage of State Paroles Discharged Successfully, by Selected Characteristics, 1990 and 1999

	Percent successful	
Characteristic	1990	1999
Gender		
Male	35.9%	39.3%
Female	37.1	47.7
Race/Hispanic origin		
White non-Hispanic	44.1%	40.9%
Black non-Hispanic	33.2	39.0
Hispanic	31.0	50.6
Other	33.6	42.2
Age at parole discharge		
17 or younger	26.2%	42.9%
18–24	33.4	36.3
25–29	34.8	42.6
30–34	34.1	39.0
35–39	36.8	38.3
40–44	38.4	39.5
45–54	46.2	43.1
55 or older	56.6	54.5
Method of release		
Discretionary parole	51.6%	54.1%
Mandatory parole	23.8	33.1
Type of release		
First release	56.4%	63.5%
Re-release	14.6	21.1
Most serious offense		
Violent	39.1%	41.0%
Property	33.8	36.5
Drug	33.7	40.9
Public-order	46.1	47.1
Time served in prison*		
Less than 12 months	74.6%	74.0%
12–23 months	67.7	68.7
24–59 months	59.1	62.7
60 months or more	49.5	62.0

Note: Based on prisoners with a sentence of more than 1 year who were released from State prison. Data are from the *National Corrections Reporting Program*.

*First releases only.

Source: Timothy A. Hughes, Doris James Wilson, and Allen J. Beck, *Trends in State Parole, 1990–2000*, (Washington, D.C.: U.S. Department of Justice, Bureau of Justice Statistics, October 2001), p. 12.

a new crime, they can be prosecuted and sentenced for the crime, it is considered a violation of their original conditional release, and they can be processed as a parole violator in addition to the prosecution for the new offense.

When either type of violation occurs, a formal revocation process begins, and includes several steps: (1) determining that there is a violation; (2) a possible stipulated agreement; (3) notice of violation; (4) possible warrant for arrest and custody; (5) preliminary revocation hearing; (6) full revocation hearing; and (7) either reprimand/modification of conditions with return to supervision or violation and return to prison. Obviously, the first step is for the parole officer to determine that

Violation

failure to follow conditions
of parole supervision

there is a **violation**, or failure to follow conditions of supervision. If the offender
has committed a new crime, the officer usually receives a notice of arrest and
charges from the local police and prosecutor. For technical violations, the officer
must make the *determination of a violation.* Violations may be obvious, in that the
offender fails a drug test or does not report to the officer as required; the officer
may also determine a violation through his or her own investigation, such as if the
offender has failed to maintain employment or has moved without notifying the
officer.

The second step is authorized in most jurisdictions. If the violation is considered minor, yet does deem that action be taken, the parole officer may discuss the
violation with the offender and propose a modification of the conditions of supervision with a continuation of parole. If the offender agrees, the officer writes a
report that is referred to as a *stipulated agreement* in many states. In the federal
system, it is referred to as an *action with consent and waiver.* In either case, since
the offender agrees to the modification, the officer merely files the report with the
parole board or supervising court. If the offender does not agree, the officer requests a hearing by the board or the court with a recommendation to modify the
conditions.

When a violation occurs and the offender does not cooperate or absconds from
supervision and cannot be found, the officer writes a *notice of violation* to the supervising authority and may request a *warrant for arrest and custody* if the officer
believes that the offender should be taken into custody. The authority then schedules a *preliminary hearing.* The offender receives a notice of the violation, with a
listing of the alleged violations and date of the preliminary hearing (usually required within fifteen days of notice of violation or arrest warrant). The purpose of
the preliminary hearing is to determine whether *probable cause* exists to believe
that the offender has committed the violation. This is particularly important if offenders have been taken into custody, as the preliminary hearing allows a timely
determination of whether they should continue to be held pending the full revo-

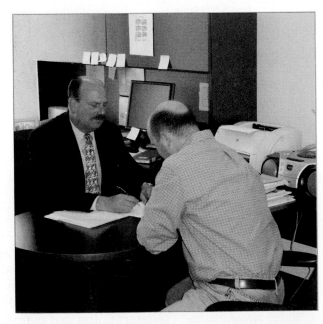

*In many jurisdictions, parole officers and parolees can agree
on a "stipulated agreement" to modify conditions, as a way
to respond to minor violations by the parolee.*
Photo by Richard P. Seiter.

cation hearing. Offenders may waive the preliminary hearing and proceed to the revocation hearing. If they choose to have the hearing, the officer presents the evidence of the violation before a hearing officer, usually an attorney employed full-time by the authority to conduct such hearings. At the hearing, offenders have limited due-process rights to have legal representation, challenge the evidence, confront witnesses, and present evidence on their behalf. If the hearing officer determines that there is probable cause, the parolee is held in custody until the full revocation hearing.

The *full revocation hearing* is similar to the preliminary hearing, except that it is more comprehensive. It is held within ninety days of the preliminary hearing, and its purpose is to determine whether a violation of parole is serious enough to warrant a return to prison. The hearing is presided over by parole board members or the sentencing court for mandatory release violators. All activities during the supervision of the offender are reviewed, to include positive adjustment as well as the violation. The board or court can take one of three actions if they determine that the offender violated conditions of release. First, they can return the offender to supervision with no modification of conditions. This is unlikely; if the violation was serious enough to warrant a revocation hearing, there is probably the need to modify the conditions. Second, the offender can be returned to supervision with a modification of conditions. Finally, the offenders' conditional release can be revoked and the offender returned to prison to serve additional time.

LEGAL ISSUES REGARDING REVOCATION

The principal case regarding parole revocation was the 1972 U.S. Supreme Court decision ***Morrissey v. Brewer***.[42] While recognizing the *Greenholz* decision that parole is a privilege and not a right and that full due process is not required, the Court noted that once parole is granted, a liberty interest is created, and offenders must have certain due process rights in actions to revoke that liberty. The limited due process that must be followed in the revocation process includes the following:

- The parolee is provided advance written notice of the alleged violation and the evidence of the violation.
- The parolee must have the opportunity to attend the hearing and present witnesses and documentary evidence.
- The parolee has the right to confront and cross-examine adverse witnesses.
- A neutral and detached body must hold the hearing.
- The parolee must receive a written decision of the hearing body, as well as the evidence relied upon to revoke the parole.

Morrissey v. Brewer

a 1972 U.S. Supreme Court decision that once parole is granted, a liberty interest is created, and offenders must have certain due process to revoke that liberty

The *Morrissey* case did not, however, establish the right to counsel during the revocation process. In 1973, in *Gagnon v. Scarpelli*, the U.S. Supreme Court did extend the *Morrissey* due process rights to probationers during revocation proceedings, and established that parolees have a limited right to counsel and that the hearing body must determine whether counsel shall be provided to the offender.[43] These two cases are the primary ones that influenced the required process for parole revocations described previously.

Effectiveness of Parole

There are varying views on the effectiveness of parole. Parole is often criticized for the wrong reasons, primarily because the public believes that parole is a lenient approach to incarceration and lets dangerous criminals out of prison early. In reality (or at least by design), when indeterminate sentences are created in the penal codes by state legislatures, the minimum time is the term determined to hold offenders accountable for their crimes and satisfy the sentencing goals of punishment, deterrence, and incapacitation. Release at any time after the minimum then considers the individual characteristics of offenders such as any aggravating circumstances of their crime, dangerousness, and potential for rehabilitation.

To examine the effectiveness of parole, a definition of effectiveness must first be agreed on, although several differing definitions are often used. First, effectiveness can be defined in terms of how many (or what percentage) of offenders successfully complete their terms of supervision. The U.S. Department of Justice reports that of the more than 464,500 parolees discharged from supervision in 2001, 46 percent had successfully met the conditions of their supervision, while 40 percent had been returned to incarceration because of either a rule violation or a new offense. An additional 9 percent had absconded and 2 percent failed to successfully meet the conditions of supervision but were discharged without incarceration. The success rate among those discharged from parole dropped from 50 percent in 1990; however, the percentage incarcerated also dropped (from 46 percent to 40 percent). These declines were offset by increases in absconders (from 1 percent to 9 percent).[44]

During 2000, there were 182,100 parole violators admitted to adult prisons in the United States. It is interesting to note, however, that only 34,948 (19.2 percent) of these violators were admitted to prison for a new felony in addition to their technical parole violation.[45] Over the past decade, there has been less tolerance for technical violations of parole, offenders are more likely to be returned for violations that do not include committing a new felony, and parole failures now constitute a growing proportion of all new prison admissions. In 1980, parole violators constituted just 18 percent of all admissions, but recent years have seen a steady increase to the point where they represented 35 percent of all new admissions in 1997.[46] Parole agencies are hesitant to take the risk of continuing offenders on parole who are not following the conditions of the release, in case they later commit a crime and the parole agency is blamed for not violating them for the technical violation.

A second definition of effectiveness considers the percentage of offenders who do (or do not) recidivate by committing new crimes or being returned to prison. The most thorough review of recidivism among released inmates was a study completed by Beck and Shipley for the Bureau of Justice Statistics in 1989. The report states, "Of the 108,580 persons released from prisons in 11 states in 1983, representing more than half of all released State prisoners that year, an estimated 62.5% were rearrested for a felony or serious misdemeanor within 3 years, 46.8% were reconvicted, and 41.4% returned to prison or jail."[47] The findings also indicate that rearrest rates were the highest during the first year (see Table 6.6). While not all of the released inmates were on parole, most states still used parole as a release mechanism in 1983. These numbers are obviously not a strong endorsement that parole works, yet the figures must be considered both in terms of the size of parole caseloads and how much supervision parolees received, as well as whether they would have recidivated at the same rate if not conditionally released on parole.

Therefore, the third and perhaps the most valid measure of effectiveness is how parole and the supervision following discretionary release compares to unconditional mandatory release without parole or supervision. In a study by Sacks and Logan to determine the effect of supervision after release, parolees who received supervision were compared to a group of court-ordered prison releasees who received no supervision, in terms of recidivism defined as conviction of a new felony or misdemeanor. After three years, the parole group recidivated at a rate of 77 percent, while the group receiving no supervision recidivated at a rate of 85 percent.[48] In addition, a federal study compared prison releasees who received supervision with those receiving no supervision after release. In a review of those who recidi-

TABLE	6.6	Recidivism of State Prisoners Released in 1983, by Time after Release		

	Percent of released prisoners who were:		
Time after release	**Rearrested**	**Reconvicted**	**Reincarcerated**
6 months	25.0%	11.3%	8.4%
1 year	39.3	23.1	18.6
2 years	54.5	38.3	32.8
3 years	62.5	46.8	41.4

Source: Allen J. Beck and Bernard E. Shipley, *Recidivism of Prisoners Released in 1983* (Washington, D.C.: U.S. Department of Justice, Bureau of Justice Statistics, 1989), p. 3.

TABLE	6.7	Percentage of Successful State Parole Discharges, by Method of Release	

		Method of release	
Year	**All discharges**	**Discretionary parole**	**Mandatory parole**
1990	44.6%	51.6%	23.8%
1991	46.8	52.6	24.9
1992	48.6	50.7	29.8
1993	46.9	54.8	33.5
1994	44.3	52.2	30.4
1995	44.3	54.3	28.0
1996	45.2	55.9	30.2
1997	43.4	55.8	30.8
1998	43.8	55.3	32.2
1999	41.9	54.1	33.1

Source: Timothy A. Hughes, Doris James Wilson, and Allen J. Beck, *Trends in State Parole, 1990–2000*, (Washington, D.C.: U.S. Department of Justice, Bureau of Justice Statistics, October 2001), p. 11.

vated and were returned to prison, the average time remaining in the community before return to prison was seventeen months for those receiving supervision, and only thirteen months for those without supervision.[49] Finally, the Bureau of Justice Statistics compares the percentage of successful discharges from parole by method of release (see Table 6.7). In each year from 1990 to 1999, inmates released under discretionary parole (by the decision of a parole board) were more successful than those under mandatory parole (those released after serving a determinate sentence with supervision to follow).

In the "A Questions of Policy" box, consider the issue of the future of parole.

A QUESTION OF POLICY

SHOULD PAROLE BE SAVED?

Parole has been commonly acknowledged to aid prisoner reentry in several ways, and with the indeterminate sentencing structure, parole served many positive functions. First, extremely dangerous inmates were often maintained in prisons longer than they would have been under a determinate sentence structure. Determinate sentences are usually shorter than

(continued)

indeterminate sentences, and parole boards regularly require dangerous, high-risk inmates to serve the maximum sentence. The State of Colorado abolished parole as a release mechanism in 1979, but reinstated it after finding out that the length of prison sentences served was decreasing, particularly for high-risk offenders.

Second, parole boards do act as a gatekeeper to ensure that inmates have solid release plans when they return to the community. Parole boards always ask inmates questions such as, "Where will you live when you get out of prison?" and "What job opportunities are available to you?" The boards also have reports available to them from parole officers who have investigated the inmates' release plans. Third, the existence of parole is an incentive for good behavior by inmates and an incentive for program participation that can be beneficial, even if not truly voluntary. There is no evidence that nonvoluntary program participation is less effective than participation with some coercion, and there is recent data indicating the benefit of a variety of prison program participation (cognitive skills training, drug treatment programs, education and work programs, and treatment of sex offenders) on reducing recidivism.[50]

Finally, parole consideration sets the framework for supervision and treatment needs following release. Parole boards create conditions under which parolees must be supervised and attend treatment programs from which they would benefit. Without parole, supervision is less individualized and based on risk rather than need, setting supervision levels based primarily on offenders' history of criminal behavior.

With these issues in mind, students should struggle with the policy question of whether parole should be continued in the states that still have it, or reestablished in states that have abolished it. There is no question that the abolition of indeterminate sentences and parole has impacted the increase in the number of prisoners. Yet there are many valid reasons why determinate sentences are seen as advantageous. List the pros and cons of parole, and decide whether you think it should be saved.

Prisoner Reentry: A Changing Phenomenon

As noted, there has been tremendous growth in the prison population in the United States, and almost 1.5 million prisoners are now in federal and state prisons. With so much attention on the number of offenders in prison, until recently little attention has been paid to the fact that many more offenders are also leaving prison and returning to the community than at any prior time in history. During 2000, there were 596,191 prisoners released by adult prisons, an increase from 409,150 in 1991.[51] In New York City alone, New York state prisons release approximately 25,000 people a year, and New York City jails release another 100,000.[52] In the State of California, 124,697 prisoners left prisons after completing their sentences in 2000, almost ten times the number of releases only twenty years earlier.[53]

Prisoner reentry

the process by which an inmate leaves prison and returns to the community

This high number of offenders returning to their communities, many without parole supervision, and some with no supervision, has created new issues regarding **prisoner reentry**. The issues of finding housing, lack of ties with family and friends, finding a job, alcohol and drug abuse, continued involvement in crime, and the impact of parole supervision were described in a study by the Vera Institute of Justice.[54] In addition, Petersilia identified six collateral consequences of imprisonment—(1) community cohesion; (2) employment and economic well-being; (3) democratic participation and political alienation; (4) family stabilization and childhood development; (5) mental and physical health; and (6) homelessness—that are the result of recycling parolees in and out of families and communities.[55] These issues and consequences make it difficult for ex-inmates to avoid a return to crime, and therefore it is critical that prisons have programs to prepare inmates for what they will face upon release and return to the communities.

The world of prisons is very different from the world inmates face when they are released, and the transition from prison to the community often seems surreal to offenders. One ex-offender characterized his experience in leaving prison and returning to the community as "like entering Disneyland," and further describes his release:

> Leaving prison after all those years was like entering a strange new world. Inside I was a respected convict. I knew where I stood with others, how to act, and what to expect. Once outside in the "free world," everything changed. Moreover, my self-concept and orientation got flipped on its head.[56]

Prisoners have been releasing from prison for more than two hundred years, yet reentry is currently very different from only a few decades ago. These differences include the following:

1. There are many more offenders released from prisons than in the past.
2. Many prisoners are released after serving a determinate sentence, and some have no supervision requirements after release.
3. Prisoners are serving significantly longer prison terms.
4. Only a small percentage of inmates receive the benefit of extensive rehabilitation or prerelease programs.
5. The communities to which prisoners return are more disorganized, their families are less likely to be supportive, and they find fewer social services available to them in the community.
6. With reduced tolerance for risk, a larger number of releasees are returned to prison for commission of new crimes or for violating the technical conditions of their parole or release supervision.

These differences result from many factors, including a tough-on-crime attitude, reduced funding for prison programs and community social services, a weakening of the traditional support structures within communities and neighborhoods, and less (sometimes zero) tolerance for lapses by prison releasees under official supervision. The changing nature of prisoner reentry has made successful transitions from prison to community more difficult. For much of the twentieth century, preparation for release was considered an important part of the prison experience, and all states used indeterminate sentences with release by parole boards to assist in determining offenders' release preparation. The medical model emphasized that prisons should provide programs to prepare inmates for release. Educational and vocational programs, substance abuse and other counseling programs, therapeutic communities and other residential programs, and prison industry work programs were important parts of prison operations.

When prisoners were nearing release, extensive efforts were made to ease their transition to the community. Parole boards closely reviewed inmates' release plans in consideration of parole, and community parole officers investigated the plans and reported on their acceptability to the parole board. If there were not acceptable plans, inmates were usually released through a halfway house so they could be assisted with issues of housing, employment, family relationships, and mental health or substance abuse counseling. Correctional officials recognized the difficulty in the prison-to-community transition, and reintegrative programs were expanded and developed to ease the transition. There was experimentation with specialized caseloads, the use of volunteers in parole, and even ex-offenders as parole officer aides. Inmates' return to the community was intensely supervised. Parole officers' primary responsibility was to guide offenders to programs and services and supervise their successful completion of parole.

CHANGES OVER THE PAST TWO DECADES

Over the past two decades, however, this traditional process began to deteriorate. The demise of the medical model, the tough-on-crime attitude of the public and elected officials, the belief that rehabilitation did not work, the reduced funding for prison and transitional programs, and the change in parole supervision from casework to surveillance changed the model of release used until the 1980s. The current model of prison operations and prisoner reentry focuses less on inmate rehabilitation and preparation for release than on punishment, deterrence, and incapacitation. Most offenders serve a determinate sentence that is much longer than in the past. Inmates are seen as making a conscious decision to commit crimes, and punishment is believed important to produce a proper deterrent effect. Prison programs are considered valuable to keep inmates busy and maintain order, more than for release preparation. Without parole boards in many states, there is no "gatekeeper" to review the inmate's preparation and release plans. After release, if the offender is under supervision, there is little tolerance for drug use, technical violations, and minor criminal behavior, and offenders are quickly returned to prison for even minor violations.

Most inmates face serious problems, and there are not enough programs within prison to deal with them. Many inmates have long histories of criminal involvement and substance abuse, are gang members, and have few marketable skills. With the decline of support for mental illness by states, a greater number of mentally ill people are being admitted to prisons and jails, as a recent survey revealed that nearly one in five U.S. prisoners report having a mental illness.[57] In 1997, only about one of six prisoners who had used alcohol or drugs in the month before the offense for which they were incarcerated received substance abuse treatment while in prison.[58]

Programs that are effective in improving prisoner reentry, such as work and prison industry programs, substance abuse counseling, sex offender programs, and release from prison through a halfway house, are available only to small numbers of inmates. On January 1, 2001, state and federal prisons reported only 120,687 inmates (12.9 percent) in drug treatment programs, a decline of more than 50,000 inmates since 2000.[59] On the same date, only 77,380 inmates (6.3 percent) were assigned to prison industries, which have been found extremely successful in improving work skills and reducing recidivism.[60] Only 12,149 inmates (3.4 percent) were enrolled in sex offender programs on January 1, 2001.[61] Only 59,180 inmates were placed in halfway houses during 2000, yet this represented only 9.9 percent of the 596,191 inmates released from state and federal prisons that year.[62] And, during 2000, only 40,164 inmates were placed in work or study release.[63]

Petersilia reports that parole and release officers also have a difficult challenge. In the 1970s, parole officers handled an average caseload of approximately forty-five parolees, but the average caseload is now more than seventy. Approximately 80 percent of all parolees are supervised on these large regular caseloads, and result in an average of less than two fifteen-minute face-to-face contacts with the parole officer each month.[64] And in 1999, nearly 100,000 prison releasees (18 percent) left prison under expiration of sentence and had no postrelease supervision.[65]

ISSUES FACED BY OFFENDERS RETURNING TO THE COMMUNITY

Many obvious issues face offenders after they serve long sentences in prison and then try to return to their communities, find jobs, support their families, and have a crime-free lifestyle. Simply finding a suitable place to live is difficult. Most ex-

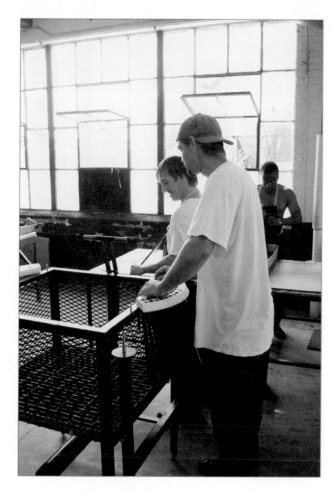

Learning a skill and developing good work habits is part of an effective program for successful reentry to the community from prison.
Photo by Richard P. Seiler.

offenders have few financial resources when they leave prison, cannot afford high monthly rents or the required deposits of first-and-last-month's rent, and therefore must look for public housing. Unfortunately, some public laws allow providers of federally assisted housing to exclude individuals with a criminal record from receiving public housing.[66]

Incarceration also disrupts relationships with offenders and their families. In a three-year study of the incarceration of males in the District of Columbia (of which 10 percent of African-American men between ages 18 and 35 were imprisoned), findings indicate that a result of the extensive use of incarceration was "injuring the families of prisoners often as much as and sometimes more than criminal offenders themselves."[67] Not only did the incarceration impact the ability of the offender to support the family and provide child care, it also diminished the relationship between husband and wife, and father and children. Most males in prison are fathers and maintain monthly contact with their children.[68] However, these men fail to offer support as a parent or serve as a positive role model for their children. Incarceration further strains these relationships and makes it difficult for families to stay together even after the prisoner is released.

Finally, it is not easy for ex-inmates to find suitable employment, particularly in difficult economic times. In these conditions, employers are less likely to hire

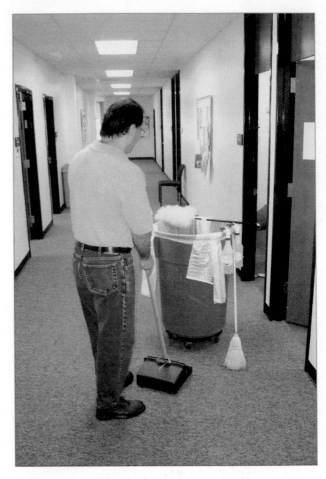

Many former offenders can find only low-paying, entry-level jobs during these difficult economic times. Employment is key to successful reentry.
Photo by Richard P. Seiter.

ex-offenders, and a larger percentage of former prisoners are unable to find and keep jobs. In the "get tough on criminals" movement, legislatures place more statutory restrictions on ex-offenders. In many states, ex-prisoners are restricted from working in the professions of law, real estate, medicine, nursing, physical therapy, education, dentistry, engineering, and pharmacology. Suitable employment for ex-offenders is difficult to find, yet we continue to recognize that employment is one of the most important vehicles for improving offender reintegration and increasing desistance from crime.[69] Uggen and Staff consider work a "turning point" for offenders, noting the research indicating a relationship between work and crime, and that the quality of employment is important for reducing recidivism.[70] The potential for obtaining quality work, finding suitable housing, and maintaining strong family relationships are all negatively affected by long terms of imprisonment. Reentry programs must address these collateral consequences to improve offenders' chances for successful and crime-free lives. The following "*A Look Into*" box illustrates many of the issues facing offenders as they come out of prison.

A LOOK INTO . . .

REENTRY FROM THE EYES OF AN EX-CON

The following interview regarding prisoner reentry was recently conducted with Dr. Charles Terry, assistant professor of criminal justice at Saint Louis University. Dr. Terry has served four terms of imprisonment (a total of approximately twelve years during the 1970s and 1980s) and has been in and out of local jails several more times.

Q: Dr. Terry, can you provide a brief history of your criminal life and incarceration?

A: I was first sent to prison at the California Rehabilitation Center (CRC) in 1975. I served fifteen months, was released, but committed another burglary to buy drugs and was returned to prison within two months. I was sent to the California Correctional Center (CCC) at Susanville for sixteen months, released, and again out for two months. I committed another crime to buy drugs, and was put in jail. Somehow I beat the case and was released. I tried to get jobs, but no one would hire me. I finally got a job as a dishwasher. I continued to use drugs, and even though I had eight dirty UAs (positive urine tests indicating the use of drugs), my parole officer believed I was not doing crimes, so she let me stay out. Finally, after the eighth dirty UA, she told me either she had to violate me, or I had to go on methadone maintenance, which was a substitute for heroin. After one and a half years on methadone and doing pretty well, I decided to get off the methadone. But as I gradually reduced the dosage of methadone, I got sick, and decided I might as well use heroin to feel better. I started to just use enough to not be sick, but it just got worse and worse. Soon, I ran out of money to buy heroin, committed another burglary, and got caught.

California by then had determinate sentencing, and I got a three-year sentence. I was sent to the California Correctional Institution (CCI) at Tehachapi, but manipulated a transfer to the Sierra Conservation Center (SCC) in Jamestown. In 1981, I was released after serving two years. I went home to Santa Barbara, but moved to Oregon to try to stay out of trouble. I stayed out three years, had a job, and was doing OK. Parole supervision in Oregon was minimal. I just had to report in; they did not do UAs. I started using heroin again, got busted, and was sent to the Oregon State Penitentiary (OSP) for six and a half years for burglaries. I got out in 1990, and have been out since.

Q: What made the difference the last time, that allowed you to stay out?

A: I started taking some education classes at OSP, did pretty well, and found that I liked to read and learn. The teachers were competent and caring people who treated us like human beings. After two years of school, I began to make a radical shift in self-concept. About ninety days before I was to be paroled, I injected a good dose of heroin, and remember wondering why I wasted so much of my life for this feeling. I then believed I could go straight without the use of heroin. My parole plans were vague, but I wanted to go to college. I knew I was institutionalized, but knew school was an institution, so I would just switch college with prison. School became a substitute for using drugs. I really don't think I would have changed if I hadn't become interested in school.

Q: What do you think is the biggest detriment to prisoners making a successful transition from prison to the community?

A: Prisonization. It is totally assimilation into the prison culture. This means you see the world through the eyes of someone adapted to the prison culture. It is not a reflection of the individual, but of the culture. The attributes of prisonization that are important for living in

(continued)

prison (don't tell on anyone, don't show weakness, mind your own business) are not those of the streets, and continuing to live the prison culture makes it more difficult to move to the street. The more time I did inside prison, the more alienated I felt around nonconvicts. Because in this culture, you are able to live with self-respect, dignity, others respect you. One of central effects of prisonization is resistance; you learn to resist everything (pains of imprisonment, authority). This is counter to the norms of a successful life on the street. For instance, you get this "I don't give a damn" attitude, and you have tattoos all over you. A convict in prison has respect, knows the system, what to expect. He knows and enjoys the routine. You leave your cell, go to work, go work out, know there will be certain food for certain meals. Once you get out, the comfortable familiarity is gone. The convict status you had in prison is seen as something strange in the community. Therefore, you experience more alienation. To me, that is the biggest obstacle to a successful transition.

Q: How did you decide to become a "convict," in prison, and adopt the culture of the prison?

A: I did not just decide to be a convict rather than square john. When I first went to prison I thought these inmates or convicts were really strange people, and I did not want to be like them. But over time, I moved more and more in this direction. I saw these guys that had adapted to the prison life, with tattoos, working out and getting big, laughing and joking, and seemed to not be having a bad time. This seemed like a magnet to me. I also wanted to not have a bad time, so I gradually started to move in that direction in terms of my behavior, appearance, and attitude. Becoming a convict took years for me, because I came from a middle-class background. If you come from the inner city, you adjust to the prison life pretty quick. I just used all the information I collected, and the lessons I learned from the guys I hung out with. I think the younger a person is when they go in to prison, the more likely they are to become prisonized. You see people go in one way, and come out very different.

Q: How do inmates overcome prisonization to be successful once they get out?

A: The more social support you have, the better your chances of staying out. If you have a support system, you feel safe. You know you have people that will take you as you are and provide you the support you need as you try to find work and, as my goal always was, "to do good." I did not know what "doing good" meant, but I always had that intention.

But regardless of what support you have, it is hard. You get a job, maybe a girlfriend, and at first it seems like things will be fine, as you are just glad to get out. But soon you realize you don't like your job, you don't like the "old lady," and gradually the excitement of getting out is not enough, and you begin to feel more and more like there is something missing. You may actually miss being with the guys in prison, working out, hanging out, and laughing and joking around. The gap between the two worlds narrows as you learn to do OK in the community or stay off drugs. I was involved in NA and hanging out with other NA guys, most of whom were also convicts. We were learning together, found out how to ask for help, and how to change the effects of prisonization.

Q: What is the most important change we can make to improve the likelihood of successful reentry for prisoners?

A: The most important thing we can do is to keep time spent in prison to the least possible time, thereby reducing the likelihood and impact of prisonization.

In addition, the focus taken by most criminologists is that the support outside is very important. That is true, but beyond that, we need a different reference group. When I go into a grocery store, I look around, and everything seems so strange. There are no guards to tell me where to go and what to do, food is everywhere, but I am always surprised that they expect me to pay for this stuff. The norms and values associated with the world outside prison are just too different from the world inside.

WHAT CAN BE DONE TO IMPROVE PRISONER REENTRY?

One of the most important elements to improving the success of prisoner reentry is to build on what we know works. In a review of research regarding prisoner reentry programs, Seiter and Kadela identified several programs that work to reduce the recidivism of released prisoners.[71] The authors first created the following definition of prisoner reentry programs:

- All correctional programs that focus on the "transition" from prison to community (prerelease, work release, halfway houses, or specific reentry programs), or
- Programs that have initiated treatment (substance abuse, life skills, education, cognitive/behavioral, sex/violent offender) in a prison setting and have linked with a community program to provide continuity of care.

The method to then identify whether a category of program was successful used the Maryland *Scale of Scientific Methods* (MSSM), developed by Sherman and colleagues in 1998 for the National Institute of Justice, in order to identify crime prevention programs that work. This scale ranks research studies from 1 (weakest) to 5 (strongest) on overall internal validity. Seiter and Kadela identified thirty-two studies that fit the definition of prisoner reentry. Each study was placed into an MSSM level, and evaluations of similar programs have been grouped into: (1) vocational training and work; (2) drug rehabilitation; (3) educational programs; (4) sex/violent offender programs; (5) halfway house programs; and (6) prison prerelease programs.

The next step was to determine whether any of these six categories of prison reentry programs were effective, using the Sherman framework definitions. For a program to be considered to be "working," at least two Level 3 evaluations with statistical significance tests must indicate that the intervention was effective and the preponderance of the remaining evidence must support that conclusion. For a program to be coded as "not working," at least two Level 3 evaluations with statistical significance must indicate the ineffectiveness of the program and the preponderance of the remaining evidence must support the same conclusion. Programs for which the level of certainty from available evidence is too low to support generalizable conclusions were defined as "promising." Any program not classified in one of these three categories is defined as having unknown effects.

Results indicate a positive result for vocational training and work release programs (found effective in reducing recidivism rates as well as improving job readiness skills for ex-offenders), for drug rehabilitation (graduates of treatment programs were less likely than other parolees and noncompleters to have been arrested, commit a drug-related offense, continue drug use, or have a parole violation), to some extent for education programs (only to increase educational achievement scores, but not to decrease recidivism), for halfway house programs (found effective in reducing the frequency and severity of future crimes), and for prerelease programs (effective in reducing recidivism rates of ex-offenders). In addition, there are promising results for sex and violent offender programs.

Even with the problems resulting from the changes over the past two decades, this analysis of prisoner reentry programs has identified several categories of programs in which there is evidence of success. Public officials should take note of these programs, implement or expand the use of vocational training and/or work release programs, drug rehabilitation programs, education programs, halfway house programs, and prerelease programs that have proven successful, and expand the use of sex and violent offender programs that show promise. These programs can be expanded significantly with only a small portion of funding that is currently used for imprisoning offenders.

Idleness in prison makes prison management more difficult, and does nothing to prepare inmates for release to the community.
Photo by Richard P. Seiter.

The nation has invested billions of dollars in locking up offenders. Policies concerning reentry have become increasingly an avoidance of risk. As a result, we have created a revolving door of offenders who will be committed to prison again and again as they fail in the community. This is not only a failure by the inmate; it is a failure of release and reentry policies. This analysis has pointed out that certain programs can improve prisoner reentry and reduce the revolving-door syndrome. With billions of dollars focused on imprisonment, it is only fitting that a few million more be focused on their return to the community.

Chapter Review

SUMMARY

During much of the history of corrections, indeterminate sentences and discretionary parole have been a cornerstone of both theory and practice. The minimum term of an indeterminate sentence satisfied the punishment, deterrence, and incapacitation sentencing goals, and a parole board of experts then examined the individual offender characteristics to determine when the goal of rehabilitation was maximized and the offender was best prepared for release to the community. However, this model came under attack and was completely abandoned in a third of the states, and seriously compromised in another third. In its place developed the use of determinate sentences that were longer than the minimum indeterminate sentence term, in an effort to make the punishment fit the crime and to hold offenders accountable for their criminal acts. Unfortunately, punishment, deterrence, and incapacitation became so predominant that rehabilitation was often ignored or seriously reduced in emphasis.

Several problems have resulted from these changes in philosophy, policy, and practice. There has been a fivefold increase in the number of prison inmates, at a tremendous cost to society, and many argue, with little benefit in the reduction of crime or successful return of offenders to the community. With criminal offenders now predominantly receiving determinate sentences, there is no parole board to act as gatekeepers between the prison and community. Some high-risk offenders actually serve shorter sentences than when a parole board could deny parole and continue them even until their maximum sentence term was met. Without a parole board, there is no review of release plans, and there is very little incentive for good behavior while in prison. Almost 80 percent of inmates were released on discretionary parole only twenty-five years ago, yet just over 20 percent are now similarly released. Most prison releasees still receive supervision as a postprison requirement, and violation of conditions results in a possibility of returning to prison. However, approximately 18 percent of prison releasees go into the community with no requirement for supervision.

Prisoner reentry has become a much more significant issue than it was twenty years ago. As pointed out by Jeremy Travis, former director of the National Institute of Justice, in referring to the recent interest and problem of prisoner reentry, "they all come back."[72] Inmates are serving longer periods of time, are older when released, are more prisonized from serving longer times in prison, are less likely to participate in prison rehabilitative programs, and enter communities that are more disorganized and unable to provide them services and assistance. Fortunately, some reentry programs have been found to help prisoners return to the community. It is critical that public policymakers build upon these findings and fund and expand those programs proven successful, while hopefully ending the negative cycle of crime-prison-release-crime.

REVIEW QUESTIONS

1. Describe the four stages of the system of release implemented by Alexander Maconochie on the Norfolk Island penal colony.

2. Describe the four stages of release implemented by Sir Walter Crofton in the Irish System.

3. How did the Elmira Reformatory move toward the implementation of a system of parole in the United States?

4. How did the Martinson findings of "nothing works" impact the use of parole and the medical model?

5. Describe some of the suggested models to replace the medical model of corrections.

6. Compare and contrast parole, supervised mandatory release, and unconditional mandatory release.

7. What two factors do parole guidelines attempt to predict?

8. Name and describe the two types of parole conditions.

9. What are the two types of parole violations?

10. Describe the process for revoking parole.

11. List the due process rights prescribed by the *Morrissey v. Brewer* decision.

12. List some of the ways in which issues facing prisoners reentering the community are different than they were in the past.

13. Describe Seiter and Kadela's findings regarding the effectiveness of prisoner reentry programs.

ENDNOTES

1. W. B. Taylor, "Alexander Maconochie and the Revolt against the Penitentiary," *Southern Journal of Justice* 3, no. 1 (1978): 18.

2. R. Hughes, *The Fatal Shore* (New York: Knopf, 1987), p. 468.

3. As cited in Norval Morris, *Maconochie's Gentlemen: The Story of Norfolk Island and the Roots of Modern Prison Reform* (New York: Oxford University Press, 2002), p. 156.

4. H. E. Barnes and N. D. Teeters, *New Horizons in Criminology* (Englewood Cliffs, N.J.: Prentice Hall, 1959).

5. A. A. Bruce, *Parole and Indeterminate Sentences* (Springfield: Illinois Parole Board, 1928).

6. M. S. Sherrill, "Determinate Sentencing: History, Theory, Debate," *Corrections Magazine*, no. 3 (September 1977): 3–13.

7. E. Lindsey, "Historical Origins of the Sanction of Imprisonment for Serious Crimes," *Journal of Criminal Law and Criminology* 16, no. 1 (1925): 9–26.

8. David Dressler, *The Parole Chief* (New York: Viking Press, 1951).

9. Margaret Werner Cahalan, *Historical Corrections Statistics in the United States, 1850–1984* (Washington, D.C.: U.S. Government Printing Office, 1986).

10. Edward J. Latessa and Harry E. Allen, *Corrections in the Community*, 2nd ed. (Cincinnati, Ohio: Anderson, 1999), p. 159.

11. Seymour Halleck, *The Politics of Therapy* (New York: Science House, 1971).

12. Norval Morris, *The Future of Imprisonment* (Chicago: University of Chicago Press, 1974).

13. John Irwin, "Adaptation to Being Corrected: Corrections from the Convict's Perspective," in *The Sociology of Corrections,* edited by R. G. Legar and J. R. Stratton (New York: Wiley, 1977), pp. 276–300.

14. Howard Abadinsky, *Probation and Parole: Theory and Practice,* 8th ed. (Upper Saddle River, N.J.: Prentice Hall, 2001), p. 218.

15. Douglas Lipton, Robert Martinson, and Judith Wilks, *The Effectiveness of Correctional Treatment and What Works: A Survey of Treatment Evaluation Studies* (New York: Praeger, 1975).

16. David Fogel, *We Are the Living Proof* (Cincinnati, Ohio: Anderson, 1975).

17. Andrew von Hirsch and Kathleen J. Hanrahan, *Abolish Parole?* (Washington, D.C.: U.S. Government Printing Office, 1978).

18. Twentieth Century Task Force on Sentencing, *Fair and Certain Punishment* (New York: McGraw-Hill, 1976).

19. Bureau of Justice Statistics, *National Prisoner Statistics* (Washington, D.C.: U.S. Department of Justice, 1977).

20. Alvin Blumstein, "Prisons: A Policy Challenge," in *Crime: Public Policies for Crime Control,* edited by James Q. Wilson and Joan Petersilia (Oakland, Calif.: Institute for Contemporary Studies, 2002), pp. 451–452.

21. J. Furniss, "The Population Boom," *Corrections Today* 58, no. 1 (1996): 38–43.

22. Camille Graham Camp and George M. Camp, *The 2001 Corrections Yearbook: Adult Systems* (Middletown, Conn.: Criminal Justice Institute, 2002), p. 1.

23. Timothy A. Hughes, Doris James Wilson, and Allen J. Beck, *Trends in State Parole, 1990–2000* (Washington, D.C.: U.S. Department of Justice, Bureau of Justice Statistics, October 2001), p. 4.

24. J. Monahan, *Predicting Violent Behavior: An Assessment of Clinical Techniques* (Beverly Hills, Calif.: Sage, 1981).

25. During the 1980s, several states were under federal court order to keep their prison population at less than full capacity. When the population grew to a certain point (perhaps 98 percent), an emergency release would be mandated, and the parole board could review all inmates within so many months of parole eligibility and release those most deserving and presenting the least community risk.

26. Hughes, Wilson, and Beck, 2001, p. 1.

27. Lauren E. Glaze, *Probation and Parole in the United States, 2002* (Washington, D.C.: U.S. Department of Justice, Bureau of Justice Statistics, August 2003), p. 1.

28. Ibid., p. 5.

29. *Greenholz v. Inmates of the Nebraska Penal and Correctional Complex,* 99 S. Ct. 2100 (1979).

30. Edward E. Rhine, William R. Smith, and Ronald W. Jackson, *Paroling Authorities: Recent History and Current Practice* (Laurel, Md.: American Correctional Association, 1991), p. 54.

31. President's Commission on Law Enforcement and Administration of Justice, *Task Force Report: Corrections* (Washington, D.C.: U.S. Government Printing Office, 1967), p. 67.

32. Hughes, Wilson, and Beck, 2001, p. 7.

33. Victoria C. Myers, currently Division Director of Human Services for the Missouri Department of Corrections, and formerly a member of the Missouri Parole Board, developed these scenarios.

34. Ohio Department of Rehabilitation and Correction, "APA Offender Classification," Policy Section 501, Number 28, February 15, 2001, p. 3.

35. Ibid., pp. 5–6.

36. Camp and Camp, 2002, p. 192.

37. Ibid., pp. 222–223.

38. Ibid., p. 220.

39. Ibid., p. 225.

40. Ibid., p. 196.

41. Hughes, Wilson, and Beck, 2001, p. 12.

42. *Morrissey v. Brewer,* 408 U.S. 471 (1972).

43. *Gagnon v. Scarpelli,* 411 U.S. 778 (1973).

44. U.S. Department of Justice, Bureau of Justice Statistics, "Probation and Parole Statistics: Summary Findings," http://www.ojp.usdoj.gov/bjs (accessed December 26, 2002).

45. Camp and Camp, 2002, pp. 60–61.

46. Joan Petersilia, "When Prisoners Return to the Community: Political, Economic, and Social Consequences," *Federal Probation* 65, no. 1 (June 2001): 3–8.

47. Allen J. Beck and Bernard E. Shipley, *Recidivism of Prisoners Released in 1983* (Washington, D.C.: U.S. Department of Justice, Bureau of Justice Statistics, 1989), p. 1.

48. Howard R. Sacks and Charles H. Logan, "Does Parole Make a (Lasting) Difference?" in *Criminal Justice: Law and Politics,* 4th ed., edited by George F. Cole (Pacific Grove, Calif.: Brooks/Cole, 1984), pp. 362–378.

49. William J. Sabol, William P. Adams, Barbara Parthasarathy, and Yan Yuan, *Offenders Returning to Federal Prison, 1986–1997, Special Report* (Washington, D.C.: U.S. Department of Justice, Bureau of Justice Statistics, September 2000), p. 6.

50. G. G. Gaes, T. J. Flanagan, L. L. Motiuk, and L. Stewart, "Adult Correctional Treatment," in *Prisons,* edited by Michael Tonry and Joan Petersilia (Chicago: University of Chicago Press, 1999), pp. 361–426.

51. Camp and Camp, 2002, p. 71.

52. Marta Nelson, Perry Deess, and Charlotte Allen, "The First Month Out: Post-Incarceration Experiences in New York City" (monograph, The Vera Institute, September 1999), i.

53. Joan R. Petersilia, "The Collateral Consequences of Prisoner Reentry in California: Effects on Children, Public Health, and Community" (monograph, April 2000), 1.

54. Nelson, Deess, and Allen, 1999.

55. Joan Petersilia, "When Prisoners Return to the Community: Political, Economic, and Social Consequences," *Corrections Management Quarterly* 5, no. 3 (2001): 4.

56. Charles M. Terry, "From C-Block to Academic: You Can't Get There from Here," in *Convict Criminology,* edited by Jeffrey Ian Ross and Stephen C. Richards (Belmont, Calif.: Wadsworth, 2003), p. 105.

57. P. Ditton and D. J. Wilson, *Truth in Sentencing in State Prisons* (Washington, D.C.: U.S. Department of Justice, Bureau of Justice Statistics, 1999).

58. Christopher J. Mumola, *Substance Abuse and Treatment, State and Federal Prisoners, 1997* (Washington, D.C.: U.S. Department of Justice, Bureau of Justice Statistics, 1999).

59. Camp & Camp, 2002, pp. 136–137.

60. Ibid., p. 117.

61. Ibid., p. 134.

62. Ibid., pp. 71, 144.

63. Ibid., p. 144.

64. Joan R. Petersilia, "Parole and Prisoner Reentry in the United States," in *Prisons,* edited by Michael Tonry and Joan Petersilia (Chicago: University of Chicago Press, 1999), pp. 479–529.

65. Hughes, Wilson, and Beck, 2001, p. 1.

66. See Gwen Rubenstein and Debbi Mukamal, "Welfare and Housing—Denial of Benefits to Drug Offenders," in *Invisible Punishment: The Collateral Consequences of Mass Imprisonment,* edited by Marc Mauer and Meda Chesney-Lind (New York: New Press, 2002), pp. 37–58.

67. Donald Burman, "Families and Incarceration," in *Invisible Punishment: The Collateral Consequences of Mass Imprisonment,* edited by Marc Mauer and Meda Chesney-Lind (New York: New Press, 2002), p. 117.

68. Christopher J. Mumola, *Bureau of Justice Statistics Special Report: Incarcerated Parents and Their Children* (Washington, D.C.: U.S. Department of Justice, 2000).

69. S. Bushway and P. Reuter, "Labor Markets and Crime Risk Factors," in *Preventing Crime: What Works, What Doesn't, What's Promising,* edited by L. W. Sherman, D. Gottfredson, D. MacKenzie, J. Eck, P. Reuter, and S. Bushway (Washington, D.C.: U.S. Department of Justice, Office of Justice Programs, 1998).

70. Christopher Uggen and Jeremy Staff, "Work as a Turning Point for Criminal Offenders," *Corrections Management Quarterly* 5, no. 4 (2001): 1–16.

71. Richard P. Seiter and Karen R. Kadela, "Prisoner Reentry: What Works, What Doesn't, and What's Promising," *Crime and Delinquency* 49, no. 3 (April 2003): 360–388.

72. Jeremy Travis, "But They All Come Back: Rethinking Prisoner Reentry," *Corrections Management Quarterly* 5, no. 3 (2001): 23–33.

Chapter 7

AFTER READING THIS CHAPTER, YOU SHOULD BE ABLE TO:

1. Identify the trend in the number of offenders under correctional supervision since the early 1980s.

2. Understand the use of incarceration rates to compare numbers of offenders over various time frames.

3. Explain the issue of racial disparity in regards to offenders under correctional supervision.

4. Describe how male offenders are assigned to various security levels of prisons and how their daily routine operates.

5. Specify the growth of female offenders under supervision and in prison and suggest reasons for the growth.

6. Identify the special needs of women inmates and how correctional agencies have responded to their needs.

7. Describe the challenge facing women prisoners as mothers.

8. Compare the classification of female prisoners with that of male prisoners.

9. Understand the impact that the *Barefield v. Leach* and *Pargo v. Elliot* court cases had on programming for female inmates.

The Clients of Adult Correctional Agencies

KEY TERMS

racial disparity
drug offenders
male offenders
general population
female offenders
parenting programs
Girl Scouts Behind Bars
substance abuse programs
Barefield v. Leach
Pargo v. Elliot

Introduction

In Chapters 3 through 6, we covered the scope of the correctional process, including pretrial services, sentencing, probation and intermediate sanctions, imprisonment, and release and reentry to the community. Each of these process descriptions included historical developments, theoretical basis for the evolution of policy and practice, and an explanation of how the process currently operates. Now we will cover correctional perspectives and address topics such as the clients of correctional agencies, distinctions of the operations of the juvenile justice system as separate from the criminal justice system, and special offender groups.

In this chapter we identify and provide a basic understanding of the clients of adult correctional systems. Questions asked include the following: What categories of clients do correctional agencies serve? What theoretical underpinnings are the bases of past and current operations? What are the backgrounds and characteristics of the different categories of correctional clients? What might make them unique and require special processing, handling, or management? Has anything in their background contributed to their criminality? For each group, characteristics that make them distinctive and influence how they are handled and managed are described. The chapter begins with an overview of offenders who make up the adult correctional system, including the numbers under supervision and their makeup by gender, offense category, and race and ethnicity. Particular note is made of the increasing number of offenders under correctional supervision, and especially the significant increase in the number in state and federal prisons over the past two decades.

The prison population today is very large and is more diverse than in the past. Much of the prison growth resulted from the incarceration of many property and drug offenders who previously did not get sent to prison. The makeup of the prison population is increasingly black and brown, as white offenders make up a continually smaller proportion of the prison population. And the prison population is no longer "middle crime age" (age 25 to 35) and physically and emotionally healthy. Many juveniles are now tried as adults and sentenced to adult prisons, the percentage of elderly offenders is increasing, mental illness among inmates is a difficult problem, and inmates experience a variety of severe health problems. This chapter identifies characteristics of the unique groups of offenders and some of the activities, policies, and programs that are used to respond to their special situations.

The clients of corrections are what corrections is all about. Corrections is not a manufacturing operation with products. Corrections is not information technology, with hardware and software to make work more efficient. Corrections is about people and about dealing with correctional clients. All too often, students of corrections study, analyze, and consider the strengths and weaknesses of the *process* rather than the *people* the process is designed to manage. This chapter provides many facts and figures that may seem impersonal and inconsistent with this admonishment to consider the people. However, using these facts and figures as a beginning point, students can then work to understand the issues that must be considered as government and correctional officials develop policies and operations to meet public safety, offender rehabilitation, and inmate security goals for various criminal sanctions and the variety of criminal offenders. It is important for students to have a clear understanding of the situations and issues that face correctional clients, and therefore how specific policies and operations will affect them similarly or differently. With that perspective, students will have both the background and sensitivity to better understand and critically assess issues described in later chapters detailing security, inmate programs, the prison environment, and management of special offenders.

Overview of Adult Offenders

The number of adults under correctional supervision (individuals on probation, in jail, in prison, or on parole) has grown dramatically over the past two decades. As indicated in Table 7.1, only 1.8 million adults were on probation and parole and in jail and prison in 1980. This number had doubled in only eight years by 1988, and by 2001, there were 6.6 million adults under the supervision of correctional agencies in the United States. Most private companies and even public agencies would welcome an increase in clients, as there is no group, business, or clients served by government agencies that have grown at anywhere near this rate over the same period of time.

As illustrated in Table 7.1, a significant part of the growth in the number of adults under correctional supervision comes from the growth in the prison population. The use of incarceration as a criminal sanction has skyrocketed over the past two decades. In 1980, the rate of sentenced inmates incarcerated per 100,000 population was only 139. By 2001, the rate of sentenced adults incarcerated per 100,000 population had reached 470.[1] While the incarceration rate increased every year during the period and more than doubled between 1980 and 1990, the rate of increase declined from 1990 to 2000. Figure 7.1 illustrates the continued growth since 1980, but also how the rate remained relatively stable from 2000 to 2001 and even declined during 2001. On January 1, 2001, the states reporting the highest incarceration rates per 100,000 population were Louisiana (783), Oklahoma (670), Alabama (664), and Mississippi (659). Those reporting the lowest incarceration rates were Minnesota (125), Maine (135), North Dakota (167), Massachusetts (167), and New Hampshire (170).[2]

TABLE 7.1	Number of Adult Offenders under Correctional Supervision			
Year	**Probation**	**Jail**	**Prison**	**Parole**	**Total**
1980	1,118,097	183,988	319,598	220,438	1,842,100
1981	1,225,934	196,785	360,029	225,539	2,008,300
1982	1,357,264	209,582	402,914	224,604	2,194,400
1983	1,582,947	223,551	423,898	246,440	2,476,800
1984	1,740,948	234,500	448,264	266,992	2,690,700
1985	1,968,712	256,615	487,593	300,203	3,013,100
1986	2,114,621	274,444	526,436	325,638	3,241,100
1987	2,247,158	295,873	562,814	355,505	3,461,400
1988	2,356,483	343,569	607,766	407,977	3,715,800
1989	2,522,125	395,553	683,367	456,803	4,057,800
1990	2,670,234	405,320	743,382	531,407	4,350,300
1991	2,728,472	426,479	792,535	590,442	4,537,900
1992	2,811,611	444,584	850,566	658,601	4,765,400
1993	2,903,061	459,804	909,381	676,100	4,948,300
1994	2,981,022	486,474	990,147	690,371	5,148,000
1995	3,077,861	507,044	1,078,542	679,421	5,342,900
1996	3,164,996	518,492	1,127,528	679,733	5,490,700
1997	3,296,513	567,079	1,176,564	694,787	5,734,900
1998	3,670,441	592,462	1,224,469	696,385	6,134,200*
1999	3,779,922	605,943	1,287,172	714,457	6,340,800*
2000	3,826,209	621,149	1,316,333	723,898	6,445,100*
2001	3,932,751	631,240	1,330,980	731,147	6,592,800*

*Totals for 1998 through 2001 exclude probationers in jail or prison.

Source: Bureau of Justice Statistics Correctional Surveys (*National Probation Survey, National Prisoner Statistics, Survey of Jails,* and *National Parole Survey.*)

INCARCERATION RATES OF ADULT OFFENDERS

FIGURE **7.1**

Incarceration rate, 1980–2001
Number of offenders per 100,000 population

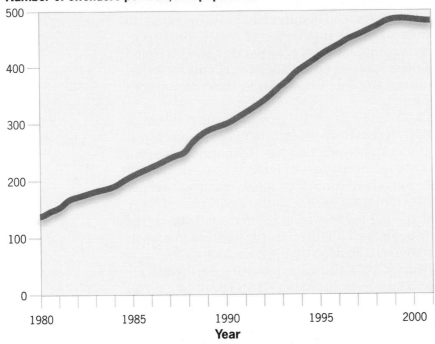

Note: Number of sentenced
inmates incarcerated under
state and federal jurisdiction
per 100,000 population,
1980–2002.

Source: Bureau of Justice
Statistics, "Key Facts at a
Glance," http://www.ojp.usdoj.
gov/bjs/glance/tables/incrttab.
htm (accessed July 27, 2003).

GENDER, RACE, AND ETHNICITY

As well as the tremendous growth in the number of individuals in prison, there has been a change in the makeup of this population by gender, race, and ethnicity. First, as reported in the *Sourcebook of Criminal Justice Statistics, 2001,* the rate of growth for females under all types of correctional supervision has grown at a more rapid rate than the number of males under supervision (see Table 7.2). From 1986 to 1997, the number of males increased 70 percent (from 2,829,100 to 4,797,200), while the number of females increased 118 percent (from 410,300 to 859,300). By 1998, an estimated 950,000 women were under the control of adult correctional agencies. The Bureau of Justice Statistics reported in 1999, "Women represent about 21% of those on probation, 11% of those in local jails, just under 6% of those in prisons, and 12% of those on parole."[3]

The gender makeup of the U.S. prison population is perhaps experiencing the greatest change. At year-end 2002, there were 97,491 women incarcerated in state and federal prisons, making up 6.8 percent of the total prison population.[4] While the proportion of the prison population that is female is still relatively small, the average annual rate of growth of state and federal prisoners has increased more rapidly for females (5.2 percent per year) than for males (3.7 percent per year) from 1995 to 2001.[5] Table 7.3 illustrates the number of women in prison, the annual percentage growth, and the incarceration rate for women. Three of the largest jurisdictions (Texas, the federal system, and California) hold more than one-third of all the female prisoners.[6]

Similarly, there has been a shift in the racial makeup of adults under correctional supervision. As indicated in Table 7.4, whites made up a majority (65 percent) of the correctional population in 1986. However, by 1997, whites represented only 60 percent of all adults offenders under supervision. A majority of the prison population are minorities. On January 1, 2001, the population of state and federal

TABLE	7.2	Correctional Populations by Gender, 1986–1997

Number of persons under correctional supervision

Year	Male	Female
1986	2,829,100	410,300
1987	3,021,000	438,600
1988	3,223,000	491,100
1989	3,501,600	554,000
1990	3,746,300	601,700
1991	3,913,000	622,600
1992	4,050,300	712,300
1993	4,215,800	728,200
1994	4,377,400	763,900
1995	4,513,000	822,100
1996	4,630,100	852,800
1997	4,797,200	895,300

Source: Bureau of Justice Statistics Correctional Surveys (*National Probation Data Survey, National Prisoner Statistics, Survey of Jails*, and *National Parole Data Survey*) as presented in *Correctional Populations in the United States, 1997* (Washington, D.C.: U.S. Department of Justice, 1998).

TABLE	7.3	Women under the Jurisdiction of State or Federal Correctional Authorities, 1995–2001

Region and jurisdiction	Number of female inmates			Percent change		Incarceration rate, 2001[b]
	2001	2000	1995	2000 to 2001	Average, 1995 to 2001[a]	
U.S. total	93,031	93,234	68,468	−0.2%	5.2%	58
Federal	10,973	10,245	7,398	7.1	6.8	6
State	82,058	82,989	61,070	−1.1	5.0	52
Northeast	9,111	9,082	8,401	0.3%	1.4%	29
Connecticut	1,447	1,406	975	2.9	6.8	46
Maine	59	66	36	−10.6	8.6	8
Massachusetts[c]	716	663	656	8.0	1.5	13
New Hampshire	129	120	109	7.5	2.8	20
New Jersey	1,628	1,650	1,307	−1.3	3.7	37
New York	3,133	3,280	3,615	−4.5	−2.4	32
Pennsylvania	1,711	1,579	1,502	8.4	2.2	27
Rhode Island	193	238	157	−18.9	3.5	10
Vermont	95	80	44	18.8	13.7	18
Midwest	14,878	14,598	10,864	1.9%	5.4%	45
Illinois	2,747	2,849	2,196	−3.6	3.8	43
Indiana[c]	1,542	1,452	892	6.2	9.6	49
Iowa	635	592	425	7.3	6.9	43
Kansas	497	504	449	−1.4	1.7	36
Michigan[c]	2,149	2,131	1,842	0.8	2.6	42
Minnesota	383	368	217	4.1	9.9	15
Missouri	2,124	1,993	1,174	6.6	10.4	73
Nebraska	342	266	211	28.6	8.4	38
North Dakota	101	68	29	48.5	23.1	27
Ohio	2,829	2,808	2,793	0.7	0.2	49
South Dakota	222	200	134	11.0	8.8	58
Wisconsin	1,307	1,367	502	−4.4	17.3	47

(continued)

TABLE	7.3	Continued

	Number of female inmates			Percent change		
Region and jurisdiction	2001	2000	1995	2000 to 2001	Average, 1995 to 2001[a]	Incarceration rate, 2001[b]
South	39,138	39,652	27,366	−1.3%	6.1%	68
Alabama	1,783	1,826	1,295	−2.4	5.5	74
Arkansas	793	772	523	2.7	7.2	57
Delaware	591	597	358	−1.0	8.7	62
Dist. of Columbia	189	356	494	—	—	—
Florida	4,281	4,105	3,660	4.3	2.6	50
Georgia	2,834	2,758	2,036	2.8	5.7	66
Kentucky	1,138	1,061	734	7.3	7.6	52
Louisiana	2,262	2,219	1,424	1.9	8.0	99
Maryland	1,207	1,219	1,079	−1.0	1.9	38
Mississippi	1,823	1,669	791	9.2	14.9	113
North Carolina[c]	2,015	1,903	1,752	5.9	2.4	35
Oklahoma	2,290	2,394	1,815	−4.3	4.0	130
South Carolina	1,509	1,420	1,045	6.3	6.3	65
Tennessee[c]	1,468	1,369	637	7.2	14.9	50
Texas	12,369	13,622	7,935	−9.2	7.7	96
Virginia	2,240	2,059	1,659	8.8	5.1	59
West Virginia	346	303	129	14.2	17.9	36
West	18,931	19,657	14,439	−3.7%	4.6%	55
Alaska	376	284	243	32.4	7.5	53
Arizona	2,168	1,964	1,432	10.4	7.2	72
California[c]	9,921	11,161	9,082	−11.1	1.5	55
Colorado	1,375	1,333	713	3.2	11.6	62
Hawaii	616	561	312	9.8	12.0	65
Idaho	563	493	212	14.2	17.7	84
Montana	363	306	112	18.6	21.7	79
Nevada	839	846	530	−0.8	8.0	78
New Mexico	517	511	278	1.2	10.9	50
Oregon	663	596	465	11.2	6.1	37
Utah	316	381	161	−17.1	11.9	26
Washington	1,079	1,065	793	1.3	5.3	35
Wyoming[c]	135	156	106	−13.5	4.1	54

—Not calculated due to transfer to the federal system.

[a]The average annual percentage increase from 1995 to 2001.

[b]The number of female prisoners with sentences of more than one year per 100,000 U.S. residents.

[c]Growth from 1995 to 2001 may be slightly overestimated due to a change in reporting from custody to jurisdiction counts.

Source: Paige M. Harrison and Allen J. Beck, *Prisoners in 2001* (Washington, D.C.: U.S. Department of Justice, Bureau of Justice Statistics, July 2002), p. 7.

prisons was 38.5 percent white, 46.2 percent black, 12.8 percent Hispanic, 1.3 percent Native American, 0.6 percent Asian/Pacific Islander, and 0.6 percent other.[7] Of the 1,829,539 individuals under probation supervision by state agencies on the same date, 52 percent were white, 33 percent were black, 13 percent were Hispanic, and 2 percent were "other."[8] The fact that white offenders make up 52 percent of probationers, yet only 39 percent of prisoners, raises further concern. And the state and federal prison populations on December 31, 2002, included more black males (586,700) than white males (436,800) and Hispanic males (235,000) with sentences of more than one year, and 10.4 percent of all black males age 25 to 29 were in prison, compared to 2.4 percent of Hispanic males and 1.2 percent of white males of the same age group.[9]

The rate of growth in the number of female offenders is even greater than that of males.
Photo by Richard P. Seiter.

TABLE 7.4	Adults under Correctional Supervision by Race, 1986–1997		
Number of adults in prison or jail, or on probation or parole			
Year	**White**	**Black**	**Other**
1986	2,090,100	1,117,200	32,100
1987	2,192,200	1,231,100	36,300
1988	2,348,600	1,325,700	39,800
1989	2,521,200	1,409,000	45,400
1990	2,665,500	1,632,700	49,800
1991	2,742,400	1,743,300	49,900
1992	2,835,900	1,873,200	53,500
1993	2,872,200	2,011,600	60,200
1994	3,058,000	2,018,000	65,300
1995	3,220,900	2,024,000	90,200
1996	3,294,800	2,083,600	104,500
1997	3,429,000	2,149,900	113,600

Source: Bureau of Justice Statistics Correctional Surveys (*National Probation Data Survey, National Prisoner Statistics. Survey of Jails*, and *National Parole Data Survey*) as presented in *Correctional Populations in the United States, 1997* (Washington, D.C.: U.S. Department of Justice, 1998).

This issue of the vast **racial disparity** within the makeup of the U.S. correctional population merits an examination of whether criminal justice and correctional policies are in some way discriminatory. It is important to examine how race (separate from social class, level of poverty, drug use, and other issues) affects discretionary decisions by police, prosecutors, judges, prison officials, and parole board members. Marc Morial, president of the National Urban League, recently identified a disturbing trend: 2002 census figures indicate that that 17 percent of blacks age 25 and older had a bachelor's degree, yet with 875,000 blacks incarcerated in the United States, one out of every seven black men age 25 to 29 are in prison or jail.[10]

Racial disparity

the condition that exists when minorities make up a greater percentage of those under correctional supervision than their makeup in the American population

Current correctional populations are made up of a large percentage of minorities. Less than 50 percent of the current prison population is white.
Courtesy of AP/Wide World Photos.

But why are these numbers disproportionate to the racial and ethnic makeup of the U.S. population? Wilbanks, in *The Myth of a Racist Criminal Justice System*, proposed that the "perception of the criminal justice system as racist is a myth," in that while there are incidents of individual racism, most studies do not show sufficient evidence of racism; he concludes that prejudice and racism are not systematic.[11] In turn, many researchers argue that the disproportion results from the fact that minorities are disproportionately involved in crime, especially violent crime, both as the perpetrators and also as the victims. Minorities in poverty-stricken, urban neighborhoods are most likely to be victims of violent crime. In a 1988 report, the Bureau of Justice Statistics noted that based on Uniform Crime Report homicide data, while 1 out of every 179 white males will be murdered, 1 out of every 30 black males will be murdered.[12]

Crime is also closely linked to poverty, drug use, and lack of opportunity for legitimate approaches to economic success. With crime more prevalent in neighborhoods where African Americans and Hispanics reside, it is not surprising that they are arrested at a higher rate than whites. Law enforcement efforts are always more intense in urban areas with high crime rates and high drug use. A study of how the police responded to the war on drugs noted that arrests for drug use and possession usually occur in the city rather than the suburbs and "have had a disproportionate effect on African Americans."[13] While it appears that the disproportionate numbers of minorities under correctional supervision have less to do with racism within the criminal justice system than with social factors influencing crime, race, and social class, these high numbers of minorities in correctional systems still create a phenomenon that can cause the perception of racism and challenges to the management of correctional agencies.

AGE OF OFFENDERS

Another factor that has changed significantly is the age of the typical prisoner in the United States. Historically, criminals often began their criminal behavior between ages 18 and 21, and were first incarcerated between ages 25 and 30. Most prisoners were age 30 to 35, with very few young or old inmates. However, the bell-shaped age curve of the prison population is leveling out (see Figure 7.2). On

THE LEVELING OUT OF PRISON POPULATION BY AGE

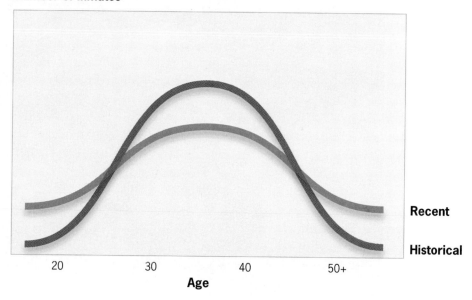

Number of inmates

20 30 40 50+

Age

Recent

Historical

January 1, 2001, there were 7.9 percent of the nation's inmates age 50 or older.[14] This is an increase from 4.9 percent in 1990,[15] which rose to 8.6 percent in 2000 before declining to the current level in 2001. Three phenomena contribute to the aging of the prison population. First, the overall U.S. population is aging, as Americans over age 50 constituted only 26 percent of the population in 1992, but this figure is estimated to reach 33 percent by 2010.[16] Second, inmates are serving longer sentences and therefore stay in prison until they are older. Finally, mandatory sentences and sentencing guidelines take away the discretion of judges who may have kept older offenders in the community on probation rather than sending them to prison, as they are not believed to be a risk to the community. Current sentencing approaches are "age blind," and offenders who may have been allowed to remain in the community because of their advanced age are now sent to prison if their crime severity warrants it.

There has also been an increasing number of offenders under age 18 in state and federal prisons. Over the past decade, many high-publicity and serious crimes have been committed by juveniles. As a result, many states enacted legislation to prosecute serious juvenile offenders as adults, with a sanction of imprisonment in adult rather than juvenile correctional facilities. On December 31, 1997, only 5,400 offenders in state prisons, (less than 1 percent of the total prison population) were under age 18. However, the number of juvenile offenders admitted to prison each year more than doubled from 3,400 in 1985 to 7,400 in 1997.[17] Since 1997, however, the number of juveniles under age 18 in adult correctional facilities has declined. As of June 30, 2002, there were 3,055 juveniles in state prisons and none in federal prisons.[18] Demographics suggest that the proportion of the nation's population age 18 and younger will increase during the first decade of the twenty-first century. With the increase in commission of violent crimes by youthful offenders, it is expected that a higher number of juveniles will be committed to adult institutions over the next ten years.

TYPES OF OFFENSES AND LENGTH OF CONFINEMENT

In addition to the preceding changes in offender populations, the types of offenses for which individuals are under correctional supervision have changed. As Table 7.5

Prisons are now housing a much larger number of elderly offenders, many with serious health problems.
Photo by Richard P. Seiter.

TABLE	7.5	Number of People in Custody of State Correctional Authorities by Most Serious Offense, 1980–2000		
Year	**Violent**	**Property**	**Drug**	**Public order**
1980	173,300	89,300	19,000	12,400
1981	193,300	100,500	21,700	14,600
1982	215,300	114,400	25,300	17,800
1983	214,600	127,100	26,600	24,400
1984	227,300	133,100	31,700	21,900
1985	246,200	140,100	38,900	23,000
1986	258,600	150,200	45,400	28,800
1987	271,300	155,500	57,900	31,300
1988	282,700	161,600	79,100	35,000
1989	293,900	172,700	120,100	39,500
1990	313,600	173,700	148,600	45,500
1991	339,500	180,700	155,200	49,500
1992	369,100	181,600	168,100	56,300
1993	393,500	189,600	177,000	64,000
1994	425,700	207,000	193,500	74,400
1995	459,600	226,600	212,800	86,500
1996	484,800	231,700	216,900	96,000
1997	507,800	236,400	222,100	106,200
1998	545,200	242,900	236,800	113,900
1999	570,000	245,000	251,200	120,600
2000	589,100	238,500	251,100	124,600

Source: *Correctional Populations in the United States, 1997,* (Washington, D.C.: U.S. Department of Justice, 1998); *Prisoners in 2001* (Washington, D.C.: U.S. Department of Justice, 2002).

The use and sale of drugs represent the primary increase in crimes during the 1990, and the principle reason for an increase in the number of inmates in prison.
Courtesy of Corbis Royalty Free.

indicates, there has been a growth in the relative number of offenders who have committed the most serious crimes. The number of people in custody for committing violent offenses increased 340 percent (from 173,300 to 589,100), while the number of those committing property offenses increased by 267 percent (from 89,300 to 238,500). Overall, the percentage of sentenced state inmates incarcerated for violent crimes increased from 46 percent to 49 percent from 1990 to 2000, while the percentage of those convicted of property crimes decreased from 25 percent to 20 percent during the same period.[19]

The most significant increases in number of prison inmates were for those sentenced for committing drug and public-order offenses, both of which increased more than 1,000 percent during the past two decades. Both of these categories were very small parts of the total population under custody in 1980, with drug offenses making up only 6.5 percent and public-order offenses 4.2 percent. However, by 2001, **drug offenders** made up 20.9 percent and public-order offenders 10.4 percent of the total population under custody.[20]

Sentence length has also been increasing. The average length of incarceration (determined by the number of months served by all prison releasees during any specific year) was 23.7 months for 1990 releases from prison, and increased by more than 25 percent to 30.0 months in 1996[21] and 30.6 months in 2000.[22] In addition, more than 300,000 inmates were serving sentences of twenty years or more or life on January 1, 2001.[23] Sentences increased through many "tough on crime" statutes that were passed since 1980. In an effort to alleviate public fear of crime, elected officials have vowed to "lock 'em up and throw away the key" for any criminal that commits serious crimes or continues a pattern of criminality. With many prisoners having no possibility for release in the distant future, prison administrators fear continuously increasing tension and violence in the nation's prisons. Order within prison does not result from physical control, numerical superiority, or intimidation by correctional staff. It results from clear and consistent enforcement of rules, and inmates perceiving they "have something to lose" if they misbehave.

Drug offenders

people convicted of crimes regarding the possession or sale of drugs

Male Offenders

As is well known, males commit the largest proportion of crimes and make up the largest proportion of the correctional population under supervision. During 2000, males made up 78 percent of all arrests by law enforcement agencies,[24] yet on January 1, 2001, males made up 93.2 percent and females only 6.8 percent of the population of state and federal prisons.[25] When the general public thinks of criminals or inmates in prisons, they have a picture in mind of a large, tough-looking male, not a small female. Even though crime rates have been decreasing over the past few years (see Figure 7.3), the role and scope of corrections in managing **male offenders** continues to increase. Some pertinent facts include the following:

Male offenders

men who are convicted and sentenced; men constitute more than 93 percent of all prison inmates

- There were 1,287,695 male inmates under the jurisdiction of state and federal departments of corrections on January 1, 2001.
- There were 645,467 male inmates admitted to adult correctional agencies during 2000.
- There were 53,207 adult male probation violators and 165,458 parole violators admitted to correctional agencies during 2000.
- There were 10,296 adult male inmates completing a boot camp program during 2000, and 6,050 male inmates in boot camps on January 1, 2001.
- Males represented 78.4 percent of all probationers and 88.9 percent of all parolees under active supervision status on January 1, 2001.[26]

MALE OFFENDERS AND VIOLENCE

Male offenders are much more linked to violence than female offenders. In 1998, males represented 78 percent of felony arrests in the United States and 81 percent of arrests for violent crime. From 1989 to 1998, male arrests rose by 2 percent overall, yet declined by 2 percent for violent crime. Yet over the past five years, male ar-

---

THE CRIME RATE HAS BEEN DROPPING

FIGURE **7.3**

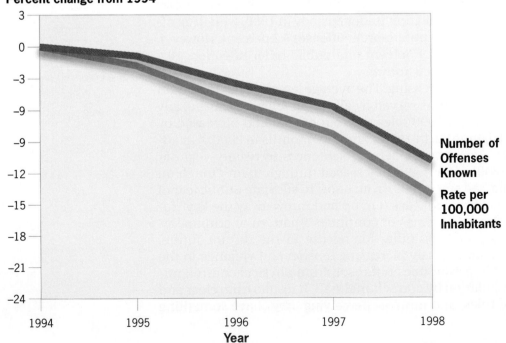

**Crime Index Total
Percent change from 1994**

Number of Offenses Known

Rate per 100,000 Inhabitants

Year

Source: Federal Bureau of Investigation, *Crime in the United States, 1998* (Washington, D.C.: U.S. Department of Justice, 1999), p. 7.

rests for all crimes increased by 2 percent, but fell 12 percent for violent crimes. Female arrests for all crimes increased by 28 percent, increased by 53 percent for violent crimes from 1989 to 1998, and increased for all crimes by 13 percent and for violent crimes by 12 percent from 1994 to 1998.[27]

Even with violent crime seemingly on the decline for males and on the incline for females, males are still predominantly involved in the commission (illustrated by the arrest totals) of violent crimes. Table 7.6 illustrates the number of violent crimes committed by adult males (over age 18) as a percentage of the total of such crimes by both male and female adults. Even though they are a minority of the population of the United States, adult males represented 88.8 percent of the murder and nonnegligent manslaughter arrests and 89.9 percent of all robbery arrests.

TABLE 7.6	Total Arrests of Adult Males in 1998 for All Index Crimes		
	Number of arrests		
Offense charged	**Total**	**Males**	**Percent male**
Total Crimes	9,508,770	7,433,618	78.2%
Murder and nonnegligent manslaughter	11,786	10,462	88.8
Forcible rape	20,608	20,370	98.9
Robbery	83,358	74,972	89.9
Aggravated assault	341,264	274,076	84.4
All violent crimes	457,016	379,880	83.1
Burglary	219,063	191,609	87.5
Larceny-theft	872,771	570,165	65.3
Motor vehicle theft	101,533	85,662	84.4
Arson	11,096	9,459	85.2
All property crimes	1,204,463	856,895	71.1

Source: Adapted from Federal Bureau of Investigation, *Crime in the United States, 1998*, Table 37 (Washington, D.C.: U.S. Department of Justice, 1999), p. 219.

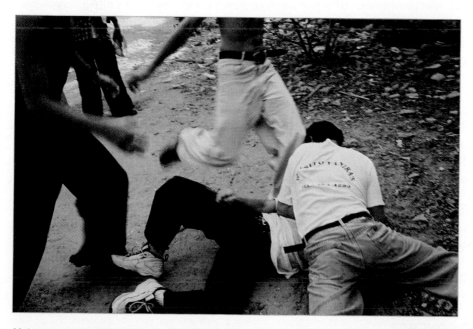

Males are much more involved in violent crimes than females and represent more than 80 percent of the arrests for violent crimes.
Courtesy of Jerome Sessini/In Visu/CORBIS-NY.

TABLE 7.7	Estimated Number of Sentenced Prisoners under State Jurisdiction by Offense and Gender, 2001		
Offense	**All**	**Male**	**Female**
Total	1,208,700	1,132,500	76,200
Violent offenses	596,100	571,700	24,400
Murder[a]	159,200	150,700	8,500
Manslaughter	16,900	15,000	1,900
Rape	30,900	30,600	300
Other sexual assault	87,600	86,600	1,000
Robbery	155,300	150,100	5,200
Assault	118,800	113,100	5,600
Other violent	27,400	25,500	1,900
Property offenses	233,000	213,100	20,000
Burglary	104,700	101,300	3,400
Larceny	45,500	39,600	5,800
Motor vehicle theft	18,000	17,300	700
Fraud	33,700	25,400	8,300
Other property	31,100	29,500	1,600
Drug offenses	246,100	222,900	23,200
Public-order offenses[b]	129,900	121,600	8,300
Other/unspecified[c]	3,600	3,200	400

Note: Data are for inmates with a sentence of more than one year under the jurisdiction of state correctional authorities. The number of inmates by offense were estimated using the 1997 *Survey of Inmates in State Correctional Facilities* and rounded to the nearest 100.

[a]Includes nonnegligent manslaughter.

[b]Includes weapons, drunk driving, court offenses, commercialized vice, morals and decency charges, liquor law violations, and other public-order offenses.

[c]Includes juvenile offenses and unspecified felonies.

Source: Adapted from Paige M. Harrison and Allen J. Beck, "Prisoners in 2002," *Bureau of Justice Statistics Bulletin,* (July 2003), Table 15, p. 10.

Only for larceny-theft are a relatively high proportion of the arrests for females, as males make up 65.3 percent of arrests for that crime.

With the violent background of so many male offenders, violence is much more likely in male prisons than in female prisons. In 2000, 49 percent of adults sentenced to state prisons were committed for violent offenses, 20 percent for property offenses, 21 percent for drug offenses, and 10 percent for public-order offenses.[28] Table 7.7 illustrates the percentage of sentenced prisoners under state jurisdiction by offense and gender in 2001. More than 150,000 male inmates were convicted of murder, more than 117,000 were convicted of rape or other sexual assault, more than 150,000 were convicted of robbery, and more than 113,000 were convicted of assault. Within all state prisons, 596,100 inmates are serving time for violent offenses.

With so many violent inmates in prisons, there is no question that staff must work in situations that can result in assault or even death. I share with you in the "An Insider's Experience" box one of my most frustrating times as a correctional administrator: how helpless I felt when an inmate killed one of the staff members who worked for me.

MALE PRISONERS

Prison systems are predominantly planned and administered around the management of male inmates. The state and federal prison systems have subcompo-

AN INSIDER'S EXPERIENCE: The Murder of a Prison Worker

What a hopeless feeling. I was director of the Ohio department of corrections. I had just received a call from the warden of the highest-security prison in the state. An inmate had murdered a staff member working in prison industries. The inmate had a history of mental health problems and had just recently gotten out of segregation for misconduct. He had been having problems at his industry job, and his supervisor had counseled him regarding his performance. The supervisor was more than sixty years old, a soft-spoken and pleasant man, and was respected by the inmates who worked for him. However, the inmate became angry that he was counseled for poor performance, found a piece of steel that was used in the factory production, and struck the industries supervisor over the head, killing him.

I had never had to deal with the death of someone who worked with or for me before. I listened to the warden describe what had happened, and told him I would get back to him. What could I do? I was 100 miles away, and didn't know what I should do in this situation. I called my old boss at the Federal Bureau of Prisons who had faced this situation. Several steps were suggested: Order all flags flown over the prisons at half-staff. Inform the prison of your intent to attend the funeral. Make contact with the family of the victim and offer your condolences. Move the inmate murderer from the prison to avoid the chance of retribution by angry staff and take away the constant reminder of the killing of the staff member. These seemed like reasonable things to do, and I quickly put them in place. However, they just seemed so insignificant for the death of someone. But I felt helpless to

do more. I talked to the warden about the security of the prison and about avoiding further violence, but he had all that under control.

I made a trip to the prison to show support for staff and assure them that the murderer would be prosecuted and we would seek the death penalty. But I found myself at a loss for words that seemed to be responsive to losing their friend and co-worker. I attended the wake and funeral for the staff person, and spent time with his family. But they didn't know me, and I know I was little comfort to them. A group of angry co-workers wanted to know what we were going to do to keep this from happening again. But there is no way to prevent it without keeping inmates in cells or handcuffs all the time. One co-worker even followed me around the funeral home to listen to everything I said—I guess thinking I would say something insensitive and he could use it to blame me. Everyone felt helpless, many were afraid, and they wanted someone to blame.

Over the next few months, we put many improvements in place at the prison that made it a more manageable and safer place for inmates and staff. But there was no way to bring back the staff member who had been killed. And over time, staff did return to normal and resumed their duties in the professional and competent way they always did their jobs. I know that I was a good leader and brought many positive reforms to the correctional department in Ohio. However, I also know how helpless I felt, and how futile the immediate actions I took seemed. But, that is probably true when experiencing the death of anyone close to you. It just brings our mortality closer to us.

---

nents of groups of offenders, including women, juveniles serving time in adult prisons, mentally ill inmates, substance abusers, and other groups that are housed and managed separately. However, the majority of adult prisons hold normal, male inmates (often referred to as the **general population**) without a particular designation requiring special housing or management. Male inmates in the general population are received into the prison systems, assessed, and classified to one of the various security level prisons to serve their sentence. Security levels of prisons are designed to match physical security, staff resources, programs, and prison operations with the risk of violence and escape by male inmates assigned to each level.

The 1,384 state and federal prisons on January 1, 2001, are divided into the following security levels: intake, community, minimum, medium, high/close, maximum, or multiple custody. Table 7.8 illustrates the numbers and percentage of all prisons in each category. Each increasing level of security has more physical

General population

the inmates in a prison who do not have any specific designation as a special type of offender

TABLE 7.8	The Makeup of Prisons by Security Level	
Institution security level	**Number of prisons**	**Percent of total**
Intake	49	3.5%
Community	194	14.0
Minimum	325	23.5
Medium	327	23.6
High/close	92	6.7
Maximum	95	12.0
Multiple	302	40.0
Total	1,384	100

Source: Camille Graham Camp and George M. Camp, *The 2001 Corrections Yearbook, Adult Systems* (Middletown, Conn.: Criminal Justice Institute, 2002), pp. 79–82.

security to reduce the potential for escapes, a higher staff-to-inmate ratio, more restrictions on inmate movement, more emphasis on security, and less emphasis on inmate programs. The overall goal of inmate security classification is to maintain homogeneity of inmates by risk of violence and escape, and therefore ensure that they are placed in prisons that are physically designed to meet these risks. Housing high-security inmates in a facility that is low or minimum security creates the danger of escape, predatory behavior, or violence against staff or other inmates.

To ensure that inmates are in the proper security level and to plan for their participation in work and programs, prison caseworkers and counselors oversee the classification and program process. The "Your Career in Corrections" box describes the role of these staff members.

YOUR CAREER IN CORRECTIONS

CASEWORKERS AND COUNSELORS

A position in prisons that is often used as an entry-level job for recent college or community college graduates is that of counselor or caseworker (sometimes called a social worker in some agencies). These professionals work directly with inmates, with the primary responsibility of classifying offenders and creating and monitoring plans for program and work participation. The plans continue throughout the period of confinement and build to the preparation for release.

A key component of the caseworker's job is security and treatment classification of an inmate. When inmates are sent to prison, they must first be classified to determine the security level of the prison in which they will be placed. The caseworker reviews the presentence investigation and any other informational documents to determine criminal and social history, sentence information, medical and psychological needs, education and work history, and other relevant preincarceration information. From this review, the caseworker usually completes an objective classification form to determine whether the inmate will be minimum, medium, or maximum security. The caseworker must continue to update the classification instrument with new information (such as prison behavior and time left to serve) to see if the security classification changes. The classification plan also assists with the assignment of work and program participation to meet identified inmate needs.

In describing the role played by these staff persons, Carlson suggests:

> Case management staffers maintain the official classification documents . . . These staff members are not only responsible for determining the prisoner's custody and security needs, but charged with helping the inmates plan their institution-based work and program assignments.[29]

Caseworkers often perform as a team with prison educators, mental health professionals, and substance abuse counselors to create treatment plans and monitor inmates' progress toward their goals. Some caseworkers actually perform counseling, but in most state and federal prisons, their principal role is to guide inmates through all aspects of their prison sentence, including the legal sanction and expectation for release, an understanding of their individual treatment needs, and the availability of prison programs to meet these needs. Caseworkers can also assist inmates with services outside the prison (job assistance, family counseling, or halfway house agencies) that will aid in their transition from prison to community.

Jobs as a caseworker require good interpersonal, decision-making, and writing skills. Most states require that applicants for these jobs have a college degree (often in the social sciences), but a few states do not require a degree if the person has experience. The type of college degree may vary with the specific job requirements of the position. Williamson writes, "The primary determinants of educational requirements are the specific job description and the states in which they are located."[30] If caseworkers perform therapeutic treatment themselves, they may be required to possess a clinical degree in mental health or social work. While the salary for most state or federal caseworker jobs is usually 15 to 20 percent higher than the starting pay for a correctional officer, caseworkers usually have less opportunity to earn additional overtime pay, and the annual earnings may actually end up being about the same. However, these are excellent jobs, providing the broad experience, the challenge of interaction with inmates, the need for planning ahead, and the ability to have an important impact on the future lives of criminal offenders.

Female Offenders

In 2000, women made up about 22 percent of all arrests by law enforcement agencies, an increase from 19.5 percent in 1994.[31] As women's involvement in crime has increased, the growth in the number of **female offenders** under correctional supervision has grown rapidly. Most of the detailed information available regarding female offenders is from Greenfeld and Snell's 1999 publication, *Women Offenders*. This study indicated that the number of women under correctional supervision increased at a greater rate (118 percent) than the number of males (70 percent) under supervision between 1986 and 1997. In 1998, women constituted approximately 16 percent of the total correctional population, including 21 percent of the probation population, 11 percent of those in jails, 6 percent of prisoners, and 12 percent of parolees.[32] As indicated in Table 7.9, women make up 17 percent of all arrests for violent offenses, 29 percent of arrests for property offenses, and 18 percent of arrests for drug offenses. A recent review by the Illinois Criminal Justice Information Authority examined cases of 2,438 adult probationers and found that female probationers were much more likely than males to have been convicted of drug or property offenses.[33]

Much of the growth in terms of women under correctional supervision can be seen from the increase in the felony convictions in state courts from 1990 to 1996 (see Table 7.10). In 1996, women accounted for about 16 percent of all felony convictions, including 8 percent of all convictions for violent crimes, 23 percent for property crimes, and 17 percent for drug offenses. The growth in the number of females convicted of felonies increased at two and a half times the rate of the growth in the number of male convictions between 1990 and 1996.[34]

Once sentenced, women have historically been given lesser sentences than men. However, as a result of sentencing guidelines and mandatory prison sentences, judges have less discretion and are now treating women more similar to men than in the past. A 1993 study in Pennsylvania reported that similar sentences were received by men and women charged with similar offenses.[35]

Female offenders
women who are convicted and sentenced; just over 6 percent of prison inmates are female

TABLE 7.9	Arrests of Females, 1998	

	Arrests of females	
	1998	**Percent of all arrests**
Total arrests	3,170,520	22%
Violent offenses	113,877	17
Murder	1,959	11
Robbery	12,130	10
Aggravated assault	99,490	20
Property offenses	521,894	29
Burglary	41,177	13
Larceny	453,277	35
Motor vehicle theft	23,585	16
Drug offenses	272,073	18
Driving under the Influence	219,514	16

Note: Violent offenses, which include rape, and property offenses are the Part I offenses in the FBI *Uniform Crime Reports. Total arrests* includes Part I and Part II offenses.

Source: Lawrence A. Greenfeld and Tracy L. Snell, *Women Offenders* (Washington, D.C.: U.S. Department of Justice, Bureau of Justice Statistics, December 1999), p. 5.

TABLE 7.10	Felony Convictions of Women in State Courts, 1990–1996				

	Estimated number of women convicted of felonies in state courts				
	1990	**1992**	**1994**	**1996**	**Percent change, 1990–1996**
Total	112,800	120,550	131,404	160,470	42%
Violent felonies	10,428	12,313	13,936	13,509	30
Murder	1,051	1,205	1,289	1,005	−4
Rape/sexual assault	202	375	630	442	119
Robbery	3,047	3,142	2,854	2,920	−4
Aggravated assault	5,043	6,152	6,906	7,786	54
Other violent	1,085	1,440	2,256	1,356	25
Property felonies	48,206	52,230	53,649	69,536	44
Burglary	5,593	5,830	6,603	6,847	22
Larceny	20,728	22,179	22,136	28,786	39
Fraud	21,885	24,221	24,910	33,902	55
Drug felonies	43,000	42,047	46,468	59,027	37
Trafficking	24,562	23,529	25,561	33,005	34
Possession	18,438	18,518	20,907	26,022	41
Other felonies	11,166	13,959	17,351	18,399	65

Note: Murder includes nonnegligent manslaughter; larceny includes motor vehicle theft; and fraud includes forgery and embezzlement. Details may not equal totals because of rounding.

Source: Lawrence A. Greenfeld and Tracy L. Snell, *Women Offenders* (Washington, D.C.: U.S. Department of Justice, Bureau of Justice Statistics, December 1999), p. 5.

Chesney-Lind reports, "Twenty years ago, nearly two-thirds of the women convicted of federal felonies were granted probation, but in 1991, only 28 percent were given straight probation."[36] The characteristics of female offenders under correctional supervision have similar traits to those of male offenders. As illus-

TABLE 7.11	Characteristics of Adult Women under Correctional Supervision			
Characteristics of women	**Probation**	**Local jails**	**State prisons**	**Federal prisons**
Race/Hispanic origin				
White	62%	36%	33%	29%
Black	27	44	48	35
Hispanic	10	15	15	32
Other	1	5	4	4
Age				
24 or younger	20%	21%	12%	9%
25–34	39	46	43	35
35–44	30	27	34	32
45–54	10	5	9	18
55 or older	1	1	2	6
Median age	32 years	31 years	33 years	36 years
Marital status				
Married	26%	15%	17%	29%
Widowed	2	4	6	6
Separated	10	13	10	21
Divorced	20	20	20	10
Never married	42	48	47	34
Education				
8th grade or less	5%	12%	7%	8%
Some high school	35	33	37	19
High school graduate/GED	39	39	39	44
Some college or more	21	16	17	29

Source: Lawrence A. Greenfeld and Tracy L. Snell, *Women Offenders* (Washington, D.C.: U.S. Department of Justice, Bureau of Justice Statistics, December 1999), p. 7.

trated in Table 7.11, while nearly two-thirds of women on probation are white, almost two-thirds of women in jail or prison are minorities. Women in prison are older than those on probation or in jail. This simply indicates the factoring of criminal history in sentencing decisions. As offenders grow older and accumulate a more extensive offense history, they are more likely to receive a prison sentence. Women under correctional supervision are more likely than the general population to have never been married, and the majority of female offenders have completed high school.

In terms of recidivism, rates for female offenders are high, yet are thought to be less than recidivism rates for comparable male offenders. In a 1983 study of 6,400 women (and more than 100,000 men) released from prison in eleven states, 52 percent of the women were rearrested, 39 percent were reconvicted, and 33 percent were returned to prison during a three-year follow-up.[37]

The most important factor in predicting recidivism for women is prior arrest history, as the greater the number of prior arrests, the higher rate of rearrest among women released from prison over a three-year follow-up. A national study reports the following:

> [A]mong women with only the one arrest for which they had been imprisoned, 21% were rearrested within 3 years. Among women with 2–3 prior arrests, 33% were rearrested; those with 4–6 prior arrests had a 47% rearrest rate; among those with 7–10 priors, 69% were rearrested; and, nearly 8 out of 10 women with 11 or more priors were rearrested.[38]

WOMEN IN PRISON

In 1925, only 3,438 women were in prison, representing 3.7 percent of the national prison population. This percentage of women in the overall prison population remained relatively stable until the 1980s, when it began to rise as many states implemented sentencing guidelines and mandatory prison sentences. The percentage of women in the prison population increased to 5.7 percent by 1990.[39] On June 30, 2002, there were 1,426,118 prisoners in state and federal prisons, of which 96,099 (6.7 percent) were women.[40] Just as with male offenders, much of the increase in the number of women incarcerated resulted from the war on drugs and expansion of arrests and prosecutions for drug offenses. In 1998, 34 percent of all women in state prisons and 72 percent of women in federal prisons had been convicted of drug offenses.[41]

The average length of prison sentence served by women is considerably less than that served by men. On January 1, 2001, men in prison were serving an average sentence of 5.22 years, while women in prison were serving an average of 3.63 years.[42] Some would argue that this indicates that women still receive less severe sentences than men. However, it is more likely the result of the fact that men in prison have more extensive criminal careers than women and commit a greater proportion of violent and serious crimes. A report by the Bureau of Justice Statistics in 1999 indicated that about 65 percent of women in state prisons had prior convictions compared to 77 percent of men in state prisons, and that "Based on self reports of victims of violence, women account for about 14 percent of violent offenders."[43] In addition, the same report noted the that consequences of male violence were more serious for the victim, in the sense of weapon use (15 percent of women used a firearm, knife, or blunt object, compared to 28 percent of men), injury to the victim (5 percent of victims of women were seriously injured, compared to 8 percent of victims of men), and average loss to the victim ($595 for victims of women and $943 for victims of men). Even though they still make up a

The war on drugs and other "tough on crime" sentencing approaches have resulted in many more women going to prison than in the past.
Courtesy of Bob Daemmrich/Bob Daemmrich Photography, Inc.

small percentage of all prisoners in the United States, when women go to prison, they have many issues and needs that are different from those of male offenders and create challenges for correctional administrators.

SPECIAL ISSUES AND NEEDS OF FEMALE INMATES

Some of the issues facing female inmates that are different from those of male inmates include health care, vocational training and work opportunities, potential of sexual abuse from staff, alcohol and drug use, and problems relating to their children. Approximately 60 percent of women in state prisons have experienced physical or sexual abuses prior to their incarceration.[44] A 1995 study by Bloom estimated that 80 percent of incarcerated women are mothers,[45] and the Bureau of Justice Statistics lists 53,600 female inmates (approximately 60 percent) in 1999 as having minor children.[46] Approximately one-fourth of the women who enter prison are either pregnant or have given birth within the past twelve months.[47] As mothers, female inmates often feel guilt for abandoning their children, and must ask other family members to care for their children during incarceration. Because a small percentage of inmates are women, there are fewer female than male prisons. Therefore, the distance from home for female offenders is usually greater than for males, making it more difficult for family and the children to visit.

Many states have created innovating programs that they believe are particularly effective in responding to the special needs of female inmates. A survey of these programs in several states identified the following innovations. The

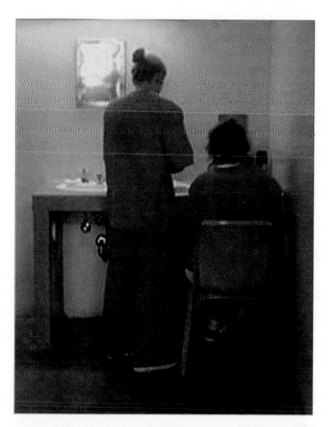

Most female inmates are mothers, and separation from their children is a difficult consequence of their imprisonment.
Photo by Richard P. Seiter.

number of programs that are operational in each category in all states is shown in parentheses.

Psychological programs (90): substance abuse, mental health counseling, and domestic violence counseling

Work programs (48): work training, prison industry programs, and other work *related programs*

Parenting programs (42): child visitation, parent education, and other parenting programs

Other programs (62): transition and aftercare programs, education programs, health programs (including HIV/AIDS education), and life skills programs[48]

In addition to establishing these programs, administrators of women's correctional facilities noted specific program elements that are key to making the programs successful (see Figure 7.4). The most important elements for success are staff characteristics, comprehensiveness of approach, and pertinence to women's

---

ELEMENTS RELATED TO SUCCESSFUL PROGRAMS FOR WOMEN

FIGURE **7.4**

Program Staff
- Staff are dedicated/caring/qualified.
- Ex-addicts or ex-offenders are on staff.
- Women staff members serve as role models.

Meeting of Specific and Multiple Needs
- Program has a comprehensive or multifaceted focus.
- Program addresses rudimentary or basic needs.
- Program establishes a continuum of care.

Program Participation
- Participants like the program.
- Inmate participation is high or self-initiated.
- Participants help run the program.

Peer Influence
- Other participants provide positive peer influence.
- Other participants provide pressure (e.g., to be a good mother).
- Other participants provide support.

Individualized, Structured
- Clear, measurable goals are established.
- Treatment plans and programming are individualized.
- Program is intensive and of appropriate duration.
- Appropriate screening and assessment are provided.

Technology, Resources
- Equipment, money, and other resources are available.
- Adequate space is available.

Acquisition of Skills
- Marketable job skills can be acquired.
- Parenting and life skills are taught.
- Education addresses thinking and reasoning.
- Anger management is taught.

Program Environment
- Atmosphere is "homey"; climate is conducive to visits.
- Communications are open; confidentiality is kept.
- Rapport with other participants is good.
- Participants are separated from the general population.
- Program enrollment is small.

Victimization Issues
- Program addresses self-esteem.
- Women are treated like human beings.
- Program addresses domestic violence.
- Program addresses empowerment and self-sufficiency.

Administrative and Staff Interaction
- Administrative support and communication are good.
- Management style is nonaggressive.
- Security staff are understanding and supportive.

Assistance from Outside the Facility
- Outside private-public partnerships exist.
- Interagency coordination exists.
- Some staff come from outside the department of corrections.

Source: Merry Morash, Timothy S. Bynum, and Barbara A. Koons, "Women Offenders: Programming Needs and Promising Approaches," *National Institute of Justice: Research in Brief* (August 1998): 7.

own interests. Of secondary importance is that these programs involve female staff, and female offenders have the opportunity to identify with these staff. Some of the specific issues that confront incarcerated women are described next.

Separation from Family and Children

In a way very different than male inmates, women inmates suffer from the separation from their family and children and feel helpless in their child-raising role. Approximately 65 percent of women held in state prisons have children under age 18 and report an average of 2.38 children per inmate. About two-thirds of these women (compared to 44 percent of male inmates) lived with their young children before entering prison.[49] While some children of female offenders are placed in foster homes, most end up with their maternal grandmothers. In only a small percent of cases of female inmates is there a husband and father of the children who is not also incarcerated. Almost 90 percent of children of male inmates live with the children's mothers. This placement seems to be the most acceptable to female inmates and gives them the most peace of mind about how their children are being treated and the ease of getting their children back after release.[50] Female offenders know that their criminal involvement has caused a hardship for and separation from their children, and feel shame and guilt for their own actions, yet anger and bitterness with the criminal justice system for their situation.

With such a large proportion of women inmates having children, visiting in prison is particularly important. However, elderly parents of inmates caring for children often have a difficult time making the trip to visit regularly. Visits are also problematic due to the long distance between the inmates' homes and the prisons in which they are incarcerated. Female prisoners make up a relatively small portion of the nation's prison population, and most states have several male prisons but only one or two female prisons. Therefore, women are placed farther from their homes than men. It is interesting that wives of male inmates regularly bring children to visit their fathers. However, when mothers end up in prison, they receive fewer visits with children due to the distances and the logistical problems those giving child care have in making visits.

Unfortunately, when women receive visits from their children, prison visiting room conditions are not conducive to fostering a parent-child relationship. Prison visiting areas usually provide seating similar to that in an airport waiting area, although many now provide a small room or area of the larger visiting room for small children with a television, videos, and books or toys for children to play with. To improve the parental relationship between women inmates and their children, many prisons have established **parenting programs**. These programs often include training classes to improve parenting skills and suggest methods to "parent" from prison. One example is how to play the role of mother as teacher, by emphasizing the mother reading to children (sometimes on audiotape) and helping children with their school homework during visits. A few programs include special visiting situations where children may be able to spend extended time or even overnight with their mothers, and may include special use (separate from other inmates) of the prison recreation or dining areas.

Another unique program to assist inmate mothers in staying connected to their children is **Girl Scouts Behind Bars**. Some female prisons have established Girl Scout chapters, have meetings with female inmates and their daughters in the visiting room, and get the inmate mothers involved in "den mother" activities such as planning meetings or providing snacks. The Girl Scout chapters are usually linked to a chapter in the community so that the children can also be involved in normal Girl Scouts activities. This program also encourages the continued involvement of mothers and daughters in Girl Scouts after the mothers' release from prison.[51]

Parenting programs
prison programs that help inmates improve their parenting skills, even while in prison

Girl Scouts Behind Bars
Girl Scout troops that have their chapter based in a prison so inmates with children can participate as Scout parents

Many prisons have added a room for children to play or for parents to read to them, so there is some semblance of normalcy as children visit their parents in prison.
Courtesy of the Ohio Department of Rehabilitation and Correction.

Alcohol and Substance Abuse

Many women offenders have a serious history and problem with alcohol and substance abuse, often even more serious and more involved in their criminality than men. About half of women inmates in state prisons were using alcohol or drugs at the time of their offense, and 40 percent of women (compared to 32 percent of men) were under the influence of drugs at the time of their crime.[52] As well, "[n]early 1 in 3 women serving time in State prisons said they had committed the offense which brought them to prison in order to obtain money to support their need for drugs."[53] The Center for Substance Abuse Treatment reports that almost 80 percent of the women in state prisons have "severe, long-standing substance abuse problems."[54] Unquestionably, women offenders are in need of programs and services to reduce their dependence on alcohol and drugs.

Unfortunately, the need for substance abuse treatment in prison is generally not satisfactorily met. On January 1, 2001, there were 120,687 male and female inmates (an average of 12.9 percent of the prison populations) participating in drug treatment programs in state or federal prisons. Of these, 40,909 were in counseling only, and the remainder were evenly divided between separate drug treatment units and additional group programs.[55] Twenty percent of women offenders report receiving drug or alcohol treatment during the period of their incarceration.[56] Another Bureau of Justice Statistics report noted that one in four inmates participate in drug treatment programs, most of which are self-help groups, and only 4 percent receive professional counseling for their abuse.[57]

It is important to increase the overall number of **substance abuse programs**, and particularly the number of those for female inmates. As well, the women's pro-

Substance abuse programs

programs that help offenders reduce their likelihood of further abuse of alcohol or drugs grams should focus on the specific issues around the reasons for female drug abuse and special circumstances around their postincarceration needs. Chesney-Lind suggests:

> Women's programs must, first and foremost, give participants strategies to deal with their profound substance abuse problems. They must also be gender-sensitive in additional ways: they must understand that most women take drugs as a form of self-medication, and they must be sensitive to women's unique circumstances (by providing such services as child care and transportation).[58]

Need for Medical Care

Medical care is very difficult to provide in a quality fashion within a prison. Moore suggests, "Problems in providing care to the incarcerated fall into two broad categories: health status of the inmate population and deficiencies in the delivery of medical care,"[59] and identifies six factors inherent in correctional settings that hamper the provision of health services:

1. not a priority of the correctional institution;
2. limited financial resources;
3. difficulties in staff recruitment;
4. absence of a current manual of health care policies and procedures;
5. isolation of the institution from community health care; and
6. lack of a constituency for inmate health services.[60]

While all inmate medical care is difficult to provide, one issue without question is that female inmates have more serious health problems than male inmates. This results not only from the need for gynecological care, but from a history of poverty, drug and alcohol abuse, poor diet and nutrition, and past neglect and lack of health care.[61] Women, of course, also have medical issues around pregnancy. Greenfeld and Snell report that 5 percent of women admitted to state prisons are pregnant, and while 90 percent of these had received a gynecological exam since their admission, only 4 percent had received prenatal care since their admission.[62] Another survey of pregnant prisoners noted that only half were provided prenatal care, 15 percent were provided a special diet or nutrition education, 15 percent received counseling regarding placement of their child after birth, and 11 percent were provided postnatal counseling.[63]

The delivery of correctional health care has improved over the past two decades. However, there is a serious need for correctional administrators to continue to make improvements, and specifically to address the challenges in providing health care for women prisoners. In describing these challenges for correctional administrators, Seiter notes,

> [T]here are unanswered philosophical questions about the quality and quantity of medical care that should be provided incarcerated felons. Costs of inmate health care continue to rise, and there is constant pressure on administrators to reduce medical spending. Prisons have never been an attractive recruiting ground for medical personnel, and competition for providers has intensified over the past decade. All of these issues require prison administrators to look for new ways to solve serious problems. Yet, there are few states that would suggest they have found the answers, and are comfortable with the cost and quality of the medical care provided in their prisons.[64]

Classification Systems for Female Offenders

One concern that has recently come to light is that objective classification systems developed for male offenders often tend to "overclassify" female offenders. In a 2001 review of all fifty states, the National Institute of Corrections examined the current classification practices used for female offenders and discovered that while many states recognized the differences by gender regarding needs and risks, few had incorporated these differences into their objective classification systems.[65] Overclassification is the placement of offenders in prisons more secure than needed for their level of risk, and results from using risk factors (such as seriousness of the offense) that were developed using predominantly male offender examples, and did not take into account the specific variables that reduced the risk posed by women.

In the early 1990s, the Federal Bureau of Prisons (BOP) reviewed its classification system based on these gender issues. The BOP found that it was placing female offenders at a higher level of physical security prisons than their risk to escape or tendency for violence warranted. In most cases, women's criminal involvement was as accomplices to men, and if the crime included the use of a weapon or violence, male offenders actually handled the weapon or resorted to violence. As well, a previously unconsidered factor was that female inmates often had children and close ties in the community, and these were important factors in predicting escape. Therefore, the BOP administratively reduced the number of points assigned for certain types of crimes (such as crimes of violence or use of a weapon during the offense) committed by women, and was able to move a large percent of the female inmate population to less secure prisons.

The "A Look Into" box describes the issues and challenges that prison staff have in dealing with female inmates.

A LOOK INTO . . . WORKING WITH FEMALE INMATES

One interesting point regarding female offenders is the differences in them as inmates from their male counterparts. I have worked as a case manager and a unit manager for female inmates, and in three other prisons that held male inmates. To develop this case study, I talked to someone who has recently been a case manager for a male and a female caseload. It is interesting to see the differences he describes in working with the two populations.

- Females need more contact with agencies outside of the prison. More women are filing for divorce and need contact with the family courts. More have children issues, and must contact the division of family services. These types of contacts often require telephone calls, as they cannot be completed only through the mail.
- Sentences for women overall are less than for men, so the turnaround is greater. More women are referred to halfway houses, and staff have to move more quickly to get referrals completed.
- Medical and mental health issues are different and more intense. Female inmates are sometimes pregnant while in prison and need prenatal care. Mental health issues seem more pronounced for female inmates, they need more psychological services, and a higher percentage seem to be on antidepressants.
- Women stay much more attached to the community than men, who seem to divorce themselves from their families and community ties. Female inmates take more responsibility in regard to their children and family, especially their parents, and are continually more stressed out about their problems in the community.
- Female inmates are very different in regard to their relationships with staff and other inmates. Women seem to need someone to talk to and will talk more freely than men to staff about their problems. They are also much more open about their sexual relationships (in prison) than men.

They may have a girlfriend; they may have a break up; and there is more fighting about these sexual relationships. A higher percentage of women seem to participate in homosexuality, or they hide it less. Men get involved in homosexual activity more for the sexual gratification, while women get involved for the emotional relationship.

■ Women are more interested in being involved in programs. There is a high demand for drug programs, and they are more willing to confront their drug use as a problem that needs attention. They work better with staff and are more willing to take orders and follow instructions.

■ One interesting issue concerns property. Men want food or snacks, but women try to accumulate hobby or craft items, to create more of a "homey" atmosphere in their cell or dormitory area than men. They try to get jewelry, and often have visitors bring them things that are not allowed. They have different demands of the commissary; they desire hair dye; skin care products, and other personal cosmetic items.

■ Race is not as much of an issue as with men. Female inmates seem less concerned about race and do not self-segregate near as much. In male dining rooms, inmates often sit at tables with only their race, while women are much less concerned about this.

■ Women have fewer disciplinary issues than men. They just seem to accept their incarceration without breaking the rules as much.

■ Female inmates, however, are far more manipulative with staff than male inmates. They are more likely to exaggerate or outright lie about a problem at home that requires immediate attention or a crisis phone call home.

■ In general, women have many more demands and take much more staff time than men. They realistically have more issues, particularly related to home, and desire immediate attention from staff. When case managers need to talk to male inmates to prepare a progress report; they almost have to order them to come in to talk and discuss their community plans. Women are lined up at the door to talk about issues at home.

LEGAL ISSUES REGARDING PARITY FOR FEMALE INMATES

Over the past ten years, correctional agencies have made many improvements in responding to the specific needs of women in prison. Many of these developments have resulted from the intervention of federal courts, noting the disparate treatment received and conditions faced by female offenders. As early as 1974, a federal court in the case of **Barefield v. Leach** found that the state of New Mexico was not providing parity in vocational training and work opportunity for female inmates, and ruled that such disparity could not be justified just because the smaller number of female inmates made it more costly to provide parity in these programs.[66] In *Butler v. Reno*, female plaintiffs who were federal inmates claimed gender discrimination due to denial of access to facilities, programs, and services available to similarly situated male federal inmates. The U.S. District Court for the District of Columbia agreed with the plaintiffs, and the parties entered into a stipulated order of settlement in 1995. In the order, the Bureau of Prisons agreed to provide programs, services and facilities for female inmates that were comparable to those offered to male inmates. This included placing minimum-security female inmates in camps with limited physical security; maintaining similar staff-inmate ratios; providing work, education, parent-child and recreation program opportunities; and providing health care comparable to that in male prisons.

In the 1995 case of **Pargo v. Elliot**, the Eighth Circuit Court found that just the fact that there are differences in programs between male and female prisons is not necessarily a violation of the equal protection clause of the Constitution. The Court suggested that five criteria should be used to examine whether differences in prison programs are discriminatory: the number of inmates in a prison, the

Barefield v. Leach
a 1974 federal court decision that a disparity of programs for female inmates could not be justified because the smaller number of female inmates made it more costly to provide program parity

Pargo v. Elliot
the 1995 Eighth Circuit Court case that determined that differences in programs between men's and women's prisons do not necessarily violate the equal protection clause of the Constitution

Female offenders have developed some of the same habits as male offenders (such as adding tattoos), and the courts have declared that they deserve parity with male offenders in programs and services.
Photo by Richard P. Seiter.

prison security level, the crimes committed by inmates, the length of sentences being served by inmates, and any other special characteristics that could be identified by the prison as reasons for program differences.[67] It is recognized that women will look for different types of jobs after release from prison, and that many need training in parenting and child-care issues that are not as critical for men.

The solution to the problem of parity has been lessened with the growth in the number of female inmates. Rafter reports that while only two to three new female prisons were opened every decade between 1930 and 1950, during the 1980s more than 34 new women's prisons were opened, by 1990 there were 71 women's prisons, and in 1995, there were 104 prisons designated for female offender.[68] With more than 90,000 women in state and federal prisons in 2001 and the opening of many new prisons for women, there are more economies of scale in providing additional categories of vocational training or other treatment programs for women inmates. New prisons also provide the opportunity to begin new types of educational, vocational, and work programs, focusing on the nontraditional roles of women offenders, and providing parity with male programs. Finally, additional prisons scattered across states enable women to be more likely housed closer to their homes than when the state had only one female prison.

ALTERNATIVES TO PRISON FOR WOMEN OFFENDERS

Many experts believe that the most effective way to prepare female offenders for success in the community is to maximize the use of alternative programs to incarceration. While the public has taken a "tough on crime" approach for male offenders, most people are willing to recognize that women present less risk (or at least are perceived to present less risk) of further victimization, and therefore are good candidates to be supervised and managed in the community.

With this in mind, nine out of ten state correctional administrators reported that they use some type of alternative to prison for women, even after they are committed to prison. Some of these programs shorten the prison stay and move female inmates into the community more quickly, while others target successful reentry of women from prison to community. Figure 7.5 illustrates the types of alternative programs that are used by states in this regard, both by number of states and by percentage of women in the alternative sanctions. The alternative used by most states is work release, in which inmates either leave the prison during the day and go into the community and work, or are moved to community residential centers (halfway houses) to find jobs and work in the community. The highest percentage of female inmates are involved in prerelease centers. An example of a state prerelease center is the Franklin County (Ohio) Prerelease Center, to which inmates are moved in their last three to six months in prison in order to participate in programs focusing on release preparation. At the center they receive training in life skills (finding a residence, opening a checking account, applying for credit) and preparation for entering the world of work (writing a résumé, interviewing for a job, and responding to the issue of their criminality and incarceration). Women also learn how to deal with the day-to-day issues in the workplace, such as the importance of quality, taking responsibility, and getting along with supervisors and peers.

Now that students have learned the issues that face women convicted of a crime, and have considered the potential for alternatives to incarceration, it is time to struggle with the challenging question of whether women should face justice for their crimes just as men do. Consider this issue in the "You Make the Decision" box.

The Franklin County Prerelease Center in Ohio is a facility to which women inmates move in their last few months of incarceration to prepare for release to the community.
Courtesy of the Ohio Department of Rehabilitation and Correction.

ALTERNATIVE SANCTIONS FOR WOMEN OFFENDERS AFTER COMMITMENT TO PRISON   FIGURE 7.5

Alternative Program

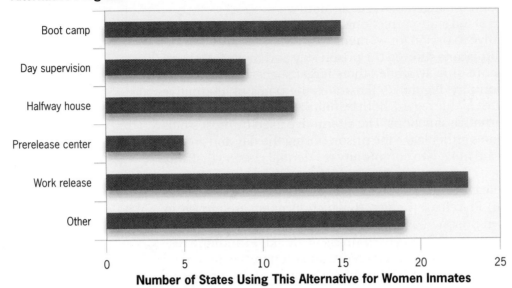

Number of States Using This Alternative for Women Inmates

Alternative Program

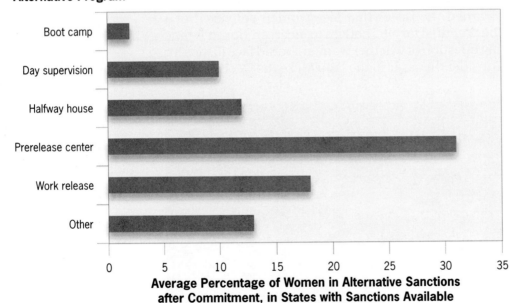

Average Percentage of Women in Alternative Sanctions after Commitment, in States with Sanctions Available

Source: Merry Morash, Timothy S. Bynum, and Barbara A. Koons, "Women Offenders: Programming Needs and Promising Approaches," *National Institute of Justice: Research in Brief* (August 1998): 5.

YOU MAKE THE DECISION . . .

SHOULD WOMEN GO TO PRISON JUST LIKE MEN?

As noted earlier, in 1925 women represented only 3.7 percent of the national prison population, but in the 1980s this percentage began to climb. By 1990, it had increased to 5.7 percent, and by January 1, 2001, 6.6 percent of the 1,372,131 prisoners in state and federal prisons were women. Historically, judges gave female offenders a break by often granting them probation instead of incarceration, thinking that they were not a risk to society and most of their crimes were as accomplices to men. With the war on drugs, the imposition of mandatory prison sentences, and the use of sentencing guidelines, women now go to prison just as frequently as men. However, the average sentence served by women is considerably less than that served by men (in 2001, men in prison were serving an average sentence of 5.22 years, while women in prison were serving an average of 3.63 years).

Women face different issues than men do when they go to prison. Eighty percent of incarcerated women are mothers, one-fourth of the women who enter prison are either pregnant or have given birth within the past twelve months, and 65 percent of women held in state prisons have children under age 18. About two-thirds of these women (compared to 44 percent of male inmates) lived with their young children before entering prison. More female inmates have a link between their criminality and substance abuse than male inmates. Approximately one-third of women inmates committed the offense that brought them to prison in order to obtain money to support their need for drugs.

It can be argued that female offenders are not as dangerous or as serious a risk as their male counterparts. In terms of recidivism, rates for female offenders are high, yet thought to be less than recidivism rates for comparable male offenders. They are less likely to be involved in violent crimes, and the consequences of male violence were more serious for the victim. This increase in women in prison, the collateral consequences faced by women, and the fact that they are less dangerous to society urges the reconsideration of the "one size fits all" sentencing approach. A question of policy is whether judges should have more discretion to consider these factors and sentence women offenders to community alternatives when they believe that such sanctions are in the public interest. Consider all of these issues and decide whether women should be sentenced differently than men.

Chapter Review

SUMMARY

In the last twenty years, the number of adults under correctional supervision has increased from just over 1.3 million to almost 6.6 million, while the number of prison inmates grew from just over 300,000 to more than 1.3 million offenders. These increases have resulted from several factors, including the war on drugs and a tremendous increase in the number of arrests for drug offenses; toughened sentencing statutes that lengthened the time offenders serve in prison, on probation, and on postprison supervision; sentencing guidelines and mandatory minimum sentences that took discretion away from judges and resulted in more female offenders being sent to prison; and a lower tolerance for risk, resulting in an increased number of parole and probation revocations.

Even though the gender makeup of offenders throughout the criminal justice system is still predominantly male, female offenders are "catching up" in that their rate of growth in most areas is greater than that of male offenders. Women now make up 22 percent of all arrests by law enforcement agencies, 16 percent of all felony convictions, and 6.6 percent of the state and federal prison population. Much of the attention and study of the criminal justice system, offenders, and their characteristics has been historically directed toward male criminals. However, with the increasing number of women offenders, the impact of gender differences on the correctional system is now an important area of study.

While much of the increase in women's criminal involvement has been linked to drug crimes, it is estimated that women commit 14 percent of violent offenses. Women in prison face a variety of different problems and therefore have different needs for programs and services. Their family ties and separation from their children make visiting and parenting programs even more critical for female than male prisoners. Many women suffer from long-term and serious substance abuse histories, which are unfortunately not being addressed in prison. Their medical needs are much greater than those of men. And the recent implementations of objective classification systems have tended to over classify them to prisons with higher emphasis on security than is necessary.

This chapter has set the groundwork for a further and more detailed examination of the makeup of the correctional population in the United States. The next chapter examines the handling of juvenile offenders, and following that, the many "special" groups of offenders who require handling or management are described. As noted at the introduction to this chapter, offenders are what corrections is all about. Corrections is not simply policy, operations, or laws. It is the management of people, and various considerations that must be taken into account as we attempt to manage a diverse group of people in an environment that is safe and secure and contributes to the long-term safety of the public.

REVIEW QUESTIONS

1. What has been the primary factor in the growth in the number of individuals under correctional supervision over the past twenty years?

2. Compare the increase in females versus males in terms of the number under correctional supervision.

3. What does Wilbanks say about the presence of racism in the criminal justice system, and what do most researchers believe is the reason for the disproportionate number of minorities under correctional supervision?

4. What percentage of people arrested for violent felonies are male?

5. What is the general overall goal of a prison classification system?

6. Why are women now sentenced similarly to male offenders.

7. What is the most important factor in predicting recidivism among offenders?

8. What percentage of the prison population is female?

9. List some of the special problems faced by female inmates.

10. Describe the impact that the case of *Barefield v. Leach* has had on the operation of female prisons.

ENDNOTES

1. Bureau of Justice Statistics, "Key Facts at a Glance," http.www.ojp.usdoj.gov/bjs/glance (accessed January 8, 2003).

2. Camille Graham Camp and George M. Camp, *The 2001 Corrections Yearbook: Adult Systems* (Middletown, Conn.: Criminal Justice Institute, 2002), pp. 26–27.

3. Lawrence A. Greenfeld and Tracy L. Snell, *Women Offenders* (Washington, D.C.: U.S. Department of Justice, Bureau of Justice Statistics, 1999), p. 6.

4. Paige M. Harrison and Allen J. Beck, *Prisoners in 2002* (Washington, D.C.: U.S. Department of Justice, Bureau of Justice Statistics, July 2003), p. 1.

5. Harrison and Beck, 2003, p. 6.

6. Ibid, p. 7.

7. Camp and Camp, 2002, p. 21.

8. Ibid., p. 186.

9. Harrison and Beck, 2003, p. 9.

10. Marc Morial, in a presentation at the 2003 Urban League annual conference, as reported in the *St. Louis Post-Dispatch*, July 28, 2003, p. A3.

11. William Wilbanks, *The Myth of a Racist Criminal Justice System* (Monterey, Calif.: Brooks/Cole, 1987), pp. 5, 6.

12. Bureau of Justice Statistics, *Report to the Nation on Crime and Justice*, 2nd ed. (Washington, D.C.: U.S. Department of Justice, 1988).

13. J. M. Klofas, "Drugs and Justice: The Impact of Drugs on Criminal Justice in a Metropolitan Community," *Crime and Delinquency* 39, no. 2 (1993): 204.

14. Camp and Camp, 2002, p. 37.

15. Camille Graham Camp and George M. Camp, *The Corrections Yearbook, 1998* (Middletown, Conn.: Criminal Justice Institute, 1999), p. 25.

16. Kenneth Moritsugu, "Inmate Chronological Age versus Physical Age," in *Long-Term Confinement and the Aging Inmate Population* (Washington, D.C.: Federal Bureau of Prisons, 1990).

17. Kevin Strom, *Profile of State Prisoners under Age 18, 1985–1997*, NCJ 176989 (Washington, D.C.: U.S. Department of Justice, Bureau of Justice Statistics, February 2000), p. 1.

18. Paige M. Harrison and Jennifer C. Karberg, *Prisons and Jail Inmates at Midyear 2002* (Washington, D.C.: U.S. Department of Justice, Bureau of Justice Statistics, April 2003), p. 5.

19. Harrison and Beck, 2003, p. 12.

20. Paige M. Harrison and Allen J. Beck, *Prisoners in 2001* (Washington, D.C.: U.S. Department of Justice, Bureau of Justice Statistics, July 2002), p. 13.

21. Camp and Camp, 1999, p. 57.

22. Camp and Camp, 2002, p. 70.

23. Ibid., p. 67.

24. Bureau of Justice Statistics, *Sourcebook of Criminal Justice Statistics, 2001* (Washington, D.C.: U.S. Department of Justice, 2003), p. 354.

25. Harrison and Beck, 2003, p. 1.

26. Camp and Camp, 2002, pp. 18, 55, 59–60, 138, 186–187.

27. Federal Bureau of Investigation, *Crime in the United States, 1998* (Washington, D.C.: U.S. Department of Justice, 1999), p. 210.

28. Harrison and Beck, 2002, p. 12.

29. Peter M. Carlson, "Case Management/Unit Management," in *Prison and Jail Administration: Practice and Theory,* edited by Peter M. Carlson and Judith Simon Garrett (Gaithersburg, Md.: Aspen, 1999), p. 83.

30. Harold Williamson, *The Corrections Profession* (Newbury Park, Calif.: Sage, 1990), p. 137.

31. Bureau of Justice Statistics, 2003; Bureau of Justice Statistics, *Sourcebook of Criminal Justice Statistics, 1994* (Washington, D.C.: U.S. Department of Justice, 1995), p. 386.

32. Greenfeld and Snell, 1999, p. 5.

33. David E. Olson, Arthur J. Lurigio, and Manus Seng, "Comparison of Female and Male Probationers: Characteristics and Case Outcomes," *Women and Criminal Justice* 11, no. 4 (2000): 65–79.

34. Ibid.

35. D. Steffensmeier, J. Kramer, and C. Streifel, "Gender and Imprisonment Decisions," *Criminology* 31, no. 3 (1993): 411–449.

36. Meda Chesney-Lind, "The Forgotten Offender, Women in Prison: From Partial Justice to Vengeful Equity," in *Exploring Corrections: A Book of Readings,* edited by Tara Gray, (Boston: Allyn & Bacon, 2002), p. 8.

37. Reported in Greenfeld and Snell, 1999, p. 11.

38. Ibid.

39. Allen J. Beck, *Prisoners in 1998* (Washington, D.C.: U.S. Department of Justice, 1999).

40. Harrison and Karberg, 2003, p. 5.

41. Greenfeld and Snell, 1999, p. 6.

42. Ibid., p. 16.

43. Greenfeld and Snell, 1999, pp. 1, 9.

44. Ibid.

45. Barbara Bloom, "Incarcerated Mothers," in *Children of Incarcerated Parents,* edited by K. Gabel and K. Johnson (New York: Lexington Books, 1995), p. 21.

46. Bureau of Justice Statistics, 2003, p. 502.

47. George Church, "The View from behind Bars," *Time* 22 (September 1990): 20–22.

48. Merry Morash, Timothy S. Bynum, and Barbara A. Koons, "Women Offenders: Programming Needs and Promising Approaches," *National Institute of Justice: Research in Brief* (August 1998): 7.

49. Greenfeld and Snell, 1999, p. 8.

50. Phyllis Jo Baunach, *Mothers in Prison* (New Brunswick, N.J.: Transaction, 1984).

51. M. Moses, "The Girl Scouts Behind Bars Program: Keeping Incarcerated Mothers and Their Daughters Together," in *Maternal Ties: A Selection of Programs for Female Offenders,* edited by C. Blinn (Lanham, Md.: American Correctional Association, 1997), pp. 35–49.

52. Greenfeld and Snell, 1999, p. 8.

53. Ibid.

54. Center for Substance Abuse Treatment, *Substance Abuse Treatment for Incarcerated Women Offenders: Guide to Promising Practices* (Rockville, Md.: Department of Health and Human Services, Public Health Service, 1997), p. 2.

55. Camp and Camp, 2002, p. 136.

56. Greenfeld and Snell, 1999, p. 9.

57. Bureau of Justice Statistics, *Substance Abuse and Treatment: State and Federal Prisons, 1997* (Washington, D.C.: U.S. Department of Justice, 1999).

58. Chesney-Lind, 2002, p. 11.

59. Jacqueline M. Moore, "Privatization of Inmate Health Care: A New Approach to an Old Problem," *Corrections Management Quarterly* 2, no. 2 (1998): 46.

60. Ibid., p. 47.

61. Robert R. Ross and Elizabeth A. Fabiano, *Female Offenders: Correctional Afterthoughts* (Jefferson, N.C.: McFarland, 1986).

62. Greenfeld and Snell, 1999, p. 8.

63. John D. Wooldredge and Kimberly Masters, "Confronting Problems Faced by Pregnant Inmates in State Prisons," *Crime and Delinquency* 39 (1993): 195–203.

64. Richard P. Seiter, *Correctional Administration: Integrating Theory and Practice* (Upper Saddle River, N.J.: Prentice Hall, 2002), p. 282.

65. Patricia Van Voorhis and Lois Presser, *Classification of Women Offenders: A National Assessment of Current Practices* (Washington, D.C.: U.S. Department of Justice, National Institute of Corrections, 2001).

66. *Barefield v. Leach,* No. 10282 (D. N.M., 1974), 196.

67. *Pargo v. Elliot,* 49 F.3d 1355 (8th Cir. 1995), 196.

68. Nicole H. Rafter, *Partial Justice: Women, Prison, and Social Control,* 2nd ed. (New Brunswick, N.J.: Transaction, 1990).

Chapter 8

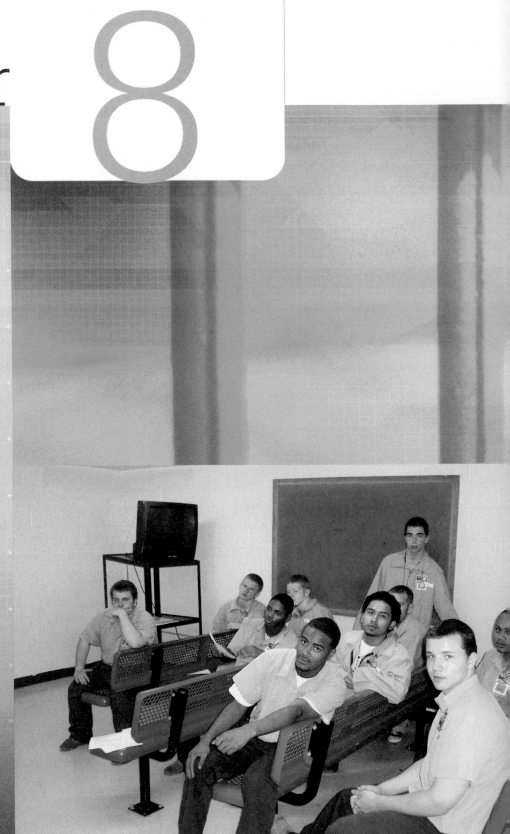

**AFTER READING THIS CHAPTER,
YOU SHOULD BE ABLE TO:**

1. Describe the problem of juvenile crime and identify any trends in such crimes.
2. Explain the development of the juvenile justice system and the concept of *parens patriae*.
3. Discuss the reasons why juveniles are waived to adult courts and the concerns about this process.
4. List and define the three categories of offenders referred to the juvenile justice system.
5. Outline the steps in the juvenile justice process and compare it with similar steps in the adult justice process.
6. Identify and specify the result of key federal court cases impacting rights of juvenile offenders.
7. Describe the problems regarding juvenile gangs and juvenile drug use.

The Juvenile Correctional System

KEY TERMS

status offense
Refuge Period
juvenile justice system
parens patriae
deinstitutionalize
superpredator
waiver to adult courts
dependent children
neglected children
delinquent children
age of original jurisdiction
juvenile detention
intake
consent decree
referral
delinquency petition
adjudicate
order
aftercare
In re Gault
juvenile gangs

Introduction

When I was director of adult corrections for Ohio, I used to tell my colleague who was director of the juvenile correctional system, "I am glad I do not have your job." Our mission was much clearer in dealing with adult sanctions. We supervised and incarcerated adult felons so that society is protected. We built secure prisons and knew how to manage inmates. But my colleague's mission was far less clear. Some people want to treat serious juvenile offenders just as we treat adults. Others argue that these offenders are still children and should not be punished as criminals, but treated as delinquents who need to be led back on the right path to mature and responsible adults. In the juvenile system, no one can decide whether correctional institutions are prisons or training schools, whether offenders are inmates or students, or whether clients and society are better off with them in institutions or maintained in the community. Unfortunately, these statements are still accurate. The juvenile justice system was originally created to deal with delinquent acts committed by individuals under age 18, in a separate system designed to deal differently with juveniles than with adults. Over the years, however, the juvenile justice system has suffered from a lack of consistency and agreement on the mission and approach.

This chapter describes the problem of juvenile crime, the history and creation of the juvenile justice system, and recent developments to ensure that the system can respond to modern challenges of criminal and delinquent behavior by youth. As well, issues regarding developing case law, drug crimes by youth, and juvenile gang membership are described. To introduce some of the problems, the "An Insider's Experience" box illustrates some of the mission confusion faced by juvenile correctional agencies.

The Problem of Juvenile Crime

Similar to adult crimes, juvenile crime rates and trends fluctuate over time, yet there is often a disconnect between actual crime data and public perception and justice policies. It often appears that media coverage of crimes and criminal activity by juveniles has more influence on policy than actual trends in the data. The Federal Bureau of Investigation (FBI) collects juvenile as well as adult crime data in the annual *Uniform Crime Reports* (UCR). Serious and violent crime trends are reviewed by monitoring four crimes in the UCR (murder and nonnegligent manslaughter, forcible rape, robbery, and aggravated assault) and the Violent Crime Index.

Over the past few years, the high number of juveniles arrested for crimes has been a serious concern. In 2000, there were 22.4 million juveniles arrested. However, this is a 5 percent reduction since 1999 and a 15 percent reduction since 1996. Table 8.1 illustrates the overall numbers of juveniles arrested for all categories of offenses during 2000.

While the volume of these numbers is alarming, they actually represent some good news. The 1,200 arrests of juveniles for murder in 2000 is a reduction of 55 percent since 1996. Since 1991, juvenile arrests for motor vehicle theft declined by 51 percent, and burglary arrests declined by 38 percent. Concerns, however, are for the increases since 1991 in the number of juvenile arrests for drug abuse (145 percent) and curfew and loitering violations (81 percent).[1] However, these increases may not necessarily indicate an increase in the volume of this type of crime, as much as law enforcement efforts targeting this type of activity. Interesting is the large number of arrests for runaway. Runaway is an example of a **status offense**, an act that is determined a violation of law for juveniles but not for adults.

Over the past several decades, the number of juvenile arrests has been relatively stable except for increases in juvenile violent crime, as murder arrests for juvenile

Status offense

an activity that is considered a crime only because the offender is under age 18 and would not be a crime if committed by an adult; includes acts such as running away from home, ungovernability, truancy, and underage drinking

AN INSIDER'S EXPERIENCE: Defining the Role of Juvenile Institutions

As noted previously, I was glad to be the director of an adult correctional rather than a juvenile agency. At no time was this clearer than when I received a call from a good friend for help. The person had recently been appointed director of the Ohio Department of Youth Services (DYS). His background had always been in juvenile corrections, and he was an accomplished and well-respected person in that field. He was having problems at a juvenile institution that was located on "the hill" in Columbus, about five miles from downtown in an area that had originally been commercial but was now highly residential. The institution, referred to as TICO, held some of the highest-risk juvenile offenders and was having a terrible problem of escapes. It may be an overstatement to call them "escapes," because the perimeter security was just a single fence with no razor ribbon, and it was easy for youthful, athletic 17-year-olds to climb it and run away.

After several escapes in a short time, the neighborhood was up in arms. They felt that these escapes by juvenile offenders were endangering them, even though no serious crimes had occurred as a result. They wanted some action that proved that DYS could stop the escapes. My friend asked our department to send some staff to look at their security and how to improve it and reduce the escapes. This was easy. We were experts at designing perimeter security, and if there was enough money and commitment, escapes could be reduced dramatically. A plan was developed to make the perimeter more like an adult prison by adding a second fence and installing razor ribbon. When presented to neighborhood groups, the plan received mixed reviews.

While some neighbors appreciated the plan and believed it would work, others were not thrilled. They felt that the secure-looking fence would be unsightly and detract from the neighborhood. Groups of youth advocates were also very upset with the plan. They argued that these were children and should not be treated as adult criminals. They worried that escaping juveniles might get cut and hurt themselves on the razor ribbon while trying to escape. When these stories were conveyed to me, I was very surprised, but should not have been. What seemed like a common-sense effective solution created strong emotions and debate about the root purpose of the juvenile justice system—to protect citizens from offenders, or to educate, train, and restore delinquents to a self-fulfilling and productive life. There are no easy answers when managing juvenile offenders.

offenders increased by 93 percent during the 1980s and arrests for aggravated assault increased by 72 percent.[2] As illustrated in Figure 8.1, between 1988 and 1994 there was a dramatic increase in the arrest rates for juvenile serious violent crimes, and public attention and concern regarding the problem of juvenile violent crime increased. Since 1994, however, these arrest rates have dropped 41 percent and reached the lowest levels since 1985.

Public concern is not only about juveniles' violent crimes, but also all crime that is being committed by juveniles. The proportion of violent crimes cleared by juvenile arrests averaged about 9 percentage of all violent crimes during the late 1980s, but climbed to 14 percent of all violent crimes in 1994. Since that year, the percentage of violent crimes committed by juveniles declined to 12 percent in 2000.[3] Table 8.2 compares the change in the number of violent crime arrests for juveniles and adults between 1991 and 2000, indicating that the decline was actually greater for juveniles than adults.

The FBI *Uniform Crime Reports* also include trends in the volume of property crimes committed by juveniles, using the four property index crimes of burglary, larceny-theft, motor vehicle theft, and arson. During the increase in juvenile violent crime from 1988 to 1994, arrest rates of juvenile property crime remained relatively constant and then began to fall after 1994, as did violent crimes. From 1994 to 2000, the juvenile Property Crime Index arrest rate dropped 37 percent to its lowest level since at least the 1960s.[4]

| TABLE 8.1 | Number of Juveniles Arrested by Crime Type, 2000 |

	2000 Estimated Number of Juvenile Arrests	Percent of Total Juvenile Arrests		Percent Change		
Most Serious Offense		Female	Under Age 15	1991–2000	1996–2000	1999–2000
Total	2,369,400	28%	32%	3%	−15%	−5%
Crime Index total	617,600	28	38	−28	−27	−5
Violent Crime Index total	98,900	18	33	−17	−23	−4
Murder and nonnegligent manslaughter	1,200	11	13	−65	−55	−13
Forcible rape	4,500	1	39	−26	−17	−5
Robbery	26,800	9	27	−29	−38	−5
Aggravated assault	66,300	23	36	−7	−14	−4
Property Crime Index total	518,800	30	39	−30	−28	−5
Burglary	95,800	12	39	−38	−30	−5
Larceny-theft	363,500	37	40	−24	−27	−6
Motor vehicle theft	50,800	17	26	−51	−34	−3
Arson	8,700	12	65	−7	−17	−7
Non-index total						
Other assaults	236,800	31	43	37	−1	0
Forgery and counterfeiting	6,400	34	12	−20	−24	−7
Fraud	10,700	32	18	−3	−15	−5
Embezzlement	2,000	47	6	132	48	11
Stolen property (buying, receiving, possessing)	27,700	16	29	−40	−33	−1
Vandalism	114,100	12	44	−21	−19	−4
Weapons (carrying, possessing, etc.)	37,600	10	33	−26	−28	−10
Prostitution and commercialized vice	1,300	55	13	−13	−4	−3
Sex offense (except forcible rape and prostitution)	17,400	7	52	−4	8	5
Drug abuse violations	203,900	15	17	145	−4	0
Gambling	1,500	4	18	−27	−30	−22
Offenses against the family and children	9,400	37	38	92	−8	2
Driving under the influence	21,000	17	3	14	13	−3
Liquor law violations	159,400	31	10	20	4	−6
Drunkenness	21,700	20	13	−3	−19	−3
Disorderly conduct	165,700	28	38	33	−9	−8
Vagrancy	3,000	23	28	−33	−7	27
All other offenses (except traffic)	414,200	26	28	35	−5	−5
Suspicion	1,200	22	23	−76	−53	−29
Curfew and loitering	154,700	31	28	81	−16	−11
Runaways	142,000	59	39	−18	−29	−6

Note: Detail may not add to totals because of rounding.

Source: *Crime in the United States 2000* (Washington, D.C.: U.S. Government Printing Office, 2001), Tables 29, 32, 34, 36, 38, and 40. Arrest estimates were developed by the National Center for Juvenile Justice. Table as illustrated in Office of Juvenile Justice and Delinquency Prevention, *Juvenile Arrests 2000,* OJJDP Bulletin (November 2002) p. 3.

Juvenile involvement in violent crimes has created a public concern resulting in rethinking many of the approaches and policies used to deal with youthful offenders.
Courtesy Chet Gordon/The Image Works.

THE JUVENILE VIOLENT CRIME INDEX ARREST RATE, 1980–2000

FIGURE **8.1**

Arrests per 100,000 juveniles ages 10–17

Violent Crime Index

Year

Source: Analysis of arrest data from unpublished FBI reports for 1980 through 1997 and from *Crime in the United States* reports for 1998, 1999, and 2000 (Washington, D.C.: U.S. Government Printing Office, 1999, 2000, and 2001, respectively); population data from the U.S. Bureau of the Census, *U.S. Population Estimates by Age, Sex, Race, and Hispanic Origin: 1980 to 1999 (With Short-term Projection to Dates in 2000)*, released April 11, 2000. Figure from Office of Juvenile Justice and Delinquency Prevention, *Juvenile Arrests 2000*, OJJDP Bulletin, (Washington, DC: US Department of Justice, Office of Justice Programs, November 2002).

Several theories suggest the reasons for the increase in juvenile violent crime from 1988 to 1994. The first is that, as in crime statistics regarding adults, the emergence of crack cocaine and the violence around its use and sale caused an increase in juvenile violent crime. Crack cocaine is an extremely addictive drug and can result in violent behavior by those using it. Crack cocaine is also considerably less expensive than powder cocaine, and its emergence created a new drug of choice in urban, poverty-ridden areas. Violent confrontations between various factions of drug sellers occurred as groups attempted to control areas of drug sales for their own group or individual profit.

TABLE	8.2	Percent Change in Arrests of Juveniles and Adults, 1991–2000	
		Percent change in arrests, 1991–2000	
Most serious offense		**Juvenile**	**Adult**
Violent Crime Index		−17%	−10%
Murder		−65	−37
Forcible rape		−26	−30
Robbery		−29	−32
Aggravated assault		−7	−1

Source: *Crime in the United States 2000*, as illustrated in Office of Juvenile Justic and Delinquency Prevention, *Juvenile Arrests 2000*, OJJDP Bulletin (November 2002), p. 11.

Second, the expansion of juvenile gang membership during this period resulted in expanded juvenile violence. Gangs lead to violence in a variety of ways. Gangs use violence to get attention, show their toughness, and recruit new members. Violence is also a way that gangs show that they are in control of an area, other gangs should stay out, and nongang youths should join them to be a member of the dominant group and avoid becoming victims themselves. Gang violence also occurs between gangs. Gangs will fight rather than let any other gang gain members or take control of their area. As well, the proliferation of weapons in possession of juveniles led to an increase in violence. The number of juvenile arrests for weapons charges increased 103 percent from 1985 to 1994; eleven large cities reported that approximately 40 percent of their juvenile males were in possession of a weapon at some time,[5] and there has been a noted increase in the use of guns by juveniles who participate in the illegal drug market.[6]

Juveniles involved in gangs contributed to the increases in violent and other crimes during the past two decades.
Courtesy A. Ramey/PhotoEdit.

Juvenile and adult gangs like to "mark" their territory, warning other gangs to stay away, and informing local residents that the gang is in control of the area.
Photo by Jeffrey J. Rojek.

Development of the Juvenile Justice System

In the late eighteenth century, as the American colonies were establishing systems of government and courts, juveniles under age 7 were seen as below the age of reason and thereby incapable of the formation of criminal intent. However, those over age 7 were handled in the criminal justice system, the same as adults. Soon thereafter, recognition of the need to deal separately with delinquent or neglected children developed. As a result, between 1824 and 1899, the **Refuge Period** developed. Houses of Refuge were created to house, train, educate, and provide good habits for these wayward children through strict discipline.[7] These houses were usually operated by charitable or religious organizations, they had few controls or standards, and the attempt to change the behavior of delinquents often resulted in harsh and brutal conditions. As the need for reform of the entire approach to managing juveniles was recognized, the Society for the Prevention of Juvenile Delinquency began to advocate for reforms to include a separation of juveniles from the adult system as early as 1825.

When John Augustus, the Boston shoemaker regarded as the "father of probation," began to bail criminals out of jail in the middle 1800s, he also persuaded judges to place wayward youth under his supervision, and he brought the distinctions between juvenile and adult offenders to the court's attention. However, the **juvenile justice system** was not created until Illinois passed the Juvenile Court Act, and the first juvenile court was established in Cook County (Chicago) in 1899. By creating a separate juvenile court, the concept of **parens patriae** was recognized as the basis for giving the court the authority to take over supervision of children when their parents failed to provide proper care and guidance. The concept of *parens patriae* means "parents of the nation" and was first established in England with the 1601 Elizabethan Poor Laws, which allowed officials to take change of delinquent children and place them in poorhouses or orphanages to gain control of them. In more modern times, this doctrine was expanded as the basis for juvenile court and correctional systems to take responsibility for educating and nurturing delinquents, with an emphasis on reform and rehabilitation.

Refuge Period
a period from 1824 to 1899 when delinquent or neglected children were placed in homes for training and discipline

Juvenile justice system
a system to handle juveniles separate from adult offenders, based on the concept of *parens patriae*, which was used as the basis for giving the court the authority to take over supervision of children when their parents failed to provide proper care and guidance

Parens patriae
"parents of the nation"; a concept established in 1601 to allow officials to take change of delinquent children and place them in poorhouses or orphanages to gain control of them; in more modern times, this doctrine was expanded as the basis for juvenile court and correctional systems to take responsibility for educating and nurturing delinquents, with an emphasis on reform and rehabilitation

During the 1800s, Houses of Refuge were operated to house wayward youths and provide them with structure and discipline.
Courtesy T. A. Carlson/CORBIS-NY.

The use of a separate juvenile court, initiated in Cook County, proved to be popular, and by 1925 all but two states had established juvenile courts or probation departments separate from their adult systems.[8] Even though the concept of *parens patriae* is no longer fully applicable in juvenile courts, the theory of nurturing and reforming juveniles continued, and mission statements for most juvenile courts still stress the benevolent nature of the system and emphasize rehabilitating rather than punishing youthful offenders. With this underlying concept, the juvenile system was much less formal and less reliant on legal precedent and due process than the adult system. Hearings were not adversarial proceedings but attempts by the court to determine what actions were in the best interest of the juvenile and society.

By 1960, these philosophies and processes began to be questioned because of concern for the impact they had on the juvenile offender. There was apprehension that the juvenile system's emphasis on treatment could result in the indefinite institutionalization of delinquents until treatment was deemed complete. There was a belief that juveniles, even for benevolent reasons, were often pulled into the system, removed from their family and community, and put into juvenile institutions without a clear ability to treat and return them in a better state. Therefore, there was a move to formalize the court processes, include more due process, and use the criminal standard of proof *beyond a reasonable doubt* rather than *by a preponderance of evidence.*

There were also efforts to remove status offenders not charged with criminal conduct from the juvenile court system. In the Juvenile Justice and Delinquency Prevention Act of 1974, the U.S. Congress required assessments of the juvenile justice system in order to identify youth who were victimized, rather than helped, by placement in juvenile facilities.[9] The juvenile institutions, which had been considered a positive environment for youths while emphasizing education and training, began to be seen as an overly aggressive sanction. Advocates for juveniles believed that they should be diverted from the justice system and could better be treated in

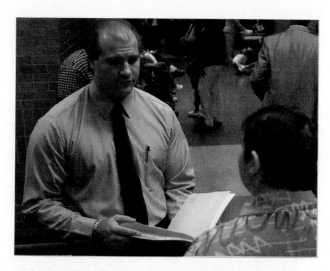

Massachusetts closed most of its juvenile institutions and moved offenders into community programs.
Courtesy of AP/Wide World Photos.

the community. The highlight of the movement to **deinstitutionalize** juvenile correctional facilities came when Jerome Miller, Commissioner of the Massachusetts Department of Youth Services, closed most of that state's juvenile institutions and placed the youths in community programs. Miller believed that institutions were more damaging to juveniles than helpful, and that they could be better treated in the community.

Since the early 1980s, however, another reform of the juvenile justice system has prevailed. This reform was prompted by concern not for the juvenile offender, but for community safety. Just as public sentiment regarding adult offenders supported punishment and offender accountability over treatment and rehabilitation, there was a similar swing in attitudes regarding juveniles. The increases in juvenile violent crime created a fear by the public of dangerous, marauding gangs of juveniles creating havoc and violence throughout the urban landscape. During the early 1990s, DiIulio even coined the term **superpredator** in warning of a coming generation of violent youths who practiced almost indiscriminate violence on the streets.[10]

As a result, state legislatures enacted laws to respond in a more punitive and public-safety-conscious manner, recreating some juvenile court processes to parallel the adult courts, establishing mandatory prison sentences for some juvenile offenses, and waiving serious juvenile offenders from the juvenile to the adult court systems. By the end of the twentieth century, nearly all states had passed laws to permit **waiver to adult courts** of serious juvenile offenders. These waivers allow the movement of serious juvenile offenders to adult courts for criminal processing. States use other terms for this process, including *certification, remand,* or *bind over,* for criminal prosecution. In Kansas and Vermont, juveniles as young as age 10 in can be tried as adults, and often prosecutors, rather than judges, have the authority to waive the case and have it transferred to an adult court.

WAIVER OF JUVENILE OFFENDERS

Transferring juveniles to adult criminal courts is not a new phenomenon, and provisions for such transfer was available in some states even before the 1920s; many other states have permitted transfers since the 1940s.[11] However, state transfer provisions changed extensively between 1992 and 1999, as forty-nine states and the District of Columbia modified their transfer provisions. Many of

Deinstitutionalize

to remove juveniles from correctional institutions and place them in community alternatives

Superpredator

a term created by DiIulio to describe a generation of violent youths who practiced almost indiscriminant violence on the streets

Waiver to adult courts

statutory exceptions granted to allow movement from juvenile to adult courts for criminal processing because of the serious nature of a juvenile offender's crime

The waiver of juvenile offenders has resulted in many juveniles now serving their time in adult prisons.
Photo by Richard P. Seiter.

these modifications instituted *mandatory waiver,* or direct assignment of specific crimes committed by juveniles to be handled in adult courts.

In *discretionary waivers* from juvenile to adult courts, juvenile courts usually decide on a case-by-case basis whether the court will waive the processing of the juvenile and allow prosecution as an adult in the criminal justice system. In this situation, the juvenile court must first find probable cause to believe that the juvenile committed the alleged act, and if so, must also find that it is in the court's best interest to waive its right to handle the case and give jurisdiction to the adult court. The process and how juvenile offenders are managed in adult prisons is described in Chapter 9.

Many correctional professionals question the efficacy of serious juvenile offenders being tried and sentenced in adult courts. The American Correctional Association (ACA) standards distinguish the juvenile justice system as having significantly different processes, procedures, and objectives from adult corrections. James A. Gondles, executive director of the ACA, adds, "We will never, in my view, solve our problems on the back end with punishments . . . Treating kids as adults solves very little; it's another quick-fix solution to a complex problem that took years to reach and will take years to resolve."[12] In the "You Make the Decision" box, you must take a position on this issue.

Categories of Juvenile Offenders

The juvenile justice system defines three categories of offenders: dependent, neglected, and delinquent. **Dependent children** have committed no legal offense but may be without a family (parent or guardian) or without support, possibly because the parent is physically or mentally unable to act in that capacity. **Neglected children** have a family or guardian but are not receiving proper care, or the situation in the home is harmful to them and their upbringing. **Delinquent children** have committed an act that would be considered criminal if committed by an adult. In many jurisdictions, a fourth category is *status offenders,* children that have committed acts that are law violations only if committed by a person of juvenile status.

Status offenses include running away from home, ungovernability (being beyond the control of parents or guardians), truancy, status liquor law violations (such as underage drinking, which also applies to young adults up to age 21), and

Dependent children

children who, while committing no legal offense, may be without a parent or guardian, possibly because the parent is physically or mentally unable to act in that capacity

Neglected children

children who have a family or guardian, but are not receiving proper care or have a home situation that is harmful to them and their upbringing

Delinquent children

children who have committed an act that would be considered criminal if committed by an adult

YOU MAKE THE DECISION . . .

SHOULD JUVENILES BE TRIED AS ADULTS?

As described previously, more juveniles arrested for serious crimes are being bound over to adult courts to be tried as adults and, if convicted, to serve an adult sentence. Since serious crimes are those handled in the criminal justice system, the sanctions usually include imprisonment. Three models of incarceration of juveniles tried and convicted as adults are used. Most states place these juvenile offenders in adult prisons with adult inmates. A few states house juveniles with adults, but require them to be housed and programmed separately. Some states place juveniles in juvenile institutions until they reach age 18, and they then are transferred to adult prisons.

In 1997, there were 5,400 juveniles in adult prisons; 92 percent were male, 61 percent were committed for violent crimes, and the average maximum sentence was 82 months. Fifty-eight percent were black, another 15 percent were Hispanic, and 2 percent were of other races. However, by 2002, the number of juveniles in adult prisons declined to 3,055 (almost all males). The original punitive attitude of the late 1990s has lessened, and many people are reconsidering the reasons for prosecuting juvenile offenders as adults.

In this exercise you are to decide whether it is good public policy to try and punish juvenile offenders as adults. Either individually or in a small classroom group, list the pros and cons for juveniles being waived to adult courts. Then come up with a decision as to whether it is good public policy. Be sure to address issues such as cost, long-term impact on the juveniles, impact on the various sentencing goals, and protection of the public. You will find that this is not an easy issue to agree on, and many good arguments exist on both sides.

other miscellaneous offenses that apply only to minors (such as curfew violations and tobacco offenses).[13] When status offenses do not constitute a separate category of juvenile offenders, states classify them in two other ways. In some states, status offenders are an "incorrigible" subcategory of delinquent children. Other states have moved status offenses from acts of delinquency to the category of dependent children, thereby removing them from the juvenile courts and placing them in a family court or child welfare agency. If the status offense behavior continues, however, the juvenile will be referred to the juvenile court.

In 1997 (the most recent data available), juvenile courts in the United States processed approximately 158,500 status offense cases, including the following:

- 24,000 runaway cases
- 40,500 truancy cases
- 21,300 ungovernability cases
- 40,700 status liquor law violation cases
- 32,100 other miscellaneous status offense cases[14]

Figure 8.2 indicates the continual increase in the number of status offense cases handled by juvenile courts in the United States. From 1988 to 1997, the number of truancy cases handled by the juvenile courts increased by 96 percent, runaways increased by 93 percent, liquor law violations increased by 56 percent, and ungovernability increased by 65 percent.

One important factor for each of these offender categories is the **age of original jurisdiction**, the upper or oldest age at which a juvenile court will have jurisdiction over categories of offenders (see Table 8.3). Each state defines juveniles by age for the various categories. For status offenses, abuse, neglect or dependency, the age of original jurisdiction varies, and may often go through age 20.[15] In almost every state, the age of delinquency (for the delinquent category) is under age 18 at the

Age of original jurisdiction

the upper or oldest age at which a juvenile court will have jurisdiction over offenders

STATUS OFFENSES HANDLED BY JUVENILE COURTS, 1988–1997

FIGURE **8.2**

Petitioned status offense cases

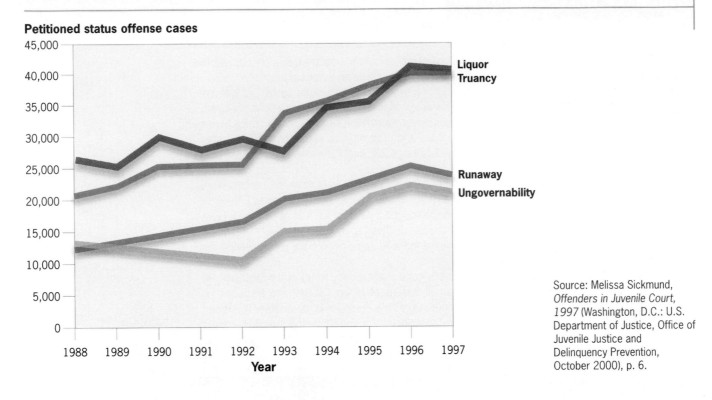

Source: Melissa Sickmund, *Offenders in Juvenile Court, 1997* (Washington, D.C.: U.S. Department of Justice, Office of Juvenile Justice and Delinquency Prevention, October 2000), p. 6.

TABLE	8.3	Age of Original Juvenile Court Jurisdiction

Age	State
15	Connecticut, New York, North Carolina
16	Georgia, Illinois, Louisiana, Massachusetts, Michigan, Missouri, New Hampshire, South Carolina, Texas, Wisconsin
17	Alabama, Alaska, Arizona, Arkansas, California, Colorado, Delaware, District of Columbia, Florida, Hawaii, Idaho, Indiana, Iowa, Kansas, Kentucky, Maine, Maryland, Minnesota, Mississippi, Montana, Nebraska, Nevada, New Jersey, New Mexico, North Dakota, Ohio, Oklahoma, Oregon, Pennsylvania, Rhode Island, South Dakota, Tennessee, Utah, Vermont, Virginia, Washington, West Virginia, Wyoming

Source: Office of Juvenile Justice and Delinquency Prevention, *Juveniles in Court* (Washington, D.C.: U.S. Department of Justice, June 2003).

time of the offense, arrest, or referral to court. However, many states have statutory exceptions to this age criterion, and allow exceptions related to the youth's age, alleged offense, and prior court history. These exceptions (called *statutory exclusions*) can place a youth under the original jurisdiction of the adult criminal court. In other states, these exceptions can place the youth under the original jurisdiction of both the juvenile and criminal courts (called *concurrent jurisdiction*). In concurrent jurisdiction, the prosecutor is given the authority to decide which court will initially handle the case.

In 2000, sixteen states set an age as the lowest level at which there can be juvenile court jurisdiction over acts of delinquency, as children below that age are presumed incapable of criminal intent. Table 8.4 illustrates these age levels.

Even with most juvenile crime reducing, many status offenses such as runaway increased between 1988 and 1997.

Courtesy of Cleo Photography/PhotoEdit.

TABLE	8.4	Youngest Age for Juvenile Court Jurisdiction over Delinquency Matters

Age	State
6	North Carolina
7	Maryland, Massachusetts, New York
8	Arizona
10	Arkansas, Colorado, Kansas, Louisiana, Minnesota, Mississippi, Pennsylvania, South Dakota, Texas, Vermont, Wisconsin

Source: Office of Juvenile Justice and Delinquency Prevention, *Juveniles in Court* (Washington, D.C.: U.S. Department of Justice, June 2003), p. 5.

The Juvenile Justice Process

In many ways, the juvenile justice process is similar to the adult criminal justice process described in Chapter 1. However, as noted in the history of the juvenile justice system, the goals and philosophies in the juvenile justice system differ from those of the criminal justice system. A good example of the differences in the two systems is a comparison of the mission statements of the adult and juvenile correctional agencies in Missouri. The Missouri Department of Corrections states its mission as follows:

> The Department of Corrections is an agency dedicated to public safety through the successful management and supervision of offenders on probation, in prison and on parole. The Department's responsibility is to administer the sentence set by the court—ranging from probation to capital punishment—in ways that promote the longest lasting public safety at the lowest cost to taxpayers. Offenders assigned to the Department are successfully managed by ensuring they are supervised at the correct custody or supervision level.[16]

The Missouri Department of Social Services, Division of Youth Services lists the following mission statement:

> The mission of the Division of Youth Services is to enable youth to fulfill their needs in a responsible manner within the context of and with respect for the needs of the family and the community. DYS programs are established to provide the mandated services enumerated, ... to include assessment, care and treatment, and education of all youth committed to its care.[17]

The adult system emphasizes public safety through managing offenders; mentions administering sentences imposed by the court, including capital punishment; and promotes carrying out responsibilities at the lowest cost to taxpayers. This mission gives readers a sense of punishment and cost-effectiveness. The juvenile agency, on the other hand, focuses on enabling youth to fulfill their needs within the context of the family and community. Assessment, care and treatment, and education of youth are seen as the most important functions. This example illustrates how most states differentiate their role in dealing with adult criminals versus juvenile delinquents. The language, processes, and steps in each justice process reiterate these differences.

The juvenile justice process usually begins, just like the adult criminal justice process, with a complaint to the police and a contact between a law enforcement officer and the offender. Table 8.5 illustrates a comparison of the juvenile and the adult criminal justice systems, while highlighting the common ground that exists between them.

STEPS IN THE JUVENILE JUSTICE PROCESS

As with adults, juveniles begin their entry or contact with the justice system with a contact with law enforcement, an investigation after a complaint has been filed that leads to a juvenile as a suspect of a crime, or through police witnessing activity that they believe to be a crime or act of delinquency. However, juveniles can also come into contact with the justice system through referrals by parents, school officials, or other citizens. Law enforcement personnel are usually the source of approximately 85 percent of delinquency referrals and 50 percent of status offender referrals to juvenile court.[18] Currently, the police are more likely to divert juvenile offenders or handle them informally than to do so with an adult. It is estimated that approximately one-quarter of juveniles arrested are handled informally and released by the police, and nearly seven out of ten are referred to juvenile court.[19] Figure 8.3 is a simplified diagram of the process by which a case travels through the juvenile justice system, although the steps vary from state to state.

Juvenile detention

the temporary care of children in physically restricted facilities pending court disposition or transfer to another jurisdiction or agency

Intake

the process in which officials determine whether a juvenile case should be dismissed, handled informally, or referred to the juvenile court

Once a juvenile comes in contact with the police, he or she may be detained for a short time to contact a parent or guardian, or while a waiting transfer to a juvenile facility. Approximately one-fifth of arrested juveniles are detained. **Juvenile detention**, as defined by the National Council of Crime and Delinquency, is the temporary care of children in physically restricted facilities pending court disposition or transfer to another jurisdiction or agency.[20] In general, juveniles will be detained if they are believed to be a threat to the community, are at risk in the community, or may fail to appear for future processing. Juveniles detained must be separated from adult offenders and must have a detention hearing within a few days (usually within twenty-four hours).

The next step in the juvenile justice process is **intake**, carried out by the juvenile probation department or prosecutor's office to determine whether the case should be dismissed, handled informally, or referred to the juvenile court. The purpose of this step is to determine whether sufficient evidence exists to formally process the allegation. At this point, approximately 40 percent of cases are

TABLE 8.5	Comparison of the Juvenile and Criminal Justice Systems

Juvenile justice system	Common ground	Criminal justice system
	Operating Assumptions	
■ Youth behavior is malleable. ■ Rehabilitation is usually a viable goat. ■ Youth are in families and not independent.	■ Community protection is a primary goal. ■ Law violators must be held accountable. ■ Constitutional rights apply.	■ Sanctions should be proportional to the offense. ■ General deterrence works. ■ Rehabilitation is not a primary goal.
	Prevention	
■ Many specific delinquency prevention activities (e.g., school, church, recreation) are used. ■ Prevention is intended to change individual behavior and is often focused on reducing risk factors and increasing protective factors in the individual, family, and community.	■ Educational approaches are taken to specific behaviors (drunk driving, drug use)	■ Prevention activities are generalized and are aimed at deterrence (e.g., Crime Watch).
	Law Enforcement	
■ Specialized "juvenile" units are used. ■ Some additional behaviors are prohibited (truancy, running away, curfew violations). ■ Some limitations are placed on public access to information. ■ A significant number of youth are diverted away from the juvenile justice system, often into alternative programs.	■ Jurisdiction involves the full range of criminal behavior. ■ Constitutional and procedural safeguards exist. ■ Both reactive and proactive approaches (targeted at offense types, neighborhoods, etc.) are used. ■ Community policing strategies are employed.	■ Open public access to all information is required. ■ Law enforcement exercises discretion to divert offenders out of the criminal justice system.
	Intake—Prosecution	
■ In many instances, juvenile court intake, not the prosecutor, decides what cases to file. ■ The decision to file a petition for court action is based on both social and legal factors. ■ A significant portion of cases are diverted from formal case processing. ■ Intake or the prosecutor diverts cases from formal processing to services operated by the juvenile court, prosecutor's office, or outside agencies.	■ Probable cause must be established. ■ The prosecutor acts on behalf of the State.	■ Plea bargaining is common. ■ The prosecution decision is based largely on legal facts. ■ Prosecution is valuable in building history for subsequent offenses. ■ Prosecution exercises discretion to withhold charges or divert offenders out of the criminal justice system.

(continued)

TABLE	8.5	Continued

Juvenile justice system	Common ground	Criminal justice system
	Detention—Jail/lockup	
■ Juveniles may be detained for their own protection or the community's protection. ■ Juveniles may not be confined with adults unless there is "sight and sound separation."	■ Accused offenders may be held in custody to ensure their appearance in court. ■ Detention alternatives of home or electronic detention are used.	■ Accused individuals have the right to apply for bond/ball release.
	Adjudication—Conviction	
■ Juvenile court proceedings are "quasi-civil" (not criminal) and may be confidential. ■ If guilt is established, the youth is adjudicated delinquent regardless of offense. ■ Right to jury trial is not afforded in all States.	■ Standard of "proof beyond a reasonable doubt" is required. ■ Rights to be represented by an attorney, to confront witnesses, and, to remain silent are afforded. ■ Appeals to a higher court are allowed. ■ Experimentation with specialized courts (i.e., drug courts, gun).	■ Defendants have a constitutional right to a jury trial. ■ Guilt must be established on individual offenses charged for conviction. ■ All proceedings are open.
	Disposition—Sentencing	
■ Disposition decisions are based on individual and social factors, offense severity, and youth's offense history. ■ Dispositional philosophy includes a significant rehabilitation component. ■ Many dispositional alternatives are operated by the juvenile court. ■ Dispositions cover a wide range of community-based and residential services. ■ Disposition orders may be directed to people other than the offender (e.g., parents). ■ Disposition may be indeterminate, based on progress demonstrated by the youth.	■ Decisions are influenced by current offense, offending history, and social factors. ■ Decisions hold offenders accountable. ■ Decisions may give consideration to victims (e.g., restitution and "no contact" orders). ■ Decisions may not be cruel or unusual.	■ Sentencing decisions are bound primarily by the severity of the current offense and by the offender's criminal history. ■ Sentencing philosophy is based largely on proportionality and punishment. ■ Sentence is often determinate, based on offense.
	Aftercare—Parole	
■ Function combines surveillance and reintegration activities (e.g., family, school, work).	■ The behavior of individuals released from correctional settings is monitored. ■ Violation of conditions can result in reincarceration.	■ Function is primarily surveillance and reporting to monitor illicit behavior.

Source: Howard N. Snyder and Melissa Sickmund, *Juvenile Offenders and Victims: 1999 National Report* (Washington, D.C.: U.S. Department of Justice, National Center for Juvenile Justice, September 1999), pp. 94–96.

STAGES IN THE JUVENILE JUSTICE PROCESS

FIGURE **8.3**

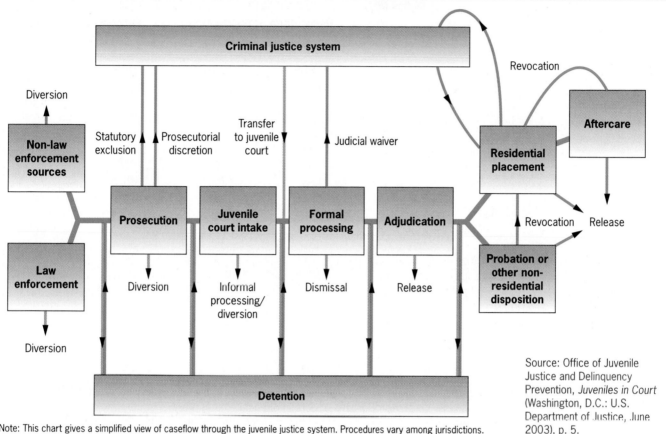

Source: Office of Juvenile Justice and Delinquency Prevention, *Juveniles in Court* (Washington, D.C.: U.S. Department of Justice, June 2003), p. 5.

Note: This chart gives a simplified view of caseflow through the juvenile justice system. Procedures vary among jurisdictions.

diverted, dismissed, or otherwise handled informally, while the other 60 percent continue in a formal manner. With informal handling, the case is often concluded with a **consent decree**, whereby the delinquent juvenile must admit to wrongdoing and agree to specific conditions of behavior (similar to pretrial diversion for adult offenders). This stage is sometimes referred to as *informal probation.* If the juvenile meets all the conditions of the consent decree, the case is dismissed and there is no formal record of delinquent action.

If during intake, the determination is to handle the case formally, or the case was originally handled informally and the juvenile does not meet the consent decree conditions, it will be formally handled in that a **referral** is made to the juvenile court. The referral is similar to charging an adult offender with a crime. In the referral, a **delinquency petition** (similar to an indictment for adults) states the delinquent acts the juvenile is alleged to have committed and asks the juvenile court to **adjudicate** or find the juvenile guilty of the delinquent act) and make the juvenile a ward of the court. A hearing is then scheduled, facts are presented, witnesses may be called, and the court determines whether the juvenile is responsible for the delinquent act. Juveniles do not universally have a right to a hearing before a jury, as do adult felons, yet a few states allow a jury to hear the case.

If the juvenile is found responsible for the delinquent act, the judge must determine what sanction or **order** (similar to the sentence for an adult) should apply. The primary orders for juveniles are for either probation or residential placement. Over the past decade, the number of delinquency cases resulting in residential placements has increased. In 1989, there were 119,700 residential placements, in 1998, there were 163,800 residential placements.[21] Table 8.6 illustrates the change in orders between 1989 and 1998.

Consent decree

an informal handling of a juvenile justice case in which the delinquent juvenile admits to wrongdoing and agrees to specific conditions of behavior; sometimes called informal probation

Referral

the formal processing of a juvenile offense through the juvenile court

Delinquency petition

a statement of the delinquent acts a juvenile is alleged to have committed; similar to an indictment for adults

Adjudicate

to find a juvenile guilty of a delinquent act

TABLE	8.6	Orders for Probation and Residential Placement, 1989–1998			
		Percentage of residential placement cases		Percentage of formal probation cases	
Characteristic		**1989**	**1998**	**1989**	**1998**
Most serious offense		100%	100%	100%	100%
Person		19	24	17	23
Property		50	41	59	45
Drugs		9	11	8	12
Public order		22	24	16	21
Gender		100%	100%	100%	100%
Male		88	85	85	79
Female		12	15	15	21
Race		100%	100%	100%	100%
White		60	61	63	66
Black		36	36	33	31
Other races		4	3	4	3
Age		100%	100%	100%	100%
12 and younger		5	4	8	8
13		9	9	10	10
14		17	17	17	17
15		25	25	23	23
16		26	27	24	24
17 and older		18	19	18	18

- Compared with 1989, the profiles of residential placement and probation cases in 1998 contained greater proportions of person offenses and females.
- Compared with the profile of cases that resulted in residential placement in 1998, cases that resulted in formal probation involved a greater proportion of property offenses (45% versus 41%), females (21% versus 15%), whites (66% versus 61%), and youth age 13 or younger (18% versus 13%)

Note: Detail may not total 100% because of rounding. Juveniles of Hispanic ethnicity can be of any race, but most are included in the white racial category.

Source: Office of Juvenile Justice and Delinquency Prevention, *Juveniles in Court* (Washington, D.C.: U.S. Department of Justice, June 2003), p. 23.

Order

the sanction for a juvenile found delinquent by juvenile court; similar to the sentence for an adult

For the past few years, in approximately 60 percent of the cases, probation was the most severe sanction ordered.[22] Juvenile probation is similar to adult probation in that there are conditions of supervision and the probation officer plays a dual role of finding appropriate treatment resources and monitoring the juvenile for compliance with conditions. While adult probation agencies have moved toward a greater emphasis on monitoring compliance, juvenile agencies still primarily focus on rehabilitating delinquents. While the juvenile justice system has very few intermediate sanctions between probation and incarceration, many jurisdictions have initiated intensive probation supervision programs that are operated very much like such programs for adults.

If the juvenile is not granted probation, the judge may elect to remove the offender from the community and place him or her under the supervision of the state department of youth services. In approximately one in four cases, the court ordered juveniles to residential placement such as training school, boot camp, drug treatment, a group home, or some other correctional facility.[23] These residential placements may be in a secure correctional facility (such as a training school or reform school) or a nonsecure group home, depending on the severity of

TABLE 8.7	Terminology in the Juvenile and Adult Justice Systems	
Juvenile justice system	**Activity**	**Adult justice system**
Delinquent	Violator of laws	Offender
Detention	Holding offenders by police	Arrest
Intake	Determination to handle case	Preliminary hearing
Consent decree	Informal handling with conditions	Pretrial diversion
Referred to court	Formal processing by the court	Charges filed
Delinquency petition	Statement of the allegations	Indictment
Respondent	Individual alleged guilty	Defendant
Adjudicate	Find responsible for act	Convict
Hearing	Review of factual issues	Trial
Responsible	Committed the act	Guilty
Order	Court determination of sanction	Sentence
Probation	Supervision in the community	Probation
Commitment	Placed in a correctional facility	Incarcerated
Resident	Institutionalized individual	Inmate
Residential placement	Correctional facility	Prison
Aftercare	Supervision after release	Parole

the act and the background of the juvenile. In some states, the sanction is for an open-ended period of time (indeterminate sentence) and the decision to release is the responsibility of the department of youth services. In other states, the judge sanctions the juvenile for a set period of time (determinate sentence) until release back to the community. After release, the juvenile is on **aftercare** supervision, much like adult parole, with specific conditions that must be followed. If these conditions are not met, the juvenile may be returned to the residential placement or placed in a more secure facility to serve additional time.

As noted earlier, the process for juveniles is similar to the adult criminal justice system. However, the terminology is distinct. Table 8.7 compares the terminology used in the juvenile and adult justice systems.

The juvenile justice process provides the opportunity for many career opportunities, including detention staff, juvenile court workers, probation and aftercare staff, and social service staff who work in juvenile correctional institutions. The "Your Career in Corrections" box describes the work of juvenile social service workers.

Legal Issues Affecting the Juvenile Justice System

As in adult correctional systems, federal courts had little involvement in the operation of juvenile correctional agencies until the 1960s. The first major case reviewed by the U.S. Supreme Court was *Kent v. United States* in 1966. In this case, a 16-year-old was charged with rape and robbery and the juvenile court waived jurisdiction to the adult court. The juvenile received a sentence of thirty to ninety years in prison as an adult. The Supreme Court acceptance of the case was the first challenge to the *parens patriae* foundation of the juvenile justice system, in that juveniles charged with offenses should not receive less due process just because the system has a greater concern for juveniles and provides a "compensating benefit." The Court ruled that juveniles must have "the essentials of due process," including the right to notice of the charges in time to prepare for trial, the right to counsel, the right to confront and cross-examine accusers, and the privilege against self-incrimination.[24]

Aftercare

supervision of a juvenile in the community, after he or she has served time in a juvenile correctional institution; similar to parole for adults

YOUR CAREER IN CORRECTIONS

JUVENILE SOCIAL SERVICE WORKERS

Juvenile social service workers are staff who work in juvenile correctional institutions. Interestingly, these individuals fill a dual role of case managers and correctional officers in adult prisons. They usually supervise delinquents, develop treatment plans, and help them prepare for release. Until the 1950s, most juvenile institutions had "house parents" who lived in the institution housing complex with the delinquents and acted as parents would in counseling, guiding, rewarding, and punishing the residents under their care. Today, the role is much more professional, usually requiring a two- or four-year college degree, some training in counseling, and much more adherence to policy rather than individual discretion.

Juvenile social service workers have challenging yet rewarding jobs. First, they have to play the role of correctional officers, as they are usually the only person supervising juvenile residents (a term used similarly to adult prison inmates) and therefore must be sensitive to security issues and maintain control and order of residents. However, they also are often responsible for counseling and program planning for residents and therefore have to play a dual role of case manager. Much of their work in this regard consists of creating a responsible living environment with the other residents of the housing unit. An important part of the management of juvenile correctional facilities is the "governing" of the housing unit. Social service workers direct and mentor residents in how to get along with one another and how to work together to reach the unit's goals of sanitation, positive program participation, and good behavior on the part of all residents. Many juvenile facilities use some type of group behavior modification program in which the housing unit as a group receives or loses privileges based on the group's performance.

Juvenile social service worker jobs can be stressful as well. It is difficult to work with 16- to 18-year-old offenders who do not have a history of responsible behavior or self-control and may resort to violence as a way to get what they want. These positions are entry-level and the pay is usually fairly low. However, these are excellent positions in which to learn how to deal with youthful offenders and use personal communication skills to gain compliance and positively influence behavior. From these positions, there are also opportunities for promotion to midlevel management positions throughout the juvenile justice system.

In re Gault

a 1967 U.S. Suprme Court case that required that in hearings in which juveniles may be committed to an institution, they must have the right to counsel, to notice of the charges against them, to question witnesses, and to protection against self-incrimination

The next year (1967), the Court accepted and decided *In re Gault*. Gerald Gault, a 16-year-old on probation, called a neighbor and made some obscene remarks. Gault did not attend the adjudication hearing and was committed to a juvenile training school for the period of his minority (to age 18). If he had been an adult, this act would have been a misdemeanor punishable by a small fine and a two-month jail sentence. The Court rejected the doctrine of *parens patriae* as giving the juvenile court unbridled discretion, and required that in hearings in which juveniles may be committed to an institution, they must have the right to counsel, to notice of the charges against them, to question witnesses, and to protection against self-incrimination.[25]

In the 1970 case of *In re Winship,* the 1971 case of *McKeiver v. Pennsylvania,* and the 1975 case of *Breed v. Jones,* the U.S. Supreme Court further clarified the due process rights of juveniles. In *Winship,* the Court determined that a finding of guilt for juveniles required more than just a preponderance of the evidence, but had to meet the adult standard of *beyond a reasonable doubt.*[26] In *McKeiver,* the Court did not further expand due process provided to juveniles, deciding that jury trials are not a requirement in juvenile courts.[27] In *Breed,* the Court found that waiver to an adult court after an adjudication hearing in juvenile court constitutes double jeopardy.[28]

In two later cases, the U.S. Supreme Court indicated that it had perhaps taken the expansion of due process rights for juveniles to a conclusion. In *Fare v.*

Michael C. (1979), the Court affirmed the conviction of murder of a juvenile who claimed he had asserted his right to remain silent. Michael C. was arrested for murder, and when advised of his *Miranda* rights, he asked to see his probation officer. The police said the officer would be contacted later, and Michael could talk to the officer then if he desired. The Court ruled that asking for a probation officer is not the same as asking for a lawyer or asserting the right to remain silent.[29] In *Schall v. Martin* (1984), the Supreme Court upheld the use of preventive detention pending trial for juveniles, stating that the protection of both the juvenile and society from pretrial crimes is not intended to punish the juvenile.[30] In addition, the Court did not rule out the importance of *parens patriae,* and reasserted the interest of the state in promoting the welfare of children.

In addition to addressing the due process rights of juveniles, the Supreme Court has also addressed the use of the death penalty for juvenile offenders. In 1982, the Court decided *Eddings v. Oklahoma,* declaring that the youthful age of a defendant should be considered a mitigating factor in deciding whether to apply the death penalty during the penalty phase of a capital punishment trial.[31] In *Sanford v. Kentucky* (1989), the Court determined that the minimum age at which a juvenile could receive the death penalty is 16.[32] In 2002, the Court refused to accept and hear the case of *In re Stanford,* which asked the Court to again address the issue of capital punishment for juveniles.[33] On January 27, 2003, the Court again declined to accept a case to reconsider the death penalty for Scott Allen Hain, an Oklahoma offender who was 17 at the time of his crime. Apparently, four justices believe that executing juveniles for murder is unconstitutional, as Justices Stevens, Souter, Ginsburg, and Breyer issued a statement that "the practice of executing such offenders is a relic of the past and is inconsistent with evolving standards of decency."[34]

Therefore, the current age of 16 for consideration of the death penalty for juveniles still stands. However, of the thirty-eight states that allow the death penalty, sixteen prohibit it by statute for offenders younger than 18 at the time of the crime. The federal government also bans the death penalty for juveniles. At least three additional states are considering legislation to eliminate the death penalty for juvenile offenders. It is likely that in the next few years, few states will allow the execution of juveniles convicted of murder, or the U.S. Supreme Court is likely to gain a fifth vote of support and will reject the death penalty for youthful offenders.

As a result of the active role the Supreme Court played in defining the due process rights of juveniles, there is now little difference in the procedural due process requirements between the juvenile and adult justice systems. Juveniles have the right to notice of charges against them, the right to counsel, the right to confront and cross-examine witnesses, the right to avoid self-incrimination, the right to a judicial hearing with full consideration of their individual case before transfer to adult court, and the right to the standard of *beyond a reasonable doubt* to be found responsible for a delinquent act. While *parens patriae* as a foundation of the juvenile court is not applicable as open discretion for actions by the court, the recognition that the court is to act in the best interests of the juvenile is still acknowledged.

Issues in Juvenile Corrections

Many aspects of the juvenile justice system are similar to the adult criminal justice system. These include the role played by juvenile gangs in street crime and the continued influence of these gangs within juvenile correctional institutions. Additionally, a major concern within the juvenile justice system is how to break the cycle of juvenile substance abuse and involvement in drug crimes. Juvenile justice administrators and policymakers attempt to look into the future to determine what new issues will confront juvenile corrections and create new approaches to effectively deal with these issues.

JUVENILE GANGS AND JUVENILE CRIME

Over the past twenty years there has been a proliferation of juvenile gangs in most large inner cities, and research indicates that gang membership intensifies delinquent behavior. From the earliest to the most recent investigations, criminologists have consistently found that, when compared to youth who do not belong to gangs, gang members are far more involved in delinquency, especially serious and violent delinquency.[35] Gang activities create a fear and perception of danger among most citizens regarding inner-city youth, make neighborhoods unsafe, and prompt a reaction by police to intensify patrolling and arrests of juveniles not only for delinquent acts, but also for loitering and other status offenses.

Juvenile gangs

groups of adolescents or young adults who see themselves as a group and have been involved in enough crime to be of considerable concern to law enforcement and the community

Juvenile gangs are defined as groups of adolescents or young adults who see themselves as a group and have been involved in enough crime to be of considerable concern to law enforcement and the community.[36] In the early 1990s, a study of thirty-five cities that had organized gang control programs estimated that there were more than 1,500 juvenile gangs with more than 120,000 members in these cities, and there is no reason to believe that the number has done anything but increase since that time.[37] Most gangs are formed within racial or ethnic groups, as law enforcement reported gang membership as 54.6 percent African American and 32.6 percent Hispanic.[38] Gangs are 95 percent male, and male members commit most gang crime. Gangs are very chauvinistic, and while many male gangs have female auxiliaries, only a few allow female members. Interestingly, new gangs are forming in smaller, more rural communities. A recent report notes that gangs that formed only within the past few years

> had younger members, slightly more females, and more of a racial/ethnic mixture; were less involved in drug trafficking; and were less involved in violent crimes, including homicides. The later onset jurisdictions were most likely to be in rural counties, smaller cities, and suburban counties with populations of less than 50,000.[39]

Gangs get involved in criminal activities to make money, to intimidate others and protect their turf, and as a part of the structure and role of members. Law enforcement officials believe that much gang violence results from their involvement in drug sales, but gangs are regularly involved in all types of index crimes. Gangs have a definite organizational structure. Individuals involved with gangs on a continued and long-term basis are "core members," who are the gang members most regularly involved in crime and violent acts. Some core members are regular or associate members who actively participate in the gang, and others are fringe members who are less involved in the gang activities and its criminal acts. The average age of arrested gang members is 17 or 18. The younger individuals who want to join the gang are called "wanna-bes," or those being recruited for membership.

Law enforcement officials attempt to control gang activity through suppression and social programs. They collect intelligence regarding gang members, their activities, their areas of operation, and their historical activities. Police then target their areas of operation and attempt to disrupt the gang's activities by patrolling and arresting gang members for loitering, curfew violations, or any crime that can get them off the streets. In addition, some cities have passed ordinances against ganglike activities, and gang members can be arrested and imprisoned for simply hanging out with the gang and violating the ordinances.[40]

Another approach to reduce gang activities is through social programs. In-school education programs inform students of the dangers of gang involvement and how to avoid being forced to enter a gang. As well, parents are provided information regarding gang activities and what to watch for to determine whether their child is getting involved in gang activities. Recreational, educational, and vocational programs target potential or even current gang members and get them working or

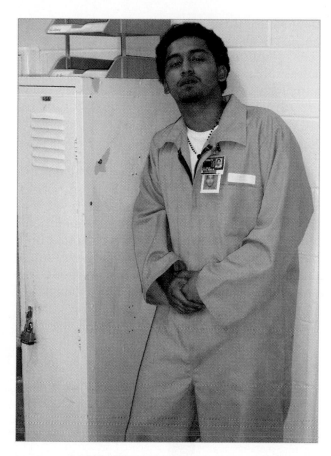

Involvement of juveniles in gangs often is the cause of their getting involved in crime and being sent to prison.
Photo by Richard P. Seiter.

using their leisure time in a noncriminal manner. While there is some evidence that suppression tactics reduce gang criminal activity, it is more difficult to determine whether social programs reduce gang membership or juvenile crimes.

RESPONDING TO JUVENILE DRUG CRIME

A serious concern regarding juveniles is substance abuse that leads to health problems, undermines family relationships, creates problems in school, and results in delinquency that often continues into adult criminality. The juvenile justice system struggles with how to break this cycle and redirect juveniles into productive and law-abiding patterns of behavior. In the early history of the juvenile justice system, the focus was on the individual juvenile and how he or she could be rehabilitated. Over the past two decades, more emphasis has gone to protecting society and victims while holding delinquents accountable for their behavior, and there is an increased use of incarceration and out-of-the-home placements. With neither rehabilitation nor juvenile accountability proving to be effective in dealing with juvenile drug crime, a blending of both into a balanced and restorative justice (BARJ) perspective has emerged. In a 2001 National Institute of Justice document encouraging the use of a balanced approach, the authors note:

> Specifically, the model strikes a balance among *offender accountability* (making amends to the victim and community), *competency development* (changing behaviors and improving functional skills), and *community safety* (protecting the community by carefully monitoring the juvenile's behavior).[41]

As indicated in Figure 8.4, BARJ integrates the goals of public safety and rehabilitation, using graduated sanctions to reward good behavior and increase punishments for improper behavior, collaboration with the juvenile justice system and other community resources such as substance abuse treatment providers, and a case management approach identifying and using community services to build on each juvenile's strengths and talents. Figure 8.4 illustrates the continuous process of entry, assessment, judicial decision making, supervision and treatment, and continuing care to move delinquents from substance abuse to successful community reintegration.

In many ways, the BARJ approach is similar to that used in adult drug courts. BARJ emphasizes collaborative (rather than adversarial) efforts by all parties within the juvenile justice system to focus on the outcome of reducing juveniles' substance abuse and criminal involvement. As well, the model is multidimensional, in that it uses treatment, punishment, psychological, social, and cultural factors to work toward freedom from drugs for juveniles. While the system must continue to deal with criminal and delinquent activity by juveniles, the model focuses on the underlying problem of substance abuse as a cause, more than as an effect (involvement in illegal behavior).

The approach of the BARJ model is also consistent with the overall vision of what is needed in the future for the juvenile justice system. In a 1998 publication,

THE BALANCE AND RESTORATIVE JUSTICE PERSPECTIVE   FIGURE **8.4**

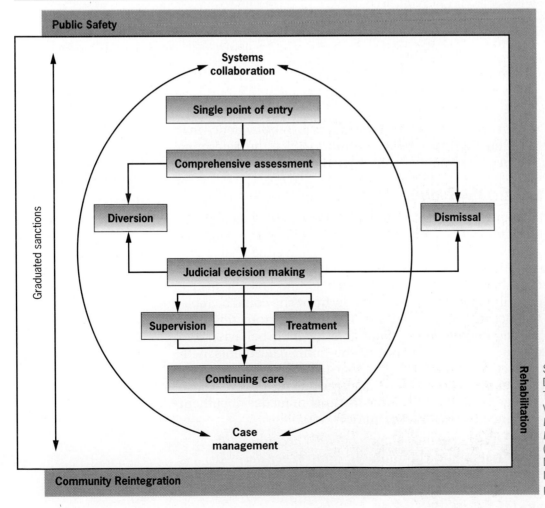

Source: Curtis C. VanderWaal, Duane C. McBride, Yvonne M. Terry-McElrath, and Holly VanBuren, *Breaking the Juvenile Drug-Crime Cycle: A Guide for Practitioners and Policymakers* (Washington, D.C.: U.S. Department of Justice, National Institute of Justice, May 2001), p. 5.

the director of the Office of Juvenile Justice and Delinquency Prevention, addressing the needs of the juvenile justice system for the twenty-first century, concluded that an effective justice system must meet three objectives: holding juvenile offenders accountable, enabling the juvenile to become a capable, productive and responsible citizen, and ensuring the safety of the community. The author concludes that

> these objectives are best met when a community's key leaders, including representatives from the juvenile justice system, health and mental health systems, schools, law enforcement, social services, and other systems, are jointly engaged in the planning, development, and operation of the juvenile justice system.[42]

The following "A Case Study" box in an illustration of how many cases in the juvenile justice system seem to result in an unsatisfactory outcome for all involved parties.

A CASE STUDY

IS THE JUVENILE JUSTICE SYSTEM "JUST"?

A recent case handled in the juvenile justice system is a good example of the challenges faced by either the juvenile or criminal justice system regarding their ability to create a "just" outcome for some cases. A group of teenagers was at a church picnic, horsing around as teenagers do. A 13-year-old was bragging about how tough he was, and how he could take a blow to the head. He had his skateboard with him, and hit himself over the head with it, laughingly telling his friends that it did not hurt. He then challenged any of them to hit him over the head with it to show how tough he was.

Another 13-year-old, but one who was much bigger and stronger than the first youth, took up the challenge. He took the skateboard and walloped his friend over the head with it. The youth fell to the ground, began to convulse, and was rushed to the hospital, where he subsequently died. The friend who hit him was taken into custody and charged in juvenile court with murder. A few months later, he pleaded guilty to involuntary manslaughter and received a sentence of one year in a juvenile detention center. There was no indication that this juvenile was a bully or had ever before been violent, and all information was that he had grown up in a typical middle-class family with no serious problems.

The case received considerable media attention, and debate raged about whether justice was served for either party. The victim had been tragically killed, and nothing could bring him back to life or provide his parents any comfort regarding their loss. The youth who hit him had to live with the fact he had killed his friend. Taking him out of his home and away from his family was going to do nothing, and would probably make it more difficult for him to deal with the result of his actions. Placing him in a juvenile correctional institution illustrated that he had to be responsible and be held accountable for his act of stupidity. Even those who argued for a strong punishment had to admit that incarceration was probably going to make it even more difficult, if not impossible, to get his own life back together. This event and the subsequent sentence will probably result in the loss of two promising lives.

Some argue that if the boy had been in adult court, with the opportunity to go before a jury and the prosecutor required to prove guilt beyond a reasonable doubt, he might have been able to argue for a lesser sentence. Some also suggested that he was too accepting of responsibility for the act, and that he should have fought the sentence more, trying to get probation, the opportunity to stay in his parents' home, and counseling and treatment regarding his own psychological issues around this event. The one thing most people agreed on is that there seems to be no "good" sentence for the individual in this case, and they questioned the ability of the juvenile justice system to provide a just outcome.

Chapter Review

SUMMARY

The juvenile justice system has a long and distinguished history. Formed to protect children who needed society's assistance and to keep juvenile delinquents separate from adult criminals, the juvenile justice system has played a valuable role in the treatment and rehabilitation of generations of the nation's youth. However, during the past two decades, this "kinder and gentler" approach has come under attack, and fear of dangerous and violent juvenile offenders has forced the U.S. Congress and state legislatures to push for reforms and make the juvenile court similar to adult courts in terms of its goals, processes, and punishments. While it is difficult to argue with the point that victims don't much care whether their vicious assailant is 17 or 19, and that the increase in violent crime does require new methods, it is only normal to think that perhaps we have thrown out the baby with the bathwater and lost some of the rational reasons for the original creation and organization of the juvenile justice system.

The juvenile justice system has had these mixed missions and inconsistent approaches for several decades, and the issues seem to get more confused rather than clearer. Crimes committed by offenders under age 18 are getting more serious. Some juvenile offenders are now bound over to adult courts and correctional systems for incarceration. Urban youths are joining gangs that encourage violence and a life of crime. Some experts think there should not be a juvenile justice system at all—that all criminals should be treated the same, regardless of their age. Yet others recognize that immaturity leads to mistakes of judgment that require considerations of age, and most people do not want to give up on youthful offenders and accept that they cannot be reformed and made into productive and law-abiding citizens.

The next decade will be an interesting time for the juvenile justice system. Will it continue in the trend toward adversarial judicial processes, waiver from juvenile to adult courts for a growing number of delinquents, and more harsh punishments to include incarceration of juveniles with adult offenders? Or will there be a realization that intervention with rehabilitation and treatment approaches is still the best opportunity society has to correct delinquent behavior and push juveniles back to an acceptable lifestyle? Most likely, the BARJ model, emphasizing a balance between a punitive and restorative approach, will be accepted and implemented in many local and state jurisdictions.

REVIEW QUESTIONS

1. What trends have resulted from the rates of juvenile crime over the past decade?

2. List three possible theories for the rise in juvenile violent crime between 1988 and 1994.

3. What was the Refuge Period?

4. Define the concept of *parens patriae.*

5. How did the term "superpredator" develop, and what does it mean for the future of juvenile violent crime?

6. What is a waiver to adult courts, and why are some juvenile offenders handled in adult criminal courts rather than juvenile courts?

7. What are the four categories of juvenile offenders and how are each managed in the juvenile justice system?

8. How does the typical mission of a juvenile justice agency differ from the mission of an adult correctional agency?

9. Describe the process followed as a juvenile moves through the juvenile justice system and compare it to the adult criminal justice system.

10. What are the two primary court orders (sentences) for juvenile offenders, and approximately what percentage of juveniles receive each one?

11. What was the most significant outcome of the U.S. Supreme Court decision in *In re Gault?*

12. Describe and list the most important court decisions regarding sentencing juveniles to the death penalty. What is the current legal position on this issue?

13. How do juvenile street gangs contribute to street crime and what two approaches are taken to control gang behavior?

14. What is the BARJ model for juvenile justice and how does it work?

ENDNOTES

1. Office of Juvenile Justice and Delinquency Prevention, *Juvenile Arrests 2000,* OJJDP Bulletin, (November 2002), p. 3.

2. John J. Wilson and James C. Howell, *Comprehensive Strategy for Serious, Violent, and Chronic Juvenile Offenders: Program Summary* (Washington, D.C.: U.S. Department of Justice, Office of Juvenile Justice and Delinquency Prevention, 1993), p. 2.

3. Office of Juvenile Justice and Delinquency Prevention, 2002, p. 11.

4. Ibid., p. 6.

5. H. N. Snyder, M. Sickmund, and Y. Poe-Yamagata, *Juvenile Offenders and Victims: 1996 Update on Violence* (Washington, D.C.: U.S. Department of Justice, 1996) p. 21.

6. Alfred Blumstein, "Youth, Violence, Guns, and the Illicit-Drug Industry," *Journal of Criminal Law and Criminology* 86, no. 1 (1995): p. 14.

7. A description of the Refuge Period and other developments in the juvenile justice system can be found in Todd R. Clear and George F. Cole, *American Corrections,* 5th ed. (Belmont, Calif.: Wadsworth, 2000), pp. 395–399.

8. Howard N. Snyder and Melissa Sickmund, *Juvenile Offenders and Victims: 1999 National Report* (Washington, D.C.: U.S. Department of Justice, National Center for Juvenile Justice, September 1999), p. 86.

9. The Juvenile Justice and Delinquency Prevention Act of 1974 (Public Law 93-415) encouraged removing status offenders from the juvenile court system.

10. John J. DiIulio, Jr., "The Question of Black Crime," *Public Interest* (Fall 1994): 3–12.

11. Melissa Sickmund, *Juveniles in Court* (Washington, D.C.: U.S. Department of Justice, Office of Juvenile Justice and Delinquency Prevention, June 2003).

12. James A. Gondles, Jr., "Kids Are Kids, Not Adults," *Corrections Today* (June 1997): 3.

13. Melissa Sickmund, *Offenders in Juvenile Court, 1997* (Washington, D.C.: U.S. Department of Justice, Office of Juvenile Justice and Delinquency Prevention, October 2000), p. 6.

14. Ibid.

15. Sickmund, 2003, p. 5.

16. State of Missouri Department of Corrections Web site, http://www.corrections.state.mo.us/overview (accessed January 2003).

17. State of Missouri Department of Social Services Website, http://www.dss.state.mo.us/dys/index (accessed January 2003).

18. Sickmund, 2000.

19. Snyder and Sickmund, 1999, p. 97.

20. National Council on Crime and Delinquency, *Juvenile Justice Policy Statement* (San Francisco: NCCD, 1991).

21. Office of Juvenile Justice and Delinquency Prevention, *Juveniles in Court* (Washington, D.C.: U.S. Department of Justice, June 2003), p. 23.

22. Ibid., p. 22.

23. Ibid.

24. *Kent v. United States,* 383 U.S. 541, 86 S. Ct. 1045 (1966).

25. *In re Gault,* 387 U.S. 1, 87 S. Ct. 1428 (1967).

26. *In re Winship,* 397 U.S. 358, 90 S. Ct. 1068 (1970).

27. *McKeiver v. Pennsylvania,* 403 U.S. 528, 91 S. Ct. 1976 (1971).

28. *Breed v. Jones,* U.S. 519, 95 S. Ct. 1779 (1975).

29. *Fare v. Michael C.,* 442 U.S. 707 (1979).

30. *Schall v. Martin,* 467 U.S. 253, 104 S. Ct. 2403 (1984).

31. *Eddings v. Oklahoma,* 455 U.S. 104 (1982).

32. *Stanford v. Kentucky,* 492 U.S. 361 (1989).

33. *In re Stanford,* 123 S. Ct. 472 (2002).

34. Quoted in Associated Press, "Supreme Court Appears One Vote Shy of Rejecting Death Penalty for Young Killers," *St. Louis Post-Dispatch,* January 28, 2003, p. 2.

35. Sarah R. Battin-Pearson, Terence P. Thornberry, J. David Hawkins, and Marvin D. Krohn, *Gang Membership, Delinquent Peers, and Delinquent Behavior* (Washington, D.C.: U.S. Department of Justice, Office of Juvenile Justice and Delinquency Prevention, October 1998), p. 1.

36. C. L. Maxson, K. J. Woods, and M. W. Klein, "Street Gang Migration: How Big a Threat," *National Institute of Justice Journal* 230 (February 1996): 26–31.

37. Irving Spergel, David Curry, Ron Chance, Candace Kane, Ruth Ross, Alba Alexander, Edwina Simmons, and Sandra Oh, *Gang Suppression and Intervention: Problems and Response* (Washington, D.C.: U.S. Department of Justice, Office of Juvenile Justice and Delinquency Prevention, October 1994), p. 1.

38. Ibid.

39. James C. Howell, Arlen Egley, Jr., and Deborah K. Gleason, ""Modern Day Youth Gangs," Juvenile Justice Bulletin (June 2002), p. 6.

40. For a description of how police organize to target the suppression of youth gang activity, see Vincent J. Webb and Charles Katz, "Policing Gangs in an Era of Community Policing," in *Policing Gangs and Youth Violence,* edited by Scott Decker (Belmont, Calif.: Thompson-Wadsworth, 2003), pp. 17–49.

41. Curtis C. VanderWaal, Duane C. McBride, Yvonne M. Terry-McElrath, and Holly VanBuren, *Breaking the Juvenile Drug-Crime Cycle: A Guide for Practitioners and Policymakers* (Washington, D.C.: U.S. Department of Justice, National Institute of Justice, May 2001), p. 2.

42. Shay Bilchik, "A Juvenile Justice System for the 21st Century," Juvenile Justice Bulletin (May 1998), p. 1.

Chapter 9

AFTER READING THIS CHAPTER, YOU SHOULD BE ABLE TO:

1. Define special offenders and describe how they require special handling under correctional supervision.

2. List and describe the three ways in which juveniles can be transferred to adult courts.

3. Identify the three approaches for incarcerating juveniles in adult correctional facilities.

4. Explain the scope and trends regarding drug offenders' involvement in the criminal justice system.

5. Identify the types of substance abuse programs provided in prisons for inmates.

6. Specify the reason why so many mentally ill individuals have been able to remain in the community since the 1960s.

7. Discuss the concerns about violence in prisons by inmates.

8. Describe the operation of supermax prisons and suggest reasons for and against their use.

9. Outline the problems facing the treatment of sex offenders under correctional supervision.

10. Identify the issues facing HIV-positive inmates under correctional supervision.

Special Offenders

KEY TERMS

special offenders
blended sentencing
straight adult incarceration
graduated incarceration
segregated incarceration
Drug Use Forecasting
antipsychotic drugs
supermax prisons
Bruscino v. Carlson
sex offenders
pedophile
containment model
human immunodeficiency virus (HIV)

Introduction

Correctional agencies, unfortunately, have become "all things to all people." The typical offender was historically young, was in good mental and physical health, was convicted of property crimes, and did not require unusual handling or management. There were only "standard" caseloads for probation and parole agencies until the 1960s, as all inmates under supervision in the community were handled similarly. Prisons built during the early 1900s were extremely large, with extensive factory space, in order to house prisoners inexpensively, while they produced goods that the prison could sell to help support itself. These standard approaches were fine until the makeup of the offender population began to change and the need for special management of certain offenders was recognized.

Special offenders

offenders whose circumstances, conditions, or behaviors require management or treatment outside the normal approach to supervision

This change in the management of smaller groups of the correctional population based on their characteristics and needs is referred to as differential handling of special offenders. **Special offenders** are those offenders whose circumstances, conditions, or behaviors require management or treatment outside the normal approach to supervision. This may be the result of some physical problem or infectious disease, a mental disorder, a tendency for violence, a history of sexual assaults, age (juvenile or elderly), or serious substance abuse. All of these circumstances require correctional officials to create special methods of managing, handling, or treating these offenders.

This chapter describes the circumstances and management approaches that result from the individual needs of a variety of special offenders. Included are offenders under age 18 who are waived from jurisdiction of the juvenile court to adult court and correctional systems, as well as offenders who have serious drug problems or a mental illness. In addition, the chapter includes descriptions of the needs and management of aging offenders (older than 50), offenders who exhibit violent and dangerous tendencies, and those convicted and sentenced for a sexual offense. Finally, the particular management and treatment of offenders with infectious diseases such as HIV/AIDS and tuberculosis are described. This chapter provides students with an understanding of the challenges and difficulties in attempting to manage all of these special populations within a correctional environment.

Juvenile Offenders in Adult Criminal Courts

As noted in Chapter 8, the past twenty years have seen an increase in the number of waivers of jurisdiction from juvenile to adult court for juveniles who commit what would be serious felony offenses if they were over 18. States had historically limited the opportunities for such waivers and protected the authority of the juvenile court to determine whether to waive jurisdiction to allow a delinquent to be prosecuted as an adult, thereby continuing to emphasize the juvenile court philosophy of rehabilitation and providing young offenders the chance to make positive changes in their lives. However, during the 1990s, all states but one expanded their statutory provisions to ease the transfer of juveniles to criminal court.[1] States have added statutory exclusions, expanded the list of offenses for which transfer is allowable, or lowered the minimum age for which a juvenile may be transferred to adult court.

Currently, all states allow juveniles who commit offenses to be waived from the jurisdiction of the juvenile court and be prosecuted in the adult criminal court system. The legal process for transferring juveniles to the adult court system varies from state to state, primarily focusing on who has the discretion to make the transfer or waiver decision. An Office of Juvenile Justice and Delinquency Prevention report outlines the three variations of how this can occur.

1. *Waiver*—The juvenile court judge is the decision maker and determines whether the offender is waived from the juvenile justice system to adult criminal court. Waivers are usually limited by age (must be above a certain age) and by offense criteria. Some states provide juvenile court judges with guidelines on the types of criteria to consider (such as the juvenile's potential for rehabilitation) while others reduce judicial discretion by presuming that the juvenile will be waived for certain types of cases.
2. *Direct file*—Fifteen states have concurrent original jurisdiction, in that the prosecutor has the discretion to file charges in either the juvenile justice or criminal justice system. In these states, the prosecutors' discretion is limited by specific age and offense criteria.
3. *Statutory exclusion*—Twenty-eight states have mandatory waiver to adult courts for specific age and offense criteria. If a juvenile is above the minimum age specified and commits a serious offense designated by statute, judges and prosecutors have no discretion; the case must be prosecuted in adult criminal court.[2]

In addition, twenty-two states allow **blended sentencing**, whereby the courts can impose juvenile or adult sentences on certain juvenile offenders.[3] In some states, the authority to blend sentences lies with the juvenile court; in other states, it lies with the adult court. Blended sentences are a middle ground between juvenile and adult sentences in that judges can choose from a broad array of both juvenile and adult sanctions. At times these offenders are given a juvenile sentence as a last chance to avoid an adult sanction.

Even with the concern for dealing with serious juvenile offenders in a punitive and public-safety-oriented approach, and with the expansion of authority to move juveniles into the adult court and correctional process, there have not been an overwhelming number of cases transferred to criminal courts. Figure 9.1 illustrates

Blended sentencing

a middle ground between juvenile and adult sentences that allows judges to choose from a broad array of both juvenile and adult sanctions

NUMBER OF JUVENILE OFFENDERS WAIVED TO CRIMINAL COURT BY CRIME TYPE, 1989–1998

FIGURE **9.1**

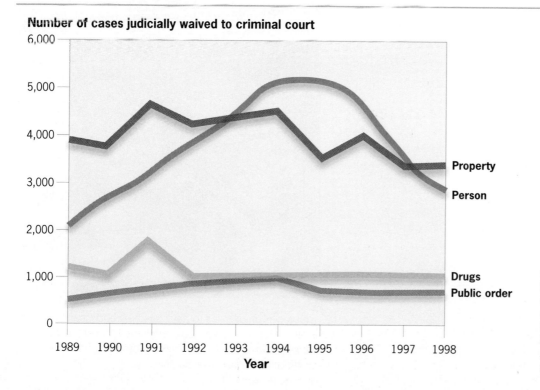

Number of cases judicially waived to criminal court

Source: Charles M. Puzzanchera, *Delinquency Cases Waived to Criminal Courts, 1989–1998* OJJDP Fact Sheet #35 (Washington, D.C.: U.S. Department of Justice, September 2001), p. 1.

the increase in the number of cases judicially waived by crime type from 1989 to 1998. Overall, "[t]he number of delinquency cases judicially waived to criminal court peaked in 1994 with 12,100 cases. This represented a 51% increase over the number of cases waived in 1989 (8,000). Since 1994, however, the number of cases waived to criminal court has declined 33% to 8,100 cases."[4] Cases most likely to be waived to adult court in 1991 were drug offenses (4.1 percent of all juvenile court cases formally petitioned), although this declined to 1.1 percent of cases in 1998. Currently, crimes against the person committed by juveniles are those most likely to be waived to criminal court.[5]

Over the past several years, the number of people under 18 held in state prisons has increased, yet remained relatively constant as a proportion of the overall prison population. From 1985 to 1997, the number increased from 2,300 to 5,400, yet the percentage of juveniles among all inmates remained at only 0.5 percent.[6] Of the juvenile inmates held in 1997, 92 percent were male, 61 percent were committed for violent crimes, and the average maximum sentence was 82 months. Twenty-five percent were white, 58 percent were black, 15 percent were Hispanic, and 2 percent were other.[7] Since 1997, however, the number of under-18 inmates in adult prisons has declined each year, and was only 3,055 (including 112 females) on June 30, 2002.[8] Eleven states had more than a hundred juvenile prisoners, twelve states had fewer than ten, and three states and the Federal Bureau of Prisons had no inmates under 18 at midyear 2002.[9]

There are three approaches for housing offenders under age 18 in state correctional systems. **Straight adult incarceration** places juveniles in adult prisons, with no separate housing or differentiation in programming or job assignment. While all but six states allow juvenile inmates to be housed in prisons with adult inmates, most separate them from adults to some extent, most often in separate housing units or in separate program assignments. **Graduated incarceration**, used in twelve states, initially places inmates under age 18 in juvenile facilities. Once they reach a certain age (usually 18), they are then transferred to an adult prison to

Straight adult incarceration

a form of incarceration in which juveniles handled by adult courts are placed in adult prisons with no separate housing or differentiation in programming or job assignments

Graduated incarceration

a system in which juveniles handled by adult courts are placed in juvenile facilities until they reach age 18; they are then transferred to an adult prison to complete the sentence

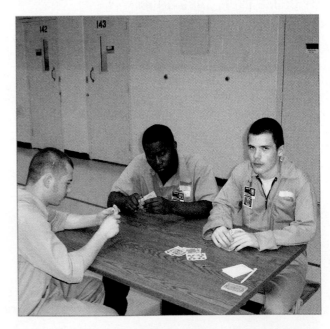

The waiver of juveniles to adult systems and incarceration in adult prisons causes difficult problems for correctional administrators who try to provide proper programs while maintaining the juveniles' safety.
Photo by Richard P. Seiter.

complete their sentence. Finally, eight states use **segregated incarceration**, in which inmates under age 18 are constantly separated from adults, even though they are housed in the same facility. The juvenile prisoners are housed separately and placed in specialized educational, vocational, life skills training, and substance abuse programs that cater to their age and needs.[10]

Many correctional officials are opposed to housing offenders under age 18 in prisons with older adult felons, and even most states that allow integration of juvenile prisoners with adults prefer to maintain some type of separation. This is sometimes difficult, especially in states that have only a handful of juvenile offenders. With small numbers, it is almost impossible to keep juveniles separate from adults, yet provide a full range of program offerings. In states with large numbers of juveniles in adult prisons, the administrative problems are less burdensome, as an entire prison can be dedicated to the youthful offenders and specialized programs developed to meet their needs.

Drug Offenders

One commonly held belief is that drug use leads to criminality. With the initiation of the war on drugs in the late 1980s, the American criminal justice system is targeting and increasing the number of people arrested and punished for selling or using illegal drugs. In fact, the war on drugs has provided substantial dollars for stopping drugs from entering the United States, prosecuting and punishing those who commit drug offenses, and treating drug addicts. In 2002, the federal drug control budget was $18.8 billion, of which 33 percent was for demand reduction, 51 percent was for domestic law enforcement, 6 percent was for international supply reduction, and 11 percent was for interdiction.[11] These budget figures do not include the cost to local and state governments for prosecuting and incarcerating drug offenders.

The U.S. Department of Justice reports a strong relationship between drug use and crime. In **Drug Use Forecasting** studies of incarcerated populations, it was discovered that in eighteen of twenty-three cities included in the study, more than 50 percent of those booked on criminal charges tested positive for some illicit drug.[12] In 1998, an estimated 61,000 convicted jail inmates said they had committed their offense to get money for drugs; one in four convicted property and drug offenders said they committed their crimes to get money for drugs.[13] Table 9.1 illustrates the high percentage of offenders who committed a variety of crimes who indicated that they committed their offense to get money and buy drugs for their own use. As well, 19 percent of state prisoners and 16 percent of federal inmates in 1997 said they committed their current offense to obtain money for drugs.[14]

Not all drug offenders are drug addicts, or even drug users. Some offenders commit drug crimes simply to make money, and avoid serious drug use because

Segregated incarceration a form of incarceration in which juveniles handled by adult courts are assigned to an adult prison, yet are housed separately and placed in specialized educational, vocational, life skills training, and substance abuse programs that match their age level and needs

Drug Use Forecasting surveys of jailed inmates by the U.S. Department of Justice to determine the extent of drug use related to criminality

TABLE 9.1	Percentage of Jail Inmates Who Committed Offense to Get Money for Drugs	
Offense	**1996**	**1999**
Total	15.8%	13.3%
Violent	8.8	11.5
Property	25.6	24.4
Drugs	23.5	14.0
Public-order	4.2	3.3

Source: Bureau of Justice Statistics, *Profile of Jail Inmates, 1996,* (Washington, D.C.: U.S. Department of Justice, April 1998) Davis James Wilson, *Drug Use, Testing, and Treatment in Jails,* (Washington, D.C.: U.S. Department of Justice, May 2000).

they know it will hurt their business and increase their chance for arrest. An estimated 21 percent of probationers without a mental health problem reported that their current offense was a drug offense.[15] Approximately 109,200 (about 22 percent) of all 1996 jail inmates were held for a drug offense, a growth of over fivefold since 1983.[16]

There is also a large proportion of state and federal prisoners serving a sentence for a drug offense. From 1990 to 1999 the number of drug offenders in state prisons increased by 69 percent from 148,600 to 251,200, but declined to 246,100 in 2001.[17] In federal prisons, drug offenses constituted the largest group of inmates, as approximately 60 percent of federal prisoners were serving a sentence for a drug offense in 2000, up from 53 percent in 1990.[18] Revisions in the federal criminal code over the past decade have resulted in mandatory sentences of either five or ten years for offenders convicted of trafficking or sale of drugs, resulting in the Federal Bureau of Prisons prison population rapidly climbing and becoming increasingly a population of drug offenders.

While the United States is targeting a tremendous amount of resources toward the arrest, prosecution, and punishment of drug offenders, the relationship between drug and alcohol use and crime is complex and lacks a cohesive conclusion. The *National Household Survey on Drug Abuse* (NHSDA) has tracked patterns of licit and illicit drug use among the general U.S. population since 1971. Findings indicate that illegal drug use, as measured by the number of people using an illicit drug in the previous month, steadily declined from 1979 to 1992, with a leveling off of the decline since that time.[19] While this seems to indicate that drug abuse is substantially less of a problem than it was two decades ago, there is no question that substance abuse remains a serious problem among criminal offenders. Many experts believe that a more general theory of deviance applies, in that individuals who commit one deviant act (substance abuse) are likely to commit another (criminal behavior). The mixed theories are perhaps the underlying reason that the public is split as what to do with drug users. In a 2001 poll, 47 percent agree with jailing people for possessing drugs, and 47 percent disagreed.[20] When asked to rate the effectiveness of selected approaches to drug use, 36 percent of Americans rate "provide drug treatment" as very effective (with only 19 percent rating it as not very effective), while 30 percent rate "arrest drug users" as very effective, while 34 percent rate it as not very effective.[21]

Without question, it is critical that prisons offer drug abuse programs. Table 9.2 illustrates the number of state and federal inmates who were involved in drug treatment programs each year. The 2001 figure of 120,687 represented 12.9 percent of the inmate population. These programs include residential units with a total environment directed toward dealing with the addictions, addiction groups, and outpatient counseling.

As an example of how a residential drug program operates within prisons, the Federal Bureau of Prisons' drug abuse program (DAP) has separate units in several prisons with the same staffing, structure, length of treatment, and programs provided. All inmate participants in the five-hundred-hour program reside in a treatment unit separate from the prison general inmate population. The program requires offenders to assume responsibility for their behavior and to make a conscious decision to avoid engaging in drug taking and criminal behavior. The treatment model is "bio-psycho-social, " emphasizing a comprehensive lifestyle change, with issues of physical well-being, family relationships, and criminality all targeted for change while participants acquire positive life skills as a vehicle to avoid future drug use.[22]

The BOP program has a five-part treatment strategy: (1) orientation screening and referral: (2) drug abuse education; (3) nonresidential drug abuse treatment services; (4) residential drug abuse treatment; and (5) transitional services. Spe-

TABLE	9.2	Inmates in Drug Treatment Programs on January 1, 1992–2001

Year	Number of inmates
1992	135,034
1993	200,980
1994	158,158
1995	130,560
1996	92,155
1997	96,078
1998	99,210
1999	172,747
2000	172,622
2001	120,687

Source: Adapted from Camille Graham Camp and George M. Camp, *The 2001 Corrections Yearbook: Adult Systems* (Middletown, Conn.: Criminal Justice Institute, 2002), pp. 136–137.

cific unit-based drug treatment is typically delivered no less than four hours a day, five days a week, supplemented by other complementary programs such as education, work skills training, recreation, disease prevention, and health promotion instruction. The BOP, in conjunction with the National Institute of Drug Abuse, is conducting an ongoing evaluation of the effectiveness of the program. In an early review of outcome, findings indicate that in high-security prisons, misconduct among inmates who completed the residential drug abuse treatment program was reduced by 50 percent. For the first six months after release from custody, inmates who completed the residential drug abuse treatment program were 73 percent less likely to be rearrested for a new offense than those who did not participate in a

These female inmates are participating in a residential drug program, and are having a full-unit meeting regarding the program objectives and their personal commitments.
Photo by Richard P. Seiter.

residential drug abuse treatment program, and were 44 percent less likely to use drugs or alcohol than those who did not participate in a residential drug abuse treatment program.[23]

While it is critical to offer drug abuse programs to inmates, it may be even more important to provide drug treatment to offenders on probation, and hopefully through treatment they can avoid further criminality resulting in a prison sentence. In New York City, the Department of Probation manages probationers with a history of drug abuse through a combination of specialized supervision caseloads and contracts for outpatient treatment programs. The specialized units have smaller-than-normal caseloads, supervising about 65 probationers, compared with the approximately 175 probationers in regular caseloads. The department contracts with an outside provider for a twelve-month outpatient treatment program that provides counseling services while working closely with offenders and reporting their progress to probation staff. Probationers receive a mandatory urinalysis within the first two weeks of entry to the program, a second urinalysis within two weeks after the first, and then random monthly testing thereafter.

Research indicates that the program is effective in that probationers receiving the drug treatment had significant reductions in recidivism, "with the greatest reduction in recidivism among those clients who were appropriately matched to outpatient drug treatment on the basis of the severity of their drug use."[24] Recidivism rates were also significantly lower for probationers who stayed in the program more than ninety days than for those who dropped out earlier, as "about half of the probationers who stayed in treatment less than 3 months were rearrested, while only about one-quarter of those who stayed longer were rearrested."[25]

Many types of drug treatment programs are delivered to correctional clients, and not every type of program has been found effective with all types of abusers. However, there is positive evidence that drug abuse programs reduce levels of rearrest and other measures of recidivism. In a recent meta-analysis of a variety of drug abuse programs, the evaluators found that therapeutic communities are effective in reducing recidivism, while boot camp and group-counseling programs did not show consistently good results.[26] Therefore, the National Task Force on Corrections Substance Abuse Strategies recommends that correctional agencies "provide a range of quality programs to meet offenders' control, supervision, and treatment needs."[27] With the high level of correctional clients that do have substance abuse problems, it is critical that correctional agencies provide substantial opportunities for involvement in drug abuse programs.

Mentally Ill Offenders

During the past half century, the United States has made tremendous progress in the treatment and management of the mentally ill. Unfortunately, reforms and improvements in the mental health field have also caused issues and problems for corrections. **Antipsychotic drugs** were invented in the 1960s, and they helped many people with mental illness remain in the community rather than be placed in mental hospitals. These drugs provided a humane alternative to the deleterious placement of patients in the old state mental hospitals, where patients often had little to do and received minimal treatment. Taking antipsychotic drugs can help most mental health patients stay in the community, and the number of patients in state mental institutions went from a high of 559,000 in 1955 to 69,000 in 1995.[28]

However, with minimal monitoring, some patients in the community stop taking their medication, as they may not like the uncomfortable side effects, think they are doing better, or just decide to stop taking the medicine. Or they may lose their insurance coverage, and cannot afford to buy the medicine. Without their medication, the symptoms of the mental illness return, and many such mentally

Antipsychotic drugs

drugs administered to mentally ill individuals to counteract the symptoms of their mental illness, often allowing them to live successfully in the community rather than being institutionalized

State mental institutions in the early 1900s were places of misery that provided little treatment for most patients.
Photo by Peter Turnley/CORBIS-NY.

ill people do not receive treatment, their behavior deteriorates, they end up committing crimes, and they become clients of the criminal justice system rather than patients of the mental health system. The Bureau of Justice Statistics (BJS) estimated that at midyear 1998, there were 283,800 mentally ill offenders in state and federal prisons and local jails (16.2 percent of the population) and 547,800 others on probation.[29]

When inmates are sent to prison, they are initially screened for mental illness. The screening is primarily a self-report by inmates as to whether they have ever experienced a mental health problem. Drawing from inmate surveys conducted as a part of the BJS report cited previously, "10.1 percent of state prison inmates reported a mental or emotional condition, and 10.7 percent said they stayed overnight in a mental hospital or program."[30] Treatment for the mentally ill in prisons generally falls into three categories: (1) twenty-four-hour residential care, (2) therapy and counseling, and (3) psychotropic medications. As of June 30, 2000, 1.6 percent of state prison inmates were receiving residential care, 12.8 percent were receiving therapy or counseling, and 9.7 percent were on psychotropic medication.[31] Overall, most inmates with identified mental health needs are receiving some level of care. Table 9.3 illustrates the level of mental health screening and treatment provided by each state prison system.

In prisons, the responsibility of assessing and treating mentally ill inmates falls to correctional psychologists. The "Your Career in Corrections" box illustrates the type of jobs available to psychologists in a prison setting.

In jails and prisons, mentally ill inmates create a dual problem of control and treatment. Since they have committed a criminal act and are often violent, they may require a high-security institutional placement, resulting in their often being housed with non–mentally ill offenders who have also committed serious offenses and are serving equally long sentences. While they must be controlled, they must also receive treatment for their mental illness and be protected from other violent and dangerous inmates.

| TABLE | 9.3 | Mental Health Screening and Treatment in State Correctional Facilities, June 30, 2000 |

Number of facilities, by type of policy

Region and state	Total*	Screen inmates at intake	Conduct psychiatric assessments	Provide 24-hour mental health care	Provide therapy/ counseling	Distribute psychotropic medications	Help released inmates obtain services	No services provided	No data reported
Total	1,558	1,055	990	776	1,073	1,115	1,006	125	39
Northeast	233	154	163	152	173	178	167	5	3
Connecticut	20	17	17	13	18	16	16	0	0
Maine	8	6	5	3	7	7	6	0	0
Massachusetts	25	20	17	15	21	20	20	0	2
New Hampshire	8	4	5	4	7	7	7	0	0
New Jersey	43	27	24	14	23	30	25	3	0
New York	69	31	52	66	53	43	40	0	0
Pennsylvania	44	36	29	32	29	40	39	2	0
Rhode Island	7	7	7	0	7	7	7	0	0
Vermont	9	6	7	5	8	8	7	0	1
Midwest	301	190	167	140	207	210	196	25	1
Illinois	48	30	30	32	31	31	34	4	0
Indiana	25	17	14	14	15	13	13	4	0
Iowa	30	11	12	12	10	21	23	2	1
Kansas	11	9	8	9	9	10	11	0	0
Michigan	70	39	43	35	40	31	32	10	0
Minnesota	9	1	1	1	8	9	8	0	0
Missouri	28	27	0	0	27	27	27	1	0
Nebraska	9	2	2	0	9	9	0	0	0
North Dakota	3	2	2	1	2	2	2	1	0
Ohio	34	34	34	26	33	32	29	0	0
South Dakota	4	2	3	1	3	4	3	0	0
Wisconsin	30	16	18	9	20	21	14	3	0
South	730	527	497	338	514	535	471	59	17
Alabama	35	16	21	13	21	26	11	3	1
Arkansas	15	12	12	12	12	12	12	3	0
Delaware	9	8	8	2	8	8	5	0	1
District of Columbia	6	2	2	3	2	3	4	2	0
Florida	106	98	90	1	88	88	85	8	0
Georgia	83	54	45	38	41	47	48	6	2
Kentucky	25	15	12	8	13	12	14	1	0
Louisiana	17	12	11	11	10	11	11	0	5
Maryland	26	12	14	13	18	18	22	2	0
Mississippi	28	12	11	5	8	9	2	9	1
North Carolina	80	49	55	31	68	73	61	0	2
Oklahoma	52	37	30	25	33	37	20	4	3
South Carolina	34	19	18	17	21	22	20	5	0
Tennessee	15	14	14	15	15	15	14	0	0
Texas	127	117	114	111	114	118	109	2	2
Virginia	61	44	34	31	34	30	29	14	0
West Virginia	11	6	6	2	8	6	4	0	0

Mentally ill inmates are more likely than other inmates to have disciplinary problems while in prison. A recent survey found that 36 percent of mentally ill state prison inmates, compared to 27 percent of non–mentally ill inmates, were involved in fights. Twenty-four percent of mentally ill state prison inmates were involved in two or more fights since admission, and 12 percent reported involvement in four or more fights. Among jail inmates, 10 percent of the mentally ill were involved in two or more fights, compared to 6 percent of those who were not

TABLE	9.3	Continued

Number of facilities, by type of policy

Region and state	Total*	Screen inmates at intake	Conduct psychiatric assessments	Provide 24-hour mental health care	Provide therapy/ counseling	Distribute psychotropic medications	Help released inmates obtain services	No services provided	No data reported
West	294	184	163	146	179	192	172	36	18
Alaska	24	16	10	6	12	19	18	1	1
Arizona	16	15	13	13	14	14	12	0	1
California	86	50	35	28	41	36	38	13	12
Colorado	47	16	30	32	34	38	35	0	3
Hawaii	10	10	9	9	10	9	1	0	0
Idaho	13	7	5	6	5	10	7	1	0
Montana	8	6	5	4	6	6	4	0	1
Nevada	20	11	10	7	10	9	9	7	0
New Mexico	10	10	10	8	10	9	8	0	0
Oregon	13	13	10	7	9	12	11	0	0
Utah	8	6	5	4	5	6	7	0	0
Washington	30	17	15	17	17	17	15	13	0
Wyoming	9	7	6	5	6	7	7	1	0

*Includes 1,295 state-operated facilities, 22 facilities under joint state and local authority, 3 facilities operated by the District of Columbia, and 238 private facilities with more than 50% of their inmates held for state authorities.

Source: Allen J. Beck and Laura M. Maruschak, *Mental Health Treatment in State Prisons, 2000*, Bureau of Justice Statistics Special Report (Washington, D.C.: U.S. Department of Justice, July 2001), p. 5.

YOUR CAREER IN CORRECTIONS

CORRECTIONAL PSYCHOLOGISTS

Corroctional psychologists do all the things associated with clinical psychology, only they do them in a correctional setting. Correctional psychology has some subspecialties such as forensic psychology (conducting evaluations to establish competency and responsibility for crimes or doing judicial evaluations that may influence sentencing), or specialty programming such as drug or sex offender treatment. The first thing that staff psychologists working in a prison do with new inmates is conduct an intake screening, to look for past histories of mental health treatment, determine current mental health status, and make program recommendations. They then conduct both individual or group counseling, advise managers on how to best manage inmates, and may be involved in the employee assistance program. They sometimes must respond to and assist with emergency situations, and may have special duties such as hostage negotiations, confrontation avoidance (trying to talk an inmate out of an action to avoid a calculated use of force), crisis interventions for inmates or staff (such as an inmate finding out that he or she has an unfaithful spouse), and working closely with medical staff to monitor inmates' compliance in taking medications.

Not everyone is suited for working as a correctional psychologist. Those considering such jobs should be able to work in a paramilitary situation in which psychology and mental health evaluations may not be the primary factor in action taken. They must also recognize that they will work in what could become an unsafe environment with the potential for violence. However, training that psychologists receive and use in a nonprison clinical practice is very similar for correctional psychologists. The correctional psychologist will treat a greater number of individuals with depression and anxiety and will see more cases of serious mental illnesses such as schizophrenia.

(continued)

For most states and the federal government, a doctoral degree is required, although some states require only a master's degree in psychology. On an individual basis, a correctional psychologist must have emotional security to work in a prison and be able to work within the structure of an organization focused on security and order. Pay, benefits, and working conditions for correctional psychologists are similar to those of other institutional settings (such as Veterans Administration hospitals or state mental hospitals). On the other hand, many individuals find that career opportunities for correctional psychologists are greater than for an outside clinical psychological practice, since working for a large organization provides not only a more extensive career ladder but also opportunities outside psychology.

mentally ill. Other disciplinary problems were also more common among mentally ill inmates. More than 60 percent of state prison inmates with mental illness had been formally charged with breaking prison rules since admission.[32]

While on probation or postprison community supervision, the mentally ill have similar problems. As a condition of their community supervision, offenders must often maintain employment, submit to drug testing, or participate in treatment. It is estimated that 13 percent of probationers had a condition requiring them to seek mental health treatment, yet in a 1997 survey of these probationers, only 43 percent of those required to participate in such treatment had done so.[33] Managing offenders in the community creates unique problems, and only recently have most probation and parole agencies created special caseloads for managing the mentally ill. These caseloads require patience, treatment expertise, and control by the officers in charge. Offenders must have a treatment program developed, must receive counseling for their mental illness, must be encouraged to continue to take their medication, and require much more time and patience in supervising than the typical criminal offender. Probation officers responsible for such caseloads require specialized training to be able to address the difficult dilemma created by the overlap of criminality and mental illness.

Mentally ill offenders are not only a problem to manage while in prison or under community supervision; they are also more likely to recidivate than other offenders. The Bureau of Justice Statistics reports the following:

> Among repeat offenders, 53% of mentally ill State inmates had a current or past sentence for a violent offense, compared to 45% of other inmates. Forty-six percent of mentally ill jail inmates and 32% of other jail inmates with a criminal history had a current or past sentence or a current charge for a violent crime. Among Federal prisoners with a prior sentence, the mentally ill (44%) were twice as likely as other inmates (22%) to have a current or prior sentence for a violent offense. Although offenders on probation had shorter criminal histories, nearly 3 in 10 of the mentally ill were recidivists with a current or past sentence for violence.[34]

Managing mentally ill offenders in the community and in prison is a difficult challenge. These offenders are not deterred by typical punishment. They may understand that they have received a long prison sentence for their crimes, yet may not be able to use that punishment as an incentive to discontinue criminal activities. While they are supervised in the community, their commission of crimes is not the result of a simple decision to recidivate, but is more likely a result of their inability to manage themselves, to maintain the use of their psychotropic medication, and to deal responsibly with problems regarding housing, employment, or relationships.

Aging Offenders

The prison population in the United States is getting older. Part of the reason for this is that the general population of the United States is also aging. Individuals age 65 and older represent the fastest-growing age group in the United States; their numbers reached 34 million in 2000. Americans over age 50 constituted only 26 percent of the population in 1992, but it is estimated that the proportion of this age group will reach 33 percent by 2010.[35] Changes in the models of sentencing is a second reason why more elderly offenders are imprisoned, as sentencing guidelines and mandatory sentencing take away sentencing judges' discretion to consider age, health issues, and risk to the community. Previously, judges would consider these factors and often grant older offenders probation for crimes and criminal backgrounds that would result in a prison sentence for younger offenders.

Finally, with the statutory lengthening of prison sentences for almost every crime over the past two decades, once someone is sentenced to prison he or she stays a longer time. As well, three-strikes and habitual-offender laws often require offenders to go to prison for life without parole. These prisoners naturally age while serving their sentence and end up dying while in prison. These factors increase the average age of the U.S. prison population. In 1990, only 4.9 percent of the inmates in state and federal prisons were age 50 or older,[36] and on January 1, 2001, there were 113,358 inmates older than age 50, representing 7.9 percent of the prison population.[37]

This increase in the average age and number of older offenders creates many management, resource, and programmatic issues for correctional administrators. Perhaps the most critical, expensive, and difficult issue is increased health care needs. A *Time* magazine article notes, "Because elderly people require more medical care, it costs nearly three times as much to incarcerate them, or about $65,000 a year per inmate."[38] Many illnesses and general health problems result from the aging process and years of risky lifestyle choices such as tobacco use, extensive drug and alcohol use, and high-risk sexual behavior. The health problems of the elderly are not only more severe than, but very different from those of younger offenders, and prison medical clinics are usually not prepared to deal with the depression, sexually transmitted diseases, tuberculosis and other infectious diseases, heart problems, and reduced circulation that occur in older inmates. Table 9.4 illustrates how medical problems relate to the age of prisoners.

There are also security, work opportunity, and program issues. Prisons were designed and operational processes created to hold young and physically active inmates. Prison architecture, recreation facilities, and types of housing were all designed without consideration for older inmates. Simple problems, such as difficulty in getting around in wheelchairs or inability to walk long distances, result from the campus-style prison architecture emphasizing space to spread out

TABLE 9.4	Percentage of Prisoners Reporting a Medical Problem since Admission, 1997		
Age of reported problem	**Total**	**Required surgery**	**Required Other Treatment**
24 years and younger	11.8%	4.1%	9.0%
25 to 34 years	14.3	5.7	10.5
35 to 44 years	21.0	9.5	14.6
45 years and older	37.4	17.7	28.5

Source: Adapted from Bureau of Justice Statistics, *Sourcebook of Criminal Justice Statistics, 2001* (Washington, D.C.: U.S. Department of Justice, 2003), p. 527.

inmates over as much area as possible. Prison recreation programs such basketball, jogging, and weight lifting do not meet the needs or interests of the elderly.
Few work opportunities can be assigned to older inmates.

Prison housing and bed arrangements often cause problems for older inmates.
Prisons usually have bunk beds. Many older inmates cannot get into upper bunks,
and assignment to lower bunks due to age causes morale problems among
younger inmates who believe they deserve these beds due to their good behavior
and time served in prison (the criteria usually considered for preferred assignments). Most prisons have two inmates assigned to each cell. Many older and
younger inmates do not want to share a cell, as they have different habits and interests in radio or television stations. Younger inmates may have little tolerance for
older inmates getting up to go to the bathroom several times per night, resulting in
tension and requests for prison managers to change housing and bed assignments. Finally, prison administrators may need to protect older inmates from being victimized by younger and stronger predators, who find older inmates easy victims from whom to steal or extort money. Prison officials are constantly challenged
with finding solutions to these problems, which have no easy or clear answers.

To remedy these problems, most prisons make allowances in standard polices
for cell and bed assignments, or even for inmate movement, and let older inmates
begin moving from one building to another before younger inmates. Some correctional agencies even use entire prisons or housing units to house older inmates
and create counseling programs and recreation that meet their needs. Prisons also
try to identify specific jobs that can be done by older inmates, and have recreation
departments create leisure activities such as stretching classes or table-game tour-
naments to occupy these inmates and meet their special needs. The "A Case Study"
box illustrates issues that result as older inmates are sentenced to prison.

A CASE STUDY — SENIOR CITIZEN INMATES

The discussion about issues facing corrections regarding the aging of the prison population
creates a question of whether all of these inmates should come to prison, and whether they
should stay for their full sentence, if their health puts them in danger of dying in prison. An interesting case involved the sentence received by a male offender in his sixties. This person had been
a law enforcement officer for more than thirty years, rising to the executive level of two different
law enforcement departments. He was respected in his community and spent several hours a
week serving his community.

Surprisingly, this person had another life. He had been sexually molesting his grandchildren
for the past several years. As the story became public, most people who knew him were shocked,
as he did not seem like someone who would do this, and they knew the good he did for the community. However, all his built-up goodwill was not enough to keep him from getting a lengthy
prison sentence for his offenses. Even his closest allies and friends could not argue against his
receiving a term in prison for molesting his grandchildren.

After the sentence, his life became very difficult. He had a double problem as an inmate. While
inmates do not usually physically abuse child molesters, as had been the case in the past, molesters are still looked down upon and receive continual harassment by the inmate population. As
well, as a past and well-known law enforcement officer, this person had personally arrested many
offenders and put them in prison. Prison administrators had to make intense efforts to protect
his safety, including placing him in a prison far away from his home with a population that was
less likely to assault him. At times, he had to be placed in administrative detention for his own
protection. His punishment of imprisonment was much greater than that of a "normal" inmate.

As time went on, the inmate's health worsened, and it became apparent that he was going to
die in the next few years, even though he still had several years to serve on his sentence. The

state in which he was incarcerated did have a policy that allowed emergency release of a dying inmate. However, due to the nature of his crime, there was little sentiment by anyone that he should be released. So, in effect, his sentence became a life sentence rather than a multiyear sentence.

The issue that becomes apparent in this situation is how a regular sentence for older offenders can become a life (some may say death) sentence for aging inmates. Yet with mandatory sentences and sentencing guidelines, a judge often cannot consider the age or medical condition of an offender. The other side of the issue is whether someone should receive a lesser sentence for the same crime due to age or infirmity. Unfortunately, there is no easy solution to this dilemma, and aging offenders cause unique problems for correctional administrators.

Violent Offenders

Needless to say, many violent individuals are under correctional supervision, and particularly in prison. In 2000, 49 percent of all adults sentenced to state prisons were committed for violent offenses.[39] However, a much smaller number and percentage of inmates are truly violent and predatory and continue violent acts even while in prison. These violent and predatory inmates think nothing of assaulting, raping, or killing other inmates, and correctional officials must take extraordinary actions to protect both staff and other inmates. The standard inmate disciplinary process described later in Chapter 13 ("Custody and Treatment") and Chapter 14 ("Legal Issues and the Death Penalty") is the procedure used to respond to inmate violence. However, some inmates exhibit extremely violent behavior in prison, are not deterred by standard inmate discipline, and cannot be allowed to remain in even high- or maximum-security prisons without being a threat to security.

For these inmates, many states and the Federal Bureau of Prisons have developed **supermax prisons**. Supermax prisons get their historical beginning with Alcatraz, the most famous prison in the world. During the crime wave that swept across the United States during the Great Depression of the 1930s, correctional administrators were first challenged with how to handle offenders with serious criminal histories of violence. As a result, in 1934 the federal government opened Alcatraz Island as the most super-maximum prison ever created in the United States. Alcatraz was designated to handle the most notorious and dangerous criminals of the era, using strict regimens of control and tight security. However, Alcatraz was very expensive to operate, with no freshwater wells and all supplies needing to be ferried across the water from San Francisco. As a result of cost, Alcatraz closed in 1963, and was replaced with the United States Penitentiary (USP) in Marion, Illinois.

USP Marion had problems adjusting to this mission to control the nation's most dangerous offenders. As a result of continuously tightening security, inmates in 1980 staged a work strike, and the Bureau of Prisons permanently closed Marion's prison factory and terminated all classes. Tensions increased between prison officials and inmates and on October 22, 1983, two inmates separately killed two correctional officers. Four days later, a prisoner was found murdered in his cell. Marion was placed on emergency status, and implemented a twenty-four-hour lockdown of prisoners in solitary cells.[40] Inmates were allowed out of their cells only five hours per week for recreation, showers, and visits with family members. Inmate programs were eliminated, except those provided over video on in-cell television sets or by program staff (such as chaplains) coming to the inmates in their cells. In 1985, inmates filed suit against the lockdown. In the case of ***Bruscino v. Carlson,*** a federal judge denied their motion, stating, ". . . the Court is of the firm conviction that this litigation was conceived by a small group of hard-core inmates

Supermax prisons
either freestanding prisons or distinct units within other prisons that provide for the management and secure control of inmates designated as violent or seriously disruptive in other prisons

Bruscino v. Carlson
a 1985 federal court decision that the lockdown of inmates at the U.S. Penitentiary in Marion, Illinois, was not a violation of the Constitution

Alcatraz. Perhaps the most famous and mysterious prison in the history of corrections.
Courtesy of the Federal Bureau of Prisons.

Warden James A. Johnson served as the first warden of Alcatraz.
Courtesy of the Federal Bureau of Prisons.

who are bent on the disruption of the prison system in general and of USP-Marion in particular."[41] The U.S. Court of Appeals upheld that decision in 1988, claiming that the conditions were not a violation of the Constitution, and in 1989 the U.S. Supreme Court let that decision stand. Marion was then free to continue the lockdown and became the model for "supermax prisons" that has since been copied by more than thirty states. A supermax prison is defined as follows:

> A freestanding facility, or distinct unit within a facility, that provides for the management and secure control of inmates who have been officially designated as exhibiting violent or seriously disruptive behavior while incarcerated. Such inmates have been determined to be a threat to safety and security in traditional high-security facilities, and their behavior can be controlled by separation, restricted movement, and limited access to staff and other inmates.[42]

USP Marion was the replacement for Alcatraz. However, its design was not secure enough for the nation's most dangerous inmates, and it was replaced in 1994.
Courtesy of the Federal Bureau of Prisons.

Security is the dominant feature of the supermax prison. All aspects of maintaining the prison, including structure of the building, education and programs, human contact, medical services, food service, property, and policies and procedures, revolve around proper security measures. When inmates do come out of their cells, they are handcuffed, often placed in leg irons, and escorted by at least two correctional officers. Human contact in a supermax prison is very limited, as inmates have minimum (or no) contact with other inmates, and have contact with medical staff, clergy, or counselors only as these staff members visit their cells. Inmates are almost always alone in solitary cells, and generally eat, recreate, and participate in programs (via video) by themselves.

Supermax prisons were created for inmates that exhibited violent and predatory behavior in other prisons. However, the use of supermax prisons has expanded; in some states, to reduce gang activity and related violence in other prisons, identified prison gang members are also removed from general-population prisons and placed in a supermax prison, even if they have not committed a violent act while in prison. Connecticut was one of the first states (beginning in the early 1990s) to move gang members and leaders to a supermax prison. The only way for gang members to get out of the lockdown situation is to refute their membership and debrief or tell correctional officials everything they know about the gang operations and membership. Once they do tell officials about the gang activities, they would not be welcome back into the gang, and would probably be assaulted or killed by other gang members if they had the chance. Since the first identification of prison gangs, California has had the most gang members and the most problems, and now uses a similar strategy, as all gang leaders are placed in the supermax prison at Pelican Bay, are kept in a single person cell, and recreate by themselves.

The purpose of the solitary isolation and extraordinary security within a supermax prison is to prevent extremely violent and dangerous inmates from harming others. Supermax prisons serve two functions in this regard. First, they control very violent and dangerous inmates. With constant diligence, security, and

A supermax cell. All the materials in the cell are built to be indestructible and unable to be used as weapons.
Courtesy of the Ohio Department of Rehabilitation and Correction.

caution, these inmates have very limited opportunity to harm others. As inmates comply with security rules and show less intent to be disruptive, they usually earn small additional privileges, such as added time out of their cells or the opportunity to recreate or eat with a small number of other inmates. Over two or three years, if they continue to behave, supermax inmates can progress in privileges and work their way out of the supermax to a traditional maximum-security prison. The second function of supermax prisons is to discourage violent behavior in general-population prisons. Correctional administrators point out that the presence of supermax prisons is an incentive for good behavior, as inmates want to avoid being sent to this type of lockdown confinement.

The overall emphasis on security has resulted in controversy surrounding supermax prisons. Correctional officials maintain that these prisons are incentives for good behavior in other prisons, as inmates detest the thought of being sent to lockdown confinement. And taking the most violent and predatory inmates out of other prisons keeps general-population institutions more peaceful and orderly. However, opponents of supermax prisons assert that the lack of human contact, the absence of work, and the deficiency of intellectual stimulation are human rights violations and have negative consequences on individuals. The Federal Bureau of Prisons has shown that violence in other federal prisons has gone down since the advent of supermax prisons. However, more research is necessary to determine the impact of these facilities on overall inmate behavior. The "You Make the Decision" box asks you to decide whether you support the operation of supermax prisons.

In a supermax prison, inmates often can recreate out of their cells only in a small caged area with a small number of other inmates.
Photo by Richard P. Seiter.

YOU MAKE THE DECISION . . .

IMPLEMENT A SUPERMAX PRISON?

Over the past ten years, supermax prisons have been "all the rage" in corrections, as most states and the federal government have expanded their use of supermax prisons. Prison systems have grown in the number of inmates; they have more inmates with a history or violence and gang involvement; and, because of longer sentences and three-strikes laws, they have more inmates who have little hope to get out of prison anytime soon and little disincentive for acting out violently or attempting escape. As a result, prison officials have found supermax prisons a seemingly good preventive approach to violence in prisons. If inmates are locked in their cells all but a few hours per week, if programs and services are brought to them instead of them going to the service, and if when they do come out of cells they are handcuffed and escorted by staff, they have little opportunity to commit further acts of violence. Prison officials also believe that with supermax prisons in operation, other prisons are more peaceful, as the most violent inmates are locked up and the supermax acts as a disincentive for serious rule violations.

However, supermax prisons are not without their downside. Opponents of supermax prisons express concern that the lack of human contact, the absence of work, and the deficiency of intellectual stimulation have negative consequences on an individual. In addition, they argue that physical violence toward inmates may be common in such a controlled atmosphere. There is also a question of the impact on staff working in such a rigid and secure facility over long periods of time. Supermax prisons are also extremely expensive to build and operate. The requirement for high-security building materials and components, elaborate electrical and technical systems, and the overlay of physical security drives construction costs up to almost double that of a normal medium-security prison. The increased staff-to-inmate ratio, the need to take services to inmates in a lockdown status, and the absence of inmate workers to carry out many functions also drives up the day-to-day operational costs.

Considering these pros and cons, decide whether you support the implementation of supermax prisons. If you do, specify the category of inmates or the acts committed by inmates that would warrant their assignment to a supermax. If you do not, specify how you would handle violent and dangerous offenders. You can do this exercise individually or in a small group.

Sex Offenders

Over the past twenty-five years, as a result of two major factors, the number of sex offenders under correctional supervision has risen significantly. First, public education regarding sex offenses has led to more victims reporting the sexual offense to police. Victims had previously been very hesitant to make their allegations public, fearing that they would not be believed, would be humiliated, and might suffer reprisal. The criminal justice system is better prepared to respond to the allegations of sex offenses, and DNA testing and other advances in forensic science have made some of them it easier to prove. Second, legislatures have passed laws to support and aid victims, to clarify definitions of sex offenses that aid in the prosecution of such crimes, and to toughen sanctions for such offenses.

Sex offenders are commonly defined as those who commit a legally prohibited sexual act, or in some states any offender who commits any crime that is " sexually motivated." For instance, an assault that was an unsuccessful rape attempt may still be classified as a sex offense. The term *sex offender* usually includes offenders convicted of rape or sexual assault. Sexual assault includes the crimes of statutory rape, forcible sodomy, lewd acts with children, and other offenses relating to fondling, molestation, or indecent practices. **Pedophile** is the term for someone who is sexually attracted to and molests children.

Females are the primary victims of sexual assaults, although both male and female children are more equally molested by pedophiles. According to the National Crime Victimization Survey, between 1992 and 2000,

> Persons age 12 or older experienced an average annual 140,990 completed rapes, 109,230 attempted rapes, and 152,680 completed and attempted sexual assaults . . . Most rapes and sexual assaults were committed against females: Female victims accounted for 94% of all completed rapes, 91% of all attempted rapes, and 89% of all completed and attempted sexual assaults.[43]

Table 9.5 illustrates the characteristics of victims of rape and sexual assault, and Table 9.6 illustrates characteristics of imprisoned sexual offenders. Both victims

Sex offenders

offenders who have committed a legally prohibited sexual act or any crime that is statutorily defined as sexually motivated

Pedophile

someone who is sexually attracted to and molests children

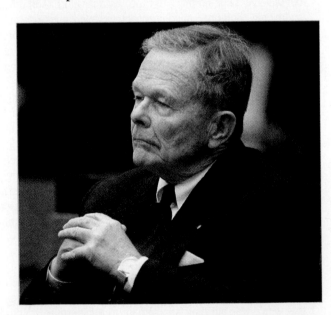

John Geoghan, a priest who was sentenced to a Massachusetts prison for child molestation, was shortly thereafter murdered by another inmate.
Courtesy of AP/Wide World Photos.

TABLE	9.5	Victims of Imprisoned Rape and Sexual Assault Offenders

	Violent offenders in state prison reporting single victims		
Characteristic	All	Rape	Sexual assault
Sex of victim			
Male	55.8%	5.5%	15.2%
Female	44.2	94.5	84.8
Race of victim			
White	64.5%	67.8%	76.4%
Black	29.8	27.6	20.1
Other	5.7	4.6	3.5
Age of victim			
12 or younger	9.9%	15.2%	44.7%
13 to 17	8.8	21.8	33.0
18 to 24	17.5	25.1	9.4
25 to 34	31.1	25.4	7.7
35 to 54	26.5	10.2	4.3
55 or older	6.3	2.3	.9
Median age	29 yrs	22 yrs	13 yrs
Relationship to offender			
Family	12.9%	20.3%	37.7%
Spouse	2.5	1.2	.6
Child/stepchild	6.1	14.0	25.9
Other relative	4.3	5.1	11.2
Intimate	5.5	9.1	6.2
Boyfriend/girlfriend	5.0	8.8	5.4
Ex-spouse	.5	.3	.8
Acquaintance	34.7	40.8	41.2
Stranger	46.9	29.8	14.9

Source: Lawrence A. Greenfeld, *Sex Offenses and Offenders: An Analysis of Data on Rape and Sexual Assault* (Washington, D.C.: U.S. Department of Justice, Bureau of Justice Statistics, February 1997), p. 24.

TABLE	9.6	Characteristics of Imprisoned Rape and Sexual Assault Offenders

	Offenders in state prison		
Characteristic	All violent	Rape	Sexual assault
Estimated number of offenders, 1994	429,400	33,800	54,300
Sex			
Male	96.2%	99.6%	98.8%
Female	3.8	.4	1.2
Race			
White	48.1%	52.2%	73.9%
Black	48.2	43.7	22.8
Other	3.7	4.1	3.3
Age at arrest for current offense			
Less than 18	3.1%	.6%	1.1%
18–24	38.1	33.7	23.6
25–29	22.1	20.9	17.0
30–34	15.0	17.7	16.3
35–39	8.8	10.9	13.4
40–44	5.0	4.1	10.2
45–49	3.4	4.8	6.6
50–54	1.7	2.9	4.4
55–59	1.5	3.2	4.2
60 or older	1.4	1.3	3.2
Average at arrest	29 yrs	31 yrs	34 yrs
Marital status			
Married	17.1%	22.1%	21.8%
Widowed	2.6	1.2	1.7
Divorced	21.4	28.5	35.0
Separated	5.6	6.2	4.9
Never married	53.3	42.0	36.6

Source: Lawrence A. Greenfeld, *Sex Offenses and Offenders: An Analysis of Data on Rape and Sexual Assault* (Washington, D.C.: U.S. Department of Justice, Bureau of Justice Statistics, February 1997), p. 21.

and offenders of sexual assault are more likely to be white. While 47 percent of all victims of violent crimes are strangers to the offender, in only 30 percent of the rapes and 15 percent of sexual assaults are victims strangers.

Data on conviction and sentencing for rape and sexual assault indicates the following:

- In 1992 an estimated 21,655 felony defendants nationwide were convicted of rape.
- Just over two-thirds of convicted rape defendants received a prison sentence, 19 percent received a jail sentence and probation, and 13 percent were sentenced to probation supervision in the community.
- For rape defendants sentenced to prison, the average term imposed was just under fourteen years. The average jail term for an offender convicted of rape

was eight months, and the average probation term was just under six years. An estimated 2 percent of convicted rapists received a term of life imprisonment.
- About a third of rape defendants had one or more additional felony convictions collateral to the conviction for rape.
- Sentences of convicted rape defendants also carried additional penalties, which included a fine (13 percent of convicted defendants), victim restitution (12 percent), required treatment (10 percent), and community service (2 percent).[44]

In 1994, sex offenders constituted approximately 4.7 percent of all offenders under correctional supervision. Table 9.7 illustrates the number and percent of sex offenders under the various sanctions. The largest group represented is sex offenders in state prisons (9.7 percent of the state prison population). Sex offenses are generally prosecuted in state rather than federal courts.

In 1980, only 20,500 sex offenders were in state prisons; by 1994, this number had climbed to 88,100,[45] and by 1997 to 107,698.[46] A 1997 publication by the National Institute of Justice reported that approximately 234,000 sex offenders are under correctional supervision on any given day, and about 60 percent of these are supervised in the community.[47] In 2001, there were 386,112 offenders in state sex offender registries, a 47 percent increase from 1998.[48] Figure 9.2 illustrates the increase in the number of sex offenders in state correctional institutions from 1980 to 1994. Once in prison, sex offenders are serving longer periods of time. In 1990, offenders convicted of rape were serving an average of 62 months in jail or prison, and those convicted of other sexual offenses were serving 36 months. By 1999, this had increased to 79 months for rape and 47 months for other sexual assaults.[49]

Containment model

an approach to managing sex offenders that includes treatment to develop internal control over deviant thoughts, supervision and surveillance to control external behaviors, and polygraph examinations to monitor conformance to treatment plans and supervision conditions

TREATMENT AND MANAGEMENT OF SEX OFFENDERS

Sex offenders present a difficult challenge for management in both community and institutional settings. Not all sex offenders share similar characteristics, and the most effective management and treatment comes from creating a program that relates to the individual characteristics of the offender. A National Institute of Justice survey of state supervision of sex offenders in the community identified a five-part containment process that "seeks to hold offenders accountable through the combined use of both offenders' internal controls and external control measures (such as the use of the polygraph and relapse prevention plans)."[50] The **containment model** is designed to use a "triangle" of supervision: "treatment to teach sex offenders to develop internal control over deviant thoughts; supervision

TABLE 9.7	Supervision of Convicted Sex Offenders, 1994		
		Sex offenders	
	Total population	**Number**	**Percent**
Probation	2,964,171	106,710	3.6%
Jail	304,274	10,345	3.4
State prisons	906,112	88,100	9.7
Federal prisons	87,515	875	1.0
Parole	690,159	27,606	4.0
Total	4,952,231	233,636	4.7

Source: Lawrence A. Greenfeld, *Sex Offenses and Offenders: An Analysis of Data on Rape and Sexual Assault* (Washington, D.C.: U.S. Department of Justice, Bureau of Justice Statistics, February 1997), p. 17.

THE ESTIMATED NUMBER OF SEX OFFENDERS IN STATE PRISONS, 1980–1994

FIGURE **9.2**

Number of offenders

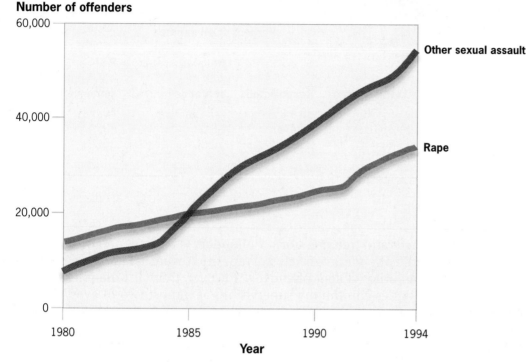

Source: Lawrence A. Greenfeld, *Sex Offenses and Offenders: An Analysis of Data on Rape and Sexual Assault* (Washington, D.C.: U.S. Department of Justice, Bureau of Justice Statistics, February 1997), p. 17.

and surveillance to control offenders' external behaviors; and polygraph examinations to help design, and to monitor conformance to, treatment plans and supervision conditions."[51] The five components of the model are as follows:

1. An overall philosophy and goal of community and victim safety.
2. An individualized case management system of sex offender–specific containment tailored to the needs of the sex offender.
3. A multidisciplinary approach of collaboration among teams of law enforcement, probation and parole, treatment providers, and prison personnel to manage the offender.
4. Consistent public policies reflecting the latest knowledge regarding effective management of sex offenders.
5. A quality-control component to monitor whether policies are being implemented as intended and that they are producing the desired impact.

SEX OFFENDER RECIDIVISM

While sex offenders are a difficult group to "rehabilitate, " the recidivism rates generally attributed to sex offenders is not as high as many people think. In examining sex offender inmates in state prisons in 1991 who were recidivists, an estimated 24 percent of those serving time for rape and 19 percent of those serving time for sexual assault had been on probation or parole at the time of the offense for which they were incarcerated.[52] In a study by the Bureau of Justice Statistics of recidivism by probationers, rapists on probation were found to have a lower rate of rearrest for new felonies (19.5 percent) than other violent probationers (41 percent) over the three-year follow-up.[53] Another three-year follow-up of recidivism of offenders discharged from prison during 1994 had similar findings. Table 9.8 illustrates the lower rearrest, reconviction, and reincarceration rates for ex-inmates who had served a sentence for rape or sexual assault, than for those who served a sentence for all violent offenses.

TABLE	9.8	Recidivism Rates of Violent, Rape, and Sexual Assault Offenders, 1994			

	Percent of all inmates			
Offenders	Rearrested	Reconvicted	Reincarcerated with new sentence	Reincarcerated without new sentence
All violent offenses	61.7%	39.9%	20.4%	49.8%
Rape	46.0	27.4	12.6	43.5
Sexual assault	41.4	22.3	10.5	36.0

Source: Bureau of Justice Statistics, *Sourcebook of Criminal Justice Statistics, 2001* (Washington, D.C.: U.S. Department of Justice, 2003), p. 508.

The management and treatment of sex offenders is difficult and often unsuccessful, even though offenders convicted of rape and sexual assault have lower recidivism rates than other violent offenders. However, there is little tolerance for sexual offenders under community supervision, as almost two of every five offenders are returned to prison, even when not committing a new crime. Intensive treatment and monitoring in the community, including the use of polygraph examinations to confirm compliance with treatment and supervision conditions, often leads to revoking supervision as a preventive approach to avoid further criminality.

Offenders with Infectious Diseases

Criminal offenders generally come from a high-risk group for infectious diseases. They usually have not had a healthy lifestyle, including poor nutrition, a lack of medical care, high stress, likelihood of involvement in violent acts, shared needles for drug use, and interaction with other high-risk individuals. Therefore, the problems of infectious diseases are often greater than in the general U.S. population, and management by correctional officials with infected offenders causes more serious problems in handling offenders and keeping disease from spreading. Infectious diseases most common to and most problematic with correctional populations include HIV/AIDS and tuberculosis.

HIV/AIDS

Human immuno-deficiency virus (HIV)

a virus that attacks the body's immune system, increasing the chance of infection and other diseases

Human immunodeficiency virus (HIV) attacks the body's immune system, increasing the chance of infection and other diseases. The HIV virus can develop into acquired immune deficiency syndrome (AIDS), which usually proves fatal after some period of time. HIV/AIDS is a serious concern for correctional agencies, especially prisons and jails, in which offenders and staff interact regularly; there is the chance of violence and blood spills, and staff and inmates fear the transmittal of the disease, even though it is passed only through body fluids (blood, semen, vaginal fluids, and other body fluids) and there is usually little likelihood of individuals contracting the disease through casual or chance contact. HIV is known to be spread by sexual contact with an infected person or by sharing needles or syringes for drug injection with someone who is infected. HIV/AIDS is a disease that is very difficult and expensive to treat and taxes the staff and budgets of correctional agencies.

It is estimated that between 800,000 and 900,000 Americans are infected with the HIV virus. The overall rate of confirmed AIDS cases among the U.S. prison

HIV/AIDS-infected inmates represent just over 2 percent of the incarcerated population, and receive counseling and medical care while in prison.
Photo by Mark Peterson/Corbis/SABA Press Photos, Inc.

TABLE	9.9	Percentage of HIV-Positive Prison Inmates by Year

Year-end	Number	Percent of Population
1995	24,256	2.3%
1996	23,881	2.2
1997	23,886	2.1
1998	25,680	2.2
1999	25,801	2.1
2000	25,088	2.0

Source: Laura M. Maruschak, *HIV in Prisons, 2000*, Bureau of Justice Statistics Bulletin (Washington, D.C.: U.S. Department of Justice, October 2002), p. 1.

population (0.52 percent) was approximately four times the rate in the general U.S. population. On December 31, 2000, there were 24,074 state prison inmates (2.2 of the population) and 1,014 federal inmates (0.8 percent of the population) known to be HIV-positive, and 5,528 were confirmed to have developed AIDS.[54] As indicated in Table 9.9, the percentage of the prison population infected with HIV has declined over the past few years, from 2.3 percent of the prison population in 1995 to 2.0 percent in 2000. During 2000, 195 inmates died from HIV-related causes. However, the 1999 rate of AIDS-related deaths in state prisons (20 per 100,000) was lower than for a comparable group in the general U.S. population (25 per 100,000).[55]

HIV/AIDS is not distributed evenly throughout the prison population. A slightly greater proportion of female inmates (3.6 percent of the prison population) as compared to male inmates (2.2 percent) in state prisons on December 31, 2000, were HIV-positive.[56] As indicated in Table 9.10, states in the Northeast had a significantly higher proportion of HIV-infected inmates (5.2 percent) than other regions, with only 2.3 percent in the South, 1.1 percent in the Midwest, and 0.9 percent in the West.

To determine whether inmates have HIV/AIDS, most states require inmates to have an HIV test. Nineteen states do such testing at admission to prison, and

| TABLE 9.10 | Inmates by Region Known to Be Positive for HIV during 2000 |

Jurisdiction	Total known to be HIV-positive[a]			HIV/AIDS cases as a percent of total custody population[b]		
	12/31/99	6/30/00	12/31/00	12/31/99	6/30/00	12/31/00
U.S. total[c]						
Reported	25,801	25,359	25,088	2.1%	—	2.0%
Comparable reporting[d]	25,801	25,067	25,088	—	—	—
Federal	1,150	—	1,014	0.9%	—	0.8%
State	24,651	25,359	24,074	2.3	2.2%	2.2
Northeast	10,030	9,779	8,721	6.0%	5.7%	5.2%
Connecticut	632	928	593	3.7	5.5	3.6
Maine	9	15	11	0.5	0.9	0.7
Massachusetts	346	499	313	3.3	4.8	3.0
New Hampshire	17	14	23	0.8	0.6	1.0
New Jersey	869	942	771	3.5	3.6	3.2
New York[e]	7,000	6,500	6,000	9.7	9.1	8.5
Pennsylvania	939	776	900	2.6	2.1	2.4
Rhode Island	203	92	90	6.9	2.7	2.6
Vermont	15	13	20	1.3	1.0	1.5
Midwest	2,171	2,479	2,252	1.0%	1.1%	1.1%
Illinois	635	653	619	1.4	1.5	1.4
Indiana	—	292	—	—	1.6	—
Iowa	30	39	27	0.4	0.5	0.3
Kansas	41	44	49	0.5	0.5	0.6
Michigan	578	404	585	1.3	0.9	1.2
Minnesota	32	42	42	0.6	0.6	0.7
Missouri	290	274	267	1.1	1.0	1.0
Nebraska	20	19	18	0.6	0.5	0.5
North Dakota	2	3	2	0.2	0.3	0.2
Ohio	391	522	478	0.8	1.1	1.1
South Dakota	5	7	4	0.2	0.3	0.2
Wisconsin	147	180	161	1.0	1.2	1.0
South	10,243	11,167	10,767	2.2%	2.2%	2.3%
Alabama	283	267	419	1.3	1.2	1.8
Arkansas	99	98	101	1.0	0.9	0.9
Delaware	170	122	127	2.6	2.2	1.9
District of Columbia	359	232	126	7.8	9.7	3.3
Florida	2,633	2,714	2,640	3.8	3.8	3.7
Georgia	846	1,166	938	2.0	2.6	2.1
Kentucky	122	118	124	1.1	1.0	1.3
Louisiana	381	526	500	2.1	2.7	2.6
Maryland	820	862	998	3.6	3.8	4.3
Mississippi	192	157	230	1.9	1.1	2.1
North Carolina	554	643	588	1.9	2.1	1.9
Oklahoma	122	215	145	0.8	0.9	1.0
South Carolina	617	574	560	2.9	2.7	2.7
Tennessee	185	206	215	1.4	1.1	1.6
Texas	2,520	2,691	2,492	1.8	1.7	1.9
Virginia	330	567	550	1.3	1.9	1.9
West Virginia	10	9	14	0.3	0.3	0.5

thirty-four require inmates to be tested if seriously assaulted.[57] Every state and the federal prison system provides educational information to inmates to inform them of the potential for inmates in the population to have HIV/AIDS, describe the types of behaviors that can lead to infection, and reduce the fear of infection from other inmates. Once inmates are determined to be positive for HIV, prisons take different approaches to the management of this population. In a survey conducted

TABLE	9.10	Continued

	Total known to be HIV-positive[a]			HIV/AIDS cases as a percent of total custody population[b]		
Jurisdiction	12/31/99	6/30/00	12/31/00	12/31/99	6/30/00	12/31/00
West	2,207	1,934	2,334	0.9%	0.8%	0.9%
Alaska	16	43	—	0.6	1.4	—
Arizona	144	183	110	0.6	0.7	0.4
California	1,570	1,179	1,638	1.0	0.8	1.0
Colorado	131	139	146	1.0	0.9	1.0
Hawaii	30	20	19	0.9	0.5	0.5
Idaho	15	21	14	0.4	0.6	0.4
Montana	10	15	11	0.7	0.7	0.7
Nevada	125	146	151	1.4	1.6	1.6
New Mexico	26	28	28	0.5	0.6	0.5
Oregon	23	39	41	0.2	0.4	0.4
Utah	34	34	37	0.6	0.8	0.9
Washington	75	83	90	0.5	0.6	0.6
Wyoming	8	4	6	0.6	0.2	0.5

—Not reported.

[a]Counts published in previous reports have been revised.

[b]Includes only those inmates housed in a jurisdiction's facilities.
Percentages are based on custody counts, except for New Mexico. In 2000
New Mexico's percentages are based on its years and jurisdiction count.

[c]Exclude inmates in jurisdictions that did not report data. National and Regional totals on 12/31/00 include 43 HIV-positive cases in Alaska reported in the midyear count.

[d]Excludes data from Indiana in the midyear 2000 count.

[e]Midyear 2000 count was estimated by averaging the year-end 1999 and 2000 counts.

Source: Laura M. Maruschak, *HIV in Prisons, 2000*, Bureau of Justice Statistics Bulletin (Washington, D.C.: U.S. Department of Justice, October 2002), p. 2.

by the Criminal Justice Institute during 2001, of the thirty-three states responding, nineteen states reported that they did not separate inmates testing positive for AIDS, while fourteen reported that they did separate those inmates from the general inmate population.[58]

Those separated are housed together, some in a medical setting and some in a standard prison housing unit, in order to reduce concern among other inmates and the potential of transmission to other inmates. Most systems that adopt a non-separation policy do not divulge the identity of inmates with AIDS, in order to avoid discrimination against them in program and work opportunities and harassment by other inmates and possibly staff. Inmates and staff are told to "take universal precautions," meaning to treat every inmate as HIV-positive by avoiding behavior by which HIV could be transmitted and handling inmates or blood spills in a way that avoids the risk of infection (such as by wearing a surgical mask and using rubber gloves when blood is visible).

Inmates who are in advanced stages of AIDS require substantial medical care. They are usually hospitalized during the terminal stage of AIDS, in order to provide them treatment and to avoid possible contagious illnesses from other inmates due to their reduced immunity and ability to fight infections. Some prisons have created "hostels" to provide a sympathetic and dignified setting for inmates who are near death and beyond the ability of medical care to save. Being in prison is difficult for many inmates, but one can only imagine the suffering by inmates who know they are dying and are unable to spend much time with family or friends.

TUBERCULOSIS

Tuberculosis (TB) was a serious medical problem during the early 1900s in the United States, declined, and then resurged in the 1980s and 1990s. It is particularly a problem in prisons and jails, as inmates have high rates and risk of TB because of their background of poverty, poor living conditions, substance abuse, and a higher level of HIV/AIDS than the general U.S. population. As well, overcrowded conditions in correctional facilities increase the potential for transmission of TB among inmates. Early in the 1990s, particular concern was raised by various outbreaks of multidrug-resistant TB in New York State and other jurisdictions. In a 1994 report by the National Institute of Justice regarding tuberculosis in prison and jails, the authors write, "Tuberculosis is an airborne disease, transmitted via droplet nuclei (e.g., the dried residue of droplets from sneezes or coughs) from patients who have pulmonary or laryngeal TB and who cough, laugh, spit, or otherwise emit sputum containing the TB bacteria (called *Mycobacterium tuberculosis*). TB can be transmitted through repeated exposure in crowded, poorly ventilated environments; it does not require intimate contact. "[59] While many individuals may test positive for TB infection, the infection may not develop into active TB.

To determine whether inmates have TB, all state and federal prison systems screen inmates at intake. During 2000, 26,968 state, federal, or District of Columbia inmates (4.1 percent of the population) were found to be infected with TB, and 291 were under treatment for active TB.[60] The screening is accomplished through a purified protein derivative (PPD) skin test. One problem, both for health care and for detection, is that there can be a false negative skin test for inmates coinfected with TB and HIV, as the skin test shows negative for TB and the individual does not receive treatment when in fact he or she has both TB and HIV.

To avoid the spread of TB in correctional facilities, the Centers for Disease Control recommend the following actions:

- Rapidly identifying, reporting, isolating, and initiating appropriate therapy for active and potentially infectious cases of TB

The Hocking Correctional Facility in Nelsonville, Ohio, was originally a TB hospital. Once TB was able to be treated with medication, those infected were no longer removed from society, and these facilities were available for other uses—such as prisons.
Courtesy of the Ohio Department of Rehabilitation and Correction.

- Ensuring the continuity and completion of therapy through direct observation and other adherence-enhancing strategies
- Rapidly identifying and evaluating contacts of infectious TB cases and initiating preventive therapy for infected people
- Identifying people with TB infection at high risk for developing active TB and ensuring that they complete a full course of preventive therapy[61]

An inmate found to have active TB is immediately removed from the rest of the inmate population, and all effort is made to prevent any staff or inmate from breathing the contaminated air around him or her. Most prisons now have negative-pressure isolation rooms in their medical areas and prison hospitals, in which the ventilation system for that room is contained and does not flow into the general ventilation system for the prison. Inmates are placed in these rooms and treated with medication until they prove no longer contagious. They will be regularly screened to detect whether they have returned to an active state.

One of the key elements to dealing with TB is multiagency collaboration and a coordinated legislative and regulatory approach. In California, a law was passed requiring notification to health departments of all TB cases, spurring collaboration with various correctional systems in developing reporting procedures. The state board of corrections has the power to regulate local and county jails, and it passed regulations to require each jail to have a communicable-disease control plan created collaboratively by jail and local health officials. A success story of managing the threat of TB occurred in New York State. As reported in a 1998 National Institute of Justice and Center for Disease Control research brief,

> Since 1988, the New York State DOH (Department of Health) Bureau of TB Control and the DOCS (Department of Correctional Services) have had extensive and . . . exemplary collaborations in screening, treatment, case management, surveillance, outbreak investigation, discharge planning, education and training of staff and inmates, and technical assistance to staff. TB cases in DOCS have declined steadily since reaching a peak in 1993. No TB outbreaks have occurred in DOCS facilities since 1993.[62]

Chapter Review

SUMMARY

Most correctional agencies are organized to manage, control, and treat the "typical" adult offender, who is relatively young, is in good physical and mental health, does not have a serious substance abuse problem, and is not a sex offender. However, it could be argued that when inmates with all of these characteristics are removed from the overall group of offenders, very few are left to be deemed "typical." Yet groups of offenders with any of these individual issues or needs are defined as "special" offenders, and require specialized treatment, handling, or management. Most community and institutional correctional agencies have unique units (or individuals) trained to deal with these offenders apart from or with different approaches than the mainstream adult offender.

Correctional agencies today face many serious management problems that they did not have in the past as a result of the increasing proportion of the correctional population that may be termed as special offenders. The increasing number and percentage of the population that are drug offenders, mentally ill offenders, violent offenders, sex offenders, older offenders, or those with an infectious disease create significant problems of control, treatment, and provision of services. Each of these special groups requires additional programs, new policies and procedures, and modified services or even housing arrangements. Such provisions seem difficult enough during times of available budgets, and almost impossible during the current times of budgetary restraints.

Another group that is growing in number and in its impact on correctional agencies well beyond the small numbers of prisoners is offenders under age 18 who have been waived into the adult criminal justice system. Once incarcerated (since most juveniles are waived to adult court for a serious offense, most end up sentenced to prison), correctional agencies struggle with the best way to manage these offenders. Most states attempt to keep juvenile prisoners as separate as possible from adults. Yet when a state has small numbers of prisoners, it is difficult to provide the scope of programs and services that these offenders require, and there seems to be no simple solution to this problem.

Special offenders will continue to be a significant problem for adult correctional agencies. They strain the budgetary resources of an agency, as their management is usually much more expensive per inmate than for non–special offenders. They strain the organizational makeup of an agency, as they require unique units of specially trained staff to manage, and with so many of these units being created, they take attention away from the central mission and role of most correctional agencies. And they put a strain on staff members, who are under more stress and have greater challenges in dealing with these special groups. Unfortunately, it is not expected that the number of special offenders served by correctional agencies will decline. As this chapter indicates, many more offenders in the correctional population are not being treated or specially managed, and require continued expansion of the special services described. Special offenders within prison cause staff members and other inmates serious problems. As we close this chapter, I want to share with you in the "An Insider's Experience" box a story that illustrates a problem we had in managing mentally ill and violent inmates that almost cost me my job.

AN INSIDER'S EXPERIENCE: I Thought I Would Get Fired

I was awakened about 3:00 A.M. As I sleepily answered, a correctional supervisor in Ohio's maximum-security prison was on the telephone, saying, "I am sorry to have to wake you up, but we just had an inmate die here at the prison after an altercation with staff. The warden is out of town, and the associate warden is on his way, but said I should call and inform you." I was now fully awake, got more information, and asked the supervisor to tell the associate warden that I would be at the prison in about two hours. I called my deputy director, and we soon left for the hundred-mile drive to the prison.

When we arrived, we received more details. An inmate with a history of mental health problems who had a history of violence and was isolated in a cell identified for mental-health-troubled inmates, had started to destroy his cell and act out about 11:00 P.M. He also jumped headfirst from the top bunk to the floor and appeared to be injured. The supervisor in charge at the time ordered a group of correctional officers to assemble, remove the inmate from his cell, and move him to another cell where he could be restrained, medicated, and checked for injuries.

When the group of eight officers was assembled, they discussed how to move the inmate. The inmate was very big and very strong, and they suspected he would not come out peacefully. They decided to use a Plexiglas riot shield, move into the cell as a group, and pin the inmate against the back wall. They would then handcuff him and move him to the other cell.

However, when they opened the cell door, the inmate came charging out at them, knocking down many of the officers. Most of the officers were untrained in self-defense, were not in good shape, and were ill-prepared to handle the inmate in this situation.

The single inmate continued to fight with the officers, and they were having a very difficult time grabbing his arms and legs to control him. Finally, they got him down on the floor and started to restrain him with handcuffs. The inmate was still struggling, flailing his head around, and making it difficult for staff to hold him still. One of the officers yelled at another to hold the inmate's head to the floor. Tired from the fight, instead of reaching down with his hands, the officer placed his foot on the side of the inmate's neck to hold his head. The inmate was successfully restrained and taken to the other cell. However, when a medical person went into the cell to check on his injuries about thirty minutes later, the inmate was dead. It was believed that the officer's foot pressed on the carotid artery, cutting off blood to the brain, resulting in death by asphyxiation. The state police were called in to investigate.

The death of the inmate under these conditions was bad enough, but the circumstances around it made it worse. Exactly one week before, an inmate had murdered a staff member at that prison. The prison had perhaps an unfair reputation of racism, but had only one black officer among five-hundred staff members. I had been on the job for less than one year and was targeting this area for change. The staff member who was murdered was a well-liked, over age 60, white staff member who worked in the prison industry area. The inmate who killed him was black, had a history of mental health problems, and was mad because the staff member had threatened to fire him from his job unless he improved his work performance.

The staff member's death rocked the spirit and morale of the prison staff. They questioned the leadership of the prison and the department, they complained that there were not enough staff for security and safety, and they threatened a union action of some type if things didn't improve. The prison was in the district of the most powerful member of the state legislature (the speaker of the house of representatives), and he had to do something to respond to his constituents. So there was already an emotional and inflamed environment at the prison at the time of the inmate's death.

When the circumstances of the inmate's death became public, there were cries from the black community and many media sources of racism and retaliation by prison staff. Another very powerful state legislator and leader of the black elected officials in the state called on the governor for action, including criminal prosecution and the firing of all officers responsible for the death. The racial issue was even more inflamed by the fact that about one month before, a black woman who was director of the department of mental retardation was fired by the governor for poor management, in part brought to light by the death of a patient who had suffered neglect by staff at one of state hospitals. The black state leadership wondered publicly how I could have a similar incident and not also be fired.

I had decided and continued to refuse to take any immediate disciplinary action against the staff involved. I did not believe there had been intent to injure the inmate, and knew that the investigation by the county grand jury would result in criminal prosecution if intent was found to exist. I also believed that the staff had not been properly trained in handling mentally ill inmates, as well as how to safely and humanely remove a violent inmate from a cell. While I did not feel that the inmate's death was racially motivated, I recognized that it was very difficult to fight that appearance, and knew we needed more black staff and training for all staff in racial sensitivity. All of these things took time to implement; however, there were continued calls for my firing for not taking what would appear to be more aggressive and immediate action.

I used the challenging situation as an opportunity to ask for additional resources and implement some changes at the prison. With the support of the speaker of the state house of representatives, I got approval to add approximately thirty new correctional officers and mental health staff to the prison. I openly and candidly discussed the racial issues with black members of the state legislature, and secured their support for recruiting black staff to apply for the new positions and for implementing racial sensitivity training at the prison. I worked with the state department of mental health to expand their services to the prison and used some of the positions to open a special unit at the prison to manage mentally ill and violent inmates. As these changes were being implemented, the county grand jury came back with a decision not to seek an indictment against the correctional officers involved in the death.

REVIEW QUESTIONS

1. What is a special offender, and why do they require special handling while under correctional supervision?
2. What forces encouraged the movement toward the waiver of juveniles into adult courts?
3. In what ways do correctional agencies deal with juveniles under confinement?
4. Explain the distinction between drug offenders and drug addicts.
5. What role have antipsychotic drugs played in the deinstitutionalization of mentally ill individuals?
6. List the reasons for the increased proportion of elderly inmates in the prison population.
7. Why have supermax prisons become such an attractive option for the management of violent or seriously disruptive inmates?
8. Why do sex offenders present such a difficult challenge for management in both community and institutional settings?
9. Identify the various categories of offenders with infectious diseases.
10. What is the rate of confirmed cases of HIV among inmates, and how does this compare to the rate of those infected with the virus in the nonprison population?

ENDNOTES

1. Howard N. Snyder, Melissa Sickmund, and Eileen Poe-Yamagata, *Juvenile Transfers to Criminal Courts in the 1990s: Lessons Learned from Four Studies* (Washington, D.C.: U.S. Department of Justice, Office of Juvenile Justice and Delinquency Prevention, August 2000), p. xi.

2. Patricia Griffin, Patricia Torbet, and Linda Szymanski, *Trying Juveniles as Adults in Criminal Courts: An Analysis of State Transfer Provisions* (Washington, D.C.: U.S. Department of Justice, Office of Juvenile Justice and Delinquency Prevention, December 1998), p. 1.

3. Melissa Sickmund, *Juveniles in Court* (Washington, D.C.: U.S. Department of Justice, Bureau of Justice Statistics, June 2003), p. 7.

4. Charles M. Puzzanchera, *Delinquency Cases Waived to Criminal Court, 1989–1998*, OJJDP Fact Sheet 35 (Washington, D.C.: U.S. Department of Justice, September 2001), p. 1.

5. Ibid., pp. 1–2.

6. Kevin J. Strom, *Profile of State Prisoners under Age 18, 1985–97* (Washington, D.C.: U.S. Department of Justice, Bureau of Justice Statistics, February 2000), p. 1.

7. Ibid.

8. Paige M. Harrison and Jennifer C. Karberg, *Prison and Jail Inmates at Midyear 2002* (Washington, D.C.: U.S. Department of Justice, Bureau of Justice Statistics, April 2003), p. 5.

9. Ibid.

10. Ibid., p. 10.

11. Bureau of Justice Statistics, *Sourcebook of Criminal Justice Statistics, 2001* (Washington, D.C.: U.S. Department of Justice, 2003), p. 16.

12. National Institute of Justice, *Drug Use Forecasting: Drugs and Crime, 1990, Annual Report* (Washington, D.C.: U.S. Department of Justice, 1991).

13. Bureau of Justice Statistics, "Drug Use and Crime," http://www.ojp.usdoj.gov/bjs/dcf/duc.htm#drugrelated, accessed May 9, 2002.

14. Bureau of Justice Statistics, *Substance Abuse and Treatment, State and Federal Prisoners, 1997* (Washington, D.C.: U.S. Department of Justice, January 1999).

15. Bureau of Justice Statistics, *Mental Health and Treatment of Inmates and Probationers* (Washington, D.C.: U.S. Department of Justice, July 1999).

16. Bureau of Justice Statistics, *Profile of Jail Inmates, 1996* (Washington, D.C.: U.S. Department of Justice, April 1998).

17. Bureau of Justice Statistics, *Correctional Populations in the United States, 1980–96* (Washington, D.C.: U.S. Department of Justice, various years); *Prisoners in 2002* (Washington, D.C.: U.S. Department of Justice, August 2001).

18. Bureau of Justice Statistics, 2003; Bureau of Justice Statistics, *Criminal Offender Statistics* http://www.ojp.usdoj.gov/bjs/crimoff, accessed January 8, 2003.

19. Substance Abuse and Mental Health Services Administration, *National Household Survey on Drug Abuse, 1995* (Washington, D.C.: U.S. Government Printing Office, 1996).

20. The Pew Research Center for the People and the Press, included in *Sourcebook of Criminal Justice Statistics, 2001* (Washington, D.C.: U.S. Department of Justice, 2003), p. 129.

21. Ibid.

22. Federal Bureau of Prisons, "Drug Treatment Programs in Federal Prisons," in *Best Practices: Excellence in Corrections*, edited by Edward E. Rhine (Lanham, Md.: American Correctional Association, 1998), pp. 427–430.

23. Ibid., p. 429.

24. Gregory P. Falkin, Sheila Strauss, and Timothy Bohen, "Matching Drug-Involved Probationers to Appropriate Drug Interventions: A Strategy for Reducing Recidivism," *Federal Probation* (June 1999): 4.

25. Ibid., p. 5.

26. Frank S. Pearson and Douglas S. Lipton, "A Meta-Analytic Review of the Effectiveness of Correctional-Based Treatment for Drug Abuse," *The Prison Journal* 79, no. 4 (1999): 384–410.

27. The National Task Force on Correctional Substance Abuse Strategies, *Intervening with Substance-Abusing Offenders: A Framework for Action* (Washington, D.C.: U.S. Department of Justice, National Institute of Corrections, June 1991), p. 27.

28. "Prisons Replace Hospitals for the Nation's Mentally Ill," *New York Times,* March 5, 1998, p. A-26.

29. Paula M. Ditton, *Mental Health and Treatment of Inmates and Probationers* (Washington, D.C.: U.S. Department of Justice, 1999).

30. Allen J. Beck and Laura M. Maruschak, *Mental Health Treatment in State Prisons, 2000*, Bureau of Justice Statistics Special Report (Washington, D.C.: U.S. Department of Justice, July 2001), p. 3.

31. Ibid.

32. Ditton, 1999.

33. Ibid.

34. Ibid., p. 5.

35. Kenneth Moritsugu, "Inmate Chronological Age versus Physical Age," in *Long-Term Confinement and the Aging Inmate Population* (Washington, D.C.: U.S. Department of Justice, Federal Bureau of Prisons, 1990).

36. Camille Graham Camp and George M. Camp, *The Corrections Yearbook, 1998* (Middletown, Conn.: Criminal Justice Institute, 1999), p. 25.

37. Camille Graham Camp and George M. Camp, *The 2001 Corrections Yearbook: Adult Systems* (Middletown, Conn.: Criminal Justice Institute, 2002), p. 34.

38. Tammerlin Drummond, "Cellblock Seniors: They Have Grown Old and Frail in Prison. Must They Still Be Locked Up?" *Time* 153, no. 24 (June 21, 1999): 60.

39. Paige M. Harrison and Allen J. Beck, *Prisoners in 2001*, Bureau of Justice Statistics Bulletin (Washington, D.C.: U.S. Department of Justice, July 2002), p. 12.

40. Robert Perkinson, "Shackled Justice: Florence Federal Penitentiary and the New Politics of Punishment, " *Social Justice* 21, no. 3 (1994): 119.

41. *Bruscino v. Carlson*, 854 F.2d 162 (7th Cir. 1988).

42. Chase Riveland, *Supermax Prisons: Overview and General Considerations* (Washington, D.C.: U.S. Department of Justice, National Institute of Corrections, January 1999), p. 3.

43. As reported in Callie Marie Rennison, *Rape and Sexual Assault: Reporting to Police and Medical Attention, 1992–2000* (Washington, D.C.: U.S. Department of Justice, Bureau of Justice Statistics, August 2002), p. 1.

44. Lawrence A. Greenfeld, *Sex Offenses and Offenders: An Analysis of Data on Rape and Sexual Assault* (Washington, D.C.: U.S. Department of Justice, Bureau of Justice Statistics, February 1997).

45. Kim English, Suzanne Pullen, and Linda Jones, *Managing Adult Sex Offenders in the Community—A Containment Approach* (Washington, D.C.: U.S. Department of Justice, National Institute of Justice, January 1997).

46. Calculated from Bureau of Justice Statistics, 2003, p. 499.

47. Greenfeld, 1997, pp. 14–15.

48. Bureau of Justice Statistics, 2003, p. 516.

49. Ibid., p. 505.

50. English, Pullen, and Jones, 1997, p. 3.

51. Ibid., p. 2.

52. Greenfeld, 1997, p. 25.

53. Ibid., pp. 25–26.

54. Laura M. Maruschak, *HIV in Prisons, 2000*, Bureau of Justice Statistics Bulletin (Washington, D.C.: U.S. Department of Justice, October 2002).

55. Ibid., p. 1.

56. Ibid., p. 3.

57. Camp and Camp, 2002, p. 50.

58. Ibid., p. 52.

59. Karen Wilcock, Theodore M. Hammett, Rebecca Wldom, and Joel Epstein, *Tuberculosis in Correctional Facilities 1994–95*, (Washington, D.C.: U.S. Department of Justice, 1996), p. 5.

60. Camp and Camp, 2002, pp. 48–49.

61. Centers for Disease Control, "Screening for Tuberculosis and Tuberculosis Infection in High Risk Populations: Recommendations of the Advisory Council for the Elimination of Tuberculosis, " *Morbidity and Mortality Weekly Report* 44, no. RR-11 (1994): 19–34.

62. Theodore M. Hammett, *Public Health/Corrections Collaborations: Prevention and Treatment of HIV/AIDS, STDs, and TB* (Washington, D.C.: U.S. Department of Justice, National Institute of Justice, July 1998), p. 9.

Chapter 10

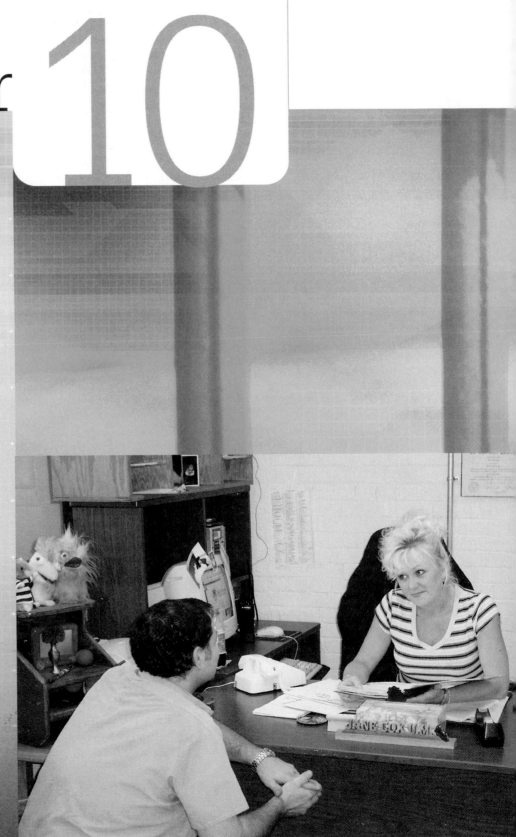

AFTER READING THIS CHAPTER, YOU SHOULD BE ABLE TO:

1. Explain how prisons are organized to accomplish their mission.
2. Describe the functions that are usually a part of the office of the director of a state correctional agency.
3. Discuss the role the inspector plays for a correctional agency.
4. Contrast the custody and treatment functions within a prison.
5. Define unit management and describe the role it plays in the management of a prison.
6. Identify the methods available to prisons to maintain inmate compliance.
7. List ways in which the classification of inmates contributes to the management of a prison.
8. Outline the way an inmate disciplinary system operates within a prison.
9. Suggest ways the staff of a correctional agency can help or hinder a prison accomplishing its mission.

The Management of Prisons

Introduction

How are prisons managed? What does it take to accomplish their mission of creating a safe and secure environment and providing inmates the opportunity for program participation that can help them reenter the community? Prisons are complex organizations, based on a tenuous relationship of greatly outnumbered staff controlling potentially violent and dangerous inmates. They must provide all services necessary for their operation in a cost-effective manner, and endeavor to change inmates' future behavior through the provision of treatment programs. None of these activities are easy in their own right, and trying to accomplish them all can seem like an impossible goal. However, modern prisons do a very good job of meeting these objectives through a combination of their organization, methods to control inmate behavior, working through their staff, and taking steps to ensure quality performance of their functions.

The first section in this chapter covers how prisons and their headquarters agencies are organized. The organization of any agency should be designed to enhance the completion of the agency mission. However, in the public sector, the agency must also address many "external" pressures and interests, which are thus reflected in the agency organization. However, the key components of a headquarters correctional organization are to help the prisons operate effectively and efficiently and to oversee the supervision of offenders in the community. The organizational charts for both a state department of corrections and a state prison are presented to illustrate and explain these functions. As well, the use of unit management as a more efficient method of managing prisons is presented and discussed.

In the second section of this chapter, the methods used to manage inmates and control behavior are addressed. These include the consistent implementation of state-of-the-art policies and procedures, a classification system to match inmate needs and security risks with staff and prisons resources, and the use of a fair and equitable system for disciplining inmates who violate rules. There are far fewer prison staff than inmates at any time in a prison. Therefore, the key to effective management of a prison is to have these types of functions in place to create expectations for staff and inmates, to divide inmates into similar groups of risks and needs so policies and practices can be tailored to each group, and to reward compliance and punish violation of prison rules by inmates.

Finally, the critical role that staff play in the management of prisons is described. No matter how good the physical security of a prison, no matter how thorough the policies, and no matter how well implemented a classification or inmate disciplinary system, if staff are not competent and professional in carrying out their duties, all of these other managerial aspects are undermined. In this regard, this chapter also describes the practices used to recruit and hire quality staff, as well as the role that collective bargaining plays in managing a prison.

The Organization of Prisons

Prisons are organized in a manner that leads toward their ability to carry out their mission of creating a safe and secure environment and providing inmates the opportunity for program participation that can help them reenter the community. While prisons could, most likely, carry out this mission independently, with no guidance or oversight by a state department of corrections, states and the federal government have found it more effective to have an umbrella agency that oversees prisons, is the link between elected officials and the prisons, and can ensure quality and consistency in the operations of all the prisons within that agency. In Chapter 5, the reasons for and stages of the development of state and the federal correctional agencies were described.

Therefore, to understand the way prisons are organized to carry out their mission, it is also important to understand the role of a state department of corrections, and the activities it undertakes to guide and assist in the effective operation of each individual prison. In the following sections, both the organizations of the umbrella agency and individual prisons are presented and described. As of January 1, 2001, the fifty states and the federal government operated 1,380 prisons, or approximately 27 per jurisdiction. The agency with the most prisons on that date was the Federal Bureau of Prisons, which had ninety-seven, and the state with the fewest prisons was North Dakota, with two.[1] These prisons had a capacity to house 1,164,843 inmates, but were operating at approximately 107 percent of this capacity.[2]

STATE DEPARTMENTS OF CORRECTIONS

The central organization that oversees state and federal prisons is often called the "central office" or "headquarters." For much of their history, American prisons were operated independently, governors appointed wardens, state legislatures appropriated the budget for each prison, and wardens ran the prison without interference and in whatever manner they saw fit. As noted in Chapter 5, most of these headquarters organizations have been established over the past thirty years, as states did not previously have a separate agency to oversee the operations of prisons and other correctional components. However, the increasing political and public interest in how states ran their prison systems, the increasing litigation by prisoners regarding conditions of confinement, and the need for quality and efficiency caused the creation of these central agencies in order to ensure consistency of standards and guide the administration of prisons.

As the numbers of prisoners and prisons have grown significantly over the past thirty years, the central headquarters of the state and federal correctional agencies have grown in the number of functions and employees required for overseeing large and complicated organizations and maintaining central control and consistency among prisons. As an example, the table of organization of the central office of the Ohio Department of Rehabilitation and Correction (Figure 10.1) is presented. Ohio is the eighth-largest correctional agency in the United States in terms of the number of inmates under supervision, with 43,562 offenders in Ohio prisons as of January 1, 2001. The seven largest in order of number of inmates on that date were California (150,609), Texas (134,574), Federal Bureau of Prisons (124,540), New York (70,152), Florida (67,408), Michigan (47,256), and Illinois (45,281).

The Ohio Department of Rehabilitation and Correction has responsibility not only for all the state prisons, but also for the parole board and parole supervision, probation services and supervision in some counties, and assistance to counties for jail inspections and developing and funding community sanctions. This department is similar to most state correctional agencies and illustrates the complexity in the management of an agency that operates thirty-four prisons, has an annual budget of $1.5 billion, employs approximately 16,000 staff, and supervises 46,500 inmates and 33,000 offenders in the community. Several key functions deserve note in review of the organizational chart for a state department of corrections.

Functions within the Office of the Director

The chief executive of a state department of corrections is usually called the **director** or secretary of the department. Many functions are attached to the office of the director. Most central correctional agencies organizationally locate the external management functions (legal services, legislative liaison, public affairs, investigations) close to the director, and sometimes reporting to the director. Correctional agencies have found that external management issues are very sensitive

Director

the chief operating officer of a state or federal department of corrections

TABLE OF ORGANIZATION FOR THE CENTRAL OFFICE
OF THE OHIO DEPARTMENT OF REHABILITATION AND CORRECTION

FIGURE 10.1

Source: Ohio Department of Rehabilitation and Correction. Reprinted with permission.

and can quickly become political or media crises, and therefore, there should be immediate access of the issue between the staff dealing with it and the director. The worst thing that can happen to a correctional agency is for an issue that is potentially sensitive to be misrepresented by lower-level staff that have not been provided input from the person in charge of the agency.

Directors of correctional agencies often become like managers of professional baseball teams in that when things go wrong, they get the blame and are replaced. This is not always because they have done a bad job, but because a change is seen as necessary to appease important groups or individuals outside the agency. Directors of state correctional agencies can lose the confidence of their elected supervisors and therefore most often lose their jobs because of the way agency policies are perceived, rather than an actual failure in the internal management of the agency. Therefore, directors of corrections do not want "surprises" when it comes to developments around sensitive external communications, and they maintain these organizational functions as components of the director's office.

The organizational entities that often reside in the office of the director include public and media affairs, legislative liaison, legal advisors, and internal affairs. As criminal justice and correctional issues have become of great interest to the public, there is a tremendous demand for information from the media. Minor incidents in one prison with local media interest are usually handled at that local prison. However, an issue of state correctional policy or a major incident will usually result in the headquarters public information section responding to requests from the media.

As state correctional agencies have grown to be one of the largest state departments and use a large percentage of the state budget, legislatures have become much more interested in correctional policy and operations, and legislative members regularly have questions about a prison in their district or an issue regarding a constituent. Therefore, correctional agencies usually have an office of legislative affairs, which responds to legislative requests and builds support for the department regarding resources and programs. Staff of the office of legislative affairs regularly brief staff from legislative offices and committees so that they know the purpose of programs and are not surprised by media reports or bills submitted by the department.

Legal sections within correctional agencies also often report to the director of corrections. Legal offices deal with three general categories of issues: (1) responding to inmate lawsuits, (2) reviewing policy for legal impact, and (3) giving general advice regarding implementation of programs in line with past legal decisions. As described more fully in Chapter 14, with the demise of the "hands-off" doctrine by federal courts, the floodgates were opened to inmate litigation. In 2000, there were 24,519 lawsuits filed against staff or adult correctional agencies, and 89 class-action lawsuits were in effect on January 1, 2001.[3] Legal staff of correctional agencies usually do not actually argue the cases in court, as that is the responsibility of the state and federal attorneys general. However, correctional lawyers must often review the lawsuits and initiate investigations to aid in the defense. As well, correctional legal staff usually review new or changed policy to identify any potential legal concerns.

The office of the director also will usually have an **inspector** or internal affairs division as a part of the organization. Ethical behavior by staff of a correctional agency is a very high priority, and the opportunity for unethical or even illegal behavior is great when staff are in daily contact with manipulative inmates. Therefore, complaints of staff misconduct by anyone (inmates, other staff, inmate families, or the general public) are investigated. An objective look by trained investigators is the best defense for staff against untrue allegations, and it is necessary to find cases in which staff have acted unethically or unprofessionally to maintain a credible and effective operation of prisons. In addition, many inmate complaints often end up in a lawsuit, so an early investigation of the complaint also creates a documented record for later use (perhaps months or even years later) when the department needs to respond to a legal suit.

Inspector
a person in a department of corrections who investigates allegations by inmates or others against staff

As noted earlier, state directors of correctional agencies have tremendous responsibilities and are often like professional baseball managers in that when things go wrong, they get fired. However, they have the opportunity to influence the lives of many people. The "Your Career in Corrections" box describes their roles and responsibilities.

Administration Functions

The central headquarters of a correctional agency usually carries out two major functions: budget development and accounting, and new prison construction. The central budget division collects information from all the prisons, other divisions, and the governor's office to create a budget that represents desired programs, growth, and continued operations. The corrections budget becomes a part

YOUR CAREER IN CORRECTIONS

CORRECTIONAL ADMINISTRATORS

There are only fifty-two jobs of this kind in the United States—in the fifty states, the District of Columbia, and the Federal Bureau of Prisons (BOP): director of a correctional agency. How do directors get this job? They have to be appointed by the governor of a state, the mayor of the District of Columbia, or the Attorney General of the United States (for the BOP). The people appointed to do these jobs usually have years of correctional experience, but with more sensitivity by elected officials regarding the political impact of correctional policies, people with no correctional experience (but close to the governor or with extensive political experience) have been appointed to these jobs more frequently.

For 2001, the average correctional administrator has responsibility for 26,500 prisoners, 8,500 staff, 40,500 community-supervised offenders, and an annual budget of $700 million.[4] They must oversee the operations of twenty–six prisons (the average in each state); create a politically supported agenda; be responsible for the safety and security of staff, offenders, and the general public; and provide rehabilitative programs to improve the chance of offenders becoming productive and law-abiding citizens. When things go well—there are no prison riots or escapes, there are no horrible crimes committed by former clients (offenders under their supervision), and there are no union complaints because of low pay or perceived unsafe working conditions—they are merely doing the job they were hired to perform. However, when any of these things happen, or when elected officials or the public are upset about specific correctional policies, how they are implemented, or how much they cost, directors get the blame. One would wonder why anyone takes such a job.

Staff that work in corrections usually do not do so because they are motivated by power or pay. They desire to make a difference, to serve the public, and to assist offenders. They work in corrections for several years and find that they have an affinity for the discipline and management and leadership talent. They see that the individuals in authority have the opportunity to initiate programs and improvements that can benefit staff, offenders, and the public. So as they move into an executive position, and the opportunity comes along to be considered for the top administrator position, they do not think of the downside of the position, but only the opportunities it brings.

Pay is not bad for correctional administrators, although similar levels of responsibility in the private sector would pay considerably more. The average salary for directors of adult correctional agencies as of January 1, 2001, was $101,872; however, the average tenure in office at that time was only 4.4 years.[5] Not too many directors stay in the job much longer than this, because with every change of governor, there is often a change in corrections director. As well, the positions are highly stressful, and when things go wrong, there is often a change in leadership.

However, these are great jobs if you enjoy a challenge and having a lot of responsibility. This responsibility is not to be taken lightly, as it can involve the safety of staff and the potential of life-threatening situations. However, the rewards of satisfaction for a job well done, of serving the public, and of helping offenders get their lives in order make this job one worth striving for.

of the entire state budget that the governor presents to the state legislature. Once a budget is approved for a correctional agency, the administrative division maintains accountability of funds and keeps current on spending levels so that the agency does not go beyond its allocated amount.

For the past twenty years of tremendous growth in the number of prison inmates, these budget requests have regularly included funds to construct new prisons. In 2000, twenty-four new prisons were opened in the United States at a cost of $1.231 billion; thirty-nine new prisons were under construction and sixty-two existing ones were expanding their capacity at a total cost of $3.4 billion; and funding for capital construction for budget year 2001 was $3.8 billion.[6] The administration division is usually charged with overseeing design and construction of these new and renovated facilities, including hiring architects, coordinating their design with the departments' correctional experts, overseeing construction, and preparing to open the new facilities.

Human Resources Functions

In some states, the central headquarters performs all human resources activities. In other states, each prison carries out the personnel functions of recruitment, hiring, evaluations, and retirement, while the broad human resources functions (labor relations, affirmative action or equal employment opportunity [EEO], and the operation of a central training academy) are carried out by the headquarters human resources division. Most states have a unionized correctional workforce, and negotiating and administering labor contracts is very legalistic and time-consuming. Therefore, the central office usually has staff with expertise in labor relations to do the negotiations and advise prison managers on labor contract issues. While each prison conducts some staff training, almost every state operates a central academy for training new hires and for providing specialty training statewide.

Community Supervision Functions

For states that still use indeterminate sentences and parole for release decisions, the parole board and postrelease supervision are usually located within the department of corrections. In some states, the probation functions are also operated by the state rather than the counties (see Chapter 3). Statewide parole and probation functions are organized into geographic regions, districts, or city offices to supervise offenders. In addition, many states carry out intermediate sanctions programs (electronic monitoring, house arrest, intensive supervision, or halfway houses) that are also coordinated by central headquarters. Finally, states sometimes provide assistance to county jails. Assistance may be in the form of grant funds to build new jails or to upgrade policies, procedures, or operations. In addition, every state has statewide jail standards, and department of corrections employees are usually responsible for inspecting jails for compliance with these standards.

Field Operations Functions

Finally, central offices have a division (or geographic regions) that directly supervises prisons. The Ohio system is divided into North and South regions that supervise the prisons. The role of the central office is to supervise the prison wardens and general operations, to create policy, and to oversee consistent implementation of policy. The following sections describe the organization of a prison and how the prison implements policies prescribed by the central headquarters of a correctional agency.

An interesting link between the headquarters of a correctional agency and the prisons is the personal role of the leaders of the department in overseeing the work of the prison. While prisons are led and managed by a warden, the director (correctional administrator) of the department sets the tone and should be a role

The director of a state prison system makes regular visits to the prison, talks to the warden and other staff, and clearly communicates expectations.
Photo by Richard P. Seiter.

model for managing the correctional institutions. The "A Look Into" box illustrates this role and some ways that correctional administrators keep in contact with what goes on in a prison under their supervision. This interview is with myself, when I was director of the Ohio Department of Rehabilitation and Correction.

A LOOK INTO . . .

AN INTERVIEW WITH A CORRECTIONAL ADMINISTRATOR

This is an interview with Richard P. Seiter, who served as director of the Ohio Department of Rehabilitation and Correction from 1983 to 1988. He had previously been a warden for the Federal Bureau of Prisons and chief of the National Academy of Corrections. He was 34 years old when he was appointed director, the youngest person ever appointed director of this Ohio department. After leaving Ohio, he served as a warden and assistant director of the Federal Bureau of Prisons until his retirement in 1999.

Q: I understand that you regularly visit the prisons in the state, and that these visits are "from dawn to dusk," covering every area and talking to every staff member in the prison. I also understand that when you are there, you do a thorough sanitation inspection, looking, as I am told, "for dust in every corner and on every ledge, for soap grime in the bathroom sinks, and at every fire extinguisher for the monthly inspection documentation." First of all, why do you make such regular and extensive visits to the prisons?

A: Well, the problem with working in a headquarters of an agency is that you get removed from the day-to-day working of the agency and its people. So, I do it so I do not forget what it is like, how hard the jobs are, and to hear from our staff firsthand how they are doing and what issues are on their mind. But, as much as anything, I do it because I enjoy it. This may sound pretty strange, but I really get a kick out of being in the prisons, and interacting with staff and inmates.

Q: Let's discuss that in more detail. Talk more about the danger of getting too far removed from the day-to-day operations of the prisons.

A: I see my job as primarily to make the job of the staff working in a prison easier. This means many things. First, I need to stay ahead of the issues that are confronting them, so the problems do not get to a point where they are out of control. Every prison has problems in management. That is just the nature of the beast. Inmates are not used to following rules and complying with authority. So every day, someone will try to avoid compliance, and staff have to deal with each situation—many will not work out as perfectly as planned. They have to take care of those issues by themselves; I can't help them with each situation. But I can understand the forces that create situations and make the prison management more difficult. For instance, if we are beginning to have a newly developing friction between some competing gangs, it is important to get on top of it as soon as possible. By being in the prisons, I can get a sense for what is happening from those having to deal with it, gather some intelligence they have picked up, and see what urgency there is to create some systemwide response.

Let me stick to that point for a second. I think an extremely underacknowledged skill of administrators is to understand when an issue has urgency, especially when the administrator is removed from the situation (in his or her prison office or in the state headquarters) and does not feel the intensity of the staff that have to react to it. Not all issues or situations (regardless of how serious they may be—for instance a murder of an inmate by another) have the urgency that requires a systemwide response. Some just need to be handled as best staff can deal with them as they come up. Others need a deliberate and thoughtful response, and the proper response can almost "bubble up" from each sequential incident. Administrators must be careful not to do the wrong thing or create the wrong response, just to react to something before they really understand the cause and underlying issues.

Finally, some issues do have real urgency, and staff are crying out for guidance and policy change or new direction. Let me go back to the example I started to reference about developing gang tensions. If I hear staff concern about this issue in one prison, it is worth having our gang staff (often called security threat groups) in headquarters survey other prisons to see if they are having similar situations. The fact that I heard about the issue from prison staff firsthand helped me understand the urgency and my responsibility for action. Otherwise, you may just read reports about a variety of incidents in a variety of prisons, and while you sense a link and ask staff to look into it, you do not do so with the sense that it is critical to the safe management of the prisons. I have talked to my colleagues about issues like this one that have gone on in a state, with staff constantly seeking help on how to deal with it. However, because the top administrators are so tied up with their own issues (budget, the legislature, media pressure about an escape), they don't jump on the importance of this to the prisons. I personally get a better sense of the urgency of an issue by being in the prisons and hearing staff talk about it. One final note: Line staff and even wardens tend to downplay certain things when talking to their bosses; they do not want to give the impression that they can't handle it. So they don't "sound an alarm" themselves, and don't often communicate a sense of urgency. That is when your own correctional experience and common sense comes into play, and you hear a sense of urgency that is not overtly communicated.

The second way I try to make the job of prison staff easier is to show them that I support them, appreciate them, and respect the job they are doing. Correctional administrators can do this in a variety of ways. They can provide an adequate level of funding for employee awards programs to recognize staff who do a good job. They can urge managers to use incentive awards and can create special awards to recognize the behaviors they think are important at any particular time. They can send notes to employees who have done some especially good job or had a significant accomplishment. They can do media interviews and make public statements of support for staff and the jobs they do. However, nothing is more important than giving staff your time, going to them and saying hello, shaking their hand and showing them you care about them personally. I received feedback from a prison in the town in which I grew up. In fact, it was told to my mother, which really made me feel good. She met a staff member of the local prison, a relative of a friend of hers in her church. The staff member told her he thought I was a pretty good guy,

(continued)

that when many "dignitaries" visited the prison where he worked and came into an area he was working, they often acted as it he were invisible and did not talk to him. The dignitaries just talked to the warden or whoever was showing them around. But the staff member told my mother that whenever I entered the area where he worked, I went straight to him, said hello, and shook his hand. This made him feel that I respected him and thought he was important. Line staff make these kinds of judgments about the administrators they work for, and those interactions are more important than creating the most effective policy and getting the most favorable budgets from the legislature. They do tough jobs, and have to know and believe that their bosses acknowledge this and acknowledge them.

Another thing I do when I go to the prisons, which I enjoy and I believe that the staff enjoy, is to challenge them. All staff take pride in their work and want it to be recognized. They feel even better if they have to work really hard and are still successful. When I made my first round of visits to all the state prisons, I checked every fire extinguisher for the required monthly inspections. Each one has a tag on it showing that it has been inspected every thirty days to ensure that it is ready for action if needed. Every prison probably has two or three hundred extinguishers and it is easy to miss a few. I always found a few that had not been checked, until I went to one prison that had an extremely dedicated fire and safety officer. I found only one or two extinguishers that had been missed in some month over the past few months that were noted on the tag. I was extremely complimentary of the fire and safety officer, and he responded that he would be sure none were missed for my next visit. So I returned the challenge, and assured him that I would check. Each time I returned I would look in one new place that I thought he might have missed—in a security tower guarding the fence or on a farm tractor. Our challenge, his attempt to be sure no fire extinguishers were missed, and my attempt to find one that had been missed became almost legendary at the prison. Staff would follow my prison tour route by radio, trying to anticipate where I would look on this visit. If I found one, everyone knew within minutes, and the fire and safety officer had to live with the ribbing of his fellow staff for days. If he won, he could bask in their still ribbing him about trying to please the boss. I would do the same thing with sanitation issues with all staff, looking for dirt or dust in some of the less obvious places, complimenting them when I found none, and poking fun at them when I found some. Seldom would I find much after the first couple of visits to a prison. Staff enjoyed the challenge, and the fact that I pushed them to be better and appreciated them when they did.

Finally, I can make their jobs easier by creating a culture with a positive work environment. Prison jobs are tough enough, without administrators second-guessing staff and the decisions they make. I can help with this by not accepting problems or mistakes, but accepting that individuals will make some. I have a saying: "Be tough on the issue, but be soft on the staff." Don't accept that things just happen and that nothing can be done to reduce the likelihood that problems will occur. But don't let it be taken personally by the staff who make the error. If they blatantly disregarded policy, they will be disciplined for that. However, if staff make an error of judgment or don't deal with a situation as well as they should, look for ways to improve the likelihood that they will do better next time. This may mean that a particular type of training should be provided. It may mean that a new policy, procedure, or response to a situation needs to be developed. It may mean that causal factors need to be found and dealt with. But it is wrong not to look for underlying issues, ask tough questions of responsible staff, and try to respond appropriately when possible. And it is wrong to overreact to a staff error with discipline of only that staff member, and to do nothing to improve all staff members' ability to be successful the next time.

Q: That was a really interesting overview of the role of an administrator in setting a tone and helping staff do their jobs. But you usually don't think of a director of corrections checking toilets for sanitation, checking fire extinguishers, or looking at farm tractors. Why do you spend so much of your prison tour time on these kinds of activities?

A: That's really a good question, and one I am not surprised you asked. It can seem odd to do these things. But I do this for a couple of reasons. First, when you enter an area of a prison and want to interact with the staff person working in the area, there are limits to what you can focus on. Many line staff working an area rotate regularly and do not have much control over policy or operational procedures. But they do have control over sanitation. So by checking this so thoroughly, you can deal with something under their control, and your few minutes with them will be focused on their work, rather than something they have no control over.

But the most important reason is for the staff and me to pay attention to detail. In corrections, there is a saying that "if you pay attention to detail, the big issues will be worked out." As strange as that seems, it is very true in this environment. Prisons work on routine and consistent following of policy and procedures. Staff and inmates come to expect certain things to happen in certain ways. Inmates also watch staff who shortcut the way they do their jobs, which often results in a security breakdown that observant inmates will take advantage of. If every staff member pays attention to detail and makes sure that each step of a procedure is done the right way every time, there are no security breaches or breaks in routine that can undermine the safe and secure environment you are trying to accomplish. There will be fewer resulting problems and, therefore, fewer big issues.

When staff see how much attention I pay to detail, they realize the importance of it. I don't just check sanitation, I check the details of the policy. I look at log books to see that they are used as required; I note how staff lock doors behind them, even if they know they are going to have to unlock the door thirty seconds later. I check how we control and keep inventories of syringes in the hospital. Staff expect me to look at the details of how they do their jobs, and they know that these things are important to me. I have seen an improvement in their attention to detail since I have been doing this. I seldom find the same thing twice in a visit to a prison. So I combine a concern for them personally with a challenge for them to do their jobs right each and every time. Through those two things, I send the messages I want to send, and do what I can to help establish the environment in the prisons that I think is necessary.

PRISON STAFF ORGANIZATION

As noted earlier, prisons are organized in a manner to carry out the mission of operating a safe and secure environment, and providing offenders an opportunity for program participation that can help them after release. Figure 10.2 is the table of organization for the Lebanon (Ohio) Correctional Institution. The chief executive officer of a prison is usually called a warden, although in some states, he or she is called a superintendent. Reporting to the warden are deputy (as in Ohio), associate, or assistant wardens. The general functions supervised by these individuals usually fall into three categories:

1. **Custody**—all of the functions that come under the security activities within a prison; includes all uniformed employees such as correctional officers and correctional supervisors
2. **Treatment**—all of the rehabilitative functions focused on keeping inmates productively engaged and preparing them for release, including counseling, religious services, substance abuse programs, or education
3. **Services**—all of the functions that are required to operate the prison such as budget and finance, maintenance of the facility, human resources management, and those that provide basic services to inmates such as food and health services, work programs, commissary, and laundry operations

The organization of modern prisons is almost as complicated as that of the central headquarters. While the mission of prisons has changed little over the past fifty years, the organizational structure has changed considerably. Organizational entities that internally control and manage staff and inmates are very much the same, but (similar to central headquarters) functional entities have been added to respond to external management needs. Included in the organization of the warden's office in Figure 10.2 are an inspector of institutional services, an institutional investigator, labor relations, and a management analyst supervisor who

Custody
the functions within a prison that come under security; includes all uniformed employees such as correctional officers and correctional supervisors

Treatment
the rehabilitative functions in a prison focused on keeping inmates productively engaged and preparing them for release, including counseling, religious services, substance abuse programs, and education

Services
the functions required to operate a prison such as budget and finance, maintenance, human resources management, food and health services, work programs, commissary, and laundry operations

TABLE OF ORGANIZATION FOR THE LEBANON (OHIO) CORRECTIONAL INSTITUTION   FIGURE **10.2**

Source: Ohio Department of Rehabilitation and Correction. Reprinted with permission.

also serves as EEO (equal employment opportunity) chairperson. None of these functions were part of a prison table of organization a few decades ago, but changing times require changing organizational focus. As noted earlier, inmate complaints against staff must be promptly and thoroughly investigated, and prisons often have inspectors or investigators to carry out this function. Since collective-bargaining and labor relations are prevalent in many correctional agencies, there is often a staff person dedicated to managing the local prison collective-bargaining agreement and dealing with grievances by union members. The general components of a prison organization are presented next.

Custody and Security Functions

The custody and security component is often referred to as *correctional services* and encompasses all of the security activities within a prison, including the duties of the security staff as well as the operations of the special housing unit (SHU), inmate transportation, and the inmate disciplinary process. Correctional services departments are sometimes also referred to as *uniformed staff*, as they are paramilitary in organization, rank, and dress (wearing uniforms that are similar to military dress uniforms). The rank of major is usually the highest-ranking uniformed officer, who supervises the security department. Captains run each eight-hour shift and coordinate security operations during that period. Lieutenants are responsible for an area of the prison, such as recreation or the SHU, and sergeants are supervisory correctional staff who either supervise a smaller area than lieutenants or are senior correctional officers assigned to work the most difficult posts.

Correctional services is the largest department (in number of staff) in a prison, ranging from 50 percent to almost 70 percent of all staff, depending on the state. In many state and federal prisons, no correctional officers are assigned to certain areas of the prison, such as education or prison industries. The non-uniformed staff who work in those areas (such as teachers and industrial specialists) carry out the security functions as well as their specialty functions. In other states, correctional officers do more than the pure security functions and may supervise recreation areas such as the gym or yard, oversee inmate leisure time activities, or even direct inmates who work in prison industries or maintenance departments.

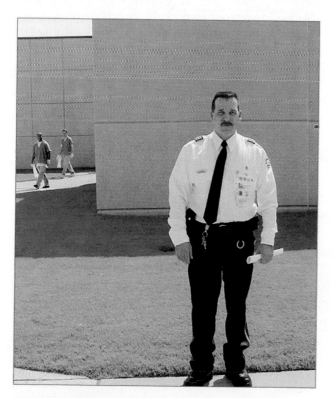

Correctional officers in most states are organized in a paramilitary fashion, wear uniforms, and have ranks of sergeant, lieutenant, or captain.
Photo by Richard P. Seiter.

Treatment Functions

The departments within a prison that are labeled as treatment or programs include education and vocational training, recreation, mental health, religious services, and substance abuse or recovery services. These functions serve the second part of the mission of a prison: to provide programs to inmates that can help them prepare for reentry to the community. In other words, they provide the rehabilitative activities within a prison. Staff that work in these departments are sometimes referred to as *professional staff,* because most of the jobs within these disciplines require a college education and specific preparation or certification to perform.

Education departments operate academic teaching, vocational training, library services, and sometimes recreation programs for inmates. These departments are managed similar to a community elementary or high school. In a few states, the prison system is actually an accredited "school district." Teachers must be certified, but teach a general topic (math, English, or science), rather than a grade. As inmates enter prison, they are tested for academic competence and work toward completion of a GED (general equivalency diploma) at their own pace under the guidance of a teacher, who usually has a class of fifteen to twenty inmates. Vocational programs include carpentry or general building maintenance, landscape or horticulture, food service, and office skills. In many states and the Federal Bureau of Prisons, recreation is also a part of the education department, while in the Ohio prison organization, recreation is a separate department. Recreation staff are assigned to areas such as the gymnasium or the recreation yard, and not only supervise the area but plan and schedule leisure-time activities to try to involve the largest possible number of inmates.

Mental health programs are provided in every prison, since (as discussed in Chapter 9) approximately 16 percent of prison and jail inmates are mentally ill. Mental health departments usually employ one or two Ph.D. psychologists to assess and counsel inmates. There may also be counselors with master's degrees to provide counseling programs. Few prisons have a full-time psychiatrist, but usually contract with one for a few hours per week to see the most ill patients who require psychotropic medication. Substance abuse or recovery programs that provide counseling for alcohol and drug abuse are sometimes a part of the mental

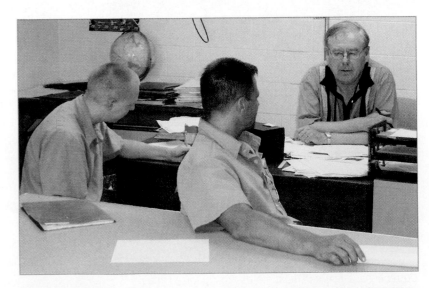

Teachers are critical to the management of a prison, as they provide inmates counseling and instruction in educational areas that are critical to their future lives.
Photo by Richard P. Seiter.

health department; in other states they are a separate department. Another critical treatment area within a prison is religious services. Prisons usually employ one or two full-time chaplains (often a Catholic priest and a Protestant minister) who hold religious services and coordinate other programs. Since all inmates have a right to practice the true tenets of their religious faith, prisons contract with clergy of other faiths (Muslim, Buddhist, Native American, or Jewish) to provide religious services and counseling to these inmates.

Service Functions

Service functions within a prison are those that deal with staff or facility issues (budget and finance, maintenance, human resources management) and those that provide services to inmates such as food and health services, work programs, commissary, and laundry operations. The functions of operating a business office and human resources department are very similar to those of other government organizations. The budget office has accountants to maintain control and record budget allocations, purchasing agents to buy necessary supplies and equipment, and financial managers to prepare budget needs and do budget projections. The human resources department follows overall government requirements for accepting and scoring applications for employment, going through the hiring process, and training new employees to prepare them for work in the prison. This department also oversees the **employee awards program** to recognize and reward staff who perform well, the evaluation of staff by supervisors each year, and the labor relations program to monitor compliance with collective-bargaining contracts and respond to labor union issues.

Employee awards program

a program to recognize and reward staff who perform beyond their expected level

The components of the organization that provide services to inmates are also similar to those that would be in place on any military base or Veterans Administration hospital. Whenever there is a relatively isolated group of individuals, basic services of food, health care, laundry, commissary, and maintenance of the facility must be provided. Staff roles in the food and health care areas are described in Chapter 12. Unique in prisons, as compared to other public or private agencies, is the work program for inmates. Work programs serve several purposes. They benefit inmates as a rehabilitative tool, as inmates learn how to work for a supervisor, follow instructions, and develop positive work habits. Work programs benefit prison administrators by keeping inmates busy and assisting in maintaining control of the prison environment. And work programs benefit the public, by selling prison products and performing other work to reduce the cost of incarceration.

Work programs in a prison are unique in how they are supervised and organized. Each area of work assignment (prison industries, building maintenance, sanitation, food services) has full-time staff who are experts in the area, but instead of doing the work themselves, they supervise inmate crews to perform the tasks. A good example is how a "plumbing shop" in a prison operates. There will be one or two plumbers who know how to do all the required plumbing tasks. The plumbers will be assigned a crew of approximately ten to fifteen inmates. The plumbers organize work in the shop for inmates to do (such as repairing damaged equipment) and take inmates into areas of the prison to do maintenance and repair work as necessary. These employees seldom are assigned inmates who are experienced or able to perform these duties without training. Therefore, the staff members have to train inmates as well as supervise them in performing these tasks.

Unit Management

Unit management is a way to organize a prison into smaller components, decentralize the authority to manage the inmate population, and make staff more accessible to the inmate population. Unit management was first established in 1966 by the Federal Bureau of Prisons (BOP) at the National Training School for Boys,

Unit management

organizing a prison into smaller components by decentralizing the authority to manage the inmate population while making staff more accessible to inmates

Maintenance workers supervise inmates in several trade areas that both maintain the prison and develop beneficial skills for inmates.
Photo by Richard P. Seiter.

in order to decentralize the management of the prison and enhance communication between staff and inmates, and has been implemented at every federal prison since that time.[7] The BOP defines a unit as a "small, self-contained, inmate living and staff office area that operates semi-autonomously within the larger institution."[8] The average prison holds approximately 1,000 inmates, and many prisons have as many as 3,000 inmates. Managing such a large inmate population is difficult, so unit management breaks the prison into more manageable units (between 200 and 300 inmates) based on housing assignments. Casework and other unit staff are assigned and located within the housing unit to be accessible and deal directly with inmates, and are given the authority to make decisions and manage the unit.

Unit management enhances staff and inmate communication. The location of staff offices in the housing unit not only makes them more accessible to inmates, but also provides staff the opportunity to monitor inmate activities and see how each inmate behaves on a daily basis. Freeman suggests that accessibility of staff in each unit provides "each [unit] with a sense of group identity, and increases the frequency of employee-staff contacts [with inmates] so that small problems can be addressed before they become large problems."[9] The "A Case Study" box is a good illustration of the practical impact that unit management can have in aiding prison security.

The unit team reviews each inmate's background, evaluates his or her needs, and determines appropriate program and job assignments. Upon their arrival, new inmates meet with their team to develop a plan for their work and program activities, and then meet with their team every six months to review progress and adjust the plan. Figure 10.3 illustrates the organization of a unit team. The team includes staff from a variety of disciplines and departments within the prison. Units are directed by a **unit manager**, and include case managers and correctional counselors. **Case managers** (called *social workers* or *case workers* in some states) have a caseload of 100 to 150 inmates, and are responsible for developing the program of work and rehabilitation for each inmate and writing progress reports that release (parole) authorities or classification staff can use when considering an inmate for a program or transfer to another prison. **Correctional counselors** are promoted

Unit Manager

the staff person who is in charge of the unit, including housing, security, and treatment issues

Case manager

sometimes called a social worker or case worker; responsible for developing the program of work and rehabilitation for inmates assigned to him or her

Correctional counselor

a former correctional officers who works with inmates on prison issues such as creating a visiting or telephone list or getting a prison job assignment

*Unit management offices are located in the inmate housing areas (see window
in lower center of picture), so that staff are accessible to inmates.*
Photo by Richard P. Seiter.

A CASE STUDY

THE EFFECTIVENESS OF UNIT MANAGEMENT

When I worked at the U.S. Penitentiary in Leavenworth, Kansas, two incidents occurred that illustrated the positive impact unit management can have on the operations of a prison. When I first arrived at Leavenworth, it was not operated under the unit management concept. There were correctional counselors, but instead of being assigned to housing units, they were assigned to areas of the prison, such as industries, the dining room, the main corridor, the recreation yard, and the segregation building. Their duties were to be accessible to inmates in those areas and help out in the management as necessary.

About a year after I began working there, we had a work strike. Several inmates were upset with a change in the telephone policy (how they were allowed to make telephone calls) and decided to organize a work strike to get the attention of the administration and try to force a change in the policy. Early on a Monday morning, when inmates were on their way to work, groups of inmates blocked them in some of the main work areas, showing knives or other prison-made weapons, and threatening inmates who did not comply with their demands to go back to their cells and not work.

We quickly discovered what was going on, and to avoid putting inmates in danger, we ordered all inmates to return to their cells. We locked down the prison and began to try to identify the organizers of the work strike. We began by interviewing inmates, and called all the correctional counselors together to see whether they had an idea of which inmates were behind the work strike. Unfortunately, we discovered the counselors did not really know the inmates and could not put together a credible list of suspects.

About six months later, we implemented unit management at Leavenworth and assigned unit managers, case managers, and correctional counselors to each of the housing units. Their offices were in the housing units, and they spent most of their day observing and talking to inmates. A few months after implementation, there was a serious stabbing in one of the cell houses, and the inmate who was assaulted died a few hours later. When he was being carried out of the cell

(continued)

house on a stretcher, a counselor asked him who stabbed him. The inmate did not know the full name of his assailant (the cell house had about 400 inmates living in it); he just said, "Tommy from California."

The unit staff quickly got together to see whether they knew who this might be. They had recently noticed some Aryan Brotherhood inmates who appeared to be talking and planning something together, and they knew that one of its leaders was named Tommy and was from California. They immediately went to his cell, found bloody clothes he had not yet gotten rid of, and found him in the shower washing off blood and evidence. Tommy was charged with and convicted of the inmate's murder. In this case, the fact that the unit staff knew the inmates, their names, and their habits led to the staff's ability to bring justice to a killer, whereas the previous management model for the prison was unsuccessful in identifying the organizers of a work strike.

TABLE OF ORGANIZATION FOR A UNIT MANAGEMENT DEPARTMENT IN A PRISON   FIGURE 10.3

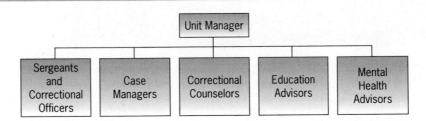

from the ranks of correctional officers and still wear officers' uniforms. Correctional counselors work with inmates on the daily issues that confront them while in prison, such as creating a visiting or telephone list, correcting an error on their account of finances held by the prison, or learning how to find a prison job or get along with other inmates. Because these staff members wear officer uniforms, the stereotype that all security personnel do regarding inmates is enforce rules and give them orders is diluted.

There are also correctional staff (sergeants and officers) that work in the housing unit. In some states, these staff report to and are evaluated by the unit manager, while in others, they report to security supervisors, and the unit manager provides input for their performance evaluations. Also considered a part of the unit team, but usually not reporting to the unit manager, are education and mental health specialists. They evaluate inmate needs and help the unit team create appropriate programs for education, vocational training, substance abuse counseling, and psychological assistance. While a goal of unit management is to enhance communication between staff and inmates, it has a secondary benefit of enhancing communication between these various groups of staff as they work together on the unit team.

Over the past two decades, most states have decided to implement unit management. Although it is generally recognized as a positive way to manage prisons, when a prison decides to implement it, there are still many questions and concerns from staff members regarding the impact on them and the types of positions that are available. Unit management can also be costly, as there may be additional positions for unit counselors and unit managers that were not in the prison prior to the unit management implementation. In Ohio, we were able to reduce the costs of perimeter security to fund unit management, but making this decision and change was still difficult. The "An Insider's Experience" box describes the change process.

AN INSIDER'S EXPERIENCE: Taking Down the Towers

Two of the things I wanted to do when I was director of the Ohio department of corrections was to implement unit management and fund it by "taking down" the towers used to secure the perimeter fences at all of the medium-security prisons. Most of these medium-security prisons had been built in the 1930s through the 1950s and used traditional methods for perimeter security to keep prisoners from escaping. The prisons usually had a set of two fences around them and armed guards in towers every hundred yards or so to watch the fence and shoot inmates who tried to escape.

The problem with these guard towers is that they are only as effective as the staff member's ability to see the fence and accurately shoot an escaping inmate. Staff members also have few alternatives to using deadly force. They cannot leave the tower and respond to the area of attempted escape. And it is a tremendous expense to have someone sit in every tower for twenty-four hours a day, seven days a week. New developments in technology now provide options to this traditional approach to perimeter security. Many medium-security prisons in the United States upgrade the fence security using layers of razor ribbon, which makes it extremely difficult for inmates to move through and get to the fences without being seriously cut and injured. In addition, electronic detection devices can be set up on the fences to alert staff to an attempted breach of the fence, even if the staff are not present or cannot see because of fog or other bad weather conditions. Finally, instead of having eight to ten guard towers around the prison fence line, two or three armed "roving" patrols can be used to complement the detection system and quickly respond to an alarm of a possible attempt to escape at any particular section of the fence line. These roving patrols are correctional officers in vehicles specially equipped with electronic pictures of the fence line that visually show the point of attempted breach. The vehicles continuously drive around the perimeter, and two or three patrols provide better coverage than eight or ten towers.

I thought the two changes could go hand in hand. I could improve the fence security, remove the towers, and use the saved staff positions to implement unit management. I first had staff research the possible replacement of the towers at the medium-security prisons in the state. The findings were that for approximately $150,000 per prison, the physical security of the fences could be improved with razor ribbon, electronic detection devices could be installed, and roving vehicles could be purchased and equipped. Two roving patrols operated twenty-four hours per day, seven days per week, could replace ten towers that also had to be operated continuously, saving eight staff posts. These eight posts required forty staff members to cover them. A post that must be covered twenty-four hours per day, seven days per week, is calculated at approximately five to one. In other words, calculating the need for around-the-clock coverage and sick and annual leave by staff, it takes five people to fill one post. At an average of $35,000 in salary and benefits (in 1985 dollars), these forty staff members not needed could save $1,400,000 per year.

I was able to find enough money to improve the fence lines over a period of about three years, and decided to invest the money in upgrading the fences and eliminate all the towers in the medium-security prisons. We would move the staff positions saved from the tower posts to implement unit management. However, when the plan for the first prison was announced, the local union objected. They suggested that the change would not be as effective as the current guard towers, and even put a full-page ad in the local newspaper stating that removing these towers would endanger the community. However, in reality, some of the correctional officers liked working alone in the towers, with no contact with inmates and little contact with their supervisors.

The prison warden developed a plan to reduce the union opposition and inform staff of the benefits of the change and of implementing unit management. First, he sent several staff members to a medium-security federal prison about seventy miles away to observe the no-tower fence system and talk to staff at that prison about its effectiveness, as well as the benefits of unit management. Second, the warden challenged the union leadership try to get through the razor ribbon and climb the fence without setting off the alarm and having the roving patrol quickly respond. They could not do it. Finally, the warden briefed local politicians about the effectiveness, benefits, and potential cost savings of the new system. These efforts were successful, and over the next few years, six medium-security prisons eliminated towers and implemented

(continued)

unit management, and each new newly constructed prison (except for the maximum-security facilities) were built without towers.

I believe this change really benefited the management and operation of the prisons throughout Ohio, and thank the warden of that first prison for taking strong leadership to successfully implement the change. I really appreciated the success of this endeavor when I read a January 2000 Associated Press article about New Jersey Governor Donald T. DiFrancesco ordering state prisons to continue manning guard towers, reversing a cost-cutting measure imposed by his predecessor, Governor Christie Whitman. The Whitman administration had previously ordered prisons to begin vacating the towers as new electronic perimeter fencing was installed, in order to save money. However, the article noted that complaints from correctional officers and community residents persuaded DiFrancesco to change course.

Controlling Inmate Behavior

The mission of a correctional institution includes creating a safe and secure environment, yet because inmates tremendously outnumber staff, they cannot control behavior (over the long term) through threats, intimidation, and physical dominance. Many activities are key in the management of prisons, contribute to the ability of staff to control inmate behavior, and move toward accomplishing the mission of safety and security. These activities include the consistent implementation of prison policies and procedures, the use of classification to match inmate risks and needs to the appropriate prison, and an inmate disciplinary system to encourage adherence to prison rules and punish inmates who fail to comply with these rules.

POLICIES AND PROCEDURES

One of the keys to controlling inmates' behavior is to have clearly written, well-communicated, and consistently implemented policies and procedures. Every organization uses fairly detailed policies and procedures to guide staff on how to perform and provide clients an understanding of what to expect from the organization. Such guidance and expectations for performance is especially critical within a prison, in which inmates are likely to sue staff for performing their duties in a way that they believe negatively effects them, and in which inmates must be held accountable for following the rules and policies of the prison. While it is almost impossible to imagine an agency not having written policies and procedures for almost any occurrence or situation, thirty years ago many prisons did not have written policy manuals or consistent implementation of procedures.

At least four conditions are necessary for prison policies and procedures to effectively contribute to the overall prison mission. First, policies must be consistent with professional standards and be written and authorized by the prison administration. The **American Correctional Association** (ACA), the major professional organization for corrections in the United States, publishes standards manuals for all types of correctional practices. These policies and practices were created through a rigorous development, review, and approval process conducted by national correctional experts. Similar to the American Medical Association or the American Bar Association, ACA standards are created by practicing professionals in the field and are used to guide and evaluate acceptable modes of operation.

Second, for policies and procedures to be effective in managing and controlling inmate behavior, they must be clearly communicated to staff and inmates. While a few "security" policies give details of how staff shall respond during a riot or other emergency situations and are not communicated to inmates, most policies are made available to inmates. Usually, these policies are available for review in the inmate library, so inmates will understand what is expected of both them and staff.

American Correctional Association

the largest professional organization for corrections in the United States

The third element of effective policy is to have procedures consistently carried out. If one correctional officer follows all policies in detail, and another officer follows only those that seem most important, it makes enforcement of the policy difficult and can cause confusion and tension among inmates and between inmates and staff. Inmates realize the need for policy, and almost welcome it. Their whole life revolves around the activities within the prison. They recognize the importance of routine in a correctional environment, and want to know what they and other inmates have to do in each situation. Inmates also recognize that if policies are not consistently implemented, or staff are not diligent in their monitoring and enforcement, some inmates will take advantage of the complacency, violate the policy, and compromise the overall safe environment for inmates as well as staff. The fourth component of effective policy is to ensure its consistent implementation in a quality fashion. The next section describes some of the quality-assurance practices used in correctional institutions.

Quality Assurance in the Implementation of Policy

Two activities used to ensure consistent implementation of prison policies are monitoring policy compliance and ACA accreditation. The method most commonly used to monitor policy compliance by staff is an active auditing program to determine the extent to which policy is effectively carried out and contributes to the mission of the prison. Prisons use a variety of auditing procedures to monitor compliance with operational policies. One of these, a **policy audit**, ascertains whether broad agency policy is in place at the prison. Policy audits match agency-required policy with local prison implementation procedures to ensure that procedures are in place at each prison to address each agency policy. In most states, the central headquarters dictates broad policy with which each prison in the state must comply. An example of a statewide policy regarding keeping contraband from entering the prison is that "all vehicles, carts, and boxes or packages must be thoroughly inspected before being allowed to enter or exit a prison." Each prison is required to develop and implement operational procedures to effect the required statewide policy. In this example, the prison describes how it will inspect the vehicles, carts, and boxes or packages, including where it will be done, who will do it, and what equipment will be necessary. A policy audit is valuable to begin an overall review of security operations, but only identifies whether the required scope of written, authorized, and mandated policies at the prison exists. It does not determine compliance with implementation, consistency in practice, or thoroughness of procedures.

Policy audit
a review to ascertain whether broad agency policy is in place at a prison

Compliance with policy is determined by a **policy implementation audit**, which identifies whether procedures are consistently being carried out by staff in their daily duties. While the policy audit is a review of written documents, the policy implementation audit is a review of actual operations. It is completed by a team of knowledgeable staff from outside the prison who observe the methods by which staff carry out their assignments and identify any lack of compliance with established policy. Even though staff members are aware that their behavior is being observed during an audit and will be sure to follow the policy as they know it, the audit still identifies weaknesses in compliance resulting from failure to train staff, improper procedures, or a misunderstanding about the policy requirements. And if staff would normally take shortcuts in following policy, the audit reminds them of the importance of following procedures.

Policy implementation audit
a review to identify whether procedures prescribed by policy are consistently being carried out by staff in their daily duties

The second method of ensuring compliance with policy is **ACA accreditation**. In the early 1970s, corrections improved its ability to be seen as professional through adopting the acknowledged approaches associated with a profession: (1) a systematic body of theoretical knowledge acquired through lengthy academic study and not possessed by those outside the profession; (2) community interests

ACA accreditation
a process to promote and recognize improvement in the management of correctional agencies through the administration of voluntary standards

rather than self-interest as a motivator of professional behavior; (3) self-regulation; and (4) a system of rewards.[10] Corrections made many progressive strides to be recognized as meeting these components, especially creating a body of knowledge (standards) of acceptable performance and a system of self-regulation. The American Correctional Association formed the Commission of Accreditation for Corrections (CAC) and standards identifying state-of-the-art practices were developed. Agencies that implement and meet these standards may then apply for consideration to be accredited by the ACA. According to the ACA, the purpose of this accreditation process is as follows:

> to promote improvement in the management of correctional agencies through the administration of a voluntary accreditation program and the ongoing development and revision of relevant, useful standards . . . The recognized benefits from such a process include improved management, a defense against lawsuits through documentation and the demonstration of a "good faith" effort to improve conditions of confinement, increased accountability and enhanced public credibility for administrative and line staff, a safer and more human environment for personnel and offenders, and the establishment of measurable criteria for upgrading programs, personnel, and physical plant on a continuing basis[11]

When a prison applies to be accredited, ACA conducts an audit to determine whether it meets the required standards. The audits are completed by a team of objective ACA-trained auditors who spend one week at the prison, review written policy, and observe procedures. If all standards identified as "life safety" and 90 percent of others are met, ACA will accredit the prison, meaning that it meets acknowledged standards of professional operations. Not every correctional administrator supports accreditation, arguing that ACA accreditation means nothing and requires a considerable amount of work to complete. Yet most recognize that it gives a professional credibility to those outside corrections (the courts, the public, elected officials), and the process is an excellent reminder and confirms the importance of consistent implementation of policy by staff.

INMATE CLASSIFICATION

Another essential prison management device for controlling inmate behavior is inmate classification. Prison classification systems help control inmate behavior in three ways. First, classification is used to determine the appropriate prison security level to which an inmate should be assigned. When inmates are initially sentenced, the correctional agency does an assessment to determine their risk of escape and potential for violence. By matching inmates' risk of escape and violence to prison physical security, security policies and procedures, and staff allocations, the potential for escape or violence is reduced. Second, once inmates are assigned to a prison, classification systems are used (in some states) to determine the type of housing assignment within a prison (single cell, multiple-inmate cell, or dormitory) that is most suitable for each inmate. Finally, the reclassification of inmates after they are assigned to a prison acts as a motivator for good behavior. Inmates' behavior is regularly reviewed and can lead to a reassignment to a higher-security prison with tighter restrictions and fewer privileges or to a lower-security prison.

Until the 1970s, most states used a clinical classification process, in which a team of experienced correctional staff interviewed inmates and reviewed their criminal, medical, psychological, and social histories. They would then decide what type of prison housing, work assignment, and treatment programs would be best for the inmate. Currently, most states use an objective classification system—

an actuarial risk assessment—to determine an inmate's initial assignment to a prison. This initial classification is based predominantly on offense history and sentence length. In describing the need for these actuarial systems, Dallao writes, "Instead of assigning offenders to certain security levels based on gut reaction and subjective discussion, this new system provided an orderly and objective way of separating violent from nonviolent inmates."[12]

The Federal Bureau of Prisons was the first correctional agency to implement such a system; in the mid-1970s it assigned a team of specialists to design a classification system that was more predictive of behavior than the early clinical approaches. The team initially identified ninety-six factors that were considered important for classification purposes and sought the opinion of correctional professionals across the country on these factors. The original list was pared to forty-seven factors, and later to six: history of escape or attempted escape; detainers; types of prior commitments; history of violence; severity of offense; and length of sentence. These factors focus on public risk by using acts that occurred prior to sentencing. Brennan suggests that these security classifications emphasize "legal variables, history of criminality, seriousness of current offense, and past escape attempts."[13]

To make the initial assignment of an inmate to a prison, a BOP staff member reviews the background of the offender and assigns a score for each of the six areas. Figure 10.4 shows the form used to determine security designations for each inmate. Inmates are assigned the points indicated on the Security Designation form, and the total points are then used to determine the security level of the prison to which the inmate is assigned. The following security point totals result in placement in the corresponding security level of federal prison:

Security point totals	Prison security level
0–7	Minimum
8–11	Low
12–18	Medium
19+	High

Since the adoption of this system by the BOP, almost every state has developed objective classification systems to assign the levels of prison security for inmates. As of January 1, 2001, 10.6 percent of all prison inmates were assigned to maximum security, 11.8 percent were assigned to close/high security, 41.7 percent were assigned to medium security, 25.3 percent were assigned to minimum security, 5.6 percent were assigned to community security, and 4.9 percent were unclassified.[14] Objective classifications reduce the tendency to "overclassify" that often resulted from clinical systems. As support for this, in 1978, 51 percent of prisoners were in maximum security, 38 percent in medium, and 11 percent in minimum-security prisons.[15]

The classification process also is useful in determining the type of housing assignment within a prison that is most suitable for each inmate. Many prisons have a variety of housing areas for inmates, which may be either individual or multi-person cells or dormitory-style housing with several (possibly hundreds of) inmates in an open area without any physical security to separate them from each other or from staff. **Internal classification systems** are instruments used to assign inmates to housing or programs after they are placed in a particular prison. However, most prisons still make these decisions based on clinical judgments, or make housing assignments only on the availability of space.

The most widely used internal classification system is the Adult Internal Management System (AIMS) developed by Dr. Herbert Quay, which classifies inmates on the analysis of life history records and a correctional adjustment checklist. These

Internal classification system

instruments used to assign inmates to housing or programs after they are placed in a particular prison

INMATE LOAD AND SECURITY DESIGNATION FORM—MALE (BP-337)

INMATE LOAD DATA	1. REG NO	2. LAST NAME	

3. FIRST NAME	4. MIDDLE	5. SUFFIX

6. RACE	7. SEX	8. ETHNIC ORIGIN	9. DATE OF BIRTH

10. OFFENSE/SENTENCE

11. FBI NUMBER	12. SOCIAL SECURITY NUMBER	

13. STATE OF BIRTH	14. OR COUNTRY OF BIRTH	15. CITIZENSHIP

16. ADDRESS-STREET	17. CITY

18. STATE	19. ZIP CODE	20. OR FOREIGN COUNTRY

21. HEIGHT—FT: IN:	22. WEIGHT	23. HAIR	24. EYES

25. ARS ASSIGNMENT

SECURITY DESIGNATION DATA

1. PUBLIC SAFETY FACTORS

A—NONE	F—SEX OFFENDER	I—SENTENCE LENGTH
B—DISRUPTIVE GROUP	G—THREAT GOVT OFFICIAL	L—SERIOUS ESCAPE
C—GREATEST SEVERITY OFFENSE	H—DEPORTABLE ALIEN	M—PRISON DISTURBANCE

2. USM OFFICE	3. JUDGE	4. REC FACILITY	5. REC PROGRAM

6. TYPE OF DETAINER	0—NONE 1—LOWEST/LOW MODERATE	3—MODERATE 7—GREATEST 5—HIGH

7. SEVERITY OF CURRENT OFFENSE	0—LOWEST 1—LOW MODERATE	3—MODERATE 7—GREATEST 5—HIGH

8. MONTHS TO RELEASE _____

9. TYPE OF PRIOR COMMITMENT	0 = NONE	1 = MINOR	3 = SERIOUS

10. HISTORY OF ESCAPE OR ATTEMPTS		NONE	>15 YEARS	10–15 YEARS	5–10 YEARS	<5 YEARS
	MINOR	0	1	1	2	3
	SERIOUS	0	3 (S)	3 (S)	3 (S)	3 (S)

11. HISTORY OF VIOLENCE		NONE	>15 YEARS	10–15 YEARS	5–10 YEARS	<5 YEARS
	MINOR	0	1	1	3	5
	SERIOUS	0	2	4	6	7

12. PRECOMMITMENT STATUS	0 = NOT APPLICABLE −3 (R) = OWN RECOGNIZANCE −3 (V) = VOLUNTARY SURRENDER

13. VOLUNTARY SURRENDER DATE	14. VOLUNTARY SURRENDER LOCATION

15. CRIM HX PTS _____	16. SECURITY POINT TOTAL

17. OMDT REFER (Y/N) _____

18. REMARKS

Source: Federal Bureau of Prisons, *Security Designation and Custody Classification Manual* (Washington, D.C.: U.S. Department of Justice, 1996), Chapter 5, p. 1.

factors identify inmates who are likely to be violent and aggressive or likely to be victimized, and therefore allow staff to separate likely victims from likely aggressors. Another system developed by the State of Illinois uses an internal classification system to make assignments within its maximum-security prisons. The Illinois system makes housing, work, and program assignments using some past criminal behavior factors from the external classification system, adding prison disciplinary conduct and history of gang activities to predict a level of institutional aggression.

Classification is an incentive for good behavior by inmates, as it is used to guide interinstitutional transfers due to security or treatment purposes. Inmates seldom stay at the prison to which they were originally assigned throughout their entire term of incarceration. Their time served and institutional behavior changes their predicted risk of violence and escape. Correctional agencies regularly reclassify and move inmates to higher- or lower-security prisons based on these changes. Objective classification systems make it very clear to inmates what they need to do to have their security level reduced, or what behavior will result in an increase in security. Most inmates strive to get to lower-security prisons throughout their term of imprisonment, and therefore work for good behavior to reduce their level or security and increase their freedom and opportunity for program involvement.

The reclassification review is scheduled at regular intervals (often three or six months). At the reclassification review, an inmate's behavior and the percentage of his or her sentence served are combined into the classification score system. If behavior is good, and as the inmate reaches certain stages in his or her sentence (so many months served or a certain percentage of the sentence completed), it may result in a lowered security score and corresponding prison assignment. Serious misbehavior by inmates can also result in reclassification, as it indicates that the inmate cannot be controlled in the current security level. An inmate who commits a serious disciplinary infraction or continues to commit less severe infractions receives extra points on the security instrument and may be upgraded to a higher-security prison.

Figure 10.5 shows the California Department of Corrections Reclassification Score Sheet. Unfavorable and favorable behavior scores are combined to recalculate

Inmates strive to work their way down to minimum-security prisons, which are often less restrictive in their movements and often have additional programs available.
Photo by Richard P. Seiter.

STATE OF CALIFORNIA | CDC Reclassification Score Sheet | DEPARTMENT OF CORRECTIONS

II. RECALCULATION OF SCORE

A. UNFAVORABLE BEHAVIOR SINCE LAST REVIEW

Last Review Date

☐☐ – ☐☐ – ☐☐ 24
mo   day   year

1. Number of serious
   disciplinaries
   dates: _____ _____ ___ x 6 = ☐☐ 30

2. Number of escapes during
   current period
   date: ___ x 8 = ☐☐ 32

3. Number of physical assaults
   on staff
   date: ___ x 8 = ☐☐ 34

4. Number of physical assaults
   on inmates
   date: ___ x 4 = ☐☐ 36

5. Number of smuggling/trafficking
   in drugs
   date: ___ x 4 = ☐☐ 38

6. Number of deadly
   weapon possessions
   date: ___ x 16 = ☐☐ 40

7. Number of inciting
   disturbance
   date: ___ x 4 = ☐☐ 42

8. Number of assaults that caused
   serious injury
   date: ___ x 16 = ☐☐ 44

9. TOTAL UNFAVORABLE POINTS = + _____

B. FAVORABLE BEHAVIOR SINCE LAST REVIEW

Number of Six
Month Periods

1. Continuous minimum
   custody ___ x 4 = ☐☐ 46

2. Continuous dorm
   living ___ x 2 = ☐☐ 48

3. No serious
   115's ___ x 2 = ☐☐ 50

4. Average or above performance in work, school, or
   vocational program ___ x 2 = ☐☐ 52

5. TOTAL FAVORABLE CREDITS = – _____

C. COMPUTATION OF CLASSIFICATION SCORE

1. Prior Classification Score = ☐☐ 54

2. Net Change in Behavior Score
   (A.9 minus B.5) = ☐☐ 57
   (+ or –)

3. Change in term points = ☐☐ 60
   (+ or –)

4. Current Classification Score = ☐☐☐ 63

III. PLACEMENT

A. SPECIAL CASE FACTORS

1. Placement Concerns
   a) Hold   b) Restricted   c) Medical Restriction
   (enter A, P, or #) Custody Suffix   (enter FULL, REST,
   Felony   INS   (enter R or *)   UNAS, or *)
   ☐ 66 ☐ 67 ☐ 68 ☐☐☐☐ 69

2. Other Placement Concerns
   a) (*)   b) (*)
   ☐☐☐ 73   ☐☐☐ 77

3. Caseworkers
   a) Counselor
   ☐☐☐☐☐☐☐ ☐ 81
   Last Name   FI

   b) Supervisor
   ☐☐☐☐☐☐☐ ☐ 90
   Last Name   FI

4. Current Custody
   ☐☐☐ – ☐ – ☐☐☐ 99

5. Current Institution and Facility
   ☐☐☐☐☐ – ☐☐☐ 107

B. CLASSIFICATION STAFF REPRESENTATIVE ACTION

1. Classification Staff Representative
   ☐☐☐☐☐☐☐ 114
   Last Name

2. Date of CSR Action
   ☐☐ – ☐☐ – ☐☐ 122
   mo   day   year

3. Administrative Determinants
   a) (*)   PRIMARY
   ☐   ☐☐ 128

   b) (*)   c) (*)
   ☐☐☐ 132   ☐☐☐ 136

4. Placement Approved   a) Cat.
                              ☐

   b) Institution and Facility
   ☐☐☐☐☐ – ☐☐☐ 141

5. Reason for Administrative or Irregular Placement
   ☐☐☐☐ 148

I. IDENTIFYING INFORMATION

A. CDC NUMBER
☐ ☐☐☐☐☐ 1

B. INMATE'S LAST NAME
☐☐☐☐☐☐☐ 7

C. Date of Current Review
☐☐ – ☐☐ – ☐☐ 15 –
mo   day   year

D. PAROLE VIOLATOR
   ADMISSION TYPE   ☐☐ 21
   (enter RTC or WNT)

an inmate's classification score. Unfavorable factors include serious rule violations, escapes, assaults on staff or inmates, drug smuggling, weapon possession, or inciting a disturbance. Favorable behaviors include maintenance of minimum custody, continuous living in dormitory-type housing, no serious rule violations, and good program performance. Inmates are reviewed every six months or whenever there is a serious rule violation.

The goal of initial classification is to have similar-risk inmates assigned to appropriate-security-level prisons, and the goal of reclassification is to maintain homogeneity of inmates by security level. Both overclassifying and underclassifying inmates can cause problems, as housing high-security inmates in a low- or minimum-security facility increases the potential for escape, predatory behavior, or other types of violence, while housing low- or minimum-security inmates in high-security prisons places them in danger of violence and intimidation and wastes correctional resources, as high-security prisons cost three to four times as much to build and operate as minimum-security prisons.

INMATE DISCIPLINE

Another key to controlling inmate behavior is a system of disincentives and punishment for violation of prison rules. Prisons create and use an **inmate disciplinary system** to respond to violation of prison rules by inmates. The disciplinary process includes an accusation of the violation, investigation of the incident, a hearing to determine guilt, and imposition of a sanction if found guilty. Inmate disciplinary systems usually include (1) a written policy documenting prohibited behavior, which is provided to all inmates; (2) a fair and equitable set of corresponding sanctions increasing with the severity of the rule violation, and a process to appeal those sanctions; (3) a way to separate inmates accused of rule violations from the general inmate population when the security of the prison could be threatened; and (4) provisions for long-term separation or special security handling for inmates who continuously threaten institutional security or against whom a serious threat of violence exists.

Inmate disciplinary system
the process required to find that an inmate committed a prohibited act; it identifies allowable punishments for each act

The first component of an inmate disciplinary system is a written policy of specific prohibited behavior. The policy also explains the process used to determine guilt and the range of punishments that result from rule violations. The purpose and scope of the BOP policy regarding inmate discipline is stated as follows:

> So that inmates may live in a safe and orderly environment, it is necessary for institution authorities to impose discipline on those inmates whose behavior is not in compliance with Bureau of Prisons rules. The provisions of this rule apply to all persons committed to the care, custody, and control (direct or constructive) of the Bureau of Prisons.[16]

Correctional agencies provide a copy of the inmate discipline policy to every inmate upon their arrival at a prison, and inmates sign that they have received, read, and understand the policy. Informing inmates and ensuring that they understand prohibited acts not only is fair, but also reduces the potential for successful appeals of inmate disciplinary actions before a federal court. Most correctional systems categorize prohibited acts by severity. The BOP policy lists four categories of prohibited acts: greatest, high, moderate, and low moderate,[17] with a specific range of sanctions authorized for each category of prohibited act. The BOP provides for a two-stage disciplinary process, with minor violations handled in a less formal manner than serious infractions, and time frames are associated with each step in the process so the inmate knows the time available for collecting evidence or seeking assistance. Figure 10.6 illustrates the disciplinary process and time limits for each step in the BOP policy.

U.S. BUREAU OF PRISONS DISCIPLINARY PROCESS

FIGURE 10.6

1. Staff become aware of inmate's involvement in incident.

Ordinarily maximum
of 24 hours

2. Staff give inmate notice
of charges by delivering
Incident Report.

Maximum ordinarily three workdays from
the time staff became aware of the inmate's
involvement in the incident (excludes the
day staff became aware of the inmate's
involvement, weekends, and holidays).

3. Initial hearing (UDC)

Minimum of 24 hours
(unless waived)

4. Discipline Hearing Officer
(DHO) Hearing

*Note: These time limits are subject to exceptions as provided in the rules. Staff may
suspend disciplinary proceedings for a period not to exceed two calendar weeks while
informal resolution is undertaken and accomplished. If informal resolution is unsuccessful,
staff may reinstitute disciplinary proceedings at the same stage at which suspended. The
requirements then begin running again, at the same point at which they were suspended.*

Source: Federal Bureau of
Prisons, "Inmate Discipline and
Special Housing Units," Federal
Prison System, Policy Statement
#5270.07 (Washington, D.C.:
U.S. Department of Justice,
December 29, 1987), Chapter
4, p. 8.

According to the BOP policy, once an incident report is issued to an inmate, an initial hearing must occur within three workdays. If the infraction is minor, the hearing panel (referred to as the Unit Disciplinary Committee or UDC) can determine guilt and impose minor sanctions such as a loss of privileges. If the violation is more serious and could result in loss of good time, disciplinary transfer to another prison, or disciplinary isolation from the general inmate population, the UDC will refer the case to an upper-level hearing panel, a Discipline Hearing Officer (DHO), who is not a staff member of the prison in which the incident took place and is therefore seen as impartial.[18] Most states have a similar two-tiered system to handle inmate discipline.

Sanctions for commission of prohibited acts can be minor, such as restriction from privileges, or serious, such as transfer to a supermax prison. The following list describes the types of sanctions in order of severity used by most correctional systems.

Warning: Some jurisdictions allow a temporary suspension of disciplinary action, with an inmate receiving a warning. If there are no further violations during the period of suspension, the rule violation may be expunged from the inmate's record.

Reprimand: A reprimand is a written admonishment against the behavior with no other sanction or punishment.

Assignment of extra duty: Assignment of additional work for an inmate, usually for a specific number of hours.

Restriction to quarters: Restriction to quarters requires the inmate to remain in the housing location for a specific period of time (such as one week) whenever he or she is not at work, meals, or an assigned program.

Impoundment of personal property: Inmates may have their personal property confiscated or impounded, and either it will be held or the inmate will have to pay to send it out of the prison.

Loss of job: When the infraction has something to do with the job assignment, inmates may lose their job and have to find or be assigned another less-favored job.

Removal from program or group activity: Similar to the loss of a job, an inmate may be removed from a program or group activity if the infraction is related to a program or activity.

Change of quarters: Inmates may be required to move from one housing unit to another.

Loss of privileges: Inmates may be restricted from specific privileges, such as participation in recreation or loss of the use of the prison commissary.

Monetary restitution: If the infraction included damaging government property or another inmate's property, the violating inmate may be required to pay for the damage.

Withholding of good time: Correctional sentences allow inmates to earn a certain number of days off their sentence for each month of good behavior, and if a violation of prison rules is serious, good time may not be granted, lengthening the term of the sentence.

Disciplinary segregation: Inmates may have to serve a sentence in segregation, in a separate facility from the general inmate population, with little time out of their cell.

Disciplinary transfer: Inmates who continually violate prison rules or commit a serious violation can be transferred to a higher-security prison.

Placement in a supermax prison: Supermax prisons (described in Chapter 9) house the most violent and dangerous inmates, and inmates who have shown an inability to follow rules in a standard prison may be transferred to a supermax prison for an indeterminate period of time.

Once there is a finding of guilt and imposition of a sanction, correctional agencies usually provide an **administrative appeals process** to allow inmates to appeal a disciplinary sanction, or to seek to remedy any other injustice they believe they have received at the hands of correctional officials. Having an appeals process promotes acceptance by inmates and avoids expensive and burdensome review of disciplinary decisions by federal courts. Administrative appeals usually have at least two levels: first a reconsideration by the warden, and if the inmate is not satisfied with the response, a second level of reconsideration by the agency headquarters. For disciplinary processes, the inmate appeal cannot dispute a finding of fact, but is limited to procedural and due process rights. Inmates usually have thirty days after notice of the decision to appeal. In describing the review process, Cripe writes:

> The records (the disciplinary offense report, the investigation report, and the written report of the hearing officer or committee) are examined, to be sure that the procedures required by the agency's disciplinary policy have been followed. The facts of the case and the sanction imposed are summarily reviewed. There must be some evidence to support

Administrative appeals process

an informal process for inmates to appeal a disciplinary sanction, or to seek remedy of any other injustice they feel they have received at the hands of correctional officials the finding of the disciplinary authority. The reviewer ensures that the sanction imposed is within the range of punishments authorized for that offense. There is a legal requirement that the hearing officer or committee record the evidence relied on to support the conclusion reached, and that the reasons for the sanction(s) imposed be given.[19]

The Role of Staff in a Prison

Everyone who works for a correctional agency recognizes that the staff is the agency's most valuable resource. Corrections is a business in which people are more important than the bars and fences, prison cells, or available technology. Correctional staff supervise offenders, monitoring and guiding their behavior toward the development of a crime-free and productive lifestyle. On January 1, 2001, state and federal correctional agencies employed almost 440,000 prison staff and over 72,000 probation and parole staff,[20] and approximately 85 percent of a correctional agency budget is spent for staff salaries.

Historically, the role of correctional staff who worked in prisons was very narrowly defined, and there was little effort to recruit, develop, or retain the most educated and professional staff. Line prison staff (such as correctional officers) had minimal discretion or decision-making authority. In 1965, Cressey wrote, "Most guards have nothing to do but stand guard; they do not use inmates productively any more than they themselves are used productively by prison managers."[21] The role of correctional staff in modern prisons has changed considerably, spurred by the emphasis on rehabilitation as a correctional goal during the 1950s and 1960s. As a part of this transformation, new professional staff, including psychologists, educators, and administrators, were brought into prisons, and the importance of the overall prison experience in inmate rehabilitation was recognized.

In addition, with the dramatic increases in the number of prisoners during the 1980s, most prisons became overcrowded, and correctional staff often felt overworked and frustrated and feared losing control. Totally outnumbered, correctional officials recognized that the authoritarian style of inmate supervision was ineffective, and staff skilled in interpersonal communications were better able to gain the compliance of inmates and maintain order. Correctional officials moved aggressively to recruit educated individuals trained in supervising and communicating with others. Many states and the BOP require candidates for correctional officer positions to have either a bachelor's degree or at least two years' experience working in a correctional or law enforcement setting. Corrections began to recognize the critical value of all staff, not just those delivering treatment programs, in accomplishing their mission.

RECRUITING AND HIRING CORRECTIONAL STAFF

Recruiting for prisons in the past was done very haphazardly or not at all. Prisons usually relied on recruitment through encouragement by relatives or friends who already worked at the prison. There was no plan by which characteristics of successful employees were identified, organizational needs considered, and an aggressive recruitment effort implemented, and correctional agencies usually accepted the hiring of a nondiverse workforce with little experience or academic preparation. Most correctional agency recruitment was all too often like that described here regarding the State of Massachusetts:

> Massachusetts in the 1970s had a depressed economy with high unemployment. At the same time, the Massachusetts prison system had a high turnover rate among officers and a chronic need for new officers.

Yet . . . corrections with its similar salary and benefits (to police and fire departments) was in reality a "walk-in" job. Screening and selection were largely limited to investigation of possible criminal records of applicants. The prison officer recruit was largely self-selected.[22]

Prompted by high turnover and the challenge of a growing workforce, correctional agencies recruitment is now much more sophisticated and has been very successful in recruiting from a variety of sources, including other criminal justice agencies, individuals leaving the military, public and private social service agencies, and community and four-year colleges. Even with quality recruiting generating a large pool of qualified applicants, there still must be effective hiring practices to screen and select the most qualified individuals from this pool. Correctional agencies identify the areas of competence that they want in prison employees and create a screening process to rate applicants' abilities. Some of the traits and abilities identified to be a successful correctional worker are the following:

- Good interpersonal skills (both oral and written)
- Ability to make sound decisions
- Lack of prejudice toward criminal offenders
- Understanding of the need to treat all clients/inmates in a fair and consistent manner
- Ability to "think on one's feet"
- Ability to supervise others
- Good presentation of oneself

Correctional agencies use several screening and rating mechanisms. Not only must candidates complete a fairly extensive application (including past education, military, and job experience), but they must also provide examples of how these past experiences are indicative of the identified traits and abilities. After the agency identifies the best group of candidates from the applications, screening usually includes a personal interview, review of a writing sample, and an integrity interview. During the personal interview, interviewers present candidates with difficult and stressful scenarios, have them describe how they would handle it, and then rate how desirable the candidate's response would be in a correctional environment working with inmates. Candidates are often required to provide a writing sample, to determine their ability to communicate in writing. And one of the most important screening mechanisms is the **integrity interview**. Since correctional staff are continually confronted with opportunities to personally benefit from giving offenders favored treatment, integrity interviews are used to determine whether candidates have issues such as financial problems, past employment problems, current drug or alcohol abuse, or other conditions that could put them in a compromising situation or make them more likely to accept a bribe to show favored treatment to an inmate.

Line staff such as correctional officers are critical to the success of a prison, but only if they are properly trained, supervised, guided, and managed. Management of prisons in the early 1900s was much simpler than it is today. An autocratic warden cannot just create and enforce rules to maintain control and punish staff who did not follow the leader's directives. Currently, prison order has more to do with fairness and equity, with leadership and empowerment, and with organization and management. As suggested by DiIulio in *Governing Prisons:*

> The answer to be offered . . . is that the quality of prison life varies according to the quality of prison management. The evidence will lead us to the conclusion that prison management is the strategic variable, one that may be subject to change with predictable and desirable consequences.[23]

Integrity interview

interview of candidates for correctional employment used to determine whether the candidates have issues or conditions that could put them in a compromising situation or make them more likely to accept a bribe to show favored treatment to an inmate

COLLECTIVE BARGAINING WITHIN CORRECTIONAL AGENCIES

While a few states (Connecticut in the 1940s, and New York and Washington in the 1960s) have had public employee unions for some time, collective bargaining is relatively new to most state correctional agencies. By the 1970s, more than twenty states had formally authorized collective bargaining by public employees, and by the end of the twentieth century, more than half of the states had collective bargaining for at least some correctional employees. Due to the mission of safety and security and the role of supervising felony offenders, collective bargaining is more complex for correctional agencies than for many other public and private organizations.

Collective bargaining is the formal recognition of employee organizations and their right to negotiate with management regarding conditions of the workplace. The purposes of collective bargaining are as follows:

- To establish and protect employees' rights
- To improve working conditions and benefits
- To establish and maintain more harmonious employer-employee relationships
- To establish a participative role for employees in management decisions that affect employees[24]

While the purposes seem non-confrontational and in line with the mission of a prison, many correctional administrators have feared that they would diminish their management authority and undermine prison security. The biggest point of debate is the role in which **seniority** of staff is considered in such things as work schedules, post assignment, and promotion. Union officials usually desire seniority to be key in determining employees' work assignments, days off, shift schedules, and even promotions. Correctional management officials want to have as much discretion as possible to place staff with unique abilities in the positions that require their strengths and create schedules to meet security needs. Over the years in which correctional agencies have used collective bargaining, the fears that it would jeopardize an agency mission have not materialized, and input by the unions representing line staff has usually resulted in improved decision making and higher morale.

Many national labor organizations represent public-sector and correctional employees, including the AFL-CIO, AFSFME (the American Federation of State, Federal and Municipal Employees), and the International Brotherhood of Teamsters. In some states, several different organizations represent different groups of correctional employees (correctional officers, nurses, professional staff), while in others, employees elect a single labor union to represent all of them. The labor organization that represents employees is able to negotiate issues of pay and benefits for public employees, and sometimes other issues, such as how staff are selected for overtime, the type of clothing provided to staff by the agency, and the number and areas of coverage by correctional officers. While collective bargaining is well entrenched in many prisons and correctional agencies and has a major impact on policy and practice, and there is usually a harmonious relationship between management and labor, in some jurisdictions there has been a lack of trust and constant battles for power and influence. Jacobs and Crotty write, "[Collective bargaining] has redefined the prison organization in adversary terms so that wardens are bosses and complaints are grievances."[25]

One historical concern by both parties has been the right to strike. Most public-safety organizations are not allowed to strike, which takes away a major union tactic to get management to accept labor's negotiating demands. While a crisis could

Collective bargaining
the formal recognition of employee organizations and their right to negotiate with management regarding workplace issues

Seniority
length of employment used to determine an employee's assignment, days off, or other job-related functions

occur if police or correctional officers were allowed to strike, unions representing these groups sometimes sanction informal job actions (the "blue flu") to get the attention of management. In the past, there have also been illegal strikes by correctional officers. In New York State, even with the Taylor Law penalties whereby strikers lose two days' salary for each day they are on strike,[26] a strike of New York state correctional officers occurred in 1979. An analysis of the strike found that collective bargaining was not well suited to resolve the problems in this situation (officers believed they had lost status and authority, and racial tension existed within the officer ranks and between officers and inmates) and may have even aggravated them.[27]

Another concern regarding collective bargaining is its impact on security and correctional efforts toward rehabilitation. During the 1960s and 1970s, the rehabilitative movement created a fear by officers that the interest in "helping" inmates would lead to a reduction of authority for correctional officers, and unionization gained strength within prisons. However, many labor and correctional officials recognize that interests of prisoners and officers are intertwined, and both groups stand to benefit from the rehabilitative philosophy. As rehabilitative programs improve inmate morale, reduce idleness, and enhance security, the workplace situation improves for prison staff.

Several states still do not authorize collective bargaining for correctional employees, fearing it will undermine security and the authority and flexibility for management to effectively operate prisons. In the *You Make the Decision* box, students are to read through the information, weigh the pros and cons, and decide (if they had the authority) whether they would implement collective bargaining in a state.

In general, collective bargaining is believed to have more positive than negative implications for corrections. When both management and labor communicate and listen to each other and are reasonable in their positions, collective bargaining can be a benefit to the overall effectiveness of a correctional organization. However, when the parties in collective bargaining stop listening, let the issues get personal, and become overly adversarial in the relationship, collective bargaining makes a difficult workplace even more tense and stressful.

YOU MAKE THE DECISION . . .   IMPLEMENT COLLECTIVE BARGAINING?

When a state or local government authorizes public employees to organize and engage in collective bargaining, the first step is for the employees to select a labor organization to represent them. A major decision that must be made early in the collective-bargaining process is how to align employee groups for representation. For instance, all correctional employees may be represented by one labor organization, or employees may be clustered into logical groups (all correctional officers, all trade employees, all treatment staff) to be represented by a union. After the employees are grouped for representation, the group votes to elect the labor organization (the AFL-CIO; the American Federation of State, Federal and Municipal Employees; and the International Brotherhood of Teamsters are some that represent correctional workers) that will represent them in negotiations and contract management.

The election process can be extremely highly contested and difficult for both management and employees, as competing unions seek to find issues and convince staff that they can best represent their interests. One state director of corrections noted the following:

The organizing and election process was horrible. We are a large state, and our employees would end up being several thousand union members. I thought management had a really good relationship with staff, and I personally spent a lot of time with line staff whenever I visited the prisons. I know they appreciated it and respected me for my concern

(continued)

and leadership. All of a sudden, the three national unions vying to represent them were campaigning and trying to find issues to get employee attention. Since there really were no major issues regarding safety or prison management, they had to make things up. It was a personal affront to me with some of the things they came up with. I couldn't believe some of the nefarious schemes they came up with to suggest why we made certain decisions.

After selecting a representative, the parties prepare for negotiations. A major issue in negotiations regarding correctional employees concerns the role of seniority. After the contract is negotiated, each prison or community corrections office must implement and administer it. Unfortunately, there are always questions that come into dispute about the true meaning of the contract. In these instances, management can make a decision, and the union can file a grievance to argue it. A grievance is a formal complaint that the decision is not within the language or intent of the labor contract as negotiated, and it must go through a formal process for resolution. One thing is clear in a collective-bargaining environment: If either or both parties want to be confrontational and argue almost every minor contract issue, they will spend a tremendous amount of time and money to resolve their disputes.

With this background information, do you think a state should implement collective bargaining? Think of both the positives and the negatives that can come up, and remember that once the decision is made to implement, it is unlikely it can ever be taken back.

Chapter Review

SUMMARY

Many questions were asked at the beginning of this chapter regarding how prisons are managed. These include how a prison manages staff and inmates to accomplish its mission, how a greatly outnumbered staff controls potentially violent and dangerous inmates, how prisons ensure quality performance of their functions, and what role staff members play in the accomplishment of the mission. In this chapter, these questions have been addressed and hopefully answered to students' satisfaction. Prisons and their oversight agencies must first organize themselves in a way to manage the staff and resources provided to have a safe and secure environment, while offering programs that help inmates return to their communities as successful and law-abiding citizens. Since prisons have become such big businesses and use such a large percentage of state taxpayer dollars, there is much more interest from the public and elected officials in how they perform than ever before. Therefore, these agencies must organize to manage both the prison's internal and external environments.

The various methods for managing inmates have also been described. Prisons must begin with professional policies and implementation procedures, com-

municate these to staff and inmates, and consistently carry them out. Since there is a considerable difference in the methods and expense of handling maximum- and minimum-security inmates, an effective classification instrument to separate inmates by needs and risks is beneficial. Prisons must have a fair and equitable disciplinary process to punish violation of prison rules, control misbehavior, and maintain order.

Finally, this chapter describes how important correctional staff members are to the management of a prison. Prisons are sometimes referred to as a "people business," meaning that they are all about people managing other people. While prisons must have sufficient physical security, they must have well-developed and state-of-the-art policies, and they must consistently implement these policies; the accomplishment of their mission is impossible without dedicated and committed professional staff. This chapter has provided information regarding how prisons recruit, hire, and manage staff, including when a collective bargaining agreement exists between management and labor. Prisons are complex organizations and require the utmost in management and leadership.

REVIEW QUESTIONS

1. Why are entities such as public and media affairs, legislative liaison, legal advisors, and internal affairs often organizationally located in the office of the director?

2. What is the role of an inspector in a department of corrections or prison?

3. Describe the three functions of custody, treatment, and services within a prison organization.

4. What is unit management and how does it contribute to the management of a prison?

5. Why is it important to consistently implement policies and procedures within a prison?

6. What processes are used to determine whether policies and procedures within a prison are being consistently applied?

7. What is an internal classification system, and what function does it play in a prison?

8. How can a classification process assist in gaining inmate compliance?

9. Define an inmate disciplinary system.

10. List five sanctions that can be taken against inmates for failure to abide by prison rules.

11. What processes are available for inmates to appeal a disciplinary decision or seek to redress wrongs done them by prison staff?

12. Why is staff recruitment and hiring so important to the accomplishment of the mission of a prison?

13. Define collective bargaining.

ENDNOTES

1. Camille Graham Camp and George M. Camp, *The 2001 Corrections Yearbook: Adult Systems* (Middletown, Conn.: Criminal Justice Institute, 2002), pp. 79–80.

2. Ibid., pp. 83–86.

3. Ibid., pp. 74–75.

4. Ibid., pp. 3, 150, 187, 100.

5. Ibid., p. 148.

6. Ibid., pp. 87, 89, 99–100.

7. For a discussion of the history of unit management in the Bureau of Prisons, see Robert Levinson and Roy Gerard, "Functional Units: A Different Correctional Approach," *Federal Probation* 37, no. 4 (1973): 8–16.

8. Federal Bureau of Prisons, *Unit Management Manual* (Washington, D.C.: U.S. Department of Justice, Bureau of Prisons, 1977), p. 6.

9. Robert Freeman, "Management and Administrative Issues," in *Prisons: Today and Tomorrow* edited by Jocelyn M. Pollack (Gaithersburg, Md.: Aspen, 1997), p. 300.

10. E. C. Hughes, "Professions," in *The Professions in America,* edited by Kenneth S. Lynn (Boston: Houghton-Mifflin, 1965), p. 4.

11. American Correctional Association, *Standards for Adult Correctional Institutions,* 3rd ed. (Laurel, Md.: American Correctional Association, 1990), p. vii.

12. Mary Dallao, "Keeping Classification Current," *Corrections Today* 59, no. 4 (July 1997): 87.

13. Tim Brennan, "Classification for Control in Jail and Prisons," in *Prediction and Classification: Criminal Justice Decision Making,* edited by Don M. Gottfredson and Michael Tonry (Chicago: University of Chicago Press, 1987), p. 343.

14. Camp and Camp, 2002, pp. 29–30.

15. Joan Mullen, *American Prisons and Jails, Volume I: Summary and Policy Implications of a National Survey* (Washington, D.C.: U.S. Department of Justice, 1980), p. 57.

16. Federal Bureau of Prisons, "Inmate Discipline and Special Housing Units," Federal Prison System, Policy Statement #5270.07 (Washington, DC: U.S. Department of Justice, December 29, 1987), Chapter 1, p. 1.

17. Ibid., Chapter 4, p. 4.

18. Ibid., Chapter 2, p. 3.

19. Clair A. Cripe, "Inmate Disciplinary Procedures," in *Prison and Jail Administration: Practice and Theory,* edited by Peter M. Carlson and Judith Simon Garrett (Gaithersburg, Md.: Aspen, 1999), p. 214.

20. Camp and Camp, 2002, pp. 150, 219.

21. Donald Cressey, "Prison Organizations," in *Handbook of Organizations,* edited by J. March (New York: Rand McNally, 1965), p. 1024.

22. Kelsey Kauffman, *Prison Officers and Their World* (Cambridge, Mass.: Harvard University Press, 1988), p. 167.

23. John J. DiIulio, *Governing Prisons: A Comparative Study of Correctional Management* (New York: Free Press, 1987), p. 95.

24. M. Robert Montilla, *Prison Employee Unionism: Management Guide for Correctional Administrators* (Washington, D.C.: U.S. Department of Justice, National Institute of Law Enforcement and Criminal Justice, 1978), p. 2.

25. James B. Jacobs and Norma Meacham Crotty, *Guard Unions and the Future of Prisons* (Ithaca, N.Y.: Institute of Public Employment, 1978), p. 41.

26. Andrew A. Peterson, "Deterring Strikes by Public Employees: New York's Two-for-One Salary Penalty and the 1979 Prison Guard Strike," *Industrial and Labor Relations Review* 34, no. 4 (July 1981): 545–562.

27. Lynn Zimmer and James B. Jacobs, "Challenging the Taylor Law: Prison Guards on Strike," *Industrial and Labor Relations Review* 34, no. 4 (July 1981): 531–544.

Chapter 11

AFTER READING THIS CHAPTER, YOU SHOULD BE ABLE TO:

1. Describe the activities within "total institutions" that Goffman suggested make it more difficult for prisoners to successfully return to and adapt to community living.

2. Define the concept of prisonization and explain its impact on inmates both while serving a prison sentence and as they return to the community.

3. Identify many of the common prison slang terms and what they mean within a prison setting.

4. Compare the different types of violent acts that occur within prisons and the forces that increase the likelihood of violence.

5. Explain the history, development, and operation of prison gangs and identify the threat they are to operating a safe and secure prison.

6. Discuss the methods that prison staff use to identify gang members and control gang activities.

7. Specify the reasons why homosexual activities are disallowed in prisons and suggest activities that can reduce their likelihood.

8. Identify the ways that illegal drugs come into prisons and evaluate the potential of various methods to limit their availability within prisons.

9. Describe the development of women's prisons in terms of management and philosophical approaches.

10. Compare the culture of women's prisons to the culture of men's prisons.

11. Define and describe the way "pseudofamilies" function in women's prisons.

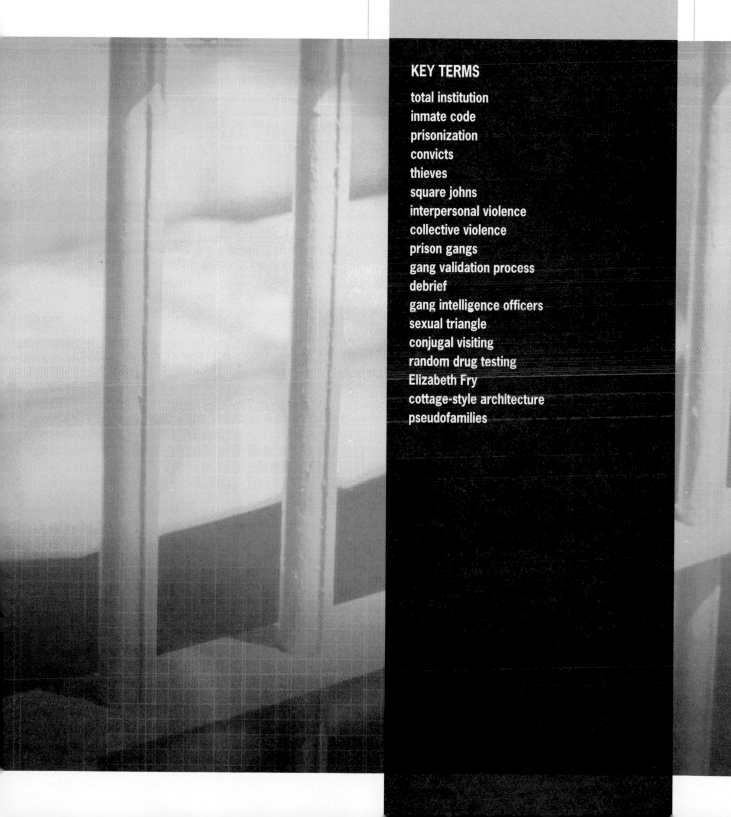

Prison Life for Inmates

KEY TERMS

total institution
inmate code
prisonization
convicts
thieves
square johns
interpersonal violence
collective violence
prison gangs
gang validation process
debrief
gang intelligence officers
sexual triangle
conjugal visiting
random drug testing
Elizabeth Fry
cottage-style architecture
pseudofamilies

Introduction

Now that we have covered the organization, functions, and models used to manage prisons, we move to a look at life for both inmates and staff within a prison environment. From the next two chapters, students will not only assimilate information and facts, they will also get a feel for what it is like to be in the closed environment of a prison; the unique relationships among inmates and between inmates and staff; and matters such as material possessions, routines, privileges, and interpersonal communications that take on much more importance in prison than in normal society. The prison world is a social realm of its own, and while it is difficult to describe to those who have not seen or experienced it, it has some structure and organization that needs to be considered and understood.

In Chapter 7, characteristics of the clients of correctional agencies were described, as well as certain activities, policies, and programs related to these characteristics. This chapter addresses the world in which inmates live and the issues of violence, inmate culture, drugs, gang activity, and homosexuality that inmates face. The chapter presents the prison environment for both male and female inmates, as institutions for each have many unique characteristics in terms of the culture, inmate relationships, and potential for violence. The male inmate's world is based more on survival, watching one's back, and getting along without creating problems that can result in assaults or other serious problems. Male inmates adapt to incarceration by isolating themselves; they try to do their time independently and avoid being involved in other inmate problems or issues. However, the existence of prison gangs often requires them to group together and protect themselves or avoid intimidation or coercion for sex or money. However, male inmates (whether in a gang or not) see these groupings only as a value for strength or financial benefit.

Female inmates, on the other hand, adjust to imprisonment by forming close relationships to other inmates, seeking relationships to provide a support structure. With less concern for personal safety than male inmates, women in prison desire a family relationship similar to what they experience outside prison, with specific roles of parent, child, or partner. They also do not mentally separate themselves from their families on the outside as men do, and their lives stay integrated into those of their outside family. The potential for abuse by staff is more of an issue with women inmates, however, and female inmate treatment programs are usually different in terms of their goals and operations than many of those in male institutions. At the end of this chapter, students should understand how inmates adapt to the culture of a prison, and how the inmate and staff structure impacts both their life in prison and influences their life when they return to outside society.

Prison Life for Male Offenders

Prisons strive to provide a balanced approach to accomplishing the multiple goals of corrections. By merely holding offenders against their will and taking away their freedoms, prisons inflict punishment. However, at the same time, they attempt to create a positive and interactive environment, providing rehabilitative programs to help offenders prepare for release and their return to their communities. However, the somewhat isolated nature of prisons through their location and separation from normal society can easily result in a punitive atmosphere in which inmates lose their identity and ability to make decisions for themselves.

In 1961, Erving Goffman, wrote of the impact a prison environment could have on those housed within the institution. Goffman described the concept of a **total institution**, a setting isolating people from the rest of society and unnecessarily manipulating them through the actions of the administrative staff.[1] He suggests

Total institution

Goffman's concept of a setting isolating people from the rest of society and unnecessarily manipulating them through the actions of the administrative staff that certain characteristics of such institutions result in isolation and inability to act for oneself:

- Staff members supervise all spheres of daily life, such as where inmates eat, work and sleep.
- The environment is highly standardized, with one set of activities for everyone.
- Rules and schedules dictate how inmates perform all aspects of their daily routine.

Prisons take on these characteristics for controlling and managing inmates' behavior, and through the use of rewards and punishments, attempt to "resocialize" inmates to a law-abiding lifestyle. However, Goffman warns that while institutions can bring about the desired change in some inmates, others become confused, hostile and bitter, and that extended periods of institutional living can actually reduce an individual's capacity for independent living.

Goffman argues that institutional activities such as making new inmates publicly strip, wear degrading striped uniforms, and shave their heads fail to resocialize inmates. Most of these actions have been recognized as problematic and have been changed in most prison systems. However, subtler, yet perhaps even more important, is the effect of the prison environment resulting from the tone set by interactions between staff and inmates. Staff are charged with consistent enforcement of rules and maintenance of control. Yet they are not to do so in a punitive or derogatory manner. This balance is sometimes difficult to carry out.

The challenge in creating and continuing positive interactions between staff and inmates is illustrated in Zimbardo's classic experiment.[2] To test the ways in

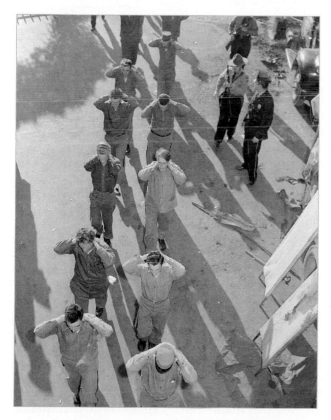

Some aspects of prison life can take away inmates' self-concept and ability to act for themselves, making a successful adjustment back to the community more difficult.
Courtesy of Corbis/Bettmann.

The experiment by Zimbardo at Stanford University illustrates how hostility can develop between staff and inmates within a prison setting.
Courtesy of Philip G. Zimbardo, Inc.

which prisons change human behavior, Zimbardo constructed a mock prison in the basement of a building at Stanford University and used students in one of his college classes to play the role of staff and inmates. Twenty-four male students were then randomly assigned to roles as either guards or prisoners. For two weeks, the prisoners were to spend time in the "Stanford County Prison," with the guards responsible for operating the prison. Soon after the experiment began, guards and prisoners became hostile toward each other; guards humiliated and yelled at prisoners, and prisoners resisted and insulted guards. The situation deteriorated to the point that after the first week, Zimbardo had to cancel the remaining week of the experiment. Zimbardo wrote that "some boys (guards) treat others as if they were despicable animals, taking pleasure in cruelty, while other boys (prisoners) became servile, dehumanized robots who thought only of escape, of their own individual survival and of their mounting hatred for the guards."[3] This experiment illustrates the type of relationship that can easily develop between staff and prison inmates; constant diligence and strong leadership by prison administrators is needed to avoid such a situation.

PRISON CULTURE AND THE INMATE CODE

To the student of corrections, nothing seems more fascinating that the formation of a separate and unique culture within prisons. For many reasons, and in a way that has changed over time, inmates construct a culture with unique values, traditions, roles, expectations, language, and customs while in prison. This culture is called the **inmate code**, the expected rules and behaviors represented by the model prisoner that reflect the values and norms of prison society. What factors influence the creation of a prison culture and inmate code, the extent to which prisonization (inmates accepting and adapting to the prison culture) occurs, and whether the inmate code still exists are topics of continued study and debate.

More than sixty years ago, Clemmer studied prisons and was one of the first to identify the special adaptation that inmates make as they spend time together in prison. He coined the term **prisonization** to describe the process by which inmates "[take] on in greater or lesser degree the folkways, mores, customs, and general culture of the penitentiary."[4] Clemmer suggested that inmates learn the behaviors of being in prison (dressing, working, new language, dependence on

Inmate code

the expected rules and behaviors represented by the model prisoner, reflecting the values and norms of prison society

Prisonization

the process whereby inmates take on the folkways, mores, customs, and general culture of the penitentiary others, degradation of status), and that this process of prisonization leads to an increased identification with criminal lifestyles and more difficulty in successfully returning and adapting to the community after release.

Over the next two decades, others who studied the effects of being in prison identified many aspects of the inmate code. The code is how those who want respect as a "con" act and behave. As a philosophy, it emphasizes loyalty to convicts and distrust of correctional officers (*hacks* or *screws*), being trustworthy, and not getting involved in other inmates' business. From the work of Sykes in the 1950s[5] and Irwin and Cressey in the 1960s,[6] several behaviors have been identified that are elements of the inmate code:

- Do your own time (don't get involved in the business of other inmates)
- Be a stand-up guy (be someone that other inmates can count on)
- Don't rat on other inmates (do not tell staff what other inmates have done or are doing—don't be a "snitch")
- Don't trust the guards (don't become overly friendly with staff, don't show them respect, and talk to them only when you have to)
- Don't exploit other inmates (don't take advantage of others or their problems or steal from them)
- Maintain dignity and respect (don't show staff a weakness and show respect to other inmates)
- Settle conflict between inmates (don't go to staff with problems between inmates, settle it yourself)
- Respect the real "cons" (the inmates who have done a lot of time, know the system, and live the inmate code deserve respect)

There are two theories on how the inmate culture becomes a part of prison life. The first is that the culture is "indigenous" to prisons; Clemmer believed that it develops as a result of the environment in which inmates find themselves. Sykes believed that the norms arise specifically in response to the deprivations and loss of liberty inherent in incarceration. The other theory is that the culture is "imported" or brought in with the values of the inmates from the outside world. Irwin and Cressey identified three types of offenders that bring characteristics to the prison setting, and the blending of these characteristics creates the prisoner subculture. **Convicts** are long-term inmates, probably beginning with youths who were in foster homes, reform schools, and then prisons. They become used to the single-sex, masculine society, and find a way to live in this environment with a minimal amount of problems and disruptions. **Thieves** have adopted a career of crime and are just doing their time in prison until they can get out and hit the "big score." **Square johns** are probably first-time offenders and have more identification with "straight" society and the norms of noncriminals.

Today, many people believe that the inmate code is dead, or at least ignored by most inmates. The older inmates talk of "young punks," inmates who are always out to exploit others, don't respect the old-timers, constantly cause trouble that brings greater supervision from staff, and use muscle and not brains to get through their prison experience. The change in adhering to the inmate culture comes from at least several developments. The first is that with a greater reliance on prison than on probation for many offenders, there are more square johns in prison, and even though they serve short sentences and turn over rapidly, they represent a larger percentage of inmates who do not adhere to the inmate culture. Second, there are many young and impulsive inmates who respect only physical power or intimidation. Finally, the fact that prisons are not as isolated as in the past undermines the solidarity and formation of the inmate code. Today, inmates talk to their family and friends on the telephone on a regular basis, they have visitors several times per

Convicts

long-term inmates who become used to the prison society and find a way to live in this environment with a minimal amount of problems and disruptions

Thieves

inmates who have adopted a career of crime and are doing their prison time until they can get out and hit the "big score"

Square johns

inmates who are usually first-time offenders and have more identification with "straight" society and the norms of noncriminals

Younger inmates don't respect the code that was followed by older inmates.
Photo by Richard P. Seiter.

The availability of telephones and other ways to communicate with the world outside prison is thought to be one of the reasons why the inmate code is dying.
Photo by Richard P. Seiter.

week, and they read newspapers and magazines and stay attuned to what is occurring in the outside world. While the inmate code has not been seen as a valued commodity by many prison staff, most staff and inmates who have been around for several years regret its demise. They feel that at least the inmate code provided an expected order, organization, and understanding of how the prison would informally work and how inmates would behave toward staff and other inmates.

As with any culture or society, a special language develops. The "A Look Into" box contains a glossary of prison terms and slang.[7]

A LOOK INTO . . .

A GLOSSARY OF PRISON SLANG

A&P	Inmate store, commissary
Bad Mammy Jammy	Good-looking female visitor
Bird bath	Taking a sponge bath in the sink in the cell
Blow	Cigarette
To blow	To get mad
Bo-hog	An inmate who bosses other inmates around and preys on weaker inmates
Bomb	Letter denying parole; also refers to rolled-up toilet paper used for cooking in a cell
Bricks	Life outside prison; a person hits the bricks when he or she leaves prison
Bull	Correctional officer or police officer
Bull sisters	A gang of predatory homosexual inmates
Bust a nut	Relief by masturbation
Buzzard	An inmate who looks out for officers on patrol
Carry a lunch pail	To hold a routine 9–5 job on the outside; something many inmates despise
Cellie	Cellmate
Convict	A tough prisoner who has proven himself in multiple encounters over the years; also referred to as a *regular, solid,* or *right guy*
Cop out	To confess; inmates claim it is unwise to cop out to anything
Crib	Inmate's bunk or cell
Crow	An inmate who watches out for officers while other inmates violate the rules
Dirty dog	Sorry, no-good inmate
Double trouble	When an inmate borrows something and must pay back twice the amount borrowed
Fishing line	Bag and rope tied together to reach something under the cell door
Free worlder	Anyone who is not an inmate
Front	To pretend to be tough
Ghetto penthouse	Top tier in the cellblock
Goon squad	Officers who dress in riot gear to quell inmate riots or extract resistant inmates from their cells
Hardcastle	Warden or any officer who acts tough
Hard stuff	Heroin or opium
Head up	One-on-one fight
Hold your mud	Not backing down in the prison setting
Hole	Isolation cell
Home boy	Inmate from your neighborhood
House	Cell
Hugging the bars	Refers to someone who wants to get out of prison quickly or doesn't want to get involved in an incident
Jamming	Fist fighting
Joint	Prison or jail
Joint converted	Inmate who finds religion
Juice	Power; an inmate who can make things happen
Keister stashed	Contraband inserted into the rectum
Kite	A letter from home, or an informant's tip to the authorities
Lowlife rouger	Someone who steals other inmates' belongings
The Man	Correctional officer
Mud water	Cell-brewed coffee
Mule	Free person who transports contraband into and out of the prison for inmates

(continued)

Off someone	To kill a person
On the Rio	Not joking, serious
P.C.	Protective custody
Peckerwood	In Georgia, refers to a white correctional officer and is an insult; in California, refers to a high-status inmate and is something to be attained
Pimp slap	Slap across the face
Pruno	Prison-made booze concocted from yeast, fruit juices, bread, or potatoes. Doesn't taste good, but does cause a buzz
Pumping iron	Lifting weights
Punk	Someone who submits sexually to a stronger inmate
Put it on ice	Don't give up information
Rabbit	Escaped inmate
Railroad	To get blamed for something you didn't do
Reruns	Inmates who return after being released
Road dog	Inmate who roams the yard looking for trouble
Screw	Correctional officer
Shank or shiv	Prison-made knife
Silent beef	Crimes suspected but not proven in court; the parole board often considers these offenses in deciding on parole
Snitch	An inmate who informs on other inmates in return for favors from the prison officials
Speeding ticket	Minor write-up, disciplinary report
Throw down	Fight
Tunk	An inmate card game
Went for a rib	Provoked an inmate into doing something

VIOLENCE IN PRISONS

As noted in Chapter 7, a large percentage of male inmates have a lengthy history of violence. In 2000, 49 percent of adults sentenced to state prisons were committed for violent offenses.[8] With such a large proportion of inmates previously involved in violent acts, it is not surprising, therefore, that violent behavior is a way of life within prisons. Many inmates just resort to violence as their normal reaction to frustration, disagreements, or lack of power. Those who are not prone to violence are constantly watchful to avoid situations that could lead to violent confrontations. Overcrowded prison conditions,[9] tensions between inmate gangs,[10] the powerlessness, boredom, and sexual frustration of inmates,[11] and the importation of street cultures of "face to face rivalries, retaliation, machismo, disrespect, and drunkenness"[12] are suggested reasons for violent acts in prisons. The simple conclusion as to why there is a high level of violence within prisons is that prisons hold violent people who act out in violent ways, and the prison culture and environment adds to the tension and threat of violence by inmates.

Hassine suggests another reason for prison violence: inmate avoidance of the reality of their incarceration. He writes,

> Violence in Graterford (a state prison in Pennsylvania) had also become a form of escape for many inmates. In creating and maintaining a predatory environment, these men were able to avoid the reality of imprisonment by focusing all their attention on fighting one another. The more hostile the environment, the more they saw themselves as victims and the less responsible they felt for their own action.[13]

With almost half of prison inmates sentenced for violent crimes, it is not surprising that violence becomes a way of life in prison.
Courtesy of Corbis Royalty Free.

In *Prison Violence in America*, Braswell, Montgomery, and Lombardo distinguish between interpersonal violence and collective violence.[14] **Interpersonal violence** occurs between two or more individual inmates, and the reason for the violence is a personal issue between the individuals. **Collective violence** is between and initiated by groups of inmates, and includes prison riots and disturbances. While collective violence is usually by inmates against prison staff and administration, large-scale gang conflicts also come under this category. Collective violence stems from the fundamental difference in values and positions of the two groups, rather than an individual conflict.

The threat of interpersonal violence causes the constant fear and tension of individual inmates in a correctional environment. Some inmates are always looking for a reason to violently act out, and others are always worried that they may be that reason. Johnson, in describing life in prison, writes,

> The convict world is populated by men who doubt their worth as human beings and who feel they must constantly find occasions to "prove" themselves . . . The convict world is a world of continuing—and generally escalating—conflict. Aggrieved parties cannot afford to back down, for then they are seen as weak and hence vulnerable to more abuse. Violence in the convict world establishes one's competence as a man who can survive in a human jungle.[15]

Terry, in *The Fellas: Overcoming Prison and Addiction*, uses interviews with inmates and ex-inmates to paint a similar view of the constant problem of violence in prisons. He notes that violence in prison is rampant and likely to continue for some time. He points out how violence occurs, even though inmates may try to avoid it. He quotes some of the "fellas" as follows:

> Doing your own time, minding your own business or staying away from trouble while serving a prison sentence . . . may be next to impossible . . .

Interpersonal violence
prison violence that occurs between two or more individual inmates; the reason for the violence is a personal issue between the individuals

Collective violence
prison violence that is between and initiated by groups of inmates; it includes prison riots and disturbances; it can be groups of inmates against staff or against one another, as this violence stems from the fundamental difference in values and positions of the two groups

what it comes down to is this—I don't care how much you try to stay out of it—nowadays, as crazy as it is, you're gonna be involved some way, some how.[16]

After experiencing an increasing level of violence within federal prisons, officials attempted to identify the types of inmates more likely to commit violent acts. Innes and Verdeyen write that there are three general categories of inmates who resort to violence:

1. *Anti-social offenders* have developed the habit of using force and coercion to get what they want. This group has used violence on the streets, and while they have the competencies and skills to act in prosocial ways, they have found that violence works successfully for them.
2. *Special-needs offenders* are those with physical or mental deficiencies. As a result of their impairments, they are unable to function satisfactorily in a prison environment, and often react to situations violently.
3. *Psychopathic offenders* are predatory, cold, and calculating, and usually act violently for no good reason. They do not feel compassion, and will be violent simply for their own enjoyment.[17]

Male inmates live in an environment with the constant threat and potential for violence. Not only are there a lot of violent people in prison, but the environment and culture creates a breeding ground for violence, with the need to act tough and not back down, prevalence of gang members and gang activities, pressure for homosexual sex from some inmates, and conflicts that result from the sale and use of drugs. Unfortunately, violence in prisons, especially in high-security prisons, is a common event. There are days without fights or serious assaults, but a prison administrator with his or her eyes open and an understanding of the environment knows that inmates are pressured and extorted every day. Prisons are full of individuals who have lived their lives violently and try to intimidate others to get what they want. It is not possible for prison administrators to stop all this from happening; their focus is (1) to provide a situation that allows inmates to protect themselves (in nonviolent ways and using legitimate means) and (2) to do everything possible to isolate the predators from potential victims.

GANGS IN PRISONS

Prison gangs not only are disruptive within a prison environment; they also contribute greatly to acts of violence and the resulting tension. Gang members stick together to intimidate other inmates, control drug sales and prostitution, and gain power and influence. In a study of the relationship between gang affiliation and violent acts in federal prisons, researchers found that both specific and generic gang indicators were statistically related to violence and misconduct,[18] and concluded that controlling gang activities has great potential to reduce tension and violence within prisons.

Prison gangs

groups that form in prison and use the threat of violence to intimidate other inmates, control drug sales and prostitution, and gain power and influence

Prison gangs were first identified in California in the early 1960s, when prison administrators realized that many of their problems—violence, intimidation of staff and inmates, and introduction of drugs—were being controlled and coordinated by organized groups of inmates. A Department of Justice report on the early development of gangs and their prison activities notes, "Their organization was so firmly entrenched (in California) before authorities understood the danger confronting them that control of the institutions was seriously threatened. This phenomenon has been repeated in numerous jurisdictions as the presence and influence of gangs has spread throughout the country."[19]

The existence of prison gangs results in intimidation of staff and inmates and leads to tension and violence within prisons.
Photo by A. Ramey/PhotoEdit.

Since that time, prison gangs have continued to grow in number and influence in the nations' prisons. A national survey in 1985 identified more than a hundred gangs, with a total membership of approximately 13,000.[20] An American Correctional Association 1993 survey identified thirty-nine different, major gangs in the nation's prisons, and estimated that 6 percent of prisoners were members of a gang.[21] In 2001, state and federal correctional agencies reported a total of 65,183 gang members in prisons, making up 5.1 percent of the prison population.[22]

Gang members in prisons usually have a more extensive history of crime than non–gang members, get in more trouble in prison, participate in fewer prison programs, and are more likely to have a substance abuse problem.[23] Several authors suggest that gangs are a natural outgrowth of large groups of criminals placed together in a prison setting. Scott suggests, "The prison gang, as both a process and an organization, facilitates the adaptation of inmates to life in the prison and, more locally, the cell block."[24] Sykes, describing the prison environment in the 1950s, noted that inmates find ways to cope with their confinement and the deprivations they encounter.[25] However, other authors describe gangs as more hedonistic than social phenomena, and note that through money and power, gang members can avoid the deprivation of property, freedom, and influence that a prison tries to accomplish. Fleisher and Decker suggest, "Motivated by a desire to make money and be at the top of an institution's inmate power structure, prison gangs exploit the inherent weaknesses resulting from overcrowded, understaffed mega-prisons."[26]

Fortunately, correctional agencies have gained sophistication in understanding prison gangs, and much more is currently known about their operations, membership, and organization. In an issue of *Correctional Management Quarterly* devoted entirely to the threat of prison gangs, Seiter writes, "Correctional administrators can never hesitate, stop gathering intelligence, or fail to stay ahead of the gangs' operations . . . For the individual correctional staff involved, their will to further the correctional mission—to provide a safe environment for staff and inmates—cannot waiver."[27]

Many prison gangs started as an extension of street gangs. When such groups as Bloods and Crips found that many of their street gang members ended up in prison, it was only natural that they continue their criminal activities while recruiting membership, intimidating other inmates, and attempting to control the drug dealing in prison. Other gangs, such as the Mexican Mafia, Dirty White Boys, and Black Guerilla Family, originated in prison as ethnic and racial groups of inmates began to band together for strength and support. They discovered that such alliances could lead to control over other prisoners, create funds, and provide members power to gain advantages in prison they might otherwise not have. The following list describes some of the current major prison gangs.

- *Aryan Brotherhood (AB):* The Aryan Brotherhood started in 1967 in San Quentin Prison, is limited to Caucasians, and is a Nazi-oriented, antiblack gang that dislikes authority and adheres to violence to gain prestige. They have no hesitancy to kill to keep their membership and organization secure, and once had a rule of "making one's bones" to get in, meaning that prospective members had to kill for the gang to show their worth. It was also said that the only way to get out of the gang was to die. The AB has been aligned with many street motorcycle gangs and has extensive prison and street networks for dealing drugs. They also have alliances with other white supremacist gangs to gain numbers and power in prison. They have (from time to time) had an association with the Mexican Mafia to expand their drug dealing and ability to perform contract killings.

- *Mexican Mafia (MM):* The Mexican Mafia is a Hispanic gang that requires members to take an oath of "blood in, blood out," meaning that prospective members must assault someone for the gang to prove themselves, and are badly beaten or even killed to get out of the gang. It originated in the Deuel Vocational Institution (California) in 1958; it has since become one of the most powerful prison gangs in the country. Having no underlying political views, the gang is focused on committing crimes to support its members in prison. The leaders organize the entire criminal activity and often rob banks to gain funds to support their prison activities.

- *Black Guerilla Family (BGF):* The Black Guerilla Family also started in San Quentin Prison, and its first leader was George Jackson, the Black Panther who was killed in a 1971 escape attempt. They follow a politically charged revolutionary philosophy, intent on destruction of the "white establishment" and overthrow of the government. They hope to coalesce all black inmates so they can "control their own destiny."

- *La Nuestra Familia (NF):* The NF ("our family") was established in the late 1960s in Soledad Prison (California), primarily by Chicano inmates from Northern California, to protect themselves from the Southern California–based Mexican Mafia. They have been at war with the Mexican Mafia (and the Aryan Brotherhood) for most of their existence, but more recently have tried to have a peace agreement. In their battles against these two gangs, they often will form an alliance with the Black Guerilla Family. A board of directors, known as *La Mesa,* controls them. Rank in the gang depends on the number of killings accomplished for the gang.

- *Mexikanemi (EME):* This gang, also known as the Texas Mexican Mafia, started in the Texas prison system in 1984. They have spread rapidly in federal prisons across the country and are also in other southwestern states. Gang members are very violent and kill enemies in and outside of prison. They usually act alone, but have aligned with the Texas Syndicate to fight the Mexican Mafia. They also are organized in military fashion with generals, lieutenants, sergeants, and soldiers. Members work their way up the organization within the prison they are in, and are elected to positions based on their leadership. If transferred to another prison, they lose their rank unless re-elected there.

■ *Texas Syndicate (TS):* This is another California-originated prison gang, started by inmates who had migrated to California from Texas. Instead of joining one of the two California Hispanic gangs, they formed their own to maintain their Texas heritage and band together to protect Texas inmates from other gangs. The TS is well organized and has a national president, with appointed chairmen at each prison. There are vice-chairmen, captains, lieutenants, sergeants at arms, and soldiers. When the early gang members were released from California prisons, they returned to Texas and established the TS in Texas and other southwestern prisons. Their primary agenda is drug trafficking and selling protection to other inmates. They have a reputation for violence and are feared by other inmates.

Prison Gang Control Strategies

In order to control the activities and violence of gangs, correctional staff focus on a variety of strategies. These include early detection of gang activities, identification of leaders and members, surveillance of gang activity, denial of gang turf or wearing of gang colors and symbols, and a variety of gang control tactics. Lesce identifies six measures to control prison gangs:

1. Transferring gang members to maximum-security prisons
2. Limiting inmates' access to money, which often plays a critical role in inmates' underground economy
3. Placing the most violence-prone gang members in special facilities
4. Developing gang intelligence
5. Recruiting informers
6. Observing inmates' daily routine activities to identify patterns of activities and associations of gang members[28]

The most important action that prison staff can take to control gangs is early detection of gang activities. Correctional staff are informed of gangs' organization, activities, and known membership at a prison, and are asked to report any intelligence regarding gang member activities. In order to identify gang leaders and other members, correctional agencies collect and maintain detailed records of gang membership, often divided into leaders, hard-core members, and marginal members.[29] Other terms to identify levels of gang involvement are *member, associate,* or *suspect.* A **gang validation process** requiring several identifiers of gang activity is used to confirm individuals' gang involvement level. Five or six different items are needed to validate an inmate as a "member," three or four items may substantiate an inmate as an "associate," and one or two identify an inmate as just a "suspect." Gang validation identifiers include inmate self-admission that he or she is a gang member; information from a presentence investigation report that the inmate has participated in street gang activities; confiscated gang documents such as membership lists, photographs, or correspondence from other gang members; violation of prison rules that indicates involvement in gang activities such as drug trafficking, gambling, extortion, or strong-arming other inmates; involvement with known gang members; or tattoos indicating gang signs.[30]

The next gang control strategy is surveillance of gang activities. After gang members are identified, their activities are closely monitored and recorded. The

Gang validation process determination of the number of identifiers of gang activity; used to confirm an individual's gang involvement level

National Major Gang Task Force of the U.S. Department of Justice recommends the following actions to monitor gang members:

- *Posted picture file:* A centralized photo and data file on significant gang members, suspects, and associates.
- *Confidential reports:* All staff report gang-related grouping activity on the daily confidential reports.
- *Gang communications:* There should be a priority with prison staff to intercept notes passed between gang members.
- *Identify gang visitors:* Visitors of gang members should be identified and their names shared with other prisons. There are often visitors of gang inmates at multiple institutions who pass along gang information and "hit contracts."
- *Gang control efforts:* Staff should watch for efforts by gangs to dominate any physical area of the institution or access to any inmate program.[31]

Another important activity to control prison gangs is to keep them from showing their power. Gangs like to show their strength to recruit members, tout themselves as controlling activities or areas, and show willingness to be violent against their enemies. To do this, gangs try to flaunt colors, hand signs, and symbols; wear clothing a certain way; and stake out turf. Prison staff need to be aware of the meaning of the different signs or colors, and prohibit inmates from wearing or showing them.

Some jurisdictions, once they identify inmates as gang members, isolate them by moving them either to a high-security prison or to a supermax prison in lockdown status. The Federal Bureau of Prisons policy requires that validated members (not associates or suspects) be assigned to a maximum-security prison. In the early 1990s, Connecticut developed a unique gang control strategy (now used by many other states), in which they moved gang members and leaders to a high-security prison in lockdown status, similar to disciplinary segregation or a supermax prison. The only way for members to get out of the lockdown situation is to

Gang members like to flaunt their power by showing displays of membership and group strength, such as tattoos, hand signs, staking out turf, or wearing clothes a certain way.
Photo by Mark Richards/PhotoEdit.

YOUR CAREER IN CORRECTIONS   GANG INTELLIGENCE OFFICERS

For students who like the idea of working in a prison, are fascinated with investigative strategies, and are challenged by the idea of trying to keep ahead of the "bad guys," gang intelligence officer might just be the job to have. Most prisons and large correctional agencies have staff who act as **gang intelligence officers** (the title varies by jurisdiction). These staff members collect intelligence and advise administrators regarding strategies to manage and contain prison gang activity. As prisons have implemented gang control strategies, gangs are increasingly becoming more secret and try to hide their illegal and strong-arm tactics from detection. Prisons do not specifically recruit and hire gang intelligence officers, but select promising individuals from their internal employee ranks and train them for these jobs. The positions are usually midlevel managers in the prison security departments, but act rather independently, as they are not in the traditional chain of command.

The primary function of gang intelligence officers is to collect and organize intelligence regarding gang activities and members. First, officers train prison staff regarding the types of behavior, dress, or other activities that could indicate gang functioning and how to report it to be included as intelligence information. Second, officers organize the information they collect to identify specific gangs and specific individuals that may be involved in the gang. Third, officers use this information to designate individuals as gang members, associates, or suspects. Once gang members are identified, staff can pay particular attention to the activities and associations of these inmates. Finally, gang intelligence officers use this information to anticipate gang activities and proactively move to thwart their implementation.

The second function served by gang intelligence officers is the development of comprehensive gang control strategies. The information they gather can be used for control or discovery of gang activities by individuals or small numbers of gang members. It can also be used to develop broader strategies that may be implemented agency-wide to subvert the formation and illegal behavior of gangs. For instance, states such as Connecticut and California have decided to place all identified gang members in a lockdown situation and not let them off lockdown unless they debrief by telling officers all that they know about the gang, its operations, and its members and leaders. Gang intelligence officers, through their experience and knowledge, are the key staff members who develop such strategies to control gang activities to make prison safe for other inmates and staff.

Gang intelligence officers
prison staff charged with collecting intelligence and advising administrators regarding strategies to manage and contain prison gang activity

renounce their membership and **debrief** or tell correctional officials everything they know about the gang operations and membership. Once inmates debrief, they can never be accepted back into the gang, and in fact, become an enemy of the gang.

Gangs are a danger to staff and other inmates within a prison, and correctional staff spend considerable time and effort to identify gang members and control their activity. If they do not, the gangs gain power, other inmates feel compelled to join a gang for their own protection, and prisons become a "war zone" rather than a secure and safe place in which inmates who desire to participate in self-improvement programs can do so. To break the cycle of crime and have any chance of returning prisoners to their communities as law-abiding citizens, prisons must control gang activities and limit potential violence. The "Your Career in Corrections" box describes the role of gang intelligence officers.

Debrief
to tell correctional officials everything a gang member knows about the gang operations and membership. Once inmates debrief, they become an enemy of the gang

HOMOSEXUAL BEHAVIOR IN MALE PRISONS

A problem that results from the operation of any single-sex prison is homosexual behavior, whether forced or consensual. It is difficult to identify the actual amount of homosexual activity in prisons, as inmates are hesitant to admit such involvement, and therefore staff are not aware of the full extent of involvement. A well-designed study by the federal prison system in the early 1980s surveyed more than three-hundred inmates regarding their sexual activity in prison and found that more than 30 percent admitted some type of homosexual experience.[32] However, less than 1 percent admitted that they were forced into such activities, and 7 percent stated that inmates who were nice to them or gave them gifts later seduced them.

All prisons have a rule against any type of sexual behavior between inmates, and if caught, inmates are punished for even consensual homosexual acts. Even though homosexual relationships are accepted in society, they are still not allowed in prisons, because there is no way to ensure that relationships are really consensual. A stronger inmate may actually be forcing a weaker inmate to have sex, while threatening to have him beaten or killed if he tells correctional staff about it. As well, many fights and stabbings in prisons result from **sexual triangles** in which two inmates become jealous and fight over another one. Most inmates who admit homosexual relationships while in prison state that they are heterosexual, but due to long periods of sexual deprivation, get involved in homosexual activity as a sexual release.

Prisons do have a problem with forced sex acts or rape. While some rapes are strictly for sexual gratification, Hassine reports that most sexual assaults (rapes) in prison are committed to "generate fear and to maintain power over the general population."[33] The most likely targets of such assaults are inmates who are young, physically small, and seen as weak and easily intimidated.[34] Inmates often watch for the newly arrived inmates ("fish") to identify likely targets of sexual aggression, and then take advantage of them while they are feeling alone and do not yet understand the avenues they can take to protect themselves from assault. These inmates are led to believe that they can later report this sexual pressure and be protected by staff.

In order to try to reduce the number of sexual assaults in prisons, correctional staff take several preventive as well as reactionary measures. First, they advise inmates during the reception process that sexual assault is a possibility and that they have the option of telling staff and being separated from the aggressors. Second, staff watch for signs of such aggressive acts and question potential targets about such pressure. Finally, staff investigate every allegation of sexual pressure or assault and will separate the inmates from one another as a precautionary measure. Even though most allegations cannot be proved because they become one inmate's word against another's, if staff fail to act to protect victims once brought to their attention, they could be held legally liable for injury or psychological trauma that later results.

One controversial approach to reducing the degree of homosexual activity in prison is to allow **conjugal visiting**, sometimes referred to as family visiting. Conjugal visiting is private visiting between inmates and their spouses, and it is expected that they will engage in sexual relations. In 2001, only six states (California, Connecticut, Mississippi, New Mexico, New York, and Washington) permitted conjugal visiting.[35] Supporters of conjugal visiting argue that it provides a normal release of sexual tension, is an incentive for good behavior as only inmates with good records earn such a visit, and reduces homosexual activity in prison. Opponents believe it can only be provided to a small number of inmates and therefore has little impact on homosexual activity. As well, it creates issues such as discriminating against inmates who are not legally married, and degrades women in that the visit becomes more sexually oriented than family- or social-oriented. There are many arguments for and against implementing conjugal visiting. In the "You Make the Decision" box, you have to decide regarding its implementation.

Sexual triangle

the relationship that exists when two inmates become jealous and fight over another inmate

Conjugal visiting

sometimes referred to as family visiting; private visiting opportunities between inmates and their spouses, where it is expected that they will engage in sexual relations

As noted previously, there are several pros and cons regarding conjugal visiting. When I worked for the Federal Bureau of Prisons (BOP), it became a heavy topic of discussion during the Carter administration, when the deputy attorney general (number two in command in the Department of Justice) was in favor of conjugal visiting for the BOP, and asked then-director Norman Carlson to consider it. The BOP had always taken the approach that conjugal visiting in prisons was not a normal situation, and the BOP would rather extensively use furlough programs to allow inmates to earn the privilege of going home for a weekend to have a more natural setting and time for a relationship with their spouse. There was also the concern that since only married inmates were allowed conjugal visits in states, it would discriminate against unmarried and homosexual inmates, and that there would likely be "jailhouse" marriages (those done out of convenience rather than for a long-term loving situation) just to get the chance for conjugal visits.

However, the deputy attorney general countered that the BOP often expressed concern for the level of violence in prisons, and it was accepted fact that a certain degree of violence resulted from forced homosexual activities and fights between sexual triangles. It was difficult to counter the bosses' argument, but the leadership of the BOP was against their implementation. Before the study was completed, there was a change in leadership in the Department of Justice, and the deputy left his position. The BOP did not pursue the issue with his replacement, and it was never raised again.

Consider what you think are the pros and cons of conjugal visiting. Try to also imagine the logistical problems that would be encountered by the implementation of such a program. Then decide, either by yourself or in a small classroom group, whether you favor or oppose the implementation of conjugal visiting.

DRUGS IN PRISONS

There are thousands of drug offenders in state and federal prisons, and a high proportion of inmates have a history of drug or alcohol abuse. The Bureau of Justice Statistics reported that in 2000, an estimated 57 percent of federal inmates and 21 percent of state inmates were serving a sentence for a drug offense.[36] The 2001 edition of the *Sourcebook of Criminal Justice Statistics* reports that more than 210,000 prisoners were serving a sentence for which their most serious offense was a drug law violation.[37] Data for 1997 indicated that 32.6 percent of state inmates and 22.4 percent of federal inmates (see Table 11.1) were under the influence of drugs at the time of their offense, and 80 percent of state prisoners and 70 percent of federal prisoners reported past drug use.[38] Therefore, as expected, drug use is a serious problem in the nation's prisons.

Prison inmates are always scheming and finding avenues to bring drugs into prisons. They look for opportunities through the mail, by bribing or paying staff to bring in drugs, by getting their visitors to bring in drugs, and through any other weakness they discover in a prison's security procedures. Once the drugs are inside, inmates sell them at a tremendous profit. The price of drugs depends on their availability, and when prison officials are doing a good job of keeping drugs out of prison, the price gets very high and inmates get much more desperate for ways to bring drugs into prisons. Money is not allowed in prison, so inmate sellers require their buyers to get family or friends to pay the seller's outside contact. If payment is not made, violence usually results. Because of the opportunity for huge profits, prison gangs usually try to control the drug trade. Dealing drugs in prison perfectly fits the gangs' desires to make money, have power, and use violence to enforce payment of debts.

TABLE	11.1	Level of Prior Drug Abuse by Selected Characteristics of State and Federal Prisoners, 1997

		Percent of prisoners reporting use of drugs			
Characteristic	Estimated number of prisoners[a]	Ever in the past	Used regularly[b]	In the month prior to offense	At the time of offense
All state prisoners	1,059,607	83.0%	69.6%	56.5%	32.6%
Sex					
Male	993,365	82.9%	69.3%	56.1%	32.1%
Female	66,242	84.0	73.6	62.4	40.4
Race/Hispanic origin					
White non-Hispanic	352,864	83.6%	70.5%	55.2%	33.9%
Black non-Hispanic	492,676	83.7	70.5	58.3	31.9
Hispanic	179,998	80.7	65.6	55.0	33.0
Other	34,069	79.0	66.7	52.7	27.8
Age					
24 or younger	209,343	84.1%	71.1%	63.2%	33.3%
25–34	404,034	86.4	72.9	60.0	35.0
35–44	311,999	86.3	73.4	56.5	34.5
45–54	103,470	70.5	55.2	40.4	22.7
55 or older	30,761	39.0	24.3	18.4	9.7
All federal prisoners	89,072	72.9%	57.3%	44.8%	22.4%
Sex					
Male	82,646	73.7%	58.1%	45.4%	22.7%
Female	6,426	62.8	47.2	36.7	19.3
Race/Hispanic origin					
White non-Hispanic	26,616	77.2%	63.5%	49.4%	28.6%
Black non-Hispanic	33,697	77.5	61.9	47.2	22.2
Hispanic	24,349	63.5	45.5	37.5	16.9
Other	4,411	64.2	50.0	38.5	18.1
Age					
24 or younger	7,933	80.4%	65.4%	57.2%	28.1%
25–34	32,634	76.0	60.6	48.5	23.0
35–44	27,259	77.2	60.6	46.8	24.7
45–54	14,501	67.6	52.5	35.2	18.8
55 or older	6,746	43.6	28.6	24.3	11.8

[a]Based on probability of selection in the sample and adjusted to June 30, 1997, custody counts.

[b]Regular use is defined as once a week or more for at least a month.

Source: Christopher J. Mumola, *Substance Abuse and Treatment, State and Federal Prisoners, 1997* (Washington, D.C.: U.S. Department of Justice, Office of Justice Programs, January 1999), p. 7.

Random drug testing

randomly selecting a percentage of inmates to urine test to see whether they have used any drug recently; a good deterrent to and source of data about prisoner drug use

Prisons attempt to reduce the use of drugs in several ways. First, they try to keep drugs from being brought into the prison by visitors or staff. Inmates are stripped and searched when they leave any contact visit, and mail and packages are checked for contraband before they are given to inmates. In addition, 23 percent of the states conduct random "frisking" of staff.[39] Second, prison staff continually search within the prison, especially inmates' cells and other living areas. Finally, the federal prison system and forty-nine states do **random drug testing** of inmates for drug use, and all do testing if an inmate exhibits traits of being under the influ-

Random drug tests, in which inmate urine is sent to a lab to be tested, are a good way to deter and detect the use of drugs in prison.
Photo by Richard P. Seiter.

ence of drugs. Most agencies test between 5 percent and 10 percent of all inmates monthly, and nine jurisdictions do random testing weekly.[40] For the forty-three state and federal jurisdictions reporting data on these drug tests, more than 2 million tests were completed during 2000, and 3.1 percent of the tests were positive for drug use.[41]

Prisons also provide drug and other substance abuse programs. Chapter 13 describes the types of treatment programs provided in prisons. Substance abuse is an important program, in light of the high number and percentage of inmates with prior drug use. Table 11.2 indicates the percentage of inmates who have participated in drug treatment and other types of drug abuse programs since their admission to prison. Unfortunately, the need for drug treatment far exceeds the provision. Since 1991 until 1997, the percentage of state inmates receiving drug treatment declined from 24.5 percent to 9.7 percent, and the percentage of federal inmates receiving drug treatment also declined from 15.7 percent to 9.2 percent.

THE FUNCTION OF HUMOR IN PRISON

One interesting note regarding prison life for inmates is the function of humor. Professor Charles Terry of Saint Louis University, who served lengthy prison sentences in both California and Oregon, writes regarding the use of humor by inmates to negotiate the gap between a normal and a convict identity.[42] Sociologists have used humor to study the cultures of various societies for years, yet its importance in the inmate culture has been less a focus of analysis. Other authors have described how humor in prisons is unique to that environment. Goffman has described inmates' use of humorous "sad tales" to account for their problemed past and reasons for failure.[43] Ungar builds on the use of humor in telling sad tales in describing inmates' use of "self-mockery."[44] And Terry suggests that inmates regularly use humor to "denigrate the system" and blame it for the conditions in which inmates find themselves.

TABLE	11.2	Drug Treatment Percentages of State and Federal Prisoners since Admission, 1991 and 1997

			Percent of prisoners reporting participation							
	Estimated number of prisoners, 1997		Drug treatment since admission				Other drug abuse program since admission			
			State		Federal		State		Federal	
Level of prior drug use	State	Federal	1997	1991	1997	1991	1997	1991	1997	1991
All prisoners	1,048,752	87,720	9.7%	24.5%	9.2%	15.7%	20.3%	15.5%	20.0%	10.1%
Prisoners who used drugs										
Ever	870,558	63,979	11.5%	31.1%	12.4%	26.3%	24.0%	19.6%	26.0%	16.9%
Regularly*	729,578	50,244	13.1	33.9	14.5	30.9	26.4	22.2	29.6	20.1
In the month before offense	592,611	39,275	14.6	36.5	15.4	33.7	28.3	23.7	31.7	22.0
At the time of offense	338,481	19,507	18.0	41.0	18.9	39.4	32.2	27.2	38.0	25.4

*Regular use is defined as once a week for at least a month.

Source: Christopher J. Mumola, *Substance Abuse and Treatment, State and Federal Prisoners, 1997*, (Washington, D.C.: U.S. Department of Justice, Office of Justice Programs, January 1999), p. 10.

Humor in prison serves many purposes. Male inmates live in an environment that makes it difficult to express their true feelings, as they constantly have to show masculinity and toughness. Through humor, they have the opportunity to show real human feelings without showing vulnerability. And, oddly enough, humor allows inmates to achieve control. Terry notes that this is accomplished in two ways:

> It is the only social mechanism within the prison environment that allows feelings to be expressed and authorities cannot control its expression . . . It (humor) acts as proof of their power and their release from domination.[45]

The world in which inmates live is very different from the world of normal society in many ways, yet in a few ways is very similar. Humor in prison, just as in society, lets one convey a sad story in a way that does not show weakness. It allows inmates, just as in society, to put oneself down, both to make others laugh and to make an excuse for certain conditions or lack of success. Yet humor in prison is in some ways a chance to get back at the correctional staff who control inmates' lives in almost every way. By laughing, perhaps much louder and longer than the story or joke deserves, in front of correctional staff, inmates in some ways think that they are annoying staff or showing that their imprisonment won't dampen their spirits. Humor is one legitimate way inmates can show staff that while their actions are controlled, their emotions are not.

All of the activities related to crimes, prison culture, gang membership, and homosexuality are different for male offenders than for female offenders. The next section describes the parallel profiles of women who commit crimes and go to prison. While they have several similar issues, there are varying ways that female prisoners group together, look for emotional support, deal with and shape the prison culture, and participate in programs and attempt to prepare for return to the community.

Prison Life for Female Offenders

In many ways, women's prisons have many of the same situations, issues, and relationships as those in male prisons. The history of women's prisons is very similar to that of men's prisons; however, there was a lag time of several decades before reforms spread from men's to women's prisons. Much of that was due to the gender-related policies that resulted in operating women's prisons to reinforce gender stereotypes by providing programming to prepare women for domestic housekeeping and parenting roles. It was more than seventy-five years after the invention of the prison in America before the first separate women's facility was opened. And it was almost another century before women received vocational training in areas other than cooking, sewing, and cleaning. However, modern prison environments for women have caught up to some extent. Facilities for both men and women are similar, there is drug abuse and homosexuality in prisons for both sexes, and prisons are not the best situation for preparing to return to the community.

THE HISTORY OF WOMEN'S PRISONS

Male and female offenders were housed in the same facilities in early American jails. Although women were separated in different cells, the institutions were not designed to provide specific security or programs to meet the special needs of female offenders. Both male and female prisoners were under the supervision of male staff, and it was not uncommon for female prisoners to be raped by their

Elizabeth Fry was a Quaker who formed the Ladies Society for Promoting the Reformation of Female Prisoners in 1816.
Courtesy of Hulton Archive/Getty Images.

guards. The need to separate male and female offenders was a concern of the Quakers, who devised and opened the first prison in a portion of the Walnut Street Jail in the late 1700s, and women were then housed in a separate section. However, while male inmates were housed in single cells and kept separate from other male inmates, female inmates did not receive the same separation, and were housed together in large cells within the jail.[46]

Over the next several decades, it was recognized that female prisoners should be housed and dealt with separately. The first of these reforms for female prisoners was prompted by an English woman named **Elizabeth Fry**, a Quaker who formed the Ladies Society for Promoting the Reformation of Female Prisoners in 1816, and tried to convince officials that the "special" needs of women required hiring female guards and making other reforms.[47] Her efforts finally resulted in Parliament's passing three of Fry's requests, but not until some thirty years after she made them. The suggestions included (1) segregation of prisoners by sex; (2) using female guards to supervise female prisoners; and (3) decreasing the amount of hard labor required of female prisoners.[48] Soon after Parliament passed these acts, the first prison for housing only female offenders was opened in England.

Fry traveled to the United States and pushed for similar reforms for female prisoners there as well. Partly as a result of her efforts, the New York House of Refuge was opened in 1825 with a totally separate building to house female juvenile offenders, who were to be supervised by female staff. A major step forward in the treatment of female offenders occurred in 1863, when Zebulon Brockway, then superintendent of the Detroit House of Correction, opened a separate unit for women and hired women as guards or matrons. Brockway also divided the inmates into small family groups, used the matrons as role models for the women, and pro-

Elizabeth Fry

a Quaker who formed the Ladies Society for Promoting the Reformation of Female Prisoners in 1816 and tried to convince officials that female prisoners should be separated from male prisoners and that female guards should be hired to supervise them

The Federal Reformatory for Women, opened in 1927, was one of the first prisons created for women, and originally had no fence or other perimeter security.
Courtesy of the Federal Bureau of Prisons.

vided domestic training.[49] He used the concepts of the reformatory movement described in Chapter 1 in creating programs for women. The emphasis was on education and training, in order to prepare inmates for release and successful return to society.

The reformatory model continued for women (as well as for youthful male offenders) for the next hundred years, and continues today for many women's prisons.[50] The Indiana Reformatory for Women and Girls, opened in 1873, was the first separate state prison for women. Soon thereafter, Massachusetts and New York opened reformatories for women, and other states gradually followed their lead and had totally separate facilities for female prisoners.

The design of the reformatories for women was different than prisons for men; it used a **cottage-style architecture**, with several small housing units holding approximately thirty inmates, and each cottage including kitchens, living rooms, and sometimes nurseries for inmates with children. The design was created as a basis to train women prisoners in the female role of domesticity, through vocational training in cooking, sewing, and cleaning.[51] These types of prisons for women continued into the middle of the twentieth century, when the continuation of promoting gender stereotypes in vocational training and the management of women's prisons was questioned, although some authors suggest that these gender stereotypes continued to influence the operation of women's prisons even into the 1980s.[52]

Over the past twenty years, women's prisons have begun to look like and be operated in a manner very similar to men's prisons. The cottage design is no longer used, although campus-style prisons (for both men and women) have housing buildings separate from other program and service buildings. Physical security has increased as well. Many early women's reformatories did not have a secure fence to keep inmates from escaping, relying instead on the inmates' being trustworthy and not a risk to the community if they did escape. Today, prisons for women have the same perimeter security, with fences, razor ribbon, and electronic detection devices to reduce escape attempts. Modern women's prisons also are built with program space to accommodate nontraditional vocational training programs such as carpentry and electronics. They also include special housing units to separate and manage disorderly and potentially violent inmates from the remainder of the population. The "An Insider's Experience" box describes the challenges faced when attempting to modernize a women's prison based on the traditional methods of managing female prisoners.

Cottage-style architecture

a style of prison design used for early women's prisons, with several small housing units holding approximately thirty inmates, including kitchens, living rooms, and sometimes nurseries for inmates with children.

AN INSIDER'S EXPERIENCE: Changing a Women's Prison

When I arrived in Ohio as director of the Ohio Department of Rehabilitation and Correction, one surprising aspect was the operation of the Ohio Reformatory for Women (ORW), the only Ohio prison for women. The prison operated on a 1950s correctional model, and it was treated as almost exempt from the department policies that governed the men's prisons. First, because the state had only one women's prison, all levels of security were housed together and the prison had no perimeter fence, although many of the inmates were classified as greater than minimum security. To make up for the lack of a perimeter fence, there was a very rigid method of inmate movement, and inmates were closely supervised during movements across the prison compound. Second, the vocational training

(continued)

programs were "traditional" for women, and included sewing and hairdressing. Third, there was a nursery, and babies born of prisoners were kept there for several weeks with other inmates acting as "nannies." Finally, male staff were not allowed to supervise any inmates. No male correctional officers worked in the housing units, and male maintenance staff were not allowed to have inmate work crews. They had to do all the work by themselves, although a bus of male inmates from a nearby prison came every day to help do some of the jobs that were considered "man's work." I recognized that while the prison was well managed and the prison staff very competent, several advantages (both in resource use and in inmate programs and services) would result from modernization of the prison.

We changed the prison in several ways. First, we had to show the staff that things could be done a different way. The warden was a wonderful woman who had worked at the prison for more than forty years and had been warden for more than twenty years. In fact, when she started work there, many staff lived on the grounds of the prison. The warden had lived there, and inmates even were used to watch the staff members' children during the day. Promotions always came from within ORW, and very few (if any) staff had worked in any other prisons; they knew nothing other than the ORW way. We began to transfer some staff in from other prisons, and encouraged ORW staff to visit other prisons. When the warden retired, I replaced her with an experienced administrator who had never worked at ORW, had been a warden at a men's prison, and had been a headquarters administrator and was responsible for implementing management changes within the department. However, when he became the first male warden of ORW, I took a lot of heat from women's groups and from the wife of the Ohio governor. I had expected some of this and cleared it with the governor first, noting that I would soon (within three months) be appointing the first two female wardens of Ohio men's prisons. I intended to break the traditions at both men's and women's prisons.

Second, ORW had been managed in a very autocratic way, and the warden had to be consulted on almost every decision. We implemented unit management (described in Chapter 10) as a way to decentralize decision making and inmate management. Three of the four new unit managers selected were from outside ORW. Third, we built a new prison industry building and implemented nontraditional work and vocational programs. We needed a new dormitory because of the inmate growth, and built a state-of-the-art building with cells and operating procedures that were just like those in the men's housing units. Inmates were classified by security level and placed in appropriate housing.

Next, we built a perimeter fence and upgraded security while encouraging prison management to relax some of the control of inmate movement within the perimeter. With the secure fence as backup, the inside could have a more relaxed environment. However, the addition of the perimeter fence and closing the compound upset several staff members, as they had been previously been allowed to drive their cars into the compound and park right next to the buildings in which they worked. Under the new system, they had to park in an employee parking lot and enter through a security building to avoid the potential of contraband coming into the prison. We also stopped the male inmate work crews, forming female inmate work crews that worked for both male and female supervisors. It was a surprise to ORW staff that the female inmates wanted to work on the carpentry, plumbing, and HVAC crews, and that they did a great job and much more work was accomplished.

Quite frankly, this job of change was one of the most difficult I encountered in Ohio. The other prisons accepted change very easily. However, the ORW operating culture was deeply rooted in staff, some of whom perceived problems with almost every aspect of the changes. And, quite frankly, some negative consequences did occur. There were instances (as in every prison) of opposite-sex staff developing romantic relationships with inmates. However, as time went on, the changes became part of the new operating culture. ORW staff realized the benefits, and ORW is now a very modern and extremely well-operated facility.

CULTURE IN WOMEN'S PRISONS

The culture in a women's prison is considerably different from that in a men's prison, with a different style of inmate communications with each other and with staff.[53] Most studies report that women also have an inmate code, emphasizing similar guidelines for women as for men, such as "do your own time" and "don't rat (tell) on other inmates." However, the code is not as important to women as to

Female inmates often form "pseudofamilies," in which each inmate plays a role as mother, father, children, and even nieces.
Courtesy of AP/Wide World Photos.

men. The important difference between male and female inmate culture is in the relationships that women form. As noted earlier, male inmates stay as independent and isolated as possible and avoid any emotional or personal relationships. Female prisoners, on the other hand, seek close personal and emotional relationships with other inmates. They also are not as concerned about being labeled a "snitch" by other inmates because of interacting with staff.

Much of the culture of a women's prison has to do with the fact that approximately 65 percent of female inmates are mothers, and much of their thoughts while in prison are about release and re-establishing their family and role as mothers. Owens notes that the importance of women's relationships with their children "has an impact on the values shaping prison culture in several ways, such as making conversations about children sacred, acknowledging the intensity and grief attached to these relationships, sanctioning those with histories of hurting children, and other child-specific cultural beliefs or behaviors."[54]

Both because women enjoy and need the support resulting from sharing personal facts regarding their children and lives with others, and because they have been socialized to play a specific role within a family structure, female inmates often tend to form what are called **pseudofamilies**. In these organizations, inmates play actual roles of parents and children. Some but not all pseudofamilies have a romantic dyad or a couple that acts as parents; there may be two mothers or a father and a mother. Parents are usually the older and more prisonwise inmates, and younger inmates take the role of children. The parental partners in these prison families are not always sexual in nature. Propper suggests that they are based on asexual pairing and do not present a greater likelihood of homosexual activity.[55] Pollock-Byrne, in describing these families, suggests that most prison lesbian relationships are based not so much on actual sexual activity as on affection with a sexual connotation.[56]

These pseudofamilies become the focus of much of the activity for family members. Family members make great effort to try to live in the same housing unit, work together on the same jobs, and recreate together. The parents act as

Pseudofamilies

family organizations formed by female inmates that have roles of parents and children mentors for the younger inmates, protect them, and maintain a discipline of order and control. The families also provide mutual support and protection, an aid network, and an opportunity for fun and laughter.[57] While most of the younger (children) inmates take on the role of daughters, some "women who take on the 'butch' or the aggressive role may be a dad, a son, or a brother, yet these designations can often be fluid."[58] Diaz-Cotto contends that these family relationships are now in decline in many prisons, primarily because inmates have more access to family, friends, and others outside prison, and therefore do not have to invest as much in prison-developed relationships.[59]

The sexual relationships that develop in a women's prison are also much different from the homosexuality that occurs in men's prisons. Men must continually show their masculinity through sexual conquest of weaker inmates, and the risk of rape is much greater in men's prisons. The male sexual aggressor is not interested in a relationship, but simply in sexual gratification, power, and dominance. Sexuality for female offenders is altogether different in that it is a search for affection, emotional support, and sharing. The desire for power and dominance and the potential for rape are minimal, and "butches" in women's prisons are sought after by women who want to play a woman's role in a relationship.[60] While early research indicated that one out of four female inmates report involvement in a lesbian relationship,[61] it has more recently been estimated that "between 30 and 60 percent of incarcerated women are in lesbian relationships."[62]

The world in which women live in prison is, in many ways, similar to that faced by male inmates. Their special needs, situations, and characteristics create unique management challenges and lead to the development of different cultures within prisons for female inmates. As described by Fleisher, Rison, and Helman after a review of the development of culture within a new women's prison, "A key issue in the development of gender-based distinctions in organizational culture is learning how to create, implement, and then perpetuate a set of organizational values and beliefs that meets women's programming needs and styles of interpersonal interaction."[63]

Chapter Review

SUMMARY

The society of a prison has a unique culture. Few if any other environments are so isolated from normal living and society that they result in such a distinct culture. This results from the forced stay, the need for routine and control by staff, the adaptation to living with many other people and many heterogeneous groups, the interdependence of inmates on other inmates, and the anger and bitterness that inmates feel as a response to their situation. As prison culture has developed over the past two centuries, in some ways it has changed little, while in other ways it has changed dramatically.

Prisons still operate with at least a cursory understanding of and sensitivity to an inmate code, particularly the tenets to "be tough" and "don't trust the guards." However, the trusted old con, who lived by the code and was respected by other inmates is a thing of the past. Younger inmates, many of whom are gang members whose loyalty is to the gang and who follow gang requirements over the inmate code, deal with issues through strength rather than guile, and do not respect the "old con," whom they see as weak and not willing to take what they want. Women's prisons have more of an accepted respect and hierarchy related to both how long and how well time is served. However, for women, the status associated with this comes not so much from adherence to the inmate code, but from knowledge and relationships and the ability to mentor and protect younger inmates.

As much as prison staff want to be aware and in control of everything within a prison, much occurs in the life of prison inmates that staff do not understand and have little influence over. While staff do not ignore drug use, gang activity and violence, or homosexuality, many honestly admit that they cannot totally control or prevent these activities. In fact, staff never find out about all of the drug use, violent acts, and homosexual activity. Well-managed institutions are said to be "controlled by staff, and not by inmates." While this is true, the actions and relationships of inmates usually have a much greater influence on the development of prison culture than the policies and procedures of staff.

REVIEW QUESTIONS

1. Describe the Zimbardo experiment and its results.
2. Describe the two theories regarding how inmate culture becomes a part of prison life.
3. How has following the inmate culture in a prison changed, and what are the potential reasons for the change?
4. List methods correctional agencies use to control prison gangs.
5. Why does Hassine suggest that most prison sexual assaults occur?
6. What do correctional officials do to prevent sexual assaults in prison?
7. What percentage of inmates in state and federal prisons are serving sentences for drug offenses?
8. How do drugs get into prisons?
9. What role does Terry suggest that humor plays in a prison environment?
10. How does the inmate culture in a women's prison differ than in a prison for men?

ENDNOTES

1. Erving Goffman, *Asylums: Essays on the Social Situation of Mental Patients and Other Inmates* (New York: Doubleday, 1961).
2. Phillip G. Zimbardo, "Pathology of Imprisonment," *Society* 9 (April 1972): 4–8.
3. Ibid., p. 4.
4. Donald Clemmer, *The Prison Community* (New York: Rinehart, 1940), p. 8.
5. Gresham Sykes, *The Society of Captives: A Study of a Maximum Security Prison* (Princeton, N.J.: Princeton University Press, 1958).
6. John Irwin and Donald Cressey, "Thieves, Convicts, and the Inmate Culture," *Social Problems* 10 (1962): 145–157.
7. This list of selected prison terms was collected by Kate King, professor of criminal justice at Murray State University.
8. Paige M. Harrison and Allen J. Beck, *Prisoners in 2001,* Bureau of Justice Statistics Bulletin (Washington, D.C.: U.S. Department of Justice, July 2002), p. 12.
9. S. Ekland-Olson, "Crowding, Social Control, and Prison Violence: Evidence from the Post-*Ruiz* Years in Texas," *Law and Society Review* 20, no. 3 (1986): 289–421. Also see Gerald G. Gaes and W. J. McGuire, "Prison Violence: The Contribution of Crowding versus Other Determinants of Prison Assault Rates," *Journal of Research in Crime and Delinquency* 22, no. 1 (1985): 41–65.
10. John Irwin, *Prisons in Turmoil* (Boston: Little, Brown, 1980).
11. James B. Jacobs, *Statesville, A Penitentiary in Mass Society* (Chicago: University of Chicago Press, 1977).
12. Mark S. Fleisher, *Warehousing Violence* (Newbury Park, Calif.: Sage, 1989), p. 198.
13. Victor Hassine, *Life without Parole: Living in Prison Today,* 2nd ed. (Los Angeles: Roxbury, 1999), p. 39.
14. Michael C. Braswell, Reid H. Montgomery, and Lucien X. Lombardo, *Prison Violence in America,* 2nd ed. (Cincinnati, Ohio: Anderson, 1994).
15. Robert Johnson, *Hard Time: Understanding and Reforming the Prison,* 3rd ed. (Belmont, Calif.: Wadsworth, 2002), p. 149.
16. Charles M. Terry, *The Fellas: Overcoming Prison and Addiction* (Belmont, Calif.: Wadsworth, 2003), p. 72.

17. Christopher A. Innes and Vicki D. Verdeyen, "Conceptualizing the Management of Violent Inmates," *Corrections Management Quarterly* 1, no. 4 (1997): 1–9.

18. Gerald G. Gaes, Susan Wallace, Evan Gilman, Jody Klein-Saffran, and Sharon Suppa, "Influence of Prison Gang Affiliation on Violence and Other Prison Misconduct," *Prison Journal* 82, no. 3 (2002): 359–385.

19. National Institute of Corrections, *Management Strategies in Disturbances and with Gangs/Disruptive Groups* (Washington, D.C.: U.S. Department of Justice, 1991), p. 2.

20. George M. Camp and Camille Graham Camp, *Prison Gangs: Their Extent, Nature, and Impact on Prisons* (Washington, D.C.: U.S. Government Printing Office, 1985).

21. American Correctional Association, *Gangs in Correctional Facilities: A National Assessment* (Laurel, Md.: American Correctional Association, 1993).

22. Camille Graham Camp and George M. Camp, *The 2001 Corrections Yearbook,* (Middletown, Conn.: The Criminal Justice Institute, 2002), p. 77.

23. Gregory Scott, "Broken Windows behind Bars: Eradicating Prison Gangs through Ecological Hardening and Symbol Cleansing," *Corrections Management Quarterly* 5, no. 1 (2001): 23–36.

24. Ibid., p. 24.

25. Sykes, 1958.

26. Mark S. Fleisher and Scott H. Decker, "An Overview of the Challenge of Prison Gangs," *Corrections Management Quarterly* 5, no. 1 (2001): 5.

27. Richard P. Seiter, "Winning a Battle of Wills: Correctional Administrators and Prison Gangs," *Corrections Management Quarterly* 5, no. 1 (2001): iv.

28. Tony Lesce, "How to Cope with Prison Gangs," *Corrections Technology & Management* 4, no. 2 (March/April 2000): 22–25.

29. National Institute of Corrections, *Management Strategies in Disturbances and with Gangs/Disruptive Groups* (Washington, D.C.: U.S. Department of Justice, 1991): p. 2.

30. Ibid., pp. 5–6.

31. Intelligence Section, Federal Bureau of Prisons, *Gang Interdiction Strategies Briefing Guide* (Washington, D.C.: U.S. Department of Justice, April 29, 1996), p. 17.

32. Peter L. Nacci and Thomas R. Kane, "The Incidence of Sex and Sexual Aggression in Federal Prisons," *Federal Probation* 47, no. 4 (December 1983): 31–36.

33. Victor Hassine, *Life without Parole: Living in Prison Today* (Los Angeles: Roxbury, 1997), p. 138.

34. T. J. Fagan, D. Wennerstrom, and J. Miller, "Sexual Assault of Male Inmates: Prevention, Identification, and Intervention," *Journal of Correctional Health Care* 3, no. 1 (1996): 49–63.

35. Camp and Camp, 2002, p. 147.

36. Bureau of Justice Statistics, "Criminal Offender Statistics," http://www.ojp.usdoj.gov/bjs/crimoff, accessed January 8, 2003.

37. Bureau of Justice Statistics, *Sourcebook of Criminal Justice Statistics, 2001* (Washington, D.C.: U.S. Department of Justice, 2003), p. 500.

38. Christopher J. Mumola, *Substance Abuse and Treatment, State and Federal Prisoners, 1997* (Washington, D.C.: U.S. Department of Justice, Office of Justice Programs, January 1999), pp. 1, 3.

39. C. W. Harlow, *HIV in U.S. Prisons and Jails* (Washington, D.C.: U.S. Department of Justice, 1993).

40. Camp and Camp, 2002, pp. 118–119.

41. Ibid., pp. 121–123.

42. Charles M. Terry, "The Function of Humor for Prison Inmates," *Journal of Contemporary Criminal Justice* 13, no. 1 (February 1997): 23–40.

43. Erving Goffman, *Asylums: Essays on the Social Situation of Mental Patients and Other Inmates* (New York: Doubleday, 1961).

44. S. Ungar, "Self-Mockery: An Alternative Form of Self-Presentation," *Symbolic Interaction* 71, no. 1 (1984): 121–133.

45. Terry, 1997, p. 24.

46. Henry Elmer Barnes, *The Evolution of Penology in Pennsylvania: A Study in American Social History* (Montclair, N.J.: Patterson Smith, 1968).

47. Russell P. Dobash, R. Emerson Dobash, and Sue Gutteridge, *The Imprisonment of Women* (Oxford, England: Basil Blackwell, 1986), p. 52.

48. Allison Morris, *Women, Crime and Criminal Justice* (Oxford, England: Basil Blackwell, 1987).

49. Nicole H. Rafter, *Partial Justice: Women, Prison, and Social Control,* 2nd ed. (New Brunswick, N.J.: Transaction, 1990).

50. Nicole H. Rafter, "Gender and Justice: The Equal Protection Issues," in *The American Prison,* edited by Lynne Goodstein and Doris MacKenzie (New York: Plenum Press, 1989), pp. 89–109.

51. Clarice Feinman, "A Historical Overview of the Treatment of Incarcerated Women: Myths and Realities of Rehabilitation," *Prison Journal* 63 (1983): 12–26.

52. Clarice Feinman, "Sex-Role Stereotypes and Justice for Women," in *Women and Crime in America,* edited by L. H. Bowker, (New York: Macmillan, 1981), pp. 383–391.

53. See Mark S. Fleisher, Richard H. Rison, and David W. Helman, "Federal Inmates: A Growing Constituency in the Federal Bureau of Prisons," *Corrections Management Quarterly* 1, no. 4 (1997): 28–35.

54. Barbara Owens, *In the Mix: Struggle and Survival in a Women's Prison* (Albany: State University of New York Press, 1998), p. 120.

55. A. Propper, "Make Believe Families and Homosexuality among Imprisoned Girls," *Criminology* 20, no. 1 (1982): 120.

56. Joycelyn M. Pollack-Byrne, *Women, Prison, and Crime* (Belmont, Calif.: Wadsworth, 1990).

57. C. B. Hart, "Gender Differences in Social Support among Inmates," *Women and Criminal Justice* 6 (1995): 67–68.

58. Ira J. Silverman, *Corrections: A Comprehensive View,* 2nd ed. (Belmont, Calif.: Wadsworth, 2001), p. 200.

59. J. Diaz-Cotto, *Gender, Ethnicity, and the State: Latina and Latino Prison Politics* (Albany: New York State University Press, 1996).

60. Katherine Stuart Van Wormer and Clemens Bartolas, *Women and the Criminal Justice System* (Needham Heights, Mass.: Allyn & Bacon, 2000), p. 66.

61. Imogene L. Moyer, "Differential Social Structures and Homosexuality among Women in Prison," *Virginia Social Science Journal* 13 (1978): 13–19.

62. Owens, 1998, p. 198.

63. Fleisher, Rison, and Helman, 1997, p. 34.

Chapter 12

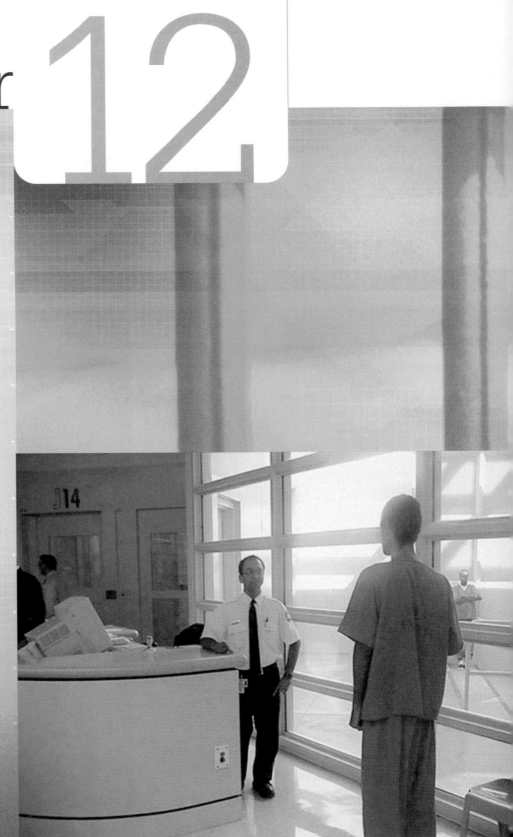

**AFTER READING THIS CHAPTER,
YOU SHOULD BE ABLE TO:**

1. Know the types and variety of jobs available in a prison.

2. Understand how prisons are organized and the role of the warden.

3. Describe the importance of organizational culture and understand how culture is formed in a prison.

4. Know the role a correctional officer plays in a prison, and consider the pros and cons of this job for yourself.

5. Know the history of female correctional officers in men's prisons and understand the challenges that face them in modern prisons.

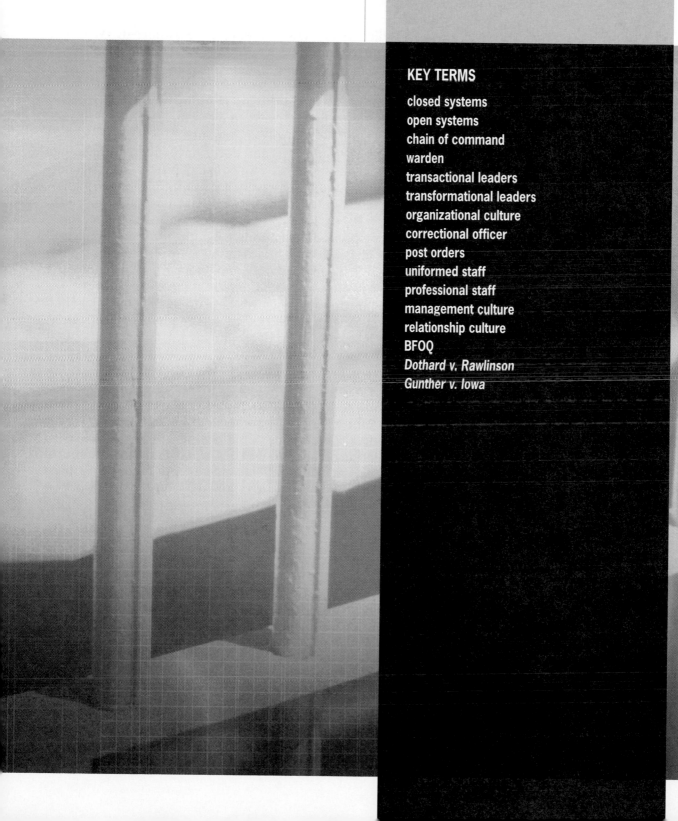

The World of Prison Staff

KEY TERMS

closed systems
open systems
chain of command
warden
transactional leaders
transformational leaders
organizational culture
correctional officer
post orders
uniformed staff
professional staff
management culture
relationship culture
BFOQ
Dothard v. Rawlinson
Gunther v. Iowa

Introduction

Just as there is a definite culture and hierarchy of status for prison inmates, there is also a culture and organizational hierarchy for prison staff. Some penologists would argue that prison staff are also influenced by the prison environment and become even more "prisonized" than inmates. That argument does not seem all that unreasonable. Most career prison staff spend more time "behind bars" than all but a small percentage of inmates. A correctional officer who works for twenty-five years prior to retirement, 2,080 hours (40 hours for 52 weeks) per year, spends a total of 52,000 hours in the prison. This is almost six full years in prison, and the impact of this time on the officer personally is extended over twenty-five years before he or she leaves the prison for good.

Consider also that most staff in prison interact extensively with inmates, to a much greater proportion than they do with other staff. Their job is to gain control and compliance without the use of weapons, threats, or intimidation. To do this requires adaptation to (not cooptation by) the prison environment and understanding the most efficient way to maintain control over inmates. The world of prisons is unlike any other social organization. Words and deeds have different meanings inside prisons than outside, and due to the need for constant interaction and communication, there is no hiding anyone's real personality or approach to the job. Inmates quickly see through staff who try to take on a demeanor that is not really them.

In a prison there is considerable and continuous stress, the threat of assault and injury, and the need to never let down one's guard or fail to be attentive to the detail of one's work assignment. Most people on their jobs can have a "bad day at the office," be unproductive, or lose their temper or handle some issue poorly or unprofessionally. However, serious problems can result from having a similar "bad day" when working in a prison. When your work consists of supervising and maintaining control over possibly a hundred offenders, who are not the most cooperative and likeable people in the world and who look for staff weaknesses and take advantage of improper behavior, having a bad day at work can put people at risk or undermine the security of a prison. Prison staff have to be professional, use their interpersonal skills, rely on one another to do their jobs well, leave the prison environment no worse than they found it, and be prepared to come back the next day to begin their eighth-hour shift all over again.

In Chapter 10 the organization of a prison was described, and the elements of the organization that make a prison operate effectively were presented. This chapter focuses on the people rather than the organization: the world in which prison staff work, the issues they face, the ways they handle them, and the culture that develops as a result of stressful and challenging working conditions. While descriptions and functions of some of the primary prison staff positions are described, the chapter focuses on the environment and culture that results from working in a prison setting.

There may be no more demanding job than working in a prison. I spent more than twenty years working for correctional agencies, was assigned to four different prisons, was warden of two prisons, was responsible for more than 30,000 inmates and 7,000 staff as director of a state prison system, and oversaw a prison industry program that employed 15,000 inmates and sold $400 million in products each year. From this work, I have a great appreciation for those staff who every day enter the world of imprisoned felons, serve the public in difficult and underappreciated positions, face uncertainty and danger, and maintain a professional approach to their jobs, the inmates, and the agencies for which they work.

The Jobs of Prison Staff

When most people think of prison staff, they think of wardens and correctional officers. However, many different positions make up the complement of prison staff. Some of these are listed here:

Chaplain	Counselor or case manager
Computer specialist	Institution administrator
Substance abuse counselor	Employee development specialist
Facility maintenance worker	Financial manager
Food service worker	Health care worker (physician/nurse)
Industrial supervisor	Laundry supervisor
Psychologist	Personnel manager
Recreation specialist	Safety manager
Secretary/clerical worker	Classification specialist
Teacher	Staff training instructor

In many ways, a prison is like a small city, requiring many of the same services and employees. Just like cities, prisons have schools, lodging accommodations, jails, eating establishments, convenience stores, places of worship, recreation facilities, sewer/sanitation/street service departments, facility and vehicle maintenance departments, barbershops, generators or electrical and power resources, laundry services, financial institutions, and administrative offices. All of the types of employees that are often found in a small community (except for many retail shops) are found in a prison, as prisons must be fairly self-sustaining and able to provide for themselves in most situations.

Each of these jobs requires specialists, both to manage the functions and to provide the service. Prisons have teachers certified to teach in the public school systems, and education supervisors who are usually accredited by the state as school principals. These supervisors carry out many of the functions of a principal

Prison staff include a variety of positions, such as correctional officer, administrator, medical person, and counselor.
Photo by Richard P. Seiter.

in creating a learning environment, supervising teachers, and maintaining discipline of students. Food services administrators must prepare menus, order food, and oversee the preparation of meals, while food service workers oversee inmates preparing and serving food. Prison physicians provide patient care and manage prison infirmaries that are very similar in operations to a typical general-practice doctor's office. In many ways, the jobs within a prison setting are very similar to the same functions carried out in the community, except that they are within a secure environment and all the clients are incarcerated felons.

The Organization of a Prison

The organization and administration of prisons is in some ways very simple, and in other ways very complex. It is simple in that there is a very clear and military-like chain of command. Yet prisons are very complex organizations in that they rely on most staff members operating individually, while following the same policies and, hopefully, subscribing to the same operational values and principles of the organization as a whole. Modern prison operations have moved well beyond the past years' emphasis on "lock them up, work them, and feed them." Expansion of inmate rights, the inclusion of rehabilitative programs, and many more prison service options have broadened the internal management puzzle for administrators to piece together. In addition, the interest of the public, the media, and other government agencies has required that prison administrators manage the "external environment" as well as they manage within the prison. Political and public interest in corrections puts additional demands on administrators, both for their time and for their sensitivity to what they do and how they do it.

Closed systems

prison systems that consist of only the internal environment, under the direct control of the warden, and without much interest or any interference from external groups

Open systems

prison systems that have frequent interactions between the organization and other groups in order to obtain resources, gain support, and accomplish goals

From their inception in the late 1800s until approximately the 1960s, prisons were closed systems. **Closed systems** consist of only the internal environment, and for prisons, that meant what happened within the walls or fences, under the direct control of the warden and without much interest or any interference from external groups. The organization of a closed system, often with autocratic leadership, is usually very simple, and the mission and goals of the organization are determined and the leader enforces compliance. However, as a result of the external interest in the management of prisons, and the fact that no modern entity operates by itself and without interacting with many others, correctional agencies have changed from closed systems to open systems. **Open systems** have frequent interactions between the organization and other groups in order to obtain resources, gain support, and accomplish goals. Snarr describes the open system, of prisons as receiving numerous inputs from external government units and being held accountable for certain expected outputs from taxpayers and elected officials.[1] Prisons today interact with the local community; with their headquarters organization; with interest groups of employees, citizens, vendors, and other public agencies; and with other providers of correctional or counseling services to offenders.

PRISON CHAIN OF COMMAND

Chain of command

the vertical hierarchy in an organization, identified in terms of authority, and the order through which people receive directives from the person immediately above them and pass these directives to the person immediately below them

Chain of command and unity of command are very critical to every organization, especially a paramilitary organization such as a prison. The chain of command in military organizations has ranks of individuals (privates, sergeants, lieutenants) relating to their place in the chain of command. The **chain of command** represents the vertical hierarchy in an organization, is identified in terms of authority, and is the order through which people receive directives from the person immediately above them and pass these directives to the person immediately below them. Most prisons have a military chain of command and use ranks such as sergeant, lieutenant, and captain. Figure 12.1 illustrates a simple prison chain of command from a warden to a correctional officer.

A PRISON CHAIN OF COMMAND

FIGURE **12.1**

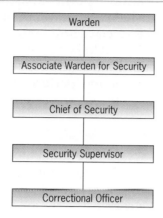

In a pure chain of command, wardens give orders to the associate warden in charge of security, who passes them on to the chief of security, who passes them on to security supervisors, who pass them on to correctional officers. While prisons are adopting more modern management practices such as staff empowerment and participatory management, they are still (and will always remain to a great extent) very structured in the use of a chain of command; one of the most revered management practices within a prison is to use and not circumvent the chain of command. Wardens certainly interact with all levels of staff and seek their input on a variety of issues. However, prison operations rely on everyone completing their responsibilities in a consistent manner, and all levels of supervision must know what others are doing. Therefore, wardens would not directly instruct a correctional officer to carry out some function without advising or passing the instruction through correctional supervisors.

In a much more complex sense, prison administrators realize that policies and orders cannot cover every act and decision that must be made by a correctional

Prison staff and prison operations have changed since these staff worked at the United States Penitentiary in Leavenworth, Kansas, c. 1895.
Courtesy of the Federal Bureau of Prisons.

officer, or the way they react to a new experience not covered by policy. Therefore, wardens attempt to instill in all levels of the organization the important principles and values that should be considered as staff act independently. Through this "empowerment," staff do not just receive orders continuously through the chain of command. They are trained in and follow policy, yet they are informed about and understand the approach and philosophy expected for carrying out their duties, and therefore make decisions and perform duties consistent with these expectations.

The Warden

The earlier era of autonomous wardens running their prisons as they desired and answering to almost no one is over. However, most people still associate that style with the role of a warden, primarily as a result of the way wardens are portrayed in movies and on television. In the classic description of the rule of a strong warden in *Stateville: The Penitentiary in Mass Society,* Jacobs described the way Warden Joseph Ragen ran that prison for more than thirty years until the 1960s.[2] Stateville is a maximum-security prison in northern Illinois, and in the middle 1900s it held almost 4,000 inmates in space designed for 1,600. The prison was filled with violent inmates and had a reputation as one of the toughest prisons in the United States.

Ragen ruled the prison with an iron fist and demanded strict adherence to rules by both staff and inmates. He maintained the prison as clean and spotless, made inmates march in straight lines when moving about the prison, and prohibited staff and inmate communication.[3] A 1996 book by Kantrowitz regarding Stateville and Warden Ragen further describes how Ragen meted out severe punishment to staff and inmates who violated his rules. Kantrowitz notes that Ragen believed his function was to synchronize men and their behavior in time and space, so the prison ran smoothly daily.[4] Jacobs further describes how Ragen was one of the last of the warden "village chieftains" who vanish as their society modernizes.

When Ragen retired, Stateville moved to a more modern management style, forced partly by federal court interventions, and shifted from discipline to rehabilitation. Unfortunately, the change was too much and too fast for the prison, and

Warden Joseph Ragen of Statesville (Illinois) Penitentiary ran this overcrowded prison with an iron fist, answering to no one and representing a management style long gone in the governing of prisons.
Courtesy of Corbis/Bettmann.

the education programs that replaced the work programs were not enough to keep inmates productively busy. By 1978, conditions had deteriorated to utter anarchy; inmate gangs ran the prison, declaring certain areas of the prison off-limits to other inmates and staff under threat of death. It took several years to get Stateville orderly, clean, and under the control of staff again. This description is not to support an authoritarian style of prison management as under Ragen, but to point out how fragile the control and authority of staff can be in prison, how inmate groups will quickly move forward to fill any void in leadership and control, and how careful wardens and administrators must be as they attempt to change the culture of such a complex organization.

THE ROLE OF MODERN WARDENS

Today, there are no Warden Ragens, and that type of management and strict adherence to discipline would no longer work. Staff control prisons, but not through threats and intimidation. Control in modern prisons is maintained through a fair and just disciplinary system holding inmates accountable for their behavior, physical security and use of technology, work and treatment programs to keep inmates busy, consistent operations according to policy, and professional staff communication with inmates.

The move away from autonomous operations of each individual prison to more of a centralization of authority has greatly influenced the organization and operation of prisons. Freeman characterizes this development as the "era of bureaucratic wardens," in which wardens must now take responsibility for maintaining a safe, secure, humane prison environment in accordance with accepted standards (constitutional mandates, centralized policies, accreditation standards of professional organizations, and so on), and suggests several specific activities for the bureaucratic warden:

1. Development of the mission statement for the organization
2. Coordination of the budget process
3. Strategic evaluation and emergency planning
4. Management of daily activities
5. Management of labor relations
6. Formulation of policy
7. Supervision and professional development of staff [5]

The modern **warden** is a manager of resources, a role model for staff, and a juggler of priorities; he or she balances custody and treatment, is firm but fair, and knows how to manage the environment external to the prison as well as that within. When people would ask me what it is like to be a warden, I used to kiddingly say, "It is simple, all you have to do is know how to say no." Seriously, however, the role of a modern warden is one of the most complex management jobs in today's society.

Currently, the public has much more interest in and much higher expectations for corrections than in the past. This requires new roles for wardens in terms of how they provide leadership to their agency. Historically, wardens had much greater control over the *internal* operations of the prison and very little *external* interference. Traditional wardens were very autocratic, not just because they wanted to be, but because processes and procedures were not spelled out in a step-by-step manner by a centralized bureaucracy. In the early years of correctional administration, there were few written policies and wardens were often left to their own devices and whims as to what should be accomplished and how it should be done. Today there are rules and regulations for every activity, from hiring staff to spending a budget to supervising an offender.

Warden
the chief executive officer of a prison, responsible for the day-to-day operations

Modern prison administrators such as Warden Jesse Williams of the Allen Correctional Institution in Ohio have complex jobs as CEOs of large organizations.
Courtesy of the Ohio Department of Rehabilitation and Correction.

Previously, wardens had few demands on them to be *external managers,* as corrections was of little interest to elected officials, the courts, or the media. Now prison administration is of interest to everyone. Crime is an important domestic priority, and the fact that we have so many prisons that require a large percentage of the annual state budgets means that their operation is of great interest to the public and elected officials. Only a few decades ago, federal courts would not get involved in correctional management issues. Today they are regularly and intensively involved in corrections and have even taken over and dictated how some correctional agencies must be managed. Media sources seldom reported on activities or occurrences in a prison. However, print and television media now regularly have stories about criminal justice and prison programs and operations.

These changes require wardens to have different skills and different leadership styles than in the past. Wardens were leaders at the top of their organizations who exercised power by giving orders and making decisions. Wardens maintained control by offering rewards and resources to staff in exchange for assistance in reaching the organization's goals, and punished those who did not. James McGregor Burns defined this type of leadership as "transactional," involving exchange relationships between leaders and followers.[6] **Transactional leaders** were the traditional authorities: those with position, power, and knowledge of a substantive area. They were able to provide answers and give direction for any issue the agency confronted. Staff respected them and looked to them for guidance and direction. Transactional leadership worked well in a prison with a relatively stable environment and with routine situations within the experience of the leader.

Transactional leaders

traditional authorities within an organization who were involved in exchange relationships between leaders and followers; they provided answers and direction for any issue the agency confronted

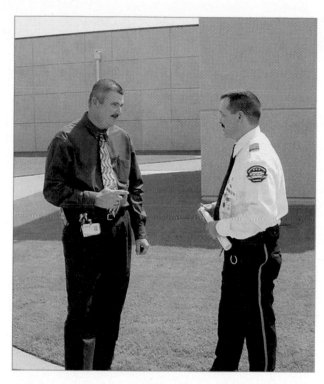

Transformational leaders communicate constantly with staff, help them to learn and understand the values of the organization, and seek their input on policies and procedures.
Photo by Richard P. Seiter.

However, the challenges of modern times within a prison are not so routine, and the environment is not so stable. Change and changing situations are more the "routine," and it is impossible to have policies to guide how to deal with every new issue. Therefore, wardens cannot be the substantive experts for everything that goes on in the prison, because there are always new issues to confront that they have never experienced before. These factors require wardens to be less transactional, and more like **transformational leaders**. Transformational leadership is much broader than transactional leadership. It is based on principles rather than practice and on motivating people to jointly address challenges and find solutions to new problems. Transformational leaders emphasize the set of values and principles to be used as guidelines in responding to issues. They help staff and the organization to learn and to work through problems in an adaptive manner. They involve staff in finding creative and innovative solutions to new problems. Wardens as transformational leaders must encourage managers and line staff to work together, and must empower staff to be able to adapt to change and deal with new challenges and issues.[7]

One of the important roles of a warden is to help set, define, and reinforce the desired culture of the prison. **Organizational culture** includes the values, beliefs, and behaviors that form the way of life within that organization. From the first day of recruiting a prospective staff member and throughout the basic training employees receive before they begin work in a prison, correctional agencies instill the desired organizational culture. For effective correctional agencies, the culture includes being professional, striving to meet high standards, being ethical, positively interacting with inmates, rewarding staff for good performance, and using state-of-the-art correctional practices. Wardens as leaders of their prisons play critical

Transformational leaders
leaders who exercise leadership based on principles, while motivating staff to jointly address challenges and find solutions to new problems

Organizational culture
the values, beliefs, and behaviors that form the way of life within an organization

AN INSIDER'S EXPERIENCE: My Job as a Warden

It's funny. Everywhere I go, people tell me, "You don't look mean enough to be a warden." I guess everyone still has the stereotypes of the old movies, where the warden was the brutal, autocratic, and power-hungry person who made everyone in the prison (staff and inmates) toe the line and do things his (there weren't many *hers* then) way. They think you have to yell and scream to be in control, and probably be a bit nutty. That probably was not too uncommon for wardens fifty years ago, when there were no state departments of corrections, wardens were appointed by the governor and received their budgets directly from the state legislature, and they did run the prison the way they wanted to with little interest or interference by anyone.

Today, a warden's job is entirely different. Prisons are run by policies and procedures, many reflecting the most recent court decisions or bills passed by the legislatures, and all created by the state department of corrections and applying to all prisons. So wardens have little discretion in how they run their prisons. Their role is to manage their resources efficiently, ensure quality and consistent implementation of policy, ensure that staff are prepared to respond to emergencies, and set the tone or climate for the prison environment.

As a warden, I see my job as consisting of two major tasks: empowering staff to do their jobs and creating a prison climate based on dignity and respect. Oh, of course I have to be sure staff are trained, know the policies and how to implement them, and go about their jobs in a quality fashion. However, this is the easy part of it. I really don't think it takes a great manager to do this. But I pride myself in being a leader—not in the old autocratic style, but in modern leadership ways of staff empowerment and setting the culture. People are often confused as to how to empower staff. It is not delegation, seeking input, or participatory management. It is recognizing that every day, correctional officers and other prison staff make dozens of decisions and take actions that are not guided by policy: How to react to an unruly inmate. How to not get lackadaisical and shortcut their jobs. What to do if they see another staff member acting unprofessional. Empowerment is getting staff to understand and support the overall vision for the prison and to use the values and principles you want as guidance for the way they do their jobs and make decisions.

I also see my role as setting the climate, tone, and culture. A warden does this in many ways: First, by getting out of the office and being in the prison, talking to staff and inmates. This shows interest and a hands-on approach. Second, by never passing by something that needs to be corrected. If you notice a security door unlocked that should be locked, get someone to lock it immediately. If you see a piece of paper on the ground, pick it up. If you see a staff member do something well, pat him or her on the back. These kinds of acts show attention to detail, high standards, and encouragement. If you as a warden don't do this, no one else will. Finally, you set a tone by the way you interact with people. You can't always be "a nice guy." Sometimes you have to chew people out, but you do it in a private and professional manner. You treat everyone with dignity and respect. I talk to every new group of inmates. I tell them I expect staff to treat them with dignity and respect, and I demand that they do the same with staff. If everyone acts this way, the prison will run efficiently and not have the constant tension that can be created without this approach. I really like my job, and spend a lot of time on these two major activities of staff empowerment and contributing to the culture of the prison.

roles in setting and reinforcing the organizational culture. Wardens are the role models for how to put the organizational culture in effect in the workplace. Staff take their cues on meeting standards, communicating with inmates, and rewarding excellence from the warden. The "An Insider's Experience" box was written when I was a warden, and illustrates this role of a modern warden.

It is sometimes thought that with all of the court intervention, political oversight, centralized control from the state department of corrections, and extensive policies and procedures, the role of a warden as a leader has been watered down, and wardens do not have as much impact today as in the past. However, one thing that never changes about organizations is that they reflect the personality of the leader. The warden sets the tone for a prison, defines professional expectations, creates the level of standards for performance, and has a tremendous impact on the morale of staff and inmates. DiIulio, in *Governing Prisons,* writes, "the individual who heads a prison, or a prison system, can shape the organization in ways that help to determine the quality of prison life."[8]

When I was a warden, I was regularly reminded of the attention that inmates and staff pay to the warden: his or her mannerisms, behaviors, tone of voice, and way of speaking. Staff and inmates watch where a warden goes and what he or she does. As I walked around the prison yard and buildings, staff monitored where I was going. I would regularly overhear on someone's communications radio (I did not carry one), "Number 1 [call sign for the warden] on his way to the recreation yard." Staff closely watch what the warden does and says. On one occasion, a correctional officer asked me, "Are you feeling okay today? You don't seem to be walking with the speed and bounce you usually have." Prisons are like most organizations in that the leader sets the tone and contributes to the culture. But prisons, probably more than most other organizations, genuinely reflect the personality and professionalism of the warden.

Life for a Correctional Officer

The role of **correctional officer** is critical within a prison, and perhaps a role unique to prisons and jails. Their role is unlike other law enforcement jobs, and unlike the treatment, services, or administrative functions within a prison. In 2001, there were 218,382 line correctional officers and a total of 259,934 uniformed staff (including correctional supervisors and officers) in state and federal prisons in the United States.[9] Correctional officers and supervisors make up approximately 60 percent of all staff in state and federal prisons. Of these line correctional officers, 77 percent were male, while 67.1 percent were white, 21.3 percent were black, 5.5 percent were Hispanic, and 6.1 percent were other minorities.[10]

Correctional officer

staff person in a prison or jail who accomplishes the institution's mission by maintaining control and order within the institution

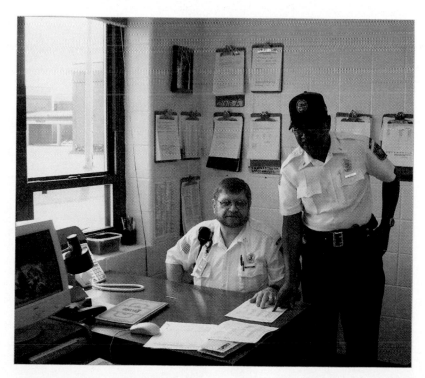

Correctional officers and supervisors make up 60 percent of prison staff. Their role of maintaining order and control is basic to accomplishing the prison's mission.

Photo by Richard P. Seiter.

The job of a correctional officer is to assist in the accomplishment of the mission of the prison by maintaining control and order within the prison. While prisons and jails have a considerably different mission, there is relatively little difference in the role that correctional officers play in the two types of facilities. Correctional officers are responsible for constant supervision of inmates and implementation of security procedures within a prison. Their world is both highly technical (in that security procedures require strict adherence to policy and attention to detail) and highly interactive (through personal communications) with inmates.

Officers have to be a variety of things to a variety of people. Their bosses expect them to be exact in performing their security duties, while being professional in their interaction with inmates. Their peers expect them to support each other and not show any weakness in how they do their job and supervise inmates. And inmates expect them to be fair and not hassle them for minor things that don't make a difference. Prout and Ross write, "The most successful [correctional officers] have a genuine interest in their work and a real desire to serve the needs of the correctional system, on the one hand, and the requirements of the inmates on the other . . . They recognize the social and political position of the prison in the larger society beyond the prison walls."[11]

THE DAILY GRIND

The job of correctional officer can become a daily grind of routine duties, while dealing with stressful and possibly dangerous situations. Routine is not a negative in a prison; in fact, it is very important to the successful operation of a correctional facility. Routine in a prison environment is the consistent, scheduled, and expected activities that make up the day within a prison. Officers have to be consis-

Correctional officers must be consistent and follow policy in the performance of their required security duties.
Photo by Richard P. Seiter.

tent in the performance of required functions, and inmates have to know what is required of them in terms of such routines as count, locking down in cells, work call, and going to meals.

Correctional officers receive a specific assignment in a prison that can be anything from supervising inmates on a work crew or in a housing area to a non–inmate contact job in a tower or control center. Lombardo lists seven different categories of correctional officer assignments:

1. Living units—officers assigned to supervise housing areas
2. Work detail supervisors—officers who oversee work details such as sanitation or lawn maintenance details
3. Industrial shop and school officers—those who provide security and inmate accountability in these areas
4. Yard officers—the patrol and supervision of inmate movement in the "compound" or center yard of a prison
5. Administration building assignments—these include checking in visitors or working in the prison control center (opening doors, watching camera monitors, and maintaining radio communications)
6. Perimeter security—the armed posts of perimeter towers or mobile patrol vehicles.
7. Relief officers—those who fill in a variety of assignments for officers who are sick or on a day off.[12]

Each specific assignment has **post orders**, a detailed description of the activities that are required to be performed throughout the day that often includes the time at which they are to occur. Post orders are different from general policies that spell out how to do an activity (such as handling security keys or conducting an inmate count) in that they are specific to the assignment and detail what to do rather than how to do it. As an example, the post orders for a housing unit officer on the day watch may include a schedule similar to the following list:

Post orders

the detailed description of the activities that are required to be performed throughout the day, often including the time they are to occur

- 7:00 A.M.—Report for duty and read the logbook of the prior shift's activities.
- 7:30 A.M.—Open the housing unit doors for ten minutes to let inmates go to work.
- 8:00 A.M.—Start sanitation assignment by inmate crew.
- 10:30 A.M.—Open the housing unit doors for inmates returning from work.
- 11:00 A.M. to noon—Allow inmates to go to the dining room for lunch.
- 12:30 P.M.—Open housing unit door for ten minutes for inmates to go to afternoon work call.
- 1:00 P.M.—Do a census count. Inmates who are off duty may be allowed to go to recreation yard.
- 3:00 P.M.—Enter day's activities into the log book, and sign over housing unit keys to evening shift officer.

The typical day for a correctional officer is a mix of routine activities and constant communication with inmates. Correctional officers' routine is described as follows: "One minute an officer is handing out toilet paper, the next he is explaining court papers. An officer is joking with two inmates playing checkers, and in an instant, he is ordering everyone to their cells."[13] Even with a regular routine of activities, there is constant tension and uncertainty as well. An officer in the Nassau County Jail thinks of his role as the following: "One unarmed correction officer and 60 inmates, the jailer and the jailed, warily taking each other's measure, sparring for control."[14] Farkas and Manning suggest that correctional work is at times routine and monotonous, and at other times it is risky and unpredictable.[15]

While most correctional officers enjoy the challenge of their jobs and have a considerable amount of pride in and loyalty for the correctional agency for which they work, there are always officers who are bitter and feel at odds with the mission of their agency. They may feel that their agency does not appreciate them, they may have been passed over for promotion, or they just may not be happy in their job. A good example of this is described in the book *The Keepers of the Keys*, in which Dickenson expresses the view of many activities within a prison from the eyes of a line correctional officer. He makes fun of the word PRIDE, the corrections department motto that stands for Professionalism, Respect, Integrity, Dignity, and Excellence. Dickenson sarcastically suggests that a better application of this motto is Perfunctory, Reaction, Indecision, Deny, and Excuse.[16]

STRESS AND DANGER

Stress is common among law enforcement personnel, and particularly among correctional officers. It is not surprising, as correctional officers must supervise individuals who are confined, yet do not want to be, and who constantly try to manipulate staff to make their confinement as interesting (many inmates enjoy the challenge of manipulating staff) and tolerable as possible. Stress results from many elements of correctional officers' working situation. In a recent review of the nature and extent of stress among correctional officers, the National Institute of Justice found the following causes of stress:[17]

- Organizational sources of stress include understaffing, overtime, shift work, and supervisor demands. Understaffing results from high turnover or officers taking excessive sick leave, and forces too much work on correctional officers in too little time, apprehension about the supervision of large numbers of inmates without potential backup support, and an inability to get time off for special occasions or family crisis. While many officers say they welcome the extra pay of overtime, too much overtime work quickly burns staff out. Officers in many states have to rotate the shifts they work (going from day to evening to night shifts), and this causes havoc with family life and problems with fatigue. And officers report that their supervisors are "always on you to do the job right, but you can't do it right [because of staff shortages]."[18]

- Work-related sources of stress include the threat of violence, inmate demands and manipulations, and problems with co-workers. Inmate assaults against correctional staff in state and federal prisons have increased. Between 1990 and 1995, the number of attacks jumped by nearly one-third, from 10,731 to 14,165, while the number of correctional officers increased by only 14 percent.[19] From 1994 to 2000, 257 employees of state and federal prisons (an average of 37 per year) died in the line of duty.[20] The constant challenge by inmates to correctional officer authority also causes stress. Problems with co-workers include competition for promotion and choice assignments, sexist attitudes from male to female officers, and concern for other officers' inappropriate or unprofessional behavior.

- There is stress from outside the system such as poor public image and poor pay. Many officers feel that their work is not understood or appreciated by the public, and low pay causes financial stress even for officers who enjoy their jobs and would like to make corrections a career.

While stress is never going to be removed from staff working in a prison, some methods and programs have been identified to reduce the damage that stress can have on both employees and their families. Those believed most successful are staff training on stress reduction, family counseling services, and postincident counseling. Most correctional agencies conduct training for staff on the causes of stress, how to attempt to avoid stressful situations, and techniques for managing your own stress levels. Staff learn the benefits of an overall healthy lifestyle of diet, exercise, and seeking stability in financial and family issues, and are trained in stress reduction techniques such as breathing exercises. Many agencies provide counseling and services for families, both so they can better understand the work environment of the officer, and to deal with stressful home situations that result in adding stress to the employee. Finally, after a critical incident such as an assault on a staff member, immediate and follow-up counseling is provided employees to give them the opportunity to recognize and manage the natural stress that results from such an incident.

GAINING COMPLIANCE OF INMATES

The most important skill for correctional officers to learn is how to gain compliance from inmates without having to resort to threats, coercion, or taking disciplinary action, and without risking the eruption of violence from an inmate refusing to abide by the orders of an officer. It is not easy to gain compliance from inmates already in prison, many of whom rebel against all authority and are serving long sentences with very little to lose. The overall prison disciplinary system creates the backdrop for gaining compliance by listing expected behavior and the penalties for failure to follow prison rules. As well, inmate classification systems provide inmates who behave the opportunity to move to less-secure prisons with more privileges for inmates. Inmates are aware of these incentives and disincentives and understand that failing to follow orders of staff can result in punishment.

Therefore, staff do not have to *individually* take responsibility for making inmates follow rules. Correctional officers know they will win any war of wills, because an inmate who continues to refuse to comply with rules or a direct order from staff will be punished through the inmate disciplinary system. This allows

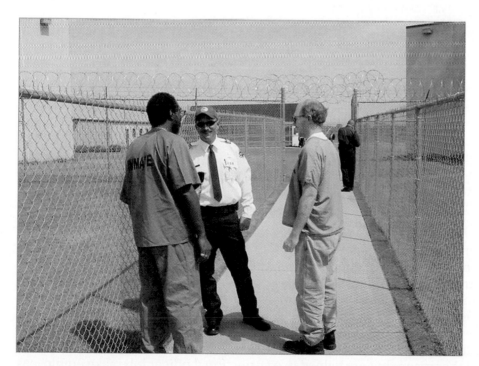

Correctional officers gain inmates compliance through communication rather than threats and intimidation.
Photo by Richard P. Seiter.

GAINING COMPLIANCE

A new, young, and aggressive correctional officer (Robert Dole) at a high-security prison wants to establish himself as tough and not willing to take anything from inmates. He is assigned as a "yard officer," and as such watches inmates move across the prison compound from one building to another. As a part of his duties, Dole is to randomly pat-search inmates (similar to "frisking" by the police). With a pat search, officers move their hands over inmates' bodies to search for concealed weapons, drugs, or other contraband under their clothing. One day, Dole sees an inmate (Jones) he wants to pat-search; he points at Jones and calls out, "Hey, you come over here," and tells him, "Hold your arms out for a pat search," in a brusque and terse manner. When finished and finding nothing prohibited, he orders the inmate, "Ok, keep moving."

Jones realizes he will be searched from time to time, but doesn't like the attitude of disrespect he believes that Dole presented. He is angry about it, and when he arrives at his work area, is confronted by his work supervisor who wants to discuss his recent poor performance with him. Jones is not a very responsible or mature person, and reluctantly begins the conversation with his supervisor. When the supervisor asks why he did not complete a task assigned the previous day, Jones angrily responds, "You guys are just looking for me to screw up, and this is a bunch of bullshit." The supervisor tries to calm him down, but Jones just seems to get madder, and starts yelling at the supervisor. Soon, other correctional staff have to intervene, and while trying to move Jones away, Jones strikes one of them. He is forced to the ground by staff, handcuffed, and taken to the special housing unit.

This incident can happen almost anytime with Jones because of his lack of maturity and responsibility. However, when correctional officer Peter Smith is working as the yard officer, there are fewer such problems. Smith has been working at the prison for a few years, and has become comfortable in gaining compliance through courtesy and respect. Smith handles pat searches as follows. When Jones approaches, and Smith decides to pat him down, he looks at Jones and says, "Mr. Jones, could you step over here please, I need to pat you down." When Smith finishes the search without discovering anything, he says, "That's it, Mr. Jones, thank you." Jones is not thrilled with being searched, but goes on feeling that Smith respects him through his courtesy. Both Dole and Smith accomplish their pat-down tasks, yet both create an outcome (Dole's bad, and Smith's good) as a result of how they did their job.

correctional officers to be relaxed and confident in dealing with inmates. Effective officers use interpersonal communication skills to simply treat inmates as individuals, or as a work supervisor would treat an employee. Inmates know what they are to do and what the rules of a prison are, and reminding them of their responsibilities usually results in proper behavior.

The "A Case Study" box illustrates a good example of the "do's and don'ts" of gaining compliance.

CORRECTIONAL OFFICER CAREERS

While many college students do not think about a career in corrections or seriously consider becoming a correctional officer after graduation, a job as correctional officer is a tremendous experience and can provide a valuable foundation for future career opportunities. In fact, many states and the federal prison system expect staff to begin their prison employment as a correctional officer, and officers with a college degree may later move into a job as a counselor or case manager. However, the skills in security, interacting with inmates, and understanding the overall functioning of the prison that are gained in a correctional officer job make employees more valuable in any other role. The "Your Career in Corrections" box describes the role and functions of a correctional officer.

YOUR CAREER IN CORRECTIONS — CORRECTIONAL OFFICERS

Correctional officers are the "front line" of prisons, jails, and other correctional facilities. Long ago, the term *guard* was used for the people in charge of overseeing inmates in prisons and jails. The role of guards, also referred to as *turnkeys* or *hacks,* was to simply guard inmates, unlock and lock their cells when necessary, march inmates from the cellhouses to another location for work or eating, and brutally enforce rules and discipline. The role of custodial staff in modern prisons has changed considerably, even to the point to which it is now a misnomer to refer to them as merely "custodial" staff. The contemporary term of *correctional officer* is used to describe the complex role of staff that carry out security functions within a prison. In 1993, the American Correctional Association (ACA) passed a resolution to encourage the use of the term *correctional officer,* because it much better describes their responsibilities of custody and control, which "require extensive interpersonal skills, special training and educations, and . . . correctional personnel are skilled professionals."[21]

Correctional officers (COs) are responsible for overseeing individuals who are detained in jail while awaiting trial, or who have been convicted of a crime and are serving a sentence in prison. Their basic responsibility is to maintain order and contribute to the secure operation of the institution. They oversee various sections of an institution, such as a housing unit, yard or compound, perimeter fence, or inmate work or program area. Many tedious custodial functions must be carried out by COs for the maintenance of security and order. They must control doors and grills and lock and unlock them to allow only approved inmate movement. They must search inmates and areas, being alert for contraband such as drugs and weapons that can endanger staff and inmates. They also must also conduct inmate counts to maintain inmate accountability and prevent escapes. They make inmates obey the rules and initiate disciplinary action when they do not. They often oversee inmate work crews, such as those assigned sanitation responsibilities, and ensure that the inmate crew performs the work at the accepted standard.

While some of the details of the CO job may seem unexciting and uninteresting, they are basics that must be accomplished. There are also many challenging roles for correctional officers. Officers must mediate between inmates, educate inmates about rules and procedures, and be a link between the inmate culture and staff management of a prison. COs cannot show favoritism in handing out discipline or enforcing prison rules or policy. Yet they also must use understanding and communication, while recognizing the individualism of every inmate. A major challenge of their role is that correctional officers must maintain order and gain compliance from offenders who are incarcerated against their will, and who have a natural inclination to resent those who try to control them. If COs have to force inmates to comply with rules by using disciplinary actions or using force on a regular basis, prisons become the tense, violent, and dangerous world that people envision. Effective correctional officers gain compliance by communicating expectations, fairly enforcing rules, and treating inmates with respect and dignity.

Correctional officers also contribute to the rehabilitation of inmates. They do this in three ways: (1) by contributing to an environment of control without threats and tension, (2) by communicating with inmates in a relaxed and professional manner, and (3) by providing human services such as overseeing the feeding of inmates, referring sick inmates to medical staff, or assisting with recreational programs. COs do not have to be counselors or treatment specialists, but they contribute to rehabilitation through the manner in which they conduct themselves and do their jobs. While correctional officers maintain order and provide security, the manner in which they perform their tasks and communicate with inmates has a major impact on the overall prison environment. A brusque and harsh manner, an unwillingness to recognize genuine inmate issues, or a lack of respect for inmates creates an environment with constant tension between inmates and staff. However, a fair and impartial upholding of prison rules, a pleasant personality, a respect for individual dignity, and an understanding of correctional officers' role in prisoner rehabilitation contribute to a relaxed environment with positive interaction between staff and inmates. The role of correctional officer has moved well beyond that of guarding inmates, and now requires knowledge, training, good interpersonal communications, and sound decision making.

(continued)

On January 1, 2001, there were 218,382 correctional officers working in state and federal prisons. Of these, 77 percent were male, 67.1 percent were white and 21.3 percent black, and approximately 20 percent of all COs worked in a prison with inmates of the opposite gender.[22] The pay of correctional officers has been increasing each year for the past decade. On January 1, 2002, the average entry-level salary for state and federal COs was $23,627; after completion of a probationary period (usually six to twelve months) the average pay was $25,861; and the average maximum pay for correctional officers was $38,232 (the highest state pay was $57,996).[23] However, correctional officers also regularly work overtime, and it is not unusual for officers to make an additional 20 percent of their base salary. Most prison systems do not require a college education for officers, but many require either experience or a two- or four-year degree. Many states and the federal prison system use correctional officer jobs as the entry level into the prison system; staff who are successful as officers gain communications and security skills that serve them well throughout their careers and often help them get promotions and additional career opportunities. Many college students do not think of using their degrees to become correctional officers. However, the job is excellent for gaining experience, developing skills, and beginning a successful career in corrections.

Not everyone will make a good correctional officer, and therefore correctional agencies must thoughtfully recruit, screen, and retain only people who have the talents and characteristics to contribute to the agency mission. It seems reasonable to believe that during good economic times, it is very difficult to recruit and hire outstanding individuals to serve as correctional officers, yet in difficult economic times, the recruitment process would be easer. The reality is that states work hard to recruit correctional officers all the time. In a recent article describing recruitment efforts by the Illinois Department of Corrections, Snyder describes the efforts of the agency to host recruitment and informational sessions to maximize the number of possible applications, yet also do rigorous physical and academic screening to ensure that individuals are appropriate candidates.[24] And Riley and Wilder point out that the key to hiring and retaining qualified officers includes the following: "Agencies must take the time at the beginning of the [hiring] process to identify the characteristics they desire in their staff."[25]

Correctional officers are the positions most critical to the day-to-day management of a prison. They constantly interact with inmates. They carry out the vital security functions that form the basis of safe operations. They set the tone for the prison by how professionally they carry out their duties. And they cannot have an "off" day without it being felt by inmates and other staff who interact with them throughout the workplace. Their jobs are challenging, stressful, and sometimes dangerous. Yet every day approximately 220,000 state and federal line correctional officers perform their jobs in a quality fashion, serve the public, and contribute to the overall criminal justice system in America.

The Roles of Other Prison Staff

As can be seen from the extensive listing of prison jobs given earlier, there are many more than the two positions (warden and correctional officer) that have now been addressed. While the warden provides leadership and sets the tone for the prison, and correctional officers are key to successfully accomplishing day-to-day activities, many other staff contribute to the accomplishment of the prison mission. Prison staff work either in an administrative capacity or in one of the three operational areas of security, programs or treatment, and service. Some of these roles are described next.

OTHER SECURITY PERSONNEL

As noted, prisons operate using a very clear chain of command, and nowhere in the prison is this clearer than with security or custody personnel. Most prisons (particularly high- and maximum-security prisons) have a deputy, associate, or assistant warden in charge of security. This is such an important part of prison operations, and includes such a high number of staff (50 to 60 percent of all staff), that it is important to have a senior manager responsible for these functions. The next level of management is a midlevel manager and highest-ranking **uniformed staff** person in the prison, often assigned the rank of major. This person supervises all security personnel and is the substantive expert on custodial policies and practices. The next level is the rank of uniformed security staff that oversee each eight-hour shift of operations in the prison. Assigned the rank of captain, they oversee the daily functioning and routine within the prison, assign work, and ensure that there are the required number of officers to cover all posts or assignments. Lieutenants are usually assigned to some of the most sensitive and explosive areas of the prison, such as the recreation area, industrial complex, and housing complex. Sergeants act either as senior correctional officers who are assigned the most difficult posts or as the direct supervisors of correctional officers, responsible for ensuring consistency and quality implementation of policies.

Uniformed staff
prison or jail staff who work in the security or custody department and are responsible for the implementation of security policies and procedures

TREATMENT AND PROGRAM STAFF

Treatment and program staff deliver programs (education, vocational, recreation, substance abuse, religious, psychological) to inmates. The following program or treatment departments are found in most prisons.

Psychological services	Education
Vocational training	Religious services
Substance Abuse	Recreation

Each department includes midlevel managers who are substantive experts and manage each of the areas, and line staff who are primarily responsible for working with inmates in their specialty areas. The education program has teachers and vocational specialists, the religious programs have chaplains, and the psychological and substance abuse programs have counselors. These are usually specialty areas that require special training and education, and some require professional certification (to do a specific type of drug or mental health counseling) to deliver the programs.

In some prisons, these staff are called **professional staff**, although correctional administrators would rather call all their staff *professional* and use *program* or *treatment* to refer to this category of staff. There is also often a deputy/associate/assistant warden of programs or treatment that supervises these functions. The role of the program and treatment staff is to deliver programs that assist inmates in their rehabilitation and preparation for reentry to the community. Inmates may take general education, English as a second language (ESL), or general equivalency diploma (GED) programs from teachers. They may receive individual or group counseling from staff psychologists. They may participate in substance abuse programs with drug and alcohol counselors. They may receive a vocational certificate from a class taught by a certified vocational instructor. Or they may participate in a religious program overseen by a prison chaplain or a contracted priest, imam, rabbi, Protestant minister, or any other religious leader.

Professional staff
prison or jail staff in a specialty area that requires distinctive training and education and may also require a professional certification to deliver a program

SERVICES STAFF

The third category of prison staff includes staff who operate departments providing inmate services within a prison. Included departments are prison industries,

Chaplains are responsible for making religious worship opportunities available to inmates. They lead services, counsel inmates, and oversee services provided by contract ministers.
Photo by Richard P. Seiter.

facility maintenance, business operations, food services, and medical care. The staff organization for each of these departments is different, but they are usually led by a deputy/associate/assistant warden for services (or operations). Service departments include the following:

Prison industries   Business administration
Facility maintenance   Human resources
Safety and sanitation   Health services
Staff training/development   Food services

Each department has a midlevel manager who provides substantive expertise and manages the budget, staff, and delivery of services within the department. Prison industries departments have factory managers to oversee the production of goods, and several industrial specialists who supervise inmate workers. Similarly, facilities maintenance departments have managers and trades supervisors (electrical, carpentry, plumbing, heating and air conditioning) who supervise inmate workers. The food services department is organized similarly, with a manager and food service supervisors responsible for overseeing inmates who prepare and serve food. In most prisons, the business offices operate the inmate commissary and laundry, and have staff who supervise inmates in providing these services. Finally, the medical services department has a chief medical officer (physician) as the department head, and nurses, pharmacy staff, and other health care delivery personnel to operate the prison infirmary.

This wide variety of jobs provides career opportunities for students with many different majors. In the "You make the Decision" box, students must weigh the pros and cons, and make a decision as to whether they would consider working in a prison.

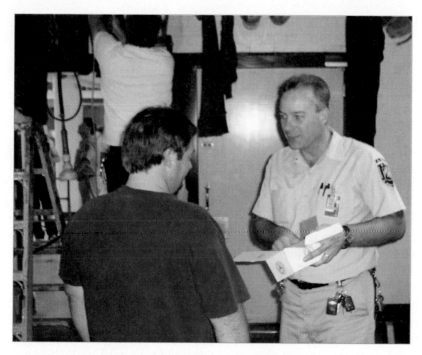

Maintenance workers train and supervise inmates in performing work to maintain the prison.
Photo by Richard P. Seiter.

YOU MAKE THE DECISION . . .   DO I WANT TO WORK IN A PRISON?

One issue that confronts students considering a career in corrections is whether they want to work in a prison. Often the first reaction is negative. Students think, "I don't want to work in a prison. I didn't get my college degree to work in that type of environment. I want a more professional job." However, after they become more familiar with prisons, their operation, the jobs and roles of various staff, and the quality of the people who work there, they often reconsider their earlier hesitancy to work in a prison.

For this exercise, you are asked to consider the pros and cons of working in a prison. Think of the various roles and issues confronted that were described in this chapter for staff who work in a prison. Create a list of all the good things that are involved with a prison job, such as stability, good benefits, and opportunities for career advancement. Then create a list of the things that are not so positive about working in a prison, such as danger, stress, and relatively low pay. After creating these lists, you may go further and do additional investigation into these topics on the Internet, in endnotes from this chapter, or in other readings, and find factual information regarding each issue.

Once you have created and investigated your list, think about what it would really be like to work in a prison. Decide (individually or in a group) whether you would consider a career that involves working in a prison.

The Prison Culture for Staff

Staff and inmates quickly learn the culture of a prison. Staff may say, "That's not the way things are done here," or tell inmates, "You need to forget how things were at your last prison, and get used to our way." They are talking about organizational culture, which is reflected in the way policies and procedures are actually carried out. State correctional agencies require the same policies to be implemented at every prison, yet, the way policy is implemented differs based on the culture of the prison. Stojkovic and Farkas suggest that there is a "nexus between prison leadership and prison culture," meaning that the leadership of the prison directly influences the culture of the prison.[26] But in some prisons, the culture may have continued so long or be so strong that leadership of the prison fails to affect it without lengthy and aggressive efforts.

Many models of prison organizational culture are based on a single focus, whether it varies by characteristics of officers, or whether multiple cultures exist within the different levels of staff.[27] In the latter, a "three-cultures" model is presented by Farkas and Manning, suggesting that values, sentiments, and modes of thinking vary between three organizational levels: the lower participant or officer segment, the middle management segment, and the top command segment.[28] In this model, the perspective from which the group looks at their jobs influences the culture of the job level. The line officer level is influenced by their union or labor organization, and most influenced by the internal organization of what occurs as they carry out the daily tasks in the prison. The middle management level identifies with either the line officer or top command level, and is influenced by the internal orientation of their jobs and working environment. The top command level is consumed with administrative duties, must respond to and is influenced by external audiences (their agency bosses, the public, politicians), and looks beyond the daily activities to longer-term objectives.

While all three levels may have a distinct culture, the levels may also influence each other so that there is a merger of cultures resulting in one blended rather than three distinct cultures. This blending is considered a positive development, and strong and visionary leaders work to bring convergence among the cultures of the three levels. A desired result is that the top command influences the other two to see the long-term good (vision) of the agency and prison, rather than reflect that of the day-to-day activities and strictly internal culture of the line officers. The most effective prisons have only one dominant culture, although there is no denying that all individuals and groups are most strongly influenced by what they desire from their job and the way they look at their work.

Two types of culture develop within a prison, one dealing with the management style of command to line staff, and one dealing with the relationship between staff and inmates. The style of **management culture** has to do with the way leadership deals and communicates with subordinate staff, and falls into a continuum between *autocratic* and *empowered*. The **relationship culture** is the style by which staff view and communicate with inmates, and falls into a continuum between *authoritarian* (gaining compliance by threats and intimidation) and *reasoned* (gaining compliance through incentives and disincentives). Both of these types of prison culture greatly affect the overall tone in which the prison is operated. Staff and inmates are aware of the culture and adapt and respond as expected, and their behavior therein perpetuates the continuation of the culture.

The management culture of a prison is represented in Figure 12.2. There is no question that the culture of Stateville under Warden Ragen was one of autocratic

Management culture

a culture based on the way prison leadership deals and communicates with subordinate staff; it falls into a continuum between autocratic and empowered.

Relationship culture

a culture based on how staff view and communicate with inmates; it falls into a continuum between authoritarian and reasoned

---

A CONTINUUM OF MANAGEMENT CULTURES IN A PRISON   FIGURE **12.2**

Autocratic	Moderate	Empowered
Staff must follow policy or check with supervisors before making decisions		Staff make decisions with full knowledge and consistent with prison principles and values

rule. Staff never made a decision that was not checked with their supervisors. In an autocratic prison culture, staff strictly follow the rules and cannot make decisions to address issues outside of policy. In an empowered culture, employees are knowledgeable about the principles, values, policies, and expected outcomes in the prison, and make decisions consistent with the expected outcome. Seiter writes,

> Empowerment involves providing employees with the principles and values of the organization, along with the desired outcomes (vision and mission), and allowing them to make decisions and respond to situations that are consistent with the principles and values, and move toward the desired outcomes.[29]

Throughout history, most prisons have operated toward the autocratic end of the management culture continuum, partly because of their development as paramilitary organizations, but also because of fear that line staff would make mistakes that could result in dire consequences of loss of life, escapes, or riots. However, a style of empowerment is important in modern prisons for several reasons. First, there is continuous change, and correctional agencies have difficulty developing routine procedures that can be counted on to work over time. Second, rapid changes result in situations that have never before been encountered, and no guidelines on how to respond are available. Third, prison employees are better educated and better trained than in the past, have experienced a world of rapid change, and are prepared to meet never-before-confronted challenges. Finally, today's employees demand to be involved in the organization, and cringe at a rigid bureaucracy that expects them to follow orders and carry out prescribed functions without knowing the reasons behind them.

The prison culture reflecting the relationship between staff and inmates is also critical within a prison environment. This cultural continuum is depicted in Figure 12.3. In the authoritarian culture, staff are threatened by inmates and believe that they cannot maintain control of the prison unless they constantly reinforce their position of authority by threats and intimidation. In such a prison, staff are seen as "weak" if they are polite or show respect and courtesy to inmates. In the reasoned culture, staff know that they have the power of sanctioning inmates with disincentives and rewarding inmates with incentives, and they maintain control through fairness in making these decisions. Therefore, they interact with inmates in a relaxed and congenial fashion, without losing authority or appearing weak. Prisons that operate on the more reasoned end of the continuum develop a less stressful and tense long-term environment.

Leaders are responsible for creating the culture within an organization. Wardens set the tone and culture by the management style they adopt and the style of staff-inmate interaction they support. The "A Case Study" box gives a good example of a warden taking a leadership role in creating a positive culture within a prison. It represents a real situation I faced after a riot at a prison where I was the warden.

A CONTINUUM OF STAFF-INMATE CULTURES IN A PRISON   FIGURE **12.3**

Authoritarian	Moderate	Reasoned
Staff demand compliance from inmates through threats and intimidation		Staff use agency incentives and disincentives for gaining compliance from inmates

A CASE STUDY | **SETTING THE TONE**

After the riot at the prison, the warden observed that staff were taking a much more authoritative approach in their interactions with inmates. More staff elevated their voice and took on a tone of discipline when talking to inmates, and statements by staff to direct an inmate to change their behavior became more like "barking orders" than reminders of the rules. While these types of interactions are necessary in certain situations and with certain noncompliant inmates, when they tend to become the regular rather than infrequent method of interaction, it sets a climate of tension and hostility that can make the environment more stressful and less stable for both staff and inmates. The warden felt that this behavior was the result of the riot, the fact that staff had witnessed a few inmates destroying property and assaulting staff, and that some staff were fearful and less confident. As a result, staff began to treat all inmates as violent and dangerous, and became more terse and disrespectful in their communications. The warden, in conjunction with his top staff, developed a plan to change this interaction style into one that was more relaxed and positive. First, he initiated activities to directly respond to staff members' fear of further victimization by inmates. This included "hardening" the prison by replacing wooden doors with metal ones and putting bars over windows to create "safe havens" for staff if another dangerous situation broke out. Staff were trained in disturbance control methods, boosting their confidence that they could handle a violent situation if one occurred.

As staff felt more comfortable with their personal safety, the warden set out to improve the positive communication between staff and inmates. Additional training was provided to staff regarding positive interactions and proper interpersonal communication. The warden made a videotape shown to all staff of him discussing the importance of positive staff-inmate interactions. On the video, the warden explained the reasons for such positive interaction, emphasizing that it was not to be "soft" on inmates, but that this approach in effect enhanced the security and safety of the institution. As well as reducing tension and lessening the likelihood of an inmate spontaneously responding with violence in a confrontational situation with staff, positive communication opened the door to inmates sharing important "intelligence" with staff about planned inmate misconduct or potential inmate gang activities. Supervisors were asked to immediately correct communication that did not comply with this approach by line staff, and use this as a key discussion point in all staff evaluations. The warden also appealed to line staff to recognize the problems that inappropriate communication caused, and to correct their fellow employees who destabilized the environment and made it more dangerous for everyone else.

These activities worked well over time. Fewer staff used harsh and authoritative tones of voice when unnecessary. More staff began to repeat the importance of positive communication, and prided themselves on their ability to gain inmate compliance without having to "bark orders" and demand it. As staff found out that they more effectively maintained order through treating inmates with courtesy and respect, while still consistently and fairly enforcing rules, they did so with increased skill and success. The overall climate of the institution returned to one of positive staff and inmate interaction, a relaxed and less stressful environment, and actually a reduced level of disciplinary infractions for failure to follow orders or insubordination by inmates.

Female Correctional Officers in Men's Prisons

Two or three decades ago, women were not allowed to work in men's prisons as correctional officers, as they were not believed to be able to perform effectively and safely. The arguments against women working as correctional officers included "(1) women weren't strong enough, (2) their presence would be disruptive to prison operations (inmates would not follow their orders or would fight for their attention and (3) the privacy of male inmates would have to be violated."[30] The only female employees in men's prisons held jobs with no inmate contact, such as clerks, secretaries, or mail workers.

However, Title VII of the 1964 Civil Rights Act, amended in 1972, proscribes employment discrimination on the basis of race, religion, sex, and national origin, and therein granted women the legal right to seek employment as correctional officers in men's prisons. Women quickly filed several cases with the Equal Employment Opportunity Commission (EEOC), claiming discrimination on the basis of sex by criminal justice agencies. A provision of Title VII, however, states that some discriminatory practices might be allowed if there is "a bona fide occupational qualification (**BFOQ**) reasonably necessary to the normal operation of that particular business or enterprise."[31] Therefore, correctional agencies hesitated to hire women for correctional officer positions, believing that the risk to security and loss of privacy for inmates would be considered an acceptable BFOQ exception.

In 1977, the U.S. Supreme Court decided the case of ***Dothard v. Rawlinson*** and first addressed the BFOQ exception.[32] Rawlinson was a woman who was denied a position as a correctional officer in an Alabama men's prison because the state prohibited women in any position that would require contact with male inmates. The Court ruled that a BFOQ prohibiting female correctional officers was allowable because of the deplorable conditions of the Alabama prisons and the presence of predatory male sex offenders as inmates. In *Dothard*, however, the Court did not address the issue of privacy for inmates in regard to the presence of female correctional officers. In 1979, in ***Gunther v. Iowa***, the U.S. District Court of Iowa did not find the same predatory environment in a medium-security Iowa prison that was believed to exist in the *Dothard* case within a maximum-security Alabama prison. The court therefore determined that inmate privacy was not a valid reason to refuse to hire women as correctional officers, finding that the state could create staffing and assignment patterns to avoid infringing on inmate privacy. The *Gunther* decision eliminated the major reason that states claimed a BFOQ in not hiring female correctional officers, and most states moved quickly to hire women. By January 1, 1992, women represented 17.6 percent of the approximately 160,000 correctional officers in state and federal prisons; by January 1, 2001, 23.9 percent of the 215,000 total U.S. correctional officers were women, and 37,834

BFOQ
a bona fide occupational qualification reasonably necessary to the normal operation of a particular business or enterprise that may allow for some discriminatory practices to occur

Dothard v. Rawlinson
a 1977 U.S. Supreme Court case regarding a woman who was denied a position as a correctional officer in an Alabama men's prison; the Court ruled that a BFOQ against female correctional officers was allowable because of the deplorable conditions of the Alabama prisons and the presence of predatory male sex offenders as inmates

Gunther v. Iowa
a 1979 case in the U.S. District Court of Iowa in which the court determined that inmate privacy was not a valid reason to refuse to hire women as correctional officers; the *Gunther* decision eliminated the major support used for the BFOQ by states in not hiring female correctional officers

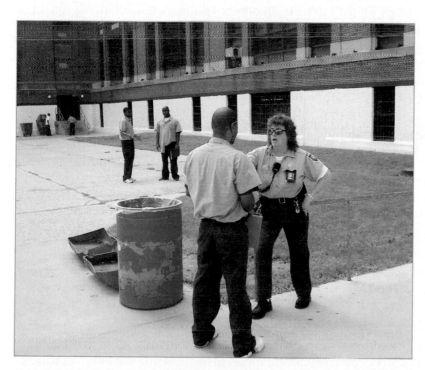

Female correctional officers are now a regular part of and play a valuable role in prisons for male inmates.
Photo by Richard P. Seiter.

(80 percent of the total employed) of these female officers worked in men's prisons.[33] This progress did not come easily, however, as the historical bias against and assumption that female officers would have different attitudes and carry out their duties differently than their male counterparts persisted. Some of the early negative reaction by male correctional officers to women working as co-workers is apparent in the following survey results:

> Out of a hundred men interviewed, only a handful were at all supportive of [women working as correctional officers] ... The most frequently voiced reasons for opposing the presence of women were that they impair the security of the institutions as a whole and jeopardize male guards' own safety.[34]

However, studies have found either no or only minor differences in relation to the attitudes and job performance of women compared to men.[35] A study of female correctional officers in California in 1983 found that women performed as well as men as correctional officers. However, men continued to perceive women as less effective when the situation required physical strength or a violent emergency existed.[36] A study within the Federal Bureau of Prisons also found no lapse in performance, but did find that female correctional officers experienced hostility and sometimes sexual harassment from male staff and inmates.[37]

Interesting findings resulted from a survey of male inmates who were asked to rate female correctional officer performance compared to male correctional officers. Cheeseman, Mullings, and Marquart found that higher-security inmates were more likely to favorably rate the performance of female officers than lower-security inmates. The authors write, "Specifically, prisoners classified as close custody were significantly more likely than minimum or medium custody inmates to agree that female staff performed as well as male staff when responding to stabbings, responding to physical fights, settling verbal disputes among inmates, and preventing riots or disturbances."[38]

In a report of interviews with female jail officers published in 1998, the findings were that female officers believed that they received paternalistic treatment, were excluded from work socialization opportunities, had higher job stress, and had more limited career prospects.[39] The findings further suggested that female correctional officers experience various problems stemming from sexism and sexual harassment by their male co-workers, which could be reduced if the jail administrators demonstrated a commitment to the thorough integration of women within the formal and informal organizational structure. With the passing of time, women have been more openly accepted into male prison environments, and in most states and county jails, women receive the same work and promotional opportunities as men.

In fact, there are many benefits to women working as correctional officers. One is that the style of supervision by female correctional officers of male inmates may bring a calming and normalized influence to a prison. Pollock writes:

> Women officers tend to ask inmates to do things rather than tell them. Female correctional officers foster personal interest in the inmate and use the relationships they develop as a technique of control. This relieves some of the tension found in prisons for men and encourages male prisoners to interact with correctional officers rather than cultivating isolation and separate subcultures.[40]

While modern correctional administrators accept women as able to effectively perform the role of correctional officers in men's prisons, some stereotypes still exist, and women in some correctional facilities are forced to endure a lack of respect that is given male officers by inmates or even other correctional officers. Even though these attitudes are not based on fact or performance, prisons for male in-

Although many women now work as correctional officers in men's prisons, they still face challenges because they are women working in a predominantly male environment.
Photo by Richard P. Seiter.

mates are very male-dominated places, and these stereotypes and perceptions will be difficult to totally overcome. The following interview with a female correctional officer working in a men's prison reflects the challenges women still face in a predominantly male environment. The "A Look Into" box presents an interview with an officer with less than one year of experience. I intentionally wanted to interview an officer who is new, still learning, and facing the challenges and developing the skills to be an effective female officer in a men's prison.

A LOOK INTO . . .

AN INTERVIEW WITH A FEMALE CORRECTIONAL OFFICER

Janel Gonzales is a correctional officer at the Madison Correctional Institution in London, Ohio. She is from Utica, New York, and moved to Ohio after being hired as a correctional officer. She had been employed for approximately nine months at the time of this interview.

Q: Janel, what made you decide to become a correctional officer, and did you decide you wanted to work in a men's prison, or were you just assigned here?

A: I had a friend who worked at the Ohio Reformatory for Women as a correctional officer (CO), and she said the job was a "piece of cake," even though she said you had to be on your toes and do your job correctly. I was looking for a career at the time, and it sounded like a stable job with good benefits. I really hadn't thought much about it before that.

(continued)

Q: Can you describe the training you received that prepared you for the job as a CO?

A: I went through the Correctional Training Academy basic course, and got all the courses on security, interpersonal skills, and self-defense. However, the most useful thing at the academy was the opportunity to spend time with two instructors who had been COs. They were really honest and told me what to expect. They said that inmates will constantly try to play with you or get things over on you. And they were right. When I started working in the dorms [as a CO supervising a housing unit], they would always tell me that they were allowed to do things outside policy, such as hang out in the television rooms, have inmates from other dorms come into the dorm to braid their hair, or leave the back fire door open for ventilation. I told them if it wasn't policy, they couldn't do it. Even if other officers allowed them to do it, I was not the other officer, I was just myself. I was glad I listened to the instructors. Because, as I checked these things out, I found that the inmates were always lying to me, just to see if they could get me to violate a minor policy. I imagine if I had done so, it would have led to more major requests for violations.

Q: How do you gain inmate compliance as a CO?

A: It is interesting how inmates will ask you the same thing several times. You just have to stick to saying no, and consistently reinforce the policies. All correctional officers are different in how they do their jobs; you have to find out and do what works for you. I am a type that if what an inmate is asking just doesn't sound right (and everything they ask isn't covered by policy), I just don't let them do it. Once they find out that you won't vary on your answers, they make it easier on you.

Q: What are the specific challenges you face as a female correctional officer working in a prison for male inmates?

A: There are different issues for women than for male correctional officers. One thing is that inmates want to get physically close to you when they talk to you. I just tell them to "get back" to talk to me. The inmates get male attention all day long, but since there are not that many female officers, they want attention. They will come up and ask questions just to talk to you: "do you have a kite?" [a form to make a request to staff], or "Has mail been delivered?" Usually they already know the answer to the question. This is not threatening, as I know why they do it. I do not feel stalked; they just want attention because I am a woman. There is stress as to the expectations of female COs. From day one you come into the prison and inmates watch and expect certain things of you. You have to be careful about joking around with inmates or spending any extra time talking to a particular inmate. They may get the wrong impression that you are being too friendly, and it doesn't take long for other inmates and staff to start wondering if there isn't something going on. That's why I won't joke around with inmates. And if you let any inmate do something outside policy, you have to do that with every other inmate. So you have to constantly follow policy.

Q: Is there some additional stress because inmates will try to become romantically involved with female staff?

A: There is some of that, but when you recognize it, you just are very careful about not doing anything that would give inmates an impression that you are that kind of person. But just the opposite is that many male inmates don't want a woman telling them what to do. They will look at you funny, or sideways, or second-guess it. I just look back and say, "Oh yeah, I said it." That never changes, because every time I go into a dorm there are new inmates. They always want to try you, and you always have to prove yourself.

Q: Have you ever been fearful for your personal safety?

A: No. I never have. Because I know I can't stop everything from happening. An inmate could walk up behind me at any time and do something. But I feel that the officers are very resourceful. We also have these "man down," or Spider alerts, and it gives you confidence. And I am just not afraid of the inmates. I don't even acknowledge it if inmates try to be intimidating. There are some times when an inmate may sit somewhere and just stare at you. In this case, I figure you have to be loud with them and embarrass them. I will ask them if they have something to ask me, and when they say no, I tell them to take their eyes off me; look somewhere else.

Q: Are there any issues that female COs face with male staff?

A: When I arrived here, I had a male CO tell me, "I disagree with women being in a male prison." I just looked at him and said, "Well, I am here." I am not worried about what others think; I am just here to do a job. But most staff just see me and the other women just as another CO.

Q: How would you advise other women who want to consider being a CO?

A: Enforce the rules consistently. While every rule can't be completely enforced, if you see something you are not comfortable with or don't like how it is going, stop it immediately and enforce the rules right there. Don't let anyone take advantage of you. Keep your eyes and ears open. If you get the skills of working successfully with inmates, you can do anything. I would encourage this as a job. It sometimes is hard to get the job, but once you get in, it is worth it.

Chapter Review

SUMMARY

In this chapter, the people who work in prisons were described and discussed. The goal of the chapter is for students to better understand the challenges these staff face, the contributions they make, and the environment and culture in which they work. While most people think of wardens and correctional officers as staff of prisons, there are many more categories of job specialties within a prison. A prison needs almost every category of specialist that it takes to operate a small city. There must be staff to maintain the facility, provide food services and health care to inmates, offer rehabilitative programs, hire and train other staff, manage the finances and budget, and maintain a secure and safe environment.

At the top of the prison chain of command is the warden. Wardens have become almost mythical individuals in the American culture. Partly because of their challenging job of maintaining order among hundreds or thousands of convicted felons, partly because they must direct a diverse workforce often represented by a union and sometimes at odds with the mission of the

agency, and partly because of the way in which they are portrayed in movies and television shows, wardens are usually thought of as autocratic, harsh and insensitive to inmates and staff, and often unethical. However, modern wardens have to be outstanding managers of people and resources, and must rely on education, intelligence, and experience more than simply a dominating personality.

Correctional officers make up the line position that is critical to the day-to-day operation of a prison and deals directly with inmates. Their job is not glamorous, not easy, and generally underappreciated. Correctional officers have challenging jobs, as inmates are constantly trying to manipulate and challenge them, and to avoid following rules. Officers must enforce security procedures, and lapses can cause escapes, assaults, and even riots. Officers are key in setting the tone of interaction between staff and inmates. They can perform their duties in a brusque and authoritative manner, or act with more respect and courtesy toward inmates. The latter is much more effective in maintaining a more relaxed and less tense environment, yet requires maturity and confidence by the officers to communicate effectively.

Two key issues in a prison are the overall culture and the role of female correctional officers in men's prisons. The culture is the approach or manner in which policies and procedures are carried out within a prison. A prison adopts a culture regarding how staff communicate with each other and how staff communicate with inmates. The warden and other leadership within a prison are critical to establishing and maintaining a positive organizational culture. The use of women as correctional officers has also become a controversial issue in men's prisons. While banned from working in men's prisons only twenty-five years ago, female officers are now recognized as valuable employees both in how they perform their jobs and in how they contribute to a positive organizational culture.

REVIEW QUESTIONS

1. Prisons have many staff other than correctional officers. List five other staff positions within a prison.

2. How does staff empowerment expand the effectiveness of prison operations beyond the traditional use of issuing orders through the chain of command?

3. How do staff control prisons in modern times?

4. How does transformational leadership differ from transactional leadership?

5. What percentage of all prison staff are correctional officers or correctional supervisors?

6. Describe the job of a correctional officer.

7. What are three causes of stress for correctional officers?

8. How do correctional officers gain the compliance of inmates?

9. What are service departments within a prison?

10. What are the two types of culture that can develop within a prison?

11. What did the case of *Gunther v. Iowa* decide, and how did it affect employment of women as correctional officers in men's prisons?

12. Approximately what percentage of state and federal correctional officers are female?

ENDNOTES

1. Richard W. Snarr, *Introduction to Corrections,* 3rd ed. (Madison, WI: Brown & Benchmark, 1996), p. 179.

2. James B. Jacobs, *Stateville: The Penitentiary in Mass Society* (Chicago: University of Chicago Press, 1977).

3. "At Stateville: The Calm Is Tense," *Corrections Magazine* 61, no. 3 (June 1980): 6–10, 15–19.

4. Nathan Kantrowitz, *Close Control: Managing a Maximum Security Prison; The Story of Ragen's Stateville Penitentiary* (Albany, N.Y.: Harrow and Heston, 1996).

5. Robert Freeman, "Management and Administrative Issues," in *Prisons: Today and Tomorrow,* edited by Jocelyn M. Pollock (Gaithersburg, Md.: Aspen, 1997), p. 279.

6. James MacGregor Burns, *Leadership* (New York: Harper & Row, 1978).

7. M. Kay Harris, "A Call for Transformational Leadership for Corrections," *Corrections Management Quarterly* 3, no. 1 (1997): 22–25.

8. John J. DiIulio, Jr., *Governing Prisons: A Comparative Study of Correctional Management* (New York: Free Press, 1987), pp. 188–189.

9. Camille Graham Camp and George M. Camp, *The 2001 Corrections Yearbook* (Middletown, Conn.: The criminal Justice Institute 2002), pp. 153, 155.

10. Ibid., p. 154.

11. Curtis Prout and Robert N. Ross, *Care and Punishment: The Dilemmas of Prison Medicine* (Pittsburgh, Pa.: University of Pittsburgh Press, 1988), p. 152.

12. Lucien X. Lombardo, *Guards Imprisoned,* 2nd ed. (Cincinnati, Ohio: Anderson, 1989).

13. Andrew Metz, "Life on the Inside: The Jailers," in *Exploring Corrections: A Book of Readings* (Needham Heights, Mass.: Allyn & Bacon, 2002), p. 65.

14. Ibid., p. 64.

15. M. A. Farkas and P. K. Manning, "The Occupational Cultures of Corrections and Police Officers," *Journal of Crime and Justice* 20, no. 2 (1997): 51–68.

16. Lee Dickenson, *The Keepers of the Keys* (Fort Bragg, Calif.: Lost Coast, 1999), pp. 142–143.

17. Peter Finn, *Addressing Correctional Officer Stress: Programs and Strategies* (Washington, D.C.: U.S. Department of Justice, National Institute of Justice, December 2000).

18. Ibid., p. 13.

19. Cited in Finn, 2000, p. 11.

20. Camp and Camp, 2002, p. 173.

21. American Correctional Association, "Resolution on the Term 'Correctional Officer,'" *Corrections Today* (April 1993): 60.

22. Camp and Camp, 2002, pp. 154–156.

23. Ibid., pp. 168–169.

24. Donald N. Snyder, Jr., "Recruitment and Retention Programs: Important during Economic Ups and Downs," *Corrections Today* (June 2000): 92–95.

25. Frank E. Riley and Beverly A. Wilder, "Hiring Correctional Staff with the Right Stuff," *Corrections Today* (June 2000): 91.

26. Stan Stojkovic and Mary Ann Farkas, *Correctional Leadership: A Cultural Perspective* (Belmont, Calif.: Wadsworth/Thompson, 2003), p. 5.

27. For a good discussion of the various models of prison organizational culture, see Stojkovic and Farkas, 2003, pp. 37–47.

28. M. Farkas and P. K. Manning, "The Occupational Cultures of Policing and Correctional Work," *Journal of Crime and Justice* 22, no. 2 (1997): 51–68.

29. Richard P. Seiter, *Correctional Administration: Integrating Theory and Practice* (Upper Saddle River, N.J.: Prentice Hall, 2002), p. 365.

30. Norman A. Carlson, Karen M. Hess, and Christine M. H. Orthmann, *Corrections in the Twenty-First Century: A Practical Approach* (Belmont, Calif.: Wadsworth, 1999), p. 441.

31. 42 U.S.C. 2000e-2 (1976), p. 703(e).

32. *Dothard v. Rawlinson*, 433 U.S. 321 (1977).

33. Camp and Camp, pp. 155, 156.

34. Lynn E. Zimmer, *Women Guarding Men* (Chicago: University of Chicago Press, 1986), pp. 53–54.

35. See Nancy C. Jurik and Gregory J. Halembia, "Gender Working Conditions and the Job Satisfaction of Women in a Non-Traditional Occupation: Female Correctional Officers in Men's Prisons," *Sociological Quarterly* 25 (1984): 551–566. Also see Lincoln J. Fry and Daniel Glaser, "Gender Differences in Work Adjustment of Prison Employees," *Journal of Offender Counseling, Services and Rehabilitation,* 12 (1987): 39–52.

36. Herbert Holeman and Barbara Krepps-Hess, *Women Correctional Officers in the California Department of Corrections* (Sacramento: California Department of Corrections, Research Unit, 1983).

37. See Kevin Wright and William Saylor, "Male and Female Employees' Perceptions of Prison Work: Is There a Difference?" *Justice Quarterly* 8 (1991): 505–524.

38. Kelly A. Cheeseman, Janet L. Mullings, and James W. Marquart, "Inmate Perceptions of Security Staff across Various Custody Levels," *Corrections Management Quarterly* 5, no. 2 (2001): 44.

39. Mark R. Pogrebin and Eric D. Poole, "Sex, Gender, and Work: The Case of Women Jail Officers," *Sociology of Crime, Law, and Deviance* 1 (1998): 105–124.

40. Joycelyn M. Pollock, "Women in Corrections: Custody and the 'Caring Ethic,'" in *Women, Law, and Social Control,* edited by Alida V. Merlo and Joycelyn M. Pollock (Needham Heights, Mass.: Allyn & Bacon, 1995), p. 111.

Chapter 13

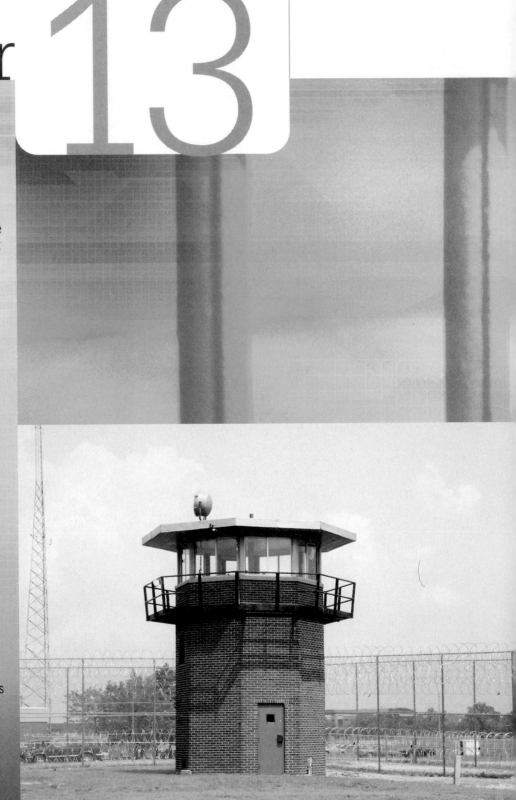

**AFTER READING THIS CHAPTER,
YOU SHOULD BE ABLE TO:**

1. List the eight types of activities that contribute to the security and custody functions within a prison.

2. Define inmate accountability and describe the activities by which prison officials ensure that inmates are accounted for.

3. Identify the three types of counts and how they are carried out in a prison.

4. Explain how contraband comes into the possession of inmates and specify procedures to prevent it from occurring.

5. Describe the two categories of inmate assignments in a special housing unit.

6. Discuss the environmental factors and precipitating events that can combine to cause an inmate riot.

7. Outline the functions and operations of the three types of emergency team in a prison.

8. Define rehabilitation and describe its evolution throughout the history of prisons in the United States.

9. Describe the various types of education and vocational programs provided in prisons.

10. Explain the scope of mental health needs of inmates and how prisons provide programs that meet these needs.

11. Identify the level of substance abuse among the inmate population and the level of program opportunities provided in prisons.

12. Trace the history of prison industry programs in terms of the way inmate labor was used and the markets that were available.

13. Describe the importance of prison religious programs and how they are delivered.

Custody and Treatment

KEY TERMS

inmate accountability
work call
controlled movement
call out
pass system
regular counts
stand-up count
census count
random count
contraband
shadow board
special housing unit
administrative detention
disciplinary segregation
environmental factors
precipitating event
hostage negotiation team
disturbance control team
special emergency response team
mandatory prison education
vocational training
Pell grants
continuum of care
lease system
state-use system
PIE Program

Introduction

As noted earlier the mission of prisons is to create a safe and secure environment, while offering inmates programs that can help them in their rehabilitation and reentry to the community. The mission has two dominant themes: custody and treatment. Custody and treatment are the principal functions within a prison, and rather than being two parallel prison functions, they often seem in total conflict with each other. To create a safe and secure environment, *custody,* the activities within a prison that control inmate behavior and maintain order, must be accomplished in a way that reduces the likelihood of escape or violence. Prisons must be secure to prevent escapes, and must be safe so that inmates and staff can live and work in the prison without constant fear of assault and injury.

The task of controlling behavior and maintaining order envisions a picture of total and absolute control by correctional officers and an environment in which inmate rights and individual characteristics must be secondary to security. Can behavior be controlled and order maintained at the same time that treatment occurs within a prison? *Treatment* is the creation of an environment and provision of rehabilitative programs that encourage inmates to accept responsibility and to address personal disorders that make success in the community more difficult. The image of treatment within prisons is envisioned as just the opposite of custody. How can prison counselors and treatment staff treat inmates in a "soft and caring" manner, get inmates to acknowledge their weaknesses, and initiate a program of rehabilitation within an environment that is totally controlled and focused on order? The reality is that neither of these suggested images of prisons is accurate. The challenge for prison management is to prudently balance custody and security with treatment and rehabilitation. This balance is not easy to accomplish, and a movement in emphasis to either custody or treatment can upset the balance and lead to serious problems.

In this chapter, the activities prison officials undertake to create a safe and secure environment and to provide inmates the opportunity to address problems and prepare for release are described. As well, the difficulty of maintaining the delicate balance between custody and treatment is explained, and the methods by which prison administrators attempt to maintain a dual emphasis on both is presented. For prisons to be safe and secure, there must be sufficient physical security, consistent implementation of security practices, methods to control behavior and prevent inmates from possessing dangerous items, and preparation to reduce the likelihood of or respond to inmate unrest. For prisons to provide effective rehabilitative services, there must be assessment of needs and provision of a variety of programs (substance abuse, mental health, religious services, education and recreation, and work opportunities) to address these needs and prepare inmates for release. And, for prisons to accomplish their dual mission in a balanced fashion, there must be skilled prison leadership guiding the delicate balance for both security and treatment.

Security and Custody within a Prison

What is "security and custody" within a prison? Most experts would suggest that it includes all of the activities that provide for the overall control of inmate behavior, in a way that reduces the likelihood of escape or violence. The most immediate goal of prison operators is to have a safe and secure prison. A safe prison is one in which staff and inmates are relatively safe from assaults or other violent acts. A secure prison is one in which inmates are prevented from escaping and unable to get to prohibited areas of the prison.

The question of how to maintain security and custody within a prison is one that many people think should be very simple, as inmates are perceived to be locked in cells most of the time; when they are out of the cells, they are perceived to be under the close supervision of many correctional staff. Yet those who work inside correctional institutions recognize that maintaining security and custody is very complicated and requires an integration of several functions and activities within a prison. In reality, inmates are in their cells only a few hours a day, and at other times, actively participate in work, programs, and leisure activities. Seiter writes,

> There are no simple solutions to creating a safe and secure environment ... Inmates are serving longer sentences, often have little hope for a quick release, and may see few incentives for positive behavior. Long sentences can also create frustration and a sense of bitterness and unfair treatment on the part of inmates toward staff. The increasing percent of the inmate population that are youthful, impulsive and gang affiliated heightens the likelihood of violence ... Maintaining a safe and secure prison involves the integration of several elements within the prison.[1]

The following eight types of activities combine to contribute to the security and custody functions within a prison, and are more fully described in this book.

1. *Effective inmate classification systems.* The goal of an inmate classification system is to separate offenders according to risk of violence and escape, and to match offender needs with correctional resources. The physical security of a prison should be designed to match these risks of violence and escape.

2. *Physical security within a prison.* Prisons are categorized as minimum-, medium-, or maximum-security in terms of the physical security provided, including the type of fences and perimeter security, housing, and construction material used. Physical security also includes the use of modern technology and physical barriers to keep inmates in or out of certain locations within the prison. While many observers tend to overrely on physical security, more than that is required to have a safe and secure prison, as prison design and technology "cannot substitute for well-trained staff and good security practices ... "[2]

3. *Consistently implemented security policies and procedures.* The importance of professionally developed and consistently implemented policies and procedures for controlling inmate behavior was noted previously. The performance of sound security practices is one of the most critical elements in accomplishing security and custody within a prison.

4. *Control of inmate movement and accountability.* Inmates are allowed to move from one prison location to another for much of the normal day. Yet these movements must be established in a manner that allows staff to maintain inmate accountability at any time during the day.

5. *Control of contraband items.* There are several items that inmates are not allowed to possess (called *contraband*), including items that can assist in an escape, are dangerous, can sabotage or subvert prison physical security, or create an unhealthy or unsanitary condition. Custody practices call for thorough procedures to keep such items from falling into inmate hands.

6. *Implementation of an effective inmate disciplinary system.* Inmates must be told what behaviors are not allowed within a prison, and must be punished and held accountable if they commit these acts. An inmate disciplinary system is therefore an important tool for controlling inmate behavior and effecting prison custody and security.

7. *Methods to separate unruly inmates or inmates at risk.* Prisons use special housing units (SHUs) to separate inmates who are being investigated for misconduct, are at risk of being assaulted, or are being punished for violating

Physical security, such as a secure perimeter fence with razor ribbon, is one of the many elements essential to a safe and secure prison.
Photo by Richard P. Seiter.

prison rules. The operation of SHUs is a key activity in the security and custody function within a prison.

8. *Control and reduction of the likelihood of a prison riot or disturbance.* The greatest fear within a prison is that inmates (who outnumber staff by perhaps twenty to one at any time) will stop following prison policy and rules, act out in a violent manner, injure prison staff, or take over control of the prison. Prison administrators go to great lengths to understand the causes of prison unrest, take action to reduce the likelihood of riots, and prepare to respond to inmate disturbance quickly and efficiently to reduce the potential of serious injury to staff or inmates and the destruction of the prison or government property.

Security and Custody Functions

As noted previously, many activities are critical security and custody functions within a prison, and eight of these have been listed. Four were described earlier in this book, and inmate accountability, control of contraband, management of special housing units, and prevention of and preparation to respond to inmate unrest and prison riots are presented shortly. Security and custody functions are often tedious and time-consuming, yet must be accomplished in a thorough and conscientious fashion in order not to undermine the overall goal of creating a safe and secure prison environment.

Inmate accountability is a principal component of a prison custody operation. While physical barriers such as fences, walls, and cells keep inmates in a specific location, the procedures used to account for them during the many hours a day they are out of their cells and involved in work or other programs are perhaps even more important in preventing escapes and maintaining prison order. A prison cannot be safely managed without control of contraband, or items that can assist in an escape or be used as dangerous weapons. Prison staff sometimes must separate inmates, either as punishment or for their protection, in special housing units (sometimes thought of as a jail within the prison). And correctional officials can never forget the potential danger that can result from inmates deciding to riot or take control of a prison and its staff, and can never waver in their efforts to prevent such incidents and prepare in case they do occur.

INMATE ACCOUNTABILITY

Henderson, Rauch, and Phillips define **inmate accountability** as "the staff's ability to locate and identify inmates at any point in time . . . the very heart of institution security, from minimum-security camps to maximum-security penitentiaries."[3] It would be simple to know where inmates are at any time if they were always locked in their cells or dormitories. However, inmates are out of their cells almost eighteen hours a day, and therefore, policies and procedures must exist to identify where inmates should be, to control their movement, to supervise them to the greatest extent possible, and to have a system of "counting" them to ensure that they are all where they are supposed to be. The following are key components of inmate accountability policies and procedures:

Inmate accountability
the staff's ability to locate and identify inmates at any point in time within a prison

- Inmates are assigned to work and programs on a daily basis. These assignments place them under the supervision of staff responsible for that program or work activity.
- There is a system of inmate movement from one location to another within the prison that reduces the likelihood that inmates can go to other than their assigned location.
- Staff provide both casual and direct inmate supervision when inmates are not in their housing units.
- There are counts of inmates at regular and random times to ensure that they are where they are supposed to be within the prison.

Program and Work Assignments

Prison work and program assignments not only aid in inmate rehabilitation, but are also critical security functions in that they keep inmates active, limit time inmates might use to plan an escape or violation of rules, and place inmates under the direct supervision of staff. For example, inmates assigned to participate in an education program are assigned to the classroom of a specific teacher, who checks inmates in as class begins and is responsible for the inmates until the end of the assignment. This contributes to security and custody, as inmates are assigned to a correctional staff member who maintains responsibility for them, supervises them, and knows where they are during that time.

Prison work and program assignments are also an important part of the normal routine of the prison day. The "A Case Study" box illustrates how a routine of work and programs contributes to inmate accountability.

Inmate Movements

As illustrated in the case study, inmates move throughout the prison during the day and evening. How they move and the way these movements are controlled and supervised is an essential element of inmate accountability. Many people imagine that inmates move individually in a prison, with at least one staff person walking with them from one point to another. However, this is not accurate, and inmates usually move in large groups from their housing units to work, meals, or education or recreation programs. To maintain inmate accountability during these mass movements, prisons use a controlled system for inmate moves.

Controlled movement is the procedure used by prisons to maintain accountability for inmates as they move throughout the prison. The most common form of controlled movement is to schedule inmates to move from one point to another at

Controlled movement
the procedure used by prisons to maintain accountability for inmates as they move throughout the prison

Work call

the time when inmates are required to move to their jobs or program assignments

A CASE STUDY THE DAILY ROUTINE

The daily routine for a prison is an important part of inmate accountability and contributes greatly to the overall security of a prison. The day begins early and continues late, as prison officials desire to have scheduled activities during which inmates are under the direct supervision of staff for as many hours a day as possible. A typical prison workday is presented here.

On workdays, inmates awake between 5:30 A.M. and 6:00 A.M., and leave their cells at 6:00 A.M. to shower and prepare for the workday. They are allowed to go to the dining hall for breakfast from 6:30 to 7:00, and must return to their housing unit by 7:15 A.M. There is a **work call** at 7:30 A.M., and inmates move to their assigned jobs or programs. They are at their assigned location until 10:30, when they are to return to their housing unit, to be released to move to the dining hall for lunch from 11:00 until 12:00 noon.

After lunch, there is an afternoon work call at 12:30, and inmates remain at their assignments until 3:30 P.M. They then return to the housing unit, have a formal "count," and then go to the dining hall for dinner. After dinner, there are evening programs and leisure activities until 8:30 P.M., when inmates return to the housing unit and are locked in. They usually have time in the unit until approximately 11:30 P.M., when they are locked in their cells until let out the next morning. The work and program routine serves as the foundation for inmate accountability. Both staff and inmates know the schedule and adhere to it. Inmates know and move to where they are to be, and prison staff know the inmates they have assigned to them and for whom they are responsible. Staff then directly supervise those inmates, and maintain their accountability during the six to eight hours per day of their assignment.

a specific time, according to the daily routine and schedule. For example, at the 7:30 A.M. work call, a controlled movement begins with the unlocking of doors to the housing units and program and work areas. The staff who unlock the doors stand by the doors and watch inmates exit and enter. Inmates usually have a short time (say, ten minutes) to move from one location to another. After the ten minutes, inmates are expected to have reached their designated destination, and the doors are all relocked. Inmates who are not in their required location are subject to disciplinary action.

Inmates are out of their cells most of the day and move across the prison compound using a variety of controlled movement methods.
Photo by Richard P. Seiter.

Controlled movement contributes to inmate accountability in that it limits the time in which inmates have freedom to move or walk around the prison, and prevents them from standing and communicating with other inmates to organize gang activities or pass information. Efficient controlled movement gives staff both real and perceived control over inmates, as it not only maintains accountability but also has specific policies and procedures to form the habit of inmate compliance with prison rules.

Even with ideal schedules and routines, there are times other than during mass movements when inmates must move individually. They may have a visit from a family member, may have an appointment with the prison doctor or psychologist, or may be required to meet with a staff member who is not their work or program supervisor. These individual movements are usually handled either through the use of a *call out* or a *pass system*. With the **call out**, inmates are scheduled for their appointments at least a day in advance. A schedule of all the appointments and required moves for the day is prepared and distributed to staff, naming the inmate, the time, and the beginning and ending point of the move. Supervising staff allow inmates to move according to the call-out schedule.

Instead of, or sometimes in addition to, a call-out system, some prisons use a pass system for individual inmate movement. A prison **pass system** is similar to that used in many high schools, as an inmate is issued a pass by the work or program supervisor to go to the scheduled appointment. The pass includes a place for staff members to write the time the inmate leaves their supervision, and for receiving staff members to write the time the inmate arrives and leaves the appointment. Upon the inmate's return to the work or program supervisor, the time of return is also written on the pass. Staff are aware of the time it takes to move from one area of the prison to another and recognize any deviation from the expected time to move. If inmates take longer than they should during the move, they are subject to disciplinary action. As well, during the time inmates are walking from one location to another, staff who see them often ask to see their pass and double-check that the inmate is in possession of a pass and is moving toward the intended destination. Through the use of controlled mass movements and either a call-out or pass system for individual movement, staff control inmate movement within the prison without having to escort them.

Casual and Direct Inmate Supervision

Casual and direct supervision of inmates by staff is another critical component of inmate accountability. Work and program supervisors are responsible for inmates during the times of their assignment, and correctional officers are responsible for inmates assigned to areas that they supervise. This supervision is *direct* in that assigned staff can directly see and watch inmates and their activities. Inmate accountability is also enhanced through *casual* supervision, or supervision by staff who are not responsible for inmates, but still have the opportunity to see their movements or activities. Prison staff are trained to constantly watch inmates and look for suspicious behavior. Staff who are walking across the prison compound see inmate movements, and even though they are not directly responsible, they monitor inmate behavior for anything unusual. Staff working in their offices look out windows and also monitor inmates' movements and activities.

Modern prisons are designed to aid in the casual supervision of inmates. For example, in the education areas within prisons, education administrators and teachers often have offices with windows with a view into the central compound of the prison and can see inmates move from one area to another. They also have windows between their offices and adjacent classrooms or library areas, so they can casually monitor inmates in those locations and see if any other staff are having trouble with an inmate. Classrooms have large windows into the corridor, into

Call out

a schedule of all the appointments and required moves for a day, including the inmate name and expected times of the move

Pass system

a form of inmate movement in which an inmate is issued a pass by the work or program supervisor to go to a scheduled appointment

Prison classrooms, staff offices, and program areas often have several large windows so that casual supervision can occur.
Photo by Richard P. Seiter.

adjacent classrooms, and on the outside of the building. Not only can teachers see inmates outside their classrooms, but other staff can also see them and their interactions with inmates in their classrooms. These easy viewing situations provide additional supervision and security and keep staff from feeling isolated, insecure, and unprotected.

Inmate Counts

Another element of inmate accountability is the actual counting of inmates at various locations and times. Counts are done to determine that all inmates are where they should be, and that no inmates either are out of bounds (in an unauthorized location) or have escaped. A series of daily counts reduces the amount of time an inmate may be unaccounted for, reducing the opportunity to escape (or quickly finding out if an escape has occurred) or to plan any other act that threatens the secure and orderly operation of a prison. Prisons use three different types of counts: regular, census, and random. **Regular counts** consist of the scheduled counting of inmates in their housing units to ensure that they are in the prison and have not escaped. At these counts, inmates must be in their cell or on their beds, and correctional officers walk by and count how many are in the housing unit. They then call in the number to a central location, at which staff add up all the counts to be sure that they have the correct number of inmates.

American Correctional Association standards require a minimum of one count per eight-hour correctional shift; however, most agencies have at least five scheduled counts during a twenty-four-hour period. With this many counts, inmates are quickly discovered missing if they have escaped or are trying to escape. Prison regular counts usually occur at midnight, at 3:00 A.M. when inmates are asleep in their cells, before work call at approximately 7:00 A.M., after return from work for the day (approximately 4:00 P.M.), and when inmates are required to return to their housing units after evening programs or recreation (approximately 9:00 P.M.). The 4:00 P.M. count is often a **stand-up count**, the most formal count of the day, at which inmates must stand at their cell door or by their dormitory bed

Regular counts

the scheduled counting of inmates in their housing units to ensure that they are in the prison and have not escaped

Stand-up count

the most formal count of the day, at which inmates must stand at their cell door or by their dormitory bed to be counted and matched to the number of inmates assigned to each housing area

Correctional officers perform counts in prison housing units by going to every cell door and counting the number of inmates to be sure that all are accounted for.
Photo by Richard P. Seiter.

to be counted and matched to the number of and identification of inmates assigned to each housing area

A second type of count is a **census count**, a less formal count conducted at program and work assignments by the staff responsible for supervising inmates. They are usually held at the beginning and end of each work period to ensure that the work and program details have the correct number of assigned inmates. A third type of count is a **random count**. Random counts are done at any time and wherever inmates are when the random count is called. The warden or a high-ranking prison official will determine that a random count is needed (just to keep everyone honest) and put out an order for all inmate movement to cease, for all doors to be locked, and for all inmates to be counted where they are at the time. Since inmates know when the regular and census counts are held, random counts keep inmates from planning to leave their assigned area right after a count and give themselves the maximum expected time between regular and census counts.

CONTROL OF CONTRABAND

A second component of prison custody and security is to control contraband. **Contraband** is defined simply as any item that inmates are not allowed to possess, and can include items that can assist in an escape (ladders or ropes), are dangerous (weapons or drugs), can sabotage or subvert prison physical security (wire cutters that can cut a security fence), or are nuisance items that create unhealthy or unsanitary conditions (unsealed food that can spoil in an inmate cell). Since contraband undermines the safe and secure operation of a prison, custody

Census count

a less formal count conducted at program and work assignments by the staff responsible for supervising inmates

Random count

a count done at any time, freezing inmates wherever they are when the random count is called

Contraband

any item that inmates are not allowed to possess, including items that can assist in an escape, are dangerous, can undermine prison physical security, or are nuisance items and security staff have many specific policies and spend considerable time implementing them to avoid possession of contraband by inmates.

Prisons have policies clearly identifying contraband items, or the limits on the number of items that inmates are allowed to have. Contraband policies also categorize contraband by risk, with the risk levels requiring different methods for storage and use. For example, tools are classified by their risk to prison security. "Class A" tools are those that can be a weapon, aid in escape, or undermine the security of a prison, and include items such as files, knives, saw blades, ladders, ropes, extension cords, lift devices, and grinders. Class A tools are only to be used under the direct supervision of staff and must be placed in a secure storage area when not in use. Class B tools are less risky, and include light pliers, short power cords, or other hand tools that are not likely to be used as a weapon or aid in an escape. They may be stored and used by inmates under less stringent conditions, but must still be controlled and accounted for.[4]

Contraband items may end up in possession of inmates in at least four ways. First, inmates may receive prohibited items hidden in mail or packages. Prisons allow inmates to send and receive letters; sometimes inmates may receive packages with reading material or other allowable items. In order to keep small items such as drugs from being mailed into a prison, inmate mail is not read, but is opened and searched for contraband items. Hardback books and magazines (in which it is easy to hide drugs or other small contraband) may be purchased and delivered only directly from the publisher, thereby reducing the opportunity for a friend or family member to hide contraband in these publications.

Second, inmate visitors may bring contraband items into the prison and give them to an inmate. Visiting by friends and family is important to maintain inmates' community ties and helps in their successful reintegration upon release. Visiting rooms are designed to allow as relaxed as possible contact and conversation between inmates and their visitors. As well, if there is no reasonable suspicion, visitors may not be searched. Visitors pass through a metal detector upon entry to the prison, and they are permitted to take only limited personal items into the visiting room, such as money and unopened packages of cigarettes. However, in the normal visiting setting, it is difficult to control the introduction of contraband such as

Class A tools such as ladders are a serious security risk in prisons, and therefore are locked so that inmates cannot take them to use as an aid in escape.
Photo by Richard P. Seiter.

drugs. During the visit, correctional staff monitor the visiting room and the conduct of inmates and visitors. Unfortunately, it is unlikely that staff (unless tipped off by another inmate) will notice passing of small contraband between a visitor and inmate. The best protection against entry of contraband through the visiting room is a thorough search of inmates after the visit and before they return to the general area of the prison. As they leave their visit, inmates are strip-searched, and when all visiting ends for the day, the visiting room is thoroughly searched before any more inmates enter the area.

Third, inmates may gain possession of contraband that is available in the prison, but should not be in possession of inmates without staff supervision. Inmates often attempt to smuggle items out of the allowed area of supervision. Some seemingly nonthreatening examples of such contraband are those that can cause a health and sanitation problem, such as food that is served in the dining room. Inmates try to obtain extra food, hide it, and take it to their housing units, sell it to others, or keep it for their own use at a later time. More serious examples of such contraband are the "Class A" tools described previously. Inmate food services workers often must be issued knives to prepare food; inmate maintenance workers may sometimes be issued tools that can cut wires or even bars. Prison contraband control procedures reduce the chance of such dangerous tools or utensils falling in an inmate's possession or being removed from the assigned area.

Class A tools and food service knives are hung on a **shadow board**, a light-colored background with the outline of the tool painted on it. This enables staff to quickly identify a missing tool or knife. When a tool or knife is issued to an inmate, a record of the staff member who issued the tool and the inmate to whom it was given is created. Before the end of the work period, all tools must be accounted for and back on the shadow board before inmates may leave the area. And, as inmates are released from a work area that uses such tools or knives, they are searched and, in some situations, must walk through a metal detector.

Shadow board

a light colored background with the outline of a tool or hazardous item painted on it; allows staff to quickly notice a missing tool or item

One way to control hazardous tools or knives is to use a "shadow board" and lock them in a cage so inmates cannot get to them.
Photo by Richard P. Seiter.

Finally and unfortunately, unethical staff may provide contraband items to inmates. Some staff may do this to make money, as inmates will arrange payment to the staff member by someone in the community if they bring drugs or possibly weapons into the prison. Other naive staff may do it "to be nice," bringing an inmate only nuisance items such as food or cigarettes that an inmate cannot get in prison. After a staff member has agreed to do this, however, manipulative inmates then threaten to tell prison officials about the staff violation of rules, knowing that the staff member will be punished for violating rules, unless the staff member agrees to bring more serious and dangerous contraband into the prison in exchange for the inmate's silence.

To deter such actions by staff, some prisons search their staff or require them to walk through metal detectors as they come to work. Since staff are well aware of these procedures and can easily avoid detection of bringing contraband into a prison, many prisons do not even attempt such searches. Instead, they rely on hiring the right kind of people and treating staff as trusted professionals, while encouraging all staff to share in the responsibility of identifying staff who may be smuggling items into the prison. Prison training programs for new staff present the dangers of providing contraband to inmates and how it undermines the safety of all staff. While these efforts work for most staff, there is always a staff member who fails to heed the warning and, whether for money or because of poor judgment, and is a target for inmates who try to get them to bring contraband into the prison.

Prison officials not only take many precautions to prevent contraband from getting into the hands of inmates, but also require regular efforts to search for contraband that an inmate may have acquired. A considerable amount of time every day is devoted to searching areas of the prison or "shaking down" inmates to find contraband and deter its possession. Correctional officers assigned to housing units have postorder requirements to search a certain number of cells every day, and teams of staff may be assigned to an area (such as prison industries or a recreation building) for a complete search. Inmates are randomly selected for shakedowns or "frisk" searches of their bodies (similar to the standard patdowns performed by police officers on criminal suspects) as they move across the compound. And all inmates leaving work areas where Class A tools are used (food services, maintenance, or industries) are patted down and may walk through a metal detector.

SPECIAL HOUSING UNITS

Special housing unit (SHU)

a temporary housing assignment for inmates who present a danger to the security of the prison, need protection from other inmates, or are being punished for violating prison rules

Administrative detention (AD)

a non-punitive confinement in an SHU; used to house inmates whose continued presence in the general population may pose a serious threat to the security or orderly running of the prison

A critical security and custody function is to be able to separate certain inmates from the rest of the general inmate population, either for their protection, as punishment, during an investigation, or because they are a threat to the orderly operation of the prison. For these situations, prisons have a **special housing unit (SHU),** similar to the operation of a jail in the community. An SHU is a temporary housing assignment for inmates who present a danger to the security of the prison, need protection from other inmates, or are being punished for violating prison rules. A stay in the SHU can be only a few days or up to twelve months. Inmates who need longer separation from a prison's inmate population are either transferred to another prison or placed in a supermax facility.

Two categories of inmates are assigned to the SHU. The first category is **administrative detention (AD),** a "non-punitive confinement used to house inmates whose continued presence in the general population may pose a serious threat to life, property, self, staff, or other inmates, or to the security or orderly running of the institution."[5] Inmates may be placed in administrative detention if they are charged with violating a serious rule in the prison and allowing them to remain in the general prison population could undermine security, or for their own safety. For a minor charge of violating a prison rule, such as the possession of nuisance contraband, inmates remain in the general population pending a disciplinary hearing. However, for more serious violations, such as fighting or possession of a weapon, they are held in administrative detention until the hearing and a determination of guilt and decision regarding punishment.

Inmates may also be placed in administrative detention for their own safety. Inmates who are being threatened or believe they are at risk of being assaulted often notify staff and seek protection—for example, if the inmate has a co-defendant in the prison against whom he or she testified, or is being pressured to participate in homosexual activity or to have a visitor bring drugs into the prison. In these situations, the inmate is placed in administrative detention, an investigation is completed, and officials decide whether to transfer the inmate to another prison. There is no predetermined time to hold inmates in administrative detention; they remain until the investigation is complete and appropriate action is taken.

The "You Make the Decision" box illustrates the difficult decision prison staff have to make regarding inmates potentially at risk in a prison.

The second category of SHU placement is **disciplinary segregation (DS),** a status of punishment after a finding of guilt for a serious prison rule violation. Disciplinary segregation is for a set amount of time established by the person or committee that considers the violation. In the Bureau of Prisons disciplinary policy, infractions of "greatest" severity can result in disciplinary segregation of up to sixty days, infractions of "high" severity can result in up to thirty days, and those of

Disciplinary segregation (DS)

a punitive assignment in an SHU after a finding of guilt for a serious prison rule violation

YOU MAKE THE DECISION . . .

LOCK HIM UP?

Inmates may be placed in AD if it is determined that there is a risk to their safety if they remain on the compound (in the general prison population). The difficulty is when to lock up inmates, or place them in the SHU, when there is no definite evidence that they are at risk. The following situation is not uncommon.

An inmate comes into the captain's office and tells the officer in charge that he is being pressured to have his wife bring drugs into the prison by a group of inmates. He thinks the inmates are in a gang. He says they told him if he doesn't do it, he will be killed. He will not identify the inmates, because he is afraid that if he does, their fellow gang members will kill him. He won't give any more or any specific information, saying that anything he says that can be traced back to him and result in the other inmates being locked up for investigation will also result in his being killed. None of the security staff have had previous encounters with this inmate, can vouch for his credibility, or have any information to support his story. His case manager, when contacted, says the inmate had been seeking a transfer to a prison closer to his home where his wife lives. The case manager told the inmate that that prison was very overcrowded, and that there was a moratorium on transfers for twelve months.

The decision seems easy; place him in AD to separate him from the threatening inmates, and transfer him to another prison. There are two problems, however. First, inmates sometimes create a story like this to get a transfer. They know that if they are at risk, they can expect to be moved to another prison, so they can manipulate the system. Second, just transferring the inmate does nothing to deal with a gang that is pressuring inmates to bring in drugs, and they will just try another inmate if this doesn't work out. You need the inmate to give more specific information to act on the allegation; yet you can't let him be at risk, even if he won't tell you more.

So, what do you do? You do not want to just put him in AD and give him a transfer without his providing more information you can use and be sure he is not just making up a story. If you do, other inmates will do the same thing. Yet you can't ignore his request. Weigh all the pros and cons you can think of, and come up with other ideas on how to handle a situation like this. Then, either individually or in a small classroom group, make a decision as to the best way to handle this situation: lock him up or not.

The inside of a cell in the SHU has minimal comforts, and inmates do not like placement there and separation from the rest of the inmate population.
Photo by Richard P. Seiter.

"moderate" severity can result in up to fifteen days.[6] Once inmates complete their disciplinary segregation time, they are returned to the general population, unless the disciplinary sanction also included a transfer to another prison.

The SHU is a separate building within a prison, usually located so that inmates in the SHU cannot communicate with general-population inmates. It is physically very secure, as cells have metal doors and metal furnishings. Furnishings include a stainless steel toilet and sink, and a bed and writing table secured to the floor or walls. Outside, but adjacent to, the SHU is a small, fenced recreation area in which inmates are allowed to exercise between five and ten hours per week. Operating procedures for the SHU are similar for both statuses. Inmates come out of their cells only when handcuffed and escorted by staff. Meals are brought to each cell. Medical and program (education or religious) staff visit inmates in the SHU, as all services are brought to the unit. SHU inmates do have access to correspondence, limited reading material, and visiting privileges.

Inmate Riots and Disturbances

The most feared event at a prison is an inmate riot or disturbance. No matter how well staff follow policy or do their jobs, emergency situations such as riots, escapes, hostage taking, and nonviolent food or work strikes can occur. Therefore, prison officials implement security and custody procedures in prisons to reduce the likelihood of such emergencies and to be prepared if emergencies do occur. Preparation includes developing contingency plans, training staff in their proper response, and creating and training special teams for hostage negotiations and responding to a disturbance.

Inmate disturbances have a devastating impact on a prison, the staff, and even the inmates. The last thirty years have seen several serious riots.[7] One of the most serious riots, and one that captured the interest of the American public, was the 1971 riot at the state prison in Attica, New York.[8] Tensions had been building at Attica for several months, as inmates complained about poor food and medical

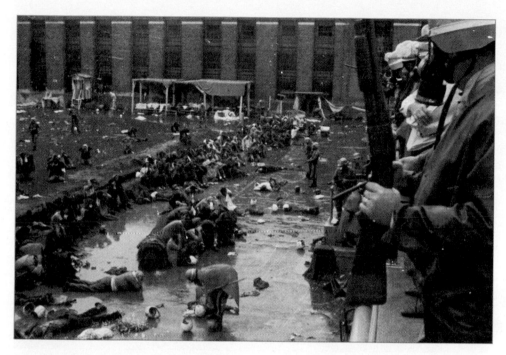

The Attica (New York) riot in 1971, one of the most deadly in the history of prisons, highlighted many factors that can create tension and increase the potential for disturbances within a prison.
Courtesy of Corbis/Bettmann.

service and discrimination by staff. A large proportion of the Attica inmates were African Americans from New York City, while staff members were predominantly white and from rural upstate New York. In September 1971, inmates took control of a large section of the prison and held several staff members as hostages. Negotiations between correctional officials and inmates continued for four days, until the governor of New York and the director of corrections decided it was time to end the siege. The New York State Police were sent into the prison and authorized to use deadly force to regain control. After they retook the prison, thirty-two inmates and eleven staff members were found killed. The investigation discovered that the state police killed thirty-nine of those during the retaking of the prison.

Another serious riot occurred in February 1980, when prisoners took over the entire prison in Santa Fe, New Mexico. Inmates held twelve staff members as hostages, controlled the prison for thirty-six hours, and caused more than $100 million in damage.[9] Inmates got control of other inmates' records and found that some had acted as informants. Rioting inmates tortured and killed thirty-three inmates they believed to have aided staff.

Another serious riot took place in 1993 at the Southern Ohio Correctional Facility in Lucasville, Ohio. In an article regarding this riot, Ohio correctional executives wrote:

> On Easter Sunday 1993, inmates returning to L-block from recreation at the maximum security Southern Ohio Correctional Facility in rural Lucasville assaulted the entry officer. Minutes later, L-block was overrun, and the longest prison siege in U.S. history where lives were lost was underway. Eleven days later the riot ended. Corrections Officer Robert Vallandingham and nine inmates had been murdered. Thirteen corrections officers had been taken hostage. Five were held for the duration of the disturbance. L-block was virtually destroyed.

Rioting inmates at the Southern Ohio Correctional Facility in Lucasville, Ohio, in 1993 did severe damage to the facility and murdered ten people.
Courtesy of the Ohio Department of Rehabilitation and Correction.

As the more than 200 media reporters packed up their cameras and satellite dishes, Ohioans breathed a collective sigh of relief that the carnage was over. But for the 11,000 employees of the Ohio Department of Rehabilitation and Correction, the end of the riot signaled fundamental changes at every level of the operation.[10]

Investigations of inmate riots and disturbances have discovered that most are not planned or precisely initiated by inmate leaders. Disturbances more often result from the coalescing of two types of factors and events. The first are **environmental factors** that create tension and an underlying unrest among inmates. They can include hot weather, reduction in budgets for recreation equipment, prison crowding, poor food service or medical care, a perceived pattern of unfairness in prison management, or poor security procedures that allow inmates to create an unsafe environment. The second is a **precipitating event**, often thought of as the "spark in the haystack," that sets off an inmate riot. It usually takes both the right environmental factors and a precipitating event to create the beginning of a prison riot.

Preventive actions that prison administrators can take to reduce inmate unrest and lessen the chance that a single precipitating event will result in a riot include the following:

- Understanding the importance to both staff and inmates of managerial visibility and approachability
- Performing effective security audits that discover security deficiencies so they can be corrected before inmates exploit them
- Consistently enforcing all rules and regulations
- Maintaining effective communications between inmates and staff, among staff, and particularly between line and supervisory personnel

Environmental factors
underlying factors that create tension and unrest among inmates

Precipitating event
the "spark in the haystack" that sets off an inmate riot

- Providing appropriate programs and services of all types (food, medical care, and so forth).
- Implementing effective management systems, such as sanitation, safety and security inspections, contraband deterrence and detection, tool and key control, and inmate accountability
- Developing sensitivity to changes in inmate actions or the institution atmosphere.
- Using risk-assessment programs to identify possible trouble spots, and correcting them as soon as possible; such systems may include the use of objective indicators (tests, review of incident data, sick call data) or more subjective elements (staff and inmate interviews) to assign levels of risk to a situation or institution[11]

The "A Look Into" box gives an example of a riot that occurred while I was the warden of the Federal Correctional Institution in Greenville, Illinois. It illustrates how environmental factors and a precipitating event can combine to result in a serious riot culminating in staff injury and major destruction of the prison.

A LOOK INTO . . .

CAUSES OF A RIOT

In October 1995, the Federal Correctional Institution in Greenville, Illinois, was a new federal prison. It was constructed using Federal Bureau of Prisons (BOP) standard medium-security guidelines, with solid wood cell doors, and card tables and folding chairs used by inmates in the housing units' common areas. The prison first accepted inmates in early 1994. The prison had just over 500 cells, but because of severe overcrowding in other federal prisons, it rapidly filled to twice that capacity to more than 1,000 inmates, with two inmates in every cell and even three inmates in some cells. Most inmates were transferred to Greenville from Southeast and West Coast federal prisons, which were experiencing the most overcrowding. These inmates were moved away from their families and friends, could not receive visits, and did not want to be in southern Illinois.

As is the practice in federal prisons, some experienced staff members are transferred to new prisons, but the majority are hired locally and have no prison experience. Procedures were new, and some were still changing and developing. The newly hired correctional officers and other staff were learning to deal with medium-security inmates, almost all of whom had been transferred from other prisons and knew how to try to take advantage of new staff and untried procedures.

Throughout 1995, there was considerable public discussion about changing the federal drug laws regarding crack cocaine. There was a ten-to-one ratio of crack to powder cocaine, meaning that to receive a mandatory ten-year prison sentence, crack cocaine offenders had to possess only one-tenth the amount required for powder cocaine offenders. Since crack cocaine was primarily used in African American communities, more than 95 percent of the crack cocaine offenders at Greenville were African American. This became an issue of racial injustice and was being reconsidered by the U.S. Sentencing Commission. In fact, in the summer of 1995, the commission recommended to Congress that the two drugs should be equalized in their weight and corresponding sentence. Through rumor, African American inmates convicted of crack cocaine trafficking believed that a change would be made, it would be retroactive, and that many would receive an immediate reduction of their sentences.

In the fall of 1995, a report issued by the U.S. Department of Justice, Bureau of Justice Statistics, noted the much higher percentage of black men between ages 19 and 30 were incarcerated at a much greater rate compared to their percentage in the overall U.S. population. This also became a rallying cry for racial injustice. Over the summer and fall of 1995, much media attention was given to a call for a "Million Man March" by Minister Louis Farrakhan, the

(continued)

controversial leader of the Nation of Islam. The Million Man March called attention to the need for African American men to take responsibility for their families. However, it also emphasized, especially in the minds of inmates, the issue of racial injustice regarding the disparity between crack and powder cocaine sentencing.

The Million Man March occurred on Monday of the third week of October. On Wednesday evening of the same week, Congress rejected the recommendation by the sentencing commission to reduce the disparity between crack and powder cocaine sentences. The next day, riots broke out in federal prisons in Alabama, Tennessee, and Pennsylvania. There was national media coverage of the fires and destruction from these riots, and inmates in Greenville watched these events unfold on television news coverage.

On Friday of that week, the Bureau of Prisons took peremptory action to prevent more riots, ordering a national lockdown of all federal prisons. At Greenville, inmates were called back to their housing units around 3:00 P.M., about one hour earlier than usual. Arriving in the housing units, inmates were told to go into their cells to be locked down. Several inmates refused to go into their cells, and began assaulting staff. Thirteen staff members were seriously injured and two housing units had massive destruction. Four or five other federal prisons also experienced smaller disturbances during the next few weeks.

Environmental factors in this riot included new staff implementing new procedures. Many inmates were extremely unhappy about being in Greenville. Feelings of racial injustice were heightened by the Million Man March, and there were expectations that the injustice would be ended by congressional action. The congressional action to maintain current sentences was unexpected by prison officials and was disappointing to inmates. The precipitating event was the attempted lockdown, when tensions were high, with inmates being locked in their cells for an unknown amount of time, when they did not know why or feel that this action was warranted.

PLANNING FOR EMERGENCY SITUATIONS

Inmate disturbances can occur in any prison. Knowing this, all prisons develop "contingency" or "emergency" plans to identify the responses and procedures to be put in place in case of a disturbance. These plans describe how to prevent disturbances and, if a riot occurs, the initial reactions, communications, staff response, the potential use of firearms and crowd control ordinances, managing the media, and postemergency actions. Emergency plans are a guide for actions in a time when emotions are high, staff and inmates may be in danger or already injured, things seem chaotic and out of control, and the warden and top prison officials may be out of the prison. The plan is detailed to the point that it provides the order of steps to take to respond to certain events. Staff are required to read the plan and are trained in its implementation in the event of an emergency. Well-coordinated, appropriate, and timely reaction at the beginning of a disturbance is critical. Boin and Van Duin write, "As prison authorities find themselves confronted with a riot, . . . [they] will have to take some sort of action in order to cope with the threat and restore a state of normalcy. It is in this stage that the actions of prison authorities may make the difference between a food strike in an isolated cell block (a riot you will never hear about) and the overtaking of an entire institution (a riot you might never forget)."[12]

EMERGENCY RESPONSE TEAMS

In preparation for inmate disturbances, emergency plans require creation, staffing, and training of at least three teams, capable of using all of the options available in crisis situations, including negotiation, controlling the disturbance, and use of deadly force. The three teams include a hostage negotiation team, disturbance control team, and special emergency response team. The key is for the decision maker to decide which team to use and how to react. It has been suggested that "negotiation, the option involving the least amount of force, is the preferred option when time permits; DCTs (Disturbance Control Teams) using less than lethal options such as chemical agents and distraction devices; and the use of deadly force through intervention by a tactical team."[13]

In some riots, staff members are taken hostage, creating a very difficult and stressful situation that eliminates or delays many of the activities that could be used to respond to a nonhostage emergency. **Hostage negotiation teams (HNTs)** are used to respond to a hostage taking. The HNT is made up of eight to ten prison employees with excellent communication skills and ability to perform under stress. The team's principal role is to open lines of communication with the hostage takers as quickly as possible, so that inmates see an option to injuring the hostage and begin to consider how to resolve the situation. The HNT goal is to preserve life and regain control of the prison and inmates. Once they open communication lines, they attempt to "reduce stress and tension with the hostage takers, build rapport, obtain intelligence, stall for time, allow hostage takers to express emotion and ventilate, and establish a problem-solving atmosphere."[14] Over the period of negotiations, a rapport builds between the negotiators and the hostage takers, and the Stockholm Syndrome develops between the captors and the hostages. The Stockholm Syndrome is thought to result in the hostages and captors beginning to identify with each other, as hostage takers see the hostages as people rather than just objects, and they are therefore less likely to physically harm or kill their hostages.

The second type of emergency team is the **disturbance control team (DCT).** The DCT has a primary mission of controlling inmates during riot situations by using defensive tactics and equipment to move them, isolate them, and get them to give up and stop the disturbance. The team wears helmets, ballistic-resistant vests, and baseball-catcher-style shin guards, and carries riot batons, gas masks, handcuffs, chemical agents such as tear and pepper gas, and ordnance such as smoke

Hostage negotiation teams (HNTs)

a team with the principal role of opening lines of communications between staff and hostage takers

Disturbance control team (DCT)

an emergency team with the primary mission of controlling inmates during riot situations by using defensive tactics and equipment to move them, isolate them, and get inmates to give up

This picture shows the burned-out center of the U.S. Penitentiary in Atlanta, Georgia, after rioting Cuban inmates took over the entire prison and held several staff members as hostages for several days in 1987.
Courtesy of the Federal Bureau of Prisons.

Special emergency response team (SERT)

an emergency team trained in the use of lethal force for when all else fails to resolve an emergency situation

grenades, stun and flash rounds, and Sting-Ball grenades. The DCT responds to a riot with a deliberate, orderly, and disciplined approach. Through this "show of force," inmates often end the confrontation, recognizing that the DCT is well trained and the inmates are likely to be hurt if they do not capitulate.

Unfortunately, some riots and hostage situations do not end successfully through negotiation or the use of the DCT. In these cases, the third type of team, the **special emergency response team (SERT),** may be called upon. A SERT, similar to a police SWAT team, is trained in the use of weapons, explosives, entry procedures, and snipers. They will be authorized to use lethal force when all else fails to resolve an emergency situation. It is a difficult decision for correctional officials to commit to the use of a SERT assault with deadly force. Hostage takers always give deadlines and threaten to kill hostages if their demands are not met. It is good strategy to have the negotiating team try to talk hostage takers past deadlines, while hoping that they will not injure hostages. Yet hostage takers may reach a point at which they are about to kill or injure hostages, and the order must be given and the SERT prepared to begin an assault.

Before the SERT assaults, they prepare a detailed plan that must receive the approval of the emergency decision maker. Once the plan is approved, the team moves into position, and stays ready to begin the assault upon receiving the "go" order. If force is necessary, it must be overwhelming, but only in the amount necessary to restore order. Prison officials goal is to develop a tactical action that ensures total control of the inmates as the final outcome, so that inmates cannot take the weapons and have SERT members as more hostages.

As a lead-in to the next section regarding treatment, I share with you the "An Insider's Experience" box regarding the shattered confidence of staff after a riot. After the riot of FCI-Greenville we realized that the prison had to return to normal operations, but in the aftermath of the riot this occurred only after changes in the style of management and improvement in the security and operation of the prison were made. Thankfully, the staff responded, and FCI-Greenville became one of the best correctional institutions in the Federal Bureau of Prisons.

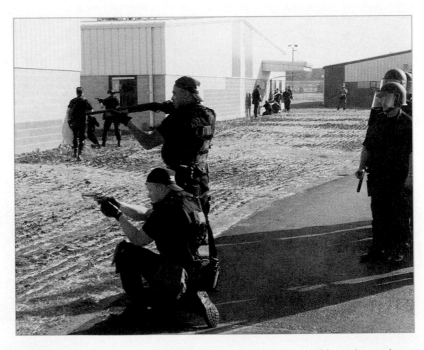

SERT members must train regularly with weapons to be used in serious prison emergency situations.
Courtesy of the Ohio Department of Rehabilitation and Correction.

AN INSIDER'S EXPERIENCE: Rebuilding Staff Confidence after a Riot

As noted previously, the riot at FCI-Greenville was during "my watch" in that I was the warden of the prison at the time of the riot, even though I was not at the prison when the riot started. Staff saw their friends being carried out of the prison injured and the new facility being vandalized by inmates. The wooden cell doors were broken down, game tables and folding chairs were used as weapons against staff, and staff were trapped in an office that was not secure enough to protect them as inmates tried to break in. Due to the quick thinking of an associate warden, shotguns were taken to the outside window of the office to threaten inmates who were trying to break down the door, and the window bars were cut to rescue the twelve trapped staff members before they were taken as hostages. It was a real shock and a rude awakening to the new staff. Their confidence was shattered—in the physical security of the prison, in their own ability to do their jobs, and in the other administrators of the prison and me.

After the riot, the employee labor union began to criticize our leadership and demanded certain changes to ensure the safety of staff. This created a divisive situation in which staff were not sure whether they should support the union or the administration. Some staff were fearful of being assaulted or taken hostage. It was not now just a case study in a training class; they knew it could happen. We had to take quick and assertive action to win back the support of the staff and rebuild their confidence.

The first thing we did was to improve the prison physical security. We replaced wooden doors with metal ones. We put bars on the staff office windows that were inside and looked into the cell houses. We got rid of the card tables and folding chairs and replaced them with metal benches that were bolted to the floor. We secured areas throughout the housing unit for staff to retreat to if trapped. We put escape hatches in many of these safety retreats so staff could be rescued quickly. And we installed cameras throughout the prison so inmates could be watched and to improve staff safety. But improving the physical security was not enough.

We changed the management style within the prison. I had always been a "hands-on" manager who got very involved in all aspects of operations and made many decisions myself. We began to emphasize staff empowerment by involving staff in decision making, pushing decisions down to the lowest possible level, authorizing midlevel managers to make decisions regarding their areas, and being very visible and open in communicating with line staff about issues, problems, operations of the prison, and why certain decisions were made. These activities seemed to be working, but we wanted to create a single focus for building a positive culture for the institution.

I organized a retreat to create a vision statement for the prison. Staff from various organizational levels and different departments, the union, and officers in the employees' club were invited to attend. We sought out opinions of each person, asking what kinds of things were important to them in the operation of the prison. As ideas came forward, we began to blend and shape them into a vision statement for the prison. We used the vision statement of having a "safe, enjoyable, and empowered workplace" as the basis for everything we did at the prison.

In addition, a line-staff advisory committee was formed to meet with me monthly. This did not take authority away from managers, as staff members who brought up issues were then empowered to go to the manager and try to work out solutions. The message was, "If we have a problem, it is everyone's responsibility to find a solution." The entire effort was directed toward changing the organizational culture so that staff took responsibility for the prison operations, improving effectiveness, and moving forward toward the organization's vision.

We found that in time, staff members began not only to return to normal, but to perform their duties with even greater confidence and professionalism. The staff believed in empowerment as more than a management "buzzword," and saw that managers welcomed their input and respected their opinions. Departments became more creative, implementing many programs and operations that were recognized as outstanding by the Bureau of Prisons, and many staff were recognized and promoted to other prisons. The riot set us all back and made us reconsider what we did and how we did it, but in the end, we were a much stronger group of staff and a much better-operating prison.

Treatment and Programs within a Prison

While creating a safe and secure environment, prisons also have the mission of providing inmates the opportunity to participate in programs that can help in their rehabilitation and successful reentry to the community. While it has always been acknowledged that rehabilitation is a valid correctional goal, support for it and the emphasis that rehabilitative programs receive in prisons has ebbed and flowed over the history of American corrections. However, the public continues to support, and correctional officials continue to encourage, programs that are designed to improve offenders' deficiencies that may have contributed to their past criminality.

Rehabilitation, at that point better termed "redemption," was a primary focus of the first American prison (the Walnut Street Jail), opened in Philadelphia in 1790. Inmates were expected to read the Bible and reflect on their wrongdoings. They were also required to work on trade products in their cells, so that these products could be sold to help support the prison. Over the next 150 years, work became the primary program within prisons, although counseling and religious services remained a mainstay of every prison. In the history of American corrections, programs for the rehabilitation of offenders have always been considered important.

The "heyday" of the goal of rehabilitation came during the middle of the twentieth century as corrections adopted a *medical model,* in which crime was believed to be the result of an underlying pathology of offenders that could be diagnosed and treated. Offenders were considered "sick" and in need of treatment to prepare them to return to the community as productive, law-abiding citizens. Correctional agencies implemented a variety of treatment programs to improve offenders and to provide them with the tools necessary to be successful members of society. The need for rehabilitation of offenders was emphasized by the Commission on Law Enforcement and the Administration of Justice, appointed by President Lyndon Johnson in 1966, which noted a need for "substantial upgrading" of the correctional system and its reorientation "toward integration of offenders into community life."[15]

By the 1980s, however, public support of rehabilitation was declining, partly the result of the publication of an early 1970s study of the effectiveness of correctional treatment. In a review of findings from 231 correctional treatment programs, Lipton, Martinson, and Wilks found no common themes in correctional interventions that consistently reduce recidivism.[16] In an earlier article regarding the review that became known as the "nothing works" conclusion, Martinson stated that "with few and isolated exceptions, the rehabilitative efforts that have been reported so far have had no appreciable effect on recidivism."[17]

During this time, correctional philosophy reverted to Darwinism and the *classical model,* in which offenders are seen as rational individuals with free will who chose to commit and are personally accountable for their crimes. With this philosophy, punishment and deterrence are considered more important as goals than rehabilitation. However, rehabilitative programs have continued in prison and community corrections settings, although medical terms such as *treatment* and *diagnosis* have been replaced with *programming* and *assessment.* In the current era of accountability, offenders must take responsibility for their criminal acts. While there is recognition of and support for self-improvement of offenders, these programs are often voluntary, prisons provide them as "opportunities" rather than treatment for deficiencies, and offenders are seen not as ill but in need of modifying their willingness to commit crimes.

Currently, the public expects criminals to be punished, yet supports providing rehabilitation programs to inmates. While the public wants to be protected, it also wants the correctional system to improve inmates' likelihood of success upon release. Innes found "no evidence in the available survey data that the general public shares the view that there is any necessary incompatibility among the goals of justice in society, punishment of criminals, and teaching or training programs for inmates."[18] In the 1995 National Opinion Survey on Crime and Justice, Flanagan writes, "Despite the primacy of the punitive sentencing goal, however, nearly one fifth of the U.S. adults favored rehabilitation as the principal goal of sentencing, and one fourth favored deterrence and incapacitation as the most important goals."[19]

In this textbook, the term *rehabilitation* will continue to be used. Rehabilitation, by definition, means "to return to a previous form." For correctional purposes, Senese and Kalinich define rehabilitation as "a programmed effort to alter attitudes and behaviors of inmates, which is focused on the elimination of their future criminal behaviors."[20] Prisons offer a variety of programs, including education, vocational training, recreation, religious, substance abuse, mental health, work, and a variety of other self-improvement modalities. These programs are valued, not only to improve the offender, but because they have been found to result in less idleness, disruption, and violence within prisons. This more practical than altruistic emphasis continued for crime-prevention purposes. Cullen and Applegate suggest that "the rehabilitative paradigm requires that government invest in lawbreakers. The goal is to improve offenders both as an end in itself and as a means of reducing recidivism and of protecting society."[21]

The following sections describe the process and programs that are ordinarily provided within prisons, which include assessing the program needs of inmates and creating a plan for them to follow during their period of incarceration. These programs can include education and vocational, recreational, substance abuse, mental health, and work programs.

Identifying Inmate Needs

Once an offender is sentenced to prison, a reception and classification process begins. Many states have correctional reception centers to which inmates are initially assigned to assess their risk of violence and escape and their need for rehabilitative programs. The risk assessment is normally done through the use of objective classification systems, with a determination of the security level of prison (based primarily on the physical security available) to which an inmate will be assigned. The identification of program needs is determined through a combination of assessment instruments, interviews with psychologists or other mental health professionals, and educational and vocational testing.

From these assessments, testing, and interviews, inmate needs for various types of programs are identified. Educational proficiency exams give an indication of an inmate's level of literacy, regardless of the grade completed in school, and indicates whether additional educational programming is needed. Psychological assessments identify any mental illness, suicide proclivity, or need for special mental health placements or programs. And through interviews and review of past histories, the need for substance abuse treatment is determined. Since most offenders have limited work histories and poor work skills, the program plan also addresses the types of vocational training or prison work experience that may help the inmate.

Once needs are identified, inmates move from the reception process to the regular incarceration stage of their sentence. If they were originally in a reception center, they are transferred to a prison to begin service of their sentence. Once transferred, inmates meet with the unit management or program team to develop a program plan to follow during their sentence. If the inmates' functional literacy is below a certain level, they are assigned to go to school. If a mental health or substance abuse problem has been identified, they are referred to the mental health department for treatment or placement in a substance abuse program. They will be assigned to a vocational program or prison job to develop work skills. And they will be informed of leisure programs and other programs within the prison believed to be of interest or assistance to them.

The unit or treatment team normally meets with inmates every six months thereafter to review the progress and current status of their program, but if an inmate requests a change in program, the team will schedule a review early. At these reviews, the team examines reports from the various program departments and discusses progress, concerns, or successes with the inmate. Most treatment programs are voluntary, yet the team may strongly suggest the inmate's involvement and commitment. Other programs may be required by statute (in several states and the federal government, inmates testing below a certain literacy level must enroll in school) or as a part of their sentence (some states allow judges to require inmates to participate in a substance abuse program during their sentence).

Types of Prison Programs

Inmates have a variety of needs, and no two inmates are exactly the same. However, there are a few inmate programs that most inmates need and participate in. Approximately half of entering prison inmates have graduated from high school. Nearly 70 percent of state prison inmates have a drug or alcohol problem. Very few inmates have an extensive work history or marketable vocational skills. And approximately 16 percent of incarcerated offenders are mentally ill. Prisons therefore attempt to create programs to meet the general needs of inmates and deal with individual requirements within these programs. Educational and vocational, mental health, substance abuse, work, religious, and recreational programs within prisons are presented next.

EDUCATIONAL AND VOCATIONAL PROGRAMS

Education is recognized as critical to everyone's success in modern American society. The achieved educational level of the general population of the United States has increased steadily in the past few decades, and criminal offenders have consistently been found significantly less educated than their law-abiding peers. Harlow reports that in 1997, only 18.4 percent of the general population had not completed high school or received a GED, while 39.7 percent of state prison inmates, 26.5 percent of federal prison inmates, 46.5 percent of jail inmates, and 30.6 percent of probationers had only some high school or less.[22] While the percentages of inmates entering prison who have not completed high school or earned a GED remained about the same between 1991 (40 percent) and 1997 (41 percent), the number of such inmates entering state prisons increased from 293,000 in 1991 to 420,000 in 1997.[23] Table 13.1 illustrates the educational attainment levels for various correctional populations and the general public.

Inmates have a significant need for educational programs, and appropriately, most prisons provide these programs. In a recent survey of adult correctional facilities, about nine in ten state prisons and all federal prisons provided educational programs for inmates.[24] As indicated in Table 13.2, prisons offer a variety of education programs, with secondary education programs to prepare inmates to take the GED the most prevalent during 2000.

A high proportion of inmates participate in education programs, as more than half (52 percent of state and 57 percent of federal inmates) report taking education classes since their most recent admission (Table 13.3). While the percentages of inmates participating in such programs decreased from 1991 to 1997, the actual number of inmates who were educated in prison increased during this period from

TABLE 13.1	Educational Attainment for State and Federal Prison Inmates in 1997 and 1991, Local Jail Inmates in 1996 and 1989, Probationers in 1995, and the General Population in 1997

| | Prison inmates | | | | Local jail inmates | | Proba-tioners | General population |
| | State | | Federal | | | | | |
Educational attainment	1997	1991	1997	1991	1996	1989	1995	1997
8th grade or less	14.2%	14.3%	12.0%	11.0%	13.1%	15.6%	8.4%	7.2%
Some high school	25.5	26.9	14.5	12.3	33.4	38.2	22.2	11.2
GED*	28.5	24.6	22.7	22.6	14.1	9.2	11.0	. . .
High school diploma	20.5	21.8	27.0	25.9	25.9	24.0	34.8	33.2
Postsecondary/some college	9.0	10.1	15.8	18.8	10.3	10.3	18.8	26.4
College graduate or more	2.4	2.3	8.1	9.3	3.2	2.8	4.8	22.0
Number	1,055,495	706,173	88,705	53,677	503,599	393,111	2,029,866	192,352,084

Note: Probationers have been excluded from the general population. General population includes the noninstitutional population 18 or older. Detail may not add to 100% due to rounding.

*General Educational Development certificate.

. . . Not available in the Current Population Survey.

Source: Caroline Wolf Harlow, *Education and Correctional Populations* (Washington, D.C.: U.S. Department of Justice, Bureau of Justice Statistics, January 2003), p. 1.

TABLE 13.2	Educational Programs Offered in State, Federal, and Private Prisons, 2000 and 1995, and Local Jails, 1999

| | State prisons | | Federal prisons | | Private prisons | | Local jails |
Educational programs	2000	1995	2000	1995	2000	1995	1999
With an education program	91.2%	88.0%	100.0%	100.0%	87.6%	71.8%	60.3%
Basic adult education	80.4	76.0	97.4	92.0	61.6	40.0	24.7
Secondary education	83.6	80.3	98.7	100.0	70.7	51.8	54.8
College courses	26.7	31.4	80.5	68.8	27.3	18.2	3.4
Special education	39.6	33.4	59.7	34.8	21.9	27.3	10.8
Vocational training	55.7	54.5	93.5	73.2	44.2	25.5	6.5
Study release programs	7.7	9.3	6.5	5.4	28.9	32.7	9.3
Without an education program	8.8	12.0	0.0	0.0	12.4	28.2	39.7
Number of facilities	1,307	1,278	*	*	242	110	2,819

Note: Detail may not add to total because facilities may have more than one educational program.

*Changed definitions prevent meaningful comparisons of the numbers of federal facilities, 1995 and 2000.

Source: Caroline Wolf Harlow, *Education and Correctional Populations* (Washington, D.C.: U.S. Department of Justice, Bureau of Justice Statistics, January 2003), p. 4.

402,500 to 550,000.[25] As noted in Table 13.3, vocational program and high school or GED programs were the most popular among inmates, with about one-third participating in vocational programs and one-fourth participating in high school classes.

Education has been a part of prison programming for more than a century. One of the most famous American penologists, Zebulon R. Brockway, argued that law-abiding behavior was attainable through legitimate industry and education, and advocated it for inmates at the American Prison Association conference in 1870.

TABLE	13.3	Participation in educational programs since most recent incarceration or sentence, for State and Federal prison inmates, 1997 and 1991, for local jail inmates, 1996, and for probationers, 1995

| | Prison inmates | | | | Local jail inmates | Probationers |
| | State | | Federal | | | |
Educational programs	1997	1991	1997	1991	1996	1995
Total	51.9%	56.6%	56.4%	67.0%	14.1%	22.9%
Basic	3.1	5.3	1.9	10.4	0.8	0.4
GED/high school	23.4	27.3	23.0	27.3	8.6	7.8
College courses	9.9	13.9	12.9	18.9	1.0	6.1
English as a second language	1.2	. . .	5.7	. . .	. . .	. . .
Vocational	32.2	31.2	31.0	29.4	4.8	7.0
Other	2.6	2.6	5.6	8.4	2.1	3.4
Number of inmates	1,046,136	709,042	87,624	53,753	501,159	2,055,942

Note: Detail may not add to total due to rounding or inmates' participation in more than one educational program.
. . . Not available.

Source: Caroline Wolf Harlow, *Education and Correctional Populations* (Washington, D.C.: U.S. Department of Justice, Bureau of Justice Statistics, January 2003), p. 4.

The current American Correctional Association standard for correctional educational programs states that

> written policy, procedure, and practice provide for a comprehensive education program, available to all inmates who are eligible, that includes the following: educational philosophy and goals, communications skills, general education, basic academic skills, GED preparation, special education, vocational education, postsecondary education, and other education programs as dictated by the needs of the institutional population.[26]

Mandatory prison education

a requirement that inmates without a high school diploma or GED must attend school

Historically, most prison education programs have been voluntary; however, many states and the Federal Bureau of Prisons (BOP) now have a requirement of **mandatory prison education** programs. In 1983, the BOP implemented the first mandatory literacy program for inmates who functioned at less than a sixth-grade educational level. The standard was raised to the eighth-grade level in 1986, and in 1991, the Crime Control Act of 1990 (Public Law 101-647) directed the BOP to have a mandatory functional literacy program for all mentally capable inmates, and the BOP raised their educational standard to the twelfth grade. Many states have since adopted such standards, and the mandatory requirement has much to do with the increasing participation over the past few years.

There have been mixed results concerning the impact of correctional education on postrelease recidivism. Several studies have indicated a positive relationship between participating in prison education programs and lower recidivism.[27] A study of postrelease recidivism of inmates released from Texas prisons during 1991 and 1992 found that inmates at the lowest levels of educational achievement benefited most from participation in academic programs as indicated by lower recidivism rates.[28] Vito and Tewksbury evaluated a program in Kentucky to increase the literacy levels of state and local inmates and to reduce recidivism. While graduates of the program increased their reading and math competencies by up to three grade levels, the educational component did not seem to have an effect on

Prison libraries are important to aid the education program and provide leisure reading opportunities to inmates.
Photo by Richard P. Seiter.

their recidivism rates when compared to nongraduates measured twelve to fifteen months after program involvement.[29]

As noted previously, most prisons also offer vocational training programs to improve inmates' vocational skills. **Vocational training** is specific training in a trade area such as carpentry, electronics, welding, office equipment and word processing, food services, or horticulture and landscaping. Vocational training has been shown to be effective in reducing recidivism. Saylor and Gaes found that "those who participated in either vocational or apprenticeship training were 33 percent less likely to recidivate through the observation period," which was as long as twelve years and as short as eight years.[30] Lattimore, Witte, and Baker also found a reduction in recidivism rates by vocational training participants in two North Carolina prisons for young offenders. Inmates who participated in the Vocational Delivery System program were less likely (36 percent) to be arrested following release from prison than the control group (46 percent).[31]

Currently, few prisons have extensive postsecondary education programs, even though several thousand inmates took college classes and earned college degrees in the past. State and federal prisons previously used **Pell grants** to fund inmate college programs. Pell grants were enacted and funded by Congress in the 1970s as a way for "disadvantaged populations" to receive funds to take college courses. Inmates met the definition of disadvantaged, and most prisons arranged with local colleges to offer courses in the prison and qualify inmates to receive Pell grant funds to pay their tuition. When I was director in Ohio between 1983 and 1988, almost every prison had more than one hundred inmates attending college classes as full-time students. These college programs were considered a productive use of inmate time, and were found to motivate inmates and improve morale.

However, in 1994, after complaints that inmates should not get a "free" college education in prison, Congress specifically eliminated inmates from receiving

Vocational training
specific training in a trade area

Pell grants
grants for disadvantaged individuals used to cover tuition costs for college courses

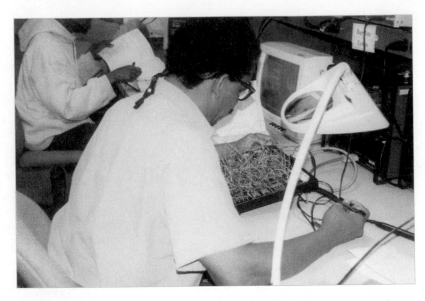

Prison vocational training classes teach inmates skills that are current and often "high-tech."
Photo by Richard P. Seiter.

Pell grants, and many active and proven college programs in prisons were eliminated.[32] Some states were able to provide limited funding and keep college-level programs going on a minimal basis. However, in 2000, the Federal Bureau of Prisons proposed modifying its own rules to make inmates responsible for all college-degree tuition costs.[33] Prisons now will help inmates arrange to take correspondence courses, but all costs must be borne by the inmate. Even ten years after the end of the Pell grants, most correctional educators still bemoan their loss as a step back in correctional education, and the ability to encourage inmates to maximize their education potential, at a time when they have little else to do.

The "Your Career in Corrections" box highlights the role that correctional educators play in prisons.

MENTAL HEALTH PROGRAMS

Providing programs for inmates with mental illness represents a very difficult problem within correctional institutions. First, a relatively high percentage of inmates have mental health problems. Second, the security demands to control these inmates can be obstacles to program efforts. Finally, correctional agencies are not designed to provide mental health programs to the same extent as mental health agencies. Unfortunately, in many states, the link between correctional and mental health agencies is often not as strong as it could be, and some mental health agencies (in many states, the mental health agencies are charged with the responsibility) do not give provision of mental health services within a prison a high priority.

A recent U.S. Department of Justice, Bureau of Justice Statistics, survey of prisoners and prisons estimated that approximately 10 percent of prison and jail inmates reported a mental or emotional condition, and 10 percent said they had stayed overnight in a mental hospital or program. Overall, an estimated 283,800 inmates (16.2 percent of all prisoners) were identified as mentally ill.[34] In another survey of the mental health services provided in prisons, Beck and Maruschak found that on June 30, 2000, 1,394 of the nation's 1,558 public and private adult prisons provided mental health services to inmates, yet only one in eight prisoners were receiving mental health therapy or counseling services.[35]

YOUR CAREER IN CORRECTIONS

CORRECTIONAL EDUCATORS

Correctional educators are the people that teach, oversee, or coordinate education and sometimes vocational training programs within prisons. Education is one of the oldest and largest programs in any prison, as most prisons have between five and ten education staff members. Correctional education formed as early as the 1800s, with prison chaplains considered the first "teachers," as they used the Bible (often the only book allowed in early prisons) to teach inmates how to read. As the earliest prison reformers began to push for improvements in the operations of U.S. prisons, one of their first initiatives was to push for more education programs to give inmates the literacy skills seen as critical to success after release.

Correctional education is a nontraditional occupation, as it is not an area that people specifically study or prepare for. Not many teachers begin thinking that they want to work in a prison; they seem to fall into it through one way or another. Most find that they love teaching, but are not completely happy with the traditional school system and begin to look for other options. They also don't always plan to make it a career, but often find it a challenging and rewarding job, and decide to continue correctional work until retirement.

Correctional educators have a nontraditional setting in that in some ways, it is like a "one-room" school. Teachers are not divided into grades, but have specialty areas such as English, math, or reading, and have students at all levels in their classes at one time. Adult learners are tested to determine their proficiency, and then work at their own level under the guidance of the teacher. Many correctional educators really like the adult learner approach as well as the structure and order of a prison education program. They find the work very rewarding, as they do not lose students each year (as they move to another grade), but see them continue until they reach a milestone of success (such as getting their GED). Most inmates enroll in school because they see it as their only means of not coming back, and they have a true motivation to learn. They (and their teachers) get almost immediate gratification, as they do not have to wait twelve years to graduate from high school, and they can get their GED in a matter of months in many cases. Another positive factor in many correctional educators' minds is that they do not worry about security in the prison environment; many say they actually feel safer teaching in a prison than in many public schools. They have control over inmates and the inmates face consequences if they misbehave.

There are also some disadvantages and frustrations teaching in a prison. First, inmates have many issues in their own backgrounds that can affect their ability to learn: special learning disorders, family problems, drug addiction, or a long sentence. One frustrating thing (especially for correctional education administrators) is that teachers are not trained in working with this type of student in a prison environment. Special training and professional development must be provided to teachers until they become accustomed to the special circumstances they will face. Even though many inmates are motivated, others are not, so teachers have to be creative with limited resources. Their students did not succeed in traditional school systems, and correctional educators must get them past this failure and do things differently. Finally, and only partly seriously, correctional educators do not get the summers off. Prison education programs go year round, unlike the traditional school calendar.

Overall, correctional educators are a very satisfied, motivated, and dedicated group of professionals. They do a difficult job, but feel that they are really helping people who understand the importance of their education and generally recognize that they do not have too many more chances to be successful. It can be a good career for those who like to teach and help others.

Most general-population prisons house inmates who are diagnosed as mentally ill and provide them treatment. A 2000 census found that 155 prisons had been created and specially operated to provide mental health programming for inmates.[36] Some of these facilities house mentally ill inmates for long periods or throughout their incarceration. Others are used to house and treat inmates who have experienced acute episodes of mental illness for short terms, stabilize them with medication and treatment, and then return them to the general-population prison. A few states have agreements with the state mental health agencies to transfer the most severely mentally ill inmates to secure psychiatric hospitals for long-term treatment. In most cases, this requires a "probate" hearing by a court to determine that the inmate's illness is so acute that he or she must be hospitalized in such a facility.

Table 13.4 illustrates the number of inmates who were receiving mental health treatment while confined in state correctional facilities on June 30, 2000. The treatment is categorized in three types: twenty-four-hour care, therapy/counseling, and receiving psychotropic medication. In the table, the percentages represent the number receiving mental health services of the total inmates housed in the prisons that provide these services. There are 16,986 state prisoners housed in a mental health unit and receiving 24-hour care. As indicated in Table 13.4, nearly 13 percent of state inmates (about 79 percent of those identified as mentally ill) receive mental health therapy or counseling services from a trained professional on a regular basis. This treatment was received by the highest percentage of female-only prisons (with more than one in four female inmates receiving therapy). Nearly 10 percent of all state inmates were receiving psychotropic medications such as antidepressants, stimulants, sedatives, or tranquilizers.

| **TABLE** | **13.4** | Inmates Receiving Mental Health Treatment in State Confinement Facilities, by Facility Characteristic, June 30, 2000 |

	Number of inmates receiving—					
	24-hour mental health care		**Therapy/counseling**		**Psychotropic medications**	
Facility characteristic	**Number**	**Percent**	**Number**	**Percent**	**Number**	**Percent**
Total[a]	16,986	1.8%	122,376	12.9%	95,114	9.8%
Facility operation						
Public	16,270	1.8%	116,296	13.0%	90,721	10.0%
Private	716	1.3	6,080	10.8	4,393	7.7
Authority to house						
Males only	13,064	1.5%	100,371	11.9%	74,736	8.7%
Females only	830	1.5	14,744	27.1	12,119	22.1
Both	3,092	5.9	7,261	14.3	8,259	15.2
Security level						
Maximum/high	6,928	2.4%	44,637	14.9%	35,069	11.5%
Medium	9,608	1.8	65,726	12.6	52,208	9.8
Minimum/low	448	0.4	11,593	9.3	7,355	5.8
Facility size[b]						
1,500 or more	6,298	1.4%	59,970	12.8%	45,283	9.3%
750–1,499	5,140	1.6	41,953	13.0	31,816	9.9
250–749	4,582	3.5	16,831	13.4	14,866	11.6
100–249	888	3.3	3,309	12.4	2,867	10.9
Fewer than 100	78	2.3	313	11.0	282	8.8

[a]Excludes inmates in mental health treatment in Florida for whom only statewide totals were reported.
[b]Based on the average daily population between July 1, 1999, and June 30, 2000.

Source: Allen J. Beck and Laura J. Maruschak, *Mental Health Treatment in State Prisons, 2000* (Washington, D.C.: U.S. Department of Justice, Bureau of Justice Statistics, July 2001), p. 3.

One of the keys to successfully providing mental health treatment to inmates is a positive partnership between state and local correctional agencies and state and local mental health service agencies. In many states, the correctional agency creates the physical setting for treatment within prisons, and the state mental health department provides staff, training, and other resources to carry out the treatment. In Ohio, a team of individuals from both the correctional and mental health agencies have developed a conceptual model of "holistic health care" that provides the following:

- Integrated medical, psychiatric, psychological, and chemical dependency service delivery
- Continuity of care within DRC (the correctional agency) and upon release
- An array of services
- Delivery of services by self-directed multidisciplinary work teams.[37]

Particularly important is the **continuum of care** to provide various levels of mental health treatment based on the intensity of needs for each inmate, as inmates prepare for movement from prison to release to the community. The most intensive level of care is an "inpatient" prison hospital, in which inmates with acute needs who represent a risk to themselves or others can receive aggressive treatment. For inmates who have severe mental illness symptoms but do not require a hospital setting, short-term crisis units are designed to stabilize their symptoms and return them to a general-population prison. The third level is a residential unit within a general-population prison, in which mentally ill inmates live and receive treatment in a therapeutic milieu, yet interact with other inmates for work, food services, and other program participation. Finally, general-population prisons provide outpatient therapy and counseling for mentally ill inmates who can live and function in a general-population prison.

Continuum of care
various levels of mental health programs based on the intensity of needs for each inmate

Mental health programs within prisons are critical to accomplishing the mission of a correctional facility. Without the types of integrative and multileveled programs described here, mentally ill inmates can be disruptive and undermine the safe and secure operation of a prison. Without effective treatment, these inmates will be unable to prepare for release and successfully reenter the community. The final step in an effective correctional mental health program is transition to the community. In preparation for release, prison and postrelease staff contact community mental health programs, identify resources for continuing mental health treatment from prison to the community, and encourage the offender to seek care from these programs.

SUBSTANCE ABUSE PROGRAMS

Substance abuse treatment programs are also critical programs within prisons because such a high proportion of inmates have a history of drug or alcohol abuse. In a recent survey of the drug and alcohol abuse patterns of incarcerated offenders, the National Center on Addiction and Substance Abuse categorized inmates based on their substance abuse involvement (see Table 13.5). Sixty-nine percent of state and 56 percent of federal prison inmates were classified as regular drug users, meaning that they had used any drug at least once per week for a period of one month or more. Most of the regular drug users (73 percent of those in state prisons and 69 percent of those in federal prisons) were regular drug users in the month prior to their arrest.[38] In addition, 9 percent of state and 5 percent of federal inmates were determined to have been involved in alcohol abuse at the time of their offense. Only 14 percent of state and 31 percent of federal inmates had no substance abuse history.

TABLE 13.5	Classification of Inmates in Custody in 1999 by Substance Involvement by Percent		
	State	**Federal**	**Jail***
Regular drug users	69% (853,168)	56% (81,433)	67% (416,170)
Alcohol-involved offenders	9 (111,282)	5 (7,271)	14 (86,961)
Non-using drug law violators	4 (49,459)	23 (33,446)	4 (24,846)
Drug experimenters	7 (86,553)	4 (5,816)	7 (43,480)
Non–drug users	10 (123,648)	9 (13,087)	7 (43,480)

*All inmates

Note: The number in parentheses is the estimated number of offenders in custody in 1999.

Source: National Center on Addiction and Substance Abuse at Columbia University, *Trends in Substance Abuse and Treatment Needs among Inmates* (Washington, D.C.: U.S. Department of Justice, National Institute of Justice, October 2002), p. vii.

Unfortunately, the treatment needs of most of these inmates go unmet while they are in prison. In a 1991 study by the U.S. General Accounting Office, it was estimated that fewer than 20 percent of identified substance abusers were enrolled in a prison substance abuse program.[39] And in a 1998 report, only 24 percent of state inmates were estimated to receive treatment over the course of a year.[40] Between 1990 and 1999, the total number of inmates needing treatment increased from 551,608 to 948,769, yet those receiving treatment increased only from 69,256 to 125,383.[41] Substance abuse treatment in prisons is critically important, as the Office of National Drug Control Policy reports that treatment while in prison and during postincarceration supervision can reduce recidivism by roughly 50 percent.[42]

Table 13.6 illustrates the types of substance abuse treatment that are provided in state and federal prisons, and the percentages of all inmates, with categories of types of substance abuse, who have received such treatment since their admission to prison. The most important figures in this table are the percentage of regular drug users and alcohol-involved offenders who receive treatment. Self-help groups such as Alcoholics Anonymous and Narcotics Anonymous are available in most prisons. Yet for regular drug users, only 26 percent of state and 16 percent of federal inmates received such treatment, while for alcohol-involved offenders, 28 percent of state and 15 percent of federal inmates received treatment.

Residential treatment is the most intensive, in which inmates live in a unit entirely focused on a substance abuse milieu, and is often considered the most effective treatment for substance abuse. In a study of Federal Bureau of Prisons residential treatment programs, only 3.3 percent of those receiving treatment (compared to 12.1 percent of a similar group that did not receive treatment) were rearrested in the first six months after release.[43] Yet only small percentages of inmates have participated in residential treatment since their admission. In light of the need for and potential positive results of such programs, Congress provided money to states in the Violent Crime Control and Law Enforcement Act of 1994 to enhance or implement residential substance abuse treatment (RSAT) programs in state prisons.

TABLE 13.6	Substance Abuse Interventions in State and Federal Prisons: Percentage of Inmates Receiving Treatment since Admission to Prison

State

Type of intervention	All inmates	Regular drug users	Nonusing drug law violators	Alcohol-involved offenders
Self-help	22%	26%	15%	28%
Drug education	12	15	8	14
Counseling treatment	5	6	1	6
Residential treatment	7	9	3	7

Federal

Type of intervention	All inmates	Regular drug users	Nonusing drug law violators	Alcohol-involved offenders
Self-help	11%	16%	3%	15%
Drug education	17	23	8	12
Counseling treatment	4	6	1	4
Residential treatment	7	11	2	4

Source: National Center on Addiction and Substance Abuse at Columbia University, *Trends in Substance Abuse and Treatment Needs among Inmates* (Washington, D.C.: U.S. Department of Justice, National Institute of Justice, October 2002), p. VI-11.

PRISON WORK PROGRAMS

Just as rehabilitative programs have been an accepted component of prisons throughout their history, so has the importance of work. In the Walnut Street Jail, inmates labored in their cells at spinning, weaving, and shoemaking. Not only was such work considered important for the inmate, but early prison labor also benefited the state, as goods were sold to help prisons be self-sufficient. In the early 1800s, state prisons leased out prisoners to the private sector. Companies would bid for control of the prison and its labor, and the winning leaseholder worked the inmates in their industrial operations and, to maximize profits, spent as little as possible to house and feed the inmates. The **lease system** ended in the early twentieth century, and states began to operate their own prison industries to keep inmates busy and make a profit from the sale of produced goods.

As prison industry programs expanded during the early 1900s, organized labor began to complain about the unfair competition resulting from prisons' sale of goods using free inmate labor. As a result, Congress passed the Hawes-Cooper Act in 1929, requiring that prison products be subject to the laws of any state to which they were shipped. Opponents of prison-made products argued that this did not go far enough, and in 1935, Congress passed the Ashurst-Sumners Act, mandating that prison products be marked as prison-made goods, and then amended the act in 1940 to fully prohibit the interstate shipment of prison goods.

These acts ended the sale of prison products on the open market, and as an alternative, prisons began to produce goods that could be used by the state and federal governments. This **state-use system** resulted in prison industries producing inmate clothing, office furniture, and other products that could be sold to government agencies. In 1934, the Congress established Federal Prison Industries (FPI) as a wholly owned government corporation to produce prison goods for sale to the federal government. FPI is currently the largest prison industry program, and is a

Lease system

a system in which state prisons accepted bids and leased out prisoners to the private sector industrial operations

State-use system

a system in which prison-made goods are sold to and used by only state and federal government agencies

Many prison inmates work in trades areas such as heating and air conditioning, learning skills that can help them find jobs after release.
Photo by Richard P. Seiter.

major producer of goods for government agencies (primarily the military) with sales of almost $500 million a year.

While thousands of inmates work in prison industries, the majority work in other areas of prison operations to help run the prison. In most prisons, staff supervise inmates who actually do the work such as preparing and serving food, doing laundry, doing electrical or plumbing work to maintain the facility, and cutting grass or doing other landscape work. The public supports prison work programs both to assist in rehabilitation and to prepare inmates for the work environment in the community. Prison officials consider work programs essential for managing a correctional institution, as they keep inmates productively busy and help maintain control and order.

Inmates are assigned to several different areas of the prison. Some work in the prison laundry washing sheets, blankets, and inmate clothing. In food service, inmates prepare food, serve it to the inmate population, and clean dishes and cooking equipment for the next meal. Other inmates work in the prison maintenance department in such areas as plumbing, electrical, heating and air conditioning, carpentry, and maintenance of prison landscaping and grounds. Finally, prisoners are used to constantly clean the prison. Sanitation is very important to prevent unsanitary conditions and the spread of infectious diseases in a prison with such large numbers of people living in congested, overcrowded conditions. Overall, between 75 to 90 percent of prisoners work in these types of job assignments to maintain the prison and its daily operations.

Prison Industries

Even with criticism from labor and trade organizations resulting in restrictions for the markets, prison industries continue to be very important to prison operations and for inmate rehabilitation. Prison industries has several benefits:

1. Industrial work assignments that are similar to private-sector operations provide inmates realistic work experience and instill positive work habits.
2. Work experience can provide valuable training and skill development that inmates can use after release.

Prison industry programs keep inmates productively busy while in prison and have been shown to reduce recidivism after release by inmate participants.
Photo by Richard P. Seiter.

3. Inmate earnings can be used to support families, pay fines and restitution, and provide inmates money to purchase their own personal items allowed in prison.
4. Earnings by the industry can be used to offset the cost of incarceration.
5. Industrial work assignments are a positive way to reduce idleness and serve as an incentive for good behavior; therefore they are valuable for inmate management.[44]

After surviving the challenges presented by the congressional acts of the 1930s, prison industry programs have grown significantly. On January 1, 2001, there were 77,380 inmates (6.3 percent of the prison population) working in prison industries in the fifty states, the District of Columbia, and the Federal Bureau of Prisons. In 2000, these programs had sales of $1,643,682,099 and profits of $33,955,681.[45] Inmates work under the supervision of staff, which must maintain a close watch over security and quality. Some of the most common products produced and sold for state use include garments and textile products, wood furniture, printing services, metal products, and other services such as laundry, warehousing, data entry, and construction. Inmates are paid between $3.03 and $8.14 per day.[46]

In addition to the state-use programs of prison industries, Congress in 1979 passed the Private Sector Prison Industry Enhancement Certification (PIE) Program, which allowed for the sale of prison goods on the open market if the program is certified as meeting several conditions, including the following:

- Paying the inmates wages comparable with similar jobs in the community
- Consulting with representatives of private industry and organized labor
- Certifying that the PIE industry does not displace employed workers in the community
- Collecting funds for a victim assistance program
- Providing inmates with benefits in the event of injury in the course of employment
- Ensuring that inmate participation was voluntary
- Providing a substantial role for the private sector.[47]

PIE Program

prison industry programs operated by private companies, with prison goods authorized to be sold on the open market if the program is certified as meeting certain conditions

Almost two-thirds of the states are involved in the **PIE Program**, in which private companies hire inmates to produce goods inside the prisons. Since they must pay inmates wages comparable to private-sector workers, the daily wage as of January 1, 2001 for inmates working in PIE ranged from $21.92 to $34.82.[48] Another requirement is that a share of the inmates' salary is withheld for fines, victim compensation, room and board, and support of families. From the beginning of the PIE Program until June 1995, more than $23 million was withheld from pay and distributed for these purposes, of which 44 percent was for room and board, 26 percent for taxes, 15 percent for victim restitution, and 15 percent for family support.[49]

Prison industry programs are an asset to prison operations, provide funds to operate, and reduce recidivism. Saylor and Gaes conducted the Post-Release Employment Project, collecting data on more than 7,000 federal offenders for a four-year period, comparing those participating in prison industries work programs with similar offenders who did not participate in this program. The results demonstrated significant and substantive effects on both in-prison (misconduct reports) and postprison (employment and arrest rates) outcome measures.[50] As beneficial and successful as prison industries is to a prison operation, it is unfortunate that such a low percentage of inmates are able to participate in these programs.

RELIGIOUS PROGRAMS

Since their inception, prisons have been places for religious reformation. Even though religion used to reform offenders is not the focus in modern prisons that it was in the Walnut Street Jail, religious programming continues to be an important rehabilitative opportunity within prisons. Whether due to the history of prisons or because the American society values religion, we will probably never give up the belief that the practice of religion is valuable for inmates, and that offenders who develop a foundation of religious beliefs are more likely to be successful upon their return to the community. Today, prisons strive to provide religious programs for any group or individual who wants to worship and follow the tenets of a recognized faith.

Most inmates are Muslim, Jewish, Protestant, or Catholic, yet there are dozens of other religious sects and worship groups. In most prisons, religious services and activities are coordinated by one or two full-time chaplains (usually Protestant and Catholic) who contract with ministers of other sects to hold services and provide religious guidance for prisoners of those faith groups. In addition to regular services, activities may include Bible study or religious discussion groups. With usually fifteen to twenty different religious groups, the schedule for religious programs is usually very full, and there are often two or three faith groups meeting on any given night. Volunteers play a particularly important role in providing religious programming, as they are used to lead study or discussion groups.

RECREATION PROGRAMS

Another important but far more controversial area of prison programming is recreation or leisure activities. While it is certainly reasonable to recognize that inmates cannot be in their cells or working the entire day, and therefore some types of organized and supervised activities are important to maintain order, the public does not like the image of inmates with too much idle time, watching color television or lifting weights. Therefore, prison officials attempt to have active recreation programs that reduce idleness, promote health and fitness, and allow inmates to "burn off steam" through exercise.

Recreation is considered critical to a controlled and orderly prison.
Photo by Richard P. Seiter.

While most inmates are required to work approximately six hours per day, five days per week, there could be far too much idle time without extensive recreational programming to keep inmates busy. Prison recreation programs include outside sports such as soccer, basketball, or softball; less-active recreation such as table games or card playing, billiards, or Ping-Pong; art and craft activities such as painting, leather crafts, or pottery making; and fitness programs such as running or calisthenics. Organized athletic activities, such as intramural teams, also have positive rehabilitative benefits, in that they require inmates to work together, develop teamwork, and follow rules and procedures. Recreational programs are also an incentive for good behavior, as inmates can be disciplined by restriction of their participation in such activities.

The most controversial recreational activity is weight lifting, which has been a staple of prisons for decades. Recently, many state legislatures, county governments, and Congress have passed legislation ending or limiting weight lifting in prisons and jails. The first effort to ban weight lifting in prison came after inmates, in a 1993 riot at the Southern Ohio Correctional Facility, used weight equipment to break into rooms in which staff were hiding and take them hostage. As a result, an Ohio congresswoman proposed legislation to ban weight lifting in prison, arguing that the elimination of weights would protect staff from harm. Along with banning weight lifting, many of these legislative acts have also banned the use of electronic musical instruments, paid programming such as HBO movies, and leisure activities such as pool and billiards.

Opponents of weight lifting in prisons argue that inmates who get stronger represent a danger to correctional and law enforcement personnel who may have to physically control them. As well, they suggest that the public does not like the image of inmates spending their time getting stronger by working out with weights, and this image reinforces the stereotypes of a leisurely prison life that does not serve as a

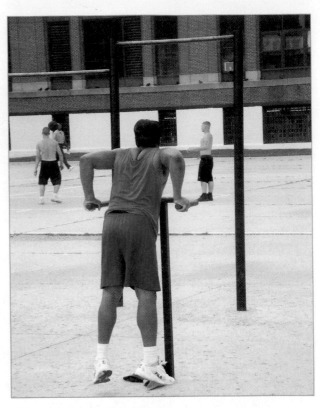

With the controversy regarding weights in prisons, several prisons have removed weights and replaced them with "dip" bars or other exercise equipment.
Photo by Richard P. Seiter.

punishment and deterrent to crime. However, most correctional officials oppose any ban on the use of weight equipment, arguing that such exercise is an important incentive for good behavior, and that there are very few cases in which staff must physically confront a stronger inmate. They point out that weight-lifting inmates seldom get into trouble, as they are usually very self-disciplined and do not want to lose the opportunity to exercise. As well, prison staff are trained not to attempt to break up a fight or get into a physical confrontation in a situation in which they do not have a definite physical advantage or in which staff greatly outnumber inmates.

Over the past decade, and partially as a result of the ban on weight lifting in many jurisdictions, prisons have started recreation programs focusing on educating inmates regarding health and diet, in order to encourage them to develop healthy lifestyles. Offenders enter prison with histories of poor medical care, nutrition, and eating habits and a lack of understanding the importance of exercise and aerobic activities to reduce fat and improve heart functioning. As prison sentences lengthen and inmates age while in prison, the costs of medical care increase significantly. Health education programs are a negligible investment in improving the long-term health of offenders and thereby reducing health care costs for inmates in the future.

Even though there is significant opposition to recreation programs for inmates, they will continue to be an important part of prison programming. There is no alternative to increased idleness if inmates have nothing to do with the time they are not at work or participating in a self-improvement program. Prison administrators fear idleness as a precursor of violence and inmate unrest, especially in today's overcrowded prisons, and forcibly argue this point to elected officials, and prisons will continue to have active recreational programs to encourage good behavior and maintain order.

Chapter Review

SUMMARY

Custody and treatment make up the two key emphases in the mission of prisons. Prisons attempt to create a safe and secure environment through the implementation of professional security policies, and provide inmates many program opportunities that can aid in their successful reentry to the community. In many ways, the two components of the prison mission seem in competition with each other. How can a prison maintain security and order while encouraging inmates to participate in self-improvement programs? And how can positive programs operate within an environment that must control every inmate activity? However, in other ways, these two emphases seem to complement and support one another, as active programs help develop self-control and encourage inmate good behavior.

In this chapter, the approaches and activities undertaken within prisons to ensure security and custody while promoting participation in inmate programming are described. Important practices for maintaining security and order include effective classification systems, adequate physical security, consistent implementation of policy and procedure, inmate accountability and control of contraband, a fair and equitable disciplinary system, methods to separate inmates when necessary, and preparation to respond to inmate disturbances and riots. Valuable program activities include education and vocational programs, mental health treatment, substance abuse programs, work activities including prison industries, religious programs, and leisure activities.

No one questions the importance of security and custody practices within a prison. Few would doubt the need to control inmate behavior and mandate compliance with rules and policies in order to create a safe environment for staff and inmates and fashion such habits among inmates. However, there is considerable controversy regarding the importance of many prison programs in terms of their cost and potential to undermine the punitive and deterrent aspects of a prison sentence. Yet prison programs reduce idleness, teach inmates to live and work in groups, open staff-inmate channels of communication, increase the confidence and self-esteem of offenders, encourage them to accept challenges and strive for success, and increase the educational and vocational skills of inmates.

Many correctional programs have proven effective in reducing recidivism. Several studies over the past decade have affirmed the value of prison rehabilitation programs,[51] and bode well for their future. Even with an emphasis on "punishment" of criminals, the public expects them to return to the community better prepared to become law-abiding citizens. Rehabilitative programs are a reasonable investment in saving money associated with continued offender criminality. We know that simply enhancing criminal sanctions and increasing the level of punishment does not reduce recidivism. However, correctly classifying offenders and providing them with quality treatment interventions result in a significant reduction in recidivism.

REVIEW QUESTIONS

1. What is the definition of custody and treatment?

2. List the eight types of activities that contribute to the security and custody functions within a prison.

3. Define inmate accountability and list the key components to maintaining inmate accountability in a prison.

4. What is the difference between controlled movement and a pass system?

5. What is a stand-up count?

6. How do random counts prevent inmates from planning escape around the other two types of counts?

7. List five Class A tools under prison security policies.

8. What is a shadow board and how is it used to control contraband?

9. What is the purpose of an SHU and what are the two categories of assignment to an SHU?

10. What does it take for a precipitating event to cause a prison riot?

11. Name the three types of teams included in prison emergency plans.

12. What is the Stockholm Syndrome?

13. What percentage of inmates have basic literacy needs?

14. How are mental health programs delivered in prisons and what is the continuum of care?

15. Define the state-use system for prison industries.

16. Outline the conditions required to be certified as a PIE Program.

17. List the arguments against weight lifting in prison.

ENDNOTES

1. Richard P. Seiter, *Correctional Administration: Integrating Theory and Practice* (Upper Saddle River, N.J.: Prentice Hall, 2002), pp. 205–206.

2. *The Security Audit Program: A "How To" Guide and Model Instrument for Adaptation to Local Standards, Policies, and Procedures* (Washington, D.C.: U.S. Department of Justice, National Institute of Corrections, 1999), p. 1.

3. James D. Henderson, W. Hardy Rauch, and Richard L. Phillips, *Guidelines for the Development of a Security Program*, 2nd ed. (Lanham, Md.: American Correctional Association, 1997), p. 21.

4. Ibid., pp. 143–144.

5. Ibid., p. 129.

6. Federal Bureau of Prisons, "Inmate Discipline and Special Housing Units," Policy Statement Number 5270.07 (Washington, D.C.: U.S. Department of Justice, Bureau of Prisons, December 29, 1987), Chapter 4, pp. 4–10.

7. For a good historical overview, see Reid H. Montgomery, Jr., and Gordon A. Crews, *A History of Correctional Violence: An Examination of Reported Causes of Riots and Disturbances* (Lanham, Md.: American Correctional Association, 1998).

8. There are several official and government reports on this riot. However, a source of interesting reading is Tom Wicker, *A Time to Die* (New York: Quadrangle/New York Times Book Company, 1975).

9. Attorney General's Office, *Report of the Attorney General on the February 2 and 3, 1980 Riot at the Penitentiary of New Mexico* (Santa Fe: State of New Mexico, Office of the Attorney General, 1980).

10. Reginald A. Wilkinson and Thomas J. Stickrath, "After the Storm: Anatomy of a Riot's Aftermath," *Corrections Management Quarterly* 1, no. 1 (1996): 16.

11. Henderson, Rauch, and Phillips, 1997, pp. 180–181.

12. R. Arjen Boin and Menno J. Van Duin, "Prison Riots as Organized Failures: A Managerial Perspective," *Prison Journal* 75, no. 3 (1995): 365.

13. Earnest A. Stepp, "Preparing for Chaos: Emergency Management," in *Prison and Jail Administration: Practice and Theory*, edited by Peter M. Carlson and Judith Simon Garrett (Gaithersburg, Md.: Aspen, 1999), p. 371.

14. Gothriel Lafleur, Louis Stender, and Jim Lyons, "Hostage Situations in Correctional Facilities," in *Prison and Jail Administration: Practice and Theory*, edited by Peter M. Carlson and Judith Simon Garrett (Gaithersburg, Md.: Aspen, 1999), p. 376.

15. President's Commission on Law Enforcement and the Administration of Justice, *The Challenge of Crime in a Free Society* (Washington, D.C.: U.S. Government Printing Office, 1967), p. 183.

16. Douglas Lipton, Robert Martinson, and Judith Wilks, *The Effectiveness of Correctional Treatment* (New York: Praeger, 1975).

17. Robert Martinson, "What Works? Questions and Answers about Prison Reform," *The Public Interest* 35 (1974): 25.

18. Christopher A. Innes, "Recent Public Opinion in the United States toward Punishment and Corrections," *Prison Journal* 73, no. 3 (1993), p. 232.

19. Timothy J. Flanagan, "Reform or Punish: Americans' View of the Correctional System," in *Americans View Crime and Justice: A National Public Opinion Survey*, edited by Timothy J. Flanagan and Dennis R. Longmire (Thousand Oaks, Calif.: Sage, 1996), p. 78.

20. J. Senese and David B. Kalinich, "Activities and Rehabilitation Programs for Offenders," in *Corrections: An Introduction*, edited by S. Stojkovic and R. Lovell (Cincinnati, Ohio: Anderson, 1992), p. 223.

21. Francis T. Cullen and Brandon K. Applegate, eds., *Offender Rehabilitation: Effective Correctional Intervention* (Aldershot, England: Ashgate, Dartmouth, 1998), p. xiv.

22. Caroline Wolf Harlow, *Education and Correctional Populations* (Washington, D.C.: U.S. Department of Justice, Bureau of Justice Statistics, January 2003), p. 1.

23. Ibid.

24. Ibid., p. 4.

25. Ibid., p. 5.

26. Commission on Accreditation for Corrections, "Comprehensive Education Program, Standard 3–34410," in *Standards for Adult Correctional Institutions* (College Park, Md.: American Correctional Association, 1990), p. 14.

27. See J. Gerber and E. J. Fritsch, "Adult Academic and Vocational Correctional Education Programs: A Review of Recent Research," *Journal of Offender Rehabilitation* 22 (1995): 199–242; M. D. Harer, "Recidivism among Federal Prisoners Released in 1987," *Journal of Correctional Education* 46, no. 3 (1995): 98–128; M. Jancic, "Does Correctional Education Have an Effect on Recidivism?" *Journal of Correctional Education* 49, no. 4 (1998): 152–161.

28. K. Adams, K. J. Bennett, T. J. Flanagan, J. W. Marquart, S. J. Cuvelier, E. Fritsch, J. Gerber, D. R. Longmire, and V. S. Burton, Jr., "Large-Scale Multidimensional Test of the Effect of Prison Education Programs on Offenders' Behavior," *Prison Journal* 74, no. 4 (December 1994): 433–449.

29. G. F. Vito and R. Tewksbury, "Improving the Educational Skills of Inmates: The Results of an Impact Evaluation," *Corrections Compendium* 24, no. 10 (1999): 1–17.

30. William G. Saylor and Gerald G. Gaes, "Training Inmates through Industrial Work Participation and Vocational and Apprenticeship Instruction," *Corrections Management Quarterly* 1, no. 2 (1997): 40.

31. Pamela K. Lattimore, Ann Dryden Witte, and Joanna R. Baker, "Experimental Assessment of the Effect of Vocational Training on Youthful Property Offenders," *Evaluation Review* 14, no. 2 (1990): 115–133.

32. John Linton, "Inmate Education Makes Sense," *Corrections Today* 60, no. 3 (1998): 18.

33. Steve Peacock, "BOP Proposes Inmates Pay All Tuition Costs for College," *Corrections Journal* 4, no. 10 (2000): 7.

34. Paula M. Ditton, *Mental Health and Treatment of Inmates and Probationers* (Washington, D.C.: U.S. Department of Justice, Bureau of Justice Statistics, 1999).

35. Allen J. Beck and Laura J. Maruschak, *Mental Health Treatment in State Prisons, 2000* (Washington, D.C.: U.S. Department of Justice, Bureau of Justice Statistics, July 2001).

36. Ibid.

37. "Mental Health Care in Ohio Corrections," (Columbus: Ohio Department of Rehabilitation and Correction, 1997), p. 4.

38. National Center on Addiction and Substance Abuse at Columbia University, *Trends in Substance Abuse and Treatment Needs among Inmates* (Washington, D.C.: U.S. Department of Justice, National Institute of Justice, October 2002), p. vii.

39. U.S. General Accounting Office, *Drug Treatment: State Prisons Face Challenges in Providing Treatment: A Report to the Committee on Government Operation, U.S. House of Representatives* (Washington, D.C.: U.S. General Accounting Office, 1991).

40. National Center on Addiction and Substance Abuse at Columbia University, *Behind Bars: Substance Abuse and America's Prison Population* (New York: National Center on Addiction and Substance Abuse at Columbia University, 1998).

41. National Center on Addiction and Substance Abuse at Columbia University, 2002, p. xvi.

42. Office of National Drug Control Policy, "The National Drug Control Strategy: 1998," (Washington, D.C.: The White House, February 1998).

43. Federal Bureau of Prisons, *TRIAD Drug Treatment Evaluation Six-Month Report: Executive Summary* (Washington, D.C.: U.S. Department of Justice, 1998).

44. Seiter, 2002, p. 126.

45. Camille Graham Camp and George M. Camp, *The 2001 Corrections Yearbook* (Middletown, Conn.: The Criminal Justice Institute, 2002), pp. 116 and 126.

46. Ibid., p. 131.

47. National Institute of Justice, *Developing Private Sector Prison Industries: From Concept to Start Up* (Washington, D.C.: U.S. Government Printing Office, 1990), p. 22.

48. Camp and Camp, 2002, p. 130.

49. Bureau of Justice Assistance, *Prison Industries Fact Sheet* (Rockville, Md.: Bureau of Justice Assistance Clearinghouse, 1995).

50. William G. Saylor and Gerald G. Gaes, "The Post-Release Employment Project: Prison Work Has Measurable Effects on Post-Release Success," *Federal Prisons Journal* 2, no. 4 (1992): 33–36.

51. Robert Martinson, *Offender Rehabilitation: Effective Correctional Intervention,* edited by Francis T. Cullen and Brandon K. Applegate (Aldershot, England: Ashgate, Dartmouth, 1998), Chapter 4; D. A. Andrews and J. Bonta, *The Psychology of Criminal Conduct* (Cincinnati, Ohio: Anderson, 1994); Paul Gendreau, "The Principles of Effective Intervention with Offenders," in *Choosing Correctional Options That Work: Defining the Demand and Evaluating the Supply,* edited by A. Harland (Thousand Oaks, Calif.: Sage, 1996), pp. 117–130; M. W. Lipsey, "Juvenile Delinquency Treatment: A Meta-Analytic Inquiry into the Variability of Effects," in *Meta-Analysis for Explanation,* edited by T. D. Cook, H. Cooper, D. S. Cordray, H. Hartmann, L. V. Hedges, R. J. Light, T. A. Louis, and F. Mosteller (New York: Russell Sage, 1992), pp. 83–127; D. S. Andrews, I. Zinger, R. D. Hoge, J. Bonta, P. Gendreau, and F. T. Cullen, "Does Correctional Treatment Work? A Psychologically Informed Meta-Analysis," *Criminology* 28 (1990): 369–404.

Chapter 14

AFTER READING THIS CHAPTER, YOU SHOULD BE ABLE TO:

1. Describe the historical development of the legal rights of inmates and the creation and then abandonment of the hands-off doctrine by federal courts.

2. Explain how the First, Fourth, Eighth, and Fourteenth Amendments to the U.S. Constitution create a basis for inmate lawsuits.

3. Identify the types of tests the courts have created to consider whether prison conditions of confinement violate the Eighth Amendment rights of inmates.

4. Specify the legal cases and tests regarding the opportunity for inmates to practice religion within prison.

5. Outline the due process rights granted inmates throughout inmate disciplinary proceedings.

6. Explain how recent court decisions and congressional actions have limited the filing of inmate lawsuits.

7. Specify the legal decisions that have affected the use of capital punishment in the United States and describe the requirements for capital trials under *Furman v. Georgia*.

8. List and describe court rulings regarding the use of capital punishment with juveniles, the mentally ill, and the mentally retarded.

9. Explain the various reasons cited by proponents of capital punishment and the counter arguments of its opponents.

10. Describe the public attitude regarding the death penalty.

Legal Issues and the Death Penalty

KEY TERMS

slave-of-the-state doctrine
precedents
Eighth Amendment
Fourteenth Amendment
balancing test
Civil Rights Act of 1871
Section 1983
Americans with Disabilities Act
totality-of-conditions test
deliberate indifference
community standards
bifurcated trial
lethal injection

Introduction

This chapter discusses the complex issues of the legal rights of inmates and the use of capital punishment. There are, perhaps, no more emotional topics than these in the overall operations of correctional agencies. Few people would argue that inmates should lose every right they have, as citizens of the United States, as a result of committing a felony and being imprisoned. It is uncomfortable to think about the unfair treatment, torture and excessive use of force, discrimination, and failure to provide basic due process to inmates that has occurred during the history of correctional institutions. While most agree that inmates do not deserve such treatment, many people also believe that inmates today receive too many rights and unduly burden correctional officials and cost taxpayers money with petty claims, and that the pendulum has swung too far in providing inmates more rights than they should have. The first section of this chapter addresses the evolution of inmate rights, the foundation for prisoner rights provided by the U.S. Constitution, a description of the specific areas of inmate rights, and some movements to limit litigation by inmates against correctional agencies and officials.

The second section of this chapter addresses another emotional issue: the use of capital punishment. While our country has a long history of the use of the death penalty as a sanction for serious crimes, the majority of the public supports it, and the U.S. Supreme Court has ruled that capital punishment in itself is not cruel and unusual, there is still deep concern and persevering debate on the topic. The historical use of capital punishment in America and the very active consideration of capital punishment laws by the federal courts over the past thirty years are presented. Arguments for and against the need for capital punishment are described, as well as the constant concern about error in conviction and the irrevocability of a sentence of death.

Legal Issues Regarding Inmates

As much as is heard about inmates suing the state, the governor, the prison warden, or any number of other prison staff, we tend to believe that lawsuits have always been a part of the history of prisons, and inmates have always had, as some people think, more rights than law-abiding citizens. However, that is not the case. The truth is that inmates are still citizens of the United States, and therefore come under the protection of the Constitution and the Bill of Rights, just like any other U.S. citizen. However, certain security and safety concerns in the operation of a prison allow prison administrators to limit inmates' full enjoyment of the rights they would have if they were not in prison.

Inmates are not hesitant to file suits against correctional agencies or prison staff. *The 2001 Corrections Yearbook* reports that in 2000, prison inmates filed 24,519 lawsuits against the agency or staff. As well, twenty-five states had eighty-nine class-action lawsuits in effect on January 1, 2001; court orders concerning conditions of confinement affected 265 prisons; and limits on how many inmates could be housed in prisons were in effect at eighty-two prisons in twelve states.[1] Since 1995, however, the average number of inmate lawsuits filed against state and federal correctional agencies has actually declined. As indicated in Table 14.1, the average number declined each year, and dropped by more than 27 percent between 1995 and 2000. It should be noted, however, that averages could be misleading. In 2000, with the average number of lawsuits filed against a correctional agency at 545, the highest number filed was against New York (5,000), and the lowest against Wyoming (4).[2]

TABLE	14.1	Average Number of Lawsuits Filed against Correctional Agencies, 1995–2000

Year	Number
1995	748
1996	682
1997	645
1998	579
1999	554
2000	545

Source: Adapted from Camille Graham Camp and George M. Camp, *The 2001 Corrections Yearbook: Adult Systems* (Middletown, Conn.: Criminal Justice Institute, 2002), p. 75.

The Development of Inmate Legal Rights

Historically, until fifty years ago, there was little consideration of the rights of people confined in correctional institutions, as federal courts did not want to intervene in the administration of prisons. This avoidance was primarily the result of the 1871 decision of *Ruffin v. Commonwealth of Virginia*,[3] in which the U.S. Supreme Court enunciated the **slave-of-the-state doctrine** holding that inmates were, for all intents and purposes, slaves of the state, and had no rights that were not granted them by the state. With this decision, the Court created what became known as the *hands-off doctrine*, and did not accept lawsuits regarding violation of inmates' constitutional rights. The Court believed it good policy to continue this approach, due to (1) the Court's lack of expertise in corrections and showing deference to the judgment of prison administrators; (2) the need for separation of powers between the judicial and the executive branches of government; and (3) a concern that accepting prisoner rights cases would open a "Pandora's box" of further litigation, and the courts would be flooded with prisoner lawsuits. The hands-off doctrine was supported in the 1948 decision of *Price v. Johnston*, when the Court ruled that convicted inmates must expect that as a part of their punishment, they lose the freedoms that free citizens take for granted.[4]

Federal courts adhered to the hands-off doctrine for most of the next two decades. However, after reading complaints by inmates that seemed like a continuing escalation of the violation of basic tenets of the Constitution, the Court decided that it needed to give some guidance to correctional officials. In 1964, it accepted and heard *Cooper v. Pate*,[5] a case regarding religious freedom in prison. Black Muslim inmates claimed that they were not being allowed to congregate, eat their prescribed religious diet, or wear distinctive items of clothing, all of which were basic tenets of their religious practice, and therefore a violation of Section 1983 of the Civil Rights Act of 1871. The Court, recognizing the Black Muslim faith as constituting an established religion, ruled that Black Muslims should be allowed to follow the prescribed practices of that religion, if those practices did not present a clear and present danger to the security and orderly running of a prison.

With their decision in *Cooper v. Pate*, the Court effectively ended the hands-off doctrine by recognizing that inmates could sue prison officials for violation of their rights under the Constitution. With this decision, the world of inmate lawsuits and legal issues for inmates changed forever. The floodgates were opened; the federal courts spend considerable time and resources handling inmate complaints, and

Slave-of-the-state doctrine

as decided in the 1871 decision of *Ruffin v. the Commonwealth of Virginia*, that held inmates were "slaves of the state," and had no rights that were not granted them by the state

NATIONAL TRENDS IN THE NUMBER OF STATE PRISON LAWSUITS

FIGURE **14.1**

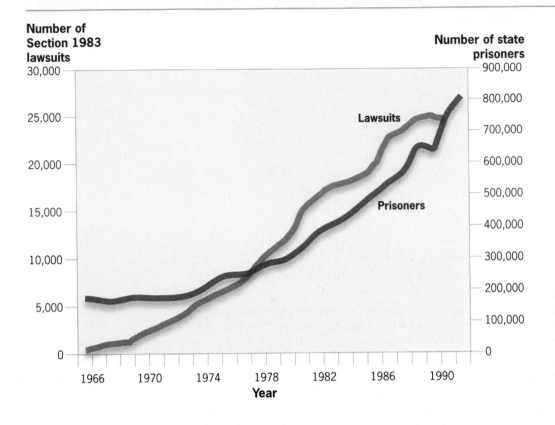

Source: Roger A. Hanson and Henry W. K. Daley, *Challenging the Conditions of Prisons and Jails: A Report on Section 1983 Litigation* (Washington, D.C.: U.S. Department of Justice, Bureau of Justice Statistics, 1994), p. 3.

Precedents

decision of courts that come before and are therefore binding on later decisions of courts within the same jurisdiction

correctional administrators must constantly stay attuned to new decisions by the courts and the impact that such decisions have on prison operations. New decisions clarify the rights that are not lost by being convicted of a felony and incarcerated and guide correctional officials in following the earlier court **precedents** and revising policies and procedures to be consistent with such decisions. As a result, instead of the early belief that inmates lose their rights, it is now believed that inmates retain their constitutional rights as citizens when incarcerated, unless the necessity for security and order in a prison deems otherwise.

Since the U.S. Supreme Court abandoned the hands-off doctrine, the number of cases filed has increased tremendously. In a 1994 review of the use of litigation by inmates under Section 1983 of the Civil Rights Act, Hanson and Daley note, "The Administrative Office of the U.S. Courts counted only 218 cases in 1966, the first year that state prisoners' rights cases were recorded as a specific category of litigation. The number climbed to 26,824 by 1992 . . . Finally, there is approximately one lawsuit for every thirty state prison inmates."[6] Figure 14.1 illustrates the increase in the number of lawsuits in comparison with the number of inmates from 1966 until 1992.

The Bill of Rights and Congressional Actions Providing Inmate Rights

The source of all inmate rights is the Constitution of the United States (ratified in 1788) and the Bill of Rights (added in 1791), just as they are the source of the rights granted to all citizens of the United States. The primary amendments that are used as a basis of lawsuits by prison inmates are the Eighth (prohibiting cruel and unusual punishment) and the Fourteenth (providing due process to individuals charged with crimes). Other amendments, as well as specific laws passed by Congress, are used less frequently, but are still the basis of many inmate rights.

The **Eighth Amendment** states that no cruel or unusual punishment may be inflicted, and is a broad opening for a variety of inmate lawsuits over aspects such as prison overcrowding, life and safety issues, use of force against inmates by staff, or poor food or medical care. It is difficult for a court or correctional administrators to determine what level of restrictions in a prison constitutes "cruel and unusual punishment." Obviously, torture or physical punishment is not allowed, but less obvious allegations of cruel and unusual punishment are more difficult to define specifically because almost every case has individual situations and presents varying facts. Over the past three decades, the federal courts have provided some guidance in defining cruel and unusual punishment in three major prisoner-rights cases.

In the 1970 case of *Holt v. Sarver,* a federal district court looked at conditions throughout the Arkansas prison system and created a standard of cruel and unusual punishment under the Eighth Amendment. Going beyond the concept of torture or physical punishment, the court found that if people of *reasonable sensitivity* found the treatment shocking or disgusting, it would also be considered cruel and unusual. The court ruled that in general terms, cruel and unusual punishment is that which "amounts to torture, when it is grossly excessive in proportion to the offense for which it is imposed, or that is inherently unfair, or that is unnecessarily degrading, or that is shocking or disgusting to people of reasonable sensitivity."[7]

In the 1979 case of *Bell v. Wolfish,* the Court reviewed conditions and practices at a federal jail for short-term offenders in New York City. Even though the jail was recently constructed, it was already overcrowded, with two inmates held in most cells at the time of the inmates' complaints leading to this decision. Inmates also complained that prohibiting them from receiving hardback books not mailed directly from a publisher, not allowing them to observe searches of their cells, and requiring them to submit to visual searches of body cavities after visits with family members or friends constituted cruel and unusual punishment. The Court ruling adopted the *punitive intent standard,* stating that the case should turn only on whether the practices in question violated detainees' right to be free from punishment, using a standard of whether the individual restrictions were punitive or merely regulatory restraints; whether the practice is reasonably related to a legitimate goal other than punishment; and whether it appears to be excessive in relation to that alternative purpose.[8]

In *Solem v. Helm,* the Court in 1983 developed the *test of proportionality,* declaring the following:

> [W]e hold as a matter of principle that a criminal sentence must be proportionate to the crime for which the defendant has been convicted. . . . In sum, a court's proportionality analysis . . . should be guided by objective criteria, including (i) the gravity of the offense and the harshness of the penalty; (ii) the sentences imposed on other criminals in the same jurisdiction; and (iii) the sentences imposed for commission of the same crime in other jurisdictions . . . [9]

The **Fourteenth Amendment** asserts that no state shall deprive any person of life, liberty, or property, without the due process of law, and also prohibits states from denying any person the equal protection of the law. When initially passed, the Constitution and Bill of Rights applied only to the federal courts and federal law in defining the relationship between citizens and government. The Fifth and Sixth Amendments guarantee due process in the course of legal proceedings, and the Fourteenth Amendment expanded these rights to states. Inmates who claim that prison officials have taken action against them for disciplinary reasons without providing them due process, or that they have not had access to legal materials and therefore access to the courts, often cite the Fourteenth Amendment.

Eighth Amendment
states that no cruel or unusual punishment may be inflicted

Fourteenth Amendment
no state shall deprive any person of life, liberty, or property, without the due process of law; states may not deny any person the equal protection of the law

Inmate lawsuits also regularly cite the First Amendment as the basis for their complaints. The First Amendment guarantees that no law shall be enacted that restricts or abridges an individual's freedom of religion, speech, and the press. These were seen by our founding fathers as such basic and fundamental rights (thus, the "First" Amendment) that the federal courts require very compelling reasons for prison officials to deny such freedoms to inmates. In the 1974 case of *Pell v. Procunier,* the U.S. Supreme Court created the **balancing test**, declaring that "[a] prison inmate retains those First Amendment rights that are not inconsistent with his status as prisoner or with the *legitimate penological objectives* of a correctional system."[10] The Court recognized that correctional officials have legitimate concerns in trying to provide security and safety within a correctional institution, and that these should be weighed (or balanced) against the restriction of rights. In more recent decisions, the courts often have required prison officials to make reasonable accommodations to practices and procedures to allow for such rights. Issues under the First Amendment of use of the mail, access to outside publications, and access to the press are described next.

Not every right was anticipated or addressed in the U.S. Constitution or the Bill of Rights. Therefore, over the years, Congress has passed several acts to protect individuals against discrimination. The earliest was the **Civil Rights Act of 1871**, which guaranteed the rights of freed slaves and provided access to federal courts for violations of the Act. **Section 1983** of the Civil Rights Act prohibits any person, acting under the color of any statute, ordinance, or regulation (color of law), from depriving another of his or her constitutional rights. The use of Section 1983 of the Civil Rights Act has expanded beyond the original use intended by Congress, and inmates regularly use it to sue government employees in their individual capacity for restricting religious practice, failing to provide proper medical care, or not protecting an inmate from assault by another inmate.

Another recent act of Congress that affects correctional institutions is the **Americans with Disabilities Act** (ADA) of 1990. The ADA prohibits any entity from discriminating against an individual with a disability in regard to employment, public services and transportation, public accommodations, and telecommunications services. The most difficult issues for correctional agencies arise in the sections dealing with employment and accommodation. Many prisons (like most law enforcement agencies) have physical conditions of employment that some disabled individuals cannot meet. And inmates can sue regarding the requirement that all areas of a prison be accessible to people with disabilities. The courts have continually (against strenuous objections by prison officials and governors from almost every state) held that the ADA applies to correctional institutions as well as other public entities. The states often argue that the ADA was not intended for prisons, but for public buildings, and that prisons, although funded with public money, are not public in that not everyone has access to them. However, at this time, prisons are not exempt from the act, and therefore must make all their areas of housing, programs, and services reasonably accessible to people with disabilities.

Specific Rights of Prisoners

The Constitution, Bill of Rights, and other acts of Congress form the basis of rights provided to inmates, and guide correctional officials as they struggle to maintain security and order in prisons without violating the basic rights of inmates. The next several sections describe specific areas in which inmate rights are often argued in courts, and in which there has been an evolution of practice in correctional facilities. These include overcrowding and overall conditions of confinement, religious freedom, medical care, freedom of speech, use of the mail and receipt of publications, access to the press, access to the courts, privacy and search and seizure, and inmate discipline.

The Americans with Disabilities Act of 1990 requires prisons to make accommodations for inmates with all types of physical disabilities.
Photo by Richard P. Seiter.

CONDITIONS OF CONFINEMENT

Inmates often complain about overcrowding and poor overall conditions of confinement (poor food, lack of satisfactory health care, unsanitary conditions) that can result from overcrowding or from simple neglect by prison officials. Courts use the **totality-of-conditions test** to determine whether the overall conditions within a prison constitute cruel and unusual punishment. The totality-of-conditions test examines the aggregate of circumstances in a prison to determine whether they, as a whole, are cruel and unusual, even if no single condition of the prison is cruel and unusual. This test was created in *Pugh v. Locke* in 1976, when Alabama prison conditions were found so debilitating that they deprived inmates of the opportunity to rehabilitate themselves or even maintain skills they already possessed.[11]

However, the U.S. Supreme Court has clearly determined that overcrowding (having more than one person in a cell) is not cruel and unusual punishment in violation of the Eighth Amendment. In *Bell v. Wolfish* in 1979, the Court held that there is no one-person, one-cell guarantee within a prison.[12] Shortly thereafter (in 1981), the Court in *Rhodes v. Chapman* determined that double celling in itself does not constitute cruel and unusual punishment, in that it does not "inflict unnecessary or wanton pain."[13] And finally, in 1991, the Court in *Wilson v. Seiter* (a significant corrections decision with the author of this text as the named defendant) noted that uncomfortable conditions are a part of the penalty that inmates pay for their criminality, and that inmates must prove that conditions are objectively cruel and unusual and that they exist due to the **deliberate indifference** of prison administrators.[14] Deliberate indifference thereafter became the standard for individual liability under conditions of confinement suits brought under Section 1983. The "A Case Study" box illustrates some of the background issues that can lead to the development of inmate lawsuits.

Totality-of-conditions test
a test created in *Pugh v. Locke* that examines the aggregate of circumstances in a prison to determine whether cruel and unusual conditions exist

Deliberate indifference
as established in *Wilson v. Seiter*, the standard that conditions at prison are not unconstitutional unless prison administrators show deliberate indifference toward inmates' basic needs

A CASE STUDY — THE DEVELOPMENT OF AN INMATE LAWSUIT

Two significant cases regarding conditions of prison confinement are *Rhodes v. Chapman* and *Wilson v. Seiter*. As director of the Ohio Department of Corrections, I was directly involved in one of these lawsuits; I became director shortly after the U.S. Supreme Court decided *Rhodes v. Chapman*. The following case study illustrates some of the issues that can lead to inmate lawsuits and affect a court decision regarding the cases.

Rhodes v. Chapman involved the Southern Ohio Correctional Institution (SOCF), located in Lucasville, Ohio. SOCF was opened in the early 1970s to replace the century-old Ohio Penitentiary (OP). Its design was to be state of the art in that it would be all single cells in three different sections, so that different groups of inmates could be separated. However, the prison opened with a large percentage of new staff, and some of the worst prisoners from the OP were transferred to the new prison. Too many inmates were transferred to SOCF too fast, and the staff competence and procedures could not keep up with the rapid growth in the number of inmates, many of whom were violent and disruptive.

The prison experienced several problems, including inmate riots, hostage takings, escapes, and staff union strikes. The upper management was changed, and while things improved, there were still many problems. Inmate Kelly Chapman and others decided to sue the Ohio Department of Corrections, complaining primarily that the prison held many more inmates than the 1,600 single cells were designed to hold. Prison officials were unconcerned about double-celling, as the cells were fairly large (approximately 80 square feet), and the prison had ample space for programs and services.

The department won the case at the federal district court level, but the inmates appealed and won in the U.S. court of appeals. Ohio decided to appeal to the U.S. Supreme Court, believing that one person per cell would not be upheld. The case was won at this level, but only because the "totality of conditions" at SOCF indicated that inmates were out of their cells all but eight hours per day, many programs (education, vocational, and work) kept inmates busy during the day, and services (food services and medical) were adequate.

In *Wilson v. Seiter*, we had opened an old tuberculosis hospital that had been closed for several years as the Hocking Correctional Facility (HCF). Housing was dormitory-style, and the prison had just over three-hundred inmates. We decided to place older inmates in the prison, as there was limited program and recreation space, believing that these inmates would need less space for such activities. While the prison seemed to meet our needs, inmates complained that the old facility was too hot (it was not air-conditioned) in the summer, and in the winter (due to rows of windows similar to an elementary school) it was not warm enough for the older inmates who lived there.

The case was quickly thrown out at the U.S. district court level, as the court did not believe that inmate "Pearly" Wilson and others involved in the lawsuit had complained about issues that reached their constitutional rights as prisoners. When the inmates appealed, the upper-level court determined that the lower court had used the wrong standard for determining that we as prison administrators had not violated the constitutional standard against cruel and unusual punishment. The case went to the U.S. Supreme Court not on the conditions that existed at HCF, but on the standard that prison administrators must be held to when conditions that were "uncomfortable" but possibly not "unconstitutional" existed. The decision by the Supreme Court that conditions at a prison are not unconstitutional unless prison administrators show "deliberate indifference" toward inmates' basic needs was a good win and very important for future defenses of inmate lawsuits by correctional agencies.

RELIGIOUS FREEDOM

As noted previously, the practice of religious freedom has been so fundamental in the founding of the United States, that courts hold correctional officials to a high standard in the restriction of the practice of inmates' duly recognized religion. The First Amendment to the Constitution states that "Congress shall make no law respecting an establishment of religion, or prohibiting the free exercise thereof. . . ."

In the 1964 case of *Cooper v. Pate,*[15] the Court determined that inmates should be allowed to practice their religion when the following conditions are met: (1) The religion claimed is a duly established religion; (2) the practices desired by inmates are part of the basic tenets of the religion; and (3) the practices do not present a clear and present danger to the security and orderly running of a prison.

Several cases since *Cooper v. Pate* have further refined this ruling. In terms of the religion being duly established, it is not for prison officials to determine which religions inmates may practice, yet inmates cannot just create some religion to subvert prison restrictions. In *Cruz v. Beto* (1972), the Supreme Court stated that inmates must be given a "reasonable opportunity" to practice their religion, even if the inmates' faith is not traditional or conventional.[16] Yet when a group of inmates at the Atlanta federal penitentiary created a new religion called the Church of the New Song (CONS) and demanded that steak and wine be included on the prison menu, the federal court disagreed (*Theriault v. Silber,* 1977), because it was not a religion entitled to First Amendment protection.[17]

If the religion is a valid one, inmates can practice activities that are determined to be based on basic tenets of the religion. For instance, prison officials must provide sweat lodges and the opportunity to use them to Native American inmates (*Hamilton v. Schriro,* 1996),[18] and Jewish inmates must be provided kosher food as a part of the prison menu (*Kahane v. Carlson,* 1975).[19] Yet the court ruled in *O'Lone v. Estate of Shabazz* (1987) that prison officials do not have rearrange inmate work schedules to allow a Muslim inmate to attend Friday worship services, even though Jumu'ah is a central part of the Islamic religious faith.[20]

When a religious practice can present a danger to the security and orderly running of a prison is difficult to generalize. In the *O'Lone* case, prison officials were successful partly because they argued that modifying the work schedules for inmates would undermine security. The courts often use a "reasonableness" test, established in the 1987 case of *Turner v. Safley,* in which the restriction of practice

Prisons must provide sweat lodges for Native American inmates to practice their religious tradition of going into a small lodge (the branches forming an igloo like structure are covered with blankets), heating rocks, and pouring water over them to sweat and clean their systems.
Photo by Richard P. Seiter.

must reasonably be related to a legitimate penological interest, such as security or safety, but possibly including conserving resources.[21] And while the court recognized that it is not practical to provide every inmate a member of the clergy (*Gittlemacker v. Prasse,* 1970),[22] Muslim inmates have been allowed to have a special meal to end Ramadan, despite prison officials' argument that provision of special food served after sunset would be cost-prohibitive (*Walker v. Blackwell,* 1969).[23]

MEDICAL CARE

The provision of adequate medical care is another basic right for inmates, established through court decisions responding to inmate suits alleging that failure to provide such care was a violation of the Eighth Amendment prohibition of cruel and unusual punishment. In 1970, the court looked at conditions throughout the Arkansas prison system, including medical care, and created a test of cruel and unusual punishment within the Eighth Amendment. Instead of including only the concept of torture or physical punishment, the court found that if people of reasonable sensitivity found the treatment shocking or disgusting, it would also be considered cruel and unusual (*Holt v. Sarver*).[24]

In *Estelle v. Gamble* (1976), the Supreme Court determined that prison officials have a duty to provide medical treatment to inmates, since inmates are dependent on them to provide for their medical needs. In this case, the Court prohibited "deliberate indifference" in responding to inmate medical needs, and neither medical staff in responding to needs, nor correctional staff by denying, interfering with, or delaying access to medical care, can be deliberately indifferent to such needs without the unnecessary or wanton infliction of pain.[25] In *Ramos v. Lamm* (1980), the court further suggested that deliberate indifference can also result from "repeated examples of negligent acts which disclose a pattern of conduct" by the correctional

Prison medical care is an area of great sensitivity to inmates, who regularly complain about it.
Photo by Richard P. Seiter.

and medical staff.[26] And in 1991, the court established that medical care in prisons must be "reasonably commensurate with modern medical science and of a quality acceptable within prudent professional standards" (*Fernandez v. United States* [1991]).[27] The principle of **community standards** seems reasonable in providing medical care, as inmates should expect to get the same quality of treatment for their health needs as they would receive if they were in the community. This does not mean that prisons must take every possible step in responding to medical needs, but they cannot deny inmates care that they would have received if not incarcerated. Medical care continues to be the topic that receives the most inmate complaints and suits. In addition to challenging a lack of adequate medical care under the Eighth Amendment, inmates often sue prison officials personally through Section 1983 of the U.S. Code, established in the Civil Rights Act of 1871.

Community standards
the test established in *Fernandez v. United States* that medical care for inmates must be reasonably commensurate with medical care they would receive if not imprisoned

FIRST AMENDMENT RIGHTS

The First Amendment of the Constitution prohibits Congress from "abridging the freedom of speech, or of the press, or the right of the people peaceably to assemble . . . " Yet in terms of freedom of speech, almost everyone has heard that "you can't yell fire in the middle of a crowded theater," and recognizes that there are some restrictions to the common citizen's rights to free speech. It is easy to imagine that many such restrictions would apply to free speech, access to the press, or freedom to assemble in a prison environment. The balancing test created in *Pell v. Procunier* is the guideline used in determining the reasonableness of restricting First Amendment Rights to inmates.

An example of the use of the balancing test is in the handling of inmate mail. Mail is recognized as important in communicating with family and friends outside prison, and such contact aids in rehabilitation and success after release. However, in the case of *Procunier v. Martinez* (1974), the U.S. Supreme Court acknowledged that there was a valid security interest in prison officials reading inmate mail, but determined that they could not censor it.[28] As well, prison officials cannot prevent inmates from writing letters that are vulgar or disparaging about prison staff (*McNamara v. Moody*, 1979).[29] In *Turner v. Safley* (1987), the Supreme Court also allowed prison officials to continue to ban inmates from writing to inmates in other correctional institutions.[30] And in regard to restricting the right of assembly, the Supreme Court in 1977 supported the ban on inmates soliciting other inmates to join an inmate union, having union meetings, and doing bulk mailings regarding the union (*Jones v. North Carolina Prisoner's Labor Union, Inc.*).[31]

Freedom of access to the press as a First Amendment right has also been the subject of many inmate legal cases. In the *Pell v. Procunier* case, California prison officials were allowed to ban press and other media interviews with specific inmates when they believed it could endanger prison security. The Court found that there were alternative channels for inmates to communicate with the media other than in-person interviews. However, most correctional agencies do allow inmates to have interviews with the press, either by telephone or in person. The greater concern regarding media interviews is the inmate's right to privacy, and prison officials usually require that an inmate request such an interview, rather than a media person seek an interview with an inmate through prison officials.

Receipt of publications (magazines and books) is also an issue of First Amendment rights. In the 1971 case of *Sostre v. Otis*, the court created the "clear and present danger" standard.[32] Because there are publications that could detail how to saw prison bars with mess hall utensils, make a bomb, or provoke a prison riot, the court noted that such material could be inflammatory or dangerous, and its presence in a prison could create a clear and present danger. A ban of publications that wardens thought were detrimental to good order and institutional discipline or that might facilitate criminal activity was also upheld in *Thornburgh v. Abbott* (1989).[33] Prison officials are also concerned about publications such as magazines and books that, due to the nature of how they are assembled, could be used to hide small contraband items such as drugs. For that reason, the courts have upheld a restriction that allows inmates to receive such publications only directly from the publisher (*Guajardo v. Estelle* [1978]).[34]

ACCESS TO THE COURTS

Another basic right for citizens of the United States is that they have access to the courts to address any injustice. This holds true for inmates. In 1969, the Supreme Court in *Johnson v. Avery* recognized that inmates, to have full access to the courts, must often have legal assistance.[35] In its decision, the Court ruled that inmates have a right to consult other inmates for legal advice if trained legal advisors are not available. And shortly thereafter, the Court added that prisons must provide sufficient legal materials to enable inmates to conduct legal research in order to have reasonable access to the courts (*Younger v. Gilmore*, 1971).[36] This was further established in 1977, when the Court decided *Bounds v. Smith*, requiring prisons to provide adequate law libraries or adequate assistance from trained legal people.[37]

FOURTH AMENDMENT RIGHTS

The Fourth Amendment provides that people be secure "against unreasonable searches and seizures." This affects prison officials, who must closely watch inmates, monitor their behavior, and control the importation of dangerous contraband (principally weapons and drugs) to maintain safety and security. The practices of searches of inmates, their belongings, and their housing areas are basic to good prison security practices. The legal issue is how much privacy from searches is reasonable within a prison. The courts have clearly ruled that inmates

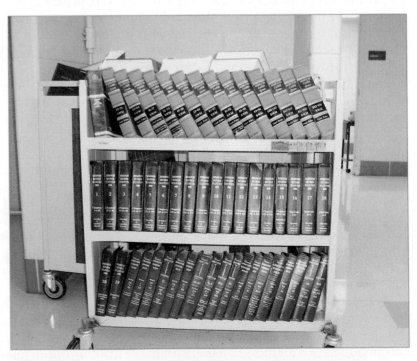

Even in jails or if inmates are held in an SHU, they have access to legal materials. Some institutions deliver legal books to these inmates on a cart.
Photo by Richard P. Seiter.

do not have an expectation of privacy while in prison. In *Hudson v. Palmer* (1984), the Supreme Court dismissed the claims of inmate Palmer that searches of his cell were just to harass him, and held that "the Fourth Amendment proscription against unreasonable searches does not apply within the confines of the prison cell."[38] Prison officials may do searches randomly and without providing specific justification. However, they are expected to leave inmates' cells orderly (not to trash them in the search), or inmates may sue under the Eighth Amendment for destruction of their property.

Inmates are also personally searched on a regular basis. In *Bell v. Wolfish* (1979), routine strip searches of inmates were deemed not to be a violation of the Fourth Amendment because they are reasonable to maintain security within a prison.[39] Searches of body cavities are more sensitive than a visual search of an inmate's naked body. However, it is not unusual for inmates to hide drugs, handcuff keys, weapons (bullets for guns), or even hacksaw blades in the rectum to smuggle them into a prison. Therefore, while these searches must be done, the courts require that there must be information that an inmate is hiding contraband in a body cavity, medical staff must conduct the search, and the search must be done in a manner that respects the inmate's dignity and privacy (*Tribble v. Gardner*, 1988).[40]

The courts have also addressed the issue of searches by prison staff of the opposite sex. In *Grummett v. Rushen* (1984), the court agreed with California prison officials that prohibiting female correctional officers from being assigned to housing areas in which inmates could be seen in partial or total nudity did not outweigh the women's equal employment opportunity rights.[41] The need for privacy can easily be accommodated by inmates wearing robes and by installing privacy screens in front of showers that do not totally block the view and therefore reduce security. Additionally, in *Johnson v. Phelan* (1995), the court also allowed searches of inmates by opposite-sex correctional staff, noting how impractical it would be to have only the same sex conduct searches of inmates.[42] However, the courts lecture against searches that may harass, humiliate, or intimidate inmates, and correctional agencies generally use same sex staff to conduct searches, unless in an emergency.

INMATE DISCIPLINE

Inmate disciplinary processes are guided by the Fourteenth Amendment, which states: "No State shall . . . deprive any person of life, liberty, or property, without due process of law." Due process as it relates to disciplinary processes for inmate misbehavior within the prison was first considered in the 1974 case *Wolff v. McDonnell*, which dealt with a claim that the state of Nebraska disciplinary processes denied inmates due process, and were therefore unconstitutional.[43] However, the Supreme Court differentiated between due process required by a defendant at trial and that of a prison inmate. While prison inmates do not receive all the due process of someone not yet proven guilty, the Court enumerated the steps required for prisoner due process when facing a prison disciplinary hearing:

- The right to receive advance written notice of the alleged infraction
- The right to have sufficient time (at least twenty-four hours) to prepare a defense
- The right to present documentary evidence and to call witnesses on his or her behalf, unless permitting this would be unduly hazardous
- The right to have assistance (by an inmate or staff representative) when the circumstances of the case are complex or if the prisoner is illiterate
- The right to a written statement of the findings of an impartial disciplinary committee of the evidence relied on to support the finding of fact and the reasons the disciplinary action was taken

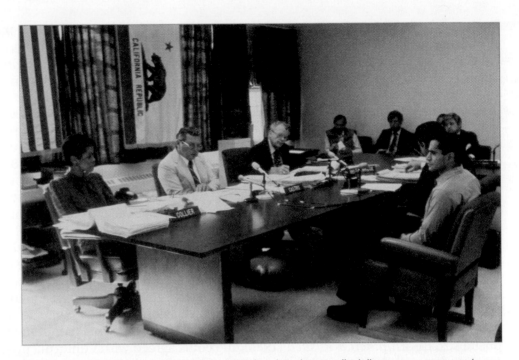

Inmates have the right to limited due process in prison inmate disciplinary processes, and hearing officers not from the inmates' prison often decide guilt and punishment.
Courtesy of the Federal Bureau of Prisons.

A later 1995 Supreme Court case clarified and gave new guidance to inmate disciplinary procedures requiring due process. In *Sandin v. Conner,* the Court, noting that the purpose of prison disciplinary actions is to maintain good prison management and achieve rehabilitative goals, determined that disciplinary actions in pursuit of those goals that do not add to the sentence being served or change the conditions contemplated in the sentence being served do not create a liberty interest and do not require due process.[44] Thus, under *Sandin,* an inmate who violates a prison rule and receives a punishment of placement in disciplinary segregation for a temporary period does not trigger the need for due process, while loss of good time that subsequently extends the sentence (by delaying the release date) does trigger the need for due process. Even with the *Sandin* decision, most prisons find it more efficient and continue to provide the full *Wolff* due process rights for handling inmate discipline.

All of these areas regarding inmate rights are constantly developing and practices are changing based on the latest legal precedent. The greatest time of change was from 1965 until 1980, the first fifteen years after the U.S. Supreme Court abandoned the hands-off doctrine. Correctional agencies began to be somewhat more proactive in dealing with issues that often were found to be of concern to federal courts. However, in the early 1990s, public sentiment indicated a frustration and disenchantment with the high number of inmate lawsuits, and Congress took action to limit lawsuits filed by inmates.

Limiting Litigation by Inmates

There are several reasons to believe that a number of actions have led to a reduction in the number of lawsuits filed by inmates. First, some Supreme Court decisions seem to have "turned the tide" of decisions away from inmates and toward support for prison administrators. The 1991 case of *Wilson v. Seiter* is considered a key decision for correctional agencies, as the Court stated that prison conditions, while they may be uncomfortable, are not unconstitutional unless administrators acted with "deliberate indifference" to the basic needs of inmates.[45] As well, the 1995 decision regarding the due process that should be provided to inmates in the disciplinary process in *Sandin v. Conner* considerably lessened the requirements of earlier cases by determining that only disciplinary actions that add to the sentence being served or change the conditions of the sentence require due process.[46]

Second, the courts have moved back toward the hands-off doctrine of allowing prisons to deal with problems themselves, rather than have inmates file lawsuits that are expensive to the correctional agencies and taxpayers. In 1980, Congress revised the Civil Rights of Institutionalized Persons Act, requiring inmates to exhaust their administrative remedies before filing a petition in federal court. If correctional agencies provide an administrative remedy process and give inmates a chance to informally resolve a problem or have a complaint dealt with by prison officials, the courts will require this process to be used before they accept an inmate lawsuit. Many federal courts require inmates to certify that they have exhausted these administrative appeals and include a copy of the response from the agency.

Finally, Congress has acted to make it more difficult for inmates to file successful suits against correctional agencies. In the Violent Crime Control Act of 1994, Congress (1) specified that federal courts find a violation of the Eighth Amendment only if the inmate filing the suit demonstrates that he or she has personally suffered from overcrowding conditions, (2) prohibited federal courts from imposing a population cap on a prison unless the "cruel and unusual punishment" is clearly harming particular identified inmates, and (3) allows a review of any court orders or consent decrees based on violations of the Eighth Amendment. In 1996, Congress passed the Prison Litigation Reform Act, requiring inmates filing prison suits to pay a filing fee unless they claim pauper status, limiting awards of attorney fees, punishing inmates with loss of good time for filing frivolous suits, and prohibiting inmates from suing for mental or emotional distress unless they have suffered a physical injury.

While these actions do not eliminate the filing of lawsuits by inmates, they have put such actions on more of a level playing field between inmates and correctional agencies. As noted earlier, the average number of inmate lawsuits filed against correctional agencies has dropped each year since 1995. The federal courts once were so actively involved in inmate legal actions that they often had to appoint a court monitor or special master to oversee their decisions. Correctional agencies now have the opportunity to thoughtfully address valid inmate claims, and do not have to spend so much time and money responding to frivolous claims.

As we conclude this review of legal rights of inmates, the "Your Career in Corrections" box describes the role of correctional attorneys.

YOUR CAREER IN CORRECTIONS

CORRECTIONAL ATTORNEYS

Although it is not a position that most people think about in a correctional agency, with all the inmate lawsuits it is obvious, that correctional agencies need attorneys to advise and represent them. In most state and federal correctional systems, the agencies have full-time staff attorneys who work with staff and administrators, and the office of the attorney general (AG) then handles the actual litigation. The role of the attorney general is to direct the case and its defense, and argue it in court if it goes that far before being dismissed or settled. The staff attorneys who work for the agencies have a very different role.

When an inmate sues a correctional agency, a big part of the function of the staff attorney is fact-finding: digging for documentation, talking to witnesses, and finding out what really

(continued)

happened. It usually takes a combination of finding the right documents and talking to people to discover the true facts. Then the staff attorney works with the AG office to assess the case and determine the legal position of the agency. In most cases, there is no or limited basis for the inmate claim, and the agency takes a position to fight the case and is usually successful in getting it dismissed before it goes to trial. In other cases, there may actually be the potential for liability, and the correctional agency must decide whether to fight the case or settle it (agree to some conditions or payment for the liability). In some cases, an inmate is asking only for a minor amount ($50 for a pair of shoes that were damaged or lost), and even though the agency does not feel responsible, it is more expensive to fight the case. Correctional agencies do not want to settle too many cases on this "nuisance value" situation, as it can encourage other inmates to file similar suits just because the agency will not fight it, but it is sometimes good practice to settle such nuisance cases.

Another role of the staff attorney is preventive, to watch for issues (policies or procedures) that may incur potential legal liabilities, and try to get the policy or procedure changed. The staff attorney brings the issue to the decision makers, expresses the legal concerns, and advise them on the potential problems. In a way, the attorney helps administrators determine the most important aspects or outcomes of the policy or procedure, and then works to find a more legally defensible way to accomplish what they want.

Correctional attorneys note that the best thing about their job is the variety of issues they address and variety of cases they work. At any time, they may have cases involving use of force, freedom of religion, medical malpractice, or conditions of confinement. In private practice, young attorneys are often pigeonholed into one particular area of the law and do nothing except work on these types of cases. The negative things about the job are that it sometimes seems as though much time is wasted dealing with minor or trivial cases, such as the nuisance value cases noted earlier.

Most people do not go to law school thinking about working for a correctional agency. Somehow they fall into the position, and once involved, most people stay with the correctional agency, obviously enjoying the variety and challenge of their work.

Capital Punishment

Many people, in discussing inmate rights, suggest that the ultimate right is to "life, liberty, and the pursuit of happiness." They go on to suggest that no discussion of the rights of inmates should fail to address the issue of *capital punishment,* the legal killing of someone by the government as punishment for serious criminal misconduct. The topic of capital punishment is one of the most hotly debated, emotionally charged, and controversial components of our criminal justice system. Some people oppose it on a moral basis, claiming that government never has the right of retribution by taking someone's life. Others argue that capital punishment is a deterrent, and that executing a few people saves many other lives. The practical-minded propose that the overall cost to the criminal justice system should be considered in any decision regarding capital punishment. However, many disagree about whether capital punishment or a sentence of life in prison is less expensive.

In this section, we examine the history of capital punishment in the United States, the legal cases and developments regarding the use of the death penalty, the current status of capital punishment, the number of people on death row, and the methods of execution that are currently used. Also described are issues regarding capital punishment, including the potential for error in the finding of guilt, execution of juveniles and the mentally ill or retarded, the deterrent value, and the cost of capital punishment versus a lengthy prison sentence. Finally, the public's view and opinion of the death penalty is discussed, and the most recent actions by state officials regarding the death penalty are described.

The electric chair has been used throughout the history of capital punishment and is still in use in some states today.
Courtesy of the Ohio Department of Rehabilitation and Correction.

The History of Capital Punishment in the United States

As noted in Chapter 1, capital punishment was used extensively in England and in the early American colonies, as many crimes (not just murder) carried a penalty of death. As well, brutal corporal punishments regularly resulted in death, as the imposition of such torture so seriously injured the offender to be a cause of his or her death. Both torture and executions were often carried out in public, as a deterrent to others with the threat of the punishment they would receive if committing similar crimes. Public executions continued until 1936, when several thousand people witnessed the execution by hanging of a black man convicted of raping and murdering a white woman in a small town in Kentucky.

With the creation of the prison as a criminal sanction, the reliance on corporal and capital punishment lessened, and the number and types of crimes that could result in capital punishment were reduced. Even though we believe that the criminal justice system became more "enlightened" and "merciful" during the twentieth century, the 1930s and 1940s still saw more than 150 executions per year. However, as indicated in Figure 14.2, the number of executions declined to zero in the late 1960s, and did not rise until the late 1970s. However, since the mid-1980s, the number of executions has climbed rapidly, and in 2002, seventy-one inmates were executed in thirteen states.[47]

EXECUTIONS OVER THE PAST SEVENTY YEARS

FIGURE **14.2**

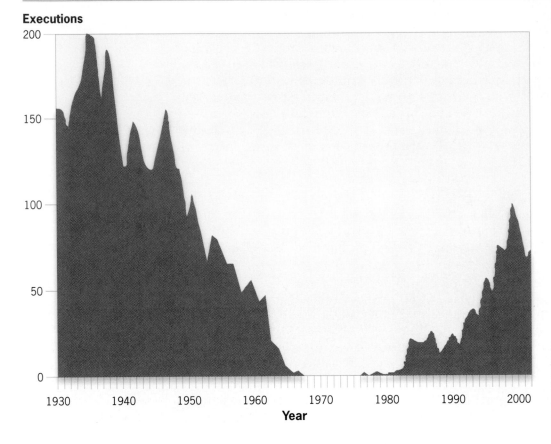

Executions

Source: Tracy L. Snell and Laura M. Maruschak, *Capital Punishment 2001* (Washington, D.C.: U.S. Department of Justice, December 2002), p. 11.

Legal and Statutory Provisions for the Death Penalty

Figure 14.2 illustrates the dramatic decline in the number of people executed from 1940 to 1967. Peaking at 199 executions in 1935, the graph looks like a mountain range with peaks up and down but a consistent decline through the next three decades. Only two executions took place in 1967, and none were performed in 1968 or for the next ten years. This decline was primarily the result of the courts' willingness to consider appeals from death row inmates and continued legal challenges to the constitutionality of the death penalty. At this time, the public was not in a "retributive" mood, as we were coming out of a war with a considerable number of fatalities, there was a strong belief in rehabilitation and that people could change, and crime was not a serious concern among the public.

The increasing amount of litigation regarding capital punishment culminated with the 1972 landmark decision by the U.S. Supreme Court in *Furman v. Georgia*.[48] Furman (a 26-year-old black man with a sixth-grade education) was burglarizing a home. When discovered by the homeowner, Furman tried to escape, shot back into the house through a closed door once outside, and killed the homeowner. Before his trial, Furman was committed to a state psychiatric hospital for evaluation. The hospital staff concluded that Furman had a mild to moderate mental deficiency, with psychotic episodes and a convulsive disorder. However, the staff concluded that Furman was not psychotic at the time of his trial, knew right from wrong, and was able to cooperate with his attorney to prepare a defense. Therefore, he was able to stand trial, and the jury found him guilty of first-degree murder and sentenced him to death.

The case was appealed and made its way to the U.S. Supreme Court, at which several critical decisions were made regarding the death penalty. First, the Court did not determine that capital punishment in itself is unconstitutional as cruel and unusual punishment, although two of the justices voted that it was. Without such a determination, the Court's decision did not put an overall ban on capital punishment throughout the United States. Second, in a 5–4 vote, the Court determined that due to the arbitrary, capricious, and unfair manner in which it was applied, the death penalty as then administered was cruel and unusual. However, the Court's decision (even with, or perhaps because of, each justice writing a separate opinion) provided no clear guidance to states as what would be considered not arbitrary and capricious. Within months after the decision, states began to rewrite their death penalty statutes to make them less arbitrary and constitutionally acceptable.

States took two approaches to try to overcome the "arbitrary" concerns of the Supreme Court. The first approach was to adopt mandatory requirements for a sanction of the death penalty when a specific crime was committed, thereby eliminating discretion altogether. Both Louisiana and North Carolina had such mandatory statutes found unconstitutional in the 1976 cases of *Robert v. Louisiana* and *Woodson v. North Carolina*.[49] Most states passed guided-discretion statutes that provided for **bifurcated trials**, in which guilt was first established at a traditional trial. If found guilty, the trial moved to a second stage of sentencing, at which the jury would decide between death and life imprisonment, using statutory guidelines to consider both aggravating and mitigating circumstances of the crime. Aggravating circumstances could include the killing of a law enforcement officer, committing murder during commission of another felony such as rape or robbery, previous convictions of murder, or multiple killings. Mitigating circumstances could be emotional stress that impaired decision making, mental deficiencies,

Bifurcated trials

used in capital cases, with guilt first established at a traditional trial, and if found guilty, a second stage of sentencing considers between death or life imprisonment

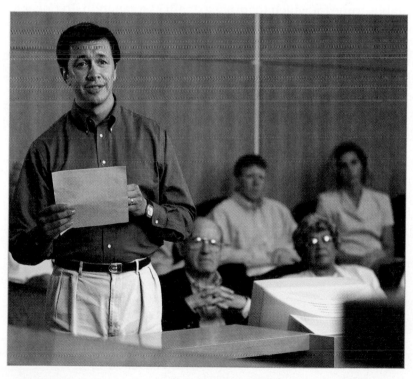

In capital punishment cases, the U.S. Supreme Court has decided there must be bifurcated trials, in which the jury first determines guilt, and then considers punishment.
Courtesy of Corbis Royalty Free.

playing a secondary or minor role in the murder, or developmental problems that bring sympathy from the jury.

The first case in which a guided-discretion statute was considered and found constitutional by the U.S. Supreme Court was the 1976 case of *Gregg v. Georgia.*[50] Through its decision in this case, the Supreme Court laid out the expected elements of a state's death penalty to pass constitutional muster:

- The death penalty can be considered only for specific and the most serious crimes.
- The trial must be bifurcated into two stages: one to determine guilt and the other to consider the sentence.
- During the sentencing stage, the jury will hear evidence regarding both mitigating and aggravating circumstances surrounding the crime, the victim, and the defendant.
- There must be an automatic appeal and review of the death sentence to consider whether the sentence could have been arbitrary due to prejudice, passion, or some other factor, whether the evidence supports the finding during sentencing of statutory aggravating circumstances, and whether the death penalty has been similarly imposed for similar crimes and similar defendants.

Since *Gregg v. Georgia* and up to 2001, thirty-eight states and the federal government have passed capital murder statutes. The District of Columbia and twelve states (listed in Table 14.2) have not passed death penalty statutes.

Several other federal court decisions have addressed the death penalty since *Gregg v. Georgia,* some clarifying and addressing the death penalty regarding certain groups of offenders. As noted in *Gregg v. Georgia,* the death penalty can be imposed only for specific, serious crimes, and several cases have dealt with the issue of what is an acceptable crime for which to impose death as a sanction. In *Coker v. Georgia* (1977), the Court said that the death penalty was excessive for rape of an adult.[51] In *Godfrey v. Georgia* (1980), the Court decided that statements of aggravating circumstances that define the crime being "outrageously or wantonly vile, horrible, or inhumane" are too broad and vague.[52] And in 1987, the Court determined that the death penalty could be imposed on offenders who do not specifically intend to kill their victims (*Tison v. Arizona*).[53] Table 14.3 indicates the specific offenses in each state that can receive capital punishment.

The U.S. Supreme Court has also considered the use of the death penalty for offenders who are insane, those with mental illness, and juveniles. In 1986, the Court considered the case of *Ford v. Wainwright* and ruled that mentally ill people cannot be executed.[54] When convicted, Ford was not judged mentally ill, and not until he was on death row did he display conditions of mental illness. The Court considered the case and concluded that executing an insane person was a violation of the Eighth Amendment, in that the accused must comprehend both the fact that he or she has been sentenced to death and the reason for the sentence.

TABLE 14.2	States That Have Not Adopted the Death Penalty	
	Alaska	Minnesota
	Hawaii	North Dakota
	Iowa	Rhode Island
	Maine	Vermont
	Massachusetts	West Virginia
	Michigan	Wisconsin

TABLE	14.3	Capital Offenses by State, 2001

Alabama. Intentional murder with 18 aggravating factors (13A-5-40(a)(1)-(18)).

Arizona*. First-degree murder accompanied by at least 1 of 10 aggravating factors (A.R.S. 13-703(F)).

Arkansas*. Capital murder (Ark. Code Ann. 5-10-101) with a finding of at least 1 of 10 aggravating circumstances; treason.

California. First-degree murder with special circumstances; train wrecking; treason; perjury causing execution.

Colorado*. First-degree murder with at least 1 of 15 aggravating factors; treason.

Connecticut*. Capital felony with 8 forms of aggravated homicide (C.G.S. 53a-54b).

Delaware. First-degree murder with aggravating circumstances.

Florida*. First-degree murder; felony murder; capital drug trafficking; capital sexual battery.

Georgia*. Murder; kidnaping with bodily injury or ransom when the victim dies; aircraft hijacking; treason.

Idaho. First-degree murder with aggravating factors; aggravated kidnaping.

Illinois. First-degree murder with 1 of 15 aggravating circumstances.

Indiana*. Murder with 16 aggravating circumstances (IC 35-50-2-9).

Kansas*. Capital murder with 7 aggravating circumstances (KSA 21 3439).

Kentucky*. Murder with aggravating factors; kidnaping with aggravating factors (KRS 532.025).

Louisiana. First-degree murder; aggravated rape of victim under age 12; treason (La. R.S. 14:30, 14:42, and 14:113).

Maryland*. First-degree murder, either premeditated or during the commission of a felony, provided that certain death eligibility requirements are satisfied.

Mississippi. Capital murder (97-3-19(2) MCA); aircraft piracy (97-25-55(1) MCA).

Missouri*. First-degree murder (565.020 RSMO 1994).

Montana. Capital murder with 1 of 9 aggravating circumstances (46-18-303 MCA); capital sexual assault (45-5-503 MCA).

Nebraska*. First-degree murder with a finding of at least 1 statutorily-defined aggravating circumstance.

Nevada. First-degree murder with at least 1 of 14 aggravating circumstances (NRS 200.030, 200.033, 200.035).

New Hampshire. Six categories of capital murder (RSA 630:1, RSA 630:5).

New Jersey. Knowing/purposeful murder by one's own conduct; contract murder; solicitation by command or threat in furtherance of a narcotics conspiracy (NJSA 2C:11-3C).

New Mexico*. First-degree murder with at least 1 of 7 statutorily-defined aggravating circumstances (Section 30-2-1 A, NMSA).

New York*. First-degree murder with 1 of 12 aggravating factors.

North Carolina*. First-degree murder (NCGS § 14-17).

Ohio. Aggravated murder with at least 1 of 9 aggravating circumstances (O.R.C. secs. 2903.01, 2929.02, and 2929.04).

Oklahoma. First-degree murder in conjunction with a finding of at least 1 of 8 statutorily defined aggravating circumstances.

Oregon. Aggravated murder (ORS 163.095).

Pennsylvania. First-degree murder with 18 aggravating circumstances.

South Carolina*. Murder with 1 of 10 aggravating circumstances (§ 16-3-20(C)(a)).

South Dakota*. First-degree murder with 1 of 10 aggravating circumstances; aggravated kidnaping.

Tennessee*. First-degree murder with 1 of 14 aggravating circumstances.

Texas. Criminal homicide with 1 of 8 aggravating circumstances (TX Penal Code 19.03).

Utah. Aggravated murder (76-5-202, Utah Code annotated).

Virginia. First-degree murder with 1 of 12 aggravating circumstances (VA Code § 18.2-31).

Washington*. Aggravated first-degree murder.

Wyoming. First-degree murder.

*Eighteen states excluded mentally retarded people from capital sentencing as of December 31, 2001: Arizona, Arkansas, Colorado, Connecticut, Florida, Georgia, Indiana, Kansas, Kentucky, Maryland, Missouri, Nebraska, New Mexico, New York, North Carolina, South Dakota, Tennessee, and Washington. Mental retardation is a mitigating factor in South Carolina.

Source: Tracy Snell and Laura M. Maruschak, *Capital Punishment 2001* (Washington, D.C.: U.S. Department of Justice, Bureau of Justice Statistics, December 2002), p. 2.

In Atkins v. Virginia, *the U.S. Supreme Court determined that executions of mentally retarded criminals were cruel and unusual punishment under the Eighth Amendment.*
Courtesy of Daily Press/AP Wide World.

The Court, in addressing the issue of the death penalty for the mentally retarded, has only recently reversed itself. In 1989, it decided *Penry v. Lynaugh.*[55] Penry had an IQ of approximately 70, yet was considered able to stand for trial. The Court decided that the execution of mentally retarded offenders does not violate the Eighth Amendment; at that time only two states (Maryland and Georgia) prohibited executing the mentally retarded. However, in 2002, the Court heard the case of *Atkins v. Virginia* and, by a 6–3 vote, determined that executions of mentally retarded criminals were "cruel and unusual punishment" under the Eighth Amendment.[56] Atkins was convicted of shooting a man for beer money in 1996. At that time, he had an IQ of 59. The majority acknowledged a reversal of *Penry,* but noted that there has been a growing national consensus since 1989 that executions of the mentally retarded may be unacceptable, even though only eighteen of the thirty-eight states that allow capital punishment had disallowed such executions. With the ruling, inmates on death row who can prove mental retardation (usually an IQ less than 70) will have their sentences commuted to life imprisonment.

The Supreme Court has also considered the use of the death penalty for juvenile offenders. In *Eddings v. Oklahoma* (1982), the Court held that the youthful age of a defendant should be considered a mitigating factor during the sentencing stage of a capital punishment trial.[57] In 1989, the Court ruled in *Stanford v. Kentucky* that the minimum age to impose a death sentence on a juvenile is 16.[58] In 2002, the Court refused to consider *In re Stanford,* declining to reconsider the issue of capital punishment for juveniles,[59] and on January 27, 2003, the Court also declined to consider the death penalty for Scott Allen Hain, a 17-year-old Oklahoma offender, even though four justices wrote that they believed that executing juveniles "is a relic of the past and is inconsistent with evolving standards of decency."[60] Therefore, 16 remains the age for which the Court has held that juvenile offenders can be considered for a sentence of death. Of the thirty-eight states that allow the death penalty, sixteen currently prohibit it by statute for offenders younger than age 18 at the time of the crime. In 2001, seven jurisdictions did not specify a minimum age for which

TABLE	14.4	Minimum Age Authorized for Capital Punishment, 2001	
Age 16 or less	**Age 17**	**Age 18**	**None specified**
Alabama (16)	Georgia	California	Arizona
Arkansas (14)[a]	New Hampshire	Colorado	Idaho
Delaware (16)	North Carolina[b]	Connecticut[c]	Louisiana
Florida (16)	Texas	Federal system	Montana[d]
Indiana (16)		Illinois	Pennsylvania
Kentucky (16)		Kansas	South Carolina
Mississippi (16)[e]		Maryland	South Dakota[f]
Missouri (16)		Nebraska	
Nevada (16)		New Jersey	
Oklahoma (16)		New Mexico	
Utah (14)		New York	
Virginia (14)[g]		Ohio	
Wyoming (16)		Oregon	
		Tennessee	
		Washington	

Note: Reporting by States reflects interpretations by State attorney generals' offices and may differ from previously reported ages.

[a]See Ark. Code Ann. 9-27-318(c)(2)(Supp. 2001).

[b]Age required is 17 unless the murderer was incarcerated for murder when a subsequent murder occurred; then the age may be 14.

[c]See Conn. Gen. Stat. 53a-46a(g)(1).

[d]Montana law specifies that offenders tried under the capital sexual assault statute be 18 or older. Age may be a mitigating factor for other capital crimes.

[e]The minimum age defined by statute is 13, but the effective age is 16 based on interpretation of U.S. Supreme Court decisions by the Mississippi Supreme Court.

[f]Juveniles may be transferred to adult court. Age can be a mitigating factor.

[g]The minimum age for transfer to adult court by statute is 14, but the effective age is 16 based on interpretation of U.S. Supreme Court decisions by the State attorney general's office.

Source: Tracy Snell and Laura M. Maruschak, *Capital Punishment 2001* (Washington, D.C.. U.S. Department of Justice, Bureau of Justice Statistics, December 2002), p. 5.

the death penalty can be imposed, and seventeen others indicated an age between 14 and 17.[61] No cases from these states have yet been an issue with the Supreme Court decisions, as the youngest person on death row at the end of 2001 was age 19.[62] Table 14.4 indicates the statutory minimum age authorized for capital punishment by state. On December 31, 2001, seventy-seven inmates on death row were age 17 or younger at the time of the offense for which they were sentenced to death.[63]

Current Statistics Regarding Capital Punishment

DEATH ROW PRISONERS

At year-end 2001, thirty-seven states and the federal prison system held 3,581 prisoners (all of whom had committed murder) under sentence of death, which were twenty fewer than at year-end 2000.[64] As can be seen in Figure 14.3, the number of inmates on death row declined immediately after the 1972 Supreme Court decision in *Furman v. Georgia,* holding that the death penalty as then administered was unconstitutional. Even with that decision, not every state emptied its death row, so the number did not reduce to zero. Soon thereafter, the number on death row began to climb significantly, as the Court in *Gregg v. Georgia* and other cases upheld the revised capital punishment laws.

NUMBER OF PEOPLE ON DEATH ROW OVER THE PAST FIFTY YEARS

FIGURE **14.3**

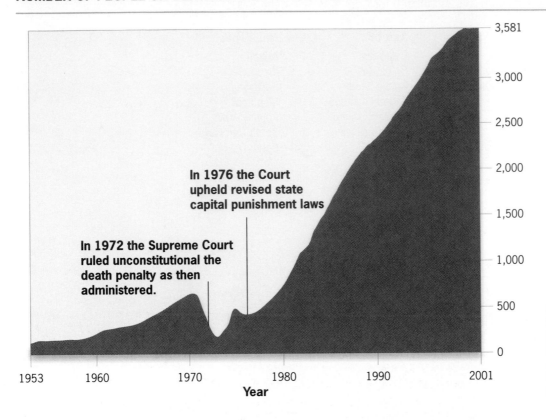

In 1976 the Court
upheld revised state
capital punishment laws

In 1972 the Supreme Court
ruled unconstitutional the
death penalty as then
administered.

Year

Source: Tracy Snell and Laura
M. Maruschak, *Capital
Punishment 2001* (Washington,
D.C.: U.S. Department of
Justice, Bureau of Justice
Statistics, December 2002),
p. 3.

Of those on death row in 2001, fifty-one were women, two-thirds had prior felony convictions and one in twelve had prior homicide convictions, and the youngest death row inmate was 19 and the oldest was 86.[65] Race has been an issue in the capital punishment debate for the past several decades, as minorities continue to be overrepresented among those sentenced to death, on death row, and executed. Of people under sentence of death in 2001,

- 1,969 (55 percent) were white,
- 1,538 (43 percent) were black,
- 28 (0.8 percent) were American Indian,
- 33 (0.9 percent) were Asian, and
- 13 (0.4 percent) were of unknown race.

As well, there were 358 Hispanic inmates (11 percent) under sentence of death.

Figure 14.4 illustrates the proportions of people on death row by race.

The fact that minorities are on death row at a rate well above their representation in the U.S. population has opened the door to an argument of the continuation of racial bias in the administration of the death penalty. However, in the 1987 case of *McCleskey v. Kemp,* the Supreme Court heard an argument of race discrimination in the death penalty. McCleskey was a black man convicted of murdering a white police officer. McCleskey's attorneys, in their arguments to the Supreme Court, used a study by Baldus, Woodworth, and Pulaski that examined the role of race in the imposition of the death penalty in Georgia. The study found that defendants charged with killing whites were 4.3 times more likely to receive the death penalty that those convicted of killing blacks.[66] The attorneys argued that this disproportionate sentencing to death of killers of whites indicated a denial of the equal protection clause under the Fourteenth Amendment, and likely an arbitrary and capricious use of the death penalty in violation of the Eighth Amendment.

PRISONERS ON DEATH ROW BY RACE, 1968–2001

FIGURE **14.4**

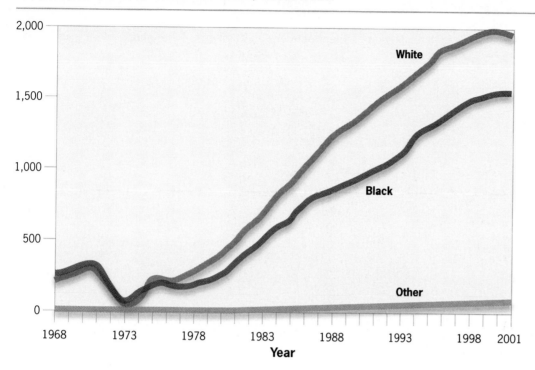

Source: Tracy L. Snell and Laura M. Maruschak, *Capital Punishment 2001* (Washington, D.C.: U.S. Department of Justice, December 2002), p. 8.

However, by a 5–4 vote, the Court rejected these claims, noting that a statistical study did not establish discrimination in this particular case.

EXECUTIONS

As indicated in Figure 14.2, the number of executions has risen over the past twenty years, and in 2002, seventy-one people were executed in thirteen states. Table 14.5 lists the number of people executed by state. Texas, by far,

TABLE	14.5	States Administering the Death Penalty, 2002

State	Number of people executed
Texas	33
Oklahoma	7
Missouri	6
Georgia	4
Virginia	4
Florida	3
Ohio	3
South Carolina	3
Alabama	2
Mississippi	2
North Carolina	2
California	1
Louisiana	1

Source: Bureau of Justice Statistics, "Capital Punishment Statistics: Summary Findings," http://www.ojp.usdoj.gov/bjs/cp.htm (accessed January 8, 2003).

TABLE 14.6	Executions by State and Method, 1977–2001					
State	Number executed	Lethal injection	Electrocution	Lethal gas	Hanging	Firing squad
Total	749	584	149	11	3	2
Federal system	2	2	0	0	0	0
Alabama	23	0	23	0	0	0
Arizona	22	20	0	2	0	0
Arkansas	24	23	1	0	0	0
California	9	7	0	2	0	0
Colorado	1	1	0	0	0	0
Delaware	13	12	0	0	1	0
Florida	51	7	44	0	0	0
Georgia	27	4	23	0	0	0
Idaho	1	1	0	0	0	0
Illinois	12	12	0	0	0	0
Indiana	9	6	3	0	0	0
Kentucky	2	1	1	0	0	0
Louisiana	26	6	20	0	0	0
Maryland	3	3	0	0	0	0
Mississippi	4	0	0	4	0	0
Missouri	53	53	0	0	0	0
Montana	2	2	0	0	0	0
Nebraska	3	0	3	0	0	0
Nevada	9	8	0	1	0	0
New Mexico	1	1	0	0	0	0
North Carolina	21	19	0	2	0	0
Ohio	2	2	0	0	0	0
Oklahoma	48	48	0	0	0	0
Oregon	2	2	0	0	0	0
Pennsylvania	3	3	0	0	0	0
South Carolina	25	20	5	0	0	0
Tennessee	1	1	0	0	0	0
Texas	256	256	0	0	0	0
Utah	6	4	0	0	0	2
Virginia	83	57	26	0	0	0
Washington	4	2	0	0	2	0
Wyoming	1	1	0	0	0	0

Source: Tracy L. Snell and Laura M. Maruschak, *Capital Punishment 2001* (Washington, D.C.: U.S. Department of Justice, December 2002), p. 16.

Lethal injection

a method of execution in which drugs are injected into a person's body, making the heart stop and causing death

leads with thirty-three, and no other state has more than seven executions. Of the persons executed in 2002, fifty-three (72 percent) were white and eighteen (28 percent) were black; sixty-nine were men and two were women; and seventy executions were carried out by lethal injection and one was carried out by electrocution.[67]

Overall, from 1977 through 2002, there have been 820 executions carried out in the United States. Table 14.6 illustrates all of the executions from 1977 through 2001, by state and method of execution. Again, Texas has by far more than any other state, and **lethal injection** is the most frequently used method of execution. Table 14.7 also illustrates the methods of execution used by various states. In some states, more than one method of execution is authorized, although currently almost every state authorizes only the use of lethal injection.

TABLE	14.7	Method of Execution Authorized by State, 2001

Lethal injection		Electrocution	Lethal gas	Hanging	Firing squad
Arizona[a,b]	Nevada	Alabama	Arizona[a,b]	Delaware[a,c]	Idaho[a]
Arkansas[a,d]	New Hampshire[a]	Arkansas[a,d]	California[a]	New Hampshire[a,e]	Oklahoma[f]
California[a]	New Jersey	Florida[a]	Missouri[a]	Washington[a]	Utah[a]
Colorado	New Mexico	Kentucky[a,g]	Wyoming[a,h]		
Connecticut	New York	Nebraska			
Delaware[a,c]	North Carolina	Oklahoma[f]			
Florida[a]	Ohio	South Carolina[a]			
Georgia	Oklahoma[a]	Tennessee[a,i]			
Idaho[a]	Oregon	Virginia[a]			
Illinois	Pennsylvania				
Indiana	South Carolina[a]				
Kansas	South Dakota				
Kentucky[a,g]	Tennessee[a,i]				
Louisiana	Texas				
Maryland	Utah[a]				
Mississippi	Virginia[a]				
Missouri[a]	Washington[a]				
Montana	Wyoming[a]				

Note: The method of execution of federal prisoners is lethal injection, pursuant to 28 CFR, Part 26. For offenses under the Violent Crime Control and Law Enforcement Act of 1994, the method is that of the state in which the conviction took place, pursuant to 18 U.S.C. 3596.

[a]Authorizes 2 methods of execution.

[b]Arizona authorizes lethal injection for people whose capital sentence was received after 11/15/92; for those sentenced before that date, the condemned may select lethal injection or lethal gas.

[c]Delaware authorizes lethal injection for those whose capital offense occurred after 6/13/86; for those whose offense occurred before that date, the condemned may select lethal injection or hanging.

[d]Arkansas authorizes lethal injection for those whose capital offense occurred on or after 7/4/83; for those whose offense occurred before that date, the condemned may select lethal injection or electrocution.

[e]New Hampshire authorizes hanging only if lethal injection cannot be given.

[f]Oklahoma authorizes electrocution if lethal injection is ever held to be unconstitutional, and firing squad if both lethal injection and electrocution are held unconstitutional.

[g]Kentucky authorizes lethal injection for people whose capital sentence was received on or after 3/31/98; for those sentenced before that date, the condemned may select lethal injection or electrocution.

[h]Wyoming authorizes lethal gas if lethal injection is ever held to be unconstitutional.

[i]Tennessee authorizes lethal injection for those whose capital offense occurred after 12/31/98; those whose offense occurred before that date may select electrocution.

Source: Tracy L. Snell and Laura M. Maruschak, *Capital Punishment 2001* (Washington, D.C.: U.S. Department of Justice, December 2002), p. 6.

OPERATIONAL PROBLEMS

People seldom think about it, but how do you manage offenders who have already proven that they have a propensity for violence and are in prison facing execution? They obviously have little to live for, and correctional administrators can threaten them with no penalty that is worse than what they already face. This creates the dilemma of to how to operate death rows. They must be secure, to protect staff and other inmates. Yet these prisoners have not (in most cases) violated any prison rule to deserve to be isolated in an SHU-type situation.

Most administrators decide to err on the safe side and operate a very secure death row, with inmates in single cells most of the time. Death row is operated like an SHU in that all services come to the unit, inmates are in their cells most of the

Lethal injection is now the most widely used method of execution.
Courtesy of the Ohio Department of Rehabilitation and Correction.

time, and they recreate and do almost everything by themselves. A few states allow inmates on death row to work, and some even have a prison industry as a part of the death row. However, security and safe operations have to be constant at all times. The "An Insider's Experience" box illustrates the danger of operating a death row.

Reasons for Capital Punishment

Proponents of the death penalty argue for its existence for several reasons, which usually include deterrence, retribution, incapacitation, and cost.

AN INSIDER'S EXPERIENCE: Hostages on Death Row

One of the most difficult situations I ever faced involving a special emergency response team (SERT) and the complex decision regarding when to end negotiations and begin an assault was when several death row inmates took two correctional officers hostage. One of the inmates had killed a jail correctional officer and vowed to kill another guard before he was executed. Obviously, these inmates had little to lose by injuring or killing the hostages. Negotiations continued for approximately thirteen hours, and several times there was a threat that someone would die if the inmate demands were not met by a certain deadline. We had the SERT prepared to use explosives to blow through a wall of the death row cell house and enter authorized to use deadly force if necessary to retake the unit.

We continued to have the hostage negotiation team talk to the inmates, and they did an excellent job of keeping them calm and talking them past the many deadlines. In the end, the negotiations were successful. The inmates gave up, and the only concession we granted them was to transfer them immediately to a county jail, as they were afraid that the correctional staff would physically abuse them when they gave up. We did this and within a few days returned them to death row and normal operations at the prison. I was never confident of a peaceful outcome of this situation until I personally saw the two hostages after they were freed. While you know that the odds of a peaceful negotiation increase with time, in this situation, we were unsure of the response by inmates who had nothing to lose, and therefore we had to be ready to use the SERT at a moment's notice.

DETERRENCE

Proponents of the death penalty argue that by having capital punishment laws, additional murders are prevented through general deterrence. Reflecting back to Bentham's hedonistic calculus that crimes will be prevented if the punishment outweighs the pleasure from the crime, it is difficult to understand how a rational person would commit a murder knowing that he or she will be executed in return. This logic seems to challenge theories of the deterrent effect of the death penalty. It can first be argued that fully rational people do not commit many murders. While a few early studies have found evidence of capital punishment as a deterrence, these have been criticized as methodologically flawed and are not recognized as credible evidence.[68] There is far more evidence that capital punishment does not deter other murders. A 1984 study by Decker and Kohfeld of homicide rates in Illinois from 1933 to 1980 did not identify any differences in rates depending on whether there was a death penalty allowed, a death penalty was allowed but not used, or the death penalty was abolished.[69] Other studies of homicide rates from various states have also not found a deterrent effect with the death penalty.[70] The general public is inconclusive in its views of the deterrent effect of capital punishment. In a 2001 public opinion poll, 42 percent responded that they believed that executing people who commit murder deters others from committing murder, 52 percent believed that it has "not much" deterrent effect, and 7 percent were not sure or refused to answer.[71]

Some proponents argue that capital punishment can be a deterrent, but will have increased deterrent value if executions are carried out in public, or at least receive a considerable amount of publicity. However, researchers argue that such publicity brings about a "brutalization" rather than a deterrent effect, in that some people identify with the executioner, and executions can promote imitation rather than deterrence for individuals already prone to violence.[72] A study by Cockran, Chamlin, and Seth and a replication of the study by Bailey of the impact of the Oklahoma capital punishment law found that a brutalization effect seems to occur as the media covers executions.[73]

RETRIBUTION

Most people believe that punishment is important to show that "bad acts result in bad outcomes." People generally do not want criminals to get off without punishment adequately matched to the severity of their crime. The concept of retribution is that offenders get their just deserts, a punishment that fits their crime (an eye for an eye). As described by Bohm in writing of capital punishment and retribution, revenge for taking a life is based on a belief that a killer deserves to be executed.[74] Many people believe that capital punishment is the only just punishment for the taking of a life. However, opponents point out that even with bifurcated trials as a result of *Gregg v. Georgia*, there is still racial and ethnic discrimination in the application of capital punishment,[75] undermining a retributive argument.

INCAPACITATION

The incapacitation argument regarding capital punishment is that the only sure-fire way to protect the public from a criminal so vicious that he or she would kill someone is to execute the person. However, it is also generally accepted that murderers have very low rates of recidivism. Studies by Sorensen and colleagues and by Vito and Wilson of inmates who had committed murder and then had their death sentences commuted indicate that offenders who commit murder have a very low rate of recidivism, and less than 1 percent later committed another murder.[76] Opponents of the death penalty also argue that life in prison without the chance of parole equally protects society through incapacitation rather than execution.

COST

A common argument when considering the death penalty is cost. Proponents of the death penalty argue that it is less expensive than life imprisonment, while opponents point out that the additional costs of a capital trial and appeals make the death penalty more expensive. Depending on the assumptions made, both sides can show evidence to support their position. Bedau[77] and Bohm[78] point out that capital punishment is more expensive due to the high cost of the trial and subsequent litigation. A 1993 study found that capital trials in North Carolina are significantly more costly than noncapital trials, and when comparing the cost of incarceration on death row for ten years, found that it was less costly than regular imprisonment for twenty years.[79] A report of several state comparisons of the cost of the death penalty compared to life imprisonment reported much greater expense for a death penalty trial and imprisonment than for a life sentence (in New York, $1.4 million compared to $602,000; in Florida, $3.2 million or six times the cost of life imprisonment).[80]

Public Opinion Regarding the Death Penalty

Over the past forty years, public opinion regarding the death penalty has changed significantly. In surveys of the American public in 1965, the Harris Poll reported that only 38 percent believed in the death penalty;[81] the Gallup Poll reported that only 45 percent were in favor of it.[82] Since that time, attitudes have continuously become more supportive of the use of capital punishment. By 2001, the Harris Poll reported that 67 percent of those surveyed believed in the use of capital punishment,[83] and the Gallup Poll, asking in 2002 about attitudes toward the death penalty for people convicted of murder, reported that 72 percent were in favor of it.[84] Over the past forty years, opinions have consistently varied by the gender and race of those surveyed. In 2000, the National Opinion Research Center reported that 63 percent of a national sample favored the death penalty for crimes of murder.[85] In the poll, 71 percent of men and 57 percent of women, and 69 percent of whites and 42 percent of nonwhites favored the death penalty.

Another interesting fact is the moderation of support for the death penalty when compared to life in prison without possibility of parole. The Gallup Poll found that in 2001, when respondents were asked, "What do you think should be the penalty for murder?" 57 percent responded "the death penalty," and 41 percent responded "life in prison."[86] The reasons that individuals favor the death penalty provide a varied response. As indicated in Table 14.8, most people support it for "just deserts" or "eye for an eye" reasons (48 percent), and 20 percent favor it because it saves taxpayer money.

The Potential for Error

One serious concern regarding the death penalty is the potential for error, or the fallibility of the death penalty. We tend to have faith in our justice system and want to believe that it makes very few errors, especially in capital murder trials when the death penalty is a possible sanction. There is considerable debate as to how many mistakes are made in findings of guilt in death penalty trials, and whether the potential for a mistake (with the irrevocability of the death penalty) puts in question the use of capital punishment. Proponents of the death penalty suggest that few errors have occurred since *Gregg v. Georgia*, with bifurcated trials and automatic reviews. However, Dieter has reviewed the risk of error, and identified several reasons that error still exists:

TABLE	14.8	Reported Reasons for Favoring the Death Penalty for People Convicted of Murder, 2001

Question: "Why do you favor the death penality for persons convicted of murder?"

<u>Reason for favoring</u>

An eye for an eye/they took a life/fits the crime	48%
Save taxpayers money/cost associated with prison	20
Deterrent for potential crimes/set an example	10
They deserve it	6
Support/believe in death penalty	6
Depends on the type of crime they commit	6
They will repeat their crime/keep them from repeating it	6
Biblical reasons	3
Relieves prison overcrowding	2
If there's no doubt the person committed the crime	2
Life sentences don't always mean life in prison	2
Don't believe they can be rehabilitated	2
Serve justice	1
Fair punishment	1
Would help/benefit families of victims	1
Other	3
No opinion	1

Note: This question was asked only of the respondents who answered "yes, in favor" to the question of whether they favored the death penalty.

Source: The Gallup Organization, http://www.gallup.com/poll/releases/pr010302.asp accessed March 2, 2001; table adapted in Bureau of Justice Statistics, *Sourcebook of Criminal Justice Statistics, 2001* (Washington, DC: U.S. Department of Justice, 2002), p. 145.

- *General reasons:* The overall expansion in the authorization of the death penalty and the fact that it has become a political issue
- *Investigative reasons:* The pressure on the police to solve murders and on prosecutors to "win" trials, along with lack of resources by defense attorneys for investigation
- *Reasons during trial:* The fact that juries are often influenced by publicity, there are mistaken identities, and the heinous nature of many murders increases the likelihood of conviction
- *Plea bargaining and failure to dismiss:* There are more guilty pleas by innocent defendants, and there are fewer dismissals of charges for innocent people[87]

A study by Bedau and Radelet reviewed thousands of death penalty cases during the twentieth century and concluded that twenty-three innocent people had been executed since 1900.[88] As well, the Death Penalty Information Center reported that between 1973 and 2003, 112 inmates under sentence of death have been released with evidence of their innocence.[89] In the past decade, the use of DNA evidence has provided a credible source for review of the guilt of some death row inmates. The use of DNA as evidence is a fairly recent technology, was not available at the time of trial for some death row inmates, but can now be used to reconsider questionable cases of guilt.

Perhaps the greatest attention to the fallibility of the death penalty has occurred in Illinois. Since 1976, Illinois has executed twelve people and released thirteen from death row due to actual innocence. Death row proponents suggest that this proves that the system and layers of appeals work. Law students at Northwestern and De-Paul Universities have for several years been researching death row cases, looking for evidence of innocence. If not for their efforts, most of these death row inmates would

In 2003, Governor George Ryan commuted the sentences of or gave pardons to all inmates on death row in Illinois, citing the risk of error by executing innocent people.
Courtesy of AP/Wide World Photos.

not have been freed. In 2000, Governor George H. Ryan declared a moratorium on executions in Illinois over concerns regarding the possible execution of innocent people. In doing so, he created a blue-ribbon task force to examine how death penalty investigations and trials worked in Illinois, and the task force made eighty-five recommendations for improvement in the administration of the death penalty.

On January 11, 2003, Governor Ryan took a dramatic step. Condemning the capital punishment system as fundamentally flawed and unfair, he announced that he was commuting the death sentences of 167 people (163 men and 4 women), primarily to life in prison. A few days earlier, he had pardoned four death row inmates, freeing them from death row and from prison. Ryan left office as governor on January 13, 2003, just two days after he emptied the state's death row, setting the stage for further debate over potential errors. There were cheers for his actions from many anti–death penalty groups and the families of those on death row. Meanwhile, there were jeers and considerable bitterness from the families of the more than 250 victims of Illinois death row inmates, pro–death penalty groups, and Illinois prosecutors and legislators. Prosecutors say that while they cannot undo Governor Ryan's blanket commutations, they plan to start refilling death row immediately. While they claim that they will not let Ryan's action hinder their pursuit of capital punishment in pending cases, they acknowledge that there will be new challenges in convincing juries that the death penalty is just and fair.

Capital punishment has been a hotly debated topic in America for years. Proponents call it just, and cite the general support of the public. Opponents call it brutal and immoral, and cite the number of innocent defendants who have been convicted and executed. While a majority of Americans continue to support its use, there is a softening of support for capital punishment, especially with more information available on potential errors in convicting innocent defendants. This perplexing dilemma is apparent in a recent speech given by Renee Cardwell Hughes, a common pleas judge in Philadelphia, Pennsylvania. Judge Hughes noted, "I am a trial judge and there are two people on death row whose commitment papers bear my signature." However, continuing the speech, Judge Hughes commented that the death penalty "is in fact a cruel and unusual form of punishment which violates the laws which assure equal protection to all of our citizens."[90] After reading the arguments for and against the death penalty, students must now struggle with their own beliefs regarding the death penalty in the following "You make the Decision" box.

YOU MAKE THE DECISION . . .

SUPPORT THE DEATH PENALTY?

The reasons for and against capital punishment related to deterrence, retribution, incapacitation, and cost are listed in the preceding sections. As well, public support and the potential for error are described. At this time, students should decide, if they do not already have a position, whether they support the death penalty. Even if you have a firm position, go through the exercise of considering all factors and see if it leads you to the same conclusion.

Either by yourself or in a small classroom group, list all the areas that are discussed as reasons for capital punishment. Then list other factors you think should be considered part of the capital punishment equation. These may be religious or humanistic, desires by the victims' families, or any other factor you think is important. Then create a list under each category of the arguments that support or weigh against capital punishment. Weigh all of these factors and decide whether you support capital punishment. This exercise is much more fun if done in a small group, and students can argue their points and try to convince others of the strength of their positions.

Chapter Review

SUMMARY

Have we as a society gone too far in recognizing the legal rights of inmates? Many people believe we have, yet few would argue that inmates should lose all protections of the Constitution and Bill of Rights because they have committed a felony and been incarcerated. This chapter has described the emergence and then abandonment of the hands-off doctrine regarding suits by inmates, and the evolution of recognition by the courts of specific rights of confined individuals. Many legal decisions have created guidelines for the provision of medical care, opportunity to practice one's religion, conditions of confinement, and due process during inmate disciplinary hearings.

For twenty-five years after the landmark decision of *Cooper v. Pate* opened a Pandora's box of inmate lawsuits, federal court decisions seemed to expand the requirements for prison officials to grant additional privileges and rights for inmates. However, over the past ten years this trend has reversed somewhat, and in fact, the number of lawsuits by prisoners has actually declined significantly since 1995. Proactive policy implementations by prison administrators, congressional actions, and some court decisions have all contributed to this changing trend.

This chapter has also addressed the complex and emotional issue of the use of capital punishment in the United States. While long a part of sentencing for serious criminal behavior, the use of capital punishment declined significantly during the 1950s and 1960s, and ended for a short period after the Supreme Court ruled in *Furman v. Georgia*. This case did not declare capital punishment in itself as cruel and unusual punishment, but did create general guidelines that must be followed for capital punishment statutes to be considered constitutional. Since *Furman*, thirty-eight states and the federal government have reenacted capital punishment statutes, and more than 3,500 prisoners are currently on death rows awaiting execution.

The reasons for support of capital punishment are also addressed. Proponents usually cite the value of capital punishment as a deterrent and provide the need for retribution, protection of society from further crimes, and reduced costs as arguments for their support. However, opponents counter these arguments, and there have been few, if any, conclusive studies on the impact of capital punishment in any of these areas. The biggest concern regarding capital punishment is its fallibility, or the chance of error in finding an innocent person guilty. Recent uses of DNA evidence have led to the exoneration and release of several inmates previously found guilty of murder and sentenced to death. For this reason, public support for capital punishment has diminished, especially when considering an option of life imprisonment without parole.

This chapter brings an end to our look into life in prisons and our examination of the world in which inmates live and prison staff work. We have reviewed the approaches taken by prison administrators to manage prisons and create a safe and secure environment while offering inmates the opportunity to participate in rehabilitative programs. In the final section of this book, we turn to recent and developing correctional challenges, including increasing correctional populations, the impact of politics on correctional policy, tightening public budgets, determining effectiveness, and future questions for correctional students and officials to deliberate.

REVIEW QUESTIONS

1. What is the hands-off doctrine, and in what case did the U.S. Supreme Court abandon it?

2. Define "cruel and unusual" punishment in regard to prison conditions.

3. What is the "deliberate indifference" test regarding conditions of confinement as established in *Wilson v. Seiter?*

4. How did *Cooper v. Pate* change the reluctance of the federal courts to get involved in prisoner lawsuits?

5. What standards are used to determine whether the level and quality of medical care provided to inmates is constitutionally acceptable?

6. List the due process principles established for inmate discipline in the case of *Wolff v. McDonnell.*

7. Define a bifurcated trial as established by *Furman v. Georgia.*

8. How many states currently have a statute allowing the death penalty?

9. Do the federal courts allow the execution of juveniles under age 18, and what legal cases form their decisions in this regard?

10. Of all death row inmates, what percentage are white?

11. Describe evidence of the deterrent effect of the death penalty.

12. What dramatic step did Governor George Ryan of Illinois take in 2003 while expressing concerns about the fallibility of the death penalty?

ENDNOTES

1. Camille Graham Camp and George M. Camp, *The 2001 Corrections Yearbook: Adult Systems* (Middletown, Conn.: Criminal Justice Institute, 2002), pp. 74–75.

2. Ibid.

3. *Ruffin v. Commonwealth of Virginia,* 62 Va. (21 Gratt.) 790, 796 (1871).

4. *Price v. Johnston,* 334 U.S. 266 (1948).

5. *Cooper v. Pate,* 378 U.S. 546 (1964).

6. Roger A. Hanson and Henry W. K. Daley, *Challenging the Conditions of Prisons and Jails: A Report on Section 1983 Litigation* (Washington, D.C.: U.S. Department of Justice, Bureau of Justice Statistics, 1994), pp. 1–2.

7. *Holt v. Sarver,* 309 F. Supp. 362 [E.D. Ark. 1970], *aff'd* 442 F.2d 304 9th Cir. (1971).

8. *Bell v. Wolfish,* 441 U.S. 520 (1979).

9. *Solem v. Helm,* 463 U.S. 277 (1983).

10. *Pell v. Procunier,* 417 U.S. 817 (1974).

11. *Pugh v. Locke,* 406 F. 2d 318 (1976).

12. *Bell v. Wolfish,* 441 U.S. 520 (1979).

13. *Rhodes v. Chapman,* 452 U.S. 337 (1981).

14. *Wilson v. Seiter,* 111 S. Ct. 2321 (1991).

15. *Cooper v. Pate,* 378 U.S. 546 (1964).

16. *Cruz v. Beto,* 405 U.S. 319 (1972).

17. *Theriault v. Silber,* 391 F. Supp. 579 (1977).

18. *Hamilton v. Schriro,* 74 F.3d 1545 (8th Cir. 1996).

19. *Kahane v. Carlson,* 527 F.2d 492 (2d Cir. 1975).

20. *O'Lone v. Estate of Shabazz,* 482 U.S. 342 (1987).

21. *Turner v. Safley,* 482 U.S. 78 (1987).

22. *Gittlemacker v. Prasse,* 428 F.2d 1 (3d Cir. 1970).

23. *Walker v. Blackwell,* 411 F.2d 23 (1969).

24. *Holt v. Sarver,* 309 F. Supp. 362 [E.D. Ark. 1970], *aff'd* 442 F.2d 304 9th Cir. (1971).

25. *Estelle v. Gamble,* 429 U.S. 97 (1976).

26. *Ramos v. Lamm,* 639 F.2d 559, 576 (1980).

27. *Fernandez v. United States,* 941 F.2d 1488 (1991).

28. *Procunier v. Martinez,* 416 U.S. 396 (1974).

29. *McNamara v. Moody,* 606 F. Supp. 2d 621 (5th Cir. 1979).

30. *Turner v. Safley,* 482 U.S. 78 (1987).

31. *Jones v. North Carolina Prisoner's Labor Union, Inc.,* 433 U.S. 119 (1977).

32. *Sostre v. Otis,* 330 F. Supp. 941 (1971).

33. *Thornburgh v. Abbott,* 109 S. Ct. 1874 (1989).

34. *Guajardo v. Estelle,* 580 F.2d 748 (1978).

35. *Johnson v. Avery,* 393 U.S. 483 (1969).

36. *Younger v. Gilmore,* 404 U.S. 15 (1971).

37. *Bounds v. Smith,* 430 U.S. 817 (1977).

38. *Hudson v. Palmer,* 468 U.S. 517 (1984).

39. *Bell v. Wolfish,* 441 U.S. 520 (1979).

40. *Tribble v. Gardner,* 860 F.2d 321 (9th Cir. 1988).

41. *Grummett v. Rushen,* 587 F. Supp. 913 (9th Cir. 1984).

42. *Johnson v. Phelan,* 69 F.3d 144 (7th Cir. 1995).

43. *Wolff v. McDonnell,* 418 U.S. 539 (1974).

44. *Sandin v. Conner,* 515 U.S. 472 (1995).

45. *Wilson v. Seiter,* 111 S. Ct. 2321 (1991).

46. *Sandin v. Conner,* 515 U.S. 472 (1995).

47. Bureau of Justice Statistics, "Capital Punishment Statistics," http://www.ojp.usdoj.gov/bjs/cp.htm (accessed January 8, 2003).

48. *Furman v. Georgia*, 408 U.S. 238 (1972).

49. *Robert v. Louisiana*, 428 U.S. 325 (1976); *Woodson v. North Carolina*, 428 U.S. 280 (1976).

50. *Gregg v. Georgia*, 428 U.S. 153 (1976).

51. *Coker v. Georgia*, 433 U.S. 584 (1977).

52. *Godfrey v. Georgia*, 446 U.S. 420 (1980).

53. *Tison v. Arizona*, 107 S. Ct. 1676 (1987).

54. *Ford v. Wainwright*, 477 U.S. 399 (1986).

55. *Penry v. Lynaugh*, 45 Cr. L. Rptr. 3188 (1989).

56. *Atkins v. Virginia*, 536 U.S. 304 (2002).

57. *Eddings v. Oklahoma*, 455 U.S. 104 (1982).

58. *Stanford v. Kentucky*, 492 U.S. 361 (1989).

59. *In re Stanford*, 123 S. Ct. 472 (2002).

60. As quoted in a story by the Associated Press, "Supreme Court Appears One Vote Shy of Rejecting Death Penalty for Young Killers," *St. Louis Post-Dispatch*, January 28, 2003, p. 2.

61. Tracy Snell and Laura M. Maruschak, *Capital Punishment 2001* (Washington, D.C.: U.S. Department of Justice, Bureau of Justice Statistics, December 2002), p. 4.

62. Ibid., p. 1.

63. Ibid., p. 9.

64. Ibid., p. 1.

65. Ibid.

66. David C. Baldus, George F. Woodworth, and Charles A. Pulaski, Jr., *Equal Justice and the Death Penalty: A Legal and Empirical Analysis* (Boston: Northeastern University Press, 1990).

67. Bureau of Justice Statistics, "Capital Punishment Statistics."

68. As an example, see Isaac Ehrlich, "The Deterrent Effect of Capital Punishment: A Question of Life and Death," *American Economic Review* 65 (1975): 397–417.

69. S. Decker and C. Kohfeld, "A Deterrence Study of the Death Penalty in Illinois," *Journal of Criminal Justice* 12 (1984): 367–377.

70. See S. Decker and C. Kohfeld, "The Deterrent Effect of Capital Punishment in the Five Most Active Execution States: A Time Series Analysis," *Criminal Justice Review* 15 (1990): 173–191; W. C. Bailey, "Desegregation in Deterrence and Death Penalty Research: The Case of Murder in Chicago," *Journal of Criminal Law and Criminology* 74 (1983): 827–859.

71. Data from *The Harris Poll* (Los Angeles: Creators Syndicate, Inc., August 17, 2001), p. 2.

72. For a discussion of brutalization theory, see W. J. Bowers and G. Pierce, "Deterrence or Brutalization: What Is the Effect of Executions?" *Crime and Delinquency* 26 (1980): 453–484.

73. See John K. Cockran, Mitchell B. Chamlin, and Mark Seth, "Deterrence or Brutalization? An Impact Assessment of Oklahoma's Return to Capital Punishment," *Criminology* 31 (1994): 107–134; William C. Bailey, "Deterrence, Brutalization, and the Death Penalty: Another Examination of Oklahoma's Return to Capital Punishment," *Criminology* 36, no. 4 (1998): 711–733.

74. R. M. Bohm, "Retribution and Capital Punishment: Toward a Better Understanding of Death Penalty Opinion," *Journal of Criminal Justice* 20 (1992): 227–236.

75. T. J. Keil and G. F. Vito, "Race and the Death Penalty in Kentucky Murder Trials," *American Journal of Criminal Justice* 20, no. 1 (Fall 1995): 17–36; R. A. Rofferty, "In the Shadow of *McClesky v. Kemp*: Discriminatory Impact of the Death Sentencing Process," *New England Journal on Criminal and Civil Confinement* 21, no. 1 (Winter 1995): 271–312; R. N. Stone, "Killing of Charles Walker: Racial Bias and the Death Sentence," *Criminal Justice* 7, no. 2 (Summer 1992): 22–27 and 54–55; J. R. Sorensen and D. H. Wallace, "Capital Punishment in Missouri: Examining the Issue of Racial Disparity," *Behavioral Sciences and the Law* 13, no. 1 (Winter 1995): 61–80.

76. J. Sorenson, R. Wrinkle, V. Brewer, and J. Mauquaut, "Capital Punishment and Deterrance: Examining the Effect of Executions on Murder in Texas," *Crime and Delinquency* 45, no. 4 (October 1999): 481–493; Gennaro F. Vito and Deborah G. Wilson, "Back from the Dead: Tracking the Progress of Kentucky's *Furman—*Commuted Death Row Population," *Justice Quarterly* 5, no. 1 (1988): 101–111.

77. Hugo A. Bedau, *The Case Against the Death Penalty*, (Washington, DC: American Civil Liberties Union, Capital Punishment Project, 1992).

78. Bohm, 1992.

79. P. J. Cook and D. B. Slawson, *The Costs of Processing Murder Cases in North Carolina* (Durham, NC: Duke University, Jerry Sanford Institute of Public Policy, 1993)

80. R. S. Spangenberg and E. R. Walsh, "Capital Punishment or Life Imprisonment? Some Cost Considerations," *Loyola University of Los Angeles Law Review* 23, no. 1 (November 1989): 45–58.

81. *The Harris Poll*, 2001.

82. Gallup Poll, http://www.gallup.com/content/default.asp?ci=6031 (accessed May 20, 2002).

83. *The Harris Poll*, 2001.

84. Gallup Poll, 2002.

85. National Opinion Research Center, *General Surveys, 1972–2000* (Storrs: Roper Center for Public Opinion Research, University of Connecticut, 2001).

86. Gallup Poll, 2002.

87. R. Dieter, *Innocence and the Death Penalty: The Increasing Danger of Executing the Innocent* (Washington, D.C.: Death Penalty Information Center, 1997).

88. Hugo Adam Bedau and Michael L. Radelet, "Miscarriages of Justice in Potentially Capital Cases," *Stanford Law Review* 40 (1987): 21–181.

89. Death Penalty Information Center, available at www.deathpenaltyinfo.org/articles.php?scid=28&did=107, accessed February 12, 2004.

90. Renee Cardwell Hughes, "The Death Penalty: A Failed System," in *The State of Corrections: 2001 Proceedings of the ACA Annual Conference* (Lanham, Md.: American Correctional Association, 2002), p. 123.

Chapter 15

AFTER READING THIS CHAPTER,
YOU SHOULD BE ABLE TO:

1. Describe the trend regarding the size of the correctional population over the past twenty years and specify the changing trend over the past two to three years.

2. Identify the forces that have caused an increase in the prison population and compare the growth of the states to the federal prison system.

3. Analyze the growth trends in jail populations.

4. List the reasons why the growth of incarcerated populations has slowed over the past few years.

5. Discuss the involvement of politics in correctional policy over the past twenty years.

6. Describe the public's attitude regarding correctional sanctions and treatment programs.

7. List and describe four approaches used by correctional agencies to reduce their overall cost of operations.

8. Compare the effectiveness of public versus private prisons.

9. Discuss the benefits of correctional accreditation.

10. Explain the importance of staff diversity for correctional agencies.

11. Describe the impact of the Martinson finding of "nothing works" and discuss the more recent advances in research methodology and findings of the reviews of correctional treatment effectiveness.

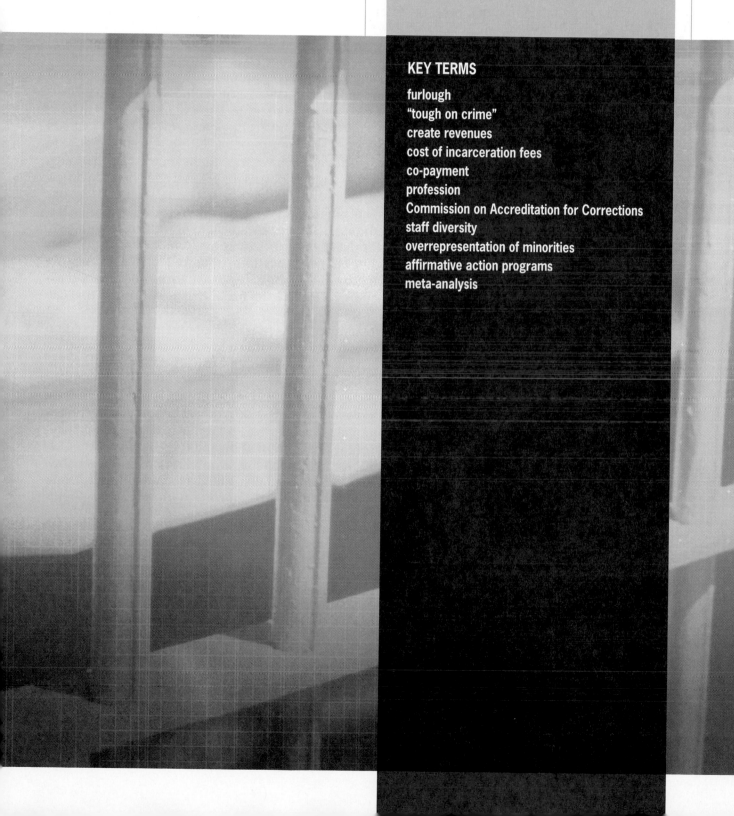

Issues in Corrections

KEY TERMS

furlough
"tough on crime"
create revenues
cost of incarceration fees
co-payment
profession
Commission on Accreditation for Corrections
staff diversity
overrepresentation of minorities
affirmative action programs
meta-analysis

Introduction

Corrections is a constantly evolving discipline. While it could be argued that we still do what was done centuries ago (incarcerate criminals and supervise them in the community), it can also be argued that everything has changed (prison architecture and management, styles of community supervision). Something certain about the field of corrections is that things do change. New issues develop. New pressures are brought to bear. New factors enter in to old problems. And, quite frankly, old issues or programs reappear, sometimes with a different name or a different "spin." Yet, often it is (as the saying goes) the same old car, just a new wax job.

In this chapter, we review some of the most recent developments, issues, and challenges facing corrections today and tomorrow. First, trends in prison and jail populations are examined. While both have continued to grow, the growth has slowed significantly for prisons and could result in a very different situation for correctional agencies in the next ten years than they faced ten years ago. Second, correctional policy has become increasingly driven by politics over the past fifteen years. Corrections and the operations surrounding it had little public importance in the political agenda just two decades ago. However, with the increase in spending, the public's concern about crime, and politicians' belief that they had to show a "tough on crime" posture, this has forever changed. Correctional policy is now, unfortunately, too often the result of political rhetoric and media sound bites than it is a thoughtful dialogue and planning based on research and prioritizing resources.

In addition, with the growth in the number of correctional clients, there has been a tremendous increase in budget allocations to correctional agencies. Yet with the downturn in the economy during the early 2000s, governments are seeking to reduce correctional spending. This chapter examines some options that can be used to reduce budget allocations.

Another issue for correctional management is the use and utility of accreditation. Developed as a means to enhance credibility and professionalism of correctional agencies, accreditation is seen by most correctional officials as a worthy endeavor, yet others see it as a bureaucratic nuisance. The accreditation process is described and the pros and cons are discussed. A critically important emphasis for correctional agencies is the diversity of staff. With a majority of clients coming from minority groups, correctional agencies have attempted to change their staff's makeup to be more reflective of the client population and thereby reduce the likelihood of problems than could result from a perception of racism and insensitivity. Finally, corrections is, now more than ever, being held accountable for the outcomes of its programs and activities. Therefore, the current understanding of the effectiveness of correctional treatment is examined.

Prison and Jail Populations

At midyear 2002, the population of the nation's prisons and jails for the first time reached two million, with 2,019,234 people incarcerated in the fifty states, the District of Columbia, and federal government prisons and local jails. One-third of these were in jails (665,475) and two-thirds were in prison (1,355,748).[1] While both prison and jail numbers indicated a growth since the previous six-month report, there has been a declining trend in the number of people incarcerated in state prisons, while populations in federal prisons and local jails have continued to increase. Overall, the total incarcerated population increased 2.8 percent since midyear 2001, with state prison populations increasing by 1.0 percent, federal prisons by 5.7 percent, and local jails by 5.4 percent. However, nine states (including most of the largest) actually had a decline in their prison population for the year ending June 30, 2002.[2]

TABLE 15.1	Incarcerated Population in State and Federal Prisons and Local Jails				
Year	Total inmates in custody	Prisoners in custody Federal	State	Inmates held in local jails	Incarceration rate[a]
1990	1,148,702	58,838	684,544	405,320	458
1995	1,585,586	89,538	989,004	507,044	601
1999[b]	1,893,115	125,682	1,161,490	605,943	691
2000[c]	1,935,919	133,921	1,176,269	621,149	683
2001[c]					
June 30	1,964,301	140,741	1,187,763	631,240	690
December 31	—	143,337	1,181,128	—	
2002[c]					
June 30	2,019,234	148,783	1,200,203	665,475	702
Percent change, 6/30/01–6/30/02	2.8%	5.7%	1.0%	5.4%	
Annual average increase 12/31/95–6/30/02	3.8%	8.1%	3.0%	4.3%	

Note: Jail counts are for midyear (June 30) and exclude people who were supervised outside a jail facility. State and federal prisoner counts for 1990–2000 are for December 31.

—Not available.

[a]People in custody per 100,000 residents in each reference year.

[b]In 1999, 15 states expanded their reporting criteria to include inmates held in privately operated correctional facilities. For comparisons with previous years, the state count 1,137,544 and the total count 1,869,169 should be used.

[c]Total counts include federal inmates in nonsecure privately operated facilities (6,143 in 2000, 6,192 in 2001, and 6,762 in 2002) and exclude District of Columbia inmates reported in both the *National Prisoner Statistics* and the *Annual Survey of Jails*.

Source: Paige M. Harrison and Jennifer C. Karberg, *Prison and Jail Inmates in Midyear 2002* (Washington, D.C.: U.S. Department of Justice, Bureau of Justice Statistics, April 2003), p. 2.

Table 15.1 illustrates the overall growth in the number of people held in prisons and jails, yet also notes a declining rate of incarceration. Between 1990 and 1995 the incarceration rate grew from 458 to 601 per 100,000 U.S. residents (31 percent) and grew another 15 percent to 691 in 1999. Since that time, the incarceration rate has been relatively constant, and was 702 per 100,000 residents on June 30, 2002.

As a subset of the overall incarcerated population, the growth of the prison population has been steadily slowing over the past several years. A U.S. Department of Justice report noted, "During 2001 the prison population rose at the lowest rate since 1972 and had the smallest absolute increase since 1979."[3] This slowdown in the growth of the nation's prison population can be somewhat misleading, however, as the federal prison population has continued to experience high growth rates, while the state prison population has been declining. Figure 15.1 illustrates the average growth in the number of state prisoners from 1995 to 2002. As can be noted, the first six months of every year has a significantly higher increase than the last six months. In fact, during the last six months of 2001, the number of state prison inmates actually decreased by 3,217 inmates (0.3 percent).[4]

As noted, the federal prison population has continued to climb. The U.S. Congress has continued to federalize several crimes that had previously been handled at the state level, with the war on drugs having the most significant effect, as additional federal law enforcement officers, prosecutors, and judges have been mobilized to investigate and prosecute drug offenses in federal court. In addition, over the past few years, the federal government has taken responsibility for inmates who were previously incarcerated by the District of Columbia, increasing

PERCENT CHANGE DURING 6-MONTH PERIODS IN THE NUMBER OF PRISONERS UNDER THE JURISDICTION OF STATE CORRECTIONAL AUTHORITIES, 1995–2002

FIGURE **15.1**

Percent change in state prison population

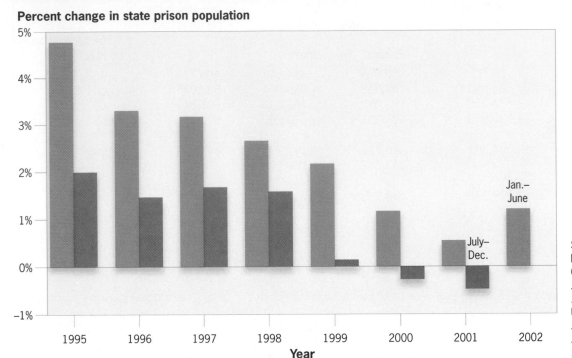

Source: Paige M. Harrison and Jennifer C. Karberg, *Prison and Jail Inmates in Midyear 2002* (Washington, D.C.: U.S. Department of Justice, Bureau of Justice Statistics, April 2003), p. 2.

the federal prison population by almost 7,000 inmates as a result. More than 40 percent of the growth in the total U.S. prison population between 2001 and 2002 has been the result of increases in the federal prison population.[5]

An interesting result of the changing prison population has been the impact on private prisons. From midyear 2001 to midyear 2002, the number of inmates held in privately operated prisons decreased from 94,948 to 86,626, a reduction of almost 9 percent.[6] As the prison population in states goes down, there is less pressure to contract with private prisons to hold inmates. As well, most states experienced tightening budgets in the early 2000s and found that they could save money by keeping inmates in state-operated prisons rather than sending them to private prisons. Continued decreases in state prison populations or a slowdown in the growth of the federal prison population will continue to affect the use of private facilities to hold prisoners. In a recent review of the status of private prisons funded by the U.S. Department of Justice, the authors projected that "[t]he number of privatized prisons is likely to increase, but not at the pace exhibited during the past decade."[7] Culp also suggests that there is considerable evidence that prison privatization is now in decline, a result of a declining incarceration rates, overbuilding of prison beds, legislation antagonistic to the private prison industry, and a number of well-publicized serious incidents.[8]

Trends in the size and growth (or decline) in local jail populations are more difficult to analyze, as the number of jailed inmates has continued to rise over the past several years, but with no consistent pattern in its growth. As indicated in Table 15.2, the total jail population has risen from 541,913 in 1995 to 737,912 by midyear 2002 (more than a 36 percent increase). This total includes both those held in jails and offenders supervised outside jails on such statuses as electronic monitoring, community service, or serving jail time only on weekends.

Figure 15.2 illustrates the inconsistent growth during each twelve-month period between 1991 and 2002. Jail incarceration rates have a trend similar to prisons

TABLE 15.2	People under Jail Supervision by Confinement Status			
	Number of persons under jail supervision			
Confinement status and type of program	**1995**	**2000**	**2001**	**2002**
Total	541,913	687,033	702,044	737,912
Held in jail	507,044	621,149	631,240	665,475
Supervised outside a jail facility[a]	34,869	65,884	70,804	72,437
Electronic monitoring	6,788	10,782	10,017	9,706
Home detention[b]	1,376	332	539	1,037
Day reporting	1,283	3,969	3,522	5,010
Community service	10,253	13,592	17,561	13,918
Weekender programs	1,909	14,523	14,381	17,955
Other pretrial supervision	3,229	6,279	6,632	8,702
Other work programs[c]	9,144	8,011	5,204	5,190
Treatment programs[d]	—	5,714	5,219	1,256
Other/unspecified	887	2,682	7,729	9,663

—Not available.

[a]Excludes people supervised by a probation or parole agency.

[b]Includes only those without electronic monitoring.

[c]Includes people in work release programs, work gangs, and other work alternative programs.

[d]Includes persons under drug and alcohol abuse treatment.

Source: Paige M. Harrison and Jennifer C. Karberg, *Prison and Jail Inmates in Midyear 2002* (Washington, D.C.: U.S. Department of Justice, Bureau of Justice Statistics, April 2003), p. 7.

ANNUAL GROWTH RATES FOR LOCAL JAILS

FIGURE 15.2

Percent change in local jail population from previous year, 1991–2002

Source: Paige M. Harrison and Jennifer C. Karberg, *Prison and Jail Inmates in Midyear 2002* (Washington, D.C.: U.S. Department of Justice, Bureau of Justice Statistics, April 2003), p. 7.

in that they rose significantly from 163 per 100,000 in 1990 to 222 per 100,000 in 1999. Since that time, however, incarceration rates stayed relatively constant, yet rose from 222 per 100,000 in 2001 to 231 per 100,000 in 2002.[9]

There are several reasons for the slowdown in the growth of incarcerated offenders that has continued (seemingly unabated) over the past twenty years. First, it is only natural that after such growth, there would be a slowdown at some time. If, as proponents of the use of incarceration argue, incapacitating offenders in prison reduces crime, then at some point a large number of potential criminals will be in jail and prison, and the increase in new admissions will have to slow down. Second, the slowdown of the economy has forced states to reconsider their continued enhancement of criminal codes that sentence more people to prison for longer periods of time. In a report regarding methods to alleviate jail overcrowding (that is also relevant to prisons), the authors noted, "Construction and operation of local jails are extremely expensive propositions. Over the years, the view that a jurisdiction can solve its jail crowding problem through building has proved to be wrong."[10]

Third, many states have increased their use of alternatives to incarceration, and these efforts are finally having some impact. There has been an increasing concern that continued increases in the use of incarceration have failed to concurrently increase public safety,[11] yet this policy has undoubtedly increased the cost to taxpayers. Therefore, many states have looked for and implemented sanctions between probation and incarceration. Many of these have proven effective and less costly, when the risk of offenders is properly identified and matched to correctional sanctions.[12] Finally, jail pretrial release programs have been added in many local jurisdictions and have also effectively slowed the increase in the number of jail inmates. The Pretrial Services Resource Center, in a review of methods used to alleviate jail overcrowding conducted for the U.S. Department of Justice, reported,

> In response to increased jail populations, probation agencies are working with other criminal justice agencies to develop alternative programs. Many counties opt for increasing the number of community-based alternatives, instead of the rate of incarceration, because the former is a more cost-effective means of alleviating jail crowding while maintaining public safety.[13]

Politics and Policy

Why has the United States prison population risen so dramatically over the past twenty years, and why may its growth be beginning to slow down? It is important to examine the impact of politics on the formation of correctional policy. While citizens would like to believe that policy is developed from painstaking research, analysis of costs and benefits, and weighing of many alternatives, unfortunately, that is seldom the case. Especially in regard to issues in which there is emotion and strong sentiment, elected officials more often respond by making decisions that will be seen by the public as the "right thing to do" and will likely win them votes and reelection.

When it comes to the use of incarceration as a sanction for criminal offending, changes in sentencing and incarceration policies had significantly more impact than other changes. Blumstein and Beck examined the growth of imprisonment between 1980 and 1996 and concluded that 88 percent was due to changes in policy, including sentencing to prison rather than probation (51 percent) and lengthening time served by offenders (37 percent). Only 12 percent of the growth was the result of changes in the crime rate or the makeup of criminal offenders.[14]

Why have elected officials moved aggressively toward "tough on crime" policies, even where there is little evidence of their effectiveness and with the knowledge that they are extremely expensive in relation to community alternative sanctions? Perhaps the watershed political event regarding politics and criminal justice

The "politicizing" of corrections was believed to have reached its watershed during the presidential campaign between George Bush and Michael Dukakis.
Courtesy of Dennis Cook/AP/Wide World Photos.

policy occurred during the 1988 presidential campaign, when Vice President George Bush successfully used the public's fear of crime as a campaign tool against his opponent, Governor Michael Dukakis of Massachusetts. Bush used campaign ads presenting Dukakis as soft on crime for allowing a Massachusetts **furlough** program and suggesting that it led to the commission of a tragic murder by Willie Horton, a furloughed inmate, while he lived in a halfway house.

Other candidates for public office saw the effectiveness of "tough on crime" policies and the dangers of being labeled "soft on crime." Therefore, campaign promises to keep dangerous offenders in prison longer became the rallying cry for elections from Virginia to California, resulting in tough sentencing laws and funding for prison construction passed by state legislatures across the country. Such legislation includes the California three-strikes law, resulting from a similar public campaign to toughen laws after the 1993 murder of 12-year-old Polly Klaas by Richard Allen Davis, who was on parole after serving only eight years of a sixteen-year sentence for kidnapping.

Another example is the nation's war on drugs, in which President Ronald Reagan pushed through legislation to toughen drug laws, allocate more resources to investigating and prosecuting drug laws, and require mandatory prison terms for federal drug offenders. The dramatic increase in the federal prison population resulted primarily from these policies, to the point that almost two-thirds of the federal prison population is currently drug offenders. A 1999 article in *Newsweek* noted, "We are developing a powerful 'prison-industrial complex,' a national growth industry exploiting today's hostility toward wrongdoers."[15]

Unfortunately, once political rhetoric forces correctional policy to move in this direction, it is difficult to change directions and turn back the clock. Increasing costs of correctional budgets usually take money from other public services, such as education, social service programs, and improvement of deteriorating infrastructures. As an example, the National Conference of State Legislatures reported that state spending on higher education experienced the highest reduction in its history during the 1990s, during which state correctional spending had its fastest growth.[16] Addressing this dilemma, Irwin and Austin argue that society must turn

Furlough

a program in which prison inmates are allowed to leave prison early to reside in a halfway house to prepare for community reentry away from the excessive use of prisons, which is diverting money from education, child care, mental health, and medical services, all of which have a greater impact on reducing crime than does building more prisons.[17]

One interesting thing in the linkage of politics and correctional policy is that the public is not nearly as strongly in favor of "get tough" policies as elected officials believe. A major result of the **"tough on crime"** political mentality has been the implementation of sentencing guidelines, determinate sentencing to replace the use of parole boards, and mandatory sentencing. All of these reduce discretion by judges and correctional professionals, resulting in an inability to distinguish among offenders by their risk and chance for successful rehabilitation. As Petersilia writes, "One of the most distinguishing characteristics of U.S. crime policy since the 1980s has been the gradual chipping away on individualized decision making and its replacement with one-size-fits-all laws and policies."[18]

Public attitudes are becoming less punitive in their belief about the most effective way to handle criminal offenders than in the past. In a recent public opinion poll conducted by Peter D. Hart Research Associates, the public favored addressing the root causes of crime over strict sentencing, by 65 percent to 32 percent. This has changed since 1994, when a Gallup poll found that only 48 percent of Americans favored addressing the causes of crime and 42 percent preferred the punitive approach. Poll respondents also favor a more rational sentencing for offenders. Only 28 percent of Americans surveyed believed that the most effective way to reduce crime is to keep offenders off the street as long as possible. Nearly two-thirds of those surveyed believed that the most effective way to reduce crime is to rehabilitate prisoners by requiring education and job training.[19]

Americans have also expressed concern with the punitive approach taken by the war on drugs. In the Hart survey, respondents recognized drug abuse as a medical problem, and 63 percent favored handling it primarily through counseling and treatment, while only 31 percent believed that it is a serious crime that should be handled mainly by the courts and prison system. Respondents also expressed concern with the overreach of three-strikes laws; 56 percent favored elimination of these policies and other mandatory sentencing laws, while giving judges more discretion to choose the appropriate sentence. In general, only 35 percent supported the direction of the nation's crime approach, and 54 percent believed we are on the wrong track.[20]

Public opinion surveys have discovered that the primary interest of the public is to be protected. They do not support sanctions that do not punish offenders and protect society. However, if they believe that community sanctions effectively protect them, the public supports the use of community sanctions over imprisonment. In an Ohio survey, when informed that prison space is scarce and expensive, the public supported the use of community corrections instead of paying for new prison construction.[21] A National Opinion Survey on Crime and Justice (NOSCJ) survey also found support for community correctional programs, as 73 percent of those surveyed indicated that intensive probation supervision was either "very effective" or "somewhat effective," 55 percent similarly supported house arrest, 73 percent supported electronic monitoring of offenders, and 78 percent supported the use of boot camps as alternatives to traditional prison sentences.[22]

Even though there is momentum to slow the growth of incarceration, continued building of new prisons, and additional increases in the budgets of correctional agencies, there are also factors that encourage a continuation of that policy. We have developed a "prison industrial" complex that requires monetary commitments and has political support for its continuation. Once the capital outlay for building a new prison is committed, it is silly to project that it will be closed and

"Tough on crime"

an attitude that criminals should be severely punished for their wrongdoings, and long prison sentences are the most effective punishment abandoned. Rural communities depend on the economic value of the jobs and purchases resulting from a prison in their area. Labor unions such as the California Correctional Peace Officers Association (CCPOA) have become a major lobbying influence for maintaining correctional officer jobs. This union has tremendous power in California politics, having contributed $2.3 million to the successful 1998 campaign of the California governor.[23] And some writers have argued that private prison companies, who will benefit from continued policies of incarceration, also influence criminal justice legislation.[24]

It will be interesting to observe whether elected officials will continue to spend money that the state does not have to further toughen criminal sanctions. Unfortunately, we often fail to learn from our past mistakes when it comes to crime policy. While it is hoped that elected officials will turn away from political rhetoric and emotion and toward research, analysis, and careful planning to shape our crime policies in the future, we have not always seen that to be the case. At this point in history, however, the difficult budget decisions facing public officials may create a backdrop for more rational decision making. The "A Case Study" box is a good example of how politics and correctional policy can clash.

A CASE STUDY

POLITICS AND POLICY REGARDING PRISON INDUSTRIES

When I was an assistant director of the Federal Bureau of Prisons, I had responsibility for Federal Prison Industries (FPI), a government corporation that manufactured products in prisons, providing inmates with real-world work opportunities, and selling the products to the federal government. The last year I was in the position, FPI had more than $400 million in sales of prison-made products. FPI was authorized by Congress in the 1930s, recognizing that inmates could not sit idly in their cells all day, the goods could be sold to the government at a fair or reduced price, and profits could be used to assist in managing federal prisons. Government agencies were to buy from FPI if they produced a product that met the agencies' specifications, could be delivered on time, and was sold at a fair market price.

FPI was the model of a government corporation for the next fifty years. It was started with a grant of buildings, machinery, and raw materials valued at approximately $3 million. Over the years, it returned some $80 million in profits back to the U.S. Treasury. There was never another penny of taxpayer dollars appropriated to its operation, as it proved profitable and able to operate successfully. Inmates received excellent training and developed valuable work skills, contributing to a reduction of recidivism for participants. The policy of operating FPI by this method seems effective and led to efficiencies in government.

However, in the late 1980s, private companies and trade associations that produced similar products as FPI, as well as labor unions, became concerned about the size of FPI in terms of sales to the government. They began to approach their members of Congress and argue that it was unfair to let inmates work and sell products that competed with the private sector, and therefore cost law-abiding citizens jobs. Even though FPI had a minuscule share of any market for the products they sold, these associations and individuals lobbied Congress to take away the "mandatory source" policy, in which agencies were supposed to first see if FPI had the product available before they purchased it from the private sector.

Members of Congress are aware that there are few if any votes to be received from supporting an inmate work program. Yet they can lose votes by not seeming to support their constituents who believe that jobs are lost due to the FPI work program. To this day, bills are annually introduced to limit the opportunity of FPI to sell inmate-made goods to the federal government. Although the merits of both the private sector and FPI arguments are debatable, this is truly a situation of politics competing with effective public policy.

Tightening Budgets

A major challenge in public policy is how to fund the continually increasing cost of correctional operations and programs. The economic downturn over the past few years has resulted in reduced tax receipts by states and the federal government. When the economy was strong and governments were experiencing budget surpluses, it was an easy decision to expand prison space and other correctional services to meet the burgeoning population under supervision. With tightening budgets, it is now a much more complicated decision as to whether to increase taxes, reduce the correctional population, or eliminate some services or supervision to meet budget shortfalls. Freeman observes, "Tax revenues are not unlimited and, as correctional budgets have grown at the expense of other state agencies, elected officials have increasingly demanded that corrections assume a proactive role in reducing the burden on the taxpayer."[25]

Over the past twenty years, the number of clients served by adult correctional agencies has grown significantly. In 2001, nearly 6.6 million individuals were under correctional supervision of either probation, prison, jail, or parole (See Figure 15.3). Correspondingly, expenditures for correctional agencies have also grown. As indicated in Figure 15.4, expenditures for all three components of the criminal justice system (police, judicial, and corrections) have expanded from 1982 to 1999. However, while police expenditures rose by 244 percent and judicial expenditures by 314 percent, corrections led the increase, rising by 442 percent. In fiscal year 1991, state and federal adult correctional agencies' budgets totaled $18.1 billion.[26] By fiscal year 2001, these budgets increased by 97 percent to $35.6 billion, representing 4.3 percent of the total budget of the jurisdiction.[27]

Local, state, and federal governments must struggle (sometimes even closing prisons) with methods to reduce their spending, since there is little hope that legislative bodies will decide to increase taxes at a level to keep up with correctional

ADULT CORRECTIONAL POPULATIONS, 1980–2001

FIGURE **15.3**

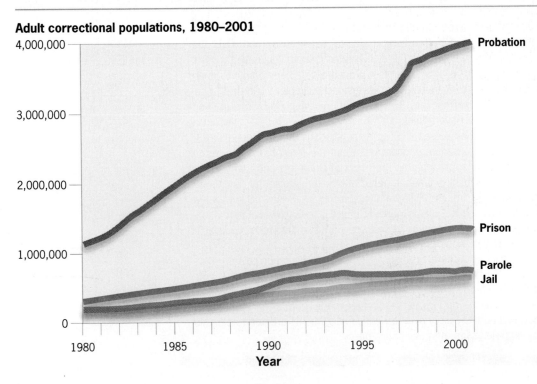

Source: Bureau of Justice Statistics Correctional Surveys (Annual Probation Survey, National Prisoner Statistics, Survey of Jails, and Annual Parole Survey) as presented in *Correctional Populations in the United States. Prisoners in 2001, and Probation and Parole in the United States, 2001.*

DIRECT EXPENDITURE BY CRIMINAL JUSTICE FUNCTION, 1982–1999

FIGURE **15.4**

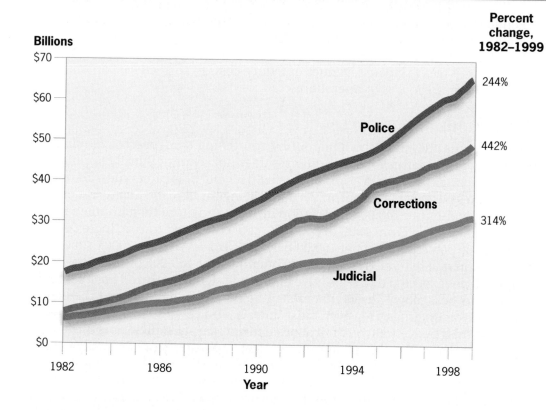

Percent change, 1982–1999

Police — 244%

Corrections — 442%

Judicial — 314%

Source: Bureau of Justice Statistics, "Expenditure Facts at a Glance," http://www.ojp.usdoj.gov/bjs/glance/exptyp.htm (accessed January 24, 2003).

The Orient (Ohio) Correctional Institution was closed during 2003 due to insufficient budgets to pay for staff salaries. Its closure resulted in increasing overcrowding at other prisons.
Courtesy of the Ohio Department of Rehabilitation and Correction.

expenditures that continue to climb. Many options are considered to reduce the cost of corrections, including the following:

- Reduce the inmate population by reducing the length of sentences or the mandatory prison terms for certain offenses
- Develop community sentencing alternatives to imprisonment.
- Charge user fees to create revenues or reduce costs of correctional operations.
- Privatize some services or operations.

REDUCING THE INMATE POPULATION

While reducing the inmate population by shortening sentences or eliminating mandatory prison terms for some offenses does not seem politically popular, recent incarceration trends do note some relief. The rate of incarceration across the United States has begun to level off. As noted in Figure 15.5, the incarceration rate was 139 offenders per 100,000 population in 1980, and more than doubled to 297 per 100,000 by 1990. From 1990 to 2000, the rate continued to rise, increasing by more than 50 percent (to 478 per 100,000) by 2002. However, from 2000 to 2001, the incarceration rate remained stable at 470 offenders per 100,000 population.

It is still not expected that legislative bodies will significantly roll back sentencing codes to "less tough" levels that existed before the mid-1980s and the beginning of the war on drugs. However, most states have a constitutional requirement to balance their budgets and are not allowed to operate at a deficit, as is the federal government. Therefore, there may be a political opportunity to minimally modify statutes to reduce the number of people in prison. In addition, there has been considerable publicity about the questionable merit of tough sentencing laws such as California's three-strikes legislation. In a review of this process, Greenwood and colleagues suggest that legislators who found voting for the legislation politically attractive later reversed themselves and found that voting against funding the act's implementation was just as politically attractive.[28]

INCARCERATION RATE, 1980–2001   FIGURE **15.5**

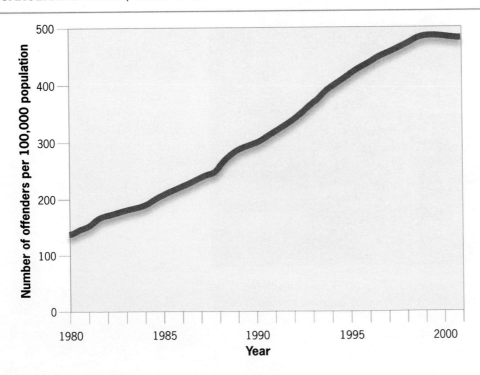

Source: Bureau of Justice Statistics, "Corrections Facts at a Glance," http://www.ojp.usdoj.gov/bjs/glance/incrt (accessed January 24, 2003).

DEVELOPING COMMUNITY ALTERNATIVES TO PRISON

A second approach to meeting tightening correctional budgets has been to expand the use of less-expensive alternatives to incarceration, such as intensive supervision probation (ISP), boot camp, and house arrest using electronic monitoring. These sanctions are still perceived as punitive by the public, yet are seen as more rehabilitative than imprisonment. These programs have been available to correctional jurisdictions for several years. However, as budgets tightened, elected officials were more willing to search for and implement alternative sanctions that cost less than prison. While evaluations of these intermediate sanctions have not always proven to reduce future recidivism by participants at a greater level than does incarceration, studies have shown that these sanctions can reduce cost without reducing public safety.

CREATING REVENUES BY CORRECTIONAL AGENCIES

A third initiative to reduce the costs of corrections has been the implementation of fees to **create revenues** or reduce the government costs for program operations. The idea of charging offenders for services is not new, particularly for community corrections. As a condition of probation, offenders have regularly been charged a fine or had to pay victim restitution. Today, many probation agencies charge offenders for services such as drug counseling, halfway house stays, or participation in work release programs, as well as for their supervision costs of electronic monitoring, intensive supervision, or drug testing. In 1980, only ten states reported charging supervision or user fees. However, by 1996, forty-one states reported using such fees.[29] Recently, many jurisdictions have approved **cost-of-incarceration fees** for prisoners housed in local jails or state and federal prisons. These fees require inmates to pay the cost of their incarceration, if they have the financial resources. However, few offenders have the means to pay these fees, and few jurisdictions have been successful at collecting the full cost of confinement from many inmates.

Create revenues

to enable governments to charge for correctional supervision or programs provided to offenders

Cost of incarceration fees

fees charged prisoners in local jails or prisons to cover the cost for their incarceration

Use of boot camps is one of many community sanctions that allow some offenders to be safely supervised in the community.
Courtesy of the Maricopa County (Arizona) Sheriff.

Co-payment

a minimal charge for inmates to see a physician or receive medical care

One fee that has been widely used is for medical care while in prison. As reported in *The Corrections Yearbook,* as of January 1, 2001, thirty-nine states charged prison inmates for medical care, charging a minimal fee or **co-payment** of two or three dollars.[30] This co-payment not only creates revenues to help cover the cost of medical care, but also reduces the demand for medical services. As one of the first states to begin to use these co-payments, Nevada found that in the first two years of implementation (from 1989 to 1991), the inmate medical utilization rate decreased by 76 percent in the maximum-security prison, and by 50 percent throughout the state.[31]

CONTRACTING WITH THE PRIVATE SECTOR

A final method used by correctional agencies to reduce their costs is to contract some services or the entire operation of prisons to the private sector. During the Reagan and George H. W. Bush presidential terms, governments began to consider use of the private sector to provide many services that had previously been provided solely by government. Some contracting for services outside government had been done for years by correctional agencies, but some ideas are relatively new. Halfway houses had historically been private, nonprofit operations, and community correctional agencies also began to contract for electronic monitoring, drug testing, and some program services. However, during the 1980s, prisons began to consider contracting with private companies to provide food services, medical and mental health care, educational programming, and substance abuse counseling. By January 1, 2001, there were 144 state and federal prisons contracting for food services and 447 for medical care for inmates.[32] Another 229 prisons had private contractors providing mental health services[33] and 190 prisons contracted for substance abuse services.[34]

As well, agencies began to consider contracting total housing, services, security, and programs for inmates with the private sector. Since the first contract with a private prison to house offenders for a public correctional agency in the early 1980s, the use of such contracts has grown significantly. On January 1, 2001, twenty-six states, the District of Columbia, and the Federal Bureau of Prisons had almost 70,000 inmates placed in 101 private prisons across the United States.[35] At an average cost per day of $43.62, these contracts equate to more than $1 billion per year.

The privatizing of prisons has been controversial, with questions being raised regarding the costs, benefits, quality of service, and ethical concerns of an offender's freedom being taken away by a for-profit company. Logan identified ten issues that are key to any deliberations regarding the use of private prisons:

1. The propriety of proprietary prisons—can the punishment of offenders be delegated to nonpublic agencies?
2. Cost and efficiency—are private prisons operated less expensively than public prisons?
3. Quality—does the profit motive diminish the drive for delivery of quality services and programs to inmates?
4. Quantity—does the involvement of the private sector to make a profit encourage the expansion of imprisonment beyond what is in the public interest?
5. Flexibility—does the fact that the private sector does not have to follow bureaucratic government policies for purchasing and personnel management increase efficiency?
6. Security—does an emphasis on profits and cost cutting undermine security for inmates, staff, and the community?

7. Liability—what impact does a government's contracting with a private firm for housing inmates have on the liability of the government for violation of inmates' constitutional rights?
8. Accountability and monitoring—how will the private contractor be monitored to fulfill requirements and be held responsible if it does not?
9. Corruption—without the restraints inherent in government to reduce the likelihood of corruption, will there be an increase in corruption in private prisons?
10. Dependence—will the public sector become dependent on the private-sector contract, and if so, how does this affect decision making?[36]

A critical issue for private prisons concerns cost efficiency. In purely monetary terms, the average cost of private-sector contracts for 2001 of $43.62 per inmate per day compares very favorably to the average daily cost per inmate in a public prison of $61.04. However, only 18 percent of private facilities (compared to 35 percent of public prisons) were multilevel or greater than medium security, which are more expensive to operate.[37] And the most expensive prisons (prison hospitals and supermax prisons) are all operated by the public sector.

Several studies have compared the cost of privately operated prisons, but few controlled for comparable security levels for the evaluated prisons. The earliest review of the Hamilton County, Tennessee, private prison suggested that it saved from 4 percent to 15 percent annually over county-operated penal farm costs.[38] A study comparing costs of public and private prisons in Kentucky and Massachusetts found that private prisons appeared to be better managed than public prisons.[39] A 1992 study comparing costs for public and private facilities housing parole violators in California found a lower cost per day for private facilities. However, the authors warn,

> While the findings of this study are preliminary, when all factors are considered, they do not appear to be more supportive of the use of either the public or private proprietary facilities . . . Considering comparative security levels, overhead, and hidden costs of [state] and [nonstate] facilities, the only conclusion at this time is that the relative costs of [these] operations are probably about the same.[40]

Several recent studies have found that private prisons house offenders at less cost than their public counterparts. A study funded by private prisons determined that between 1999 and 2001, "states that have some of their prisoners in privately owned or operated prisons experience lower growth in the cost of housing their public prisoners."[41] A *Harvard Law Review* article concluded that "what imperfect empirical evidence there is suggests that private prisons cost less than public prisons and that their quality is no worse."[42] However, Segal and Moore, in a review of the costs of outsourcing correctional services, conclude, "Policymakers should be wary of over-reliance on cost-comparison data in making privatization decisions, and be certain that cost analysts do not take it upon themselves to make policy assumptions in determining cost figures."[43]

Another reason correctional agencies turn to privatization is to eliminate having to appropriate funds for the enormous capital outlay required to build prisons. During the period of tremendous growth in the inmate population during the late 1980s and 1990s, the private sector was able to build and provide prison beds more rapidly than the public sector. Austin and Coventry note that because private companies are not subject to government regulations regarding construction of buildings, the private sector can build prisons for nearly 25 percent less and in half the time compared to public governments.[44] Culp also notes that some states were approaching their debt ceilings or did not have the time to issue bonds to fund new prison construction.[45]

Several studies have examined postrelease outcomes between public and private prison inmates, with mixed reviews. Results from a Florida study comparing recidivism of releasees from private and public prisons favored the private prisons. Recidivism of releasees from the private prisons was lower than for those released from public prisons, and of those who reoffended, the crimes were less serious for the private prison releasees.[46] However, when the General Accounting Office (GAO) conducted a comprehensive review of five outcome studies of private prisons completed since 1991 in Texas, New Mexico, California, Tennessee, and Louisiana, analysts did not believe that three of these studies were sufficiently designed to use results, but found that outcomes from the remaining two indicated minimal or no differences between the public and private prison operations.[47] Other studies have also failed to find any significant differences between the outcomes of offenders released from public versus private prisons.[48] And in a national survey to compare private and public prison operations that analyzed the types of inmates, inmate misconduct, and general characteristics of prisons and their staff, Camp and Gaes concluded that private prisons had higher escape rates and more positive results from drug tests, and did not enhance staff or community safety.[49]

There has not yet been a sufficient number of "apples to apples" comparisons of quality and cost between public and privately operated prisons to draw decisive conclusions. Opponents of the use of private prisons cite the lack of firm data as undermining the argument by the private sector that they can be more effective than their public counterparts. However, proponents suggest the evidence proves that the private sector can operate prisons as effectively as the public sector, and there are many other reasons (including cost) why the private sector plays a valuable role in providing correctional services across the nation. Even without firm cost and quality comparisons, it is expected that the use of contracts by public correctional agencies with the private sector will continue at a substantial level for the foreseeable future.

The "You Make the Decision" box asks students to decide whether they would turn to the private sector to house prisoners for their state agency.

YOU MAKE THE DECISION . . . **USE THE PRIVATE SECTOR TO OPERATE PRISONS?**

You are the director of a state department of corrections with no history of contracting entire prison operations to the private sector. Several of your fellow state administrators have used the private sector to house their inmates, and no one has expressed a serious concern about price or quality. You are aware of several serious incidents (riots, escapes, and inmate brutality) that have occurred in a few private prisons across the country and are sensitive to the negative publicity that these incidents brought. You are also aware of all of the studies that are inconclusive in terms of the benefits of the private sector in comparison to the public sector for cost and outcome.

Yet your legislative budget committee is pushing for the state to try privatization. They cite tightening budgets and the need to find better and less expensive ways to manage the burgeoning correctional population in the state. At the same time, you have had a good relationship with the labor union representing state correctional officers, and they are firmly opposed to privatization, as few of the private prisons allow collective bargaining. You feel caught in the middle of the positions of the budget committee and the labor union in terms of where you come down on supporting privatization. You are going to make one of them very unhappy with whatever decision you make.

You have decided to go through the preceding list of ten issues regarding privatization, weigh these factors as good or bad, and decide whether you will support privatizing a new prison in your state. For this exercise, either by yourself or in a small classroom group, go through each of these ten issues, determine whether they are favorable or unfavorable to the private sector, and then "score" your overall view either for or against the privatization of prisons. Use this score to decide whether you will support privatizing a state prison and what statement you will make as to your reasons for the decision. Finally, determine how you will deal with the party (budget committee or labor union) you will anger with your decision.

Accreditation of Correctional Programs

As noted in Chapter 1, in the first 150 years of corrections, correctional institutions and agencies usually lacked professional standards, central management, and consistency of operations. Therefore, as correctional organizations moved to improve their performance, professionalism, and perception by the public, a process was created to identify operational procedures that met modern professional standards. The aspects subscribed to a **profession** include the following: (1) a systematic body of theoretical knowledge acquired through lengthy academic study and not possessed by those outside the profession; (2) community interests rather than self-interest as a motivator of professional behavior; (3) self-regulation; and (4) a system of rewards.[50] Correctional agencies desired to follow the model of the American Bar Association and the American Medical Association by furthering the professional development of members while guiding and regulating their performance to the greatest extent possible.

Profession
to be seen as a profession, correctional agencies create standards for ethical behavior and self-regulation

In this regard, the American Correctional Association (ACA) has been instrumental in encouraging professional development and accrediting correctional agencies. The ACA is the major correctional professional organization, with more than 30,000 members internationally. An important element of being self-regulating is to have a professional code of ethics. As illustrated in Figure 15.6, the ACA Code of Ethics lists expectations of professional performance and practice by correctional professionals.

In addition, the ACA was used as the vehicle to create standards for professional practice of corrections as a profession, and the **Commission on Accreditation for Corrections** (CAC) was formed to administer a national accreditation programs for all components of adult and juvenile correctional agencies in the early 1970s. The first step was to develop standards that are the accepted professional practice for correctional agencies. Groups of correctional professionals were recruited to write dozens of standards that apply to correctional operations. For instance, the most recent version of the standards for adult correctional institutions identifies 463 standards regarding operational facets such as staff training, safety and emergency procedures, food services operations, health care, inmate programs, security procedures, and correctional industries.[51]

Commission on Accreditation for Corrections
a group formed to administer national accreditation programs for adult and juvenile correctional agencies

Correctional agencies must decide whether they believe that adopting these standards and using them as the basis for their own policies and procedures is in their best interests. According to the American Correctional Association, the purpose of the standards and accreditation process is

to promote improvement in the management of correctional agencies through the administration of a voluntary accreditation program and the

ACA CODE OF ETHICS

FIGURE **15.6**

The American Correctional Association expects of its members unfailing honesty, respect for the dignity and individuality of human beings, and a commitment to professional and compassionate service. To this end we subscribe to the following principles.

Relationships with clients/colleagues/other professions/the public—

- Members will respect and protect the civil and legal rights of all clients.
- Members will serve each case with appropriate concern for the client's welfare and with no purpose of personal gain.
- Relationships with colleagues will be of such character to promote mutual respect within the profession and improvement of its quality of service.
- Statements critical of colleagues or their agencies will be made only as these are verifiable and constructive in purpose.
- Members will respect the importance of all elements of the criminal justice system and cultivate a professional cooperation with each segment.
- Subject to the client's right of privacy, members will respect the public's right to know, and will share information with the public with openness and candor.
- Members will respect and protect the right of the public to be safeguarded from criminal activity.

Professional conduct/practices—

- No member will use his or her official position to secure special privileges or advantages.
- No member, while acting in an official capacity, will allow personal interest to impair objectivity in the performance of duty.
- No member will use his or her official position to promote any partisan political purposes.
- No member will accept any gift or favor of such nature to imply an obligation that is inconsistent with the free and objective exercise of professional responsibilities.
- In any public statement, members will clearly distinguish between those that are personal views and those that are statements and positions on behalf of an agency.
- Members will be diligent in their responsibility to record and make available to review any and all case information which could contribute to sound decisions affecting a client or the public safety.
- Each member will report, without reservation, any corrupt or unethical behavior which could affect either a client or the integrity of the organization.
- Members will not discriminate against any client, employee, or prospective employee on the basis of race, sex, creed, or national origin.
- Members will maintain the integrity of private information, they will neither seek personal data beyond that needed to perform their responsibilities, nor reveal case information to anyone not having proper professional use for such.
- Any member who is responsible for agency personnel actions will make all appointments, promotions, or dismissals only on the basis of merit and not in furtherance of partisan political interests.

Source: American Correctional Association. Adopted at the 105th Congress of Corrections in 1975.

ongoing development and revision of relevant, useful standards . . . The recognized benefits from such a process include improved management, a defense against lawsuits through documentation and the demonstration of a "good faith" effort to improve conditions of confinement, increased accountability and enhanced public credibility for administrative and line staff, a safer and more human environment for personnel and offenders, and the establishment of measurable criteria for upgrading programs, personnel, and physical plant on a continuing basis.[52]

If an agency decides that it wants to be accredited, it first must apply to the ACA for consideration. The ACA and CAC will send a team of evaluators to the agency or institution to conduct a comprehensive evaluation of the agency's operations in line with the documented standards. To be accredited, an agency must meet all mandatory standards (those representing life safety issues) and 90 percent of all

ACA standards are very specific regarding all areas of prison operations, and even include the number of seats required (as a percentage of the inmate population) in the dining room so that meals can be served in a reasonable time.
Photo by Richard P. Seiter.

nonmandatory standards. If the agency is accredited, there is a reaccreditation process in which a less intensive evaluation occurs every three years thereafter to ensure that the agency continues to meet these professional standards in its operation. Agencies often use their accreditation as a defense to inmate lawsuits and to demonstrate to constituents or political oversight groups that they are performing at an acceptable level of professional operations.

The first accreditation of correctional agencies occurred in 1978. By January 1, 2001, 564 state and federal prisons in twenty-seven state or federal correctional agencies (65 percent of the total number of state and federal prisons open on that date) had been accredited by the ACA.[53] Even though many others are not accredited, this does not mean that they are not being operated professionally or do not meet constitutional standards. Many agencies simply do not believe that the accreditation process is necessary or worth the time and effort to go through the process. Accreditation is strictly voluntary, as the ACA has no regulatory authority. The disadvantages to accreditation include cost, time, stress, and extra work by the staff to prepare for the process.[54] While it is believed to be beneficial for those agencies that have gone through the policy, others recognize the standards as an indication of quality, yet choose to forgo the time-consuming process to become accredited.

Importance of Staff Diversity

An extremely important factor within the operation of correctional agencies is **staff diversity.** Having a staff that is diverse in terms of gender, race, and ethnicity is important for many reasons. First, having women within a correctional workforce brings a calming and normalized influence to men's prisons and doubles the available pool for recruiting talented individuals. Second, with such a large percentage of offenders under correctional supervision being minorities, race and ethnic diversity aids in the management of prisons and community correctional agencies. Finally, staff members constantly learn from each other. Diversity in

Staff diversity

having a representative workforce in terms of gender, race, and ethnicity terms of gender, race, and ethnicity provides experiences for staff that make them better able to more effectively supervise a diverse group of offenders. The role of women working in men's prisons was described in Chapter 12, and issues of staff diversity in terms of race and ethnicity are presented next.

Over the years, there has been a shift in the racial makeup of adults under correctional supervision, and there is now an **overrepresentation of minorities** under correctional supervision. In 1986, whites made up a majority (65 percent) of offenders under correctional supervision (in prisons and jails and under community supervision). However, by 1997, whites represented only 60 percent of all adult offenders under supervision.[55] If ethnic background (Hispanics) is taken out of the number of white offenders, whites are a minority of all offenders under correctional supervision. In 1997, only 2 percent of all whites, compared with 9 percent of blacks, in the U.S. population were under correctional supervision.[56]

This proportion of minorities increases when considering the seriousness of the criminal punishment. Of the 2,014,500 inmates in prison and jail on June 30, 2002, 699,500 (34.7 percent) were white, 884,500 (43.9 percent) were black, and 367,900 (18.3 percent) were Hispanic.[57] This disproportionality becomes even more apparent when examined by age and rates of incarceration. In examining the makeup of offenders in prison or jail on the same date, the Bureau of Justice Statistics reported that "among males age 25 to 29, 12.9% of blacks were in prison or jail, compared to 4.3% of Hispanics and about 1.6% of whites."[58]

This disproportionate number of minorities in prison and jails makes it important that correctional agencies aggressively recruit minority staff in order to have the staff be somewhat representative of the offender makeup. The problems resulting from an almost all-white workforce supervising an inmate population that was primarily minority became expressly clear after the riot in the New York State Penitentiary in Attica in 1971. In a review of the causes of the riot, one significant problem was found to be the guarding of urban black and Hispanic inmates by rural white staff, who were separated by culture, mistrust, and a lack of communication. Not only was the staff from the rural area of New York State in which Attica is located, but also they had no understanding of the culture of the urban black and Hispanic inmates. Neither side made much effort to communicate; they let the cultural and racial differences grow into hostility and inmates believed race and discrimination to be the basis for many of the prison policies.

Even though there is no conclusive evidence that the criminal justice system is inherently racist in practice or policy, the high numbers of minorities in correctional systems create a phenomenon that causes management problems for correctional officials. In response, correctional agencies have created **affirmative action programs** to recruit and develop a workforce that mirrors, to some extent, the client base. While race and ethnicity do not have to be a barrier to communication between inmates and staff, a diverse workforce enhances the potential for positive communication by reducing the perception by offenders that the system is racist, and taking away one rationale of inmates that they have a "right" to misbehave or not follow prison rules.

The people who are responsible for implementing affirmative action programs (as well as a variety of other staff functions) for a correctional agency are human resources managers. The "Your Career in Corrections" box describes the functions of these positions.

Since the Attica riot, there has been progress in the hiring of minority staff by correctional agencies. On January 1, 2001, of the total of 439,788 staff employed by adult correctional agencies, 73.2 percent were white, 17.8 percent were black, and 4.9 percent were Hispanic.[59] While these percentages are still predominantly white, the percentage of nonwhite employees has climbed from 27.4 percent in 1993 to 34.9 percent in 2000.[60] Probation and parole agencies have done even bet-

---

Overrepresentation of minorities

the condition that exists when there is a greater percentage of certain racial and ethnic groups in the correctional population than in the general U.S. population

Affirmative action programs

activities to recruit and provide employment opportunities to women and minorities

YOUR CAREER IN CORRECTIONS

HUMAN RESOURCES MANAGERS

As noted previously, professional staff are critical to a successful correctional agency, and most of the budget dollars go toward staff salaries. The people responsible for all the administrative and personal contacts to hire staff are human resources managers (HRMs). These people were called *personnel managers* several years ago, but the more descriptive term is *human resources*. This is because the role of human resources is so varied and broad, including payroll (making sure staff members get paid correctly), benefits (life and health insurance, retirement), staffing (recruiting and hiring), labor-management relations, classification (determining the correct levels for pay of positions), staff training, performance evaluations, staff development, and affirmative action. There are so many different areas that an HRM has to be a generalist and knowledgeable in many different areas.

Although a few corrections HRMs major in human resources in college and then look for jobs, most do not begin their careers with a plan to work in this field. As entry-level HR jobs become available, HRMs look for individuals with good people, computer, and organizational skills to move into HR jobs as assistants, where they learn a lot about this area through specific training and work on the job.

HRMs note that the good things about the jobs include the variety, as there are not many routine, day-to-day things; they get to work on all the previously listed areas. As well, they enjoy dealing with staff, helping them with benefits, working out problems, and planning their retirements. HR staff get to know all the other staff, as they work with them on many issues. The "not so good" things about the job include having to deal with disciplinary actions (when staff members violate rules and are penalized) and having to actually deal with some very good people who just made a mistake and may be ashamed, humiliated, or even angry.

The kind of person who makes a good HR staffer has a lot of patience, is a little outgoing but not aggressive, and is seen as approachable, dependable, and reliable. HRMs give important advice to people—staff members who are planning to retire, wardens considering a new policy, managers who need to hire someone for a job—so they must be seen as credible. HRMs represent another correctional job that people seldom think about, but that plays a critical role in the success of a correctional agency.

ter than prisons. For sixty probation and parole agencies surveyed, it was reported that on January 1, 2001, they employed 72,066 people, of whom 67.3 percent were white, 23.2 percent were black, and 6.8 percent were Hispanic.[61]

These advances have not always been easy. Irwin points out that when minority staff were first recruited to rural prisons with predominantly white staff, some white staff felt that the nonwhite, urban officers would be more pro-inmate and less trustworthy and might undermine security, and did not easily accept them.[62] Some studies have suggested that nonwhite correctional officers experience more stress than their white counterparts, and black officers are more likely to quit their jobs than white officers, primarily because of conflicts with their supervisors.[63] Just as inmates become bitter and perceive many actions as racist when there is not a diverse workforce, minority staff can have some of the same feelings when they represent a small minority of the staff and do not feel fully accepted into their workplace.

Today, very few jurisdictions experience tension among their staff due to differences in race or ethnicity. While there will always be charges of discrimination even within diverse correctional staffs, the issue of the importance of diversity is not in question, and correctional staff recognize the safety needs to work together regardless of background, attitude, or philosophies. The challenge of supervising offenders is the common ground for all correctional staff and binds them as one to accomplish their mission.

The "An Insider's Experience" box illustrates the challenges I faced in trying to increase diversity in the Ohio department of corrections.

AN INSIDER'S EXPERIENCE: Increasing Minority Staff

When I became the director of the Ohio department of corrections, I inherited a department that had a very low proportion of minority staff. It was not that the department had a racist attitude or discriminated against minorities; there just had not been a focus on improving this issue. Almost all of the prisons were in rural locations, and there was no pool of minority applicants from which to hire. As well, with so few minorities already working at the prisons, there was no informal recruitment by family and friends encouraging good candidates to apply for jobs. The department also had no minorities as senior administrators in the headquarters and no minority wardens.

Governor Richard Celeste, for whom I worked, had come into office with a commitment to increase minority employment in the state, and was well aware of the poor record in my department. A large percentage of his cabinet was African Americans, and he quickly put in place an affirmative action hiring program. In one of my first major personnel moves (within a few weeks after becoming director), I promoted a current warden as my chief deputy, and replaced him with an outstanding black staff member. His appointment was welcomed by the black community and by our staff, who knew him to be extremely capable and deserving.

Nowhere was the lack of minority employees worse than at the maximum-security prison in Lucasville, at the most southern tip of Ohio, at which there was only one black person in a staff of more than five-hundred employees. Lucasville was the sole maximum-security prison for adults; more than 50 percent of inmates were black, and more than half were from Cleveland and other northern Ohio cities, more than two-hundred miles from Lucasville. At my first visit to the prison, I heard a story about the warden disciplining a correctional officer for making a racist comment over the loudspeaker as he called for all inmates to leave the yard and return to their cells.

To guide our affirmative action program, I hired a black human resources professional from Dayton who had experience and good ties with community action programs providing job and training assistance for urban minorities. Fred was full of energy and immedi-

ately set out to build ties between the prisons and the closest communities with a substantial minority population. He began to hold job fairs in communities, using local community action groups to host them and encourage attendance by minorities. I attended many of these job fairs myself, as a show of the department's commitment to hiring minority staff.

When we held the job fair in Portsmouth, a town about ten miles from Lucasville, we got an earful. Fred had organized the event, and the chief of personnel for the Lucasville prison and I attended. There was a really good turnout, with approximately fifty people (mostly African American) attending. Fred started with an overview of the types of jobs available and the reasons we were reaching out to the minority community in our recruitment efforts. But he was quickly interrupted with questions and complaints about our past hiring practices. There were allegations of racism in hiring and of driving off black staff members—allegedly in one case by putting sand into the gas tank of his car. I was really taken aback and could only reaffirm our commitment to do things differently at this point. The people there were not convinced, but simply said they would encourage applicants and see how we responded.

I am pleased to say that we were successful. As noted in an earlier "An Insider's Experience" box regarding the Lucasville prison, we received additional staff positions, and targeted adding minority employees with these additional positions. By the time I left Ohio, Lucasville had more than fifty black employees and was well on its way to ending the history of a predominantly white staff supervising a predominantly black inmate population. I even received a nice compliment in an interview that Congressman Louis Stokes, a senior black member of the U.S. Congress who had been very critical of the hiring practices of the department, did with the *Cleveland Plain Dealer* (the city's newspaper). I was not aware he was going to do it, but Congressman Stokes praised my leadership and cited the overall growth in the number of minority employees in the department. We had come a long way since that contentious job fair in Lucasville.

Effectiveness of Treatment Programs

One issue that has created controversy and influenced correctional policy over the past twenty-five years is the evaluation of the outcome of correctional treatment programs. While the public supports the concept of rehabilitation, and correctional officials value treatment programs for the stabilizing effect they have on offender populations, the bottom line is that there is an expectation that such programs reduce recidivism. Elected officials and advocates and opponents of rehabilitation all agree that in exchange for the dollars they are spending on such programs, there should be a crime reduction payback.

Support for rehabilitation dwindled after an early 1970s review by Lipton, Martinson, and Wilks of the effectiveness of correctional treatment. While finding a few isolated correlations between a treatment program and a reduction in recidivism, they identified no consistent findings that any single treatment program significantly reduced recidivism.[64] Therefore, their conclusion that "nothing works" led to the abandonment of the medical model of corrections and began the momentum for many states to move from indeterminate sentencing with a focus on changing the individual offender to determinant sentencing with an emphasis on deterrence and incapacitation.

There have been many methodological concerns about the early work of Martinson and the ability to actually evaluate correctional treatment programs based on recidivism. Many question the validity of using recidivism as a measure of the effectiveness of correctional programs, considering it unfair to expect correctional treatment to have a long-term impact by reducing recidivism. Recidivism can have varying definitions, including the commission of any new crime, commission of a felony during the period of community supervision, and return to prison. A reasonable length for posttreatment follow-up is also a concern. Can a correctional sanction or program be expected to have an impact on an offender for three or even five years after the termination of the sanction or program? Another concern is that social science research designs often have difficulty controlling for the many external and internal factors that can impact recidivism rates.

In a recent review of the effectiveness of correctional treatment, Cullen and Gendreau point out several limitations in the review by Martinson.[65] First, since the initial study, there have been developments in researchers' abilities to quantitatively synthesize and assess the impact of research findings, particularly through the use of **meta-analysis.** Meta-analysis statistically measures the average effect an intervention has on recidivism across all studies, while identifying and controlling for various conditions such as the characteristics of the offenders treated, the type of setting, and the study methodology. Second, while the review by Lipton, Martinson, and Wilks was comprehensive for that time, there were a limited number of studies per treatment category: "7 for casework/individual counseling; 15 for skill development; 12 for individual psychotherapy; 19 for group methods; and 20 for milieu therapy."[66] Third, the Lipton, Martinson, and Wilks review did not include cognitive-behavioral therapy programs, which have been found to be successful treatment approaches for offenders.[67] Finally, the review did not consider any impact or outcome other than recidivism, such as prison behavior or educational achievement.

Meta-analysis

a statistical measure of the average effect an intervention has on recidivism across all studies

Later studies revisit and question the "nothing works" concept regarding correctional treatment. In a 1975 analysis of the studies reviewed by Martinson, Palmer noted that 48 percent of the studies cited found a positive effect on recidivism.[68] And in 1990, Andrews and colleagues found that of the better-controlled studies, 40 percent found that treatment had a "positive effect."[69] In addition, the more recent use of meta-analysis has identified positive success of correctional treatment programs in reducing recidivism. A meta-analysis allows a much more sensitive consideration of the results of several studies considered together. Rather than, as Martinson and colleagues did, just tallying the number of studies that showed a statistically significant impact on recidivism caused by the correctional intervention, the computations of a meta-analysis allow the calculation of the effect of all studies, even if they individually do not result in a statistically significant outcome.

In a 1993 analysis of the impact of correctional treatment, Lipsey and Wilson reviewed ten meta-analyses and identified a 25 percent reduction of recidivism by psychological, educational, and behavioral correctional treatment programs.[70] And in 1995, Losel reviewed thirteen meta-analyses and found that the average impact from the treatment intervention would result in a recidivism rate of 45 percent for the treatment group and 55 percent for the control group.[71]

These findings make one reconsider the 1972 Martinson conclusion that "nothing works." However, in an era of tightening budgets, the question for the future is whether such findings will lead to increased funding for rehabilitative programs. This future issue is addressed in Chapter 16.

Chapter Review

SUMMARY

It is interesting to theorize why the growth in the prison population has been slowing. As a result of "tough on crime" legislation to send more offenders to prison for longer times and initiatives such as the war on drugs, the prison population in America grew by almost 600 percent in twenty years. Yet several factors now seem to be slowing that trend. Whether it is simply a demographic change with a lower percentage of the nation's population in the high-crime age, a need to find alternatives to incarceration to reduce budget demands, the incapacitative effect of incarcerating so many people, or a combination, for the first time in decades some states are actually experiencing a reduction in their prison population.

One definite truth is that the formation of correctional policies has become much more politicized than in the past. Elected officials (or those seeking office) are constantly espousing how they will take aggressive actions to protect citizens from dangerous criminals. Such rhetoric encourages sending more people to prison and makes it more difficult for those under community supervision to stay out of prison. Some individuals speculate that tightening budgets may force officials to reconsider constantly arguing for increased use of incarceration as a criminal sanction. Yet a variety of activities (enhancing the use of community alternatives, creating revenues, and contracting with the private sector) are being considered to try to reduce the budget crunch in order to fund correctional agencies.

Two very positive developments in corrections over the past twenty years that are expected to continue into the next decade are accreditation of correctional agencies and an increasing number of minority staff. During the late 1970s, correctional agencies searched for methods to increase their credibility and professionalism, both for management purposes and in the minds of the courts and with other public officials. The formation of a process of self-regulation and certification of meeting professional standards was developed and has been adopted by a large percentage of agencies and institutions. Yet this process is expensive and time-consuming, and several agencies have not yet decided that it is worth the investment.

As a result of riots, charges of racism, and an increasing sensitivity to the fact that correctional clients are predominantly minority group members, correctional agencies have aggressively targeted the recruitment and hiring of minority staff. This development is recognized as an effective management tool to better and more fairly handle offenders.

The results of more recent research into the effectiveness of correctional treatment programs are also significant for the future of corrections. The next question to be answered is, "If correctional treatment reduces recidivism and crime, is it not wise to invest more funds into treatment programs for offenders?" This significant question is further addressed in Chapter 16 regarding the future of corrections.

In the final chapter of this text, we look further into the future to investigate how these and other developments will affect correctional management and operations in the next two decades. The current paradigms are challenged and promising new approaches are examined. While many believe that the past twenty-five years represented a step backward in correctional thought and invention, many also believe that the future is very promising for those who want to shake up the status quo, reverse the "lock 'em up" mentality, and find new ways to better manage criminal offenders.

REVIEW QUESTIONS

1. What has occurred in regard to the size of the state prison population over the past three years?

2. What is the definition of *federalize* and how has federalization affected the populations of state and federal prisons?

3. List the reasons for a slowdown in the growth in the number of incarcerated offenders.

4. Who is Willie Horton and what role did he play in politicizing correctional policy?

5. What is the public's opinion regarding correctional sanctions and treatment programs?

6. What are four ways that correctional agencies use to reduce their operating costs?

7. In what ways can correctional agencies raise revenues from providing their services?

8. What is the role of the Commission on Accreditation for Corrections?

9. Why is it said that minorities are "overrepresented" in the correctional population?

10. What is a meta-analysis?

ENDNOTES

1. Paige M. Harrison and Jennifer C. Karberg, *Prison and Jail Inmates in Midyear 2002* (Washington, D.C.: U.S. Department of Justice, Bureau of Justice Statistics, April 2003).

2. Ibid.

3. Paige M. Harrison and Allen J. Beck, *Prisoners in 2001* (Washington, D.C.: U.S. Department of Justice, Bureau of Justice Statistics, July 2002), p. 2.

4. Harrison and Karberg, 2003, p. 2.

5. Ibid.

6. Ibid., p. 4.

7. James Austin and Garry Coventry, *Emerging Issues on Privatized Prisons* (Washington, D.C.: U.S. Department of Justice, Bureau of Justice Assistance, February 2001), p. xi.

8. Richard F. Culp, "The Rise and Stall of Prison Privatization" (paper presented at the Academy of Criminal Justice Sciences, Boston, Mass., March 2003).

9. Harrison and Karberg, 2003, p. 8.

10. Pretrial Services Resource Center, *A Second Look at Alleviating Jail Overcrowding: A Systems Perspective* (Washington, D.C.: U.S. Department of Justice, Bureau of Justice Assistance, October 2000), p. 2.

11. For a good review of this issue, see Joseph W. Rogers, "The Greatest Correctional Myth: Winning the War on Crime through Incarceration," in *Public Policy, Crime, and Criminal Justice*, 2nd ed., edited by Barry W. Hancock and Paul M. Sharp (Upper Saddle River, N.J.: Prentice Hall, 2000), pp. 308–321.

12. For a description of intermediate sanctions that have proven effective, see Richard P. Seiter, *Correctional Administration: Integrating Theory and Practice* (Upper Saddle River, N.J.: Prentice Hall, 2002), pp. 446–447.

13. Pretrial Services Resource Center, 2000, p. 66.

14. Alfred Blumstein and Allen J. Beck, "Population Growth in U.S. Prisons: 1980–1996," in *Prisons: A Re-view of Research*, edited by Michael Tonry and Joan Petersilia (Chicago: University of Chicago Press, 1999), pp. 17–62.

15. Rufus King, "It's Time to Open the Doors of Our Prisons," *Newsweek*, April 19, 1999, p. 10.

16. Sam C. Proband, "Corrections Leads State Budget Increases in FY 1997," *Overcrowded Times* 8, no. 4 (1997): 4.

17. John Irwin and James Austin, *It's About Time: America's Imprisonment Binge* (Belmont, Calif.: Wadsworth, 1994).

18. Joan Petersilia, *When Prisoners Come Home: Parole and Prisoner Reentry* (New York: Oxford University Press, 2003), p. 221.

19. Peter D. Hart Research Associates, *Changing Public Attitudes toward the Criminal Justice System* (New York: Open Society, February 2002).

20. Ibid.

21. S. E. Skovan, J. E. Scott, and E. T. Cullen, "Prison Crowding: Public Attitudes toward Strategies of Population Control," *Journal of Research in Crime and Delinquency* 25, no. 2 (1988): 150–169.

22. Barbara A. Sims, "Questions of Corrections: Public Attitudes toward Prison and Community-Based Programs," *Corrections Management Quarterly* 1, no. 1 (1997): 54.

23. Daniel Weintraub, "State Prison Guards Set to Ratify Rich New Contract," *Sacramento Bee*, February 10, 2002, p. E5.

24. See Joe Hallinan, *Going Up the River: Travels in a Prison Nation* (New York: Random House, 2002); Joel Caplan, "Policy for Profit: The Private-Prison Industry's Influence over Criminal Justice Legislation," *ACJS Today* 26, no. 1 (January/February 2003): 15–20.

25. Robert M. Freeman, *Correctional Organization and Management: Public Policy Challenges, Behavior,*

and Structure (Boston: Butterworth-Heinemann, 1999), p. 108.

26. Camille Graham Camp and George M. Camp, *The Corrections Yearbook, 1998* (Middletown, Conn.: Criminal Justice Institute, 1999), p. 87.

27. Camille Graham Camp and George M. Camp, *The 2001 Corrections Yearbook: Adult Corrections* (Middletown, Conn: The Criminal Justice Institute, 2002), p. 100.

28. Peter Greenwood et al., "Estimated Benefits and Costs of California's New Mandatory Sentencing Law," in *Three Strikes and You're Out,* edited by David Shichor and Dale K. Sechrest (Thousand Oaks, Calif.: Sage, 1996).

29. C. S. Baird, D. A. Holien, and J. A. Bakke, *Fees for Probation Services* (Washington, D.C.: U.S. Department of Justice, National Institute for Justice, 1986).

30. Camp and Camp, 2002, pp. 105–106.

31. M. Nolan, "Medical Co-Payment System: Nevada Department of Prisons" (paper presented at the annual conference of the American Correctional Health Services Association, Salt Lake City, Utah, April 1992).

32. Camp and Camp, 2002, p. 107.

33. Ibid., p. 109.

34. Ibid., p. 110.

35. Ibid., pp. 111–112.

36. Charles Logan, *Looking at Hidden Costs: Public and Private Corrections* (Washington, D.C.: National Institute of Justice, 1989).

37. Camp and Camp, 2002, pp. 82, 106.

38. Logan, 1989, pp. 52–54.

39. J. Hackett et al., *Issues in Contracting for the Private Operation of Prisons and Jails* (Washington, D.C.: U.S. Department of Justice, 1987).

40. Dale K. Sechrest and David Shichor, "Comparing Public and Private Correctional Facilities in California: An Exploratory Study," in *Privatization and the Provision of Correctional Services: Context and Consequences* edited by G. Larry Mays and Tara Gray (Cincinnati, Ohio: Anderson, 1996), p. 135.

41. James F. Blumstein and Mark A. Cohen, *The Interrelationship between Public and Private Prisons* (Corrections Corporation of America and the Association for Private Correctional and Treatment Organizations, April 2003), p. 1.

42. "Developments in the Law of Prisons: A Tale of Two Systems: Cost, Quality, and Accountability in Private Prisons," *Harvard Law Review* 115, no. 7 (May 2002): 1891.

43. Geoffrey F. Segal and Adrian T. Moore, *Weighing the Watchmen: Evaluating the Costs and Benefits of Outsourcing Correctional Services* (Los Angeles: Reason Public Policy Institute, January 2002), p. 17.

44. J. Austin and G. Coventry, *Emerging Issues on Privatized Prisons* (San Francisco: National Council of Crime and Delinquency, March 1999).

45. Culp, 2003.

46. Lonn Lanza-Kaduce, Karen F. Parker, and Charles W. Thomas, "A Comparative Recidivism Analysis of Re-leasees from Private and Public Prisons," *Crime and Delinquency* 45, no. 1 (1999): 28–47.

47. U.S. General Accounting Office, *Private and Public Prisons: Studies Comparing Operational Costs and/or Quality of Service* (Washington, D.C.: GAO, 1996).

48. Studies showing little evidence of cost savings include A. Cheung, *Prison Privatization and the Use of Incarceration* (Washington, D.C.: Sentencing Project, January 2002); P. Mattera and M. Khan, *Jail Breaks: Economic Development Subsidies Given to Private Prisons* (Washington, D.C.: Institute on Taxation and Economic Policy, October 2001).

49. Scott D. Camp and Gerald G. Gaes, "Growth and Quality of U.S. Private Prisons: Evidence from a National Survey," *Criminology and Public Policy* (July 2002): 427–449.

50. E. C. Hughes, "Professions," in *The Professions in America,* edited by Kenneth S. Lynn (Boston: Houghton-Mifflin, 1965), p. 4.

51. American Correctional Association, *Standards for Adult Correctional Institutions,* 3rd ed. (Lanham, Md.: American Correctional Association, 1990).

52. Ibid., p. vii.

53. Camp and Camp, 2002, pp. 96–97.

54. Elizabeth Ward, "Accreditation: A Positive Step toward Facility Improvement," *Corrections Today* (February 1995): 78–80.

55. Bureau of Justice Statistics, *Correctional Populations in the United States* (Washington, D.C.: U.S. Department of Justice, 1997).

56. Bureau of Justice Statistics, "Correctional Populations in the United States," http://www.ojp.usdoj.gov/bjs/glance/tables (accessed January 8, 2003).

57. Harrison and Karberg, 2003, p. 11.

58. Ibid.

59. Camp and Camp, 2002, p. 150.

60. Ibid., p. 151.

61. Ibid., p. 219.

62. John Irwin, "The Changing Social Structure of the Men's Correctional Prison," in *Corrections and Punishment,* edited by D. Greenberg (Beverly Hills, Calif.: Sage, 1977), pp. 21–40.

63. Susan Philliber, "Thy Brother's Keeper: A Review of Literature on Correctional Officers," *Justice Quarterly* 4, no.1 (1987): 9–33.

64. Douglas Lipton, Robert Martinson, and Judith Wilks, *The Effectiveness of Correctional Treatment and What Works: A Survey of Treatment Evaluation Studies* (New York: Praeger, 1975).

65. Francis T. Cullen and Paul Gendreau, "Assessing Correctional Rehabilitation: Policy, Practice, and Prospects," in *Policies, Processes, and Decisions of the Criminal Justice System,* edited by Julie Horney (Washington, D.C.: U.S. Department of Justice, National Institute of Justice, 2000), pp. 109–175.

66. Ibid., p. 127.

67. See D. A. Andrews, Ivan Zinger, Robert D. Hoge, James Bonta, Paul Gendreau, and Francis D. Cullen, "Does Correctional Treatment Work? A Clinically Relevant and Psychologically Informed Meta-Analysis," *Criminology* 28 (August 1990): 369–404; D. A. Andrews and James Bonta, *The Psychology of Criminal Conduct,* 2nd ed. (Cincinnati, Ohio: Anderson, 1998).

68. Ted Palmer, "Martinson Revisited," *Journal of Research in Crime and Delinquency* 12 (July 1975): 133–152.

69. Andrews et al., 1990, p. 374.

70. Mark W. Lipsey and David B. Wilson, "The Efficacy of Psychological, Educational, and Behavioral Treatment," *American Psychologist* 48, no. 12 (1993): 1181–1209.

71. Friedrich Losel, "The Efficacy of Correctional Treatment: A Review and Synthesis of Meta-Evaluations," in *What Works: Reducing Reoffending,* edited by James McGuire (West Sussex, England: Wiley, 1995).

Chapter 16

AFTER READING THIS CHAPTER, YOU SHOULD BE ABLE TO:

1. Identify some of the key questions facing corrections in the next ten years.

2. List the pros and cons of our current approach to sentencing criminal offenders.

3. Describe the problems with the current approach and discuss whether it can be successful and continue as is.

4. Identify the recent methodological advancements that aid researchers in determining whether correctional treatment programs are successful.

5. Outline current strategies for supervising offenders in the community and discuss forces that will push them to continue as is or change in some manner.

6. Define restorative justice and list its benefits over current sentencing approaches.

7. Explain how prisonization is an obstacle to successful reentry to the community.

8. List methods and changes in procedures that will counteract or reduce the impact of prisonization on inmates.

9. Identify the positive benefits of a career in corrections.

10. Decide whether a career in corrections is right for you.

Questions Regarding the Future of Corrections

KEY TERMS

accountability
rebirth in rehabilitation
invisible policy
global positioning system
reparation
parallel universe
career in corrections

Introduction

At this point in the textbook, we have covered all of the basic operational approaches and issues facing corrections today. In Part 1 of the text ("Putting Corrections into Perspective"), we reviewed the history of crime and punishment and our traditional and current approaches to sentencing. In Part 2 ("Correctional Policy and Operations"), we examined how correctional programs and policies developed and are currently operated, including jails, probation, intermediate sanctions, prisons, postrelease supervision, and prisoner reentry. In Part 3 ("Correctional Clients"), we learned about adult males and females, juveniles, and other special clients of correctional agencies. Part 4 ("Prison Life") was written to give students a realistic appreciation for life either working or living in a prison. Topics included how prisons are managed and how inmates and staff cope with the authority and control necessary for accomplishing the mission of prisons. We also read about the approaches for providing custody and treatment within a prison, the legal issues in prison operations, and the controversies around the imposition of the death penalty. In Part 5 ("Correctional Challenges"), we examined the current issues facing corrections and will try to answer some of the most critical questions regarding the future of correctional operations.

Correctional textbooks take a variety of approaches in examining the future of corrections. Most identify issues that are unresolved or continue to confront correctional policymakers and practitioners. Others recite facts and figures regarding crime and correctional practice and leave it to the reader to interpret what these mean. In this textbook, a different approach is taken; we address some of the most critical questions regarding the future of corrections including the following:

- Can our current approach to sentencing and corrections be successful and continue?
- Will rehabilitation continue as a primary correctional goal?
- Will supervision of offenders in the community change in approach?
- Do we need a new paradigm for sentencing and corrections?
- Can we reduce the impact of prisonization and improve the successful reentry of prisoners to the community?
- Is corrections a good career choice for me?

To consider these questions, students are given the opportunity to review relevant data and developing controversies. These questions are addressed fully and then an answer is given. There are no assurances that this is the "right" or "correct" answer, and only the future will reveal the true result. However, by asking and then answering these questions, students, instructors, and others have an avenue to debate for themselves how these issues will be addressed. We know for certain that corrections will continue to change. We also may be able to project the forces that will affect change in corrections. What is less certain is the result of correctional operations and how these questions may be shaped in the future. For that matter, it is even somewhat uncertain that these questions will continue to be critical issues ten or fifteen years from now. The challenge (and fun) is speculating and developing contingencies for the future of corrections.

Can Our Current Approach to Sentencing and Corrections Be Successful and Continue?

The answer to this question first depends on what we are trying to accomplish. As suggested in Chapter 1, the five goals of punishment, deterrence, incapacitation, rehabilitation, and restitution have varied in emphasis over the years. The past two centuries have seen many swings in sentencing approaches and philosophies. During the 1800s, sentencing was a mix of punishment and rehabilitation. For offenders considered to have the potential to be productive and law-abiding citizens, probation was granted, with an emphasis on helping them find work and deal with the problems that led to their criminality. More hardened criminals were sent to prison for determinate terms, subject to hard labor and strict discipline, with few rehabilitative programs to prepare them for release.

By the 20th century, the concept of parole was being adopted in most states, and with that came the emphasis on rehabilitation. Over the last two decades, an emphasis on offender accountability has precipitated the reemergence of determinate sentencing as the primary sentencing approach. While this emphasis continues, there has more recently been additional consideration of the victim and focus on restitution as a sentencing goal and correctional practice.

Currently, the predominant approach to sentencing and corrections is based on punishment, deterrence, and incapacitation. Many states have opted to abolish indeterminate sentencing and have abandoned the rehabilitative philosophy. Sentences are continually enhanced, with the belief that if we lengthen sentences, at some point potential offenders will recognize that crime does not pay, and they will be deterred from future criminality. Even if deterrence does not work, advocates suggest that long sentences will at least incapacitate offenders and result in their inability to commit further crimes against society. As a result of these changes, state and federal prison populations grew more rapidly than in any other period since prisons were first established, and reached 1,355,748 at midyear 2002.[1]

This approach to sentencing has placed far more people under correctional supervision than we have ever had in the past, and the incarceration rate has continued to climb. By the end of the twentieth century, more than six million offenders were either in prison, in jail, or under supervision in the community. The Bureau of Justice Statistics Correctional Surveys report a 252 percent increase in the number of offenders on probation, a 243 percent increase in the number of offenders in jail, a 316 percent increase in the number of inmates in prison, and a 231 percent increase in the number of offenders on parole between 1980 and 2001.[2]

With the increase in the number of offenders has come a comparable growth in the dollars committed to operate correctional agencies. In fiscal year 1991, the combined budgets for state and federal adult correctional agencies totaled $18.1 billion. By fiscal year 2001, these budgets increased 67 percent to $35.6 billion and represented 4.3 percent of the total budget of state and federal governments.[3] The Bureau of Justice Statistics reports that from 1982 through 1997, spending for corrections increased 381 percent, far exceeding the increase in police and judicial spending. Correctional agency spending is expected to continue to increase. There were 83,000 new prison beds under construction in 1998, 41,368 in 1999, and 47,476 in 2000, with $2.8 billion allocated to new prison construction in 2000 and another $2.7 billion budgeted in 2001.[4]

The bottom line is that the current "tough on crime" approach to sentencing has significantly increased the number of prisoners, the number of people under correctional supervision, and the budgets allocated to correctional agencies. But has this policy made citizens safer or less likely to be victims of street crime? From 1991 to 2000, crime decreased significantly, from a Crime Index rate of 5,897 to 4,124 offenses per every 100,000 citizens (a decrease of 30 percent), reducing it to rates not seen since 1975.[5] Unfortunately, primarily due to extensive media coverage of crime, citizens continue to believe that crime is increasing.[6] But should the credit for the decrease in crime be attributed to the deterrent or incapacitative effect of current sentencing practices, or are there other reasons why crime rates have decreased?

In an interesting analysis of the impact of the increased use of incarceration on the decline of crime rates during the 1990s, Spelman estimates that about

The increase in the number of inmates has led to the construction and opening of several new prisons across the United States
Courtesy of the Ohio Department of Rehabilitation and Correction.

one-quarter of the declining crime rates during the 1990s can be attributed to the increase in the number of offenders incarcerated during that period.[7] Other authors suggest that the rest of the crime drop is attributable to making it more difficult for potential youthful offenders to obtain guns, a reduction in the number of new users of crack cocaine and therefore a reduction in the demand (and therefore number of dealers) for the drug, and a good economy with available employment for those who want to work.[8]

The answer to the question of whether this sentencing approach can be successful is, "yes, marginally." There is no question that by locking up all the people whom we have imprisoned over the past fifteen years, we do reduce crime to some extent. However, these sentencing practices and the budget required to maintain them come at a very high cost. Not only are taxpayers pouring billions more dollars into the correctional system than two decades ago, but there is high "opportunity cost" as well. Every dollar that must be directed to correctional agencies cannot be directed toward programs believed to prevent future crimes, such as prenatal care, improved nutrition for poor families, improvements in educational opportunities and achievement, substance abuse treatment, enhanced job training and employment development, and mental health treatment.

The further question of whether these sentencing approaches will continue is intermingled with the first answer. During the 1990s, when the economy was strong and the federal government and most states had a budget surplus, legislatures did not have to make tough budget choices of what to fund. However, with the downturn in the economy, lower tax revenues, and spending deficits running across almost every governmental unit, these budget decisions are much more difficult. Government officials are now seeking **accountability**; they are challenged to consider how to get the best "bang for their buck" and must take into account how

Accountability

holding one responsible for accomplishing objectives in a cost-efficient manner effective programs are in achieving their overall goals. Today, federal, state, and local governments are looking for ways to reduce the cost of corrections and are more willing to consider alternatives to incarceration or even different sentencing approaches that result in shorter time served for nonviolent offenders.

On August 9, 2003, in a speech to the annual meeting of the American Bar Association in San Francisco, U.S. Supreme Court Justice Anthony M. Kennedy became the most visible and prominent individual to question the efficacy of our sentencing practices. Justice Kennedy, a moderate conservative appointed to the Court by former President Ronald Reagan, stated, "Our resources are misspent, our punishments too severe, our sentences too long."[9] Kennedy described the fifteen-year-old federal sentencing guidelines that give judges a narrow range of punishments for crimes as leading to longer terms than were previously common and needing to be revisited and revised downward.

The current budget challenge and an increasing number of views such as those by Justice Kennedy are likely to result in a marginal change to the current "tough on crime" approach and overall reliance on deterrence and incapacitation. The minimal reduction of crime and the high cost of imprisonment and community supervision require a reconsideration of the success of current sentencing practices. The answer to the second part of the question, "Can our current approach to sentencing and corrections be successful *and continue?*" is no, it cannot continue. It is poor public policy to continue an approach that returns to the taxpayer so little for the resources committed. That leads to an even more difficult question—what can replace the current sentencing approach? One area receiving attention and consideration (described in the next section) has been the potential to decrease crime and recidivism through rehabilitative programs.

Will Rehabilitation Continue as a Primary Correctional Goal?

As noted in Chapter 15, since Martinson and colleagues reviewed the success of correctional treatment programs and concluded that "nothing works" in the early 1970s, rehabilitation gradually took a backseat to other correctional goals such as punishment, deterrence, and incapacitation.[10] The reasoning was simple and difficult to argue. Corrections had been following the medical model of corrections for the previous twenty years. Under this model, it was believed that offenders have underlying problems that are the cause of their criminality that must be diagnosed and treated. However, if there is no evidence that correctional treatment results in a reduction of recidivism, why continue to invest dollars and staff resources in it? Why not give up on rehabilitation, let potential offenders know that they will be held accountable for their criminal acts, and punish law violations severely with lengthy periods of incarceration? It is obvious that society is best protected when offenders are removed from the community and put in prison. Therefore, incapacitating offenders through imprisonment enhances public safety in the short term. And in the longer term, it was argued that public safety is enhanced by the deterrent value that these lengthy sentences have both on individual offenders and on society as a whole.

Proponents of rehabilitation and the medical model in the late 1970s and early 1980s found that they were losing ground. Many elected officials and policymakers met their arguments that we cannot give up on rehabilitation with understanding. However, with continuous media reports on the increase in violence and other crimes during this period resulting in an increased fear of crime and anger toward criminals by the public, these elected officials were not likely to risk their chances of reelection by arguing against longer sentences for criminals. As a result, fifteen states and the federal government ended the use of indeterminate sentencing and parole, twenty states severely limited the parole-eligible inmate population, and only fifteen states continued the use of full discretionary parole. In 1977, more than 70 percent of prisoners were released on discretionary parole. Yet by 1997, only 28 percent of inmates were released by a parole board after serving an indeterminate sentence.[11]

Since the mid-1980s, criminal sentencing has focused on public safety rather than on changing behavior through treatment of the offender. And indeterminate sentencing has been replaced with determinate sentencing, often based on the justice model, in which the individual characteristics of the offender are unimportant in the sentencing decision; the sentence is based almost totally on the severity of the crime and the past criminal history of the offender. As well, many states implemented mandatory minimum sentences, three-strikes laws, and truth-in-sentencing provisions in their sentencing codes.

Mandatory minimum sentences require that for certain crimes (violent crimes, crimes using a gun, distribution of narcotics) or certain types of offenders (habitual criminals, sexual predators), there must be a sentence to prison for a minimum term. The sentencing judge does not have an option to impose a sentence of probation or a fine, or to suspend the sentence. Three-strikes laws are a legislative mandate that judges must sentence third-time felons to extremely long or life prison sentences. These laws were intended to protect society from habitual law violators by incapacitating them with long sentences in prison. And truth-in-sentencing (TIS) laws require inmates to serve 85 percent of their sentence before they are eligible for release. TIS statutes dramatically reduce the amount of good time that prison officials may grant inmates as incentives for good behavior or program participation.[12] The purpose of these laws is again to satisfy the public that offenders are getting their "just deserts" from their criminal law violation, and not getting their sentences cut short through administrative decisions by prison administrators or parole boards.

The result of these sentencing changes has been a gradual reduction in the proportion of inmates serving an indeterminate sentence and a change in philosophy to deterrence and incapacitation rather than rehabilitation. Inmates are serving significantly longer prison terms and participate in fewer rehabilitative or prerelease programs. Lynch and Sabol found that the average time served by inmates released in 1990 was twenty-two months; those released in 1998 served an average of twenty-seven months.[13] The authors also examined program participation between 1991 and 1997 prison release cohorts. They found that from 1991 to 1997, the percentage of inmates participating in vocational training declined from 32 percent to 27 percent, while education participation declined from 42 percent to 34 percent.

In addition, a recent survey indicated that a relatively small percentage of inmates are currently participating in rehabilitative programs. On January 1, 2001, state and federal prisons reported only 120,687 inmates (12.9 percent) in drug treatment programs, a decline of more than 50,000 inmates since 2000.[14] On the same date, only 77,380 inmates (6.3 percent) were assigned to prison industries, a program extremely successful in improving work skills and reducing recidivism.[15] Only 12,149 inmates (3.4 percent) were enrolled in sex offender programs on January 1, 2001.[16] Only 59,180 inmates were placed in halfway houses during 2000, only 9.9 percent of the 596,191 inmates released from state and federal prisons that year.[17] And during 2000, only 40,164 inmates were placed in work or study release.[18]

Even with this reduction in the number of inmates participating in rehabilitative programs, there have been positive developments for advocates of rehabilitation. First, there is still public support for rehabilitation. Over the past two decades, as a punitive attitude about crime, sentencing, and offenders developed, there has never been a total withdrawal of support for rehabilitation. In a 1996 survey, 53 percent of citizens ranked retribution as the most important purpose of sentencing adult criminals, although 21 percent still ranked rehabilitation as most important.[19]

There is also public acceptance of treatment programs for offenders. A 1997 survey of citizen attitudes in Ohio indicated strong support for correctional treatment programs and for rehabilitation as the primary purpose for a sentence of imprisonment.[20] Additionally, results from the National Opinion Survey of Crime and Justice provided evidence for support for rehabilitative programs, as 93 percent support prisoners learning a skill or trade, 94 percent support requiring offenders to be able to read and write before release from prison, and 88 percent support inmate work programs.[21]

Second, there is increasing evidence of positive results from treatment programs. This evidence has come from additional evaluations of the success of rehabilitative programs, as well as improved methods of measuring the effect of such research outcomes. The Martinson study found 231 evaluations in which the result was examined independently, with the conclusion that "with few and isolated exceptions, the rehabilitative efforts that have been reported so far have had no appreciable effect on recidivism."[22] However, the use of more sophisticated techniques for reviews of research has provided evidence of the success of correctional treatment. One technique is the use of meta-analysis to quantify research results. As noted in Chapter 15, meta-analysis allows researchers to examine many different outcome studies of programs, identify their individual indicators of success, and link those to each other to determine overall success of any particular treatment modality. Gendreau, Goggin, and Smith explain what meta-analysis is:

> Consider how one would assess an individual's academic performance. . . . If the grades were poor, was it due to poor study habits, "tough" courses, and so on? In order to obtain a more accurate assessment of the magnitude of the results (i.e., average grade) and how they may vary by age, study habits, and so forth across all undergraduates, then the data could be assessed on a sample of 100 students. Essentially, this is what meta-analysis does, but in this case, the individual represents one "research study."[23]

Another new approach to analyzing the effect of correctional treatment is the use of systematic reviews of evaluations, identifying studies on a particular modality, and analyzing their modality impact through the group of studies. Farrington, Petrosino, and Welsh describe how systematic reviews can be useful in identifying key indicators of treatment success across several studies.[24] Finally, researchers have also begun to measure the quality of correctional programs in assessing their effectiveness. High-quality treatment programs are based on identified offender needs, are targeted at high-risk offenders, are delivered outside the correctional environment, are fully implemented, and include follow-up after completion of treatment.[25] Using techniques to quantify the quality of a treatment program and include quality as a variable influencing program outcome has provided additional evidence of the success of high-quality treatment programs. Using these updated methods, many reviews of treatment programs now conclude that certain categories of treatment programs are effective when implemented in a quality fashion.[26]

The new information regarding the effectiveness of correctional treatment has led to increased support by elected officials and policymakers and to a **rebirth in rehabilitation**. The public wants criminals punished but is sympathetic to rehabilitative programs. Elected officials recognize this and are willing to fund rehabilitation programs that make a difference. However, rehabilitative programs have to prove that they are cost-effective and save the government at least as much money

Rebirth in rehabilitation a return to support for correctional treatment programs

Rehabilitative programs such as training in computers and office skills are important to prepare inmates for work and success after release.
Courtesy of the Ohio Department of Rehabilitation and Correction.

as they cost. It is much easier for a correctional official to argue for expending funds for correctional programs by citing data that illustrate how investing in the program reduces recidivism and protects society. Elected officials find it easy to promote and vote to fund programs on this basis, rather than because they may help offenders improve their deficiencies. Therefore, it is expected that rehabilitation will experience a rebirth, receive additional funds, and expand in its importance as a goal of corrections and as an essential element of correctional operations. The "An Insider's Experience" box provides readers with a little background in forming my personal opinion regarding rehabilitation.

AN INSIDER'S EXPERIENCE: Education Really Does Work

I guess I am like a lot of other people in that I did not have a real knowledge of or opinion on the question of whether correctional treatment works when I first began work in a prison. At my first prison in Pleasanton, California, the inmates were all young and pretty unsophisticated in their criminal histories. Although some had committed serious crimes, they were not what you would call hardened criminals. Quite frankly, I thought most of them got wrapped up in their criminal activities without intent to be a criminal, as most had been arrested for importing drugs and were just doing it to make a fast buck. I did not see that too many of them would have a problem being productive and law-abiding citizens after their release. So I never really thought too much about the impact of the programs that we offered at Pleasanton.

My next job was as the U.S. Penitentiary at Leavenworth, Kansas. These guys were just the opposite; they were hardened criminals with a long history of crime, most of them violent crimes. They looked and acted prisonized, never showing weakness, living the prison lifestyle, and not wanting to act too interested in programs unless they thought it would look good to the parole board. I was the assistant to the warden. It was a great job—somewhat of a training position in that I had the opportunity to get involved in almost every area of the prison, yet without the responsibility to supervise anything. The warden gave me several responsible assignments, such as implementing unit management in a very traditional prison.

On one of my assignments, I began to spend a lot of time in the education department. I got to know and spent time with Lonnie, the supervisor of education. Lonnie had had a very successful career, becoming a warden of two different federal prisons before he retired and became a warden for a private correctional company. Lonnie was the first person who really described for me how correctional education operated. He told me about the mandatory program in which inmates testing below a 6.0 grade level on a literacy assessment test had to enroll in school for ninety days, and then they could opt out if it was not for them. At that time, Leavenworth had a very active college education program, as Pell grants could be used to pay for college classes, and several inmates were attending classes offered by a local college.

Lonnie pointed some things out to me. He walked me around some of the GED and college classrooms, asking me if I recognized any of the inmates. At that time, Leavenworth held about 1,800 inmates, so I would not have been surprised if I did not recognize any. However, I was surprised that I did recognize many, and extremely surprised as to why. Many of the inmates actively involved in classes were known to me to have been some of the serious troublemakers

and "tough guys" in the prison. I wondered if they were involved in some type of scam that brought them to the education department.

Lonnie went on to tell me about how so many inmates who had previously been troublemakers came to education because they had to for the first ninety days. They had been kicked out of or quit traditional schools because they just didn't fit in. Yet in prison they could work at their own pace, everyone there was like them, and they did not act out or goof off just to play a role. They began to make progress, passed tests, and then earned their GED. He told me about several guys who had been disciplinary problems in prison, but were now working on their college degrees, and he showed me the long list of inmates who were going to earn an associate's degree, and a few who were earning a bachelor's degree.

I was sold. It was obvious to me that education provided the turning point in these guys' lives. They had always been a failure at everything in the community, in school, in their jobs, and with their families. Now they were succeeding at something, and this success was leading to more success. I began to think of these guys almost like the inmates at Pleasanton. I could not imagine them not becoming productive and law-abiding citizens after they got out of prison.

Will Supervision of Offenders in the Community Change in Approach?

While many more offenders are supervised in the community than are in prison and jail, the style of supervision is changing, affecting the number of revocations and subsequent imprisonment. Current supervision strategies show little tolerance for risk, special surveillance and types of conditions have expanded, and offenders are classified and supervised as aggregate groups of risk categories rather than as individuals. These changes have some very negative collateral consequences, yet it is difficult to envision how these changes can be reversed. Throughout history, probation and parole supervision used a casework approach; officers considered it their responsibility to work with offenders in finding jobs, getting into treatment programs, dealing with problems, and successfully completing supervision. However, the casework focus of helping offenders has been slowly transitioning into one in which officers use a surveillance approach to supervision of community offenders. This approach emphasizes monitoring and enforcing compliance with the conditions of supervision, timely detection of violations, and expeditious revocation when violations occur.

This transition has occurred for many reasons. First, more conditions are placed on offenders under community supervision, and therefore a violation and its detection are more likely. Adams and Roth found that between 1987 and 1996, the percentage of federal offenders with at least one special condition (participation in substance abuse, drug testing, electronic monitoring) increased from

One example of additional conditions and methods of surveillance is the regular use of a Breathalyzer to detect whether an offender supervised in the community has been drinking.
Photo by Richard P. Seiter.

67 percent to 91 percent.[27] During 2000, states involved in probation and parole supervision reported conducting 6,549,519 drug tests and revoked 16,598 offenders as a result of a positive test for drug use.[28] As well, on January 1, 2001, these agencies reported supervising 113,742 offenders on intensive caseloads, 16,366 on electronic monitoring, and 158,941 on special caseloads.[29]

Second, there is very limited tolerance for risk to the community. Instead of focusing on rehabilitation and characteristics of individual offenders, parole and probation agencies now use actuarial methods to classify offenders and manage risk for aggregate populations. There are many positives to these actuarial methods, such as matching offender risk to reoffend to the allocation of resources. However, these actuarial assessments can result in a psychology of adding surveillance techniques rather than treatment programs to an individual's supervision.

Third, the hiring and training of community supervision officers has changed. Historically, officers had a social work or clinical background and were trained in counseling and rehabilitation of offenders. Today, the majority of entering officers have a college degree with a major of criminal justice, with less than one-third majoring in psychology, sociology, or social work.[30] Training and orientation for officers is increasingly in line with that of law enforcement officers. In a recent survey, forty-three of sixty responding agencies authorize their parole or probation officers to carry weapons;[31] in twenty-eight of fifty-eight agencies, probation and parole officers have full peace officer status, carrying weapons and having arrest powers.[32]

Finally, community officers and supervisors must be sensitive to public safety. Even the most professional staff are cautious when it comes to handling even minor technical violations by community offenders. There is limited benefit, yet significant risk, if an officer tries to work with an offender, allowing a minor violation, in an attempt to deal with a more significant issue such as substance abuse. If that offender later commits a serious crime, the actions of the officer for not acting on the minor violation will be called into question, and in some jurisdictions, the officer or agency can be liable to the victim of a subsequent crime.

As a result of these changes in community supervision, the rate of revocations and resulting incarcerations has increased significantly, and most revocations are for only technical violations of supervision rather than commitment of a new felony. In a recent survey of state correctional agencies, thirty-five responding states admitted 728,296 offenders to prison during 2000. Of this number, 63,404 (8.7 percent) were probation violators, 182,100 (25 percent) were parole violators, and 15,638 (2.1 percent) were violators of some other type of postrelease supervision.[33] Overall, approximately one in three of all prison admissions were offenders revoked from community supervision. And in 1998, the Bureau of Justice Statistics identified 170,253 reported parole violators, representing more than 23 percent of new state prison admissions.[34] Yet in 1980, parole violators constituted only 18 percent of all admissions.[35] In addition, of all recent probation or parole violators, only about one in five are for commission of a new crime, and the rest are for technical violations only.[36]

This trend of moving community supervision more toward a surveillance approach and the resulting increase in the number of violations and revocations represents an **invisible policy**, not passed by legislatures or formally adopted as a policy by correctional agencies. More so, these practices result from a natural and gradual move in emphasis by individual officers to avoid risk and lessen the likelihood of criticism or legal responsibility. While it can be argued that this is a positive development for public safety, it can also be argued that it is expensive and short-sighted. Violating offenders for minor violations and returning them to prison usually results in their returning to prison for only ninety days to one year. Once released, offenders are no better prepared for successful reentry and have probably done little to reduce any personal problem such as substance abuse, poor work habits, or family problems. This is a catch-22 for community officers who do not want to risk a chance of new crimes by those they supervise, yet recognize that such revocations do little to reduce recidivism in the long run.

While it is difficult to answer the question of whether supervision of offenders in the community will change, it is proposed that this approach to supervision will have to change for many reasons. First, no level of supervision in the community can prevent offenders from committing further crimes. We have created intensive supervision caseloads with only twenty-five offenders under the supervision of an officer. We have used electronic monitoring to know when offenders are not at home. We have begun to use **global positioning systems** (GPSs) to track offenders throughout their community. However, the role of probation, parole, or other community sentences is not to "incapacitate" offenders and totally prevent them from committing crimes. Offenders placed in the community are there either because they are not such a serious criminal or serious risk to society as to warrant incarceration or because they have served their prison sentence and are ready to return to the community. An understanding of community supervision is that these offenders have a level of responsibility (reinforced with supervision) that reduces the likelihood of their committing crimes. It is impractical to expect community supervision to stop determined offenders from committing more crimes, no matter what intensity of supervision or what technologies are used.

The second reason we must change our supervision approach is that it is resulting in too much expense with no proof that it is worth the cost. Through our increase in the intensity of supervision, we discover more technical violations of probation, parole, or other community placement. These technical violations, without commission of a new crime, therefore result in thousands of offenders being sent to prison each year. It is difficult to say how many would have committed a serious crime if allowed to remain in the community. However, we do know that these incarcerations are costing taxpayers hundreds of millions of dollars each year. We must reconsider what price we are willing to pay to potentially prevent future crimes, particularly when the violation and imprisonment lasts only a few

Invisible policy
a practice that is not formalized in statute or written policy, but which develops through a consistent set of pressures and influences

Global positioning system
a system that uses a satellite to receive a signal from a transmitter and identify its location to a monitoring station

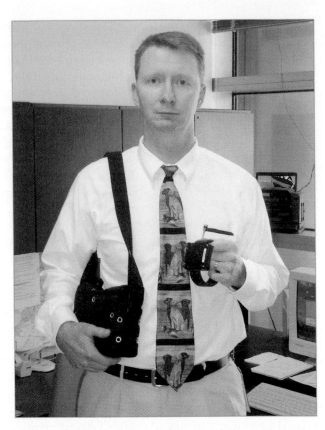

The use of GPSs is not unusual in modern supervision of offenders in the community. The only equipment needed for the offender is a somewhat larger ankle bracelet and small bag, as illustrated by this probation officer.
Photo by Richard P. Seiter.

months and then we must again face the issue of successfully supervising the same offender in the community.

Changing the approach to community supervision will not be easy. We have created a "prison recycling monster," in that it is often considered irresponsible for community officers to not act on these technical violations, and can even result in the agency being found legally and financially responsible for further crimes committed by an offender whose supervision is not revoked after technical violations. Therefore, we send violators to prison, because we have so few options. Yet a change in supervision will occur. It will be based on the finding that success in the community measured by reductions in recidivism is more likely through a balance of casework or treatment and monitoring than by increases in surveillance.[37] Therefore, community supervision will gradually move back toward the casework style, in which officers emphasize treatment for meeting offender needs but still hold offenders accountable for their failure to meet conditions of their community placement.

Do We Need a New Paradigm for Sentencing and Corrections?

In many people's minds, we do need a new paradigm for sentencing and corrections. We have been using the same sentencing model for two centuries, and over the past twenty years, we have increasingly relied on incarceration as a sanction for crimes. This continued reliance on imprisonment is costing society a tremendous amount of money, wasting lives, and doing little to prepare offenders to be successful in the community. But what options make sense in meeting the many goals of corrections? One model that seems to deserve consideration is the use of community justice or restorative justice.

Community or restorative justice is an alternative model for sentencing offenders. *Restorative justice* is a sentencing approach that is future-oriented, focuses on restoration for the victim and society, and is less expensive for the taxpayer. This model is seen as more desirable than traditional sentencing and punishing offenders, which does little for society and the victims of crimes and focuses only in a reactive way on offenders. Victims have historically been left out of the criminal justice process, and only recently have there been programs to assist victims and ensure that their voices are heard throughout the process. Restorative justice also looks to avoid the high cost to taxpayers of imprisonment, particularly for nonviolent offenders. Instead of spending large amounts of money to punish and incarcerate those offenders who represent little risk to their communities, restorative justice emphasizes that they "make right" the harm they have caused.

Restorative justice sentencing models shift the focus from being reactive and punishment-oriented, from cost to the taxpayers, and from a lack of involvement by the victims. The first of two major elements of restorative justice is to hold offenders accountable for the harm they have done and find ways for them to repair the damage. With restorative justice, offenders are forced to face and understand the damage their crime has caused and to actively participate in repairing the injury from their crime. The second element is the active involvement of the victim in determining the proper sanction for the crime. Minnesota was one of the first jurisdictions to implement restorative justice sentencing, and describe this victim focus as follows:

> Restorative justice is a philosophical framework that . . . balances the needs of three primary stakeholders: the victim, the offender, and the community. This is contrasted with a justice system that seeks as its primary aim to catch, convict, and punish offenders . . . Restorative values include responsibility, accountability, and participation by all who have a stake in the outcome, repairing the harm, making things right, and supporting the victim.[38]

In a pure restorative justice model, the offender and victim both participate in the decision regarding sentencing for the offense, focusing on what the offender can do to repair the damage. The victim provides input, in that he or she may want an apology, restitution, or a punitive sentence of imprisonment. The offender must accept responsibility, recognize the harm he or she has caused, and agree to a reparative approach to correct the harm. Some victims are hesitant to be fully involved in the process, or particularly to have any direct interaction with offenders. Therefore, it is not necessary for the parties to be together to discuss **reparation**, yet a face-to-face discussion is believed to go a long way in furthering the feeling of involvement by the victim and forcing the offender to put a face to the crime committed.

An interesting sidebar of the use of restorative justice is the benefit it can have in the public's confidence in the justice system. In the mid-1990s, the Vermont Department of Corrections recognized that it had a lack of confidence and support from the general public and implemented a restorative justice sentencing model with one objective to improve its image. Vermont created "two kinds of sentencing tracks, each to address a different sentencing purpose."[39] As illustrated in Figure 16.1, offenders who commit serious crimes are placed in the risk management track, which focuses on "incapacitating" the offender by providing a range of security, treatment, supervision, and surveillance to manage that risk and protect the public.

Reparation
the acts by offenders to repair the damage done by their crimes

VERMONT DEPARTMENT OF CORRECTIONS SENTENCING TRACKS   F I G U R E **16.1**

	Probation	Intermediate Sanction	Prison
Risk Management	Supervision Counseling Referral	Day treatment center Intensive substance abuse Life management Supervision Community restitution	Incapacitation and treatment (violent, sex, education, mental health)
Reparative	Reparative board Apology Restitution Community service	Reparative board, supervised Community service Work crew	Community Service work Camp

Source: John G. Perry and John F. Gorczyk, "Restructuring Corrections: Using Market Research in Vermont," *Corrections Management Quarterly* 1, no. 3, (1997): 33.

Nonviolent offenders are placed in the reparative track. Community boards create programs and sanctions that can be used to repair damage from the crime while holding offenders accountable for their offense. Probation sanctions include acts such as making an apology, paying restitution to the victim, and performing community service. Intermediate sanctions include more intensive community supervision under the supervision of the parole board. Offenders failing to perform the reparative acts or meet the conditions of this community supervision are violated and sent to prison. In the reparative track, a sentence of imprisonment is usually in a minimum-security facility, and even the imprisonment maintains a focus on reparation through community work.

Several states and local jurisdictions are now using community boards to help create sanctions for offenders to target reparation of the harm they have done.
Courtesy of AP/Wide World Photos.

These inmates are performing community service work to build a home for Habitat for Humanity.
Courtesy of the Ohio Department of Rehabilitation and Correction.

Apart from the overall sentencing process included in the restorative justice model, restoration and community justice can also be emphasized throughout the correctional process. Most correctional agencies have implemented ways to inform victims regarding the offenders' classification, assignments, and potential release from prison. For most states and the Federal Bureau of Prisons, victims are notified of the impending release of an offender. Some states provide the opportunity for victims to make their views known before a parole hearing, or even to attend the hearing and make a personal statement. In addition to continued involvement of victims in the correctional process, many jurisdictions find other ways for offenders to focus on reparation during their sentence.

The Federal Bureau of Prisons (BOP) has been very successful in collecting fines and restitution from inmates and from offenders under community supervision. Inmate financial responsibility is considered in decisions regarding preferred housing or job assignments. Ohio is one of many states that extensively use prison inmates for community service. Over the first eight years of this program, it was reported that Ohio inmates performed 4.2 million hours of community service work.[40] In addition to the benefits of performing this work, a study of Ohio inmates performing community service indicated a "positive statistical significance with regard to participation in community service and recidivism. In essence, prisoners with *any* experience in community service were reimprisoned less often than those who had none."[41]

Restorative justice concepts have the support of and are seen as effective by the general public. Restorative justice models are seen as more proactive than traditional sentencing, focusing on the community rather than just the offender, and emphasizing repairing the damage from the crime more than punishing the offender. In a recent review of the success of the Vermont community justice model, Karp found that 81 percent of offenders successfully completed their reparative probation. Only 31 percent of reparative probationers were rearrested within one year, and only 1.5 percent were rearrested for violent offenses.[42] Because community or restorative justice approaches have the support of the public and are promising in their effectiveness, they represent a new paradigm for sentencing and corrections that will be expanded in the future.

This inmate is involved in a community service program that repairs and rebuilds wheelchairs to ship to impoverished foreign countries, where those unable to afford them can be granted the gift of mobility. The program is called "Wheels for the World."
Photo by Richard P. Seiter.

Can We Reduce the Impact of Prisonization and Improve the Successful Reentry of Prisoners to the Community?

One of the most debilitating problems undermining offenders' successful return to the community is the impact of prisonization. As described in Chapter 11, Clemmer noted that inmates take on the customs and cultures of the prison, and as they identify with and incorporate these behaviors, they find it increasingly more difficult to return to the community and adapt to the behaviors of free society.[43] Terry describes how inmates actually become bound by an informal set of inmate rules called the inmate code. Inmates who live by the inmate code are said to have a convict identity.[44] This convict identity is difficult to shed when returning to the community, and makes the free world and the behavior of law-abiding citizens seem even more surreal than would be expected.

Is there a way to reduce the likelihood of prisonization and taking on a convict identity, and thereby improve the transition from prison to community? This area is difficult to study and has received little research attention over the past decade. However, there are many theories about how the prison experience and the community transition can be changed to improve the likelihood of success in reentry. These include finding ways to have inmates practice community-based values and customs, utilizing transitional programs to assist in preparation for release, and shortening prison sentences to the minimum necessary to provide appropriate punishments.

First, prison operations should be guided by a principle of encouraging inmates to practice values and customs that are important in the community. Prisons have significantly changed for the better since the 1960s, when Goffman wrote about "total institutions" and how their isolated nature, location, and separation from normal society resulted in inmates losing their identity and ability to make decisions for themselves.[45] Goffman had suggested that the overwhelming control of inmates' behavior can result in some inmates becoming confused, hostile, and bitter, and can actually reduce an individual's capacity for independent living. In the late 1950s, Cressey noted that staff authority required inmates to spend most of every day with other inmates with whom they do not choose to associate, and that the control of their activities gives them little chance to succeed or fail.[46]

Today's prisons are not nearly so regimented and authoritarian as to isolate inmates from their own identity or their ability to make decisions. Yet meeting the prison goals of custody and control forces prisons to operate in a way that is naturally very different from independent living in the community. However, it is possible to operate prisons with a clear emphasis on encouraging the types of behaviors that make for success in the community. The Missouri Department of Corrections recently adopted an approach it calls the **parallel universe** to accomplish this.

The department recognized the problems with successful reentry and attempted to recreate its prisons similar to the outside world, through interacting with the environment outside prisons and replicating the requirements and rewards of the free world. The goal for the parallel universe is to "cultivate in offenders the skills that yield civil, productive conduct. Essentially, the parallel universe is a corrections-based reentry program."[47] The parallel universe encourages inmates to make choices and assume responsibility, by putting them in situations that are similar to real-life in the community. There are four interactive strategies:

> First, every offender is engaged during work and nonworking hours in productive activities that parallel those of free society. In work hours, offenders go to school and work and, as applicable, to treatment for sex offenses, chronic mental health problems, and drug and alcohol dependencies. In nonworking hours they participate in community service, reparative activities, and recreation. Second, every offender must adopt relapse prevention strategies and abstain from unauthorized activities, including drug and alcohol consumption and sexual misconduct. Third, most offenders can earn opportunities to make choices and are held accountable for them. Fourth, offenders are recognized for good conduct and can improve their status by obeying the rules and regulations.[48]

The Missouri program is not unique in how most modern correctional agencies operate. Yet it is unique in that the department's total focus is to change the prison culture in a way that is designed to improve the chance of successful reentry rather than be an obstacle to it.

Other ways that prisons can reduce the difficulty in the community transition include efforts to maintain family and community ties, maintain work skills, and have inmates associate with citizens other than inmates and correctional staff. Prisons encourage visiting and allow telephone calls to family members and friends. However, these do not go far enough to avoid losing touch with the real issues facing inmates as family members or parents. Parenting programs as described previously are important in this regard. Yet it is also important to create programs that maintain inmates' conscious involvement in the issues that face their families. Why is my son having problems in school, and what can we as parents do about it? Now that my daughter is of dating age, what should she know about sex and the chance of contracting a sexually transmitted disease? Inmates feel unable to deal with these types of issues, and therefore do not try to get involved in most normal family and parenting decisions. Yet being involved in the struggle about how to address these types of concerns is exactly what can help them stay linked to the community rather than to the problems of prison life.

Parallel universe

an approach to operating prisons that puts inmates in situations that are similar to real life in the community

As inmates stay in prison for long periods of time, they lose any positive work habits and skills they may have. When they return to the community, they feel even more unable to perform or compete in the world of work, and often quickly give up trying. Prison industry programs are extremely valuable in maintaining or developing skills, creating good work habits, and building confidence in one's ability to produce in the competitive working environment. As well, it has been shown that work in prison industries not only improves prison behavior, but also reduces recidivism rates following release.[49] Unfortunately, on January 1, 2001, only 6.3 percent of the prison population was working in prison industries in the fifty states, the District of Columbia, and the Federal Bureau of Prisons.[50]

Inmates also need to associate with individuals who are not inmates or prison staff. Most prisons have volunteer programs in which citizens come into the prison to assist with education, religious, substance abuse, or other programs or activities. Volunteers in this regard can be excellent mentors and role models for inmates. It is not necessary that they work with individual inmates. Just the association gives inmates an opportunity to talk about normal issues in the community and avoid the focus on the prison that results from conversations with other inmates or prison staff.

The second way to reduce the effect of prisonization is through the use of transitional programs in preparation for release. As noted earlier, several programs have been found effective in improving the success of prisoner reentry and reducing recidivism. Vocational training and work release programs are effective in reducing recidivism and improving job readiness skills for ex-offenders. Drug rehabilitation programs are effective in reducing arrests, drug-related offenses, continued drug use, and parole violations. Halfway house programs reduce the frequency and severity of future crimes. As well, there are promising results for sex and violent offender programs. Unfortunately, as noted earlier in this chapter, these programs still are not provided to a high percentage of the inmate population.

The final method for reducing the impact of prisonization is to shorten prison sentences to only a term that meets the need for society to be assured that inmates receive appropriate punishment for their crime, and not to go beyond this point to reflect society's anger and frustration over our inability to solve the crime problem. During the past twenty years, we have attacked the crime problem through enhancing sentences. Each time there was a high-publicity crime or when criminal sentences became a political issue, legislatures responded by lengthening the term served by offenders. Unfortunately, this usually occurred without any firm evidence that the enhancement would reduce crime, and often without an estimate of the cost of the enhancement. As a result, and as noted earlier, the time served by released offenders increased more than 20 percent (from twenty-two to twenty-seven months) from 1990 to 1997.[51]

The impact of this approach to sentencing has been addressed previously, and crime has been reduced by lengthening criminal sentences. However, the question addressed in this section is how to reduce the impact of prisonization on inmates so that it is less of an obstacle to successful reentry. When asked to cite the most important change that can be made to improve the likelihood of successful reentry for prisoners, Terry responded, "to keep time spent in prison to the least possible time, thereby reducing the likelihood and impact of prisonization."[52] This is only common sense. Even with the suggested modifications in prison programs and operations to reduce the likelihood and strength of prisonization, there will still be a continued idealization of the prison way of life the longer someone lives in a prison environment.

The answer to the question of whether we can reduce the impact of prisonization and improve the successful reentry of prisoners to the community is "yes." We can if we find ways to have inmates practice community-based values and customs, utilize transitional programs to help inmates prepare for release from prison, and shorten prison sentences to the minimum necessary to provide appropriate punishments. The key feature to successfully implementing these approaches is to have an objective of minimizing the deleterious effect of imprisonment on inmates. A program such as the "parallel universe" in Missouri is an excellent example of how this can be accomplished.

The concept of prisoner reentry brings to mind the integration of correctional, community, and social services resources that are also necessary to aid in the successful reintegration of prisoners returning to the community. Many staff positions in community and social service agencies also contribute to the reentry of offenders and are the topic of the "Your Career in Corrections" box.

YOUR CAREER IN CORRECTIONS

COMMUNITY SOCIAL SERVICE STAFF

Throughout this textbook, students have been provided ideas and information for careers working for correctional agencies. However, corrections cannot operate in a vacuum and successfully punish offenders, treat them, and deter them from committing further crimes. The relationship of offenders to many other factors (employment, family, their environment in the neighborhood, availability of drugs, mental competence) all affect whether they will avoid further criminal behavior. In this regard, many other types of jobs work with correctional agencies and may be of interest to students of corrections.

First are the many community and social service agencies that work with offenders. Every community has job training and development agencies, community mental health departments, family counseling organizations, and substance abuse counselors. Some of these are private organizations that receive grants or contract with public agencies. Some are religious organizations, linked to and supported by churches. Others are federal, state, or local public agencies created to help disadvantaged citizens find jobs or receive counseling or treatment. Students majoring in criminal justice or corrections often do not consider these public or quasi-public social service agencies. However, there are many jobs as counselors or program developers in all of these types of agencies who work with correctional clients and do work similar to correctional staff. Finding these jobs is not as easy as applying to work for a large public correctional agency, as they are often small agencies that do not have a central job clearinghouse, and therefore students must develop networks through internships and faculty contacts to hear of the availability of jobs and know where and how to apply for positions.

A second category of jobs that relate closely to correctional staff positions are the other two elements of the criminal justice system: the police and the courts. While traditional police work is similar in some ways to the security functions of correctional officers, their role is substantially different. The work of correctional staff is based on using interpersonal skills in dealing with clients over a significant period of time. While police officers use many of the same skills, their interactions with citizens or clients of the criminal justice system are usually made up of single transactions or situations. However, police departments usually have school patrol officers or community relations officers who have a role that is more long-term and preventive in nature. These staff learn to work with the community or school, getting to know the citizens and students and often advising or counseling them on issues regarding criminal justice. As well, courts have victim services officers and drug court staff who play a very similar role to correctional staff.

Finally, many other social and community service positions may appeal to someone interested in a career in corrections. People drawn to corrections usually have an interest in helping others and in serving the public; they enjoy interacting with people, like jobs with a lot of variety that are not "desk-bound," and want a career that has opportunities for advancement and can lead to a variety of different career moves. Family and children's services, housing, public assistance, recreation, and legal services are a variety of agencies that need these kinds of people to work and perform roles very similar to correctional staff. If you are drawn to correctional work, your job possibilities are only as endless as your imagination.

Is Corrections a Good Career Choice for Me?

This text has presented various jobs that are available to those seeking a career in corrections. There have been discussions regarding the pay, working conditions, challenges, benefits, and issues that people face while working in corrections. With this information, it is time for students to consider whether a **career in corrections** is right for them. Correctional jobs are difficult to perform, and not every person who expresses an interest in corrections is suited for this type of work.

It is important to seriously consider the roles and specific duties of these jobs before applying for a job and committing to a career in corrections.

Corrections is a people business, meaning that it is not the bars, fences, policies, or equipment that successfully carry out the goals of a correctional sanction. It is the staff. Positive, professional correctional staff can make any program or policy effective. Yet unprofessional, poorly trained, or uncaring staff will cause any policy or program to fail. Because of the mission of corrections, the role of staff in correctional agencies is even more critical than the role of staff in most other public agencies or private-sector companies. Correctional agencies are responsible for protecting the public by limiting offenders' freedoms. This is a serious responsibility. When correctional staff fail to effectively do their jobs, innocent citizens may be victims of crime. Correctional staff have considerable discretion in how they carry out their duties and take away offenders' individual freedoms. Therefore, staff members doing these difficult jobs must follow the highest of ethical standards.

It is not unusual for people to apply for and get a job with a correctional agency and then determine that it is not the right type of position for them. This leads to a high turnover of correctional staff, especially during the first few months of employment, and especially in the difficult role of correctional officer. As indicated in Table 16.1, turnover rates for correctional officers between 1993 and 2000 increased from a low of 11.6 percent to a high of 16.1 percent.[53] Wright examined correctional turnover and suggests, "Prisons experience high rates of turnover among employees, averaging 16 percent nationwide and reaching over 40 percent in some settings."[54]

Career in corrections

beginning work for a correctional agency with the intent of working in corrections until retirement

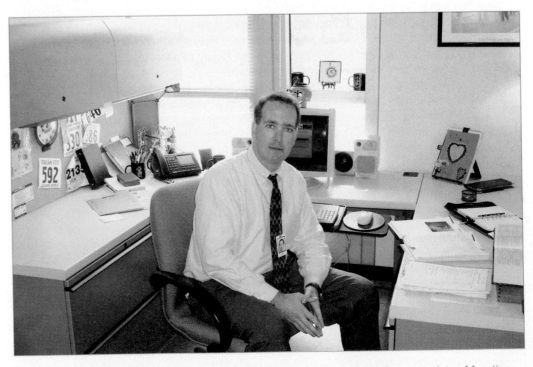

Probation and parole officers have interesting jobs and officers get to perform a variety of functions.
Photo by Richard P. Seiter.

This substance abuse counselor provides programming that assists in preparing inmates to return to the community and stay drug-free.
Photo by Richard P. Seiter.

One of the reasons for a high turnover rate in these and other correctional jobs is the stressful and dangerous nature of the positions. Correctional staff in prison and the community work with difficult clients who regularly challenge them, attempting to avoid compliance and detection of violations. As well, there is always the risk of assault and serious injury. Although most correctional personnel indicate that they do not fear for their safety, the number of assaults on prison staff increased from 10,731 in 1990 to 14,165 by 1995, a jump of almost one-third.[55] The American Correctional Association reported that the number of correctional officers climbed only 14 percent during this period, leading to the conclusion that assaults against correctional staff have increased in frequency.[56] Although many job-related functions led to stress for correctional workers (understaffing, rotating shift work, inmate demands and manipulations, and poor public image), officers

TABLE	16.1	Correctional Officer Average Annual Turnover Rate, 1993–2000

Year	Percent
1993	12.0%
1994	11.6
1995	12.7
1996	12.9
1997	14.9
1998	15.4
1999	16.0
2000	16.1

Source: Adapted from Camille Graham Camp and George M. Camp, *The 2001 Corrections Yearbook: Adult Systems* (Middletown, Conn.: Criminal Justice Institute, 2002), p. 171.

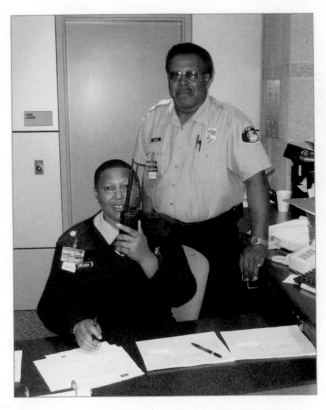

Correctional officers make up the highest percentage of jail and prison staff, and conduct a variety of custody and security functions.
Photo by Richard P. Seiter.

mentioned the threat of violence more frequently than any other single feature of their occupation.[57]

Even with these challenges and concerns, there are many reasons to consider corrections as a career. First, there are many available jobs. The *Sourcebook of Criminal Justice Statistics, 2001* reports that there were 715,573 correctional staff working at the federal, state, and local levels in the United States in 2001.[58] This is almost a 30 percent increase since 1992, when there were 556,500 correctional employees.[59] Second, these jobs are very stable, and there are many career opportunities. Seldom does a correctional agency have a layoff or have to reduce its number of staff. As well, staff with the proper educational requirements who work hard and do a good job will be promoted and given opportunities for advancement. With the growth that has occurred in corrections over the past two decades, there is a continuous requirement for new staff. As new staff are hired, those currently working are considered for promotion to take the new middle-management positions.

Third, the pay is better than most people believe, and the benefits are very good. Pay for a variety of correctional jobs has been addressed in several earlier chapters. And pay has continued to increase for most correctional positions. The average starting salary for correctional officers (without considering overtime) on January 1, 1994, was $19,305.[60] It increased each year, and on January 1, 2001, it was $23,627 for average starting pay; a few states (Massachusetts, New Jersey, Alaska, and Colorado) start correctional officers at more than $30,000.[61] The average entry-level salary for probation and parole officers on January 1, 2001, was $28,436.[62] Public-sector agencies usually have excellent vacations, days off, and health care coverage. Many have a special retirement system, similar to those of

These two jail counselors obviously enjoy their jobs.
Photo by Richard P. Seiter.

law enforcement agencies, in which employees can retire after twenty-five to thirty years of service at any age. This seems like a long time for students today thinking about a career, but retiring at age fifty or fifty-five is an outstanding benefit.

Finally, corrections is an interesting and enjoyable career. There is seldom a boring day in a correctional job. You deal with people, you face new challenges, and you have to make decisions as you go. While corrections is not a career for everyone, it is a career for people who do not want to be desk-bound, who enjoy working with people, who are not afraid of a challenge, and who want to serve the public. People with these characteristics will be making the right choice to select a career in corrections. This textbook was written to provide students a real-life understanding of what corrections is really all about. Students should seriously consider all of the issues raised in this book as they consider whether a career in corrections is right for them. But the answer, in this author's opinion, to the question of whether corrections is a good career choice is a definite "yes." I have enjoyed it for more than twenty-five years, and would recommend it to anyone.

Chapter Review

SUMMARY

With this summary, your study of an introduction to corrections is coming to a close. Corrections has an interesting history, currently faces significant challenges, and has a difficult-to-predict future. One thing that is known about the future of corrections, however, is that the discipline will continue to grow in importance, vis-

ibility, and interest to the public. Only fifty years ago, the public and elected officials had little interest in or knowledge of correctional operations. Today, it is one of the most hotly debated areas of public policy.

In this final chapter, six questions have been proposed. First, can our current approach to sentencing and corrections be successful and continue? The answer to this question is yes and no. The "tough on crime" approach to sentencing, with lengthy sentences and an emphasis on deterrence and incapacitation, can reduce crime, but only marginally. It cannot continue, however, if taxpayers demand a greater return on the tremendous amount of money they are pumping into the nation's correctional system.

Second, will rehabilitation continue as a primary correctional goal? The answer to this question is yes, it will continue, and will even expand in importance. The public supports rehabilitation programs, and there is increasing evidence of their success in reducing recidivism. Therefore, rehabilitation will experience a rebirth in importance as a correctional goal of correctional operations.

Third, will supervision of offenders in the community change in approach? A change in supervision will occur. Just as evidence of the success of rehabilitation will prompt its reemphasis, there is evidence of potential reductions in recidivism through a balance of casework and monitoring. These findings will lead to a gradual move back toward the casework style rather than a focus on surveillance.

Fourth, do we need a new paradigm for sentencing and corrections? The old paradigms have been relatively unchanged over two hundred years, and we do need to find new approaches. Community justice or restorative justice represents just such an approach. It is supported by the public, appears promising in effectiveness, and is a new sentencing and correctional paradigm that warrants expansion in the future.

Fifth, can we reduce the impact of prisonization and improve the successful reentry of prisoners to the community? Again, the answer to this question is yes. Through finding ways to have inmates practice community-based values and customs, utilizing transitional programs to assist in preparation for release, and shortening prison sentences to the minimum necessary to provide appropriate punishments, we can reduce the negative effects of prisonization and increase the chance of successful reentry to the community.

Sixth, and perhaps the most important question for readers, is corrections a good career choice? The answer is a resounding yes. In regard to this question, I admit a lack of objectivity and a total bias to the positive. I have had a career working in corrections for more than twenty-five years. I have found fulfillment from meeting difficult challenges and disappointment from failures. However, I have seldom had a dull moment, and never a second thought about whether corrections was the right choice for me. Correctional jobs are available, they are stable, they pay better than most people think, and they are interesting and enjoyable. You meet hundreds of dedicated people, and you make plenty of friends. Hopefully, by reading this book and studying corrections, students will agree that it is an honorable career that deserves a close look as a possible future.

To conclude our look into the future of corrections, students are to read the "You Make the Decision" box, and consider the answers to the six questions posed in this chapter as well as others they consider important to the future of corrections.

YOU MAKE THE DECISION . . . WHAT WILL THE FUTURE BRING?

In this chapter, six questions regarding the future of corrections have been asked:

- Can our current approach to sentencing and corrections be successful and continue?
- Will rehabilitation continue as a primary correctional goal?
- Will supervision of offenders in the community change in approach?
- Do we need a new paradigm for sentencing and corrections?
- Can we reduce the impact of prisonization and improve the successful reentry of prisoners to the community?
- Is corrections a good career choice for me?

As author, I answered them from my perspective, providing some of the data and situations that I believed would lead each of the questions to be answered as I did. However, it is now time for you to try to provide answers to these same questions *and* identify other questions you think are relevant for the future.

In this "You Make the Decision," box you are to discuss each question in a small group. List the three or four arguments for and against answering the question the way I answered it. Then, decide whether you agree with the answer I provided, and the reasons why you agree or disagree (you may agree but for an entirely different reason). If you disagree, give the answer you think is most likely to happen, and the reasons you believe it to be true.

Then think back on our study of corrections throughout this book and consider what other questions you believe are important to ponder for the future. I picked only six "big picture" issues. You can add to that, or get more "micro" in your questions, such as, "Will supermax prisons incur any successful 'cruel or unusual' legal challenges?" or "Will correctional agencies have to significantly increase salaries in order to attract qualified staff in the future?" As I noted previously, there may be no right or wrong answers to your questions. However, the fun is in thinking about the future, the types of issues that will occur, and what you think the outcome will be.

REVIEW QUESTIONS

1. What current correctional goals most influence sentencing policy and how has a focus on these goals influenced the number of offenders under correctional supervision?

2. How can tightening budgets and a focus on accountability influence future sentencing policies?

3. How has the development of meta-analysis influenced researchers examining the effectiveness of correctional treatment?

4. What has been the result of a movement toward surveillance of offenders in the community?

5. What is the definition of restorative justice?

6. How are sentences determined within a restorative justice approach?

7. Why do inmates become prisonized?

8. How does the process of prisonization negatively affect the successful reentry of inmates to the community?

9. What are the positive and negative factors of working in corrections?

10. Is a career in corrections right for you?

ENDNOTES

1. Paige M. Harrison and Jennifer C. Karberg, *Prison and Jail Inmates at Midyear 2002* (Washington, D.C.: Bureau of Justice Statistics, April 2003).

2. Bureau of Justice Statistics Correctional Surveys, 1980–2001: *National Probation Survey, National Prisoner Statistics, Survey of Jails,* and *National Parole Survey* (Washington, D.C.: U.S. Department of Justice).

3. Camille Graham Camp and George M. Camp, *The 2001 Corrections Yearbook: Adult Systems* (Middletown, Conn.: Criminal Justice Institute, 2002), p. 100.

4. Camp and Camp, 2002, pp. 76, 83–85.

5. Frank Schmalleger, *Criminal Justice Today,* 7th ed. (Upper Saddle River, N.J.: Prentice Hall, 2003), p. 46.

6. Gallup Poll, http://www.gallup.com/pol/content/default.asp?ci=9559&p9=1 (accessed October 2001).

7. William Spelman, "The Limited Importance of Prison Expansion," in *The Crime Drop in America,* edited by Alfred Blumstein and Joel Wallman (Cambridge, Mass.: Cambridge University Press, 2000).

8. Alfred Blumstein and Joel Wallman, ed., *The Crime Drop in America* (Cambridge, Mass.: Cambridge University Press), 2000.

9. As reported by the Associated Press, "Supreme Court Justice Says Prison Terms Are Too Long," *St. Louis Post-Dispatch,* August 10, 2003, p. A7.

10. Douglas Lipton, Robert Martinson, and Judith Wilks, *The Effectiveness of Correctional Treatment and What Works: A Survey of Treatment Evaluation Studies* (New York: Praeger, 1975).

11. Bureau of Justice Statistics, *National Prisoner Statistics* (Washington, D.C.: U.S. Department of Justice, 1977 and 1997).

12. P. Ditton and D. J. Wilson, *Truth in Sentencing in State Prisons* (Washington, D.C.: U.S. Department of Justice, Bureau of Justice Statistics, 1999).

13. James P. Lynch and William J. Sabol, "Prisoner Reentry in Perspective," http://www.urban.org/url.cfm?ID=410213 (accessed September 18, 2001).

14. Camp and Camp, 2002, pp. 136–137.

15. Ibid., p. 117.

16. Ibid., p. 134.

17. Ibid., pp. 71, 144.

18. Ibid., p. 144.

19. Timothy J. Flanagan and Dennis R. Longmire, eds., *Americans View Crime and Justice: A National Public Opinion Survey* (Thousand Oaks, Calif.: Sage, 1996).

20. Brandon K. Applegate, Francis T. Cullen, and Bonnie S. Fisher, "Public Support for Correctional Treatment," *Prison Journal* 77, no. 3 (1997): 237–258.

21. Barbara A. Sims, "Questions of Corrections: Public Attitudes toward Prison and Community-Based Programs," *Corrections Management Quarterly* 1, no. 1 (1997): 55.

22. Robert Martinson, "What Works? Questions and Answers about Prison Reform," *Public Interest* 35 (1974): 25.

23. Paul Gendreau, Claire Goggin, and Paula Smith, "Generating Rational Correctional Policies: An Introduction to Advances in Cumulating Knowledge," *Corrections Management Quarterly* 4, no. 2 (2000): 56–57.

24. David P. Farrington, Anthony Petrosino, and Brandon C. Welsh, "Systematic Reviews and Cost-Benefit Analyses of Correctional Interventions," *Prison Journal* 81, no. 3 (2001): 339–359.

25. For discussions of qualitative assessments of treatment programs and matching of offenders to program services, see Sharon Levrant, Francis T. Cullen, Betsy Fulton, and John Wozniak, "Reconsidering Restorative Justice: The Corruption of Benevolence Revisited?" *Crime and Delinquency* 45 (1999): 3–27; Edward J. Latessa and Alexander Holsinger, "The Importance of Evaluating Correctional Programs: Assessing Outcome and Quality," *Corrections Management Quarterly* 2, no. 4 (1998): 22–29; Paul Gendreau and Donald Andrews, *The Correctional Program Assessment Inventory*, 5th ed. (Saint John, Canada: University of New Brunswick, 1994); Paul Gendreau, Claire Goggin, and Paula Smith, "Generating Rational Correctional Policies: An Introduction to Advances in Cumulating Knowledge," *Correctional Management Quarterly* 4, no. 2 (2000): 52–60.

26. For examples of studies that indicate a positive treatment effect, see Francis T. Cullen and Brandon K. Applegate, ed., *Offender Rehabilitation: Effective Treatment Intervention* (Aldershot, England: Ashgate, 1997); Gerald G. Gaes, "Correctional Treatment," in *The Handbook of Crime and Punishment*, edited by Michael Tonry (New York: Oxford University Press, 1998), pp. 712–738; Vernon L. Quinsey, "Treatment of Sex Offenders," in *The Handbook of Crime and Punishment*, pp. 403–425; Douglas S. Lipton, "Prison-Based Therapeutic Communities: Their Success With Drug-Abusing Offenders," *National Institute of Justice Journal* (February 1996): 12–20; William G. Saylor and Gerald G. Gaes, "Training Inmates through Industrial Work Participation and Vocational and Apprenticeship Instruction," *Corrections Management Quarterly* 1, no. 2 (1997): 40; Federal Bureau of Prisons, *TRIAD Drug Treatment Evaluation Six-Month Report: Executive Summary* (Washington, D.C.: U.S. Department of Justice, 1998).

27. William Adams and Jeffrey Roth, *Federal Offenders under Community Supervision, 1989–96* (Washington, D.C.: U.S. Department of Justice, Bureau of Justice Statistics, 1998).

28. Camp and Camp, 2002, p. 201.

29. Ibid., p. 191.

30. In a study of St. Louis parole and probation officers, Seiter and West found that 54.1 percent of respondents majored in criminal justice, 1.1 percent in psychology, 9.0 percent in sociology, and 4.5 percent in social work. Other majors included education, business, art, and history. See Richard P. Seiter and Angela D. West, "Supervision Styles in Probation and Parole: An Analysis of Activities," *Offender Rehabilitation* (forthcoming).

31. Camp and Camp, 2002, p. 203.

32. Ibid., p. 224.

33. Ibid., pp. 59–61.

34. A. Beck and C. Mumola, *Prisoners in 1998* (Washington, D.C.: U.S. Department of Justice, Bureau of Justice Statistics, 1999).

35. Joan Petersilia, "When Prisoners Return to the Community: Political, Economic, and Social Consequences," *Federal Probation* 65, no.1 (June 2001): 3–8.

36. See Camp and Camp, 2002, which reported 23.1 percent of violations for new crimes in 1998 and 19.2 percent in 2000.

37. Francis T. Cullen, John Paul Wright, Paul Gendreau, and D. A. Andrews, "What Correctional Treatment Can Tell Us about Criminological Theory: Implications for Social Learning Theory," in *Social Learning Theory and the Explanation of Crime: A Guide for the New Century*, edited by Ronald L. Akers and Gary F. Jensen (New Brunswick, N.J.: Transaction, 2003), pp. 339–362.

38. Mark Carey, "Overcoming Fear, Misunderstanding, and NIMBY through Restorative Covenants," *Corrections Management Quarterly* 4, no. 3 (2000): 12.

39. John G. Perry and John F. Gorczyk, "Restructuring Corrections: Using Market Research in Vermont," *Corrections Management Quarterly* 1, no. 3 (1997): 27.

40. Reginald A. Wilkinson, "The Impact of Community Service Work on Ohio State Prisoners: A Restorative Justice Perspective and Overview," *Corrections Management Quarterly* 4, no. 3 (2000): 30.

41. Ibid.

42. David R. Karp, "Does Community Justice Work?" *Perspectives* 27, no. 1 (2003): 32–37.

43. Donald Clemmer, *The Prison Community* (New York: Rinehart, 1940).

44. Charles M. Terry, "The Function of Humor for Prison Inmates," *Journal of Contemporary Criminal Justice* 13, no. 1 (February 1997): 23–40.

45. Erving Goffman, *Asylums: Essays on the Social Situation of Mental Patients and Other Inmates* (New York: Doubleday, 1961).

46. Donald Cressey, "Contradictory Directives in Complex Organizations: The Case of the Prison," *Administrative Science Quarterly* (June 1959).

47. Dora Schriro, "Correcting Corrections: Missouri's Parallel Universe," in *Sentencing and Corrections: Issues*

for the 21st Century (Washington, D.C.: U.S. Department of Justice, National Institute of Justice, May 2000), p. 3.

48. Ibid., p. 4.

49. William G. Saylor and Gerald G. Gaes, "The Post-Release Employment Project: Prison Work Has Measurable Effects on Post-Release Success," *Federal Prisons Journal* 2, no. 4 (1992): 33–36.

50. Camp and Camp, 2002, pp. 116, 126.

51. Lynch and Sabol, 2001.

52. Charles M. Terry, interview by author, St. Louis University, July 28, 2003.

53. Camp and Camp, 2002, pp. 170–171.

54. Kevin N. Wright, *Effective Prison Leadership* (Binghamton, N.Y.: William Neil, 1994), p. 47.

55. J. J. Stephans, *Census of State and Federal Correctional Facilities, 1995* (Washington, D.C.: U.S. Department of Justice, Bureau of Justice Statistics, 1997).

56. As reported in Peter Finn, *Addressing Correctional Officer Stress: Programs and Strategies* (Washington, D.C.: U.S. Department of Justice, National Institute of Justice, December 2000), p. 11.

57. Ibid., p. 14.

58. Bureau of Justice Statistics, *Sourcebook of Criminal Justice Statistics, 2001* (Washington, D.C.: U.S. Department of Justice, 2003), p. 19.

59. Bureau of Justice Statistics, *Sourcebook of Criminal Justice Statistics, 1994* (Washington, DC: U.S. Department of Justice, updated March 2003), p. 26.

60. Camp and Camp, 2002, p. 169.

61. Ibid.

62. Ibid., p. 226.

ACA accreditation
a process to promote and recognize improvement in the management of correctional agencies through the administration of voluntary standards

accountability
the state of being held responsible for accomplishing objectives in a cost-efficient manner

adjudicate
to find a juvenile guilty of a delinquent act

administrative appeals process
an informal process for inmates to appeal a disciplinary sanction, or seek remedy of any other injustice they feel they have received at the hands of correctional officials

administrative detention
a nonpunitive confinement in an SHU; used to house inmates whose continued presence in the general population may pose a serious threat to the security or orderly running of the prison

administrative form of sentencing
a sentencing model in which administrative bodies (correctional officials and parole/release boards) have primary discretion in granting good time and determining the release time of offenders

affirmative action programs
activities to recruit and provide employment opportunities to women and minorities

aftercare
supervision of a juvenile in the community after he or she has served time in a juvenile correctional institution; similar to parole for adults

age of original jurisdiction
the upper or oldest age at which a juvenile court will have jurisdiction over offenders

Alexander Maconochie
the superintendent of the British penal colony on Norfolk Island from 1841 to 1844 who created a system of marks for good behavior that could lead to a graduated release from prison

American Correctional Association
the largest professional organization for corrections in the United States

Americans with Disabilities Act
a law that prohibits any entity from discriminating against an individual with a disability in regard to employment, public services and transportation, public accommodations, and telecommunications services

antipsychotic drugs
drugs administered to mentally ill individuals to counteract the symptoms of their mental illness, often allowing them to live successfully in the community rather than needing to be institutionalized

asset forfeiture
the authorized seizure by the government of money, negotiable instruments, securities, or other things of value that were obtained through illegal activities

atavism
the existence of features common in the early stages of human evolution

Auburn System
the congregate and silent operation of prisons in which inmates were allowed to work together during the day, but had to stay separate and silent at other times

bail
the pledge of money or property in exchange for a promise to return for further criminal processing

balancing test
established in *Pell v. Procunier,* finding that prison inmates retain those First Amendment rights that are not inconsistent with their status as prisoners or with legitimate penological objectives

Barefield v. Leach
a 1974 federal court decision that a disparity of programs for female inmates could not be justified because the smaller number of female inmates made it more costly to provide program parity

Bell v. Wolfish
a 1979 U.S. Supreme Court case in which the punitive intent standard was adopted for considering violations of the Eighth Amendment regarding jail operations

BFOQ
bona fide occupational qualification; a qualification reasonably necessary to the normal operation of a particular business or enterprise that may allow for some discriminatory practices to occur

bifurcated trials
used in capital cases, with guilt first established at a traditional trial, and if found guilty, a second stage of sentencing considered between death or life imprisonment

blended sentencing
a middle ground between juvenile and adult sentences that allows judges to choose from a broad array of both juvenile and adult sanctions

boot camp/shock incarceration
alternatives to traditional incarceration that are operated similar to a military boot camp; offenders are required to have short hair, shine their shoes, wear uniforms, do extensive physical exercise, and perform hard physical labor; at times, these are complemented with education or drug programming, but the major components of boot camps are military regimentation, discipline, exercise, and hard work

brig
a military term meaning a correctional facility

Bruscino v. Carlson
a 1985 federal court decision that the lockdown of inmates at the U.S. Penitentiary in Marion, Illinois, was not a violation of the Constitution

Bureau of Immigration and Customs Enforcement (BICE)
formerly the U.S. Immigration and Naturalization Service (INS); responsible for housing illegal aliens pending a hearing or deportation back to their home country

call out
a schedule of all the appointments and required moves for a day, including the inmate name and expected times of the move

capital punishment
punishment for the most serious crimes (generally first-degree murder); most states and the federal government provide for the death penalty

career in corrections
beginning work for a correctional agency with the intent of working in corrections until retirement

case manager
sometimes called a social worker or caseworker; responsible for developing the program of work and rehabilitation for inmates assigned to him or her

casework style of supervision
a style of supervising community offenders that places emphasis on assisting the offender with problems, providing counseling, and ensuring that the offender successfully completes supervision

census count
a less formal count conducted at program and work assignments by the staff responsible for supervising inmates

Cesare Beccaria
an Italian theorist who in the eighteenth century first suggested linking crime causation to punishments and became known as the founder of the Classical School of criminology

Cesare Lombroso
the Italian physician who in the nineteenth century founded the Positive School

chain of command
the vertical hierarchy in an organization, identified in terms of authority, and the order through which people receive directives from the person immediately above them and pass these directives to the person immediately below them

Civil Rights Act of 1871
this act of Congress guaranteed the rights of freed slaves, and provided assess to federal courts for violations of the act

Classical School
the theory linking crime causation to punishment, based on offenders' free will and hedonism

closed systems
prison systems that consist of only the internal environment, under the direct control of the warden, and without much interest or any interference from external groups

collective bargaining
the formal recognition of employee organizations and their right to negotiate with management regarding workplace issues

collective violence
prison violence that is between and initiated by groups of inmates; it includes prison riots and disturbances; it can be groups of inmates against staff or against one another, as this violence stems from the fundamental difference in values and positions of the two groups

Commission on Accreditation for Corrections
a group formed to administer national accreditation programs for adult and juvenile correctional agencies

community classification systems
risk assessments that predict the chance of new crimes being committed; they are used to determine the level of supervision an offender will receive in the community

community corrections
criminal sanctions that involve community supervision of offenders, use correctional and program resources available in the community, and require offenders to abide by specified conditions to remain in the community

community residential centers
houses in which offenders live in the community that provide supervision, room and board, and some treatment as an alternative to prison

community service
an economic sanction used when offenders do not have funds from which to pay a fine or make restitution; referred to as a "fine on their time," so that indigent offenders do not have to serve prison or jail time merely because they lack the fiscal ability to pay a fine

community standards
the test established in *Fernandez v. United States* that medical care for inmates must be reasonably commensurate with medical care they would receive if not imprisoned

concurrent sentences
sentences that run at the same time

conjugal visiting
sometimes referred to as family visiting; private visiting opportunities between inmates and their spouses where it is expected that they will engage in sexual relations

consecutive sentences
sentences that run one after the other

consent decree
an informal handling of a juvenile justice case in which the delinquent juvenile admits to wrongdoing and agrees to specific conditions of behavior; sometimes called informal probation

containment model
an approach to managing sex offenders that includes treatment to develop internal control over deviant thoughts, supervision and surveillance to control external behaviors, and polygraph examinations to monitor conformance to treatment plans and supervision conditions

continuum of care
various levels of mental health programs based on the intensity of needs for each inmate

contraband
any item that inmates are not allowed to possess, including items that can assist in an escape, are dangerous, can undermine prison physical security, or are nuisance items

controlled movement
the procedure used by prisons to maintain accountability for inmates as they move throughout the prison

convicts
long-term inmates who become used to the prison society and find a way to live in this environment with a minimal amount of problems and disruptions

co-payment
a minimal charge for inmates to see a physician or receive medical care

Cornell Correctional Companies
a private correctional company that operates sixty-nine correctional facilities

correctional counselor
former correctional officers who work with inmates on prison issues such as arranging visits

correctional officer
staff members in a prison or jail who accomplish the institution's mission by maintaining control and order within the prison

Correctional Services Corporation
a private correctional company that operates thirty-three correctional facilities

corrections
the range of community and institutional sanctions, treatment programs, and services for managing criminal offenders

Corrections Corporation of America
the largest of the private prison corporations that opened the first private, for-profit correctional facility in 1984 in Tennessee; currently operates seventy correctional facilities

cost of incarceration fees
fees charged prisoners in local jails or prisons to cover the cost for their incarceration

cost of supervision
costs associated with their supervision in the community that offenders must pay for, such as drug testing or electronic monitoring

cottage-style architecture
a style of prison design used for women's prisons, with several small housing units holding approximately thirty inmates; each cottage includes a kitchen, living room, and sometimes a nursery for inmates with children

create revenues
to enable governments to charge for correctional supervision or programs provided to offenders

custody
the functions within a prison that come under the security activities within a prison; includes all uniformed employees such as correctional officers and correctional supervisors

debrief
to tell correctional officials everything a gang member knows about the gang operations and membership. Once inmates debrief, they become an enemy of the gang

deinstitutionalize
to remove juveniles from correctional institutions and place them in community alternatives

deliberate indifference
as established in *Wilson v. Seiter*, the standard that conditions at prison are not unconstitutional unless prison administrators show deliberate indifference toward inmates' basic needs

delinquency petition
a statement of the delinquent acts a juvenile is alleged to have committed; similar to an indictment for adults

delinquent children
children who have committed an act that would be considered criminal if committed by an adult

dependent children
children who, while committing no legal offense, may be without a parent or guardian, possibly because the parent is physically or mentally unable to act in that capacity

determinate sentences
sentences of fixed terms

direct supervision
a style of inmate supervision with staff located in direct contact with inmates; requires staff to continuously supervise and communicate with inmates, reducing tension and avoiding the development of conflicts between inmates or inmates and staff

director
the chief operating officer of a state or federal department of corrections

disciplinary segregation
a punitive assignment in an SHU after a finding of guilt for a serious prison rule violation

discretionary parole
release of inmates in which the decision to release is made by a parole board

disturbance control team
an emergency team with the primary mission of controlling inmates during riot situations by using defensive tactics and equipment to move them, isolate them, and get them to give up

Dothard v. Rawlinson
a 1977 U.S. Supreme Court case regarding a woman who was denied a position as a correctional officer in an Alabama men's prison; the Court ruled that a BFOQ against female correctional officers was allowable because of the deplorable conditions of the Alabama prisons and the presence of predatory male sex offenders as inmates

drug courts
an alternative to traditional court models to deal with the underlying drug problem as the basis of the offenders' criminality

drug offenders
people convicted of crimes regarding the possession or sale of drugs

Drug Use Forecasting
surveys of jailed inmates by the U.S. Department of Justice to determine the extent of drug use related to criminality

economic sanction
a requirement that an offender pay a fine or restitution to the victim as a part of his or her sentence

Eighth Amendment
no cruel or unusual punishment may be inflicted

electronic monitoring
the use of technology to monitor an offender's location

Elizabeth Fry
a Quaker who formed the Ladies Society for Promoting the Reformation of Female Prisoners in 1816 and tried to convince officials that female prisoners should be separated from male prisoners and that female guards should be hired to supervise them

Elmira Reformatory
the first reformatory in the United States; it was opened in 1876 and used the principles of the Irish System, indeterminate sentences, and parole

employee awards program
a program to recognize and reward staff members who perform beyond their expected level

environmental factors
underlying factors that create tension and unrest among inmates

Federal Bureau of Prisons
an agency within the U.S. Department of Justice charged with housing and managing federal law offenders

federalize
to make an act that was a violation of a state penal code a violation of the federal penal code

felony
a crime that is punishable by a year or more of incarceration

female offenders
women who are convicted and sentenced; just over 6 percent of prison inmates are female

fines
money that offenders must pay to the court as punishment for committing the offense

first-generation jails
jails in which a linear design was used for housing inmates; cells are aligned in long, straight rows, with walkways in the front of the cells for jail correctional officers to walk intermittently to observe what is going on in the cells

Fourteenth Amendment
no state shall deprive any person of life, liberty, or property, without the due process of law; states may not deny any person the equal protection of the law

furlough
a program in which prison inmates are allowed to leave prison early to reside in a halfway house to prepare for community reentry

Gagnon v. Scarpelli
a 1973 U.S. Supreme Court decision that created the due process requirements for revoking probation

gang intelligence officers
prison staff charged with collecting intelligence and advising administrators regarding strategies to manage and contain prison gang activity

gang validation process
a determination of the number of identifiers of gang activity; used to confirm an individual's gang involvement level

gaol
an early English term for a jail

general deterrence
the recognition that criminal acts result in punishment, and the effect of that recognition on society that prevents future crimes

general population
the inmates in a prison who do not have any specific designation as a special type of offender

Girl Scouts Behind Bars
Girl Scout troops that have their chapter based in a prison so inmates with children can participate as Scout parents

global positioning system
a system that uses a satellite to receive a signal from a transmitter and identify its location to a monitoring station

good time
a reward that affords inmates the opportunity to reduce the time until their eligibility for release by good behavior in prison

graduated incarceration
a system in which juveniles handled by adult courts are placed in juvenile facilities until they reach age 18; they are then transferred to an adult prison to complete the sentence

Gunther v. Iowa
a 1979 case in the U.S. District Court of Iowa in which the court determined that inmate privacy was not a valid reason to refuse to hire women as correctional officers; the *Gunther* decision eliminated the major support used for the BFOQ by states in not hiring female correctional officers

hands-off doctrine
an avoidance by the U.S. Supreme Court of judicial intervention in the operations of prisons and the judgment of correctional administrators

hearing officers
correctional professionals who are not appointed members of the parole board, yet for efficiency they hold parole hearings and make a recommendation to the parole board regarding inmates' release

hedonistic calculus
the idea that the main objective of an intelligent person is to achieve the most pleasure and the least pain, and that individuals are constantly calculating the pluses and minuses of their potential actions

hostage negotiation team
a team, with the principal role of opening lines of communications between staff and hostage takers

house arrest
a form of supervision in which offenders live at home and must be at home except when they are to be at work or participating in other activities approved by their probation officer

human immunodeficiency virus (HIV)
a virus that attacks the body's immune system, increasing the chance of infection and other diseases

imprisonment
a sentence in a prison of a year or more

In re Gault
a 1967 U.S. Supreme Court case that required that in hearings in which juveniles may be committed to an institution, they must have the right to counsel, to notice of the charges against them, to question witnesses, and to protection against self-incrimination

incapacitation
reducing offenders' ability or capacity to commit further crimes

incarceration rate
the number of people per 100,000 U.S. residents who are in jail or prison

indeterminate sentences
sentences that have a minimum and maximum time to be served; a decision by a release authority determines the actual time served within that range

Industrial Prison Era
a period in which prison operations emphasized having inmates work and produce products that could help make the prison self-sustaining

inmate accountability
the staff's ability to locate and identify inmates at any point in time within a prison

inmate code
the expected rules and behaviors represented by the model prisoner, as seen from inmates' point of view, and reflecting the values and norms of prison society

inmate disciplinary system
a policy that clearly prescribes the process required to find that an inmate committed a proscribed act and identifies allowable punishments for each act; a key to controlling inmate behavior

inspector
a person in a department of corrections who investigates allegations by inmates against staff

intake
the process in which officials determine whether a juvenile case should be dismissed, handled informally, or referred to the juvenile court

integrity interview
a type of interview of candidates for correctional employment used to determine whether candidates have issues or conditions that could put them in a compromising situation or make them more likely to accept a bribe to show favored treatment to an inmate

intensive supervised probation
supervision of community offenders with higher-than-average risk, through smaller caseloads and very close monitoring of activities

intensive-supervision caseload
a caseload for offenders with too high a risk or need to be on regular supervision; created as an alternative to sending these offenders to prison

intermediate sanctions
midrange dispositions that fall between probation and imprisonment

internal classification system
instruments used to assign inmates to housing or programs after they are placed in a particular prison

interpersonal violence
prison violence that occurs between two or more individual inmates; the reason for the violence is a personal issue between the individuals

invisible policy
a practice that is not formalized in statute or written policy, but develops through a consistent set of pressures and influences the practice

Irish System
a four-stage system of graduated release from prison and return to the community; the stages were solitary confinement, special prison, open institution, and ticket of leave

jails
locally operated correctional facilities that confine people before or after adjudication

Jeremy Bentham
creator of the hedonistic calculus suggesting that punishments outweigh the pleasure criminals get from committing their crime

John Augustus
the Boston shoemaker who became the "father" of probation

John Howard
the sheriff of Bedfordshire, England, who encouraged reform of English jails in the late 1700s

judicial form of sentencing
a sentencing model in which judges have primary discretion in creating the sentence

just deserts model
a sentencing model proposed by von Hirsch to have fixed sentences for each crime, while letting the punishment fit the crime

justice model
a sentencing model proposed by Fogel that would use flat, determinate sentences; eliminate parole boards; and make all treatment voluntary

juvenile detention
the temporary care of children in physically restricted facilities pending court disposition or transfer to another jurisdiction or agency

juvenile gangs
groups of adolescents or young adults who see themselves as a group and have been involved in enough crime to be of considerable concern to law enforcement and the community

juvenile justice system
a system to handle juveniles separate from adult offenders based on the concept of *parens patriae*, which was used as the basis for giving the court the authority to take over supervision of children when their parents failed to provide proper care and guidance

lease system
a system in which state prisons accepted bids and leased out prisoners to the private sector

legislative form of sentencing
a sentencing model in which legislative bodies create very structured sentencing codes and therefore have primary discretion in the length of time served by offenders

length of stay
the time served in a jail or prison by any inmate

lethal injection
a method of execution in which drugs are injected into a person's body, making the heart stop and causing death

lockup
a few cells commonly located in police stations; they hold people for only a short time, usually no more than 48 hours

male offenders
men who are convicted and sentenced; men constitute more than 93 percent of all prison inmates

management culture
a culture based on the way that prison leadership deals and communicates with subordinate staff; if falls into a continuum between autocratic and empowered

mandatory minimum sentences
a requirement that for certain crimes or for certain types of offenders, there must be a sentence to prison for at least a minimum term

mandatory prison education
a requirement that inmates without a high school diploma or GED must attend school

Manhattan Bail Project
a program started in the 1960s to help judges identify individuals who were good candidates to be released on their own recognizance without commercial or monetary bond

mark system
credits against a sentence that allowed inmates to be released once they earned the required level of marks through work and good behavior

medical model
a theory of corrections that offenders were sick, inflicted with problems that caused their criminality, and needed to be diagnosed and treated, and that rehabilitative programs would resolve offenders' problems and prepare them for release to the community able to be productive and crime-free

meta-analysis
a statistical measure of the average effect an intervention has on recidivism across all studies

misdemeanor
a crime that is punishable by less than a year of incarceration.

mission
a statement of an organization's major function and what it is to accomplish, or its basic purposes, including general outcomes that it is committed to achieving

Morrissey v. Brewer
a 1972 U.S. Supreme Court decision that once parole is granted, a liberty interest is created, and offenders must have certain due process to revoke that liberty

neglected children
children who have a family or guardian, but are not receiving proper care or have a home situation that is harmful to them and their upbringing

Neoclassical School
a compromise between Classical and Positive Schools; while holding offenders accountable for their crimes, allowing for some consideration of mitigating and aggravating circumstances

net widening
the overlapping of criminal sanctions and added supervision for community-placed offenders, rather than diversion of offenders from prison

new-crime violations
violations of a condition of probation that results from the commission of any additional crimes

new penology
an emphasis on rational and efficient deployment of control strategies for managing and confining high-risk criminal populations

"nothing works"
a conclusion by Robert Martinson that no correctional treatment programs reduce recidivism; it effectively spelled the end to the medical model

objective classification systems
statistical approaches to considering the risk of escape and violence by inmates

offender restitution
a requirement that offenders repay society for the harm created by the offense

open systems
prison systems that have frequent interactions between the organization and other groups in order to obtain resources, gain support, and accomplish goals

order
the sanction for a juvenile found delinquent by juvenile court; similar to the sentence for an adult

organizational culture
the values, beliefs, and behaviors that form the way of life within an organization

overrepresentation of minorities
the condition that exists when there are a greater percentage of certain racial and ethnic groups in the correctional population than in the United States general population

parallel universe
an approach to operating prisons that puts inmates in situations that are similar to real life in the community

parens patriae
"parents of the nation"; a concept established in 1601 to allow officials to take change of delinquent children and place them in poorhouses or orphanages to gain control of them; in more modern times, this doctrine was expanded as the basis for juvenile court and correctional systems to take responsibility for educating and nurturing delinquents, with an emphasis on reform and rehabilitation

parenting programs
prison programs that help inmates improve their parenting skills, even while in prison

Pargo v. Elliot
the 1985 Eighth Circuit Court case that determined that differences in programs between men's and women's prisons do not necessarily violate the equal-protection clause of the Constitution

parole
conditional release of inmates by a parole board prior to the expiration of their sentence

parole guidelines
similar to sentencing guidelines; guidelines that use predictive factors to determine offenders' risk to the community and chance for success; they prescribe a presumptive time to be served based on the seriousness of the crime and the factors predictive of success for each inmate

pass system
a form of inmate movement in which an inmate is issued a pass by the work or program supervisor to go to a scheduled appointment

pedophile
someone who is sexually attracted to and molests children

Pell grants
grants for disadvantaged individuals that could be used to cover tuition costs for college courses; since 1994, inmates are no longer eligible for these grants

penal code
a legislative authorization to provide a specific range of punishment for a specific crime

Pennsylvania System
the "separate and silent" system of prison operations emphasizing reformation and avoidance of criminal contamination

penology
the study of the use of punishment for criminal acts

Period of Transition
an era of prison operations in which enforced idleness, lack of professional programs, and excessive size and overcrowding of prisons resulted in an increase in prisoner discontent and prison riots

PIE Program
prison industry programs operated by private companies, with prison goods authorized to be sold on the open market if the program is certified as meeting certain conditions

plea bargaining
an agreement in which the defendant enters a guilty plea in exchange for a reduced sentence in comparison to the sentence allowable for the charged offense

podular designs
a design of prisoner housing that provides common dayroom areas in the center of the unit to allow inmates to watch television or play table games, thereby getting out of their cells and reducing idleness and tension; podular designs make it easier for officers to view inmate activities in the cells and the dayrooms from one central location

policy audit
a review to ascertain whether broad agency policy is in place at a prison

policy implementation audit
a review to identify whether the procedures prescribed by policy are consistently being carried out by staff in their daily duties

positive contact
a face-to-face contact between a parole officer and an offender

Positive School
the belief that criminals do not have complete choice over their criminal actions and may commit acts that are beyond their control

post orders
the detailed description of the activities that are required to be performed throughout the day, often including the time they are to occur

precedents
decisions of courts that come before and are therefore binding on later decisions of courts within the same jurisdiction

precipitating event
the "spark in the haystack" that sets off an inmate riot

presentence investigation
a report used during the sentencing process that details the background of a convicted offender, including criminal, social, education, employment, mental and physical health, and other significant factors

presumptive parole date
a date on which the inmate can expect to be released on parole, even if it is five or ten years later than the hearing

presumptive sentencing
a predetermined range of a minimum, average, and maximum term for a specific crime for a "typical" offender, with allowances for mitigating and aggravating circumstances to be considered

pretrial diversion
the suspension of criminal process while the offender is provided the chance to participate in treatment programs and avoid further criminal activity

preventive detention
detaining an accused person in jail to protect the community from crimes the person is likely to commit if set free pending trial

prison gangs
groups that form in prison and use the threat of violence to intimidate other inmates, control drug sales and prostitution, and gain power and influence

prisoner reentry
the process by which an inmate leaves prison and returns to the community

prisonization
the process whereby inmates take on the folkways, mores, customs, and general culture of the penitentiary.

prisons
institutions designed to house convicted adult felons serving a sentence of one year or more

private prison
any secure correctional facility operated by other than a governmental agency and usually in a "for profit" manner that contracts with a governmental entity to provide security, housing, and programs for adult offenders

probation
a prison sentence that is suspended on the condition that the offender follow certain prescribed rules and commit no further crimes

probation supervision
the role of a probation officer in monitoring an offender's behavior through office visits; contacts with family, friends, bosses, or treatment providers; and visits to the offender's home or place of work

profession
to be seen as a profession, correctional agencies create standards for ethical behavior and self-regulation

professional staff
prison or jail staff in a specialty area that requires distinctive training and education and may also require a professional certification to deliver a program

pseudofamilies
family organizations formed by female inmates that have roles of parents and children

punishment
the correctional goal emphasizing the infliction of pain or suffering

racial disparity
the condition that exists when minorities make up a greater percentage of those under correctional supervision than their makeup in the American population

random count
a count done at any time, freezing inmates wherever they are when the random count is called

rebirth in rehabilitation
a return to support for correctional treatment programs

recidivism
the state of relapse that occurs when offenders complete their criminal punishment and then continue to commit crimes

referral
the formal processing of a juvenile offense through the juvenile court

Reformatory Era
an environment emphasizing reformation that expanded education and vocational programs and focused offenders' attention on their future

Refuge Period
a period from 1824 to 1899 when delinquent or neglected children were placed in homes for training and discipline

regional jail
a jail that serves more than one county and is overseen by a regional jail commission

regular caseload
a caseload made up of standard probationers requiring no special program or supervision

regular counts
the scheduled counting of inmates in their housing units to ensure that they are in the prison and have not escaped

rehabilitation
a programmed effort to alter the attitudes and behaviors of inmates and improve their likelihood of becoming law-abiding citizens

Rehabilitative Era
an era of prison management emphasizing the professionalizing of staff through recruitment and training and implementation of many self-improvement programs of prison management

reintegration
a belief that after offenders complete their treatment in prison, they need transitional care, and that the community must be involved in their successful return to society

relationship culture
a culture based on how staff view and communicate with inmates; falls into a continuum between authoritarian and reasoned

release on recognizance
release from jail based only on the defendant's promise to appear for further court procedures

reparation
acts by offenders to repair the damage done by their crimes

restitution
acts by which criminals make right or repay society or their victims for their wrongs

restorative justice
models of sentencing that shift the focus away from punishment of the offender and emphasize the victim by holding offenders accountable for the harm they caused and finding opportunities for them to repair the damage

retribution
infliction of punishment on those who deserve to be punished

Retributive Era
an era of corrections that emphasized holding offenders accountable for their acts and being tough on criminals while keeping them isolated from law-abiding citizens and making them serve "hard" time

Rhodes v. Chapman
a 1981 U.S. Supreme Court decision that overcrowded conditions resulting in two inmates housed in cells designed for one person was not a violation of the Eighth Amendment right of protection from cruel and unusual punishment

salient factor score
a point determination for each inmate for use with parole guidelines; the score is based on factors predictive of success on parole

Sanford Bates
the first director of the Federal Bureau of Prisons

second-generation jails
jails that use podular housing designs and remote supervision; officers are located in a secure control room overlooking the cells and dayroom, with electronic controls to open and close individual cell doors

Section 1983
a section of the Civil Rights Act that prohibits any person acting under the color of any statute, ordinance, or regulation (color of law) from depriving another of his or her constitutional rights

security classification
a system for matching offenders to institutions that have the physical security and staff resources to prevent escapes and control their behavior

security levels
levels such as minimum, low, medium, high, or maximum; they are distinguished by features such as the presence of towers and other perimeter security barriers (fences or walls) with detection devices, the type of housing for prisoners (cells or dormitory), and the staff-to-inmate ratio

segregated incarceration
a form of incarceration in which juveniles handled by adult courts are assigned to an adult prison, yet are housed separately and placed in specialized educational, vocational, life skills training, and substance abuse programs that match their age level and needs

selective incapacitation
incarceration of high-risk offenders for preventive reasons based on what they are expected to do, not what they have already done

seniority
length of employment used to determine an employee's assignment, days off, or other job-related function

sentencing
imposition of a criminal sanction by a judicial authority

sentencing guidelines
a system of structured sentences, based on measures of offense severity and criminal history, that is used to determine the length of the term of imprisonment

Sentencing Reform Act of 1984
an act of Congress that abolished parole, established determinate sentencing, and reduced the amount of good time available to federal offenders

services
the functions required to operate a prison such as budget and financial, maintenance, human resources management, food and health services, work programs, commissary functions, and laundry operations

sex offenders
offenders who have committed a legally prohibited sexual act; in some states, any offender who commits a crime that was statutorily defined as sexually motivated

sexual triangle
the relationship that exists when two inmates become jealous and fight over another inmate

shadow board
a light-colored background with the outline of a tool or hazardous item painted on it; allows staff to quickly notice a missing tool or item

sheriff
the elected official who oversees both policing activities within the county and the operation of the jail

shock incarceration/ boot camp
alternatives to traditional incarceration that are operated similar to a military boot camp; offenders are required to have short hair, shine their shoes, wear uniforms, do extensive physical exercise, and perform hard physical labor; at times, these are complemented with education or drug programming, but the major components of boot camps are military regimentation, discipline, exercise, and hard work

shock probation
a short period of imprisonment to "shock" the offender, with a return to the community within a few weeks to continue supervision on probation

short-term confinement
a sentence in a jail for one year or less

Sir Walter Crofton
the director of the Irish prison system, appointed in 1854, who began to implement many of the ideas of Maconochie's work

slave-of-the-state doctrine
a doctrine created in the 1871 decision of *Ruffin v. Commonwealth of Virginia*; the courts held that inmates were "slaves of the state" and had no rights that were not granted to them by the state

special caseload
a caseload made up of offenders with a particular type of problem, such as substance abuse, mental illness, or a history of sex offenses

special conditions of probation
conditions of probation tailored to meet the needs of a particular offender; they can be imposed to meet specific risks or needs

special emergency response team
an emergency team trained in the use of lethal force for when all else fails to resolve an emergency situation

special housing unit
a temporary housing assignment for inmates who present a danger to the security of the prison, need protection from other inmates, or are being punished for violating prison rules.

special offenders
offenders whose circumstances, conditions, or behaviors require management or treatment outside the normal approach to supervision

specific deterrence
the effect of punishment on an individual offender that prevents that person from committing future crimes

split sentence
a combination of a short jail sentence and then return to the community on probation

square johns
inmates who are usually first-time offenders and have more identification with "straight" society and norms of noncriminals

staff diversity
having a representative workforce in terms of gender, race, and ethnicity

stand-up count
the most formal count of the day, at which inmates must stand at their cell door or by their dormitory bed to be counted and matched to the number of inmates assigned to each housing area

state-use system
a system in which prison-made goods are sold to and used by only state and federal government agencies

status offense
an activity that is considered a crime only because the offender is under age 18 and would not be a crime if committed by an adult; status offenses include running away from home, ungovernability, truancy, and underage drinking

standard conditions of probation
conditions that must be followed by every probationer

straight adult incarceration
a form of incarceration in which juveniles handled by adult courts are placed in adult prisons with no separate housing or differentiation in programming or job assignments

street crimes
crimes with little sophistication required, such as murder, robbery, burglary, assault, and theft

substance abuse programs
programs that help offenders reduce their likelihood of further abuse of alcohol or drugs

suicide prevention programs
jail and prison programs that include early detection of suicide risks, staff education to recognize signs of potential suicide, and procedures for managing inmates who are now suicidal

suicide watch
management of suicidal inmates who are placed in a specially designed cell and have constant supervision

supermax prisons
either freestanding prisons or distinct units within other prisons that provide for the management and secure control of inmates designated as violent or seriously disruptive in other prisons

superpredator
a term created by Dilulio to describe a generation of violent youths who practiced almost indiscriminant violence on the streets

supervised mandatory release
a type of release in which inmates serve a determinate sentence and then are released, but with a period of supervision to follow

supervised pretrial release programs
programs in which offenders are supervised while released on their own recognizance, similar to supervision while on probation

surety
a person who is legally liable for the conduct of another; someone who guarantees the accused person's appearance in court

surveillance style of supervision
a style of supervising community offenders that emphasizes monitoring and enforcing compliance with the rules of supervision and detecting violations leading to revocation and return to custody

technical violations
violations of conditions of community supervision without commission of a new crime

test of proportionality
the result of the 1983 case of *Solem v. Helm;* a test used to guide sentencing based on the gravity of the offense and consistency of the severity of punishment

thieves
inmates who have adopted a career of crime and are doing their prison time until they can get out and hit the "big score"

third-generation jails
jail designs without remote control centers, in which correctional officers are located in the housing unit in direct contact with inmates

Three Penitentiary Act
the 1891 act of Congress that authorized the construction of the first three federal prisons

three-strikes laws
a legislative mandate that judges sentence third-time felons to extremely long or life prison sentences

ticket of leave
a form of release used by Maconochie; once prisoners earned the required level of marks, they received a conditional pardon and were released to the community

total institution
Goffman's concept of a setting isolating people from the rest of society and unnecessarily manipulating them through the actions of the administrative staff

totality-of-conditions test
a test created in *Pugh v. Locke* that examines the aggregate of circumstances in a prison to determine whether cruel and unusual conditions exist

"tough on crime"
an attitude that criminals should be severely punished for their wrongdoings, and long prison sentences are the most effective punishment

transactional leaders
traditional authorities within an organization with involved exchange relationships between leaders and followers; they provide answers and direction for any issue the agency confronts

transformational leaders
organizational leadership based on principles, while motivating staff to jointly address challenges and find solutions to new problems

treatment
the creation of an environment and provision of rehabilitative programs that encourage inmates to accept responsibility and to address personal disorders that make success in the community more difficult

truth in sentencing
a sentencing model that requires completion of 85 percent of the sentence before prisoners are eligible for release

unconditional mandatory release
a form of release in which inmates serve the full portion of their sentence and have no supervision after release from prison

uniformed staff
prison or jail staff who work in the security or custody department and are responsible for the implementation of security policies and procedures

unit management
organizing a prison into smaller components by decentralizing the authority to manage the inmate population while making staff more accessible to inmates

unit manager
the staff member who is in charge of the unit, including housing, security, and treatment issues

victim compensation
a form of restitution in which offenders repay their victims directly for their losses and harm caused by the offense

victims' movement
the criminal justice system's recognition that victims should be involved in the process of sentencing criminals

violation
failure to follow conditions of parole supervision

vocational training
specific training in a trade area

Wackenhut Corrections Corporation
a private correctional company that operates fifty-seven correctional facilities

waiver to adult courts
statutory exceptions granted to allow movement from juvenile to adult courts for criminal processing because of the serious nature of a juvenile offender's crime

Walnut Street Jail
the first penitentiary in America

war on drugs
an initiative by President Reagan to reduce the availability of and dependence on illicit drugs through interdiction, criminal sanctions, and treatment

warden
the chief executive officer of a prison, responsible for the day-to-day operations

work call
the time when inmates move to their assigned jobs or program assignments

Zebulon R. Brockway
a leading American penologist in the mid-1800s who was a proponent of adopting the Irish System in the United States, and who became the first superintendent of the Elmira Reformatory

Index

A

ACA (American Correctional Association)
  accreditation and, 323, 495
  code of ethics and, 495–496
  creation of, 23
  and the juvenile justice system, 250
  standard for educational programs, 426
  standards manuals, 322
Accountability
  budget choices and, 510
  of inmates, 404, 405–409
Accreditation, 323, 324, 495–497
Acquired immune deficiency syndrome (AIDS), 292–295
Action with consent and waiver, 190
Actuarial risk assessment, 325
Adjudication, 257
Administrative appeals process, 331–332
Administrative detention (AD), 412–413
Administrative sentencing, 52–53
Adult Internal Management System (AIMS), 325
Affirmative action programs, 498
AFL-CIO, 334
AFSFME (American Federation of State, Federal and Municipal Employees), 334
Aftercare supervision, for juveniles, 259
Age of original jurisdiction, 251–253
Aggravated assault, 242
Aggravating circumstances, 17, 55
Aging offenders, 281–283
Alcohol abuse. See Substance abuse
Alcoholics Anonymous, 432
American Prison Association, 167, 425
Anger management, 29
Antipsychotic drugs, 276
Antipsychotropic drugs, 90
Arson, 243
Aryan Brotherhood (AB), 350
Ashurst-Sumners Act, 23, 433
Assault, 142
Assessment. See also Classification systems
  actuarial risk, 325

and mental health screening, 90
for preventing disturbances, 417
probation and, 111–112
of treatment programs, 501
Atavism, 17
Auburn system, 22
Augustus, John, 100

B

Bail
  alternatives to, 40–41
  bonds, 40
  bondsmen, 40
  as a diversion program, 36, 37, 38–39
  early system of, 19
  history of, 39–40
Banishing, 18
Barefield v. Leach, 233
BARJ (balanced and restorative justice), 263–265
Bates, Sanford, 144
Bearden v. Georgia, 107
Beatings, 17–18
Beccaria, Cesare, 16
Bell v. Wolfish, 26, 89–90
Bentham, Jeremy, 17, 27
BFOQ (bona fide occupational qualification), 393
Bind over, 249
Black Guerilla Family (BGF), 350
Blended sentencing, 271
Bonds, 40, 41
Booking, 36
Boot camps
  budget issues and, 13, 491
  Bureau of Prisons and, 148
  versus imprisonment, 486
  for juveniles, 258
  probation and, 101
  as shock incarceration, 123–124
Branding, 17–18, 19
Brank, 19
Breed v. Jones, 260
Brigs, 154
Brockway, Zebulon R., 167, 360–361, 425
Broken windows probation, 111
Bruscino v. Carlson, 134, 283–284
Budget development and accounting division, 308–309
Budgets
  accountability and, 510–511
  creating revenues to reduce, 491

increases in, 9–10, 13, 52, 142, 486, 488
  within prisons, 317
  probation costs and, 110
  War on Drugs and, 139
Bureau of Immigration and Customs Enforcement (BICE), 153–154
Burglary, 142, 243
Bush, George H.W., 485, 492
Business administration, 388
Butler v. Reno, 233

C

CAC (Commission on Accreditation for Corrections), 324, 495
Call out, 407
Capital punishment
  as an early public response to crime, 18, 19
  definition of, 48
  for juvenile offenders, 261
  public opinion on, 132
Careers
  caseworkers, 222–223
  correctional administrators, 308
  correctional educators, 429
  correctional officers, 384–386
  corrections as a choice of, 526–527
  counselors, 222–223
  gang intelligence officers, 353
  halfway house staff, 121–122
  human resources managers, 498
  increases in jobs in corrections and, 9, 13
  juvenile social service workers, 260
  parole officers, 187
  policy analysts, 10
  pretrial release officers, 43
  wardens, 136
Caseloads
  intensive-supervision, 103
  parolees and, 185
  regular, 103
  special, 103
Case manager, 317
Caseworkers, 222–223
Casual supervision, 407–408
CCPOW (California Correctional Peace Officers Association), 487
Census count, 409

Certification, 249
Chain of command, 372–374
Classical School, 16, 422
Classification systems
  for controlling inmate behavior, 324–329
  in federal prisons, 146, 148
  for female offenders, 232
  internal, 325
  in jails, 73–74
  as a means for gaining compliance, 383
  for probation, 111–112, 115
  for security and custody, 403
  in state prisons, 152–153
Client Analysis Scale-Risk, 112
Closed systems, 372
Collateral, 41
Collective bargaining, 314, 334–336
Collective violence, 347
Commissary, 317
Commission on Law Enforcement and the Administration of Justice, 422
Communication
  of policies and procedures, 322
  race as a barrier to, 498
Community classification systems, 112
Community policing, 111
Community service, 47–48, 117
Community supervision
  fees and, 491
  functions, 309
  future of, 515–518
  residential centers, 119–121
Compliance. See Discipline
Comprehensive Crime Control Act, 39
Concurrent jurisdiction, 252
Concurrent sentences, 49
Conditions of parole, 182, 185
Conditions of probation, 103
Congregate and silent system, 22
Conjugal visiting, 354–355
Consecutive sentences, 49
Consent decree, 257
Construction. See New prison construction
Containment model, 290–291
Contingency plans, for disturbances, 418
Continuum of care, for mental illness, 431

Contraband, 403, 409–412
Controlled movement, 405–407
Convicts, 343. *See also* Inmates
Cooper v. Pate, 24
Co-payments, for prison medical care, 492
Cornell Correctional Companies, 156
Corporal punishment, 17–18, 132
Correctional Services Corporation, 156
Corrections
  community, 100, 491
  correctional centers and, 65
  correctional counselors and, 317
  and the correctional funnel, 8–9
  correctional officers in, 75, 379–386
  and correctional psychologists, 277, 279–280
  correctional services and, 315
  defining, 4–5
  future of, 509–511
  history of, 4–32
  importance of studying, 9–15
  mission of, 5–6
  new paradigm for, 518–522
  as part of the criminal justice system, 6–8
  policy, 8–9
  role of, 36
  sentencing goals of, 25–31
Corrections Corporation of America, 156
Correspondence courses, 427
Cost-of-incarceration fees, 491
Costs. *See also* Budgets
  intermediate sanctions and, 125
  of supervision, 117
Cottage-style architecture, 361
Counseling
  cost of, 117
  mental health, 430
  programs for, 316
  rehabilitation and, 29, 135
Counselors, 222–223, 317, 318
Counts
  census, 409
  random, 409
  regular, 408
  stand-up, 408–409
Courts, 6, 36, 42–43
Crack cocaine, 245
Crime
  decrease in, 14
  early public responses to, 17–20
  public perception of increase in, 14–15

theories of, 16–17
"tough on crime" policies, 69, 485, 486–487, 509, 511
Crime Control Act of 1990 (Public Law 101-647), 426
Crofton, Walter, 22, 165–166
Culture
  management, 390–391
  organizational, 377–379
  of prisons, 342–346, 362–364, 370
  relationship, 390–391
  staff, 389–391
  wardens and, 377–379
Custody. *See* Security and Custody

D

Darwinisim, 422
Davis, Richard Allen, 485
Deadly force, 418
Death penalty. *See* Capital punishment
Debriefing, 353
Decision-making skills, rehabilitation and, 29
Deferred prosecution, 37
Deinstitutionalization, 249
Delinquency petition, 257
Delinquent children, 250
Dependent children, 250
Deportation, 18
Detention facility, 65
Determinate sentencing
  definition of, 51–52
  growth of the prison population and, 137
  and the Neoclassical School, 17
  and prisoner reentry, 195
  problems with, 175
Determination of a violation, 190
Determinism, 17
Deterrence
  as a correctional goal, 132
  as crime prevention, 8, 27
  general, 27
  specific, 27
Direct file, 271
Director, 305
Direct supervision, 84, 407–408
Discipline
  correctional officers and, 383–384
  disciplinary segregation (DS) as, 413–414
  disciplinary systems for, 329–332
  as a function of security and custody, 403
  policies for, 329
  sanctions and, 330–331
Discipline Hearing Officer (DHO), 330
Discretionary parole, 171
Discretionary waiver, 250

Discrimination
  bail process and, 40
  overrepresentation of minorities and, 498–499
Disturbance control team (DCT), 418, 419
Disturbances. *See* Riots and disturbances
Diversion
  advantages of, 38
  bail or release on recognizance, 37
  intermediate sanctions and, 125
  as a part of corrections, 6
  recidivism rate and, 38
  substance abuse treatment programs, 37
  before trial, 36
Diversity
  inmates, 208
  staff, 75, 497–500
Dothard v. Rawlinson, 393
Drugs. *See* Substance abuse
Drug Use Forecasting, 273
Ducking stool, 19
Due process, 39, 248, 259, 261
Dukakis, Michael, 485
Dyer Act, 145

E

Economic sanctions, 47, 115–117
Eddings v. Oklahoma, 261
Education
  BOP mandatory prison education requirement, 426
  college programs, 427–428
  departments, 316
  prisoner reentry and, 201
  programs for, 72, 424–427
  program staff and, 387
  rehabilitation and, 29
EEO (equal employment opportunity), 314
Electronic monitoring
  budget issues and, 13, 491
  cost of, 117
  as a form of incapacitation, 28
  house arrest and, 118–119
  versus imprisonment, 486
  parole and, 185
Elmira reformatory, 167
Emergency response teams, 418–420
Employee awards program, 317
Employment, and prisoner reentry, 197
England
  bail in, 40
  early response to crime in, 17, 19
Environmental factors, for tension and unrest, 416

Ethics, 495–496
Ethnicity. *See* Minorities
Evaluation, of treatment programs, 501
External operations, 375

F

Facility maintenance, 388
Families
  and conjugal visiting, 354
  female inmates and, 227, 229
  and prisoner reentry, 197
  pseudofamilies as, 363
  visiting with, 72
Fare v. Michael C., 260–261
FBI (Federal Bureau of Investigation), 242
Federal Bail Reform Act, 41
Federal Bureau of Prisons (BOP), 135, 144–148, 232, 305, 325
Federal Bureau of Prisons drug abuse program (DAP), 274–276
Federal government, role in correctional systems, 6
Federalization, 143
Federal Prison Industries (FPI), 433–434
Federal prisons. *See also* Federal Bureau of Prisons (BOP)
  versus state prisons, 142, 148
  Three Penitentiary Act, 143
Fee system, 19
Felony, 36
Field operations functions, 309–310
Fines, 65, 115, 116
First-generation jails, 79
Fogel, David, 170
Food and health services, 317, 388
Forfeiture of assets, 115
Fraud, 142–143
Free will, 16
Frisking, 412
Fry, Elizabeth, 360
Full revocation hearing, 191
Furlough, 485

G

Gagnon v. Scarpelli, 108, 191
Gangs
  control strategies for, 351–353
  drug sales and, 262
  gang intelligence officers and, 353
  gender in, 262
  juvenile crime and, 246, 261–263
  overview of, 348–351
  and prisoner reentry, 196
  validation process for, 351

Gaol, 19, 64
Gault, Gerald, 260
Gender
    female inmates, 148, 219,
        223–237
    female parolees, 175
    gangs and, 262
    juvenile inmates and, 272
    males, 150, 218–222
    mental health treatment and,
        430
    parity for female
        correctional officers,
        392–397
    parity for female inmates,
        233–234
    and prison population
        makeup, 210–214
    rape and, 288
    and sexual harassment of
        female correctional
        officers, 394
    stereotypes, 361
General population, 221
Girl Scouts Behind Bars, 229
Global positioning system (GPS),
    517
Goffman, Erving, 340–341
Good time, 51–52
Graduated incarceration,
    272–273
Greenholz v. Inmates of the
    Nebraska Penal and
    Correctional Complex, 176,
    191
Gunther v. Iowa, 393

H

Hacks, 343
Hain, Scott Allen, 261
Halfway houses
    as community residential
        centers (CRCs), 119–121
    for female inmates, 235
    history of, 25
    and prisoner reentry, 195,
        196, 201
    security levels and, 148
    staff of, 121–122
Hands-off doctrine, 24
Harrison Narcotic Act, 145
Hawes-Cooper Act, 23, 433
Health care
    for female inmates, 227
    staff for, 388
Hearing officers, 180
Hedonism, 16–17
Hedonistic calculus, 17, 27
Homosexual behavior, 353–355
Hoover, Herbert, 144
Horton, Willie, 485
Hostage negotiation teams
    (HNTs), 418, 419
House arrest, 28, 101,
    118–119, 486, 491
House of corrections, 65
Houses of Refuge, 247

Howard, John, 19–20, 64
Human immunodeficiency virus
    (HIV), 292–295
Human resources
    management, 309, 317
    staff, 388, 498
Humor, 357–358

I

Immigration and Naturalization
    Service (INS), 153
Imprisonment, definition of, 48
Incapacitation
    as a correctional goal, 132
    as crime prevention, 8,
        27–29
    criticism of, 29
    selective, 28–29
Incarceration
    current trends in rates of,
        490
    lifetime chances of, 139
    rate of, 67, 139
Incentives
    as a means for gaining
        compliance, 383
    recreation as, 437
Indeterminate sentencing
    alternatives to, 172–173
    definition of, 51
    and early reformers, 22, 23
    and growth in the prison
        population, 137
    and prisoner reentry, 195
    problems with moving away
        from, 175
Industrial Prison Era, 23
Infectious diseases, 292–297
Inmates
    accountability of, 405–409
    age of, 214–215
    antisocial offenders, 348
    classification of, 324–329
    controlling behavior of,
        322–324
    disciplinary system for,
        329–332
    diversity of, 208
    elderly, 208
    ethnicity of, 210–214
    female, 359–365
        classification systems
            for, 232
        family and, 227, 229
        in federal prisons, 148
        halfway houses for, 235
        health care for, 227
        medical care for, 231
        parenting programs for,
            229
        parity for, 233–234
        parolees, 175
        prerelease centers for,
            235
        sexual abuse and, 227
        substance abuse and,
            223, 227, 230–231

    vocational training and,
        227
    work release and, 235
    gender of, 210–214
    heterogeneity of, 133
    increase in, 9–10,
        135–140, 142, 209,
        480–484
    and the inmate code, 342,
        362–363
    of jails, 66–69
    juveniles, 208
    male, 150, 340–358
    mandatory minimums for,
        53–54
    mental illness in, 90, 208
    minorities, 150–151, 210
    movement of, 405–406
    psychopathic offenders, 348
    reentry into the community
        of, 194–202
    security and custody of,
        402–421
    special needs offenders,
        348
    treatment of, 422–439
In re Gault, 260
In re Stanford, 261
In re Winship, 260
Inspector, 307, 313
Intake, 254
Integrity interview, 333
Intensive supervised probation
    (ISP), 101, 112, 117–118,
    491
Intermediate sanctions,
    115–126
Internal affairs, 307
Internal classification systems,
    325
Internal operations, 375
International Brotherhood of
    Teamsters, 334
Interpersonal violence, 347
Investigator, 313
Invisible policy, 517
Irish system, 23, 165–166

J

Jails
    design of, 75–84
    history of, 64–65
    legal issues for, 88–90
    versus lockups, 65
    mentally ill offenders in,
        90–91
    operations of, 65–75
    overcrowding in, 88
    as a part of corrections, 6,
        133–134
    preventing suicides in,
        92–95
    supervision in, 75–84
    trends in populations of,
        480–484
    Walnut Street Jail, 20
Johnson, Lyndon, 422

Judicial discretion, 51, 52–56,
    223
Just deserts model, 170
Justice model, 170
Juvenile Court Act, 247
Juvenile crime
    and adult criminal courts,
        270–273
    categories of juvenile
        offenders and, 250–253
    death penalty and, 261
    and development of the
        juvenile justice system,
        247–250
    drug-related, 261, 263–265
    gang-related, 261–263
    increases in, 215, 242–246
    and the juvenile justice
        process, 253–260
    legal issues and, 259–261
    privatization and, 155–156
    substance abuse and, 263
Juvenile Justice and Delinquency
    Act of 1974, 248–249

K

Kennedy, Anthony M., 511
Kent v. United States, 259
Klaas, Polly, 485

L

Labor relations, 313, 314
La Nuestra Familia (NF), 350
Larceny-theft, 243
Laundry operations, 317
Leadership
    autocratic and empowered
        continuum, 390
    reasoned and authoritarian
        continuum, 390
    transactional, 376–377
    transformational, 376–377
Lease system, 433
Legal advisors, 307
Legal issues
    juvenile justice system,
        259–261
    overcrowding, 89
    parity for female
        correctional officers,
        392–397
    parity for female inmates,
        233–234
Legislative liaison, 307
Legislative sentencing, 53
Length of stay, 70
Lesbian relationships, 363–364
Life skills, and prisoner reentry,
    201
Local government, role in
    correctional systems, 6
Lockups, 65
Lombroso, Cesare, 17

M

Maconochie, Alexander, 22, 51,
    165

Maintenance, 317
Management analyst supervisor, 313–314
Mandatory minimums, 36, 53–54
Mandatory prison education, 426
Mandatory waiver, 250
Manhattan Bail Project, 41
Mark system, 165
Martinson, Robert, 25, 170, 501
McKeiver v. Pennsylvania, 260
Media, 307, 509
Medical care
    for aging offenders, 281
    co-payments for, 492
    for female inmates, 231
    HIV/AIDS and, 295
    for tuberculosis, 296–297
Medical model
    beginning of, 24, 422
    change from, 133
    parole and, 167–171
    and prisoner reentry, 195
Mempa v. Rhay, 108
Mental health
    mentally ill offenders, 90, 276–280
    and prisoner reentry, 196
    prison programs for, 316, 428–431
Meta-analysis, of treatment programs, 501–502
Mexican Mafia (MM), 350
Mexikanemi (EME), 350–351
Military prisons, 154
Milken, Michael, 116
Minorities
    changes in the prison population and, 210–214
    correctional officers, 379
    females, 225
    incarceration rate in jails and, 67
    on jail staffs, 75
    juvenile gangs, 175
    juvenile inmates, 272
    overrepresentation of, 498–499
    parolees, 175
    in state prisons, 150–151
Misdemeanor, 36
Mission, 5–6, 135
Mission statement, 6
Mitigating circumstances, 17, 54–55
Montesquieu, 16
Morial, Mark, 213
Morrisey v. Brewer, 191
Motor vehicle theft
    data on, 242
    juveniles and, 243
Murder, 142, 242
Mutilation, as an early public response to crime, 17–18

N
Narcotics Anonymous, 432
National Household Survey on Drug Abuse (NHSDFA), 274
National Prison Association, 23
National Task Force on Corrections Substance Abuse Strategies, 276
National Urban League, 213
Neglected children, 250
Negotiation, 418
Neoclassical School, 17
Net widening, 125
New-crime violations
    of parole, 188
    of probation, 107
New penology, 138
New prison construction
    costs of, 132
    division of, 308–309
    jails and, 84
    politics of, 486
"Nothing works," 25, 170, 501, 511
Notice of violation, 190

O
Objective classification systems, 73–74
Offender restitution, 116, 509
Open systems, 372
Order, in juvenile court, 257
Organizational culture, wardens and, 377–379
Organized Crime Control Act of 1970, 117
Outsourcing. *See* Privatization

P
Parallel universe, 523
Parens patriae, 247–246, 259, 261
Parenting programs, female inmates and, 229
Pargo v. Elliot, 233–234
Parole
    alternatives to indeterminate sentencing, 171–173
    beginnings in the United States, 167, 509
    boards, 167, 176, 178–179
    current status of, 175–176
    and determinate sentencing, 175
    early use of, 22–23
    effectiveness of, 191–193
    guidelines for, 172
    hearings, 180–182
    history of, 164–165
    and its place in the correctional system, 6
    Maconochie and the mark system and, 164–165
    and the medical model, 167–171
    monitoring during, 138
    officers, 187
    operations of, 176–179
    and prisoner reentry, 194–202, 195
    revocation of, 188–191
    supervision and conditions of, 182–185
    terminating supervision of, 188–191
    Walter Crofton and the Irish system of, 165–166
Parole Commission and Reorganization Act, 172
Participatory management, 373
Pass system, 407
Pedophiles, 288
Pell grants, 427
Penal code, 6
Penitentiary, 5
Penitentiary Act of 1779, 20, 64–65
Pennsylvania System, 21–22
Penology, 4, 5
Period of Transition, 24, 134
Personal recognizance, 40
Pillories, as an early public response to crime, 18
Plea bargaining, 42–43
Podular jail design, 80
Police, 6, 36
Policy
    analysts, 10
    audit, 323
    contraband control and, 410
    for controlling inmate behavior, 322–324
    disciplinary, 329
    implementation audit, 323
    invisible, 517
    new construction costs and, 159
    politics and, 484–487
    as a process, 9
    for security and custody, 403
Politics, and policy, 484–487
Positive contact, 185
Positive School, 17
Post orders, 381
Post-Release Employment Project, 436
Precipitating event, for tension and unrest, 416–417
Preliminary hearing, 190
Prerelease, 201, 235
Presentence investigation (PSI), 43–47, 152
Presentencing, 43–47
President's Commission on Law Enforcement and Administration of Justice, 132
Presumptive parole date, 181
Presumptive sentencing, 54–55, 170
Pretrial correctional activities, 36–38
    bail, 39–41
    and the decrease in state prison populations, 484
    jail detention, 38–39
    service programs, 41–42
Pretrial diversion. *See* Diversion
Pretrial release officers, 43
Preventive detention, 39
PRIDE, 382
Prisoner reentry, 194–202, 522–525
Prison-industrial complex, 485, 486
Prison industries
    benefits of, 434–435
    PIE programs, 435–436
    staff for, 387–388
Prisonization, 342–343, 370, 522–525
Prison population. *See* Inmates
Prisons. *See also* Federal prisons; Inmates; Staff; State prisons
    adult systems in the United States, 142–143
    Auburn system, 22
    building designs of, 140–141
    current status of, 132–133, 482
    definition of, 132
    development of, 20–22
    drugs in, 355–357
    federal, 143–148
    growth of population of, 135–142
    history of women's, 359–362
    homosexual behavior in, 353–354
    humor in, 357–358
    immigration facilities, 153–154
    military facilities, 153–154
    organization of, 304–336, 372–374
    Pennsylvania system of, 21–22
    private (*See* Privatization)
    role and mission of, 133–135
    in the 1800s and 1900s, 22–25
    state, 148–153
    territorial facilities, 153–154
    and their place in the correctional system, 6
    violence in, 346–348
Private Sector Prison Industry Enhancement Certification (PIE), 435–436
Privatization
    for-profit facilities, 156
    halfway houses, 154–155
    Industrial Prison Era and, 23
    and jail crowding, 86–87

juvenile facilities, 156
politics and, 487
private correctional
companies, 156–157
to reduce costs, 492–494
Probable cause, 190
Probation
classification systems,
111–112, 115
conditions of, 48, 103,
105–106
current approach to, 509
definition of, 48
drug treatment for offenders
on, 276
effectiveness of, 109–110,
125–126
history of, 100–101
informal, 257
intermediate sanctions, 115
community residential
centers, 119–121
economic, 115–117
house arrest, 118–119
intensive supervised
probation, 117–118
shock incarceration/
boot camp, 123–124
shock probation,
124–125
split sentences, 123
and its place in the
correctional system, 6
juvenile, 258
modern operations,
101–102
monitoring, 138
officers, 45
reform of, 110–111
revocation of, 106–108
supervision, 102–103
without adjudication, 37
Profession, 495
Professional staff, 387
Program assignments, 405
Program staff, 387
Property crime, 69, 133, 223,
243
Prosecution, plea bargaining
and, 42
Pseudofamilies, 363
Psychological services, 387.
See also Counseling
Psychotropic medication, 316,
430
Public affairs, 307
Public safety
perception of, 486
prison growth and, 132
probation and, 100, 111
Punishment
as a correctional goal, 26,
132
retribution as, 26
test of proportionality and, 26
Puritans, response to crime of,
18

Q
Quakers, 20, 132, 360
Quality assurance, 323
Quay, Herbert, 325

R
Race, 210–214. See also
Minorities
Ragen, Joseph, 374–375
Random count, 409
Random drug testing, 356–357
Rape
data on, 242
of female prisoners by
guards, 359–360
homosexual, 354
in lesbian relationships, 364
Reagan, Ronald, 485, 492, 511
Recidivism
boot camps and, 124
correctional education
programs and, 426–427
diversion programs and, 38
drug courts and, 58
drug treatment to offenders
on probation and, 276
and evaluation of treatment
programs, 501–502
of female offenders, 225
intermediate sanctions and,
125
parole and, 192–193
privatization and, 494
probation and, 110
rehabilitation and, 29–30
of sex offenders, 291–292
substance abuse programs
and, 432
Reclassification, 327
Recreation
programs for, 316,
436–438
staff for, 387
Reentry. See Prisoner reentry
Referral, 257
Reform
John Howard and, 19–20
probation and, 110–111
Quakers and, 20
William Penn and, 20
Reformatories, 361
Reformatory Era, 23, 51
Reform school, 258
Refuge Period, 247
Regional jail, 66
Regular count, 408
Rehabilitation
anger management and, 29
counseling and, 29
decision-making skills and,
29
definition of, 423
education and, 29
future of, 511–515
as a goal of corrections,
29–30, 422

indeterminate sentences
and, 51
juvenile, 258
medical model and, 24
new paradigm for, 511–515
and prisoner reentry, 196
rebirth of, 513–514
recidivism and, 29
sensitivity training and, 29
substance abuse and, 29
Rehabilitative Era, 24, 100
Reintegration, transitional care
and, 24–25
Reintegrative Era, 100
Release on recognizance (ROR),
37, 41
Religion
prison services in support
of, 316, 317, 436
rehabilitation and, 135
staff for, 387
Remand, 249
Reparation, 519–521
Residential community
placement. See Halfway
houses
Residential substance abuse
treatment (RSAT) programs,
432
Residential treatment, for
juveniles, 258
Restitution
as an intermediate sanction,
115
as a goal of corrections, 30
victims' movement and, 30
Restorative justice
as an alternative sentencing
model, 519
restitution and, 30–31
Retribution, as punishment, 26
Retributive Era, 25
Revocation, of parole, 188–191
Rewards systems, 324
Rhodes v. Chapman, 134
RICO (Racketeer Influenced and
Corrupt Organization) statute,
117
Right to strike, 334–335
Riots and disturbances
control of, 404, 414–421
during the Period of
Transition, 24
Risk assessment. See also
Classification systems
for preventing disturbances,
417
probation and, 111–112
Robbery, 142, 242
Routines, 405–407
Runaway, as a status offense,
242
Rush, Benjamin, 20

S
Safety and sanitation, 388
Salient factor score, 172–173

Sanctions
disciplinary, 330–331
economic, 47
intermediate, 47
Sanford v. Kentucky, 261
Schall v. Martin, 260–261
Screws, 343
Second-generation jails, 80, 83
Security and custody
activities, 402–404
functions of, 313, 404–422
in jails, 77–80, 83–84
and needs of inmates, 423
security levels, 221–222
in the federal prison
system, 146, 148
in state prisons, 152
staff organization for, 315
third-party, 41
Segregated incarceration, 273
Self-regulation, 324
Seniority, 334
Sensitivity training, rehabilitation
and, 29
Sentencing
concurrent sentences, 49
consecutive sentences, 49
definition of, 36
determinate (See
Determinate sentencing)
drug courts, 56, 58
future of, 509–511
guidelines, 36, 55–56
increase in length of, 217
indeterminate (See
Indeterminate sentencing)
judicial discretion in, 51,
52–56
models, 50–52
options, 47–49
plea bargains and, 42–43
presentencing, 43–47
presumptive, 170
Sentencing Reform Act of 1984,
145
Separate and silent system,
21–22
Service functions, 317
Services, 313, 387–389
Sex offenders
mandatory minimums for,
53–54
and prisoner reentry, 196,
201
recidivism of, 291–292
special issues concerning,
288–292
treatment and management
of, 290–291
Sexual abuse, female inmates
and, 227
Sexual harassment, of female
correctional officers, 394
Sexual triangles, 354
Shadow board, 411
Shaking down, 412
Sheriff, 66

Shock incarceration/boot camp, 123–124
Shock probation, 101, 124–125
Short-term confinement, 48
Slang, 345–346
Society for the Prevention of Juvenile Delinquency, 247
Solem v. Helm, 26
Special emergency response team (SERT), 418, 420
Special housing units (SHUs), 403–404, 412–414
Special offenders
  aging, 281–283
  drug offenders, 273–276
  juveniles in adult criminal courts, 270–273
  mentally ill, 90, 276–280
  offenders with infectious diseases, 292–297
  sex offenders, 288–292
  violent offenders, 283–286
Split sentences, 69, 123
Square johns, 343
Staff
  collective bargaining and, 334–336
  contraband and, 412
  correctional officers, 75, 379–386
  diversity of, 75, 497–500
  employee awards programs for, 317
  empowerment of, 373
  functions within the office of director, 305–313
  human resources managers, 498
  of jails, 74–75
  jobs of, 371–372
  organization of, 313–322
  for pretrial services, 37
  prison culture of, 389–391
  professional, 316
  professionalizing of, 24
  recruiting and hiring, 332–333
  role of, 332
  services, 387–388
  training of, 24
  treatment and program, 387
  uniformed, 315, 387
Standards, 322, 495–496
Stand-up count, 408–409
State prisons
  versus federal prisons, 142, 148
  inmates in, 150–151
  organization of, 149–150
  security classifications in, 152–153
  states' role in correctional systems, 6
  trends in population of, 480–484
State-use system, 433
Status offense, 242, 250–251

Statutory exclusion, 252, 271
Stigma, pretrial diversion programs and, 38
Stipulated agreement, 190
Stockholm Syndrome, 419
Stocks, 18
Straight adult incarceration, 272
Street crimes, 142, 261
Stress
  correctional officers and, 370, 382–383
  female correctional officers and, 394
  nonwhite correctional officers and, 499
Substance abuse. *See also* War on Drugs
  cost of testing for, 117
  drug courts and, 56, 58
  drug offenders and, 133, 273–276
  female inmates and, 227, 230–231
  females and, 223
  gangs and, 262
  increase in number of offenders and, 217
  juveniles and, 242, 259–261, 263
  in male prisons, 355–357
  mandatory minimums for, 53–54
  offenders in federal prisons, 148
  offenders in jails, 69
  offenders in state prisons, 151
  and prisoner reentry, 196, 201
  programs for, 72, 316–317, 357, 431–432
  random drug testing for, 356–357
  rehabilitation and, 29, 135
  treatment for, 13
  treatment for juveniles, 258
  treatment staff, 387
Suicide
  prevention programs, 92
  watch, 92, 94–95
Summons, 40
Superintendent, 313
Supermax prisons, 283–287
Superpredator, 249
Supervised mandatory release, 171
Supervised pretrial release programs (SPTR), 41
Supervision
  administrative, 115
  casework style, 102
  casual and direct, 407–408
  intensive, 112
  minimum, 112, 115
  probation and, 102–103
  regular, 112
  surveillance style, 102
Surety, 40

T
Tarde, Gabriel, 17
Technical violations
  of parole, 188
  of probation, 107
Territorial prisons, 154
Terry, Charles, 357
Test of proportionality, 26
Texas Mexican Mafia, 350–351
Texas Syndicate (TS), 351
Theft, 142, 242, 343
Third-generation jails, 83–84
Three Penitentiary Act, 143
Three-strikes laws, 36, 54, 485, 490
Ticket of leave, 165, 166
Title VII of the 1964 Civil Rights Act, 392–393
Torture, 17–18, 19
Total institution, 340
"Tough on crime," 69, 133, 485, 486–487, 511
Training school, for juveniles, 258
Transactional leaders, 376
Transformational leaders, 377
Transition, 24–25, 51, 201
Transportation, as an early public response to crime, 18
Treatment Alternatives to Street Crimes (TASC), 37
Treatment and treatment programs
  functions in jails, 72
  functions in prisons, 313, 316–317
  history of, 313
  staffing of, 387
Truth in sentencing (TIS), 51–52, 137
Tuberculosis, 296–297
Twentieth Century Task Force on Sentencing, 170

U
Unconditional mandatory release, 171
Uniform Crime Report (UCR), 242
Uniformed staff, 315, 387
Unintended consequences, 53–54
Unions. *See* Collective bargaining
Unit Disciplinary Committee (UDC), 330
United States v. Birnbaum, 108
United States v. Salerno, 39
Unit management, 317–320
Unit manager, 317

V
Victims
  compensation for, 116–117
  programs for, 30
  restitution and, 30, 491

restorative justice and, 30–31
sentencing and, 30
and victim impact statement, 46
Violations
  of parole, 188–191
  of probation, 107
Violence
  in federal prisons, 148
  increase in, 217
  juveniles and, 242–243
  males as, 218–220
  mandatory minimums for, 53–54
  and prisoner reentry, 201
  prison gangs and, 348–353
  in prisons, 346–348
  special issues concerning, 283–286
  in state prisons, 151
  and violent offenders, 133
Violent Crime Control and Law Enforcement Act of 1994, 432
Visits
  conjugal, 354–355
  contraband control and, 410–411
  jail inmates and, 72
  noncontact, 72
Vocational training
  female inmates and, 227
  and prisoner reentry, 201
  programs for, 316, 427–428
  recidivism and, 427
  staff for, 387
  for women, 361
Volstead Act, 145

W
Wackenhut Corrections Corporation, 156
Waivers, 249–250, 271
Walnut Street Jail, 4, 20, 65, 422, 436
Wardens, 136, 313, 374–379
War on Drugs, 69, 138–139, 273, 481, 486
Warrant for arrest and custody, 190
Weapons, juveniles and, 246
Weight lifting, 437–438
White collar crime, 143
White Slave Act, 145
Williams, Jerry, 54
Williams v. New York, 46
Work assignments, 405
Work call, 406
Workhouses, 65
Work programs, 72, 317, 434
Work release, 201, 235

Z
Zimbardo, Philip, 340–341